Social Problems

Sixth Edition

James M. Henslin

Southern Illinois University, Edwardsville

Prentice
Hall

Upper Saddle River, New Jersey 07458

Library of Congress Cataloging-in-Publication Data

Henslin, James M.
  Social problems / James M. Henslin.—6th ed.
    p. cm.
  Includes bibliographical references and index.
  ISBN 0-13-110556-6
  1. Social problems. 2. Deviant behavior. 3. Equality. 4. Social
  change. 5. Symbolic interactionism. 6. Functionalism (Social sciences)
  7. United States—Social conditions—1980– I. Title.
  HM585.H45 2003
  361.1—dc21
                                                           2002014482

Publisher: Nancy Roberts
Director of Manufacturing and Production: Barbara Kittle
Executive Managing Editor: Ann Marie McCarthy
Production Liaison: Fran Russello
Editorial/Production Supervision: Bruce Hobart (Pine Tree Composition)
Marketing Director: Beth Mejia
Senior Marketing Manager: Amy Speckman
Marketing Assistant: Anne Marie Fritzky
Manufacturing Manager: Nick Sklitsis
Prepress and Manufacturing Buyer: Mary Ann Gloriande
Administrative Assistant: Lee Peterson
Creative Design Director: Leslie Osher
Art Director: Kathryn Foot
Interior Design: Kathryn Foot
Cover Designer: Kathryn Foot
Media Editor: Kate Ramunda
Media Production Project Manager: Jennifer Collins
Media Manager: Lynn Pearlman
Director, Image Resource Center: Melinda Lee Reo
Manager, Rights & Permissions: Zina Arabia
Interior Image Specialist: Beth Boyd-Brenzel
Photo Researcher: Melinda Alexander
Cover Image Specialist: Karen Sanatar
Image Permission Coordinator: Tara Gardner
Manager, Art: Guy Ruggiero
Art Illustrations: Maria Piper; Dartmouth Publishing Inc.
Artist: Mirella Signoretto

 © 2003, 2000, 1996, 1994, 1990 by James M. Henslin
© 1983 by James M. Henslin and Donald W. Light

Pearson Education, Inc.
Upper Saddle River, New Jersey 07458

Printed in the United States of America
10 9 8 7 6 5 4 3 2

ISBN 0-13-110556-6

Pearson Education LTD., London
Pearson Education Australia PTY, Limited, Sydney
Pearson Education Singapore, Pte. Ltd
Pearson Education North Asia Ltd, Hong Kong
Pearson Education Canada, Ltd., Toronto
Pearson Educación de Mexico, S.A. de C.V.
Pearson Education—Japan, Tokyo
Pearson Education Malaysia, Pte. Ltd.
Pearson Education, Upper Saddle River, New Jersey

For those yet to come onto this scene not of their own making—
may they live in a better world.

Contents

PART II   NORM VIOLATIONS IN SOCIAL CONTEXT

3   Prostitution, Homosexuality, and Pornography   48

4   Alcohol and Other Drugs   86

◆ 5 Violence in Society: Rape and Murder   130

◆ 6 Crime and Criminal Justice   166

PART III   PROBLEMS OF SOCIAL INEQUALITY

◆ *7*   Economic Problems: Wealth and Poverty   211

14 The Environmental Crisis 467

15 War, Terrorism, and the Balance of Power 508

Boxes

Thinking Critically About Social Problems ◆

Census 2000 ◆

Preface

Scope and Coverage of This Book

Social Problems is an enjoyable course to teach, and many students find it to be the most exciting course in sociology. Certainly the topics are fascinating, ranging from such controversial matters as prostitution and pornography to such deeply embedded problems as poverty and racism. Some of the issues are intensely personal, such as abortion; others, such as war, center on global stratification. All are significant, vital for our present and for our future.

The benefits of this course for students are similarly wide-ranging. Not only do students gain a sociological understanding of social problems, but also they are able to explore—and evaluate—their own opinions about the problems and controversies that affect their lives. As the course progresses, students become aware of the social forces that shape their views, gaining insight into how their particular situation in life penetrates their thinking and shapes their view of the world.

The Sociological Task: The Goal of Objectivity

This process of insight and self-discovery—so essential to good sociology—is one of the most rewarding aspects of teaching Social Problems. But teaching this class is also a challenge, for it requires objectivity in the midst of deep controversy, something very difficult to achieve. Students are a captive audience, and in my opinion using the classroom to promulgate particular points of view on social problems is unfair. It seems to me that the sociological task is to present competing views on what makes something a problem and what can be done about it. The instructor's view of the best solution—or of why a particular aspect of life is a social problem in the first place—is a matter of opinion. It is difficult to push one's own opinions aside, and yet this is precisely what objectivity requires.

In this text, I have tried to do precisely this—to present both sides of issues fairly and objectively. I have no hidden agenda, no axes to grind. I know, of course, that total objectivity, no matter how ardently it is desired or pursued, is impossible, but I think that objectivity should be the hallmark of Social Problems, and I have tried to attain it. The most obvious example is found in Chapter 1, where I use abortion as the substantive issue by which to illustrate basic sociological principles. Beginning with this topic jump-starts the course, placing us squarely in the midst of one of the most debated and heated issues in U.S. society. It also brings deep-seated attitudes to the surface. Used creatively, this approach allows us to illustrate the social origin of ideas, which is so essential to understanding social problems. To be fair to students, however, instructors need to take a neutral stance—no matter how strong their own attitudes may be. (This is extremely difficult in such emotional and volatile matters as abortion, and from time to time, we need to remind ourselves that our attitudes, too, are rooted in social structure.)

If I have been successful, both students and instructors who are on the extreme opposite ends of this issue—those who favor abortion on demand and those who oppose abortion under any circumstances—should feel that their position is adequately represented. They also will likely feel that I have somehow represented the other side too favorably. To check whether I had succeeded in attaining objectivity in this crucial matter, I asked national officers of both pro-choice and right to life organizations to comment on this first chapter. *Both sides* responded that I had been "trapped" into being too fair to the other side. I also asked my classes, after they had read the chapter, where they thought I stood on abortion. I was astonished—and pleased—when half replied that I was pro-choice and half that I was right to life.

The goal of this book, then, is to objectively present the major research findings on social problems, to explain their theoretical interpretation, and to describe clearly the underlying assumptions and implications of competing points of view. In endeavoring to reach this goal, I have strived to present the best of the sociology of social problems and to introduce competing views fairly. To again use Chapter 1 as an illustration: I use the terms *proabortion* and *antiabortion,* which, though far from perfect, are more neutrally descriptive than those preferred by proponents of either position—*prochoice* or *freedom of choice,* on one hand, and *prolife* and *right to life* on the other. While not everyone will be happy with my choice of terms—and they certainly cannot do justice to the many nuances and positions inherent in both sides of this critical issue—I feel that they are the more neutral and objective labels.

If I have been successful, readers should find themselves content when they encounter views with which they are in agreement and uncomfortable as they confront those with which they personally disagree. This should hold true for readers of all persuasions, whether "radical," "liberal," "conservative"—or any other label currently in fashion. It should also make for a more exciting class.

Method of Presentation: Incorporating Theory into the Discussions

Readers will find this book more theoretical than many. As one reviewer said, most texts in social problems simply mention theory in an initial chapter and then dispense with it thereafter, whereas this text follows through with the "theoretical promise" of its introductory chapters. Theory, however, can be vague, abstract, and difficult to understand. This is not necessary, and to overcome this problem I embed the theory in clarifying contexts. For example, when I introduce the three basic theories in Chapter 2—symbolic interaction theory, functional theory, and conflict theory—I make them concrete by applying each to the social problem of discrimination against the elderly in U.S. society. In the following chapters, I consistently apply these theories to *each* social problem. This approach helps give students a cohesive understanding of what otherwise might appear to be a disparate collection of problematic events and issues. The effect is cumulative, allowing students to broaden their understanding of these perspectives with each new chapter. (The single exception to applying each theory to each social problem is Chapter 3. Here I treat three social problems, and, because at this point students are becoming familiar with these theories, it seems more effective to apply a single theory in greater detail to each of the social problems.)

Chapter Organization and Features

A major impediment to learning is the seemingly whimsical way in which authors of textbooks present social problems. In the typical case, the analysis is jumbled—the order differs markedly from one chapter to the next, with no regularity of structure. To overcome this, I utilize a consistent structure within the chapters. This provides a "road map" that guides students through each social problem and lets them know what to expect in any given chapter. After the first three chapters, I use the following framework to analyze each social problem:

Opening Vignette Intended to arouse student interest in the social problem and to stimulate the desire to read more, this brief opening story presents essential elements of the social problem.

The Problem in Sociological Perspective Here I present a broad sociological background that sets the stage for understanding the social problem.

The Scope of the Problem This section presents basic data on the extent or severity of the problem. It allows students to grasp the problem's wider ramifications.

Looking at the Problem Theoretically Here I present a theoretical analysis of the problem or some major aspect of it. I consistently begin on the more personal level, with symbolic interaction theory, move from there to functional theory, and conclude with the perspective of conflict theory.

Research Findings Both current and classic sociological studies—and, where relevant, studies from other academic disciplines as well—are discussed here. To allow students to become more familiar with primary research, I present many sociological studies in detail.

Social Policy This section focuses on actions that have been taken or could be taken to try to solve the social problem. I often spell out the assumptions on which these policies are based and the dilemmas they create.

The Future of the Problem Because students are intensely interested in knowing what their future will bring, I conclude with an overview of the direction that the problem is likely to take, given what is now known about the problem's dimensions and trends.

Summary To reinforce what the students have just learned, I provide a succinct point-by-point summary of the main ideas in the chapter. Students will find this summary helpful for review purposes, especially in preparing for tests. They can also use it as a *preview* of the chapter; many of my students find it useful to read the summary *before* they read the chapter.

Key Terms As each term first appears in the text, it is set in bold type and is defined in context. Key terms are also listed and defined at the end of each chapter.

Thinking Critically Questions At the end of each chapter are several questions designed to help develop students' ability to evaluate what they have read. These questions can also be used for class discussions.

Suggestions for Using This Text

Authors of social problem texts, as well as instructors of this course, must always decide whether they want to begin with the more "micro" or the more "macro" problems. Each approach is popular and has much to commend it. In my own teaching, I prefer to begin at the micro level. I begin by focusing on problems of personal concern to students—issues about which they are already curious and have questions they want answered. After students are familiar with the sociological perspective and sociological theory, I move to an examination of broader social problems. This is only my preference, of course, and it is equally logical to begin with problems involving large-scale social change and then to wrap up the course with a focus on more individualistic problems. Instructors who wish to begin with problems affecting the largest numbers of people can simply move Part II of this text to the end of their course. Nothing else will be affected.

Because this book is written for students, I have resisted the urge to insert qualifying footnotes, the kind that read: "A fuller amplification of this position would include reference to the works of so-and-so," or "This theoretical position is really much more complex than I can describe here but because of lack of space. . . ." Such qualifiers are directed to a professional audience, and though they might serve to fend off some potential attack on the work, such "disclaimers" do not benefit students.

Request for Feedback / Invitation to Respond

This text flows from years of teaching this basic course in sociology, especially from reactions of my students, who questioned and reconsidered their view of social problems. It also incorporates feedback that was graciously provided by instructors. The text is intended to help make your course more successful, to bring greater rewards from teaching the sociological perspective. Results count, however, not intentions, and how the book actually works in the classroom is the real test. I greatly appreciate your feedback. Whether positive or negative, because it is based on your own classroom experience, I will find it useful. My e–mail address is listed below.

Acknowledgments

Finally, as is the custom in prefatory rituals, I wish to acknowledge the contributions of those without whose help this book would never have been written. First and foremost among them is my wife, Linda Henslin, who was of inestimable help in the first two editions. Each successive edition is still informed by her penetrating insight into social problems. I must also acknowledge that this edition exists largely because of her willingness to support my compulsion to continue what I began years ago—even though traveling would certainly have been a less taxing diversion.

I wish to thank Nancy Roberts for overseeing the project and working to resolve issues. Thanks also go to Sharon Chambliss and Lee Peterson for coordinating matters. Finally, I wish to thank the following for their valuable assistance in reviewing manuscripts:

Reviewers of previous editions:
Gary Burbridge, *Grand Rapids Community College*
Carole A. Campbell, *California State University—Long Beach*
Al Cook, *Trinity Valley Community College*
David D. Friedrichs, *University of Scranton*
Michele Gigliotti, *Broward Community College*
Charles Hall, *Purdue University*
Rosa Haritos, *University of North Carolina at Chapel Hill*
Rachel Ivie, *South Plains College*
Cardell Jacobson, *Brigham Young University*
Joseph F. Jones, *Portland State University*
Victor M. Kogan, *Saint Martin's College*
Paul Magee, *North Lake College*
Marguerite Marin, *Gonzaga University*
John Mitrano, *Central Connecticut State University*
Sharon Erickson Nepstad, *University of Colorado—Boulder*
Richard P. Rettig, *University of Central Oklahoma*
Edwin Rosenberg, *Appalachian State University*
K. S. Thompson, *Northern Michigan University*
Richard T. Vick, *Idaho State University*

Reviewers of this edition:

Barbara L. Richardson, *Eastern Michigan University*
Dennis L. Peck, *The University of Alabama*
Kevin R. Ousley, *East Carolina University*

Preface   **xxi**

Rosalind Gottfried, *San Joaquin Delta College*
Cheryl Childers, *Washburn University*

Finally, my heartfelt best wishes to both instructors and students. May this text prove useful, and may it provide understanding and insight into the major problems facing our country, many of which have global ramifications.

May our children live in a better world!

Jim Henslin
Professor Emeritus
Department of Sociology
Southern Illinois University
Edwardsville, Illinois 62026

henslin@aol.com

TO THE INSTRUCTOR

A wide variety of supplements to aid you in using this text is available from Prentice Hall. These supplements include:

- An **instructor's resource** and testing manual that includes chapter outlines, objectives, discussion questions and over 1500 test questions;
- A **computerized version of the test questions,** available in both Windows and Macintosh formats;
- **ABC News videos** on topics discussed in this text;
- A student study guide that includes chapter reviews and practice tests;
- A **Companion Website**™ with study questions, chapter outlines, and links to related topics on the internet;
- A *New York Times* **student newspaper** supplement highlighting current issues;
- A **searchable electronic database** that resides on Prentice Hall's *Research Navigator*™ website;
- Additional instructor materials, including **PowerPoint slides,** reside on Prentice Hall's *Sociology Central* website.

Please see your local Prentice Hall representative or visit Prentice Hall's online catalog to learn more about these supplements.

How Sociologists View Social Problems

The Abortion Dilemma

But you don't understand! It's not a baby!" Lisa shouted once again. She had reached the point of desperation. The argument with her grandmother seemed to have gone on forever.

With tears in her eyes, her grandmother said, "You don't know what you're doing, Lisa. You're taking the life of an innocent baby!"

"No! There's only one life involved here—mine!" replied Lisa. "It's my body and my life. I've worked too hard for that manager's job to let this pregnancy ruin everything."

"But Lisa, you have a new responsibility—to the baby."

"Don't judge my life by your standards. You never wanted a career. All you ever wanted was to raise a family."

"That's not the point," her grandmother pressed. "You're carrying a baby, and now you want to kill it."

"How can you talk like that? This is just a medical procedure, like when you had your gallstones removed."

"I can't believe my own granddaughter is saying that butchering a baby is like having gallstones removed!"

Lisa and her grandmother looked at each other, knowing they were worlds apart. They both began to cry inside.

◆ The Sociological Imagination ◆

When people have problems, they usually see them in highly personal—and often, emotional—terms. Their perspective is limited primarily to their immediate situation, and they fail to see the broader context in which those problems arise. Because people seldom connect their personal lives with the larger social context, they, like Lisa and her grandmother, tend to blame themselves and one another for their troubles.

What the Sociological Imagination Is

The term **sociological imagination** refers to looking at people's behavior and attitudes in the context of the social forces and institutional arrangements that shape them. C. Wright Mills, the sociologist who developed this concept, emphasized that change in society exerts direct, profound influence on the people living in it. As with Lisa and her grandmother, when a society changes, people get caught on various sides of social issues. Less than three decades ago, legal abortions were unavailable in the United States, and almost everyone sharply disapproved of abortion. Changes in our laws, however, allowed doctors to perform abortions, and many people's attitudes changed.

Applying the Sociological Imagination

If we view **personal troubles,** the individual's experience of a social problem, through the lens of the sociological imagination, the larger forces that underlie those troubles become visible. Let's see how the sociological imagination (also called the **sociological perspective**) applies to Lisa and her grandmother. Lisa's values reflect recent developments in our society; they were not part of her grandmother's consciousness when she grew up. The women's movement has stressed that each woman has the right to make choices and exercise judgment about her own body. This view holds that a woman has the right to terminate her pregnancy. In the extreme, proponents of this view state that a woman's right in this area is absolute, that she can choose to have an abortion at any point in her pregnancy—without informing her husband if she is married or her parents if she is a minor.

The sociological perspective also sensitizes us to the social forces that shaped Lisa's grandmother's point of view. When she was growing up, not only were there

no legal abortion clinics—but also, abortion was considered so shameful that people did not even talk openly about it. Every woman was expected to become a mother, and almost all girls grew up with motherhood as their foremost goal. Like Lisa's grandmother, almost everyone agreed that abortion was murder; and women who sought abortions had to keep their crime a secret. Some rode to their destination blindfolded in a taxi and endured kitchen-table surgery that carried a high risk of postoperative infection.

Yet neither Lisa nor her grandmother sees this finely woven net that has swept them up and turned their lives upside down. Instead, the impact of social change hits them on a personal level—affecting what they think and feel and how they relate to one another.

More on How the Social Context Influences Our Attitudes and Behavior

In contrast, the sociological imagination invites us to look at our lives afresh in order to understand how the broader context affects us. The sociological perspective points to the social context that shapes our ideas and behaviors—from our gender, race, religion, social class, and even the era in which we grew up to the smaller *social locations* in which we find ourselves, such as our age and marital status.

Table 1-1 illustrates how social location applies to abortion. Note that age, race, marital status, and even the region of the country make a difference in whether or not a woman has an abortion. As you can see, girls under the age of 15 who get pregnant are the most likely to have an abortion, followed by other teenagers and women in their early 20's. As you can also see, African Americans are more likely to have an abortion than are whites, as are residents of the West and Northeast compared with midwesterners and southerners. The most striking difference, however—cutting across age, race/ethnicity, and geography—is marital status: Unmarried women are five times more likely than married women to obtain an abortion.

Suppose, then, that you were born into a white family in the Midwest, that you are a teenager, unmarried, and pregnant. Can you see how much less likely you would be to have an abortion than if you were an unmarried, pregnant, African-American teenager in the Northeast?

No one is a robot, of course. We all have our own minds, and we use them. But as Table 1-1 makes apparent, we tend to make up our minds along predictable, well-traveled social avenues.

In Sum

Sociologists stress the need to use the sociological imagination to understand social problems—to make visible how the times and our social locations influence our ideas, behaviors, and personal troubles. To use the sociological perspective is to see how our views of what is or is not a social problem, and of what action we think ought to be taken, are shaped by broad social and historical forces.

◆ What Is a Social Problem? ◆

THE ESSENTIAL ELEMENTS OF A SOCIAL PROBLEM

Objective Conditions and Subjective Concerns

Basically, a **social problem** is an aspect of society that people are concerned about and would like changed. Social problems begin with an **objective condition,** some aspect of society that can be measured or experienced. With abortion, this objective condition includes whether abortions are legal, who obtains them, and under what circumstances. The second key element of a social problem is **subjective concern,** the concern that a significant number of people (or a number of significant people) have about the condition. Subjective concern about abortion includes some people's distress that abortion is not more freely available and that some women must give birth to

Table 1-1 Who Has Abortions?

	Number of Abortions	Percent of All Abortions	Abortions per 1,000 Births
Age			
Under 15	11,000	1	496
15–19	254,000	19	345
20–24	420,000	32	306
25–29	313,000	23	225
30–34	189,000	14	175
35–39	109,000	8	207
40 and over	34,000	2	290
Race/Ethnicity[1]			
White	773,000	58	200
Black and other	555,000	42	405
Marital Status			
Married	253,000	19	87
Unmarried	1,074,000	81	459
Region			
Northeast	346,000	25	506
West	349,000	26	446
South	440,000	32	323
Midwest	229,000	17	287
Weeks of Gestation			
Less than 9	732,000	55	NA[2]
9–10	292,000	22	NA
11–12	146,000	11	NA
13 or more	157,000	12	NA
Number of Prior Abortions			
None	680,000	51	NA
1	376,000	28	NA
2 or more	271,000	20	NA

[1]The total number of abortions for race/ethnicity is higher than the total for other categories because Table 116 of the source used an earlier year.
[2]Not Applicable.

Source: Statistical Abstract 1998:Tables 116, 125, 126, except for abortion ratio by region, which is from the 1994 edition. Updates from Statistical Abstract 2001. (2002 publish date) Table 93.

unwanted children. It also includes other people's distress that any woman would terminate the life of her unborn child. To see how subjective concerns about abortion differ in another part of the world, see the Global Glimpse box on the next page.

Social Problems Are Dynamic

As society changes, so do objective conditions and subjective concerns. This means that social problems change. For example, before the *Roe v. Wade* decision of 1973 by which the U.S. Supreme Court legalized abortion, this social problem had a different focus. It centered on the people who performed illegal abortions, the women who died from these underground abortions, and the women who wanted abortions but could not get them. As growing numbers of people became concerned about such matters, they worked to change the law. When they were successful and abortion became legal, the problem was transformed. At this point, some people became concerned about legal abortion. Convinced that abortion is murder, they

A GLOBAL GLIMPSE

Sex-Selection Abortion in India

As you know, science has provided physicians with prenatal tests that reveal the sex of the fetus. In amniocentesis, which can be done during the second trimester of pregnancy, a sonogram locates the fetus precisely. The physician inserts a needle through the abdomen and withdraws amniotic fluid from the uterus. In CVS (chorionic villi sampling), which can be done as early as the tenth week of pregnancy, the doctor uses a catheter to remove cells from the developing placenta. Now combine these powerful diagnostic tools with a society that is pro-son and anti-daughter.

"May you be the mother of a hundred sons" is the toast made to brides in India, where the birth of a son causes rejoicing and the birth of a daughter sadness.

Why? A son continues the family name, preserves wealth and property within the family, takes care of aged parents (there is no Social Security there), and performs the parents' funeral rites. Indeed, Hinduism even teaches that a sonless father cannot achieve salvation.

In contrast, a daughter is a liability. Men want to marry only virgins, and the parents of a daughter bear the burden of always having to protect her virginity. At marriage, they also must pay a dowry to her husband. A common saying in India reflects the female's low status: "To bring up a daughter is like watering a neighbor's plant."

With these new diagnostic techniques, in some areas the abortion of girls has replaced female infanticide, which, though illegal, is still practiced. Some clinics have put up billboards that proclaim, "Invest Rs.500 now, save Rs.50,000 later," meaning that by paying Rs.500 (500 Indian rupees) now to abort a female, a family can save a dowry of 50,000 rupees in years to come.

Some mothers-to-be resist, of course. To overcome their reluctance, nurses in one clinic pull out the fetuses of twin girls that they keep under the counter. The thought of double vigilance and two dowries is usually sufficient.

Then an accident happened. In one clinic, a *male* fetus was unintentionally aborted. This made national headlines, and protests spread across India. The Indian legislature then passed a law forbidding doctors to tell would-be parents the sex of their fetuses. Physicians who violate the law can be sent to prison and banned from their profession.

An eminent physician disagrees with the law. He says, "The need for a male child is an economic need in our society, and our feminists who are raising such hue and cry about female feticide should realize that it is better to get rid of an unwanted child than to make it suffer all its life."

What do you think?

Based on Kusum 1993; Holman 1994.

began a campaign to change the law. Each step they take is opposed by those who favor legal abortion. In short, social problems are dynamic.

SOCIAL PROBLEMS ARE RELATIVE

Social Problems Involve Competing Definitions

As you can see from the example of abortion, what people consider a social problem depends on their values. *A social problem for some may be a solution for others.* The *Roe v. Wade* decision of 1973, for example, was a solution for some but a disaster for others. Similarly, mugging is not a social problem for muggers. The billions of dollars spent on warfare are not a social problem for Boeing and other corporations that profit from arming the world. Nuclear power is not a social problem for the corporations that use it to generate electricity. From the Divided Society box on the next

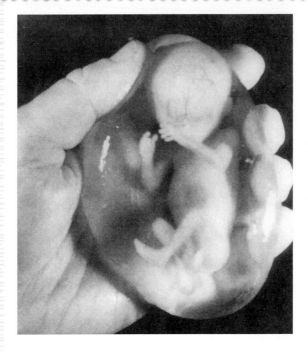

Pictured is a fetus of about eleven weeks gestation. Those on one side of the abortion controversy use terms such as "product of conception," while those on the other side call it a baby. How people define the status of the unborn is the essence of their position on abortion.

page and from Table 1-2, you can see that how people define abortion leads to contrasting views of this social problem.

In a dynamic world of contrasting definitions, whose definition of a social problem wins? The answer centers around **power,** the ability to get one's way despite obstacles. After abortion became legal in 1973, most observers assumed that the social problem was over—the opponents of abortion had lost, and they would quietly fade away. As you know, this assumption was naive. Feelings were so strong

Table 1-2	How Definitions of Abortion Affect People's Views				
	The Resulting Views				
Who Does the Defining?	**What Abortion Is**	**What Is Aborted**	**The Woman**	**The Act of Abortion**	**The One Who Performs the Abortion**
People Who Favor Abortion	A woman's right	Unwanted pregnancy	Independent individual	A service to women	Skilled technician
People Who Oppose Abortion	Murder	Baby	Mother	Killing a baby	Murderer
People Who Do Abortions	Part of my work	Fetus	Client	A medical procedure	Professional

Source: Modified from Roe 1989.

The Relativity of Social Problems

Whether people view something as a social problem depends on their view of what is involved. Thus, people who agree on many aspects of life can disagree sharply about a particular social problem. And because people are exposed to different ideas and information, over time their position on a social problem can change.

This relativity is illustrated in the case of abortion, whose central issue is how one defines the status of the unborn. Is the fetus a human being, as the antiabortionists believe, or only a "potential" human, as the proabortionists believe?

What do you think?

THE FETUS IS NOT A HUMAN BEING

This is the position of most people who believe that abortion is a woman's right. "The fetus is a potential person that looks increasingly human as it develops" (NARAL). If follows, then, that abortion is not killing but merely a medical procedure. It is the woman's right to have an abortion for whatever reason she desires—from financial pressures to health problems—as well as to help attain goals, whether those be to limit family size, to finish school, to win a promotion at work, or to fulfill other plans for the future. The state, therefore, should permit abortion on demand.

THE FETUS IS A HUMAN BEING

This is the position of most people who oppose abortion. It follows, then, that abortion is murder, a killing of unborn babies. To simply want an abortion cannot justify killing a baby. A woman has no right to abortion, for it is not just her body that is involved but also the life of another human—her own child. The exception is when another human life, the mother's, lies in the balance. The state, therefore, should not permit legalized murder, and abortion should be illegal.

---

that groups that had been hostile to one another for centuries, such as Roman Catholics and Baptists, began to work together to oppose abortion. Shocked at what they considered the killing of babies, they took to the streets and to the courts, fighting pitched battles over an issue that lies at the heart of social divisions in U.S. society.

In Sum　　Abortion makes it clear that social problems do not spring up full-blown. Rather, they develop in stages that sociologists call *the natural history of a social problem*. Let's continue with the example of abortion to see how this process occurs.

◆ The Natural History of Social Problems ◆

In an unprecedented move, Hawaii legalized abortion in 1970. Several states had liberalized their abortion laws but still kept abortion illegal except under special circumstances, such as when pregnancy endangered the mother's health. Hawaii's law, in contrast, defined abortion as a private, noncriminal act.

What made Hawaii receptive to such radical change? Before we look at the natural history of abortion, let's take a brief look at the Hawaiian situation (Steinhoff and Diamond 1977). First, more than three quarters of the population lived on the island of Oahu, where they had a tradition of personally knowing their politicians and regularly participating in political hearings. Second, two-income families were common, and half the women over age 16 worked. Finally, during an epidemic of German measles in 1964 and 1965, many Hawaiian obstetricians had aborted fetuses to prevent them from being born with deformities. This was a turning point for the physicians, and the rate of abortion never fell back to its pre-1964 level.

Now, let's trace how this issue developed in Hawaii, as well as in the United States as a whole. We shall see that social problems go through four stages.

THE FIRST STAGE: DEFINING THE PROBLEM, THE EMERGENCE OF LEADERS, AND BEGINNING TO ORGANIZE

For a social problem to come into being, people have to begin to view some objective condition as a problem. This involves a shift in outlook, a questioning of something that had been taken for granted. This can come about in a number of ways. For example, if values change, an old, established pattern won't look the same. This is what happened with abortion. The 1960s brought extensive, wrenching social change to the United States. Established values were challenged, and many new ones were adopted. The women's movement challenged many established ideas. As this movement became popular, more and more women felt that they should not have to become criminals to terminate a pregnancy. They began to believe that they had the right to legal abortions.

As people discussed their concerns, leaders emerged who helped to crystallize the issues. State Senator Vincent Yano, a Roman Catholic and the father of ten, argued that if abortion were a sin, it would be better to have no abortion law than to have one that allowed it under certain circumstances (Steinhoff and Diamond 1977). This reasoning allowed Yano to maintain his religious opposition to abortion while favoring the repeal of Hawaii's law against abortion.

Another leader emerged. Joan Hayes, a former Washington lobbyist, felt that liberalizing the laws against abortion would mean ducking what she saw as the major issue: the right of a woman to choose whether or not to have a baby. Hayes understood the use of power—and the value of arousing a concerned public. She invited leaders in medicine, business, labor, politics, religion, and the media to a citizens' seminar on abortion sponsored by the American Association of University Women.

THE SECOND STAGE: CRAFTING THE OFFICIAL RESPONSE

The stages of a social problem overlap. In this case, between 1967 and 1968, several bills had been introduced to soften the law against abortion. They did so by redefining abortion in certain ways. Thus, the stages of defining the social problem and officially responding to it were intertwined. The turning point came when Senator Yano announced that he would support the repeal of the abortion law. Other official responses soon followed as organizations, from the Chamber of Commerce to the Roman Catholic church, began to endorse or reject the repeal.

Public forums and legislative hearings were held, and the publicity they generated was the vital bridge between the public at large and the advocates of repeal. In just a few months, Hawaiians grew keenly aware of the abortion issue. Polls showed that most wanted to repeal the law against abortion, and in 1970 Hawaii did so.

THE THIRD STAGE: REACTING TO THE OFFICIAL RESPONSE

Official Response Engenders Controversy and Opposition

(A Note on Unsatisfactory Terms)

As sometimes happens, the official response to a social problem becomes defined as a social problem. This is what happened with abortion, especially after 1973, when the U.S. Supreme Court concurred with the Hawaiian legislation and struck down all state laws that prohibited abortion. Indignant about what they saw as murder, antiabortion groups advertised, picketed, and used political pressure to try to sway public opinion and turn legislative defeat into victory.

In this highly sensitive area of abortion, the terms used in discussing the issues often represent specific attitudes and positions and provoke strong emotional responses. Although they are not entirely satisfactory, and neither side prefers them, I shall use the term *antiabortion* to refer to those who oppose the legal right to abortion and *proabortion* to refer to those who favor it. These terms, intended to be neutral, are less value-laden than *prochoice* and *prolife*, which the two sides prefer. If I have succeeded in my intentions in this chapter, even if readers do not like this choice of terms, both those who favor the legal right to abortion and those who oppose it will feel that I have fairly presented their side.

Besides inspiring new opposition, official response also can change the definition of the social problem that is held by those who promoted the reform in the first place. In this case, proabortion groups noted that despite their Supreme Court victory, most counties did not offer abortions, and perhaps half a million women who wanted abortions could not obtain them (Forrest et al. 1978). Consequently, they began to promote abortion clinics to make abortion more readily accessible.

Figure 1-1 shows the success of these efforts. In 1973, the first year of legal abortion, 745,000 abortions were performed. This number quickly climbed to one million,

FIGURE 1-1
Abortions and Live Births
(Source: Statistical Abstract 1988: Tables 81, 103; 1994: Tables 104, 111; 1998: Tables 104, 115.) *Population Today,* 27, July/August 1999:6. 1997: *Vital Stats Report,* vol. 49(4) June 2001.

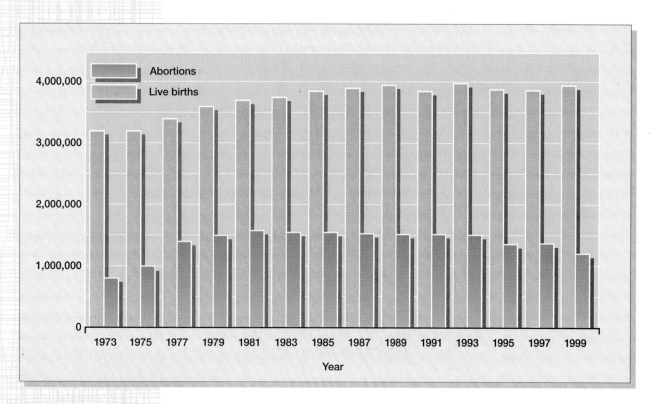

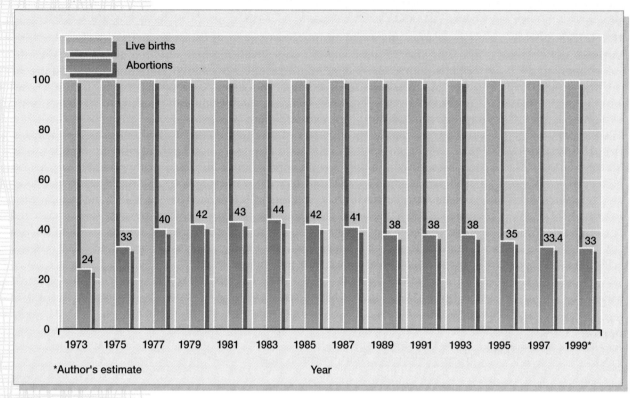

FIGURE 1-2

Number of Abortions per 100 Live Births

(*Source: Statistical Abstract* 1988: Tables 81, 103; 1994: Table 111; 1998: Tables 104, 115.) 1997: *National Vital Stats Report,* vol. 49(4) June 2001.

Alternative Strategies Pit Group Against Group

then to a million and a half, where it reached a plateau. From 1979 to 1994, the total ran between 1,500,000 and 1,600,000 each year, but beginning in 1995 the number dropped below 1,400,000. Figure 1-2 presents another overview of abortion. There you can see that the abortion ratio climbed sharply, plateaued for ten years, and then dropped. Today, for every 100 live births there are about 33 abortions.

THE FOURTH STAGE: DEVELOPING ALTERNATIVE STRATEGIES

The many abortions after the Supreme Court's ruling led to a pitched battle that still rages. Let's look at some of the alternative strategies developed by the pro- and anti-abortion groups.

Antiabortion groups have tried to persuade states to restrict the Supreme Court's ruling. They also have succeeded in eliminating federal funding of abortions for military personnel and their dependents, federal prisoners, and workers with the Peace Corps, and eliminating health insurance coverage of abortions for federal employees. Their major victory on the federal level took place in 1976, when opponents of abortion persuaded Congress to pass the Hyde Amendment, which prohibits Medicaid funding for abortions except to save a woman's life. When the Supreme Court upheld this amendment in 1980 (Lewis 1988), the number of abortions paid for by federal funds plummeted from 300,000 a year to just 17. Despite repeated attempts to change the Hyde Amendment, the antiabortion forces have succeeded in retaining it.

The antiabortion groups have also pursued other alternative strategies. One of their more effective ones is a national network of "crisis pregnancy centers." Women who call "pregnancy hot lines" (sometimes called life lines or birth lines) are offered

The nine men and women who serve for life on the U.S. Supreme Court determine the constitutionality of the laws passed by the states and the U.S. Congress. Because their interpretations of the U.S. Constitution are not objective (although they are supposed to be) but are, instead, biased by their political and personal views, their rulings on matters concerning abortion are uncertain. Consequently, when nominees of the president come before the U.S. senate for confirmation, their views on abortion become a matter of concern and controversy.

Moderates and Radicals in Social Problems

free pregnancy testing and are directed to counselors who encourage them to give birth. The counselors inform women about fetal development, talk to them about the social support and financial help available to them during pregnancy, and advise them about finding adoptive parents or obtaining financial support after the birth. Some activists also operate maternity homes and provide adoption services.

Neither side on this social problem is a single, organized group. Rather, this is a social movement, and it has swept up people from every background, some of whom are moderate, others radical, and most somewhere in-between.

The moderates choose moderate alternative strategies. They run newspaper ads and write their representatives. Those in-between picket abortion clinics. Some have taken their cue from the civil rights movement of the 1950s and practice passive resistance; lying immobile in front of abortion clinics, they allow the police to carry them to jail. In the late 1980s, antiabortion groups began to practice massive nonviolent civil disobedience, and thousands of demonstrators were arrested. This social movement is so large and active that more abortion protesters have been arrested than the number of people arrested in the entire civil rights movement (Allen 1988; Lacayo 1991; Kirkpatrick 1992).

Radical activists, however, lean toward radical methods. They have thrown blood on abortion clinics, pulled the plug on abortion machines, jammed locks with superglue, set off stink bombs, and telephoned women at night with recordings of babies screaming. Radical activists also have burned and bombed abortion clinics. In the town in which I taught, Edwardsville, Illinois, a group kidnapped a physician and threatened his life if he did not shut down his abortion clinics. Radical activists have shot and killed three abortion doctors (Yardley 1998), acts that have been condemned by both proabortionists and antiabortionists alike.

Proabortion groups, too, have developed alternative strategies. Their counterattack has taken three primary forms: campaigning for proabortion politicians, lobbying lawmakers to vote against restrictive legislation, and seeking broad-based support by publicizing their position. They have stressed a dual message: Abortion is a

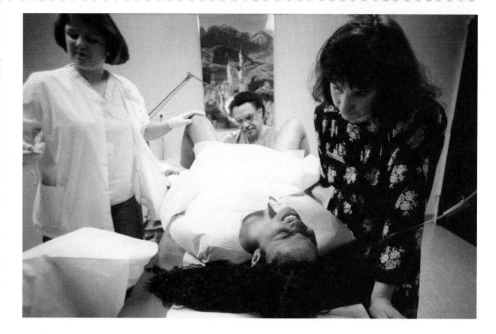

Abortion is a difficult experience for any woman to go through. She must often make excruciating decisions about her life situation, relationships, and future. The pain evident on this woman's face may be due as much to the difficulties underlying her decision as to the physical pain she is experiencing.

private decision in which government should not be involved, and "without the right to choose abortion, any other guarantees of liberty have little meaning for women" (Michelman 1988). Women who had abortions when it was back-alley business have spoken nationwide to alert the public to what it would be like if the right to abortion were taken away: rich women flying to countries where abortion is legal, poor women victimized by unqualified underground abortionists, and thousands of women dying from illegal abortions (Krieger 1985).

Mutual Accusations

Each side paints the other as grotesque, uncaring, and evil. Proabortionists accuse antiabortionists of being concerned about fetuses but not about the women who bear them, and then point to the killing of physicians as evidence of hypocrisy. Antiabortionists accuse proabortionists of supporting the murder of children and of suppressing information about the health risks of abortion.

The U.S. Supreme Court remains the final arbiter of abortion, for short of a constitutional amendment, no matter what laws the states, or even Congress, should pass, the Supreme Court decides whether those laws are constitutional. Consequently, each side has tried to influence how the Senate votes on Supreme Court nominees. Under the Reagan and Bush presidencies, antiabortionists weakened Supreme Court support for *Roe v. Wade*. The Clinton presidency, in turn, supported nominees who favor the proabortion position. We can expect this stacking of the Court to continue.

The 1989 Webster Decision

Three Supreme Court decisions since the 1973 *Roe v. Wade* are especially significant. The first is *Webster v. Reproductive Services*. In 1989, by a 5-to-4 vote, the Supreme Court ruled that

1. States have no obligation to finance abortion: They can prohibit the use of public funds for abortions and abortion counseling, and they can ban abortions at public hospitals.

2. States have a compelling interest to protect fetal life: Before doctors can abort a fetus that is 20 weeks or over, they must perform tests to determine its viability (capacity to live outside the uterus).

Chapter 1 How Sociologists View Social Problems

**The 1992 Casey v.
Planned Parenthood
Decision**

**The 1993 Freedom
of Access to Clinic
Entrances Act**

No Middle Ground

**Cutting Through
Emotion**

**Five Contributions
of Sociology to
Understanding
Social Problems**

The second significant decision is *Casey v. Planned Parenthood*. In 1992, by a vote of 6 to 3, the Supreme Court upheld a Pennsylvania law requiring that a woman under age 18 obtain the consent of at least one parent, that a 24-hour waiting period between confirming a pregnancy and having an abortion be enforced, and that the woman be given materials describing the fetus, as well as a list of agencies offering adoption services and alternatives to abortion. By a 5-to-4 vote, however, the Court also ruled that a wife has no obligation to inform her husband of her intention to have an abortion. *Casey* allows states to pass laws that restrict abortion—unless such laws impose an "undue burden" on a woman's ability to have an abortion.

A third significant legal decision occurred in 1993, this time in favor of the proabortion forces. In that year, they won a major victory when Congress passed the Freedom of Access to Clinic Entrances Act. This law impedes demonstrations, for it requires picketers and other demonstrators to remain 300 feet away from the entrance to abortion clinics or to face three years in prison. The Supreme Court has ruled that this Act does not violate freedom of speech.

Neither the proabortionists nor the antiabortionists can be satisfied, as there is no middle ground. Both sides consider their alternative strategies as only nibbling at the problem. Each wants total victory. The antiabortion groups advocate a constitutional amendment that would define human life as beginning at conception and abortion as murder. In almost a mirror image, the proabortion groups want Congress to pass a Freedom of Choice Act that would remove all state restrictions on abortion.

The activists in this ongoing social problem illustrate the sociological principle that interest groups develop alternative strategies and line up on opposing sides of a social problem. In this case, the final results are still unclear, and probably never will be final. On both sides are highly motivated people. Each side considers the other unreasonable. Each is rationally, and emotionally, dedicated to its view of morality: One talks about killing babies, the other about forcing women to bear unwanted children, even those conceived from incest and rape. With no middle ground to bridge the chasm, there is no end in sight to this determined struggle.

✦ The Role of Sociology in Social Problems ✦

SOCIOLOGY AS A TOOL FOR BREAKING
THROUGH EMOTIONS AND DEFENSES

Sociology, the study of social behavior, helps us see past the passions that surround a social problem. Most people think of their world in psychological and moral terms. For example, Lisa, in the chapter's opening vignette, may think that her grandmother is narrow-minded, and her grandmother may wonder how Lisa acquired such casual morals. Psychological defenses and moral viewpoints are real, but they cannot explain social problems.

There are five ways by which sociology can penetrate such emotions and defenses to yield a better understanding of social problems. The first is to determine the extent of a social problem by *measuring its objective conditions*. For abortion, sociologists can gather information on the number of abortions performed in clinics and hospitals. They can also determine why women have or do not have abortions, how women adjust to their decision to abort or to bear a child, and how their husbands or boyfriends react.

Second, sociologists can *measure subjective concern;* that is, they can determine people's attitudes about social problems (Becker 1966). Such information is useful in

As described in the text, sociologists use a variety of methods in their research. The purpose, always, is to add to our knowledge. To understand abortion, it is just as important to study women who choose not to have an abortion as it is to study those who decide to have one. Studying both gives us insight into how they make their decisions. Which research method would you choose to study this woman?

evaluating potential policies. To establish sound public policy involves much more than measuring public opinion, of course, but accurate measurements can guide policy makers. An example of measuring subjective concern is Table 1-3, which shows Americans' attitudes about abortion. Note how attitudes change, especially based on age, education, income, and region of country.

Third, sociologists can *apply the sociological imagination;* that is, they can place social problems into their broad social context. For example, abortion is related to extensive changes in attitudes about sexuality and sex roles. Abortion is also related to profound differences of opinion about privacy, what human life is, when life begins and ends, the role of the medical profession in terminating life, the role of religious institutions in a pluralistic society, the concept of individual freedom versus responsibility to the group, ideas about desirable standards of living and parenting, and what is and is not moral (Lerner et al. 1990).

Fourth, sociologists can *identify different ways to intervene* in a social problem, *and,* fifth, they can *evaluate likely consequences of social policies* (Becker 1966). For example, sociologists can estimate how different social policies on abortion will affect the birth rate, population growth, and expenditures for welfare and education.

These five tasks are much more easily listed than performed. Although sociologists gather extensive information on social problems, making accurate predictions from those data is difficult. People often change their behaviors unexpectedly, which can throw off the best predictions of social scientists. Sociology, however, is especially useful for clarifying issues in social problems. Clarification, of course, requires facts, which leads to the question of how sociologists get dependable information. Can they simply depend on common sense?

Table 1-3   Attitudes Toward the Legality of Abortion (by demographic characteristics, United States, 2002)

Question: "Do you think abortions should be legal under any circumstances, legal only under certain circumstances, or illegal in all circumstances?"

	Always Legal	Legal Under Certain Circumstances	Never Legal
National	26%	54%	18%
Sex			
Male	23	58	17
Female	29	51	18
Race			
White	26	56	16
Nonwhite	26	50	23
Black	27	54	19
Age			
18 to 29 years	31	44	24
30 to 49 years	27	56	16
50 to 64 years	23	60	14
50 years and older	23	59	16
65 years and older	23	57	18
Education			
College post graduate	38	51	9
College graduate	35	49	15
Some college	27	56	16
High school graduate or less	19	56	23
Income			
$75,000 and over	36	52	11
$50,000 to 74,999	30	54	14
$30,000 to 49,999	26	55	18
$20,000 to 29,999	19	60	20
Under $20,000	19	58	22
Community			
Urban area	30	52	16
Suburban area	28	53	17
Rural area	17	60	22
Region			
East	35	53	10
Midwest	21	56	21
South	19	56	22
West	33	51	16
Politics			
Republican	19	59	20
Democrat	29	58	13
Independent	31	48	19

Note: See Note, Table 2.114. The "no opinion" category has been omitted; therefore percents may not sum to 100. For a discussion of public opinion survey sampling procedures, see Appendix 4.

Source: Table constructed by SOURCEBOOK staff from data provided by The Gallup Organization, Inc. Reprinted by permission.

People have "gut feelings" about the world. Based on their experiences, they "just know" what is and is not true. **Common sense,** the ideas common to a society (or to some group within a society) that are used to make sense out of experience, include ideas about social problems. Everybody develops opinions about what causes a social problem, and what ought to be done about it.

Common Sense Is Not Enough

Common sense, though, is not enough, for it is based on impressions that may not be correct. Let's see how common sense holds up when it comes to abortion. Common-sense views about abortion include the ideas that abortion is a last resort, that women who get abortions do not know how to use contraceptives, and, certainly, that women who get abortions did not want to get pregnant.

Although these three common-sense ideas appear obvious, they are not necessarily true. For example, abortion is not always a last resort. In Russia, abortion is a major means of birth control, and the average Russian woman has six abortions during her lifetime (Yablonsky 1981; Eberstadt 1988). Abortion is so common in Russia that for every live birth there are two or three abortions (Feshbach 1981; Library of Congress 1999).

Sociological Research Probes Beneath the Surface

Nor is it that women who have abortions don't know how to use contraceptives. Sociologist Kristin Luker (1975), who studied an abortion clinic in California, found that many women did not use contraceptives, even though they knew how to use them and did not want to get pregnant. They avoided them, Luker discovered, to protect their self-concept. If they used contraceptives, they would think of themselves as "available" or promiscuous, but without them they could look at sex as something that "just happened." Other women ignored contraceptives because they interfered with intimacy, were too expensive, were disapproved of by their boyfriends, or caused adverse side effects. Luker's study shows that some women who have abortions take chances—and they get pregnant.

Sociologist Leon Dash (1990), who studied youthful pregnancy in Washington, D.C., found that the third common-sense idea is also not necessarily true. Some girls get pregnant deliberately. Some want children so that "I can have something to hold onto that I can call my own." Others are urged on by their boyfriends, who say that they want to "feel like a man." And, as Luker discovered, some women get pregnant to test the boyfriend's commitment. But then something happens, and the young women decide not to bear the child. In short, contrary to a middle-class perspective, many poor, young, unmarried women get pregnant because they *want* to.

Life takes many twists and turns, and is sometimes stranger than fiction. Shown here is Norma McCorvey, the "Jane Roe" of the landmark 1972 *Roe v. Wade* U.S. Supreme Court decision. Though she won the right to have an abortion, McCorvey is now pro-life and works with anti-abortion groups. This photo was taken at a rally in Dallas, Texas.

Principles underlying the sociological approach. Luker's and Dash's studies illustrate how common-sense ideas may not be correct, and why we must have sociological investigations to provide a deeper understanding of social problems. Sociology, in contrast, can provide the understanding we need to deal with social problems. This is because sociologists

1. *Do not base their conclusions on emotions or personal values,* which obscure our perspective and prevent us from seeing things objectively. Even if sociologists discover things that contradict their personal values, they are obligated ethically to report those findings.

2. *Use the sociological imagination.* To discover the underlying causes of social problems, sociologists interpret them from the framework of the larger picture. In contrast, common sense usually locates causes in individuals, rather than in larger social patterns.

3. *Use scientific methods* to provide objective, systematic investigations, rather than basing their findings on personal experience and opinion.

As you study social problems in this text, you will read about numerous findings that are based on sociological research. Let's take a look at how sociologists do their research.

METHODS FOR STUDYING SOCIAL PROBLEMS

How Do Sociologists Study Social Problems?

To investigate social problems, sociologists choose from several **methods** (ways of doing research). Which method they choose depends both on the questions they want to investigate and on what is practical. First they must determine what they want to find out about a social problem, for the method depends on the goals. For example, sociologists who want to find out how people form their ideas about abortion will use a different method from that used by sociologists who want to find out whether college-educated women have fewer abortions than do high-school dropouts. In this short review, we shall first distinguish how sociologists design their studies, then describe how they gather their information.

Designing a Study: Research Begins with a Problem to Be Solved

Research begins with a problem, something that you want to solve. Let's say that you want to learn why married women get abortions. The first question you need to ask is, Whom should I study? All married women? Only married women who are pregnant? Only women who are above or below a certain age? Should I compare them with single women? With divorced women?

Four Basic Research Designs:
1. Case Studies

Most studies fall into one of four common **research designs:** case studies, surveys, experiments, and field studies. Let's look at each.

The **case study** is intended to gain in-depth information. As the name implies, the researcher focuses on one *case*—an individual, an event, or even an organization such as an abortion clinic. Suppose that you want in-depth information about how women experience abortion, from making the decision to undergoing the procedure. You want to know what conflicts and emotions women experience as they wrestle with the decision, who they talk to about it, how they feel during the abortion, and how they adjust afterward. A case study could provide this type of detail, but it would not reveal whether one woman's experience is similar to those of other women who had abortions.

2. Surveys

The **survey** overcomes this limitation. The survey utilizes a **sample** of the group you want to study. Samples are intended to represent the entire group that is being

studied (your **population**). Professional surveys often use a **random sample,** one in which everyone in your group (or population) is supposed to have an equal chance of being included. Often, sociologists want to **generalize**—that is, to apply the findings to people who were not included in the sample. National surveys on attitudes toward abortion poll only about 1,500 people; yet, chosen correctly, this sample can accurately represent the opinions of 265,000,000 Americans.

3. Experiments

In **experiments,** people with certain characteristics (such as Latinas between ages 18 and 21 with two years of college) are divided into two groups. Half of them are exposed to some experience (these people are called the **experimental group**) to see how their reactions differ from those of the other half, who do not have the experience (the **control group**). How the experimental group responds is thought to be generalizable to people who share their characteristics.

Experiments are rare in the study of social problems, partly because ethics do not allow sociologists to create problems for people. For example, sociologists cannot randomly assign some pregnant women to give birth and others to obtain abortions in order to study their reactions. Sociologists, however, can use experiments in more limited ways. For example, if sociologists wanted to learn how information affects people's attitudes toward abortion, they could measure a group's attitudes, have a random half of that group listen to a woman tell about her abortion, and then measure the attitudes of both groups.

4. Field Studies

In **field studies** (or **participant observation**), sociologists enter the setting they want to learn about. (This is called "going into the field.") For example, Magda Denes (1976) wanted to know what an abortion hospital was like—for the women and the staff—so she obtained permission to be present and observe. The result was a moving book, *In Necessity and Sorrow.* Denes believes that women should be able to choose abortion, but in the abortion hospital she found sadness everywhere. She describes picking up fetuses from the trash barrel, their little arms broken, cut, and bleeding. A doctor tells her how the fetus stops moving about half an hour after he injects the saline solution, but the women rarely mention this change within them. A single woman talks about her affair with a married man who does not know that she is aborting their baby. No other research method could obtain information like this.

Because each research design has its strengths and weaknesses, sociologists often use more than one design. Luker and Denes, for example, each studied a limited number of women in one abortion clinic. Their studies could be followed up with surveys of women from many abortion clinics.

Four Techniques of Gathering Information

After choosing the research design, sociologists decide how to gather their information. Four basic methods are available: interviews, questionnaires, documents, and observations.

1. Interviews

Sociologists who use **interviews** ask people questions on the topics they want to explore. (The Thinking Critically box on the next page, about the guilt that women experience, is based on interviews.) There are two basic types of interviews. In a **structured interview,** the researcher asks everyone the same questions (for example, "What is your relationship to the man who made you pregnant?"). In an **unstructured interview,** the researcher lets people talk about their experiences in depth, but makes certain that everyone covers specific areas (contraceptive history, family relations, why abortion is desired, and so on).

2. Questionnaires

In the second method, **questionnaires,** people answer written questions. The questions can be either *closed-ended,* so that people must choose from a set of answers, or *open-ended,* allowing people to answer in their own words. A closed-ended

question might ask, "What is your relationship to the man who made you pregnant?" and list these choices: husband, boyfriend, casual acquaintance, other. An open-ended form of this question would not provide any specific choices. Each type has its advantages and disadvantages. The answers to closed-ended questions are easier to compare, but open-ended questions tap a richer world, often eliciting comments and even topics that the researcher cannot anticipate.

3. Documents

The use of **documents,** written sources or records, can be vital to the study of a social problem. Kristin Luker, for example, analyzed the records of 500 women who came to the abortion clinic that she studied. Diaries and letters can also reveal people's attitudes and provide insight into how they cope with troubles. Documents also help measure how a social problem has evolved.

4. Observation

The fourth method, **observation,** is just what the term implies: Sociologists observe what is occurring in a setting. They look and listen for the significant things that are taking place and record their observations, including conversations and statements that people make. When observation is *overt,* sociologists identify themselves as researchers; when it is *covert,* people in the setting are unaware that sociologists are studying them.

Sociologists often combine these methods. For example, Luker not only observed what was happening in the clinic, but she also interviewed women who were having abortions and examined the clinic's records on its patients.

Striving for Accuracy and Objectivity

Sociologists strive for objectivity. They do not want their data to be biased. For example, it is obvious that if they asked, "What is your opinion about killing babies by abortion?" the study would be biased in an antiabortion direction. No one, whether proabortion or antiabortion, favors killing babies. That sort of question would not constitute scientific research. It would be merely the playback of the researcher's own opinion about the issue. Nor can the researcher bias the answers the other way, such as by asking, "What is your opinion on forcing a woman to have a baby when she wants an abortion?" To be neutral, in a closed-ended form a sociologist might ask, "Do you favor or oppose abortion?" In an open-ended form, he or she might ask, "What is your opinion about abortion?" In either case, the researcher might specify the trimester being considered. The safeguard against prejudicial research—for sociologists, too, have opinions about social problems—is the publication of research results, including details on the method used. Other sociologists examine these publications, and are quick to point out any flaws.

SHOULD SOCIOLOGISTS TAKE SIDES?

Sociology Cannot Decide Moral Issues

These research designs and methods allow us to gather objective information, but they do not reveal what attitude or social policy is "correct." Abortion, for example, is interwoven with thorny philosophical and religious issues of morality, freedom, responsibility, life, death, and ultimate existence. Sociologists can study people's ideas about these topics, but the ultimate meaning that may underlie such issues cannot be determined by science.

What, Then, Should Be the Role of Sociologists?

To take a position on a social problem is to take sides—and because sociology is not equipped to make judgments about values and morality, it cannot tell us what side to take. Even so, the question of taking sides on social problems is hotly debated among sociologists, for, like other thoughtful people, sociologists have their own concerns and ideas about social problems.

The issue is clear-cut. Should sociologists, because they are scientists, forget their concerns and strive to remain detached and value-free? If so, they would merely report the facts, and not take sides on the social issues that affect our society. Or should they use their professional authority to promote the side of an issue that they see as right? For example, should they try to help the "oppressed," the "down and out," the poor, and others on the receiving end of social problems?

The Arguments in the Debate Over Neutrality versus Commitment

Those who support neutrality feel that sociologists enjoy no superior vantage point from which to make moral judgments. They do have knowledge and skills to offer, but not morality. In their study of social problems, sociologists should indicate the potential consequences of different social policies, but not promote a policy or solution as correct. To do so is to hide a moral position under the guise of sociology.

Those who defend commitment, in contrast, stress that sociologists are in a strategic position to relate the surface manifestations of a social problem (such as poverty) to deeper social causes (such as the control of a country's resources by the wealthy and powerful). Sociologists should do their studies—and side with those who are being hurt and exploited. The more extreme add that sociologists also have the moral obligation to make the oppressed aware of their condition, and to organize them to do battle against those who oppress them. If sociology is not useful for helping to reform society, they ask, of what value is it?

Besides this vital and unanswered issue, there is yet another question about the role of sociologists in the study of social problems. We turn to it now.

SHOULD SOCIOLOGISTS DEFINE SOCIAL PROBLEMS?

Agreement Can Camouflage the Issue

What if a sociologist is concerned about a problem that most people ignore? According to our definition (pages 3–5), this would not be a social problem, because a social problem requires not only an objective condition (the "facts") but also subjective concern (people's desire to change those conditions). Some sociologists, however, argue that sociologists are in a better position than most people to spot the serious problems in society and that they should bring them to the public's attention (Merton and Nisbet 1976; Young 1985). For example, when sociologist Donald Cressey (1967) served on the National Task Force on Organized Crime, he urged the task force to arouse public concern.

Few who study organized crime would fault Cressey. After all, organized crime can harm our society. Because most of us probably agree with Cressey on this issue, we may fail to recognize the controversy it entails.

Uncovering the Issue

To make this hidden value evident, consider controversial matters. What if a sociologist were convinced that we should require abortion for all unmarried pregnant teenagers? Arguments can be made for and against this position, but should sociology promote such a point of view? Or consider even more extreme cases. What if a sociologist were convinced that we should permit child pornography? Or that we should euthanize the physically and mentally handicapped, or everyone over the age of 80, or any other group? Would professional activity on behalf of these views be appropriate?

THE WORKING CONSENSUS

The Debate

This question of taking sides as *professionals* divided U.S. sociology during the Vietnam War. Some sociologists felt that the American Sociological Association should make public antiwar pronouncements, while others felt that such a position was out of order. Today, the issues have changed, but the broad cleavage among sociologists remains. Some say that sociologists should work toward changing society in order to help the less powerful; others are just as convinced that sociology's proper role is to investigate and report objectively. They say that if sociologists want to take sides on any issue, they should do so as *private citizens,* not as sociologists.

The Value of the Debate

This debate keeps sociologists sensitive to the boundaries between objectivity and partisanship. Although there is little room for middle ground, sociologists attempt to resolve this dilemma by separating evidence on social problems from their own opinions or personal positions. What they observe and measure, they attempt to report dispassionately and to analyze as accurately as possible. They try to be explicit when they move from neutral description to a value position.

Areas of Agreement

Despite their disagreements about taking sides on social problems, sociologists agree that they are in a unique position to study social problems and that they should produce thorough and objective studies. Sociologists do possess the tools to provide such studies, but they do not possess the expertise or moral superiority to serve as "social problem gurus." Sociological solutions must be exploratory, matching the best knowledge we possess about a social problem with the likely consequences of intervention. As the author of this book, it is my sincere hope that the coming chapters help you acquire a sociological imagination to allow you to work toward creative solutions for the pressing problems we face.

A Personal Note

◆Summary

1. Sociologists use what is called the *sociological imagination* (or perspective) to view the social problems that affect people's daily lives. This means that they look at how people's behavior and attitudes are shaped by their social location.

2. A *social problem* is some aspect of society that people are concerned about and would like changed. It consists of *objective conditions,* things that are measurable, and *subjective concerns,* the feelings and attitudes that people have

about those conditions. Social problems are relative—one group's solution may be another group's problem.

3. Social problems go through a *natural history* of four stages that often overlap: defining the problem, crafting an official response, reacting to the official response, and pursuing alternative strategies.

4. Sociologists are able to make five contributions to the study of social problems: to help determine the extent of a social problem; to clarify people's attitudes toward

social problems; to apply the sociological imagination to social problems; to identify potential social policies for dealing with social problems; and to evaluate likely consequences of those policies.

5. The sociological understanding of a social problem differs from a common-sense understanding because the sociological perspective is not based on emotions or personal values. Instead, sociologists examine how social problems affect people, view the causes of social problems as located in society rather than in individuals, and use scientific methods to gather information about social problems.

6. To study social problems, sociologists use four major *research designs: surveys, case studies, experiments,* and *field*

studies. Sociologists gather information in four basic ways: *interviews, questionnaires, documents,* and *observations.* These methods are often used in combination.

7. Because social problems can be viewed from so many vantage points, sociologists disagree on whether they should choose sides as professionals. Nor do sociologists agree on whether they should attempt to shape people's ideas of what their social problems really are. They do agree, however, that sociological studies must provide objective, accurate, and verifiable data.

◆ Key Terms

Case study   A type of research design that focuses on a single case. The case or subject of the study can be an individual, an event, or an organization, such as a church, hospital, or abortion clinic.

Common sense   The ideas common to a society or to some group within a society that are used to make sense out of human experience. Common-sense ideas are often narrow and based on emotions and personal values.

Control group   See *Experiment.*

Documents   Written sources or records used as a source of information.

Experiment   A research design that divides a group into an *experimental group* (those who are exposed to some experience) and a *control group* (those who are not so exposed); measurements are taken before and after to determine the effects of the experience.

Experimental group   See *Experiment.*

Field study   (or *Participant observation*) Making direct observations in a setting that one wishes to study.

Generalize   To apply to other groups the findings that were learned from one group of people.

Interview   A method of gathering information whereby the researcher asks questions. In a *structured* interview, specific questions are

asked, while in an *unstructured* interview, people are simply encouraged to talk about their experiences, with the researcher making certain that specific areas are covered.

Methods   (or Methodology) Ways of doing research.

Objective condition   An aspect of society that can be measured or experienced. See also *Subjective concern.*

Observation   A means of gathering information whereby the researcher directly observes what is occurring in a setting. In the *overt* form, people know they are being studied; in the *covert* form, they do not.

Participant observation   See *Field study.*

Personal trouble   An individual's own experience of a social problem.

Population   The group one wishes to study.

Power   The ability to get one's way despite obstacles.

Questionnaire   The use of written questions to gather information. The *closed-ended* questionnaire provides specific choices, while the *open-ended* questionnaire allows people to answer in their own words.

Random sample   A sample that gives everyone in the group being studied an equal chance of being included in the study.

Research design   Any of four major approaches sociologists use to

study social life. See also *Case study, Experiment, Field study,* and *Survey.*

Sample   A relatively small number of people intended to represent a larger group.

Social problem   An aspect of society that people are concerned about and would like changed.

Sociological imagination   A framework of thought that looks at the broad, social context of what happens to people. This perspective helps people transcend personal values and emotions in order to see the larger picture that affects their situation. Also called *Sociological perspective.*

Sociological perspective   See *Sociological imagination.*

Sociology   The overarching social science in which the emphasis is on the effects of groups on human behavior.

Structured interview   See *Interview.*

Subjective concern   The concern felt by a significant number of people (or a number of significant people) about some aspect of society. See also *Objective condition.*

Survey   A type of research design that involves the selection of a sample of respondents from a population. The sample is intended to represent the larger group from which it is selected.

Unstructured interview   See *Interview.*

Social Problems: Official journal of the Society for the Study of Social Problems, the organization for sociologists and other social scientists concerned about social problems. Available in most college libraries, the journal presents major research and theorizing on social problems.

Sociological Abstracts: A standard reference item, containing summaries of articles published in sociology journals.

Mother Jones: A magazine with radical and muckraking reporting that covers highly controversial aspects of social problems.

The Public Interest: A journal whose less sensational coverage balances the approach of *Mother Jones.*

◆ Critical Thinking Questions

1. Identify a social problem you have observed and apply the sociological imagination to it.
   - What makes this situation/condition a social problem? (Explain how it matches the definition of a social problem outlined in this chapter.)
   - What are the social values of the people involved in this social problem? (Be sure to look at *both* sides of the problem.)
   - What are the social forces that shaped the parties' points of view?
   - What conditions have changed that bring this problem to the surface?

2. Who do you think is winning the battle between the proabortion and antiabortion activists? Why? Use the laws and court decisions cited in your book to support your answer.

3. Identify a social problem you have observed. Which methods for studying this social problem do you think would be most appropriate? Why? Which method do you think you would personally enjoy as a researcher?

4. Do you think sociologists have a responsibility to take sides on a social problem they are involved in researching? Why or why not?

Interpreting Social Problems

Aging

*I*n 1928, Charles Hart, who was working on his Ph.D in anthropology, did fieldwork with the Tiwi, a preliterate people who live on an island off the northern coast of Australia. Because the Tiwi are uncomfortable around people who do not belong to a clan, they assigned Hart to the bird (Jabijabui) clan and said that a particular woman was his mother. Hart describes the woman as "toothless, almost blind, withered," and says she was "physically quite revolting and mentally rather senile." He then describes this remarkable event:

How seriously they took my presence in their kinship system is something I never will be sure about. However, toward the end of my time on the islands an incident occurred that surprised me because it suggested that some of them had been taking my presence in the kinship system much more seriously than I had thought. I was approached by a group of about eight or nine senior men all of whom I knew. They were all senior members of the Jabijabui clan and they had decided among themselves that the time had come to get rid of the decrepit old woman who had first called me son and whom I now called mother. As I knew, they said, it was Tiwi custom, when an old woman became too feeble to look after herself, to "cover her up." This could only be done by her sons and her brothers and all of them had to agree beforehand, since once it was done they did not want any dissension among the brothers or clansmen, as that might lead to a feud. My "mother" was now completely blind, she was constantly falling over logs or into fires, and they, her senior clansmen, were in agreement that she would be better out of the way. Did I agree? I already knew about "covering up." The Tiwi, like many other hunting and gathering peoples, sometimes got rid of their ancient and decrepit females. The method was to dig a hole in the ground in some lonely place, put the old woman in the hole and fill it in with earth until only her head was showing. Everybody went away for a day or two and then went back to the hole to discover to their surprise, that the old woman was dead, having been too feeble to raise her arms from the earth. Nobody had "killed" her; her death in Tiwi eyes was a natural one. She had been alive when her relatives last saw her. I had never seen it done, though I knew it was the custom, so I asked my brothers if it was necessary for me to attend the "covering up." They said no and they would do it, but only after they had my agreement. Of course I agreed, and a week or two later we heard in our camp that my "mother" was dead, and we all wailed and put on the trimmings of mourning (Hart 1970:154).

I was shocked when I first read Hart's account. Today I am dismayed that some in our society suggest that we devise a modern form of "covering up." Like the senior members of the Jabijabui clan, they agree that the time comes when those who have become "a burden" should "leave." Instead of digging a hole in the ground, they would have doctors open a small hole in a vein and pump in measured amounts of poisons—"humanely and with dignity," of course. They would give the act an appropriately dignified name such as "physician-assisted suicide." From my point of view, it is fortunate that we don't live in that type of society—although we may soon. Once we initiate such a process (at first only for those who desire it), we find ourselves on a slippery slope that could lead to the practice of having committees define who has become a "burden" to society. In the hands of some, this could lead to genocide.

The Frail Aged: A Universal Problem

Apart from the morality of Hart's agreeing that the old woman should be "covered up"—and he seems more concerned about not having to watch his "mother's" death than he is about agreeing to it—what is of interest is that every society must deal with the problem of people who grow old and frail. You may have noted that the Tiwi "cover up" only old women. It is common throughout the world for females to be discriminated against—in some places, even in death. This topic is so significant that we shall spend an entire chapter (9) on gender discrimination. For now, let's consider how theories help us to understand social life.

◆ Sociological Theories and Social Problems ◆

What Is a Theory?

To interpret social problems, sociologists use theories. A **theory** explains how two or more concepts are related, such as age and suicide, or age and attitudes of self-worth. The way a theory explains how age and suicide are related, for example, gives us a framework for organizing facts about the suicide of the elderly. A theory, then, is a way of interpreting reality.

The Theories That Sociologists Use

In this chapter, we shall look at the three main theories that sociologists use—symbolic interactionism, functionalism, and conflict theory. These theories are summarized in Table 2-1. Because each theory focuses on only a "slice" of a social problem, each provides a different perspective on the problem. As you study these theories, keep in mind that each theory is like a spotlight shining onto a dark area, illuminating only a particular part of the landscape. Taken together, these theories throw much more light on problems that we want to understand.

Table 2-1　A Summary of the Theories

	Symbolic Interactionism	Functionalism	Conflict Theory
What is society?	People's patterns of behavior; always in flux	Groups within the same social system whose parts work together to benefit the whole	Groups within the same social system competing with one another
What are the key terms?	Symbols Interaction Communication Meanings Definitions	Structure Function System Equilibrium Goals	Competition Conflict Special Interests Power Exploitation
What is a social problem?	Whatever a group decides is a social problem is a social problem for that group	The failure of some part to fulfill its function, thereby interfering with the smooth functioning of the system	The natural and inevitable outcome as interest groups compete for scarce or limited resources
How does something become a social problem?	One set of definitions becomes accepted; competing views are rejected	Some part of the system fails, usually because of rapid social change	Authority and power used by the powerful to exploit the less powerful

✦ Symbolic Interactionism and Social Problems ✦

Images and Meanings of Old Age

Biologically, old age creeps up on us all. Sociologically, however, it comes suddenly—at retirement, with the first Social Security check, or upon admittance to an old-age home. Our images of old age are largely unpleasant. We envision old and sick, old and crabby, old and dependent, old and useless. Take your pick. None is pleasant.

Symbols Change: How the Meaning of Old Age Changed in the U.S.

Yet there was a time when to Americans "old" suggested kindliness, wisdom, generosity, even graciousness and beauty. How did old age come to have such negative meanings in our society? To find out, Andrew Achenbaum (1978) traced the history of old age in the United States. He found that in the early 1800s old people were valued. At that time, few Americans reached an advanced age, so people admired those who did. They also considered the elderly to be guardians of virtue who possessed valuable knowledge about life. To quit working simply because of age was considered foolish, and the elderly, being more skilled at their jobs, were respected by younger workers.

The rise of modern industry in the late 1800s turned the situation on its head. Improved sanitation and medical care meant that more people reached old age, so being elderly was no longer a distinction. New machinery and mass production techniques changed people's ideas about the uniqueness of the elderly's knowledge and experience: It didn't take long to learn how to run the new machines, so the old workers were no more knowledgeable or productive than the young. Often the elderly resisted change, clinging to the old ways. As the social value of the elderly declined, the meaning of old age also changed. It began to suggest uselessness rather than usefulness, foolishness rather than wisdom, and it went from being an asset to being a liability.

Symbolic Interactionism Defined

Old age, then, means different things to different people—which brings us to the essence of the symbolic interactionist perspective on social life. We all see the world through **symbols,** things to which we attach meaning and that we then use to communicate with one another. **Symbolic interactionism** is the sociological theory that examines the symbols people use to communicate with one another.

Today, when we first see a person advanced in years, we tend to classify him or her as an "old person." We then see the characteristics that our culture has assigned to this symbol—wrinkled, unstylish, over the hill. Because people internalize the symbols that dominate their culture, many elderly also see themselves in such terms. In contrast, someone from a culture in which old age symbolizes wisdom or power or privilege tends to perceive an old person in a different light—and so does the old person.

Symbols Affect Perception

In short, symbolic interactionists stress that symbols, such as the terms we use to classify people, give us our view of the world. We use the symbols that our culture provides to communicate with one another, and we tend to perceive both ourselves and others according to these symbols. The images on television, the printed and spoken word, our body language, our gestures, our tone of voice, our clothing, even our hairstyles—all are symbols by which we communicate ideas.

Social Problems from a Symbolic Interactionist Perspective

As we saw in the case of the elderly, symbols change as society changes. Because the term *social problem* is also a symbol, the things we consider social problems also change. *From the perspective of symbolic interactionism, then, social problems are what people in a society define as social problems.* What we now take for granted, we may later see as a problem; what we now see as a problem, we may later take for granted.

How Problems Change: From Personal to Social Problem

Old age also provides an excellent example of how social problems change. Earlier in our society, when many people died young, some people survived the odds and reached advanced age. If they had problems because of their age, that was for them or their family to handle. It was no one else's responsibility. Old age was a *personal* problem, not a *social* problem. Now that the numbers of elderly have grown, we are more likely to perceive of them as a group. We tend to lump them together with others who have similar characteristics and needs, and we consider social action (laws and policies) to be appropriate for solving their problems. In short, *what was once a personal problem has become a social problem.*

In Sum

When they look at social problems, then, symbolic interactionists stress the changing definitions that underlie them. To understand any social problem, we must search for the underlying definitions, or symbols, by which people view their social worlds.

THE DEVELOPMENT OF SYMBOLIC INTERACTIONISM

Symbols Are Essential for Social Life

Symbolic interactionism began with the pioneering psychologist William James (1842–1910), who analyzed how people use symbols to describe their experiences (Turner 1978). Symbols are essential for our lives, because they allow us to think about other people and objects even when they are not present. We also symbolize our own self (that is, we think about our self in a certain way, such as young, attractive, and personable). How we symbolize our self affects our behavior. For example, as we saw in Chapter 1, some women risk unwanted pregnancy because to use contraceptives would conflict with their self-image.

The Looking-Glass Self

To such insights, Charles Horton Cooley (1864–1929) added that by interacting with others, *people learn to see themselves as they think others see them.* He summarized this point in the following couplet:

> Each to each a looking-glass
> Reflects the other that doth pass.

Cooley argued that our interactions with others create a **looking-glass self.** By this he meant that our self has three elements: (1) how we think we appear to others; (2) how we think others feel about this image of us; and (3) how we feel about this reflected image. According to Cooley, our self-esteem depends on this looking-glass self. In a society that reflects a negative image to its old people, the elderly tend to resign themselves to the low esteem they are accorded and to think of themselves negatively.

Taking the Role of the Other

George Herbert Mead (1863–1931) observed that symbols are the foundation of our self-concept, and that without symbols there would be no social life as we know it. Mead concluded that our self-concept evolves during childhood as we learn to **take the role of the other.** That is, as we become able to put ourselves in someone else's shoes, we learn to empathize with how that person feels and thinks and to anticipate how he or she will act. The next stage in acquiring a self is learning to take the role of people in general, which Mead called the **generalized other.**

The Generalized Other

To illustrate these terms, consider a baseball game, one of Mead's favorite examples. Suppose that you are at bat, and the bases are loaded. From playing baseball, you understand not only how the pitcher feels as he or she winds up at this critical moment (taking the role of the other), but also how others in general—your teammates, the opposing team, and the fans will feel if you strike out or get a hit (the generalized other).

As symbolic interactionists stress, our age does not contain built-in meanings. Whatever meanings a particular age has depends on culture. Consequently, the meanings of being old vary from one society to another (and, within large societies such as the United States, even from one group to another). Shown here is an elderly man in the African country of Burkina Faso. In his tribe, the elderly remain incorporated in their extended families and occupy positions of respect.

**Symbols Are
Social Creations**

Each of us must make sense out of life, and the symbols that our culture provides are the key for how we fit things together. Consider the onset of "old age." Our cultural symbols are so significant that decisions about when old age begins are more rooted in social experiences than in biology. As symbolic interactionists emphasize, there is nothing about turning 65, or any other age, that automatically makes someone "old" and disqualifies that person from certain activities. This arbitrary benchmark can be traced to Otto van Bismarck (1815–1898), the architect of the German empire. In order to weaken the appeal of socialism in Germany, Bismarck pioneered the idea of social security. He arbitrarily chose 65 as the mandatory retirement age, partly to force some of his generals out of power. Bismarck's decision, rooted in a nineteenth-century political situation, continues to affect our twenty-first-century perception of age.

**The Social
Construction
of Reality**

Symbolic interactionists stress that we do not automatically or unthinkingly label our experiences. Rather, we all want to make sense of what happens to us in life, so we reflect on those events. As we choose from among the many symbols available to us, we decide on what meaning to give our experiences. This process of making sense of life is called the **social construction of reality.**

**Constructing the
Meaning of Suicide**

To help make this idea clearer, let's look at suicide. After someone commits suicide, the surviving family members and friends wrestle with why it happened. To find the answer, they ask such questions as, "Am I to blame for not picking up on hints of suicide?" "Should I feel guilty?" "What could I have done differently?" As the survivors are developing answers to such questions, they are socially constructing their reality; that is, they are trying to bring order to their experience—and as they do so they use the symbols their culture provides.

In one of the suicides that I studied, a middle-aged woman tried to figure out why her elderly father had taken his life (Henslin 1970). After struggling with this question, she decided that he wanted to be with his wife, who had died about six months earlier. Similarly, a husband decided that his wife committed suicide because of her love for him, to spare him the burden of hospital bills that her terminal illness would have entailed.

In Sum

Although our situations are different, we, too, socially construct reality. In fact, this is an ordinary part of everyday life. We try to make sense out of our experiences—whether that means figuring out why we received an A or an F in this class, why we got promoted—or fired—at work, or even why we like or dislike some television program. In short, reality does not come with built-in meanings, and we all use the symbols provided by our culture to make sense out of life.

APPLYING SYMBOLIC INTERACTIONISM

Social Problems Depend on Definitions

The idea discussed in Chapter 1, that an objective condition of society may be considered a social problem by some groups but not by others, embodies the symbolic interactionist perspective. Social problems do not exist like stones, independent of whoever observes them. Rather, from among all the objective conditions in society, people pick some out and define them as problems. As we have seen, the aged do not automatically constitute a social problem. It depends on how they are viewed. The aged can be admired and respected—or regarded as worthless.

And, as we discussed, meanings change over time, and thus what people define as social problems also changes. Just as the meaning of being old once made a major shift, so it could again. If the elderly were to grow wealthier and more powerful, for example, then more positive features of social life would be associated with old age, and the elderly would receive admiration and respect. They would no longer be considered a social problem.

Effects of Labels on Perception and Behavior

Symbolic interactionists stress the significance of **labeling**—stereotyping or putting a tag on someone or something and acting accordingly. For example, the label "old age" is sometimes used to explain certain health problems. Medical professionals may write off an elderly man's mental or physical problems as being due to his age (perhaps using the label "senility") and thus feel comfortable in not treating him. They may think, "What else can you expect with such an old man?" In many cases, medical treatment could alleviate the problems that are written off as "that's-the-way-people-are-when-they-get-old." For example, using the labels "malnutrition" and "Alzheimer's disease" (a chemical disorder of the brain) to account for someone's memory loss and confusion implies the need to search for physiological causes and treatment. In contrast, the labels "old" and "senile" do not imply such a search. Labels, then, affect how we perceive and react to problems.

SYMBOLIC INTERACTIONISM
AND SOCIAL PROBLEMS: A SUMMARY

In Sum

Symbolic interactionists stress that social problems are symbols; that is, they do not exist independent of the people who identify and label them, and who use them to define their worlds. Social problems are socially constructed as people determine whether to consider some objective condition a social problem. To understand social problems, then, we must focus on how objective conditions become socially constructed into social problems. Symbolic interactionists also stress that to understand any social problem, we must take into account what that problem means to those involved in it.

◆ Functionalism and Social Problems ◆

Functionalism Defined

The second major theory sociologists use to interpret social problems is **functionalism** (or **functional analysis**). Functionalists compare society to an organism or a machine that is composed of various parts. Each part fulfills a *function* that contributes to society's equilibrium. When working properly, each part contributes to the stability of the whole.

The Parts of Society Are Interrelated

Consider just two services that are designed to help the elderly. Of the vast sums spent on the elderly's health care, some goes into medical research. This, in turn, benefits people in other age groups. Similarly, it is not only the 34 million retired and disabled workers who collect Social Security that benefit from this program but also the 64,000 people who work for this federal agency (*Statistical Abstract* 2001: Tables 481, 527). Their families also gain, and their spending, in turn, benefits businesses across the nation. In other words, functionalists stress how one part of society contributes to other parts of society.

Social Problems from a Functionalist Perspective

Think of society as a single machine with many parts. If each part does its job, the machine runs smoothly. If one part fails, the whole machine can suffer. Functionalists call these failures **dysfunctions.** If a dysfunction creates instability or disequilibrium in society, it is a social problem. *From the functionalist perspective, then, a social problem is the failure of a part, which then interferes with society's smooth*

Functionalists analyze functions and dysfunctions of human actions. One of the latent (unintended) functions of some medical research has been to enable more people to live into old age. This, in turn, has both functions (positive consequences) and dysfunctions (negative consequences) for other parts of society.

functioning; that is, that same social condition impedes society's goals. For example, one component of the social problem of the aged is the red tape they confront when they try to get help. Red tape impedes the allocation of resources to the elderly. Another problem is "rip-off" nursing homes that siphon money from those who are most dependent among the elderly in order to put it in the pockets of unscrupulous operators.

THE DEVELOPMENT OF FUNCTIONALISM

Comte: Society Is Similar to a Biological Organism

Functionalism is rooted in the origins of sociology (Turner 1978). Auguste Comte (1798–1857), who is called the founder of sociology, developed his ideas during the unrest following the French Revolution. Comte concluded that society is like an organism: Just as a biological organism has tissues and organs that are interrelated and function together, so does society. For a society to function smoothly, its parts must be in balance.

Spencer: Structure and Function

Herbert Spencer (1820–1903) emphasized that the parts of society work together in a **structure.** As with each part of an organism, each part of society helps to meet the needs of the structure. Spencer called the part's contribution its **function.** Because the parts fit together in a larger system, a change in one part brings about changes in other parts.

Durkheim: Normal and Pathological States

Emile Durkheim (1858–1917) further developed the idea that a society has needs that must be met if it is going to function well. When its parts fulfill their functions, he said, society is in a "normal" state; if they do not, society is in an "abnormal" or "pathological" state. To understand society, functionalists say that we need to look at both **structure**—how the parts of a society are related to one another—and **function**—how each part contributes to society.

Merton: Functions and Dysfunctions

The final functionalist I shall mention is Robert Merton (b. 1910). Merton defined **functions** as the beneficial consequences of people's actions. Functions help a social system to maintain equilibrium, such as by helping it adapt to social change. Functions can be either manifest or latent. A **manifest function** is an action that is *intended* to help some part of the system. For example, Social Security is intended to make life better for the elderly. Improvement of life, then, is a *manifest* function of Social Security. Merton emphasized that our actions also have **latent functions;** these consequences help a system adjust, but are *unintended.* For example, the salaries paid to the tens of thousands of employees of the Social Security Administration help to stabilize our economy. Because this beneficial consequence of Social Security is not intended, however, it is a *latent* function.

Merton (1968) stressed that human actions also have **dysfunctions,** consequences that disrupt a system's equilibrium. A part that fails to meet its functions contributes to society's maladjustment and is part of a social problem.

Social Problems as Maladjustment of Parts

Because consequences of people's actions that disrupt a system's equilibrium usually are unintended, Merton called them **latent dysfunctions.** For example, the Social Security Administration has hundreds of rules dealing with incredible details. If the thousands of employees of this agency were to follow each procedure exactly, the resulting red tape would interfere with their ability to serve the aged. The rules are not intended to have this effect, however, so they are *latent* dysfunctions.

In Sum

Functionalist theory sensitizes us to think in terms of systems, to see whatever we are studying as part of a larger unit. When we examine one part, we look at its functions to see how it is related to other parts of the system. Let's apply these terms of functionalism to the social problem of aging.

APPLYING FUNCTIONALISM TO SOCIAL PROBLEMS

How a Change in One Part of Society Creates a Social Problem in Another Part

From the functionalist perspective, society is viewed as a social system composed of interconnected parts that function together. When those parts work well, each contributes to the equilibrium of society. When they do not, we have a social problem.

We already have seen how economic changes caused a shift in the meaning of old age. When machine production made many of the elderly's skills outdated, the elderly came to be seen as a dependent group that needed to be taken care of. From the functionalist perspective, a change in one part of society (in this case, production) changed an interrelated part of society (elderly workers), and a new social problem arose.

Disengagement Theory

Now let's see how "functions" applies to this social problem. Some functionalists stress that society needs to pass its positions of responsibility (jobs) from one group (the elderly) to another group (younger people). To entice the elderly to leave these positions, they are offered Social Security benefits and pensions. In return, the elderly transfer their jobs to younger people. In this view, called **disengagement theory,** the elderly get paid for not working and, in return, the younger people get their jobs (Cumming and Henry 1961; Cockerham 1991). Everyone benefits by the exchange—the self-regulating machine makes the proper adjustments.

Nursing Homes as a Functional Adjustment to Social Change

Nursing homes, too, have functioned to help society adjust to social change. Care of the elderly used to fall primarily upon women's shoulders. Because women worked at home and few people made it to old age, this was not a general problem. But then, just when more women were beginning to work outside the home, life expectancy was increasing and there were more frail elderly who needed care. Nursing homes were developed to replace the daughters and daughters-in-law who were unavailable to care for the increasing numbers of frail elderly. Again, the machine adjusted to change.

Latent Functions of Nursing Homes

As they analyze social problems, functionalists also look for *latent* functions. Researchers interviewed the adult children of the residents of a well-run middle-class nursing home. Forty-five percent of the children reported that their affection had been strained by the burden of caring for a parent who had physical or mental problems. After their parent entered the nursing home, the professional care relieved this burden. Care in the nursing home uncovered the love that had been obscured by duty. As one 57-year-old daughter reported: "My mother demanded rather than earned respect and love. We had a poor past relationship—a love/hate relationship. Now I can do for her because I want to. I can finally love her because I want to" (Smith and Bengston 1979:441). Because this function is unintended, it is a *latent* function.

Dysfunctions of Nursing Homes

Functionalists also study *dysfunctions*. Unlike the nursing home in this study, which was middle class, few nursing homes are pleasant places. They sometimes are called "houses of death" or "human junkyards." After being admitted to a nursing home, most elderly people decline physically and psychologically. A chief reason is dehumanized treatment: being segregated from the outside world, being denied privacy, and being subjected to rigid controls. Nursing home residents often are controlled chemically, through the use of psychotropic drugs such as Thorazine and Mellaril. These drugs keep elderly patients quiet, but reduce them to an empty shell of their former selves (Olson 1994). This particular dysfunction, elderly people being abandoned in abusive nursing homes, is concentrated among the poor elderly who have no close family and friends.

Research on nursing homes shows that abuse is not unusual. Sociologists Karl Pillemer and David Moore (1989) surveyed nursing homes in New Hampshire. Thirty-one percent of the staff reported that during the past year they had seen physical abuse—patients being pushed, grabbed, shoved, pinched, kicked, or slapped. Eighty-one percent said they had seen psychological abuse—patients being cursed, insulted, yelled at, or threatened. When asked if they themselves had ever abused patients, 10 percent admitted that they had physically abused them, and 40 percent admitted to psychological abuse. Pillemer and Moore found that the most abusive staff members were those who frequently thought about quitting their jobs and those who thought of patients as being childlike.

A GLOBAL GLIMPSE

The Coming Tidal Wave: Japan's Elderly

With one of the world's lowest birth rates, Japan's population is aging faster than that of any other nation. In 1950, only 66 Japanese turned 100. Now 1,700 a year do. Sixteen percent of all Japanese are age 65 or older, and by the year 2020, it is expected that one of every four Japanese will be 65 or over.

Percent of Japan's Population Age 65 and Older

1950	1970	1990	2000	2020
4	7	12	16	24

Japanese policymakers are concerned about what these numbers mean for health care, especially since about half of the Japanese elderly will be 75 and over. Shortly, more than 1 million elderly Japanese will be bedridden, and another million will be senile. Japan's medical bill is expected to be six times higher than it is now. How will Japan be able to meet the health needs of this coming tidal wave of elderly?

This question must be placed within the context of Japanese culture, specifically, the obligations of one generation to another. The Japanese believe that because parents took care of children, children are obligated to care for parents. Unlike in the United States, *most* aged Japanese live with their adult children. As the proportion of elderly mushrooms, will the Japanese family be able to carry on its traditional caregiving and protective roles?

When Japanese leaders studied Europe's welfare system, they did not like what they saw: a lower work ethic, high taxes, reduced savings—all leading to less ability to compete in global markets. The Japanese then worked out their own plan. To reduce inequality among the aged, the government has begun to unify the country's pension systems and has increased spending for social security. To accommodate the elderly who have no families and those who are the sickest, the government is building nursing homes. To improve the quality of life for all elderly, the government is going to build 10,000 day service centers, provide transportation to physiotherapy centers, and offer testing for the early detection of cancer and heart disease. The government also has created a new position called "home helper." After passing a government examination, 100,000 specialists will help the elderly at home.

These government-funded services and facilities are not designed to replace the family's care but, rather, to supplement the family's efforts at caring for the elderly, thus strengthening the family.

Gnawing at these ambitious plans, however, is economic reality. Japan has moved into a depression that they can't budge. With growing federal deficits and persistent unemployment, some of these plans will have to be shelved. The tidal wave of elderly, nevertheless is on its way, and will arrive on schedule—regardless of changing economics.

Based on Freed 1994; Nishio 1994; Otten 1995.

The publicity given to problem nursing homes by magazines and television has made the public painfully aware of such dysfunctions. Consequently, the decision to place an elderly family member in a nursing home can be agonizing. Even though the individual may be too sick to be cared for at home, placing an aged parent in a nursing home is often seen as a callous denial of love and duty. One result is that of all Americans over 65, only 5 percent live in nursing homes (*Statistical Abstract* 2001:Tables 12, 175). Most nursing home residents are *not* typical of older people: They are likely to be ill, very old, or to have no family. To see how two major units of society, the government and the family, can work together to provide high-quality care for the elderly, see the Global Glimpse box on the preceding page.

FUNCTIONALISM AND SOCIAL PROBLEMS: A SUMMARY

In Sum

For an overview of functionalism, see Table 2-2. Note that functionalists begin by looking at one aspect of a social system, in this case, the column marked "Action." This action occurs in some part of the social system, such as business or government. The manifest function is the intended beneficial consequence of the action. If a beneficial consequence was not intended, it is a latent function. If there is an unintended harmful consequence, this is a latent dysfunction.

Functionalists assume that society is like a self-adjusting machine, and they examine how the parts of that machine (or social system) are interrelated. When a change occurs in some part of a social system, it affects other parts. A social problem

---

Table 2-2 Old Age: A Functionalist Overview

Related Parts of the Social System*	Action	Manifest Function	Latent Function	Latent Dysfunction
Economic (business)	Pension and retirement benefits	Provide income and leisure time for the aged	Jobs for younger workers	Displacement of the elderly; loss of self-esteem; loss of purpose
Political (government)	Social Security system	Stable income for the aged; dignity in old age	67,000 persons employed by the Social Security Administration	Income is inadequate; many recipients live on the edge of poverty
Medical	Technological developments; gerontological specialties	Longer lives for the population	A longer proportion of the elderly in the population	Makes the Social Security system much more expensive
	Medicare and Medicaid	Provide good health care for the elderly	Financing bonanza for the medical profession	"Rip-off" nursing homes
Family	Separation of parents from grown children (the nuclear family)	Independence of both younger and older generations	Institutionalized care for the elderly; greater mobility for younger workers	Isolation of the aged; loneliness and despair

*As used here, "parts" of the social system are social institutions.

---

arises when some part or parts of society do not adjust to these changes, and are not functioning adequately.

◆ Conflict Theory and Social Problems ◆

The Essence of Conflict Theory

The parts of society are *not* harmoniously working together, reply conflict theorists. What is really happening is that the parts are competing with one another, and some are ready to erupt in open conflict. Life is a struggle, and each person, each group, and each nation strives for what it can get. The guiding principle of social life is disequilibrium and change, not equilibrium and harmony, as the functionalists say.

Competition is not just an element of the marketplace; instead, it underlies all social life. For example, as we shall review shortly, old people are competing with younger people for scarce resources. If they get them, their victory must come at the cost of those younger people. The future may bring a conflict between the young and the elderly that will throw society into turmoil.

Social Problems from a Conflict Perspective

From the conflict perspective, social problems are the natural and inevitable outcome of social struggle. No matter what a social problem may look like on the surface, at its essence is a conflict between the powerful and the powerless. As the powerful exploit society's resources and oppress the powerless, they create such social problems as poverty and discrimination. As the exploited react to their oppression, still other social problems emerge: street crime, escapist drug abuse, suicide, homicide, riots, revolution. To understand social problems, then, we first need to understand that they are the natural state of society. Then we need to penetrate their surface manifestations and expose the basic conflict that underlies them.

THE DEVELOPMENT OF CONFLICT THEORY

Marx: Capitalism, Oppression, and the Struggle of Workers

Karl Marx (1818–1883), called the founder of conflict theory, witnessed the industrial revolution that transformed Europe. Cities mushroomed as peasants left the land to seek work. The new industrialists put the peasants—and their children—to work at near-starvation wages. As poverty and exploitation grew, political unrest followed, and upheaval swept across Europe.

Shocked by such suffering and inhumanity, Marx concluded that the hallmark of history is a struggle for power, that one group is always trying to oppress another. He also concluded that a major turning point in this fundamental struggle occurred when **capitalism** became dominant in the Western world—that is, when a small group of people gained control over the means of production and made profit their goal. As machinery replaced workers' tools, the **capitalists,** or owners of the factories and equipment, gained an exploitive advantage.

Because they owned the means of production, the capitalists were able to hire workers at starvation wages—and to fire them at will. When workers rebelled, the capitalists used the police power of the state to control them. In this struggle, which is still ongoing, capitalists sometimes make concessions to workers. Concessions are not signs of cooperation but, rather, strategic devices designed to confuse workers and weaken their political solidarity. The day of reckoning will finally come, and it will be bloody. The workers will overthrow their oppressors and establish a classless society in which the goal will be not profits for the few, but, rather, the good of the many.

In Marx's time, workers were at the mercy of their employers. They lacked what we take for granted today—a minimum wage, eight-hour workdays, five-day work weeks, paid vacations, medical benefits, sick leave, unemployment compensation,

**Simmel:
Subordination,
Superordination,
and Exchange**

**Positive Features
of Social Conflict**

**Coser: Close
Relationships
Breed Conflict**

**How a Social
Problem Was Born:
Industrialization
Pits Two Groups
Against One
Another**

**Fighting Back:
The Townsend
Movement**

pensions, Social Security, even the right to strike. Conflict theorists remind us that such benefits exist not because of the generosity of the benevolent rich but because workers fought for them—sometimes to the death.

Other sociologists have extended conflict theory beyond workers and capitalists. Sociologist Georg Simmel (1858–1918), for example, analyzed the relationships of people who are in higher positions (superordinates) and people in lower positions (subordinates). He added that because subordinates have some power, the more powerful must take them into consideration as they make decisions designed to protect their positions of privilege (Coser 1977). Consequently, subordinate-superordinate relationships are marked not by one-way naked power but by exchange. If employers wish to lower the benefits of a pension plan, for example, they must get unions to agree—and the workers will insist on a trade-off, such as increased job security.

Conflict, noted Simmel, also has positive features. For example, if the members of a group face an external threat, they tend to pull together. Similarly, if several groups face a common enemy, they tend to become more cohesive (Giddens 1969; Turner 1978). In times of war, for instance, workers and employers often shelve their differences in order to work together for the good of the nation. Workers may give up their right to strike, as U.S. workers did during World War II, while employers may agree to binding arbitration on all disputes.

Sociologist Lewis Coser (b. 1913) emphasized that conflict is especially likely to develop between people who have close relationships. This is because they are connected by a network of power, responsibilities, and rewards. New decisions, which are constantly necessary, often upset the precarious balances they have worked out. For example, workers and bosses are closely related, and what happens to a business or factory is of vital importance to both. Their relationship is precariously balanced, however, and actions by either party can easily upset it.

APPLYING CONFICT THEORY TO SOCIAL PROBLEMS

As we apply the conflict perspective to the elderly, let's see how Social Security came about. In this drama, the three major groups are elderly workers, younger workers, and employers. The fourth group is Congress, which, from this perspective, represented the interests of the employers.

From the point of view of conflict theory, old people became a social problem when those in power found it advantageous to push them aside. When the industrial revolution spread across the United States, owners of big business found old people a nuisance. They earned more than young workers, and they were not as docile. The owners found a natural alliance with young workers, who wanted the jobs of the older workers, and they fired many of the elderly.

One of the more startling statistics from the 1920s, the period before Social Security, is that two thirds of all Americans over 65 could not support themselves (Holtzman 1963; Hudson 1978). Most of the elderly who lost their jobs, then, became dependent on whatever someone might give them. In short, industrialization transformed the aged from a productive and respected group to a deprived and disgraced group.

Then the Great Depression struck the nation, and many elderly suffered even more pitifully. In 1930, in the midst of national despair, Francis Everett Townsend, a physician, started a movement to rally the elderly into a political force. He soon had one third of all Americans over 65 enrolled in his Townsend clubs, demanding benefits from the government (Holtzman 1963). His plan was for the federal

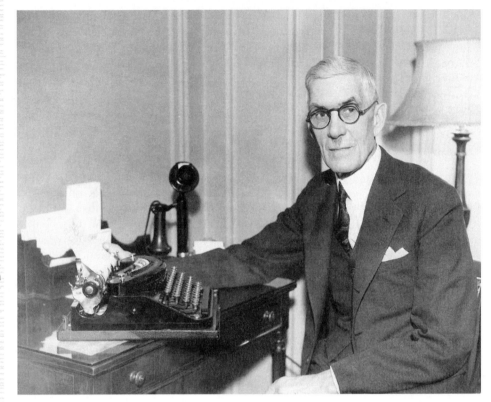

The U.S. elderly, who must be reckoned with by today's politicians, were not a political force until they were organized by Dr. Francis Everett Townsend in the 1930s. Townsend, a retired physician, gained national prominence when he proposed a $200-a-month pension plan for all the nation's elderly. He also spearheaded a campaign against congressional members who objected to his plan.

In Sum

government to impose a national sales tax of 2 percent in order to provide $200 a month for every person over 65 (the equivalent of over $2,000 a month today). Townsend argued that increased spending would generate new businesses and lift the nation out of the depression.

By 1934, the Townsend clubs had gathered hundreds of thousands of signatures on petitions, and the Townsend Plan went before Congress. In this election year, Congress felt vulnerable to a grassroots revolt by old people. But the Townsend Plan called for a high monthly pension, and the country was already strapped for money. Many also feared that it would sap people's incentive to work and save (Schottland 1963). Congress looked for a way to reject the plan without appearing to be opposed to old-age pensions. When President Franklin Roosevelt announced his own, more modest Social Security plan in June 1934, Congress embraced it.

Although the Townsend clubs had not gotten their plan passed, they had forced Congress to pass Social Security. The clubs then fought to improve Social Security. Benefits were not scheduled to begin until 1942, and millions of workers would be left uncovered. As the depression lingered, dragging even more old people into poverty, the clubs stepped up their political pressure. As a result, Congress voted to begin paying Social Security benefits in 1940, and to increase old-age assistance grants (the amounts paid to the destitute elderly).

When conflict theorists analyze a social problem, they look for conflict between competing interest groups. In this example, they emphasize that our Social Security benefits are not the result of generous hearts in Congress, but of the elderly who banded together to push their own interests. Congress gave as little as it thought it could get by with, and only when the elderly continued to put political pressure on

Congress did it reluctantly increase benefits. And for those benefits the elderly paid a dear price—their removal from the work force. A mandatory retirement age was set at 65, so out of this struggle employers also won their goal of a younger work force (Williamson et al. 1985).

CONFLICT THEORY AND SOCIAL PROBLEMS: A SUMMARY

Competition, Power, and Exploitation Make Social Problems, Natural and Inevitable

Conflict theorists view social problems in terms of competition, power, and exploitation. Groups in society conflict with one another as they pursue their interests, especially as they attempt to maintain or to gain control over scarce resources. This makes social problems inevitable, for conflict is inevitable. Thus, conflict theorists stress that when you examine a social problem you should look at the distribution of power and privilege, for social problems center on the conflicting interests of a society's groups.

Trade-Offs Are Designed to Protect the Powerful

Conflict theorists also look for the trade-offs that the powerful make as they deal with the less powerful. They regard social policies that benefit the less privileged as concessions that were forced from the powerful. Viewing such policies as strategies devised to help keep the privileged in power, conflict theorists examine them to see what the powerful gain. Social Security, for example, was voted in when the stability of the U.S. government was threatened by an army of unemployed workers.

Two Types of Social Problems

From the conflict perspective, then, social problems come in two forms. One is the troubles experienced by people as they are exploited by the powerful. The other is the troubles experienced by the powerful when the exploited resist, rebel, or appeal to higher values. Although their resources are limited, the exploited do find ways to resist. Some go on hunger strikes or campaign for political office. Others attack those in power. As we saw with the Townsend movement, the aged—a weak group in and of itself—were able to seize the initiative during a troubled period and force a change in their circumstances.

Most conflict is limited: It involves not a battle to the death but an orderly, focused contest. For example, retired Americans have not battled in the streets, but they have formed a political lobby that competes effectively with other groups. Understanding the nature of the underlying conflict in a social problem—and the limitations of power and strategies—helps pinpoint what a social problem is all about.

Social Change Brings Social Problems

Conflict theorists also point out that social change brings social problems, for it often leads to a realignment of society's groups. How a problem unfolds, what groups line up on which sides, and what solutions are developed to deal with conflict tell us much about how a society is evolving.

In Sum: Each Theory Highlights Different Aspects of a Social Problem

As I pointed out earlier, because conflict theory, symbolic interactionism, and functionalism are perspectives, each produces its particular picture of a social problem. Before we consider the future of the problem of aging in U.S. society, look at the Thinking Critically box on the next page, which stresses the different understandings that these theories yield.

◆ The Future of the Problem: The Pendulum Swings ◆

Positive Changes

Images of poor, ill, neglected grandparents have been used to promote programs designed to benefit elderly Americans. But such images are no longer broadly accurate. Economic growth and the expansion of federal programs have reduced the poverty

THINKING CRITICALLY ABOUT SOCIAL PROBLEMS

Applying the Theories: Understanding the Intergenerational Battle

Theories often appear vague and abstract. To help overcome this obstacle, as I have introduced each theory I have applied it to the social problem of aging in U.S. society. To better understand these theories, which will be used throughout this text, let's apply them to the potential battle between the generations—since you are likely to experience this cutting edge of the social problem of aging.

Each theory yields a unique interpretation of a social problem. Let's review the three theories to see the different understandings they give us of the intergenerational struggle.

Symbolic Interactionism: Symbols are the essence of social life, including social problems. Our interpretations of life come from the symbols that we use. If we use different symbols, we understand our experiences differently. Just as the meaning of old age shifted during industrialization, so this symbol is again shifting. Because people see that today's elderly are more affluent than they were just a generation ago, their ideas of the elderly are changing. The elderly are choosing new lifestyles: Their condos, motor-homes, and air travel to exotic destinations make their new affluence highly visible. As our symbol of the aged changes, so does our interpretation. The struggle that is shaping up will provide a new set of symbols, one that will guide how we think about and act toward old people.

Functionalism: We can look at the elderly and the young as two major parts in the same social system. Because each part must mesh together smoothly if society is to function efficiently, these parts must also fit together well. If one of them absorbs too much of a society's resources, an imbalance is created. Whenever an imbalance develops among the parts, adjustments must be made for the larger unit (in this case, society) to attain equilibrium. Just as an adjustment was made by giving more resources to the elderly during the past two generations, so now, if those resources have become disproportionate, another adjustment will occur. Although the adjustment process will be difficult, both the elderly and the young are essential parts of society. The final result will be a harmonious balance between them.

Conflict Theory: Of course, there is a battle shaping up. All groups struggle for their own interests. The American Association of Retired Persons (AARP) will push its own advantage and take as many resources as it can get, regardless of how its gains may affect younger people. Younger people will do the same as they pursue their interests. Each group has limited resources and will resent the other's gains. The struggle is likely to be fierce, and the group with more power will win. Regardless of its current outcome, conflict will continue in future generations.

rate for the aged to the point that it is now *below* the nation's average. To get an idea of how tremendously their poverty has dropped, consider this: In 1970, 25 percent of the elderly were poor, but today it is just 10 percent (*Statistical Abstract* 1989: Table 737; 2001: Table 683).

A Disturbing Trend

The turnaround is so remarkable that some people now think that the elderly are receiving more than their share—an attitude that reflects a primary shift in this social problem. Although people are pleased that poverty among the elderly has declined, they think that the decline may have come at the cost of other groups. Figure 2-1 shows that while the proportion of the elderly who live in poverty has dropped, the proportion of poor children who live in poverty has risen. The elderly reply that their moving out of poverty has not caused anyone else to move into poverty, that no one should live in poverty, and that they want to reduce the poverty of all age groups.

More Than Their Fair Share?

Some, however, feel that the elderly are demanding—and getting—more than their fair share of society's resources. For example, as shown in Figure 2-2, Medicare and Medicaid costs for the elderly have skyrocketed past the wildest projections of

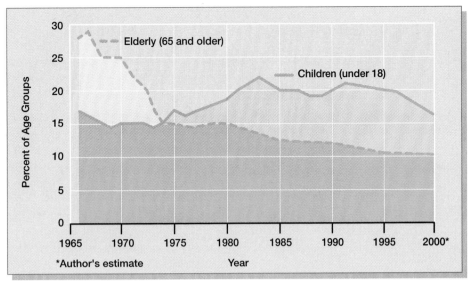

FIGURE 2-1
Comparing the Poverty Rates of Children and the Elderly
(*Source: Congressional Research Services: Statistical Abstract* 1994:Tables 728, 731; 1998:Tables 757, 760; Table A. U.S. Census Bureau: Poverty in the U.S.: 2000.)

Changes in Our Population Mix

Choices Between Children and Old People?

The Emerging Struggle

Social Security as a Gigantic Chain Letter

earlier years. It is the same with Social Security, which ran only $784 million in 1950, but today totals $408 billion. The current payout is *500 times* the amount paid in 1950 (*Statistical Abstract* 1998 and 2001:Table 527). If the Social Security payout were to continue to increase at this rate, in about 33 years the annual payout would run about $140 trillion (*Statistical Abstract* 1998:Table 716). This is an impossible figure, as the entire annual income of the United States is about $7 trillion—and that includes all salaries, interest, rents, and profits to businesses and corporations!

Yet there is no sign that the costs of Social Security—as well as Medicare and Medicaid—will diminish, for, as Figure 2-3 (on page 44) illustrates, the proportion of the elderly in our population is growing steadily. Soon one of four Americans will be age 55 or older. This growth is coming from two directions: Not only have improved sanitation and health care allowed people to live longer, but abortion and other forms of birth control are also having pronounced effects on our population mix. Elderly Americans now comprise 12.4% of the total U.S. population (U.S. Census Bureau, 2001, Table DP1).

This changing balance of age groups exacerbates the problem. The data shown in Figure 2-1 make some fear that Congress has chosen old people over children. Such people want to trim Social Security, Medicare, and other programs for the elderly on the basis that they go beyond the nation's ability to pay. Some reductions have been made. Social Security income, for example, used to be tax-free but is now taxable.

To protect their gains, older Americans have organized a powerful political lobby. This group, the American Association of Retired Persons (AARP), boasts 33 million members and a staff of 1,200. Could a battle between younger people and the elderly be on its way? The AARP has begun to arouse resentment; the activities of the Gray Panthers, whose position is summarized in the Issues box on page 46, also may indicate a coming generational conflict.

Some form of conflict does seem inevitable, for the interests of younger and older groups are on a collision course. There are two major problems. The first is

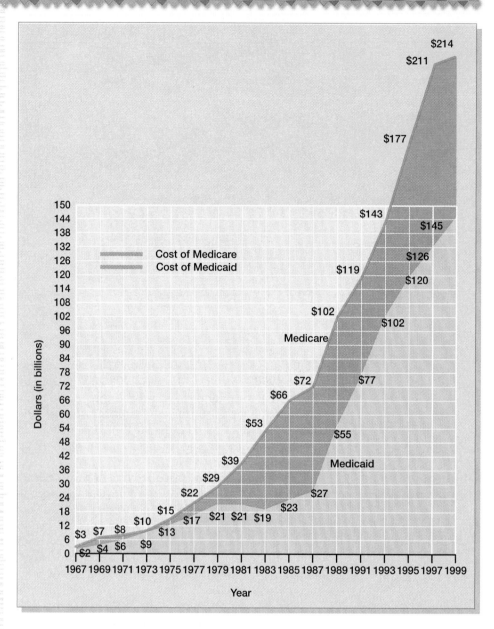

FIGURE 2-2
Health Care Costs for the Elderly (and Disabled)

Medicare funds are provided to the elderly and disabled by the federal government. Medicaid is intended for the needy and is financed by federal, state, and local governments. Although these two programs began at modest levels, their costs have increased dramatically. By 1997, Medicare and Medicaid were 60 to 70 times as costly as in 1967.

(*Source: Statistical Abstract* 1992:Table 147; 1994:Table 159; 1996:Tables 166, 167; 1997:Tables 164, 165; 1998:Tables 174, 175. 2001: Table 120.)

that the money a worker "contributes" to Social Security is not put into the worker's own account. Instead, as money comes in, it is paid out to those who are already retired—a sort of chain-letter arrangement by which the young support the old. The second problem is that the number of people who collect Social Security benefits is growing, but the proportion of working people—those who pay for these benefits out of their wages—is shrinking. We are seeing a major shift in the **dependency ratio,** the number of workers compared with the number of Social Security recipients. Presently, just under five working-age Americans pay Social Security taxes to support each person collecting Social Security. In about a generation, this ratio will drop to about 3 to 1 (Melloan 1994).

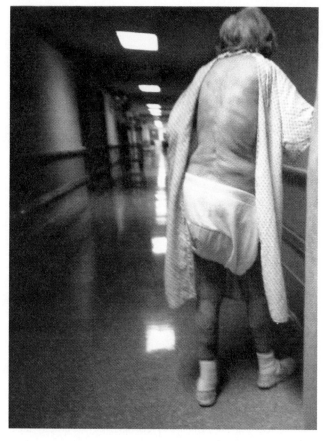

As the numbers of elderly increase, so do the costs of their health care. Cost is only one issue. Another is the quality of care, including the need to retain respect for the elderly. In some medical settings, as is evident in the care of this woman, even their basic dignity is stripped from them.

The U.S. elderly have become a group, in the sociological sense: They think of themselves as belonging together, and they consider the characteristics that make them distinctive to be significant. The elderly now make up a political force that wields a great amount of power in U.S. politics.

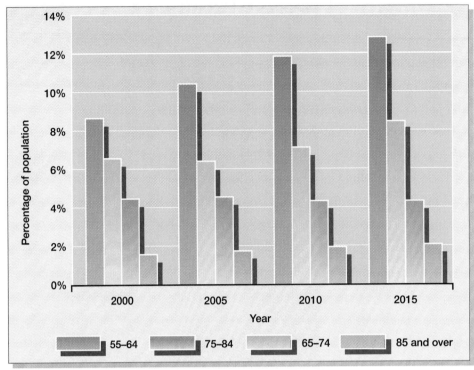

FIGURE 2-3
The Graying of America
(*Source: Statistical Abstract* 1998: Table 24. Updated projections from *Statistical Abstract* 2001: Tables 11 (2000 data) & 13.)

Coming: An Intergenerational Showdown

Many are counting on the Social Security Trust Fund to prevent an intergenerational showdown. This fund consists of several trillions of dollars that have been collected in Social Security taxes in excess of payments to retirees. The problem is that the trust fund exists in name only. Those trillions of dollars disappear as fast as they come in, for the federal government "borrows" them and spends them on whatever it desires (Henslin 1999). The day of reckoning between the generations can't be far off.

◆ Summary

1. The frameworks that sociologists use to interpret their findings are called *theories*. To interpret social problems, sociologists use three major theories: *symbolic interactionism, functionalism,* and *conflict theory.* Each theory provides a different interpretation of society and social problems. No one theory is "right." Rather, these perspectives, taken together, give us a more complete grasp of the whole.

2. Symbolic interactionists see social problems not as objective conditions but as definitions or views that are collectively held; that is, if people view something as a social problem, it is a social problem. As people's definitions or symbols change, so do their ideas about social problems.

3. Functionalists see society as a self-correcting, orderly system. Its parts work together to bring the whole into equi-

librium. Each part performs a function (hence, the term *functional* analysis) that contributes to the system. When a part is functioning imperfectly, it creates problems for the system. Those dysfunctions are called social problems.

4. Conflict theorists see social problems as a natural outcome of power arrangements. Those in power try to preserve the social order and their own privileged position within it. They take the needs of other groups into consideration only when it is in their own interest to do so. As they exploit others, the powerful create social problems, such as poverty and discrimination. Other social problems, such as revolution, crime, suicide, and drug abuse, represent reactions to oppression by those who've been exploited.

CENSUS 2000

While the poverty rate of the elderly has declined considerably in the last few decades, there is still much income inequality by sex and family type among older Americans. The table below shows two main inequalities revealed by the 2000 Census. First, you can see that the elderly who are not married are much more likely to be poor. Second, note that of the elderly who are unmarried, it is women who are more likely to be poor.

These inequalities mirror differences between men and women of other age groups. Regardless of age, women's economic situation is worse than that of their male counterparts.

Family type and poverty status

	Percent below poverty level		
	55–59	60–64	65+
married couple families	4.8	6.0	4.0
male householder, no spouse	10.8	10.6	9.8
female householder, no spouse.	13.8	17.5	10.6

◆ Key Terms

Ageism   Discrimination against people on the basis of their age; this concept is not limited to older people.

Capitalism   An economic system based on private ownership of property and the investment of capital for the purpose of profit.

Capitalists   Owners of the means of production (land, factories, tools) who buy the labor of workers.

Conflict theory   A sociological theory that views society as a system in conflict and change. Each group in society attempts to further its own interests, even at the expense of others. These interests come into conflict with one another, making the social order unstable. Those in power exploit people and resources for their own benefit. Social problems stem from exploitation and resistance to exploitation.

Dependency ratio   The number of workers compared with the number of Social Security recipients.

Disengagement theory   The view that society prevents disruption by having the elderly vacate (or disengage from) their positions of responsibility so that the younger generation can step into their shoes.

Dysfunction   When some part of a social system disrupts the equilibrium of the system or interferes with the functioning of another part in the system, it is a dysfunction. See also *Functionalism*.

Function   The contribution of a part to a system; or, people's actions that contribute to the equilibrium of a social system. See also *Functionalism*.

Functional analysis   See *Functionalism*.

Functional perspective   See *Functionalism*.

Functional theory   See *Functionalism*.

Functionalism   A sociological theory that views society as a system of interconnected parts, each contributing in some way to the equilibrium of the system. The contribution of each part is called its function; hence the term *functionalism*. Functionalists view social problems as the failure of some part of the system to function correctly (also called *functional analysis*, *functional theory*, and the *functional perspective*).

Generalized other   Basically, the community or groups in general that an individual considers important, and whose views and attitudes the individual takes into account as he or she considers a course of action.

Labeling   Stereotyping, or putting a tag on someone, and treating him or her accordingly.

Latent dysfunctions   The unintended consequences of people's actions that disrupt the equilibrium of a system or the adjustment of its parts. See also *Functionalism*.

ISSUES IN SOCIAL PROBLEMS

The Gray Panthers

WHO WE ARE

We are a group of people—old and young—drawn together by deeply felt common concerns for human liberation and social change. The old and young live outside the mainstream of society. **Ageism**—discrimination against persons on the basis of chronological age—deprives both groups of power and influence.

Besides being a movement of older and younger persons, as Gray Panthers we consider ourselves distinctive in the following ways:

We are against ageism that forces any group to live roles that are defined purely on the basis of age. We view aging as a total life process in which the individual develops from birth to death. Therefore, we are concerned about the needs of all age groups and ageism directed at any age group.

We have a strong sense of militancy. Our concern is not only for education and services, but for effective nonviolent action with an awareness of timing and urgency.

We advocate a radical approach to social change by attacking those forces that corrupt our institutions, attitudes, and values, such as materialism, racism, sexism, paternalism, militarism, and extreme nationalism.

WHAT WE WANT

1. To develop a new and positive self-awareness in our culture that can regard the total life span as a continuing process in maturity and fulfillment.

2. To strive for new options for life-styles for older and younger people that will challenge the present paternalism in our institutions and culture, and to help eliminate the poverty and powerlessness in which most older and younger people are forced to live, and to change society's destructive attitudes about aging.

3. To make responsible use of our freedom to bring about social change, to develop a list of priorities among social issues, and to struggle nonviolently for social change that will bring greater human freedom, justice, dignity, and peace.

4. To build a new power base in our society uniting presently disenfranchised and oppressed groups, realizing the common qualities and concerns of age and youth working in coalition with other movements with similar goals and principles.

5. To reinforce and support each other in our quest for liberation and to celebrate our shared humanity.

Reprinted by permission of The Gray Panthers.

Latent functions The unintended consequences of people's actions that contribute to the equilibrium of a social system or the functioning of its parts. See also *Functionalism*.

Looking-glass self Our self-images are dependent on what we think others think of us. We see ourselves, in other words, as a reflection in the eyes of others; hence the term *looking-glass self*.

Manifest function The consequences of people's actions that are intended to contribute to the adaptation, adjustment, or equilibrium of a system or its parts. See also *Functionalism*.

Social construction of reality The attempt to make sense of life by giving meaning to one's experiences.

Structure The interrelations between the parts or subunits of society.

Symbol Items of social life to which we give meaning and that we then use to communicate with one another. They include signs, gestures, written and spoken language, and even our posture and appearance.

Symbolic interactionism A sociological theory that views society as consisting of the patterns common to a group of people. Because these patterns depend on people's symbols or definitions, and because people's views change, society is always in flux. Within this framework, social problems are not considered objective conditions but simply the issues that people have decided to call social problems.

Taking the role of the other To put oneself in another's place, seeing how things look from that perspective and anticipating how that person will act.

Theory An explanation of the relationship between two or more concepts, such as age and suicide or age and attitudes of self-worth. Looking at any particular fact or event from a theory's framework provides a unique way to interpret that fact or event. Important theories in the study of social problems include symbolic interactionism, functionalism, and conflict theory.

◆Critical Thinking Questions

1. Of the three main theories identified in this chapter as the ones used by sociologists, which one do you think does the best job of explaining sociological problems? Why?

2. Imagine something that you consider a personal problem between two people. Describe the problem.
   - How would symbolic interactionism explain this problem?
   - How would functionalism explain the problem?
   - How would conflict theory explain the problem?

3. What do you think are the biggest problems we are likely to face in the United States regarding the aging of the population? Why?
   - What do you think we should do about them?
   - Why do you feel your solutions might work?
   - What might prevent your solutions from working?

Prostitution, Homosexuality, and Pornography

"Don't nobody move!" the police shouted, guns drawn, as they burst into Wiggles in the East Flatbush section of Brooklyn. The topless women gyrating on the tables quickly covered their breasts with their hands. The ogling patrons, horrified, sat frozen in their seats.

Uniformed officers also burst into El Coche in the Bronx and Sharks on Staten Island. The police didn't make any arrests, but they ordered the dancers and patrons to leave the buildings, then padlocked the doors and pasted bright orange stickers on them that said, "Closed by Court Order."

Times Square, in Manhattan, which had been the center of pornography and prostitution, has also been "cleaned up."

The man who ordered these raids is Rudolph Giuliani, the former mayor of New York City. Giuliani, who had national political aspirations, ordered the raids after polls showed that a crusade against pornographers and prostitution would score points with conservative voters.

Based on Allen 1998.

◆ Sexual Behaviors as Social Problems ◆

A basic sociological principle is that sex is never only a personal matter.

Societies Channel Sexual Behavior

All societies control or channel human sexual behavior. A major way they do this is through the social institutions of marriage and family, which shape people's ideas of right and wrong. As children learn the norms of their society, they learn what sexual behaviors are approved. As this learning experience recedes from their awareness, they come to see these behaviors as "simply natural." Most Americans, for example, grow up learning that it is "natural" to fall in love and marry one person of the opposite sex. In contrast, traditional Crow Indians grew up learning that love is "dishonorable" (Lowie 1935). In other groups, people grow up learning that it is "natural" for a man to marry many wives.

Why Are Violations of Sexual Norms a Social Problem?

Most people learn to identify strongly with the sexual norms of their group. Not everyone conforms, of course, but *what is it that makes violations of sexual norms a social problem*? Why aren't they just personal matters? After all, every society tolerates many behaviors that violate its ideals. The difference is this: When a society perceives behaviors as a threat, especially to the family, they are likely to consider them a social problem. While Americans often tolerate adult prostitution and pornography, for example, they recoil in horror at child prostitution and pornography.

In a society as pluralistic as ours, with its many diverse groups and contrary opinions, there is probably nothing about which everyone agrees. Consider two extremes: Some people find adult prostitution a serious threat; others approve of child prostitution. This underscores a major point of the symbolic interactionist perspective, noted in Chapter 1: Social problems are relative, and what is considered a social problem varies from group to group and changes over time.

As symbolic interactionists also stress, the objective conditions of a social problem need not be harmful; it is sufficient that people perceive them as undesirable and want to do something about them. The objective conditions of prostitution, homosexuality, and pornography are relatively straightforward: Some people rent their bodies for sexual purposes, some people have sexual relations with others of the same sex, and objects that people call "pornography" do exist. Whether or not these

As discussed in the text, attitudes toward prostitution vary widely among societies and in different historical periods. This 2,000-year-old depiction of a prostitute is in the Archeological Museum in Athens, Greece.

Attitudes Toward Prostitution

objective conditions are harmful is not important in determining whether they are social problems. What is significant are the subjective concerns that people have about them. As with abortion, these concerns center on issues of morality—people's ideas of right and wrong.

Prostitution, homosexuality, and pornography, then, are social problems for exactly the same reasons that other issues are social problems—because large numbers of people are concerned about them and would like to see them changed. As with abortion, Americans are divided on these matters. Sociology cannot pronounce moral judgments, but it can report on attitudes and social controversy—the concerns that make contemporary society so exciting.

Our job in this chapter, then, is to examine three social problems that are mired in controversy, more so, perhaps, than any social problem other than abortion. To understand these social problems better, we shall apply one of the three theories to each. We shall view prostitution through the lens of functionalism, apply conflict theory to homosexuality, and use symbolic interactionism to analyze pornography. As usual, we shall attempt to present fairly both the scientific evidence and the controversial positions involved.

◆ Prostitution ◆

BACKGROUND: GETTING THE LARGER PICTURE

It is no accident that **prostitution,** the renting of one's body for sexual purposes, has been called "the world's oldest profession." Accounts of prostitution by both females and males reach back to the beginnings of recorded history. It exists in one form or another almost everywhere.

Attitudes toward prostitution vary immensely. The ancient inhabitants of the Mediterranean area, Asia Minor, West Africa, and southern India held an attitude that is startling to contemporary Westerners (Henriques 1966). There, prostitution was part of religion. It took place in the temple, as a type of service to their gods. In one form of **temple prostitution,** every woman was required to perform an act of prostitution before she could marry. In another, a woman was dedicated to the gods of the temple as a sacred prostitute—either for a specific time or, more commonly, for life.

In ancient Greece, high-class prostitutes, called *hetairae,* were respected. Their portraits and statues were placed "in the temples and other public buildings by the side of meritorious generals and statesmen" (Henriques 1966:64).

Today, in many Latin countries prostitution is seen as a necessary evil—something that keeps hot-blooded men away from the pure and innocent. Although many Spaniards, Italians, Mexicans, and South Americans may consider prostitution disgusting, they are also convinced that prostitutes indirectly protect the virtue of their own wives and daughters.

The attitudes of Americans toward the legalization of prostitution are shown in Table 3-1 (on page 52). They provide an interesting profile. Those most likely to favor its legalization are white male college graduates with high incomes who live in the West. Those least likely to favor legal prostitution are black female high school graduates with low incomes who live in the Midwest. A surprise is that those between the ages of 50 to 64, usually a very conservative group, are the most likely to favor the legalization of prostitution.

How Many Prostitutes?

Prostitution has flourished in the United States. No one knows how many prostitutes there are, and estimates range from 84,000 to a half million (Winick and Kinsie 1971; Sheehy 1973; Pottêrat et al. 1990). Although a half million may seem surprisingly high, during the supposedly prudish Victorian period, prostitutes in London may have been 50 times as common—in proportion to the general population—as they are in the United States today.

Even if there is proportionately less prostitution today, prostitution is certainly alive and well. Some prostitutes have 400 customers a month (Forney et al. 1992), although the average prostitute probably engages in about 40 sexual acts a week (Sheehy 1973). If these estimates are anywhere near accurate—and we really don't know—in the United States there are between 3 million and 20 million acts of commercial sex per week. This comes to somewhere between 200 million and 1 billion a year.

Legal Prostitution

The only place in the United States where prostitution is legal is Nevada. There, prostitutes are permitted to sell sex in all but the urban counties of Reno, Las Vegas, and Lake Tahoe, where city officials believe legalized prostitution might drive away "family-type" gamblers. Illegal prostitution also thrives, as evidenced by police files on more than 10,000 prostitutes who have worked Las Vegas (Reichert and Frey 1985).

Changes in Prostitution

Prostitutes have kept up with the times. Even though the elaborately furnished "whorehouse" of bygone days is indeed bygone, massage parlors, call girls, and escort services have taken its place. Under cover of a legitimate service, "massage parlors" offer sex for sale. So do escort services: For a set fee a client arranges a date and privately negotiates the inclusion of sexual services. In Spain, "masseuses" make house calls. Their newspaper and magazine ads mention their qualifications, such as "19 years old, blue eyes, and just arrived from Germany."

Another variation is corporate prostitution. In one version, a corporation hires prostitutes for its customers. Nynex, a New York telephone company, for example, held what its executives called "pervert" conventions. In these week-long, raucous sessions, prostitutes provided sex for the company's suppliers (Carnevale 1990). In a second version, a regular employee of a corporation provides sex for clients of the firm. In the Issues box on pages 54–55, one of my students explains how she became a corporate prostitute.

In short, we can note that prostitution changes along with other aspects of society and that it serves social functions—from playing a role in religious rituals to helping corporations grow. In the following section, we shall examine the social functions of prostitution in more detail.

PROSTITUTION VIEWED THEORETICALLY: APPLYING FUNCTIONALISM

The Social Functions of Prostitution

On the most obvious level, prostitution flourishes because it satisfies sexual needs that are not met elsewhere. This, of course, is precisely why it can never be eliminated. In a classic article, sociologist Kingsley Davis (1937, 1966), a functionalist, concluded that prostitutes provide a sexual outlet for men who

Table 3-1   Attitudes Toward the Legalization of Prostitution

Question: "In your opinion, should prostitution involving adults aged 18 years of age and older be legal or illegal in your state?"

	Legal	Illegal	Don't know/ refused
National	26%	70%	4%
Sex			
Male	32%	63%	5%
Female	21%	77%	2%
Race/Ethnicity*			
White	27%	70%	3%
Black	20%	79%	1%
Age			
18 to 29 years	25%	74%	1%
30 to 49 years	28%	68%	4%
50 to 64 years	32%	65%	3%
65 years and older	18%	77%	5%
Education			
College graduate	28%	69%	3%
High School	21%	76%	3%
Income			
$50,000 and over	33%	64%	3%
$30,000 to $49,999	26%	70%	4%
$20,000 to $29,999	27%	71%	2%
Under $20,000	18%	80%	2%
Region			
East	28%	68%	4%
Midwest	20%	78%	2%
South	24%	75%	1%
West	34%	58%	8%

Source: Sourcebook of Criminal Justice Statistics 1997: Table 2–99.
*Only these two groups are listed in the Source.

1. Have difficulty in establishing sexual relationships (such as the disfigured or handicapped).

2. Cannot find long-term partners (such as traveling salesmen and sailors).

3. Have a broken relationship (such as the separated or divorced).

4. Want sexual gratification that is defined as immoral—and is thus out of bounds for wives and girlfriends.

Other researchers (Freund et al. 1991; Gemme 1993) have added that prostitutes provide a sexual outlet for men who

5. Desire quick sexual gratification without attachment.

6. Are curious.

7. Are sexually dissatisfied in marriage.

The Functionalist Conclusion: Prostitution is a Form of Social Control Over Male Sexuality

Although these observations may seem obvious, the conclusion that functionalists draw from them is not. They conclude that by meeting such needs prostitution functions as *a form of social control* over sexual behavior. By this they mean that prostitution channels sexual desires away from unwilling partners to partners who are willing to satisfy them for a price. For example, some sexual deviants (whom prostitutes call "kinkies," "weirdos," "sickies," "freaks," or "heavies") achieve sexual gratification by inflicting pain (**sadists**) or by having pain inflicted on them (**masochists**). Others combine the sex act with fantasy role playing; they may wear costumes or even have sex in a coffin (Hall 1972; Millett 1973; Prus and Irini 1988).

Most customers of prostitutes (called "johns" or "tricks") are not sexual deviants. Rather, they are regular Joe Six-Packs—married, middle-aged men (Wells 1970; Freund et al. 1991). Why do married men patronize prostitutes? Perhaps the two most common reasons are that they find their wives sexually unreceptive, or they desire a sexual variety that their wives are unwilling to provide—especially "frenching" (fellatio or oral sex), apparently the act most requested of prostitutes (Melody 1969; Heyl 1979; Gemme 1993).

Functionalists, then, see prostitution as a means of controlling or channeling sexual behavior. Prostitutes meet the needs of the sexually unattached and of those who desire sexual acts that are not otherwise readily available to them. Prostitutes also provide access to sexual variety in an inexpensive, nonemotional, and fleeting relationship. Furthermore, unlike dates, prostitutes do not threaten the male ego—the john won't be "turned down."

Symbiosis and the Sexual Black Market

Functionalists stress that when people demand a service that is not supplied by legitimate sources, an extralegal, subterranean arrangement will develop to meet the need. The underground channeling of illegitimate services to clients, called a **black market,** is built on **symbiosis** (a mutually beneficial relationship). Those who purchase a service, those who provide it, and, often, those who are supposed to suppress it depend on and benefit from one another. The clients of prostitutes purchase what they want; prostitutes work with a minimum of legal hassles (even calling their occasional fines the price of "licensing"); pimps and organized criminals earn untaxed income; and police who are "on the take" look the other way.

A Contrasting Feminist Conflict Perspective

Feminists provide an interpretation that contrasts with functionalism. Using a conflict framework, they emphasize that most women depend on men for their livelihood. This makes women exploitable by men who want to use them as objects for their own pleasure. From this point of view, prostitution is one of many ways that men degrade and exploit women in a sexist society. See the Global Glimpse box on page 57.

In line with the conflict perspective, we can add that politicians also exploit prostitutes. As we saw in our opening vignette, when it is in a politician's interest to suppress prostitution, he or she will do so. When it isn't, he or she will allow prostitutes to be exploited by pimps and owners of night clubs.

RESEARCH ON PROSTITUTION

Types of Prostitutes

Besides the masseuses, escort girls, and corporate prostitutes we have discussed, other forms of prostitution also reflect modern society—from its patterns of employment to its electronic communications. Let's see what they are. (We shall discuss male prostitutes later.)

Call girls, the elite of the prostitutes, can be selective in choosing their customers, and they have steady repeat business. They usually meet their customers at

Me, a Prostitute?

Many women are initiated into prostitution over a period of time through a gradual step-by-step process, as illustrated by this account written by one of my students who wishes to remain anonymous. The account has been set according to the original paper, including typos and misspellings.

I am a average looking blond with blue eyes. I am a female of twenty years of age. My mother is a elementary school teacher with a doctorit degree. My father is the head of instramention for a large oil company. He write books, makes movies and teaches around the world. I have one sibbling. She is 10 years old. My parents are very old fashioned. they are strickt with both my sister and I. We are Hard-Shell-Baptist, and attend church no-matter-what. They've instilled wonderful values in me. We live in the country on a farm (pleasure, we don't grow things). Our home is large and because both of my parents work we have a maid that comes three days a week to clean. I've always had to work around the house. Cooking meals, cleaning and doing farm chores such as, feeding the horses and cows, have always been a part of my dayly routine. Yet, there's never been anything I've ever done without. Anything that could be bought was automatically mine, just for the asking. Our entire family is close. We visit one another frequently and have get-togethers regularly.

I am from a family with an average annual income of over $100,000.00. My parents have never neglected me. No one has ever abused me. I've caused my share of trouble, but it was all jouvenile, never anything against the law of the state. I've never been a misfit. I was one of the "cool" kids. I was in with the "popular" crowd. I was in Student Government and Peer Leadership in High School. I was elected Snow Queen my junior year. I never had any problems with guys. There was always plenty around my house. I just could never get attached to guys my age, they came and they went . . . no big deal! I had a taste for older men even then.

When I was seventeen, I met a guy who was twenty-two. He was exciting and fun. He was my first love. He was also the first guy I'd ever had sex with. Kinky wouldn't even begin to explain him. We went out for about a year and a half. Through him I met Jesse. A gorgeous Spaniard, queer as a three dollar bill, but one of the nicest people you'll ever meet. Jesse is a "BIG" record promoter for a famous record corporation. We've been friends since the day we met. We call each other all the time and "dish" on guys.

I called Jesse up one day and asked if he'd get me tickets to go to a concert I wanted to see. He said sure as he had a million times before. Only this time he too had a request. He said, "I'm in a bit of a bind. I need someone to pick up a client and show him around town Friday!" "Cool!" I said. Jesse went on to explain, "You'll be given $200.00 to buy him dinner, go dancing, or whatever else he may want to do . . . what's left is yours to keep." "Wow, thats great," I exclaimed! I thought to myself, what could be better, a date in which we can do anything, the sky's the limit . . . you get payed for playing!!! What could possibly be better than that?

I made about $70. I had a wonderful time and so did the client. I told Jesse I loved being a escort and to fix me up as often as he liked. I was assigned many men after that. I'd say a good 75% wanted to finish off

their own place or at the client's. To keep up with appointments, they use cell phones, pagers, fax machines, and e-mail.

Convention prostitutes, as the name implies, specialize in conventions. These women pose as secretaries or sales promoters and roam hotel lobbies, display rooms, and cocktail parties. Some develop strong opinions about which professionals spend the most money, and they try to concentrate on their conventions. In the symbiotic manner referred to earlier, the organizers of a convention may make arrangements for prostitutes to be available.

Chapter 3 Prostitution, Homosexuality, and Pornography

their evenings with sex. Some even would get quite insistent. I asked Jesse what to do. Jesse said do what you want to do, guys will offer you their own money (as a write off to their own company as entertainment). To sleep with me, I thought. He said, "Do what you want to do, if you want the money, go for it! If you don't keep standing firm!" I told Jesse I couldn't do it. So, he began to filter my dates more so and more so. He was always careful not to set me up with the weirdo's or the real wild party hardy guys. I mostly got the married with three kids and a dog type from then on.

I worked at the pace of picking up $20–$100 per date, for about three months; about 60 guys total. Then I met with a client from Europe for the second time. He was a very attractive man of 40. His black hair was salted with a whitened silver. He was a family man. Though, as was the story with many of the men I escorted, he was having alot of problems with his wife. While sitting at a bar he whispered in my ear, "Would you please consider being with me tonight?" Knowing I'd turned him down the last time he was in town, he reached into his pocket for inspiration. $500.00 in crisp $100.00 bills he waved out like a fan and placed on the table. I looked at him and shook my head "No" I said. He put his hand on my arm and said, "How much do I have to offer you, $600, $700?" At this point I was getting pissed! In order to control my temper I flew off to the restroom in a rage. I remember standing at the sink, looking into the mirror, and thinking who in the hell does this man think he is!! I don't need his money! But still that much money, for sex?! . . . how could it be? I went back to the table with thousands of thoughts running through my mind. He looked at me and said, "I'm sorry if I upset you, but, I'm willing to give you all the money I have with me, $1000 dollars. Hows that sound?" My initial thought was to slap the crap out of him, however, the things I could do with $1000 cash. I agreed and it wasn't hard. No commitments, no future to worry about, and no love to get in the way of habitions. I went home that night with 10 crisp $100 dollar bills and two $20's left over from the date, in my coat pocket. There's nothing to it. I can spend $100 on myself and stick the rest in a savings account. It's no biggy!

I told Jesse about it. I told him I couldn't believe how easy or how much money I made. He laughed and asked me if I had plans of ever doing this again. I said sure, it's no problem. He started throughing me that "kind" of clients. I made over $10,000 in the 4 mths to follow. Enough to buy me a new car. I never have made $1000 in a evening again but, it became a game to me. How high can you raise the bid? How much will it take to make this man make an offer straight up? How much teasing can you get buy with, without having him drop his attention?

I've worked more than 2 yrs. I've totally mellowed out of the games. If it looks good to me, and if I find the man attractive I'll do it. I've become very secure financially. I have multiple CD's, bonds and ect. I have three savings accounts and alot of money tied up in the stock market. My only regrets are I have to keep it a complete secret from everyone. My parents, who mean more to me than the world, my family, and even my dearest friends. I miss out on the average evryday social life of a college student. I have to lie to practically everyone I meet. But, nowhere will I find a job in which I can save as much money for my future. Or for that matter when I get out of college and get a respectable job in advertising, make that kind of money. But, my life will be back to a "normal" one. One in which I can be proud of, one which I can share with my friends and family, one in which I can make a "honest" living.

Apartment prostitutes rent an apartment and set up a business at which they work set hours. Some apartment prostitutes are married women who attempt to match their apartment hours to their husband's working hours. A husband who is ignorant of his wife's activities is likely to think that she has a regular job.

Stag party workers serve as topless waitresses or put on strip shows at stag parties, that is, parties for men only. They arrange to meet customers after the party or, sometimes, in a side room during the party.

Sociologists use several criteria to classify prostitutes, including the locations at which they solicit customers. Some prostitutes specialize in conventions, where they mingle with the conventioneers. The women shown here are not prostitutes.

Hotel prostitutes work out of a hotel and share their fees with the bell captain, desk clerk, or bell boys who steer johns to them (Reichert and Frey 1985; Prus and Irini 1988). Because this "added service" attracts male guests, the hotel sometimes provides their room free or at a cut rate.

House prostitutes work in a house of prostitution or "whorehouse." Although this form of prostitution has declined, during the 1800s and early 1900s almost all large U.S. cities and many small ones had brothels, which were located in an area known as the "red light district." By means of a red bulb shining from a window or house front, passersby were informed of the nature of the establishment.

Barbara Heyl, a sociologist who has studied house prostitutes, reports that after making a selection from the women who gather in the living room, a john retires to a bedroom with the prostitute. The manager of the house, or "madam," keeps from 50 to 60 percent of the prostitute's earnings. Heyl reports that house prostitutes must learn how to persuade customers to spend more than they intend. She (1979:120) adds that this is especially difficult for the novice, "because the woman must learn to discuss sexual acts, whereas in her previous experience, sexual behavior and preferences had been negotiated non-verbally."

Bar girls, also known as "B-girls," wait in a bar for customers. Some pay or "tip" the bartender for being able to use the bar as their headquarters. Others hustle drinks (are friendly to bar patrons in order to get them to buy overpriced drinks) and receive a set fee for each drink they sell.

Streetwalkers have the lowest status among prostitutes. They are also the most frequently arrested. They are visible to the public, as they "work the street" in open view of police and customers. In some U.S. cities, streetwalkers are aggressive, hailing passing cars and opening the doors of cars that have stopped at traffic lights. Many are drug addicts who are also involved in larceny.

Another type of prostitute has emerged recently. In common parlance they are known as *parking lot lizards*. These prostitutes frequent truck stops, furtively moving from one truck to another in search of clients.

A GLOBAL GLIMPSE

The Patriotic Prostitute

A new wrinkle in the history of prostitution is the "patriotic prostitute." Patriotic prostitutes are young women who are encouraged by their government to prostitute themselves to help the country's economy. Patriotic prostitution is part of global stratification, the division of the world's countries into "have" and "have-not" nations. Some have-not, or Least Industrialized Nations, encourage prostitution to help pay their national debt. A notorious example is Thailand, where in a country of 55 million, perhaps a million women are prostitutes. About 20,000 are under the age of 15.

In some countries, government officials tell prostitutes that they are performing a service to their country. In South Korea, prostitutes are issued identification cards that serve as hotel passes. In orientation sessions, they are told, "Your carnal conversations with foreign tourists do not prostitute either yourself or the nation, but express your heroic patriotism."

With such an official blessing, "sex tourism" has become a global growth industry. Travel agencies in Germany advertise "trips to Thailand with erotic pleasures included in the price." Japan Air Lines hands out brochures that advertise the "charming attractions"

of Kisaeng girls, advising men to fly JAL for "'a night spent with a consummate Kisaeng girl dressed in a gorgeous Korean blouse and skirt."

The advertising, often showing beautiful young women with "come hither" smiles, fails to mention the underlying misery. Many of the prostitutes have been sold as children. Many are held in bondage while they pay off their families' debts. Some are locked up.

The enticing ads also leave out AIDS. In Nairobi, where about 10,000 prostitutes serve this growing industry, perhaps half are infected with AIDS. Nor is the destruction of children mentioned. Although customers pay more for young girls and boys, especially those who are advertised as virgins or "clean," the children are vulnerable to infection from lesions and injuries during intercourse.

This global sex trade is a new form of slavery. Poor women and boys and girls are commodities to be traded, bartered, haggled over, smuggled, and sold.

Based on Gay 1985; Shaw 1987; O'Malley 1988; Srisang 1989; Muecke 1992; Hornblower 1993; Montague 1996.

Male prostitutes who service women are known as "gigolos." In 1980, sociologist Ed Sagarin concluded that this "is an infrequent behavior, for which there is little demand and probably more folklore than reality." With changing sexual norms, it is likely that instances of women paying men for sex are now more common. I have to say "likely," because we don't have studies that prove this, but the indications are provocative. *How Stella Got Her Groove Back* is a movie about a woman who rediscovered the joy of life with a Jamaican man half her age. After this movie appeared in 1998, the number of single women tourists to Jamaica increased—especially in a beach area where older women "rent" young men ("Movie Spurs Jamaica Tourism").

Becoming a Prostitute

Researchers focus on prostitutes who are the most easily accessible—primarily the poor and those who have been arrested. (Those arrested also tend to be poor.) Prostitutes who come from higher social class backgrounds, such as the student of mine featured in the Issues box on pages 54–55, engage in forms of prostitution that make them less accessible to the police—and to sociologists. Keeping in mind this huge gap in the research, let's see why women become prostitutes.

The simplest answer to why someone becomes a prostitute is money—to make as much of it as easily as possible. This is an oversimplification, however, for running

Because their activities are illegal, prostitutes cannot advertise their services in conventional ways. To attract customers, they use symbols of their intention: dress, stance, and location. While these symbols accomplish their desired effect, they also announce their intention to an unwelcome audience—police and uninterested passersby.

through the accounts that prostitutes give of their early home life are themes of emotional deprivation and sexual abuse (James and Meyerding 1977; Davis 1978; James and Davis 1982; Silbert and Pines 1982, 1983; Williams and Kornblum 1985). Sociologist Robert Gemme (1993), who interviewed Montreal street prostitutes, found that before they became prostitutes one third had been raped and about half had been sexually abused.

From the conflict perspective, this pattern of abuse is significant. Abused as children, when they had no power, and most often by men, these women become locked into a way of life in which they continue to be victimized by men—by pimps who exploit their bodies for profit and by "johns" who use them for sexual pleasure.

The Three Stages in Becoming a Prostitute:

1. Drift

As you saw in the box "Me, a Prostitute?" becoming a prostitute is usually a gradual process. Nanette Davis, a symbolic interactionist who interviewed prostitutes in three correctional institutions in Minnesota, discovered that prostitutes go through three stages. In the first stage, they *drift* from casual sex to their first act of prostitution. "The 'drift' is a series of forks in the road where certain choices or events channel the young woman in a direction conducive to prostitution" (James and Davis 1982:348). Circumstances that may lead to drifting include a broken home, dropping out of school, pregnancy, drug use, and a juvenile record.

One event that sets up the drift into prostitution is having sex at a young age. On average, these women first had sex when they were $13\frac{1}{2}$ (the youngest was age 7, the oldest 18). For about four years, the girls engaged in casual sex and then drifted to selling sex. One of Davis' informants described it this way:

> I was going to school and I wanted to go to this dance the night after. I needed new clothes. I went out at ten o'clock and home at twelve. I had three tricks the first time, and fifteen dollars for every trick. (Davis 1978:206)

2. Transition

3. Professionalization

The Pimp and the Prostitute: A Counter Culture

[handwritten margin notes: WHAT ABOUT KEEPING THE FAMILY TOGETHER?? FAMILIES THAT OTHERWISE WOULD HAVE BROKEN APART? THE CHILDREN]

[handwritten margin note: SEX = POWER]

Davis calls the second stage *transitional deviance*. During this stage, which lasts an average of six months, girls experience **role ambivalence;** that is, they are not sure if they want to be a prostitute. They both want the role and do not want it. To help overcome their ambivalence, many try to **normalize** their acts; that is, they try to think of what they are doing as normal. For example, although they sell sex, they may call it something else. As one girl said:

> I'm a person who likes to walk. There's nothing wrong with picking somebody up while you're walking. I always like walking around at night, and girls will be tempted. Girls like the offer. They like to see what a guy is going to say. (Davis 1978:203–209)

To "normalize" selling sex is to turn the deviance into a normal act. In effect, this girl is saying: "I'm just doing a normal thing, walking. It's the guy who makes the offer. If a girl is tempted—well, that's only natural, too."

Davis calls the third stage *professionalization*. During this stage, the girls no longer tell themselves that their behavior is normal, and they come to think of themselves as prostitutes. They begin to build their lives around this identity. They also defend their involvement in prostitution. Some sound as though they have read the functionalist perspective; they claim that they help wives by giving husbands a sexual outlet that reduces tensions in their marriage. Others, such as a madam who wrote a book about her life, say that prostitution helps to prevent rape. Note how closely what this madam says resembles the analysis of the functionalist Kingsley Davis:

> As to my claim about performing a useful social service, every lusty, tourist-jammed town like San Francisco needs safety valves and outlets for its males. Shut down a town and the rape rate soars higher than an astronaut. (Stanford 1968: 206–207)

From a symbolic interactionist framework, prostitutes eventually come full circle. They begin by defining their activities as normal, denying that they are prostituting themselves. Then, in this last stage, they again use normalization, acknowledging their prostitution but defining it as beneficial.

To see how young some prostitutes are (as well as how old), look at Table 3-2. The involvement of children in commercial sex is what especially upsets people. We shall return to this topic in the section on children and pornography.

Why would a woman rent her body, gamble on not being hurt by sadists, even risk death by AIDS, and then turn the money over to a man? Let's see how the three sociological perspectives help explain this.

Functionalism looks at the services pimps provide. Presumably, pimps locate customers, try to screen out sadists, and bail the woman out of jail when she is arrested. However, we know that, in actuality, pimps are more likely to make the woman chase up her own customers, to be unconcerned if she is beaten by a john, and to be unavailable when she is arrested. For this reason, we have to move beyond functionalism for an explanation.

The conflict perspective provides a different answer. Simply put, pimps have the power. They, not the prostitutes, control the streets. To control women, they use their greater physical strength, and they are ruthless. Consider what a former prostitute said:

> I saw a girl walk into a bar and hand the pimp a $100 bill. He took it and burned it in her face and turned around and knocked her down on the floor and kicked her and said, "I told you, bitch, $200. I want $200, not $100." Now she's

Table 3-2	Arrests for Prostitution in the United States, by Age	
Age	Percent	Number
Under 15	.2	120
15–17	1.3	804
18–24	18.5	11,408
25–44	68.3	41,943
45–54	8.9	5,443
55–64	2.0	1,211
65 and older	.7	454
Total arrested:		61,383

Note: Because these figures also contain arrests for "commercilized vice," they include a large proportion (40 percent) of males. Due to rounding, the percentages total 99.9.

Source: Tabulated from *Uniform Crime Reports* 2000: Table 38.

gotta go out again and make not another hundred, but two hundred. (Millett 1973:134)

The third answer is provided by symbolic interactionists, who attempt to attain a "view from within." Let's explore the insights provided by this perspective more fully. We need to begin by asking what a pimp means to a prostitute. To understand this, the typical background of prostitutes, which we discussed earlier, is significant, for being victimized as a child makes one emotionally dependent, and pimps are experts at playing on this weakness. Many offer affection and tenderness. Others promise marriage, children, even a home in the suburbs after they have saved enough money from the woman's earnings. Pimps, however, are exploiters, and a pimp may be making the same promises to several women. He may tell each that she is the special one in his life, cautioning her not to tell the others so the two of them can use the earnings of the other women to fulfill their plans.

Pimps are unconcerned about the welfare of their women, except as it affects their earnings. The women are mere money machines, objects to be used or abused at will. The pimp's real interest is in the prestige he gets from other street males. His status depends on the number of women he controls in his "stable"; on how aloof he can remain from women while still making them bend to his will; and on his personal grooming, jewelry, cars, leisure, and free-spending ways.

Pimps and prostitutes form a **counterculture,** a subculture in which the values of the dominant culture are turned upside down. In this world, say anthropologists Christina and Richard Milner (1972), the women provide the income; the men spend it. The women work during the night and sleep during the day. The men don't work; they are conspicuous consumers. *Polygyny,* the union of one man with more than one woman, is the norm. The women can have sex with other men (not just the johns), and the pimps do not express jealousy. And when a woman gets pregnant, neither she nor her pimp cares who the father is.

Symbolic interactionists stress that to understand people we need to grasp their definitions of the situation. We need to see how their norms influence their behavior—just as our norms influence ours. When one takes an insider's view, the world looks like a different place—and it is. And that is the point, to see from within in order to understand human behavior—especially when it contradicts one's own standards and experiences.

Homosexual Prostitution

Before we consider why prostitution is a social problem, let's turn to the selling and buying of sexual acts between people of the same sex. Homosexual prostitution often takes place in areas known as "meat racks," public settings such as street corners, parks, and bars. A study in Rome found that some homosexual prostitutes have 1,500 sexual partners a year (Gattari et al. 1992). A study in Chicago by sociologist David Luckenbill (1986) found that male prostitutes have a hierarchy. At the top rank are escort prostitutes, those who work for modeling or dating agencies. At the lowest rank are street hustlers, and at the middle are bar hustlers. The charge per trick goes up with each level.

Prostitution by teenage boys has become more open since sociologists first studied it in the 1950s. In some urban areas known as "meat racks," boy prostitutes gather in search of customers. They use the same symbols as female prostitutes to advertise their intentions: dress, stance, and location. Shown here are four homeless boys who have become prostitutes in New York City.

Houses of Male Prostitution (rare)

Sociologist David Pittman (1971), who studied a house of male prostitution in St. Louis, found that the "madam" (a male) advertises for male models. When young men apply, he explains why he really wants to hire them. He photographs them nude and shows a catalog of his "models" to customers. With youth being so highly valued and customers insisting on a continuous supply of fresh bodies, these male prostitutes face intense pressure. Many turn to stimulant drugs, become depressed, and drink heavily. Their sexual performance flags, they lose customers, and are fired.

Boy Prostitutes

In a classic study from the 1960s, sociologist Albert Reiss, Jr. (1961) found that teenagers who were paid by homosexuals to receive oral sex maintained a heterosexual identity. As you can imagine, this required an intricate balancing act. The boys accomplished this by (1) allowing no emotional involvement with the adult fellator, (2) making money the only purpose of the act (not sexual gratification, which they reserved for females), (3) tolerating no sexual act other than receiving fellatio, (4) never seeing a homosexual socially, and (5) openly having a girlfriend.

Prostitution by boys has become more open since Reiss studied it, and probably more common as well (Morse et al. 1991; Cates and Markley 1992). Many of the boys are runaways from lower-class or welfare families (Lloyd 1976). Some prostitute themselves to survive, others simply to have extra money (Cates and Markley 1992). The apparent increase in boy prostitution is seen by many as a social problem in and of itself. A related problem is the frequency of AIDS among homosexual prostitutes.

Prostitution as a Social Problem

Why is prostitution considered a social problem? The primary objection, which has been constant throughout our history, is morality (Brace 1880:123–131). Some see prostitution as immoral because it involves sexual behavior between people who are not married to one another, it is the selling of sex, and prostitutes (along with their customers, of course) perform oral and anal sex acts, and other more unusual sexual acts. The second objection is that prostitution exploits women's bodies, degrades their spirit, and subjugates them to men. A third objection is that prostitution ruins "good" neighborhoods and depresses property values by bringing in unsavory characters and illegal activities such as drug dealing. Fourth is the view that prostitution is a social problem because it is a crime. Victimless or not, prostitution is illegal, and that makes it part of a larger social problem. A fifth view pinpoints the symbiotic nature of prostitution as the social problem: Prostitution corrupts police and judges, uniting these "enforcers of morality" with pimps and madams; prostitution also feeds organized crime. Finally, some people object because prostitutes spread disease. AIDS has given this last objection special urgency. Related to this is the disgust and fear people feel when they see used condoms and tissues left in public places, including schoolyards. In summary, people object to prostitution on the grounds of immorality, exploitation, practicality, criminality, corruption of officials, and the transmission of disease.

We now consider a second sexual activity to which many also object.

✦ Homosexuality ✦

Why are people sexually attracted to members of their own sex? How many people are homosexuals? How do people become homosexual? Do some people who are not homosexual have sex with others of their own gender? Such questions are common. As we answer them, we shall look first at the broader scope of this social problem, then apply conflict theory to homosexuality in the United States, and finally examine specific research findings.

BACKGROUND: GETTING THE LARGER PICTURE

Homosexual Behavior vs. Homosexuality

Attitudes toward **homosexual behavior**—sexual *relations* between people of the same sex—vary widely around the world. One of the most startling attitudes—to Western ears—is that of the Keraki of New Guinea. During puberty rites, which are kept secret from females, each boy is initiated into sodomy (anal intercourse). The following year, the boy continues to play a passive role with older boys and unmarried men. After that, until he marries (a woman), he, too, sodomizes the younger boys (Ford and Beach 1972). Another group in New Guinea, the Sambia, believe that a boy will remain small and weak if he does not ingest semen. To prevent this, Sambian boys have oral sex with men, and their homosexual behavior is considered a passage to "masculinization." The boys go on to a heterosexual life of marriage and procreation (Gilmore 1990).

Attitudes also vary toward **homosexuality,** the sexual *preference* for persons of one's own sex, but here cross-cultural attitudes are more consistent. No society in the world considers exclusive, or even predominant, homosexuality in adulthood to be the norm. As sociologist Arno Karlen (1978:241) summarized this point, "Like sanctions against incest, adult-child coitus, and rape, the sanction against *predominant adult* homosexuality is universal."

Possible Reasons for Negative Sanctions and Disapproving Attitudes

Why do these universal sanctions exist? From a functionalist viewpoint, the primary reason centers on the role that the family plays in human societies. Every culture expects adults to become parents, and all societies build the family around some form of mother, father, and children. To tolerate or approve general homosexual behavior would upset this fundamental biologically based arrangement.

Attitudes in the U.S.

In recent years, Americans have become more tolerant about homosexuality and homosexual behavior (Smith 1990; Marsiglio 1993; Cantril and Cantril 1994; NORC 1994). As you can see from Table 3-3, 54 percent of Americans think that homosexual relations between consenting adults should be legal. Forty-two percent of Americans, however, want homosexual relations to be illegal. From this table, you

Table 3-3   Attitudes Toward the Legality of Homosexual Relations

Question: "Do you think homosexual relations between consenting adults should or should not be legal?"

	Legal	Not Legal	No Opinion
National	54%	42%	4%
Sex			
Male	49	46	5
Female	57	39	4
Race			
White	54	41	5
Black	51	48	1
Age			
18 to 29 years	65	33	2
30 to 49 years	58	39	3
50 to 64 years	49	45	6
50 years and older	42	51	7
65 years and older	33	58	9
Education			
College post graduate	71	25	4
College graduate	68	30	2
Some college	59	37	4
High school graduate or less	40	55	5
Income			
$75,000 and over	69	28	3
$50,000 to $74,999	57	39	4
$30,000 to $49,999	53	43	4
$20,000 to $29,999	50	44	6
Under $20,000	45	51	4
Community			
Urban area	60	37	3
Suburban area	54	40	6
Rural area	45	52	3
Region			
East	59	37	4
Midwest	56	40	4
South	45	50	5
West	56	39	5
Politics			
Republican	38	57	5
Democrat	57	40	3
Independent	64	32	4

Source: *Sourcebook of Criminal Justice Statistics* 2000, page 182. Table constructed by SOURCEBOOK staff from data provided by The Gallup Organization, Inc. Reprinted by permission.

can sketch a profile of those who are most likely to support the legalization of homosexual relations: younger white women who have a post-graduate education, who live in an eastern city and who make over $75,000 a year. Those most likely to want homosexual relations to be illegal are elderly black male high school graduates with low income who live in rural areas. Attitudes follow the expected age pattern, with the younger more likely to favor the legality of homosexual relations.

Some of these attitudes are rooted in the Judeo-Christian heritage, which condemns homosexuality as a perversion of God's creation. Many Americans fear that if homosexuality were tolerated, homosexuals would attempt to recruit their sons and daughters. Others fear that if they tolerate homosexuality, they will then be forced to take the next step—giving it their approval. (**Toleration** is allowing something to exist, regardless of how you feel about it; **approval** implies positive acceptance.)

Homosexuals and the Law

The social institutions of U.S. society presume the norm of **heterosexuality,** the sexual preference for persons of the opposite sex (Law 1988; Arriola 1990). Accordingly, they are aligned against homosexuals and homosexual behavior. For example, what homosexuals do sexually, even in private, has been called "an act against nature" and until 1966 was legally prohibited in every state (Reinig 1990). Today, private, consensual sex between people of the same sex is still illegal in most states. The U.S. Supreme Court has upheld Georgia's law that makes sodomy punishable by up to 20 years in prison (Wermiel 1986a). In no state is it legal for homosexuals to marry.

Hate Crimes

Over the years, homosexuals have been the victims of violence because of their sexual orientation. Until recently, however, there was no way of knowing the extent of their victimization. This changed in 1990 when Congress passed the *Hate Crime Statistics Act,* which authorized the FBI to collect data on "crimes that manifest evidence of prejudice based on race, religion, ethnicity, and sexual orientation. . . . **Hate crimes** are not separate, distinct crimes, but rather traditional offenses motivated by the offender's bias" (*FBI UCR* 2000:1). In 2000, 1,277 incidents comprising 1,464 offenses were committed against homosexuals (*FBI UCR Hate Crime Report* 2000:7). The actual total is larger, because not all victims have made reports and not all police agencies have reported these data to the FBI.

Given the prevailing attitudes in U.S. society, most homosexuals remain "in the closet"; that is, they pretend to be heterosexuals on the job and in most of their social relations. In some fields, however, notably the arts, homosexuals are more open about their sexual preference.

Homosexuals and Occupations: Islands of Acceptance

Although we do not have space to detail how the linkages between one particular professional field and homosexuality developed, we can note the following principles. As people participate in a specialized activity, they tend to develop values, ideas, and even myths that set them apart from the mainstream. In short, they develop a **subculture.** People in the arts (including painting, poetry, sculpture, acting, creative writing, and so on) try to develop new ways of expressing reality. This makes them more receptive to nontraditional ideas—including that of accepting homosexuality as an alternative lifestyle. Myths also develop (such as that of homosexuals being more creative than heterosexuals) that facilitate the acceptance of homosexuals in certain occupations. Finally, if homosexuals are accepted and do well in an occupation, more homosexuals are attracted to it.

Current Changes

The overall situation of homosexuals in U.S. society has changed. Due to the activities of gay liberation groups and the American Civil Liberties Union, homosexuals face less occupational discrimination than they used to. The Civil Service Com-

Homosexuals in the United States have become more open about their sexual orientation in recent years. Shown here are New York City police officers who are members of Gay Officers Action League. They are participating in Gay Pride Day.

mission no longer denies federal employment to homosexuals. Similarly, such multinational corporate giants as AT&T and IBM follow strict policies of not discriminating against homosexuals in hiring or promotion. San Francisco even purposely recruits homosexuals as members of its police force. Homosexuals used to be easy targets of politicians who wanted to ingratiate themselves with voters and further their own political ambitions. Today, for a politician to verbally attack homosexuals would be to risk his or her political career. (Instead, as we saw in our opening vignette, politicians find prostitutes and pornographers easy targets.)

Such changes do not mean the end of open discrimination. The FBI and CIA, for example, will not hire known homosexuals. And although the Defense Department follows a "Don't Ask, Don't Tell" policy, soldiers who are discovered to be homosexual are discharged from the military. This policy has been upheld by the Supreme Court (Lambert 1994).

To understand homosexuality as a social problem better, let's look at it through the lens of conflict theory.

HOMOSEXUALITY VIEWED THEORETICALLY: APPLYING CONFLICT THEORY

Hostilities

Let's begin with incidents on college campuses. At Colorado State University, a dead rat was thrown at the dormitory door of Ethan Cordova, who was trying to organize a homosexual fraternity. In case the message wasn't clear, his assailants also wrote on his door, "Go Home Faggot!" Anonymous death threats also appeared on Cordova's answering machine. These were especially frightening because of the recent death of Matthew Shepard, a gay student at the University of Wyoming at Laramie, who died after he was brutally beaten, burned, and tied to a fence (Gladstone 1999). At Yale University, heterosexual students who wanted to mock their school's "Gay Awareness Week" held "Bestiality Awareness Days." And at the University of Massachusetts, students held a "Heterosexuals Fight Back Week" (Johnson 1987).

THINKING CRITICALLY ABOUT SOCIAL PROBLEMS

Should Homosexuals Be Declared a Minority Group?

This issue divides Americans. Many people feel strongly about it and land squarely on one side or the other. Where do your opinions fall? Why? Do you accept all the arguments of one of these positions? How does your position differ?

THEY SHOULD:

Homosexuals are victimized throughout society, and they deserve the same legal protection as those given to other minority groups. Anyone who refuses to rent to someone because that person is a homosexual should suffer legal consequences. So should anyone who refuses to hire a homosexual who is qualified for a job—and that includes active duty in the military.

But the matter is more than avoiding and overcoming discrimination. Schools also have a duty to discuss homosexuality in order to reduce negative stereotypes and homophobia. Children should be given the option of exploring their potential homosexual orientation within an accepting environment, not fed stereotypes and other negative images that make them ashamed of such desires.

In short, we are not asking for tolerance. Tolerance implies superiority on the part of those granting it. We demand that homosexual identity and sexual behavior be viewed as viable, legitimate, and normal as are heterosexual identity and sexual behavior.

THEY SHOULD NOT:

Homosexuals are not a minority group, and awarding them special legal rights is a misplaced idea. Racial and ethnic minorities, and males and females, become members of a group through birth. They have no choice about belonging, nor does their membership imply any immoral behavior. Homosexuals, in contrast, have chosen their lifestyle. They deserve no more legal protection for choosing to have sex with each other than does anybody else for their sexual preference. Does someone who prefers adultery deserve legal protection because of that preference? Even if some people are predisposed to homosexuality, is this any different from some people being predisposed to lying? We don't make lying an acceptable behavior and assign liars a minority status.

Anyone who believes that a homosexual lifestyle is immoral should not have to rent to homosexuals. Nor should churches be forced to ordain them, schools or other employers to hire them, or the military to accept them.

Based on Farney 1994.

Political Activism

To combat discrimination, homosexuals have become active politically. They campaign for legal reform, march in public demonstrations, and demand more social rights and political participation (Cooper 1989–90; Fisher 1992; Navarro 1998). In some cities, such as San Francisco and New York, homosexuals have become a potent political force. They have also become active as a group in national politics, and often it is at their own risk that politicians ignore the homosexual vote.

Many homosexuals have *come out of the closet,* that is, have publicly asserted a homosexual identity, but the open advocacy of homosexuality as an alternative lifestyle has generated some hostility. Gay advocacy has become a hot issue in schools and in work settings. As homosexuals have publicized their demands, homosexuality has become a charged political and social issue in the United States. Major facets of this issue are summarized above in the Thinking Critically box on whether homosexuals should be declared a minority group.

Conflict is inevitable when opposing interest groups jockey for position. The results can be positive, however: Conflict can create shifts in power alignments, force a

re-evaluation of commitments, thrust smoldering issues to center stage, and compel new trade-offs between dissenting groups. To keep the peace, such groups often make trade-offs, with each giving up something that it desires. As conflict theorists stress, however, the resulting truce can be uneasy, for the coexistence of antithetical values usually means that conflict will eventually surface. All it takes is for one side to try to shift the terms of the uneasy and often unspoken alignment.

An Uneasy Truce

Viewing homosexuals and heterosexuals as participants in an uneasy truce, conflict theorists anticipate ongoing confrontation and conflict. The conflict will endure, they stress, for many basic values and orientations of these groups are opposed to one another. At any time, those differences could erupt into open conflict. That homosexuals have been assigned most of the blame for AIDS makes that possibility more real.

RESEARCH ON HOMOSEXUALITY

The Kinsey Research

Let's turn now to a brief overview of sociological studies of homosexuality. Alfred Kinsey and his associates included homosexuality in their monumental study *Sexual Behavior in the Human Male* (1948). To understand the Kinsey findings of more than a half century ago, keep in mind the distinction made earlier between homosexual behavior and homosexuality. Based on case histories of about 5,300 males, Kinsey found that 37 percent of U.S. males have at least one sexual experience with a same-sex partner that results in orgasm. Such experiences, however, do not make people homosexuals. As Kinsey pointed out, these homosexual acts are a form of experimentation, and almost all of these males go on to live heterosexual lives. Kinsey also concluded that about 4 percent of U.S. males are exclusively homosexual throughout life.

Kinsey's findings shocked the U.S. public and unleashed a storm of criticism in the academic community. The primary problem is that Kinsey used a biased sample, and there is no scientific way to generalize from his findings. Kinsey recruited some subjects from prisons and reform schools whose inmates hardly represent the general population. He also interviewed only whites, and he had too high a percentage of the lower class (Himmelhoch and Fava 1955).

The Laumann Research

The most accurate research on U.S. sexual behavior has been carried out by a team of researchers headed by sociologist Edward Laumann (1994). Because Laumann interviewed a representative sample of the U.S. population, we can generalize his findings to the entire U.S. population. As you can see from Figure 3-1, Laumann found that over a five-year period, 4.1 percent of U.S. men and 2.2 percent of U.S. women had sex with a same-sex partner. If the time period is extended to include all the previous years of their lives, these figures increase to 3.8 percent of the women and 7.1 percent of the men. This is a far cry from Kinsey's 37 percent for men. These totals also balance the statement that is sometimes bandied about in the popular press—that "10 percent of all American males are homosexuals" (Wertheimer 1988).

As Figure 3-1 also shows, 1.4 percent of U.S. women and 2.8 percent of U.S. men identify themselves as homosexuals. These percentages are almost identical to those who report that they have had sex with a same-sex partner during the past year (1.3 percent of the women and 2.7 percent of the men). Even these figures may be slightly high, as the Laumann researchers included as homosexuals people who identify themselves as bisexuals.

As you will recall from Chapter 1, sociologists use more than interviews to do their research. Although Laumann's sampling technique gives us data from which we

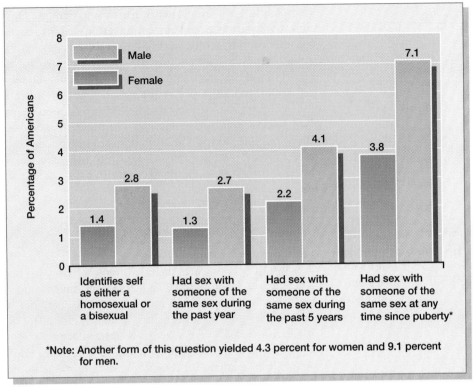

FIGURE 3-1
Homosexual Identity and Sex with Someone of the Same Sex
(*Source:* Laumann et al. 1994:293–296).

*Note: Another form of this question yielded 4.3 percent for women and 9.1 percent for men.

can generalize, some sociologists desire more qualitative data. They want information that describes what occurs when people interact.

The Humphreys Research

To get qualitative information on homosexual behavior, sociologist Laud Humphreys devised an ingenious but widely criticized method. Knowing that some male homosexuals meet for impersonal sex in public rest rooms ("tearooms," to use the homosexual vernacular), Humphreys (1970) began hanging around these rest rooms. He took the role of "watch queen," the one who gives warning when strangers approach, and observed what went on. He saw that these men used a system of gestures to initiate sex at the urinal and then moved to a toilet stall for fellatio (oral sex). Their quick, anonymous sex usually occurred without the exchange of a single word. Another sociologist, Edward Delph (1978), confirmed the silence surrounding these sexual encounters.

Humphreys found something else that was surprising: 38 percent of the men he observed having tearoom sex were married and identified themselves as heterosexuals. Why did these heterosexual men engage in homosexual behaviors? It turns out that they were sexually frustrated with their wives. In tearooms they found a sexual outlet that did not require socializing and emotional commitment. In essence, the tearooms functioned for them as a free house of prostitution: There they could obtain oral sex at no charge. Their quick stop at a park rest room just off the highway jeopardized neither their work nor their commuting schedules. Sociologists Jay Corzine and Richard Kirby (1977) found that similar behavior occurs at truck stops: Heterosexual truckers have sex with homosexuals who search out partners at highway rest areas.

The term *situational homosexual behavior* refers to sexual behavior between people of the same sex that is induced by the situation. Typical examples are same-sex boarding schools, and prisons, such as this one in California.

The Question of Research Ethics

You may have wondered how Humphreys knew how many of the men he observed having tearoom sex were married. What he did was to write down these men's license plate numbers and then trace their home addresses. A year later, he visited the men's homes in the guise of a researcher conducting a health survey. For being deceptive, Humphreys was severely criticized. At first Humphreys vigorously defended himself, but in the second edition of his book (1975) he agreed that he should have identified himself as a researcher.

Situational Homosexual Behavior: The Prison

Certain places, such as prisons and boarding schools, induce **situational homosexual behavior** in people who do not otherwise practice it. George Kirkham (1971), a sociologist who studied homosexual behavior in the state prison at Soledad, California, identified three types of participants: the "queen," the "punk," and the "wolf."

In this men's prison, "queen" refers to an inmate who prefers male sexual partners. The queen, then, does not engage in situational homosexual behavior, for, in prison or out, "she" prefers male partners. To attract fellow prisoners, the queen exaggerates aspects of female sexuality. She may adopt a feminine nickname ("Peaches," "Dee-Dee"), tear the back pockets from tight prison denims to make them more form-fitting, use cosmetics made from medical and food supplies, and wear jewelry produced in hobby shops. The queen lets her hair grow as long as the guards allow, and has an exaggerated "swish" as she walks.

When they first enter prison, most men find queens despicable. As the months pass, however, the queen evokes the memory and longing for women, and some change their mind. Some heterosexual men even enter into long-term relationships with queens. Their relationships resemble marriage, including the expectation of sexual fidelity and emotional exchange. Most queens are promiscuous, however, and these relationships are brittle. Some queens become prison prostitutes and end up working for a prison pimp. Some are even sold to other pimps to settle debts. The queen is accorded some social status, for she is thought to be following her natural inclinations.

Next to the "rat," or informer, the "punk" has the least social status among prisoners. There are two types: "canteen punks," who offer anal intercourse or fellatio in exchange for candy, cigarettes, money, or personal favors, and "pressure punks," who perform the same services in response to threats or violence. Both are despised by prison inmates: canteen punks because they sacrifice their manhood to obtain goods or services, and pressure punks because they show weakness in the face of violence.

How do men become pressure punks? Some are gang raped and then forced into this status for the rest of their prison term. Most, however, are tricked into it. Some "fish" (a new inmate), unacquainted with prison ways, accept cigarettes, money, or help of some sort from an experienced inmate. Others are the victims of a rigged gambling game. In either case, if the fish cannot pay when the experienced inmate demands settlement of the debt, he is told that he must give sex as payment. At this point, the fish has just two choices—to submit or to fight. A fish who submits is marked as a punk from then on and must continue to provide sex for the rest of his prison term.

The "wolf" has sex with punks, but he does not lose his status as a "man." To remain a "man" and still engage in sex with other men, however, he must present an image of exaggerated toughness. Force and rape match this image, and the more violence that surrounds the wolf's sexual acts, the more he is seen as masculine. He must also keep his sexual acts emotionless and impersonal. Some wolves "own" punks and prostitute them for cigarettes or drugs.

Forming a Homosexual Identity

Situational homosexual behavior disappears when the situation changes—for example, when a male prisoner leaves prison and again has sex with women. This reminds us again of the distinction made earlier between homosexuality and homosexual behavior. But what do we know about the causes of homosexuality—the *preference* for someone of one's own sex?

In spite of many theories and thousands of studies, we do not know the answer. Although it is possible that genetics in the form of DNA markers or the organization of the brain may underlie human sexual orientation, researchers have found no chemical, biological, or even psychological differences that distinguish homosexuals and heterosexuals (Hooker 1957, 1958; Masters and Johnson 1979; Paul et al. 1982; Hamer et al. 1993; LeVay 1993; Laumann 1994). Because of this, sociologists do not view homosexuality as the result of genetic predispositions, or even consider it to be due to certain types of family relations, such as a "weak," aloof father and a close, "dominant" mother.

For reasons currently unknown, then, some people feel erotic desires for members of their own sex. We know that erotic desires are insufficient cause for people to label themselves homosexual, however, for many people who experience such desires continue to identify themselves as heterosexuals (cf., Laumann 1994). How, then, do people develop an identity as homosexual? Sociologist Vivienne Cass (1979) found that this transition centers on self-labeling. Utilizing case studies and symbolic interactionism, Cass identified six stages:

Six Stages in the Process of Developing a Homosexual Identity

1. **Identity confusion** Finding his or her feelings or behaviors at odds with heterosexual orientations, the individual is confused and upset. He or she asks, "Who am I?" and replies *"My behavior or feelings could be called homosexual."*

2. **Identity comparison** The individual begins to feel "different," as though he or she does not belong. He or she makes the first tentative commitment to a homosexual identity by saying, *"I may be a homosexual."*

3. **Identity tolerance** The individual turns the self-image further away from a heterosexual identity and more toward a homosexual identity. The conclusion at this point is, *"I probably am a homosexual."*

4. **Identity acceptance** The individual moves from tolerating a homosexual self-image to accepting a homosexual identity. After increasing contact with others who define themselves as homosexual, he or she concludes, *"I am a homosexual."*

5. **Identity pride** The individual thinks of homosexuality as good and heterosexuality as bad. He or she makes a strong commitment to a homosexual group, which generates a firm sense of group identity. The individual may become politically active and thinks, *"I am a homosexual and proud of it."*

6. **Identity synthesis** The individual decides that the "them and us" philosophy is false. He or she begins to feel much similarity between himself or herself and some heterosexuals—as well as much dissimilarity between himself or herself and some homosexuals. Although homosexuality remains essential to the individual's identity, it becomes merely one aspect of the self. The individual may say, *"I am a homosexual—but I am also a lot of other things in life."*

Self Identities Are Not Fixed

In line with symbolic interactionism, Cass stresses that people construct their own self-images. Individuals who have begun to interpret their feelings and behavior in terms of homosexuality may stop at any stage. They may even move back toward a heterosexual identity. For example, in stage 1, faced with the possibility that their behavior *could* be called homosexual, people can stop the behavior. They can also continue it, but define it as situational rather than as part of their sexual orientation. People in the third stage may feel positive that they "probably" are homosexual and eagerly move to the fourth stage—or they may dislike this probability and move away from a homosexual identification. In metaphorical terms, one can continue the journey, get off the train at the station marked "Identification Stops Here," or get off at the station called "Return to Heterosexuality." To have begun the journey does not mean that one must continue it to a final destination called "Homosexuality" (Bell et al. 1981).

Confirming Sexual Identities

As people are acquiring a sexual identity, they try to confirm that identity. Often they associate with others who reinforce it. When people who feel they are heterosexual associate with heterosexuals and do "heterosexual things," and people who feel they are homosexual associate with homosexuals and do "homosexual things," both are confirming their developing identities. The heterosexual and homosexual worlds overlap, however, and the point at which they cross can present a challenge to those identities.

Challenging Sexual Identities

Although our sexual identity may be tenuous during childhood, over time it becomes more firmly rooted. By the time we are adults, we seldom question it. Not everyone's sexual identity, however, is firm. While some homosexuals and heterosexuals apparently never question their choice, others are filled with self-doubt. As sociologist Rose Weitz (1991) found in her study of AIDS, some homosexuals are plagued with guilt, and AIDS challenges their sexual identity. Some then reaffirm the social norms that condemn homosexual activities, ask their families, churches, and God to accept their apologies and to forgive their sins, and then assert a "new self." Some even try to convince others that this was their "real self" all along. To continue our earlier analogy, a few adult homosexuals get back on the train and take it to an earlier station in their sexual identity. Weitz also found that for some people whose identity as homosexual made them uneasy, AIDS is a catalyst that makes them more comfortable with their identity. For them, the train stops at a station in which they embrace a homosexual identity.

In Sum

According to symbolic interactionism, identities, including one's sexual identity, are not fixed in nature or inherent in one's birth. Instead, we are born with an undirected sexual potential that becomes channeled by our experiences into a homosexual or heterosexual direction. A heterosexual or homosexual identity does not unfold automatically from within—like an acorn that can become only an oak tree. Rather, sexual preferences are learned, and people acquire sexual identities to match.

DIFFERENCES BETWEEN MALE AND FEMALE HOMOSEXUALS

What differences have researchers found between male and female homosexuals? (The term for female homosexuals, **lesbian,** apparently first referred to the Greek island of Lesbos, home of the poet Sappho, who wrote lyric poetry celebrating the love of woman for woman.)

Incidence and Promiscuity

You have already seen that homosexuality is more common among males than females, a finding that is supported by all researchers who have reported on this matter. Let's see what other differences they have found. One of the most significant is that lesbians are more likely to seek lasting relationships, place a premium on emotional commitment and mutual fidelity, and shun the bar scene (Wolf 1979; Lowenstein 1980; Peplau and Amaro 1982). Consequently, while most male homosexuals have "cruised" (sought impersonal sex with strangers), fewer than 20 percent of lesbians have done so. As a result, lesbians tend to have fewer sexual partners than do male homosexuals. Psychologist Alan Bell and sociologist Martin Weinberg (1978) interviewed about 1,500 homosexuals. They found that almost half the white and one third the African-American homosexual males had at least 500 different sexual partners. About 28 percent of the white sample had more than 1,000 different partners. Although their sample is large, it is not representative of homosexuals, because their research focused heavily on bars and steam baths. In these settings, people are looking for sex, so the sample is skewed toward people who have many sexual partners. We need balancing studies of homosexuals who are committed to a partner. Bell's and Weinberg's findings do, however, support other studies indicating extensive promiscuity among male homosexuals.

Since the appearance of AIDS, promiscuity can mean a death sentence, as it has for so many. Consequently, many homosexuals have changed their sexual practices and reduced their number of sexual partners (Siegel et al. 1988; Siegel and Glassman 1989).

Why are there such substantial differences in promiscuity and commitment between male and female homosexuals? Symbolic interactionists would argue that the chief reason can be traced to differences in their socialization. Girls are more likely to learn to associate sex with emotional relationships, and, like their heterosexual counterparts, lesbians tend to conform to this basic expectation. Similarly, boys tend to learn to separate sex from affection, to validate their self-images by how much sex they have, and to see fidelity as a restriction on their independence (Prus and Irini 1988). In short, homosexuals reflect the broad-based gender expectations of our culture.

Like prostitution, homosexuality is a social problem because of subjective concerns, because of the way large numbers of people evaluate the behavior. Most Americans think that homosexual behavior is wrong—a perversion of the natural sexual order between men and women. Many are concerned that it threatens the family and basic decency and values. As with prostitution and pornography, however, Americans are divided on this issue. Some view homosexuality as a permissible alternative lifestyle, with the problem being that created by heterosexuals who insist on imposing their sexual orientations on others. Like other social problems, homosexuality draws its share of extremists. Those on one side argue that homosexuals should be punished with legal and social sanctions, while extremists on the other side argue that homosexuality should be encouraged among our youth. We shall return to these contrasting positions in the section on social policy.

◆ Pornography ◆

BACKGROUND: GETTING THE LARGER PICTURE

The Definition of Pornography

Originally, pornography referred to the writings of prostitutes or to descriptions of the life of prostitutes. (*Porna* is Greek for "prostitute.") For our purposes, **pornography** may be defined as writings, pictures, or objects that people object to as being filthy or depraved.

Pornography in Ancient Civilizations

Materials intended to cause sexual excitement go far back in history. Pornography abounded in the Roman Empire, as shown by excavations of the Mediterranean resort city of Pompeii, which was destroyed by an eruption of Mount Vesuvius in A.D. 79. There, archeologists have uncovered brothels decorated with mosaics of men and women in various sexual acts. The *Kama Sutra*, an Indian religious book dating from the eighth century after Christ, which is explicit about sex, includes suggestions on how prostitutes can please their customers (Henriques 1966).

Difficulties in Deciding What Is Pornographic

Deciding what is pornographic is difficult, for, like beauty, pornography lies in the eye of the beholder. For example, are nude statues pornographic? Some think so. Are movies that depict sexual intercourse pornographic? More would probably say they are. Are movies or photos that depict oral sex pornographic? Again, probably a larger number would say yes. Are movies that show sex between an adult and a child

Sex sells, and pornography has grown into a highly lucrative business. However, it remains offensive to the majority of people within the United States. Here, demonstrators carry a large red banner in Times Square saying "Women Against Pornography— Stop Violence Against Women."

Table 3-4 American Attitudes About the Distribution of Pornography

	Should Be Illegal for Everyone				Should Be Illegal Only for Persons Under 18				Should Be Legal for Everyone			
	1980	1990	1996	2000	1980	1990	1996	2000	1980	1990	1996	2000
NATIONAL	40%	41%	38%	36%	51%	52%	58%	60%	6%	6%	3%	3%
Sex												
Male	31%	33%	25%	24%	60%	59%	70%	72%	8%	6%	5%	3%
Female	47%	47%	48%	45%	45%	47%	48%	51%	5%	5%	2%	3%
Race/Ethnicity												
White	41%	42%	39%	36%	52%	51%	56%	60%	6%	5%	3%	3%
African American	35%	34%	31%	34%	51%	57%	64%	59%	10%	7%	3%	5%
Education												
College	31%	36%	36%	31%	59%	57%	63%	65%	8%	7%	3%	3%
High School	42%	44%	46%	41%	52%	51%	57%	55%	5%	5%	2%	3%
Age												
18–20	12%	17%	23%	18%	79%	65%	70%	77%	9%	13%	3%	4%
21–29	23%	29%	25%	17%	69%	67%	72%	78%	7%	3%	2%	4%
30–49	32%	36%	30%	29%	60%	60%	66%	68%	7%	4%	3%	2%
50 and over	40%	53%	54%	52%	50%	36%	39%	43%	8%	8%	4%	4%
Religion												
Protestant	45%	46%	45%	44%	48%	48%	51%	53%	5%	5%	2%	2%
Catholic	40%	39%	30%	31%	52%	56%	65%	66%	6%	4%	2%	2%
Jew	25%	20%	24%	19%	59%	53%	63%	79%	9%	20%	5%	2%
None	8%	22%	18%	16%	74%	66%	73%	76%	15%	9%	7%	7%

Source: Sourcebook of Criminal Justice Statistics 1992:Table 2–98; 1997:Table 2–97.
*Only these two groups are given in the sources.

Agreement on Restriction

or between a human and an animal pornographic? At this point, the rate of agreement would increase sharply.

On one matter, almost everyone agrees—pornography, whatever it is, should be restricted. As shown in Table 3-4, 60 percent of Americans think that the sale of pornography to teenagers should be banned, and another 36 percent would outlaw pornography altogether—a total of 96 percent who favor broad legal restrictions. Attitudes toward censorship follow broad social avenues. Those most likely to want to ban pornography are females, those with only a high school education, older people, and Protestants. Those least likely to oppose its distribution are males, college graduates, younger people, and Jews. The gap in attitude between whites and African Americans has closed in recent years, and it is now too close to call.

Child Pornography

The portrayal of sex with children especially angers people. One reporter who surveyed pornography back in 1988 said:

> What the trade calls "chicken porn" is a specialty that uses [children of] both sexes, with the larger share actually concentrated on young males. (There are some 260 magazines catering to the male gay market, including one featuring only twin boys in sexual acts.) The little girlie magazines star models as young as 4 and as old as 15 or 16, with the most interest focused on prepubescents from 8 to 10. The publications bear titles on the order of *Lollitots* and *More Lollitots* and *Moppets*. . . . The raunchiest material is on film: mini-orgies between mini-partners, sex between

adults and children, sometimes stimulated by one urinating or defecating on the other, and, now and then, sex with a dog. (Dubar 1980:236)

With the passage of legislation that hands down prison terms not only to those who produce child pornography but also to anyone who possesses it, this form of pornography has gone underground again. In the early 1990s, child porn was easily available on the Internet, but this, too, has become clandestine. Pictures of heterosexual sex, homosexual sex, and of humans having sex with animals, however, remain easily accessible on the Internet.

Pornography as Big Business

From its beginnings as a marginal, underground cottage industry, pornography has grown into an open and aggressive $10 billion-a-year business. Porn videos alone bring in $4 billion a year (Stein 1998). Behind today's pornography lies an extensive network of people who profit from it: writers, publishers, actors, and filmmakers; owners of bookstores, video stores, theaters, and cable TV—and their workers; corner newsstands and supermarket chains; banks and financiers. Behind the scenes are well-known and respected U.S. business firms—and organized crime (Meese Commission 1986; Grasso 1994). To the extent that people subscribe to Internet Service Providers in order to gain access to pornography, even AOL and Compuserve get their share. Like politics, pornography makes strange bedfellows.

PORNOGRAPHY VIEWED THEORETICALLY: APPLYING SYMBOLIC INTERACTIONISM

Roth v. U.S.

The controversy about what is and is not pornographic—and what should be done about it—is one we have inherited from the past. One era's decisions may make little sense when viewed from a later historical perspective. In 1957, in the landmark *Roth v. U.S.*, the U.S. Supreme Court ruled that materials are pornographic or obscene when

1. "Taken as a whole," the "dominant theme" appeals to "prurient interest" in sex.

2. The material affronts "contemporary community standards."

3. The material is "utterly without redeeming social value."

Slippery Symbols and Muddled Meaning

Instead of settling anything, however, the key terms of the *Roth* decision (which are placed in quotes above) added fuel to the fire. *Prurient*, for example, means "lewd or impure." But what is lewd or impure to one person is not to another. The guidelines, which were supposed to clear up matters, merely muddied the waters. If the terms were clear, they were clear only to the Court.

As symbolic interactionists emphasize, all terms are empty of meaning until people determine for themselves what they mean. If two people watch the same movie containing nudity or sexual intercourse, one may see the beauty of art and the other the filth of pornography. What, then, does a phrase like "redeeming social value" mean? If an item contains explicit sexual content, where does it leave us if I decide that its other features have "redeeming social value," but you do not?

And so the war of symbols goes on. Some claim that certain materials violate "contemporary community standards," whereas others say that those same materials reflect community standards. Still others say there are no community standards! With the Internet, the matter has become even more complicated. Do those who exchange sexually explicit materials on the Internet form a community?

After the Roth decision, prosecutors had difficulty in obtaining convictions for pornography, and in 1973 the matter was brought again before the Supreme Court. In *California v. Miller*, the Court tried to remove the ambiguities of its earlier decision. It kept the dominant "prurient" theme, said that "contemporary community standards" meant the local community, and eliminated the criterion of "redeeming social value" (Lewis and Peoples 1978:1071).

In the *Miller* decision, the Court acknowledged the central premise of symbolic interactionism, that the same thing can have different meanings to different people:

> Nothing in the First Amendment requires that a jury must consider hypothetical and unascertainable "national standards" when attempting to determine whether certain materials are obscene. . . .
>
> It is neither realistic nor constitutionally sound to read the First Amendment as requiring that the people of Maine or Mississippi accept public depiction of conduct found tolerable in Las Vegas or New York City. . . .
>
> People in different States vary in their tastes and attitudes, and this diversity is not to be strangled by the absolutism of imposed uniformity. (Lewis and Peoples 1978:1068)

The controversy continued, of course, because the description and depiction of sexual acts mean different things to different people. In communities where pornography symbolized filth and depravity to significant numbers of people (or to a number of influential people), pornography was either banned or restricted to outlets in designated areas. Pornographers vigorously resisted, and again the matter was brought before the Supreme Court. In 1976 (*Young v. American Mini Theaters*) and 1986 (*Renton* case), the Court ruled that it was constitutional to restrict the location of adult movie theaters (Sitomer 1986).

Later, the Court ruled that "tasteful" nudity is permissible, such as in theater productions and art, but nudity is not allowable in "low-art" forms, such as striptease dancing (Heins 1991). Such a ruling brings us back to the original question, of course: Whose "taste" determines the matter? As conflict theorists would point out, it is not surprising that Supreme Court justices rule that their own class-based preferences for nudity are not pornographic, but those of the lower classes are.

CONTROVERSY AND RESEARCH ON PORNOGRAPHY

Like homosexuality, pornography has become a controversial and emotional issue. The fear that pornography corrupts people so concerned Americans that in the 1960s President Johnson appointed a National Commission on Obscenity and Pornography. In 1970, the commission concluded that pornography affects some people more than others—that it stimulates the young more than the old, the college educated more than the less educated, the religiously inactive more than the religiously active, and the sexually experienced more than the sexually inexperienced. Unlike Kinsey (1953), who reported that males were considerably more aroused than females by erotic materials, the commission found that women and men are about equally aroused by watching pornography (Schmidt and Sigusch 1970).

As pornography increased during the 1970s and 1980s, concern grew. President Reagan asked the attorney general to appoint another commission to study the matter. The Meese Commission (1986:39) concluded:

> the clinical and experimental evidence supports the conclusion that there is a causal relationship between exposure to sexually violent materials and an increase in aggressive behavior directed towards women . . .

This, the Commission said, "will cause an increase in the level of sexual violence directed at women."

The commission's more specific findings (McManus 1986) include the following:

1. Of 411 sex offenders, the average had 336 victims.
2. Rape increases where pornography laws are liberalized.
3. Rapists are much more likely than nonoffenders to have been exposed as children to hard-core pornography.
4. Pornography makes rape seem "legitimate."
5. States with higher sales of pornography have higher rates of rape.
6. Males exposed to pornography that features sexual violence ("slasher films") become desensitized and see rape victims as "less injured and less worthy."

Is It Just Common Sense?

The commission (1986:39) also said that a "common-sense" approach makes the causal connection between pornography and sex crimes evident. But, as we saw in Chapter 1, common sense and science are often a mismatch. It is precisely that jump from the evidence (the frequency of pornography among sex offenders) to the conclusion (pornography causes sex crimes) that was attacked when the commission published its report. Critics said that the commission was predisposed to see pornography as evil and as the cause of crime. Therefore, it misinterpreted the evidence and ignored studies that contradicted its preconceptions (Baron 1987; Brannigan 1987; Linz, Donnerstein, and Penrod 1987).

Causation v. Correlation

Both the commission's report and its rebuttals need to be taken seriously. But we are still left with the thorny question, Does pornography *cause* sex crimes? Or are sex criminals, such as rapists and child molesters, just more likely to use pornography? There may be a cause/effect relationship, but researchers have been able to document only **correlations** (two or more things occurring together). For example, although sex offenders tend to use more pornography than do nonoffenders, not all sex criminals do so. In addition, noncriminals use pornography. Scientific proof (objective, consistent, verifiable) of a causal relationship, then, remains elusive.

More Controversy: The Danish Experience

Some researchers say that the Danish experience provides an answer. Denmark legalized hard-core pornography in 1965. Berl Kutchinsky (1973) a criminologist from the University of Copenhagen, reported that while the incidence of rape was unaffected, the incidence of sex offenses against children plummeted. To explain why, he suggested that only about a quarter of child molesters actually prefer children. Most take children as substitutes because they are unable to relate sexually to adults. For them, masturbating to pornography provides another substitute. Other researchers, however, have challenged Kutchinsky's statistics. They say that rape and attempted rape as a proportion of total sex offenses increased in Denmark (Meese Commission 1986:260). In turn, however, *their* statistics and conclusions have been challenged (Brannigan 1987).

Science at Work

This is science at work. When a study is published, it enters what we might call the "court" of science, where it is judged by critical scientific peers. Researchers report their results, and other researchers meticulously examine those studies. They challenge the data, and repeat the studies or reanalyze the original data and publish their own conclusions. Out of these investigations of social life and challenges of researchers' conclusions emerges knowledge that overcomes researchers' biases and either replaces or confirms our commonsense notions about social problems.

THINKING CRITICALLY ABOUT SOCIAL PROBLEMS

Should We Censor Violent Pornography?

As the following quotations indicate, feminists are divided on the issue of pornography. What do you think about these issues? Should pornography, especially that which shows sexual violence against women, be banned?

YES

The same people who defend pornography in the name of "sexual liberation" and freedom of speech, strenuously oppose all portrayals of Jewish or Third World men that are anti-Semitic or racist. Imagine the public outcry that would occur if there were special movie houses where viewers could see whites beating up Blacks, or Christians beating up Jews. But if it's called pornography and women are the victims, then you are seen as a prude to object.

—Diana E. H. Russell, feminist researcher

The newer research . . . demonstrates that pornography desensitizes men to violence against women and in fact can be considered pro-rape propaganda . . . pornography is not a "victimless crime." . . . It is a social phenomenon in which men are socialized into an insensitivity to female needs and are reinforced in their inaccurate fantasies about women. . . . Women who oppose this state of affairs (by supporting anti-pornographic ordinances) should be viewed as defending the freedom of the oppressed and ending the silence of those who have been silenced by pornography.

—Pauline B. Bart, Linda Freeman, and Peter Kimball, feminist researchers

NO

Despite the ugliness of a lot of pornography, despite the fact that I don't want to defend pictures of little girls being molested, I believe that censorship only springs back against the givers of culture—against authors, artists, and feminists, against anybody who wants to change society. Should censorship be imposed again, . . . feminists would be the first to suffer.

—Erica Jong, feminist writer and poet

As with Nazi rantings about Jews or racist trash spread by the Ku Klux Klan, speech graphically depicting the sexual humiliation and subordination of women is protected by the First Amendment because we have learned as a free people that it is impossible to censor speech we hate without imperiling the system of free expression upon which our political and social structure rests.

—Harriet Pilpel, feminist attorney

Based on Russell 1977; Bart, Freeman, and Kimball 1985; Blakely 1985.

Some people find this rigorous and exacting process too slow. Feeling a pressing need to act, and convinced that severe consequences are at stake, they want to take a stand now. And based on their ideas about what is right and wrong and what they find offensive, they do take a stand.

The Feminist Position

For example, feminists have become upset about how pornography portrays women. They are convinced that it teaches men to view women as "pieces of meat." Whether pornography causes sex crimes is not the point, they insist, for this portrayal degrades women and thus is an element in their victimization in society. They conclude that pornography—at least the type that shows violence against females—should be banned. The Thinking Critically box on the next page provides further information on this controversy among feminists.

There is no doubt that pornography does influence people. To think otherwise would be absurd. Sociologists Donal MacNamara and Edward Sagarin (1977:205) stated this point succinctly:

> To say that pornography cannot influence a person is to contend that books and the printed word, graphics, art, and slogans cannot move people and cause changes in their thoughts and hence their actions.

But Safety Valve or Trigger?

The question, then, is not whether pornography influences people but, rather, how. Is the **safety valve theory** of pornography right? That is, does pornography protect society by providing the private release of sexual fantasies? Or is the **trigger theory** right? That is, does pornography trigger sexual offenses by stimulating sexual appetites, often for deviance and violence?

Unfortunately, researchers have been unable to settle the question of causation. Until they can, social activists—on whichever side of the issue—will continue to struggle for what they see as a better social world, based on conviction and not irrefutable evidence.

◆ Social Policy ◆

CRIMINALIZATION OF CONSENSUAL ACTS

Difficulties in Enforcing Laws Against Consensual Acts

Sociologists use the term **victimless crimes** to refer to illegal acts to which the participants consent. The crime has no victim because the people agree to do something with or for one another. A man pays a woman for sex; two people of the same sex agree to participate in a sexual act; someone sells or buys pictures of adults involved in sexual acts—all may be illegal, but they occur with the consent of the people involved.

In most crimes, someone does something against the will of someone else. There is a victim and a perpetrator. When a victim reports a crime, the police know where and when it happened, and who the victim is. Without a victim, however, the police end up spending precious public resources attempting to determine that a crime occurred in the first place, and then prosecutors have difficulty in obtaining convictions because the people involved consented to what took place. Unless there is a public outcry, both the public and the police prefer that law enforcement dollars be spent in pursuing criminals who have victims—thieves, muggers, rapists, and murderers.

More Than Victimless Crimes

Not all prostitution, homosexuality, and pornography are victimless crimes, however. There can be force, coercion, or less than informed consent. If there is force, it is rape, a different matter entirely. If there is less than informed consent,

THINKING CRITICALLY ABOUT SOCIAL PROBLEMS

Should We Legalize Prostitution?

<table>
<tr><td align="center">YES</td><td align="center">NO</td></tr>
<tr><td valign="top">

1. Prostitutes perform a service for society. They provide sex for people who otherwise cannot find sexual partners. They even help marriages by reducing sexual demands on wives.

2. To keep prostitution illegal is dysfunctional. It stigmatizes and marginalizes women who want to work as prostitutes. It also corrupts many police officers, who accept bribes to allow prostitutes to work. Some prostitution is run by organized crime, with women held in bondage. Legalization of prostitution will eliminate these problems.

3. If prostitution is declared a legal occupation, the government can regulate it. If the government licenses prostitutes, it can collect taxes and require prostitutes to have regular medical checkups. Prostitutes can be required to display a dated and signed medical certificate stating that they are free of sexually transmitted diseases.

</td><td valign="top">

1. Prostitution is immoral, and we should not legalize immoral activities. The foundation of society is the family, and we should take steps to strengthen the family, not tear it apart by approving sex as a commercial transaction outside the family.

2. The legalization of prostitution will not stop sexually transmitted diseases. For example, the contraction of AIDS occurs before the disease shows up in blood tests. Even though prostitutes are licensed, they will spread AIDS during this interval.

3. Prostitution degrades women. To legalize prostitution is to give the state's approval to their degradation. Women will still be renting their bodies to men, who represent the dominant sector of society. Most prostitutes will still come from the working class and serve as objects to satisfy the sexual desires of men from more privileged classes.

</td></tr>
</table>

there is also a victim. Child pornography, for example, is not a victimless crime. The children are not of age to give their consent, and child pornography often involves the abuse of adult authority.

To deal adequately with social policy, we must separate such instances from those involving full consent.

ALTERNATIVES TO CRIMINALIZATION

Criminalization, or making these behaviors illegal, has certainly failed. What, then, can be done?

Decriminalization

One alternative is **decriminalization,** removing a matter from the criminal law. These behaviors would not then be a part of the criminal code, nor would they be subject to legal control when they occur between consenting adults. They would be considered private acts over which the law has no jurisdiction.

Legalization

While decriminalization is appealing in its simplicity, the sexual behaviors we have reviewed are not all the same. Because prostitution, for example, is a commercial transaction—a business—some argue that **legalization** is the answer: Since we license and tax businesses, why should we exempt prostitution? Proponents of legalization point out that prostitution will persist and suggest that it is time for the state to regulate it. For pro and con arguments on the legalization of prostitution, see the Thinking Critically box above.

Both decriminalization and legalization would eliminate bribes, a major source of police corruption, and both would free the police to concentrate on other areas of law enforcement. A major advantage of legalization is that the community can maintain control over the activity. It can determine zoning, licensing, taxation, and restrictions on age participation. Licensing requirements for houses of prostitution or massage parlors, for example, could include mandatory health checks.

The Matter of Privacy

Central to deciding social policy is the issue of privacy. The argument is that if adults want to have sex in private, anyone may judge the morality of the act, but why should it concern the state? It may be a sin, but it should not be a crime. But there is another side to the privacy argument—the right of *privacy from* people involved in sexual acts. Those who find such activities morally repugnant should not have to see them. If the law were to permit these sexual acts, it should also prohibit street solicitation by prostitutes, sex in public places, and the display of sexual acts on the covers of magazines in supermarkets and other stores.

Segregation

To allow people to engage in these acts *and* to make it so that other people do not have to witness them, some suggest **segregation**—limiting these activities to specified areas. They also would insist on preventing blatancy in even those areas. For example, if prostitutes were segregated to a certain area, they could advertise for customers through ads in newspapers or by a red light in an apartment window, but they could not walk the streets. Gay bars would be allowed, but sexually explicit advertising prohibited. Nor could pornographic outlets show sexually explicit marquees or movie stills. This would allow the patrons of prostitutes, those cruising for same-sex partners, and the consumers of pornography to be able to carry out their consensual activities in semiprivate, while respecting the privacy of the majority from these activities.

ISSUES IN SOCIAL PROBLEMS

Applying Sociology: Taking Back Children from the Night

Lois Lee isn't afraid to apply her sociological training to social problems. Lee did her master's thesis on the pimp-prostitute relationship and her doctoral dissertation on the social world of the prostitute. After receiving her Ph.D. in sociology from United States International University in 1981, Lee began to work with adult prostitutes. They told her, "You know, it's too late for you to help us, Lois. You've got to do something about these kids. We made a choice to be out here . . . a conscious decision. But these kids don't stand a chance."

Lee began by taking those kids, the teenagers who were prostituting themselves, into her home. In three years, she brought 250 home, where she lived with her husband and baby son. Lee then founded "Children of the Night," which reaches the kids by means of "a 24-hour hotline, a street outreach program, a walk-in crisis center, crisis intervention for medical or life-threatening situations, family counseling, job placement, and foster home or group place-

ment." By providing alternatives to prostitution and petty crime, Lee estimates that Children of the Night has helped over 5,000 young runaways and prostitutes to get off the streets.

Lee's work has brought her national publicity and an award from the president. She credits her success to her sociological training, especially the sensitivities it gave her "to understand and move safely through intersecting deviant worlds, to relate positively to police and caretaking agencies while retaining a critical perspective, to know which game to play in which situation."

As Lee said during a CBS interview: "I know what the street rules are, I know what the pimp game is, I know what the con games are, and it's up to me to play that game correctly. . . . It's all sociology. That's why when people call me a social worker I always correct them."

Based on Buff 1987.

The use of children in these activities is an entirely different issue. Here we are treating behavior that should be criminalized, for if the purpose of the law is not to protect the least defenseless of our society, what is its purpose? I suggest that the law should be as harsh as our citizens feel it ought to be, and that lawmakers should rely on surveys of public opinion when they consider penalties. As the Issues box on page 81 shows, private citizens can help to protect children from sexual victimization.

No social policy will please everyone. And these suggestions are no exception. In each chapter, however, I shall make suggestions for social policy that, based on the research findings and the current orientation of our society, appear to make sense. Not all will be without controversy.

◆ The Future of the Problem ◆

No one can say for certain what will happen with these sexual behaviors. A wave of political repression could curtail civil rights and drive prostitution, homosexuality, and pornography underground. But assuming that present trends continue, I foresee the following.

PROSTITUTION AND THE FUTURE

Perhaps the easiest forecast in the entire book is this first one: The demand for the services of prostitutes will continue. Always there will be sexually deprived people who want to patronize prostitutes. Additionally, the demand for "specialized sexual services" that prostitutes satisfy will continue.

In spite of changing attitudes, homosexuality remains a matter of social controversy. It is likely that homosexuals will become more open as popular stars such as Rosie O'Donnell make their sexual orientation public.

Tolerance and AIDS

Although it will continue to flourish, prostitution will remain illegal in almost all areas. The police will overlook all but the most blatant acts both because they have better things to do and because many of them are convinced that it is a harmless activity. AIDS, however, is the joker in the deck. On the one hand, AIDS may lead to an outcry to suppress prostitution due to its role in spreading this lethal disease. On the other hand, AIDS could serve as a stimulus to legalize prostitution, for then authorities can require prostitutes to pass medical examinations.

HOMOSEXUALITY AND THE FUTURE

Two Issues

Two primary issues are generating controversy. The first is the political struggle by homosexuals to be designated by the federal government as a minority group that would be eligible for legal recourse against discrimination. The second issue involves homosexuals' efforts to serve as role models—to be openly homosexual and to occupy positions that mold the orientations of youth, such as public school teachers, scout leaders, and so on. The vast middle ground between those who espouse homosexuality and those who fear or despise it is likely to be occupied by those who believe that homosexuality should be discouraged but that homosexuals should not be oppressed.

TECHNOLOGY AND SOCIAL PROBLEMS

Pornography on the Internet

Pornography vividly illustrates one of the sociological principles discussed in this chapter—that people adapt their sexual behaviors to social change. It was not long after photography was invented that photographic pornography appeared. Today a major issue is pornography on the Internet.

What is the problem? Why can't people electronically exchange nude photos with one another if they want to? If that were the issue, there would be no problem. The real issue, however, is something quite different. What disturbs many people are the photos that show bondage, torture, rape, and bestiality (humans having sex with animals). Judging from the number of such sites, apparently a large number of people derive sexual excitement from such photos and from the sites that portray such acts live, such as the much-ballyhooed broadcasts from Amsterdam, Moscow, and other places.

The Internet abounds with "news groups" (people who "meet" online to discuss some topic). No one is bothered about the news groups (or "chat rooms") that center on Roman architecture or rap music or turtle racing. But news groups that focus on how to torture women are another matter. So are those that focus on how to seduce children—or on the delights of having sex with preschoolers.

Any call for censorship raises the hackles of civil libertarians who see all censorship as an attack on basic freedoms. Censorship, they say, is just the first step toward a totalitarian society. The extreme among them defend the right to display and exchange photos of children being sexually abused. But only the extremists. Most civil libertarians appear to reluctantly draw the line at child pornography, but they don't want the line drawn any further.

Granted that such news groups will be allowed to continue, the issue then is how to protect others from being exposed to them. For example, should school and public libraries be allowed to install Internet filters that screen out designated sites? One side insists that this violates the guarantee of the First Amendment's right of free speech, the other that it is only a reasonable precaution to protect children.

What do you think?

Based on Clausing 1998; Etzioni 1998; Kaplan 1998; Mendels 1998; O'Connell 1998.

Movement to the Mainstream

Pornography is likely to increase in popularity and, with its huge profitability, to be adopted by the mainstream media. Cable television, which offers subscribers XXX options, is likely to become even more explicit and to present live sex programs. As each new communication technology appears, pornography will be adapted to fit it. With the popularity of home video cameras, more people will make their own "home porno flicks." As pornography becomes more mainstream, the line between pornography and art will become even more blurred. It will become difficult, for example, to distinguish between pornography and regular Hollywood films. See the Technology box on electronic pornography on page 83.

Potential Clashes

Such trends could fuel the movement against pornography, creating an even greater clash between the pro- and antipornography forces. Some continuing struggle is inevitable, for the values of these groups are contrary, and each desires to control the media. But pornography has become so entrenched in our society in recent years that it is likely that those who oppose pornography will limit themselves to an occasional statement decrying the fall of American values and then retreat into enclaves of people who agree with their views.

◆ Summary

1. All societies attempt to channel sexual behavior in ways they consider acceptable. When the violation of sexual norms is felt to be a threat to society, especially to the family, it is considered a social problem.

2. Examining *prostitution* through the lens of functionalism, we see that prostitution persists because it serves social functions. By servicing customers who are sexually dissatisfied or whose sexual desires are deviant, prostitutes relieve pressures that otherwise might be placed on people who are unwilling to participate. The three stages in becoming a prostitute are (1) the drifting period (drifting from casual sex into selling sex), (2) the ambivalent transition period, and (3) the professionalization period. Some male prostitutes manipulate symbols to maintain heterosexual identities.

3. In applying conflict theory to *homosexuality*, we see that fundamental tensions exist between homosexuals and heterosexuals, their adjustment to one another is uneasy, and conflict is never far from the surface. Symbolic interactionists have analyzed how a homosexual identity is learned through interaction with others. The process by which people take on a homosexual identity appears to involve identity confusion, comparison, tolerance, acceptance, pride, and finally synthesis.

4. Almost all Americans agree that the distribution of *pornography* should be restricted. Women favor greater restrictions than do men. Deciding what is and is not pornographic has confused many, including the U.S. Supreme Court, which, in the tradition of symbolic interactionism, has ruled that what a community decides is pornographic is pornographic—for them.

5. Social scientists have attempted to determine the social effects of pornography. Depending on their conclusions, researchers are accused either of liberal or conservative bias. Feminists are concerned that, by dehumanizing women, pornography generally encourages men to see women as objects to be manipulated and exploited. Social activists take action on the basis of their convictions, not on the basis of proof about causation.

6. *Victimless crimes* are illegal acts to which the participants consent. Prostitution, homosexuality, and pornography are classified as victimless crimes by sociologists when adults are involved, but not when children participate, as they cannot give full consent. Criminalizing these acts produces police corruption. Two alternatives are *decriminalization,* that is, removing them entirely from legal controls; and *legalization,* allowing them to operate under legal controls. Either solution would be opposed by those supporting the criminal status of these acts.

7. With the sexual liberalization of U.S. society, prostitution, homosexuality, and pornography are likely to become more acceptable. The interests of people who approve and disapprove of these activities are likely to continue to clash, but those who disapprove of them are likely to be fighting rear guard actions. Pornography, as it becomes adapted to technological advancements, will be more widely available than ever.

Approval Positive acceptance of something as good. See also *Toleration*.

Black market The underground channeling of illegitimate goods or services.

Correlation Two or more things occurring together.

Counterculture A subculture in which the values of the dominant culture are turned upside down.

Criminalization Making something illegal.

Decriminalization Removing a matter from the law.

Hate crimes Crimes that are motivated by prejudice based on race, religion, ethnicity, or sexual orientation.

Heterosexuality The sexual preference for people of the opposite sex.

Homosexual behavior Sexual relations between people of the same sex.

Homosexuality The sexual preference for people of one's own sex.

Legalization Permitting an activity but setting up legal controls over it.

Lesbian A female homosexual.

Masochists People who receive sexual gratification by having pain inflicted on them. See also *Sadists*.

Normalization (of deviance) To think of one's deviant acts as normal.

Pornography Writings, pictures, or objects that are considered filthy or depraved.

Prostitution The renting of one's body for sexual purposes.

Role ambivalence Feeling indecisive, or both positive and negative, about one's role.

Sadists People who receive sexual gratification by inflicting pain. See also *Masochists*.

Safety valve theory (of pornography) The view that pornography protects people by providing the private release of sexual fantasies. See also *Trigger theory*.

Segregation In terms of deviance, confining a legal activity to a certain geographical area.

Situational homosexual behavior Homosexual behavior by someone with a heterosexual identity; often occurs in same-sex settings such as prisons or boarding schools.

Subculture A group within a society that is set apart by distinct values and other characteristics.

Symbiosis A mutually beneficial relationship.

Temple prostitution Prostitution that takes place in a temple, as a type of worship.

Toleration Allowing something to exist, no matter how you feel about it. See also *Approval*.

Trigger theory (of pornography) The view that pornography triggers sexual offenses by stimulating the sexual appetite. See also *Safety valve theory*.

Victimless crime An illegal act to which the participants consent.

◆Critical Thinking Questions

1. This chapter begins by claiming, "A basic sociological principle is that sex is never only a personal matter." It goes on to explain that all societies control human sexual behavior. Why do you think this is true? What is it about sex that makes us inclined to control the sexual behavior of others? Be sure to base your explanation on the group aspects of society, not on personality or individuals.

2. Do you think there should be a separate category of "hate crimes"? Explain.
   • Does your answer depend on whether we refer to sexual orientation, race, or some other category?

3. Should it make a difference for social policy whether homosexuality is learned or genetic? Explain.
   • If you believe it should make a difference, then how should the policies be different?

Alcohol and Other Drugs

4

"D ebbie! What's this?"

Seeing the familiar plastic bag, Debbie felt her face redden. Why hadn't she put it away as she always did? She swallowed, then burst out defiantly:

"My purse! You've got no business snooping in my purse!"

"I was just looking for a match—but I found a lot more! I never expected a daughter of mine to be a drug addict."

"Drug addict, huh? That's funny! Just because someone smokes grass doesn't mean she's a drug addict."

"Everybody knows marijuana is just the first step to heroin."

"Mom, it's you who's hooked. The first thing you do in the morning is light up a cigarette and have a cup of coffee. And after that you start popping Prozac."

"Don't you compare my medicine with your drugs. My doctor prescribes Prozac for my nerves."

"Okay, then what do you call your martinis? And I know why you went in my purse for a match—it's because you're hooked on cigarettes."

"Don't you talk back to me, young lady. Ever since you started college you think you know it all. Just wait 'til your Dad gets home."

"Yeah, sure. Then you'll do the same thing you do every night—talk about it over a drink."

◆ The Problem in Social Perspective ◆

Just as Debbie's mother was shocked to discover that her daughter smoked marijuana, so hundreds of thousands of parents have had similar rude awakenings. Long an element of culture in the Far and Middle East, using drugs for pleasure has become common in the West: on college campuses, in the suburbs, and in the executive suite. One of the presidents of the United States even admitted to smoking marijuana, although he said that he "didn't inhale."

Drug Use in Ancient Societies

The use of drugs has a long history. Back in 2737 B.C., a Chinese emperor recommended marijuana for "female weakness, gout, rheumatism, malaria, beriberi, constipation and absentmindedness" (Ray 1998). About 400 B.C., the famous physician Hippocrates recommended mandrake, taken with a little wine, to relieve depression and anxiety (Blum et al. 1969). And when the Spanish Conquistadors landed in South America, they discovered that the natives chewed coca leaves for the stimulating effects of cocaine (DeRios and Smith 1977; Goode 1989).

Drug Abuse Defined

Just as drug use goes far back in history, so does **drug abuse**—using drugs in such a way that they harm one's health, impair one's physical or mental functioning, or interfere with one's social life. Noah, who is listed as the ninth descendant of Adam, was the first person in the historical record to get drunk. After the flood, he planted a vineyard, made wine from its first harvest, and drank himself into a stupor (Genesis 9). What is considered drug abuse, of course, depends on social norms: In our culture, smoking a joint of marijuana is generally considered drug abuse, while drinking a glass of beer or wine is not.

The Social History of Drugs

It is important to emphasize that *no drug is good or bad in and of itself* (Szasz 1975). If a drug is considered good or bad, this is simply a matter of social definition—how a group of people view the drug and react to it. And such perspectives change. For example, in contrast to our view of tobacco today—a view that has led to posting health warnings on cigarette packages—Americans once viewed tobacco

If a drug is in high demand, laws passed against its usage will not stop that demand; they merely drive the use of the drug underground. There, a black market develops, one that connects users and suppliers in an intricate, illegal relationship. Although coffee is broadly socially acceptable today, in some societies it was once an illegal drug, and severe penalties were attached to its possession and consumption.

The Failure of Prohibitions and Punishments

as good for their health. Tobacco companies even used to advertise that doctors recommended their cigarettes.

But let's reach back a little further in tobacco's social history. When Christopher Columbus arrived on these shores, he found that Native Americans smoked a strange substance. He took this substance back with him to the Old World, and smoking tobacco became common. King James of England disliked this new habit, and in 1604 he wrote a pamphlet, warning his subjects that tobacco was "harmful to the brain, dangerous to the lungs." Like many people today, he was not one to let health concerns interfere with business, and when tobacco growing became profitable he declared its trade a royal monopoly (Ray 1998). Other rulers who saw tobacco as evil went far beyond just issuing warnings. In 1634, the Czar of Russia ordered the noses of tobacco smokers slit. About the same time, the rulers of China and Turkey ordered tobacco smokers put to death—those in China faced decapitation (Goode 1989). All these antidrug campaigns failed.

While some people will risk their neck for a good smoke, others will do the same for the beverage that may or may not be good to the last drop. After coffee was introduced in Arabia in the 1500s, Islamic priests became upset when people drank coffee to help them stay awake during long religious vigils. Thinking that coffee was intoxicating and was therefore prohibited by the Koran, the priests ordered coffee dealers beaten across the soles of their feet. These antidrug measures, too, failed (Brecher et al. 1972). A century later, in 1674, in a pamphlet entitled "The Women's Petition Against Coffee," a group of Englishwomen complained that their men were leaving "good old ale" in order to drink "base, black, thick, nasty, bitter, stinking, nauseous" coffee. Their real complaint? The coffee, they said, was making their men sexually less active (Meyer 1954).

Changing Social Definitions

And how attitudes toward drugs in the United States have changed. In the 1800s, it was legal to buy opium and morphine in drugstores, grocery stores, and general stores. If this were inconvenient, you could order them by mail. Opium was advertised as a cure for diarrhea, colds, fever, teething, pelvic disorders, even athlete's foot and baldness (Inciardi 1986). Opium was so common that each year U.S. mothers fed their babies about 750,000 bottles of opium-laced syrup. To smoke cigarettes or drink alcohol was far more offensive than to use opium (Isbell 1969; Duster 1970; Brecher et al. 1972).

People project their fantasies and fears onto drugs. They may at one time define a drug as a holy gift, but later define it as part of a social problem. This drives home the point made in Chapter 1 about objective conditions and subjective concerns. It is not the *objective conditions* of drugs—such as whether or not they are harmful—that makes their use a social problem. Rather, it takes *subjective concerns*. As we just saw, what is considered normal drug use at one time in history may be looked at as drug abuse at another time. Just as with abortion, prostitution, homosexuality, and pornography, drugs are a part of social controversy; people learn different definitions and line up on different sides of the issue.

In Sum: Objective Conditions and Subjective Concerns

In short, *the view that a drug is good or bad depends not on objective conditions but on subjective concerns. It is a matter of how people define matters. People's definitions, in turn, influence how they use and abuse drugs, whether or not a drug will be legal or illegal, and what social policies they want to adopt* (see Table 4-1). This is the central sociological aspect of drug use and abuse, one that we shall stress over and over in this chapter.

◆ The Scope of the Problem ◆

"Mine" vs. "Yours"

Debbie, in our opening vignette, is like the eleven million other Americans who have smoked marijuana during the past month (*Statistical Abstract* 2001:Table 190). To Debbie, marijuana isn't a drug. It's just something that makes her feel good and is "no big deal." Debbie's mother is also like the many millions of other Americans who drink coffee and alcohol, smoke cigarettes, and otherwise ingest a variety of substances that *they* have a hard time thinking of as drugs.

Table 4-1   Legal Status and Use of Drugs

| | Use of Drugs | |
	Legal Use	Illegal Use
Legal Drugs	a. Prescription b. Over the counter c. "Over the bar" and in vending machines	a. Forged prescriptions b. Black market sales of prescription drugs c. "After-hours" sales "Underage" sales
Illegal Drugs	a. Marijuana prescribed for medical problems b. Cocaine for surgery	a. Crack, heroin, etc.

Drugs Defined

Like marijuana, alcohol and nicotine are drugs. A substance does not have to be sold in an alley or in some secretive manner to be a drug. A **drug** is a substance that is taken in order to produce a change in one's bodily functions, behavior, emotions, thinking, or consciousness. *The essential difference is not which substance is taken, but which drugs are socially acceptable, and which are not.*

Americans Are Prodrug

Almost all Americans use drugs. We are born with the aid of drugs, and our dying is eased by them. We use drugs for sickness and for pleasure, to relieve anxiety, queasy stomachs, and headaches, and for all sorts of other pains and discomforts. As with alcohol, we take drugs to increase sociability. And as with cigarettes, coffee, and colas, we take them routinely, unthinkingly, and habitually. (Yes, coffee, Coke, and Pepsi contain a drug. This drug, caffeine, is addictive, and some people "just can't get going" in the morning without several "fixes.") Far from being an antidrug society, then, we are actually highly prodrug.

Personal vs. Social Problem

Most of us take such drug use for granted. To us, it is like eating popcorn or munching on potato chips. When drug use interferes with someone's health or economic or social functioning, however, we begin to question it. At that point, it becomes drug abuse, but it is a *personal* problem. If large numbers of people become upset about a drug and want to see something done about the matter, that drug then becomes part of a *social* problem. As we consider two common drugs, alcohol and nicotine, note how much more important subjective concerns are than objective conditions.

Alcohol as a Social Problem

Alcohol is far more dangerous than its broad social acceptability would imply. A dramatic example is motor vehicle accidents, which kill 42,000 Americans each year. Alcohol is involved in 38 percent of these accidents, bringing the death toll for alcohol-related accidents to 16,000—about 44 a day (*Statistical Abstract* 2001:Table 1098). This is the equivalent of two jumbo jets, each loaded with 165 passengers and crew, crashing each and every week of the year.

Abusers of alcohol are also more likely to be murdered or to commit suicide (Haberman and Natarajan 1986). As indicated by the thousands who die annually from cirrhosis of the liver, they are also more likely than nonabusers to destroy their vital organs. Overall, each year another 20,000 Americans die of such alcohol-induced causes. Most are men (2 or 3 to 1), as men abuse alcohol (and most other drugs) more than women do (*Statistical Abstract* 2001:Tables 106, 108).

Nicotine as a Social Problem

Nicotine is an even more deadly drug, and the consequences of nicotine abuse—to addicts and to society—are even more staggering. Although nicotine leads to billions of dollars being spent annually on health care and being wasted in lost production and wages, the main problem is that smoking kills. The two-pack-a-day smoker is about 20 times more likely than a nonsmoker to die from lung cancer. With its link to many cancers and diseases of the heart and lungs, smoking is responsible for about 400,000 deaths in the United States each year (Ravenholt 1990).

This is a cold statistic, and it is difficult to grasp its enormity. Again, think of jets, but this time think of jumbo jets that can carry 1,000 passengers plus a crew of 90. Each day, these fully-loaded jets take off from major airports around the country. And each and every day one of them goes into a tailspin and crashes to the ground, killing everyone on board. The crashes continue without letup, day after day, year after year. The passengers *know* that one of the jets will crash that day; yet they climb aboard anyway, thinking that it won't be *their* jet that crashes.

Obviously no one would allow such a thing to continue. But it does continue with cigarette smokers. Smokers know that nicotine is lethal. They also know that

Noted throat specialists report on 30-day test of Camel smokers ...

NOT ONE SINGLE CASE OF THROAT IRRITATION due to smoking CAMELS!

For generations, U.S. tobacco companies worked to get Americans hooked on nicotine. This ad from the 1950s urged people to give Camels a 30-day test, plenty of time to get people hooked on this drug. Nicotine's effects are deadly, but slow, and it may take 30 years or longer for nicotine to kill. During that time, the cigarette companies make huge profits from their victims. Nicotine, a legal drug, kills more people than the number who die from all illegal drugs combined.

smoking-related deaths are lingering and painful, a burden to both the victims and their families. Yet they continue to put this deadly poison to their lips, thinking that they won't be on the plane that goes down. This drug is so lethal that the total number of deaths from U.S. accidents, suicides, homicides, and even AIDS is only *half* the number of those killed by nicotine (*Statistical Abstract* 1998:Tables 140, 144 and 2001: Table 105).

Drug Addiction Defined

A serious problem with some drugs is **addiction,** or **drug dependence.** That is, people come to depend on the regular consumption of a drug in order to make it through the day. When people think of **drug addiction,** they are likely to think of addicts huddled in slum doorways, the dregs of society who seldom venture into daylight—unless it is to rob someone. They don't associate addiction with "good," middle-class neighborhoods and "solid citizens."

Nicotine Addiction

But let's look at drug addiction a little more closely. Although most people may think of heroin as the prime example of an addictive drug, I suggest that nicotine is the better example. I remember a next-door neighbor who stood in his backyard, a lit cigarette in his hand, and told me about the operation in which one of his lungs was removed. I say "remember," because soon after our conversation he died from his addiction.

Smoking also causes emphysema, a disease in which breathing becomes increasingly difficult, until death eventually occurs from respiratory failure. You'd think this would be enough to make smokers quit, but chest specialists report that "even during the last months of their ordeal, when they must breathe oxygen intermittently instead of air, some of them go right on alternating cigarette smoke and oxygen" (Brecher et al. 1972:216).

Buerger's disease is another example:

> In this disease the blood vessels become so constricted that circulation is impaired whenever nicotine enters the bloodstream. When gangrene sets in, at first a toe or two may have to be amputated. If the person continues to smoke, the foot may have to be amputated at the ankle, then the leg at the knee, and ultimately at the hip. Somewhere along this gruesome progression gangrene may also attack the other leg. Patients are told that if they will stop smoking, this horrible march of gangrene up their legs will be curbed. Yet surgeons report that some patients vigorously puff away in their hospital beds following even a second or third amputation (Brecher et al. 1972:216).

Avoiding Withdrawal

Why don't drug addicts just quit? People use drugs even under dire circumstances in order to avoid **withdrawal,** the intense distress—nausea, vomiting, aches and pains, nervousness, anxiety, and depression—they feel when they abstain from the drug. Withdrawal involves **craving,** an intense desire for the missed drug. Craving may last for months or even years, and is especially strong in moments of emotional distress. Even after the physical habit is broken and craving is over, people may experience an occasional desire for the drug. This is referred to as **psychological dependence.** (A personal note: After I quit smoking I would have recurring dreams that I was smoking cigarettes. These dreams were so real that I would awaken abruptly in the middle of the night—feeling guilty for having fallen back into the habit.)

◆ Looking at the Problem Theoretically ◆

Why do we make it legal for people to use such lethal drugs as alcohol and nicotine, and yet send people to prison for using much milder drugs? This question points up how subjective concerns outweigh objective conditions, how the meanings we assign to drugs go far beyond their pharmaceutical characteristics. In order to understand the *social* significance of drugs, let's look at drugs through our three theoretical lenses.

SYMBOLIC INTERACTIONISM

Differing Definitions of Drugs

The meaning of a drug depends on who is considering it. A physician may perceive a drug as a tool to help patients; a drug dealer may view the same drug as a high-demand, high-profit product; the police may see it as an evil substance to be stamped out; users may see it as an adventure, a religious experience, a "high," a break from routine, a mild diversion that can be done without, or an absolute necessity for getting through the day. The meaning of a drug, then, does not depend on the drug, but on how people interpret the drug.

The U.S. Temperance Movement as a Symbolic Crusade

Alcohol, for example, has been associated with Americans from the time this country began (see the Issues box on the next page). How, then, could this beverage ever have been outlawed, as it was in 1919? In his account of the U.S. temperance movement, *Symbolic Crusade,* sociologist Joseph Gusfield (1963) focuses on alcohol as a symbol. He examines how abstinence became associated with power and respectability.

The Pilgrims, Beer, and Thanksgiving

The *Mayflower* had completed its historic voyage. Now the Pilgrims faced the daunting task of settling the wilderness of the New World. They found the Indians friendly enough, but the harsh winter of 1620 was something else. Samoset, a tribesman, helped them survive that first threatening winter.

But beer also helped.

When winter hit, the colonists' buildings were only half-finished. To continue work on them, they had to brave the icy February winds and ferry back and forth from the *Mayflower*, which tossed at anchor on the frigid ocean. Life was becoming unbearable and death common from pneumonia, scurvy, and exposure.

Adding to their misery was the first beer crisis in the New World. It wasn't as though the Pilgrims lacked foresight. They were planners, and they had brought with them a large supply of beer. Like other Europeans, they distrusted water, and thought alcohol essential for good health. A stiff drink kept off chills and fevers, aided digestion, made work easier to bear, and warmed the body on cold nights. The Pilgrims considered nondrinkers to be "crank-brained."

But the trip had taken longer than expected, and so had their efforts at establishing a beachhead in the wilderness. They had run out of beer, and now they were forced to drink water. Seeing their plight, the captain of the *Mayflower* shared his own beer supplies with them. He could do this only so long, however, for he had to leave enough for his own crew to drink on the long journey back to England. Eventually, he had to stop sharing.

For the Pilgrims, the situation had become desperate. William Bradford, who became the governor of Plymouth, pleaded for just one "can" of beer. He was refused. With more deaths, the Pilgrims continued to plead for beer. The captain of the *Mayflower* again took pity on them. To alleviate their suffering, from his own supplies he gave beer "for them that had need for it," particularly the sick.

With prayers, the help of Samoset, the *Mayflower's* captain, and beer, the Pilgrims made it through that first bleak winter. And, unlike our grade school images, during their first Thanksgiving feast, the Pilgrims drank beer—and Samoset joined their merrymaking, for by this time he, too, had developed a taste for this frothy, heart-warming liquid.

Based on Lender and Martin 1982.

The temperance movement, Gusfield says, was a response to social change. In the 1820s, millions of poor immigrants arrived from Italy, Germany, and Ireland. This new urban poor brought with them customs that were alien to the New England "aristocracy," which was made up of Anglo-Saxon Protestants. They brought with them a different religion (Roman Catholicism) and the custom of drinking a lot of wine, beer, and spirits. The Anglo-Saxons viewed these new arrivals, who were mostly uneducated, as ignorant Catholic drunkards, and they saw their own power decline as more and more of them arrived. The "aristocracy" reasoned that if they no longer could control the politics of the country, they at least could control its morals. They then founded the temperance movement, with the goal of turning Americans into clean, sober, and godly people whose customs would reflect the moral leadership of New England.

Drinking and abstinence then became contrasting symbols that served to identify people as members of one of two major groups. Abstinence, which was associated with morality and respectability, symbolized a hard worker, a person who was established and respectable. Drinking symbolized an unreliable drifter, an

uneducated immigrant of questionable background. To abstain from alcohol became a requirement for anyone who strived for higher social standing.

The United States continued to grow more urban, secular, and Roman Catholic, and Protestants saw their power and values slipping even further away. They intensified the temperance movement, and in 1919 they rejoiced when the Eighteenth Amendment to the Constitution was passed. Overnight it became illegal to buy even a glass of beer in the United States. Prohibition, Gusfield says, marked the victory of middle-class, Protestant, rural values over working-class, Roman Catholic, urban values. But like all other antidrug laws before it, Prohibition didn't cause people to stop using the drug of their choice. Gradually, the anti-Catholic and antiurban forces weakened, and in 1933 the Eighteenth Amendment was repealed.

It is difficult for us today to see how emotionally charged the issue of drinking a glass of beer was. But this illustrates how our understanding of any drug must center on discovering the social meanings attached to it. Cocaine use, for example, appears decadent to many, but for some it represents sophistication. Marijuana, too, involves contrasting and changing meanings. As long as marijuana was confined to "bohemian" or marginal groups, it posed no cultural threat. But in the 1960s, rebellious middle-class youth formed a subculture that was alien to their parents' world of hard work and straight living. To show their rejection and separation of the middle-class world, they promoted marijuana and other psychedelic drugs. At that point, the meaning of marijuana changed—and a social problem was born.

FUNCTIONALISM

When functionalists study a drug, whether it be legal or illegal, they examine its functions and dysfunctions. Recreational drugs such as alcohol and marijuana "loosen" people up, or otherwise help remove tensions that interfere with sociability. They also, of course, are functional for those who make money from growing, processing, distributing, and selling them. These same drugs are dysfunctional for people who abuse them. Similarly, prescription drugs are functional both for the medical profession and for the patients they serve. They, too, are dysfunctional for those who abuse them.

A striking example of the functionality of prescription drugs is their use with mental patients. In the 1950s, more than a half million Americans were locked in mental hospitals. Since then, our population has doubled, and if the rate of committment had stayed the same about a million Americans would be locked in asylums. But in the 1950s, psychiatrists began to prescribe mood-altering drugs (the psychopharmaceuticals), and in just a few years the number of patients confined to mental hospitals shrank by several hundred thousand. For these people, drugs were functional.

Prescription drugs are also dysfunctional. Drug therapy can be used to put patients in "pharmacological straitjackets." Instead of examining what is wrong with the patient or with the patient's social environment, the physician takes the easier road and prescribes drugs. Drug therapy also exacts a price. Some patients become "doped up" or lethargic. Others suffer neurological damage.

In short, when drugs interfere with people's physical or social functioning, they are dysfunctional for those people. As we saw in the example cited earlier of Buerger's disease, nicotine addiction provides a striking example of the dysfunction of a drug. Alcohol abuse is also dysfunctional, leaving behind a trail of impaired health, poverty, broken homes, and smashed dreams. Similarly, heroin, the

Changing Meanings: The Example of Marijuana

Social Functions of Drugs

Dysfunctions of Drugs

Chapter 4 Alcohol and Other Drugs

barbiturates, and other addictive drugs create severe problems for addicts and their families and friends.

The dysfunctions of drug abuse also extend far beyond the individual. Although difficult to measure, these large-scale costs involve drug-related crimes, such as burglaries and muggings that are committed in order to support an addiction; increased welfare—the result of unemployment; extensive medical costs due to illness and disease; the spread of AIDS among addicts who share needles; the harm done to victims of automobile accidents; and the loss to society of a vast reservoir of human potential as people retreat into drugs.

Latent Functions of Drug Control

Functionalists also identify a latent function that is associated with making a drug illegal, one that runs contrary to common-sense ideas about the purposes of drug laws: To make a drug illegal is to strengthen the agencies that have been established to control them (see the Issues box on sociology and common sense on the next page). Without these laws, some government agencies would go out of business. It is not surprising, then, that to protect their jobs, some bureaucrats are eager to define many more drugs as dangerous to the public's welfare.

The Example of Marijuana

Marijuana illustrates this principle. In 1930, Harry Anslinger was appointed to head the new Bureau of Narcotics in the Treasury Department. With the Great Depression, his budget was cut, and Anslinger saw marijuana as an opportunity to strengthen his faltering organization (Dickson 1968). Marijuana, however, was legal, so Anslinger embarked on a relentless campaign to get a federal law passed against marijuana. He became a **moral entrepreneur,** a crusading reformer who wages battle to enforce his or her idea of morality. As often happens with moral entrepreneurs, Anslinger received support from an unexpected source, in this case, the liquor interests who feared inroads would be made into their market if marijuana became popular (Rockwell 1972). With the help of his new ally, Anslinger was victorious, and Congress passed the Marijuana Tax Act in 1937. Anslinger's campaign to frighten people is recounted in the Issues box on page 97.

The Marijuana Tax Act (which improperly classified marijuana as a narcotic) was functional for the Bureau of Narcotics (which is still going strong). It was dysfunctional, however, for the hundreds of thousands of young Americans who became caught in its enforcement web. When marijuana became popular with middle-class youth and it became impossible to enforce abstinence among millions of smokers, this did not stop the drug enforcers from searching out and arresting offenders. It was drug use that kept them in business. This illustrates a central tenet of functional analysis: What is functional for some is dysfunctional for others.

CONFLICT THEORY

Drug Laws as Tools for Social Control

Conflict theorists emphasize how drugs are used as a political tool. To criminalize the use of a drug that is common among groups who are perceived as a political threat is to unleash the state's police power against those groups. Let's look at some examples.

The Example of Marijuana

In the 1920s the United States experienced an economic boom, and workers from Mexico were valued as a source of cheap labor. Then came the Great Depression of the 1930s. These same people were now competing for scarce jobs (Galliher and Walker 1977). They were also the main group that smoked marijuana. This presented an ideal opportunity for Anslinger to crack down on marijuana use, and he began a campaign to label this now-feared and unpopular group as dangerous drug abusers. In the article quoted in the box on page 99, Anslinger refers to "a hot tamale salesman pushing his cart about town . . . peddling marijuana cigarettes." The Marijuana Tax Act of 1937 was a political tool that was used against an ethnic community in an attempt to drive unneeded Mexican workers back across the border (Helmer 1975).

The Example of Opium

Drug laws were also used against Chinese immigrants. In the 1800s, thousands of Chinese men came to the United States to help build the railroads. They brought opium with them, a legal drug at the time. When the railroad was completed, thousands of Chinese were thrown into the job market. This coincided with a depression in the early 1870s and with a national financial panic in 1873. The men, who were willing to work cheaply, posed a threat to white workers, who beat, threatened, and killed them. In 1875, San Francisco and other West Coast cities began to prohibit opium dens. These laws did not target opium, but, rather, the Chinese men who threatened the economic security of the white working class (Morgan 1978). Even the U.S. Congress got into the act. In 1887, it passed a law that prohibited the importation of opium *by the Chinese* but not by white Americans (Szasz 1975).

Heroin as a Means to Pacify the "Dangerous Classes"?

Conflict theorists also stress that drugs are a weapon used to control what are called "the dangerous classes," those that produce rebels and potential revolutionaries. When oppressed people seek refuge in addictive drugs, their anger and their revolutionary impulses are diverted. Drugs, not social change, become their passionate concern, their rallying cry in life. Contrary to the impression given by news reports, which imply that society is about to explode in a paroxysm of drug violence, drugs such as heroin and crack actually stabilize a society. They divert the attention and

Marijuana: Assassin of Youth

Marijuana became illegal in the United States in 1937, largely due to a ruthless campaign spearheaded by a moral entrepreneur, Harry Anslinger. Anslinger called marijuana smokers "immoral, vicious, social lepers" who needed swift, "impartial" punishment (Reasons 1974). He also used dramatic accounts and exaggeration. To frighten people, he wrote articles for popular magazines. In one of them, he tells this story:

There was this young girl. . . . Her story is typical. Some time before, this girl, like others of her age who attend our high schools, had heard the whispering of a secret which has gone the rounds of American youth. It promised a new thrill, the smoking of a type of cigarette which contained a "real kick." According to the whispers, this cigarette could accomplish wonderful reactions and with no harmful aftereffects. So the adventurous girl and a group of her friends gathered in an apartment, thrilled with the idea of doing "something different" in which there was "no harm." Then a friend produced a few cigarettes of the loosely rolled "homemade" type. They were passed from one to another of the young people, each taking a few puffs.

The results were weird. Some of the party went into paroxysms of laughter; every remark, no matter how silly, seemed excruciatingly funny. Others of mediocre musical ability became almost expert; the piano dinned constantly. Still others found themselves discussing weighty problems of youth with remarkable clarity. As one youngster expressed it, he "could see through stone walls." The girl danced without fatigue, and the night of unexplainable exhilaration seemed to stretch out as though it were a year long. Time, conscience, or consequences became too trivial for consideration.

Other parties followed, in which inhibitions vanished, conventional barriers departed, all at the command of this strange cigarette with its ropy, resinous odor. Finally there came a gathering at a time when the girl was behind in her studies and greatly worried. With every puff of the smoke the feeling of despondency lessened. Everything was going to be all right—at last. The girl was "floating" now, a term given to marijuana intoxication. Suddenly, in the midst of laughter and dancing, she thought of her school problems. Instantly they were solved. Without hesitancy, she walked to a window and leaped to her death. Thus can marijuana "solve" one's difficulties.

Anslinger never tired in his campaign against this vicious drug that threatened the youth of America. Here's another story that he told.

It was an unprovoked crime some years ago which brought the first realization that the age-old drug had gained a foothold in America. An entire family was murdered by a youthful addict in Florida. When officers arrived at the home they found the youth staggering about in a human slaughterhouse. With an ax he had killed his father, his mother, two brothers, and a sister. He seemed to be in a daze. . . . He had no recollection of having committed the multiple crime. The officers knew him ordinarily as a sane, rather quiet young man; now he was pitifully crazed. They sought the reason. The boy said he had been in the habit of smoking something which youthful friends called "muggles," a childish name for marijuana. . . .

[People need to be] told that addicts may often develop a delirious rage during which they are temporarily and violently insane, that this insanity may take the form of a desire for self-destruction or a persecution complex to be satisfied only by the commission of some heinous crime. (Anslinger and Cooper 1937)

If these stories didn't do it, Anslinger had an ace up his sleeve. He said that this killer weed—his term—caused the loss of reproductive powers (Galliher and Walker 1977).

All things considered, it is little wonder that Anslinger's campaign resulted in Congress passing the Marijuana Tax Act in 1937.

energy of the exploited away from their oppression so that they no longer demand social change. In this theoretical light, sociologist Andrew Karmen (1980:174) says that heroin users become

> too passive when nodding and too self-absorbed when they aren't high to fight for community control over the schools, to organize tenants for a rent strike, or to march on City Hall to demand decent jobs for all who want to work. Since narcotics pacify those who suffer most from mental and physical degradation, it's likely that some astute members of the ruling circles have decided its benefits outweigh its costs.

How Illegal Drugs Are Functional for the Powerful

One does not have to agree that society's elite masterminds the trade in heroin and crack cocaine to see that drugs can serve the interests of the powerful in society. An old ploy sometimes used by groups in power to protect their position is to focus attention on some supposed threat posed by a disfavored group. This diverts attention from internal problems and makes people feel that they are all in the same boat—and that they had better bail together, because the boat is leaking.

Fingering the "Enemy" Behind "Bad" Drugs

Our history provides numerous examples of how those in power have used drugs to consolidate sentiment against disfavored groups. During the 1800s, Chinese opium dens were pictured as outposts of corruption and seduction. By World War I the "enemy" had changed, and heroin was supposedly being smuggled into this country by German pharmaceutical firms and anarchists. With the outbreak of World War II, Japan was identified as the power behind the narcotics trade. Then during the Cold War of the 1950s, the Soviet secret police were fingered as the sinister heroin supplier. During the Korean War, China became the culprit, and during the Vietnam War, North Vietnam and the National Liberation Front were singled out as masterminds of the narcotics trade (Karmen 1980). Vietnam, Cuba, Bulgaria, and the Soviet Union also have been called sinister drug menaces (Toai and Chanoff 1984; Kleiman 1985; Ehrenfeld and Kahan 1986). As conflict theorists would stress,

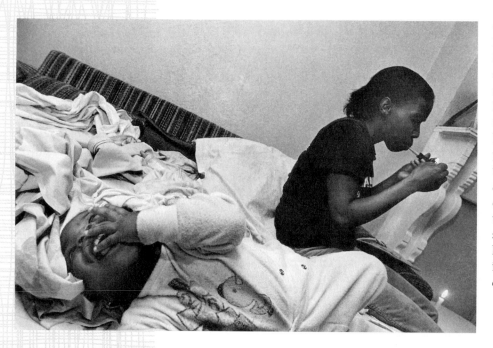

Conflict theorists point out how laws against drugs have been used as tools to control the oppressed classes. Laws against crack, like those against the use of opium, marijuana, and heroin, have served this purpose well. One reaction to oppression is to flee into addiction. Those who do so can harm themselves and their loved ones, as Denise, shown here, has done. She has neglected her children in favor of her addiction to crack.

now that the Cold War is over we can expect the government to implicate a new enemy supplier—which, inevitably, will be some group that is out of favor with the U.S. power elite.

In Sum

Each theory contributes a unique understanding of drugs as a social problem. Symbolic interactionists stress how drugs become powerful symbols that affect social life, as was the case with alcohol and the great drug experiment known as Prohibition. Functionalists examine the functions and dysfunctions of drug use: For example, some mental patients benefit from legal mood-altering drugs, but those same drugs impair the physical or social functioning of other patients. Conflict theorists examine drugs as part of a social order in which a privileged few are in control: For example, because drugs have been manipulated in the past for the purpose of enhancing power and control, this same process may underlie the heroin and cocaine trade today.

✦ Research Findings ✦

In this section, we shall examine the medicalization of human problems, consider why the effects of drugs are not always the same, and present an overview of different types of drugs. We also will deal with the common assumptions that narcotics cause crime, destroy people's incentive to work, and devastate their health.

THE MEDICALIZATION OF HUMAN PROBLEMS

The King had a difficult time getting through the day—and the nights were no better. Middle age, unwelcome by almost everyone but especially dreaded by celebrities, had settled in, bringing a paunch and double chin that the Hollywood magazines ridiculed. To make matters worse, the breakup of his marriage had torn his only child from him. Throughout these ordeals, a longtime friend, Dr. George Nichopoulos, had been a great help. During the past 31 months he had prescribed 19,000 stimulants, depressants, and painkillers, some of which were highly addictive.

Now the King of Rock and Roll lay dead on his bathroom floor. The official report stated that Elvis Presley had died from heart disease. Other medical examiners, however, claimed that death could have resulted from the interaction of the many drugs in his system. Presley's body contained toxic levels of the sedative methaqualone, ten times more codeine than was needed for therapy, and low levels of ten other drugs: morphine, Demerol, and phenyltoloxamine (painkillers); amobarbital, phenobarbital, and amitriptyline (sedatives); pentobarbital (a sedative and sleep-inducer); Valmid and Placidyl (sleep-inducers); and Valium (a muscle relaxant).

At his trial for overprescribing—for which he was found not guilty—Dr. Nichopoulos testified that Presley was under a drug plan that called for drugs to reduce his appetite, drugs to stimulate his bowels, drugs to help him urinate, drugs to relieve itching, drugs to help dizziness, drugs to relieve pain, and drugs to help him relax.

The Pharmacological Revolution

Medicalizing Human Problems

Though extreme, Elvis Presley's death pinpoints a major U.S. drug problem, *the legal abuse of legal drugs*. Since the 1930s, when the pharmaceutical industry began to manufacture psychoactive drugs, we have been caught up in a pharmacological revolution (Conrad 1975). One result is that physicians prescribe drugs for conditions that used to be thought of as a normal part of life. Anxiety and distress, feeling upset or uncertain, wrestling with perplexing problems, not fitting in, being dissatisfied—such things have been redefined as medical problems. If the old attitude was

Like that of many performers who have become addicted to drugs, Robert Downey, Jr.'s career has been marred by public arrests.

that these are problems of living that require coping skills, today's attitude is that they call for drugs. Sociologists call this **medicalization of human problems,** offering a medical "solution" for personal problems.

Valium

Valium (generic name diazepam) is a case in point. As advertised, Valium seemed a magical drug. Touted as medicine for housewives who were "always weary," Valium was even helpful in rearing children, for it could relieve "anxiety and tension in parent-child relationships" (*Use and Misuse* 1980:395). Valium quickly became the best-selling drug in the United States. Sales plummeted, however, when Hoffman-LaRoche's patent expired in 1980, and other companies were allowed to sell generic versions of the drug.

Other "Mind Candies": Xanax and Prozac

When Valium sales dropped, drug companies promoted Prozac and Xanax, "mind candies" that quickly shot to the top of the sales charts. Prozac and Xanax are prescribed for anxiety, irritability, sleeplessness, restlessness, inability to concentrate, and a pounding heart. The serenity gained through popping a pill is elusive, however, and Prozac and Xanax have side effects—from forgetfulness to suicidal thoughts. They are also addictive.

A generic version of Xanax sells for $15.56, quite a lot less than Xanax at $73. But drug companies promote the drugs on which they hold patents and can make huge amounts of money ("High Anxiety" 1993). Consequently, they aggressively promote Xanax and Prozac, and each pulls in over a *billion* dollars a year. (Lest you think that pharmacists lose out when physicians prescribe the generic version—although they charge $15.56, they pay just $.78 [Tanouye 1998]).

We are talking about big business, one in which drug companies, physicians, and pharmacists have a symbiotic interest. They all benefit by keeping the public believing that modern medicine holds the answer to their personal problems, that "popping a pill" is *the* way to cope with the problems of life. As a result, patients demand relief from their physicians, who, motivated to help patients and to line their own pockets, respond precisely as the drug companies want them to. And with such huge profits, pharmacists eagerly fill these billions of prescriptions.

But why are women the main consumers of tranquilizers (Bowe 1992)? Sociologist Jane Prather (1980) suggests that this is because women are more likely than men to describe their physical health in emotional and psychological terms. Drug companies usually portray women patients in their ads for tranquilizers, reinforcing the cultural stereotype that psychic distress is "feminine." As a result, doctors are likely to see women's stress as calling for a pill.

This broad tendency to medicalize human problems—to think of them not as normal aspects of daily life, but as a matter of "sickness"—now applies to children's rowdy behavior. Children who disrupt their classroom used to be called *unruly,* but now they are called *sick*—as though there were some sort of illness inside them that medicine can cure. Consider what happened to Douglas, a 9-year-old fourth-grader:

> Douglas would not sit quietly like the other children. He often talked out of turn and made what his teacher considered to be inappropriate remarks. His teacher sent Douglas to the school psychologist, who, in turn, sent him to a pediatrician who was just setting up practice. The pediatrician sent Douglas back to school with a note that seemed almost a reprimand to the school authorities: "This child is clearly within the normal limits of neurological maturation, and has no problems that are not within the purview of the school."
>
> Douglas continued to be disruptive, and his desperate teacher sent him back to the school psychologist, pleading that "something be done—I'm at my wit's end." This time the psychologist sent Douglas to the pediatrician the school usually used, one who had 2,000 patients on Ritalin, Dexedrin, and similar drugs: amphetamines, or "speed," which, paradoxically, calm hyperactive children. This doctor wrote Douglas a prescription for Ritalin, convinced, as he put it, that he was helping to "shape the lifestyle of this child and his family." (Schrag and Divoky 1975)

There is, of course, nothing new about teachers and parents complaining that children are difficult to teach or control. What *is* new is for teachers and doctors *to turn behaviors into illnesses.* When a child's unacceptable behavior is given a name— whether it is called **hyperkinesis,** *hyperactivity, attention deficit disorder,* or its most recent version attention deficit-hyperactivity disorder (ADHD)—it sounds as though the child *has* something. (The doctor or teacher solemnly looks at the alarmed parent and pronounces, "She has ADHD.") How frightening—and how untrue. What the child really has is a bogus "psychiatric disease" (Vatz 1994).

Just as unruly children are unacceptable to those in authority, so are political dissenters. And like the children, political dissenters also have been defined as mentally disturbed and have been given drugs to control their behavior. In the former Soviet Union, scholars, scientists, and artists who spoke out against oppression were isolated in medical facilities and given "drug therapy." The drugs produced disorganized thinking, which, in turn, "proved" that the dissenters were "crazy." Psychiatrists who objected lost their jobs or were imprisoned.

The functions of medicalizing disruptive behaviors are obvious. The "drug therapy" helped Soviet authorities justify the arrest of dissenters. Most of the hundreds of thousands of U.S. children who are given Ritalin for their "illness" sit still longer and appear to pay attention. But there also are dysfunctions, such as the stigma and loss of liberty of the political dissenters who were labeled "crazy." It also is dysfunctional to label children as mentally ill and to give them Ritalin, which can cause brain damage, cancer, tics, lethargy, depression, and addiction (Breggin 1998).

In Sum

Because pills seem such a handy answer to problems that perplex us, however, medicalizing human problems has become a standard feature of contemporary life. If only we could find the perfect pill, all personal and social problems would disappear as we dip into the pharmacological wellspring of medical miracles.

THE EFFECTS OF DRUGS

Why Drug Experiences Differ

Drugs have different effects on different people, and even on the same person at different times. Drugs do not simply "excrete" experiences, and there is no such thing as *the* drug experience (Zablocki et al. 1991; Ray 1998). What someone experiences from a drug depends on several factors. The *pharmacological* characteristics of a drug cause certain effects, but because most drugs act at many different places in the brain, even these effects differ. The *amount,* or dosage, also plays a part. Higher dosage usually amplifies a drug's effects, but it also may change the quality of the experience. The person's *psychological* state, such as anxious, depressed, or relaxed, is significant. Additionally, *physiological* characteristics of the person taking the drug, such as body weight and metabolism, are important. And, as recently discovered and for reasons yet unknown, drugs also affect men and women differently (Cimons 1999).

Social factors, such as the social setting and subculture, also affect people's drug experiences. Sociologist Howard S. Becker (1967) reported that when LSD (lysergic acid diethylamide) first began to be used, news accounts reported many psychotic reactions and suicides. Then these accounts became rare. Becker concluded that people who first took LSD had the idea that it might create panic—and they were likely to experience panic. As a subculture grew around LSD, however, people's expectations changed—and so did their experiences. When those who had used LSD introduced friends to the drug, they told them what to expect. When first-time users saw strange colors—or even walls breathing or felt a unity with plants—these "trip guides" assured them that this was normal, that it was temporary, and that they should relax and enjoy the sensations. As a result, negative LSD experiences dropped sharply.

In short, expectations influence people's experience with drugs. This is especially the case with drugs that people use to alter their perceptions, to change their mood, or to make them more sociable—drugs that we shall now consider.

THE RECREATIONAL MOOD ELEVATORS

Patterns of Alcohol Consumption

The main drugs that Americans use for sociability are alcohol, nicotine, and marijuana—and in fewer instances, cocaine. Alcohol is the "standard" drug for sociability, and each year the per capita consumption of alcohol for Americans is 36.4 gallons of alcoholic beverages—about 31.9 gallons of beer, 2.7 gallons of wine, and 1.8 gallons of hard liquor (*Statistical Abstract* 2001:Table 204). The actual consumption of those who drink alcohol is about twice this amount, since about half—52 percent—of Americans drink alcoholic beverages.

Figure 4-1 and Table 4-2 are based on a sample so good that we can generalize the findings to all high school students in the United States. As Figure 4-1 shows, during the past month half of all U.S. high school seniors drank alcohol. During this time, one third got drunk; 1 of 9 got drunk six or more times (Johnson et al. 1998). Table 4-2 gives an overview of drug use by high school seniors.

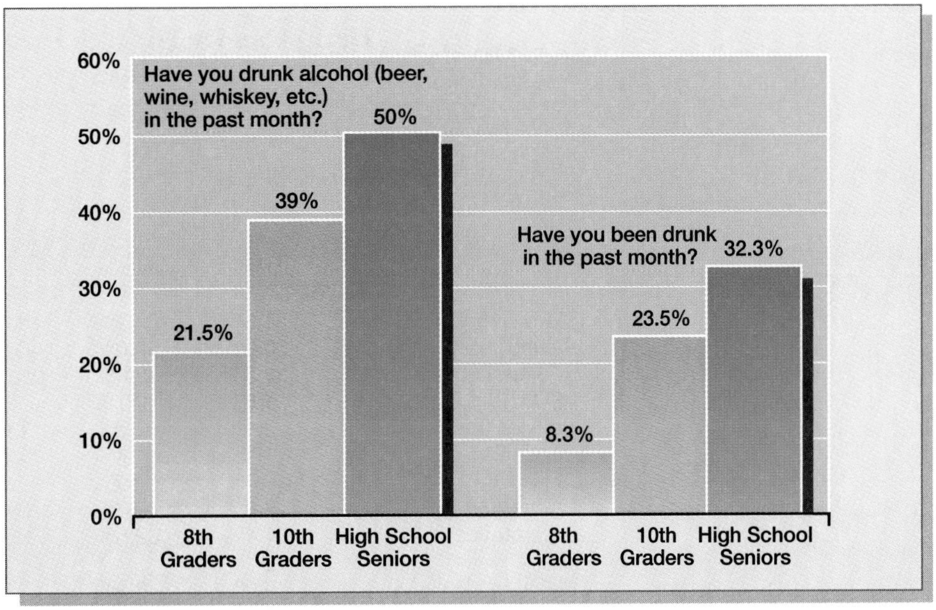

FIGURE 4-1
**Who Drinks
Alcohol?**
(*Source:* Johnston et al. 2001:Table 2
and Table D-43.)

The chart shows two sets of bars. The first set, titled "Have you drunk alcohol (beer, wine, whiskey, etc.) in the past month?", shows: 8th Graders 21.5%, 10th Graders 39%, High School Seniors 50%. The second set, titled "Have you been drunk in the past month?", shows: 8th Graders 8.3%, 10th Graders 23.5%, High School Seniors 32.3%.

**Alcohol
Consumption as a
Social Problem**

**Drunk Driving
and Sexuality**

**Health
Consequences:
Positive
and Negative**

These are objective conditions, of course, which serve as a background factor but are not adequate to make a social problem. We also have to have subjective concerns. And the subjective concerns about alcohol consumption are extensive, centering on alcoholism, underage drinking, drunk driving, and health consequences.

Of the 80 million drinkers in the United States, about 10 million are considered **alcoholics,** people who have severe alcohol-related problems. Relatively few such persons become derelicts on **skid row,** the urban area inhabited by panhandling alcoholics. Rather, almost all—whether working or middle class—continue with their routines but suffer impairment of work, family, and other social relationships.

As noted earlier, each year about 17,000 Americans die in alcohol-related motor vehicle accidents. Most of the drivers are young, male, and drunk. Why aren't just as many young women—or older Americans—involved in these accidents? Social psychologist Stanton Peele (1987) points out that in our culture, getting drunk is seen as *macho,* a symbol of male potency. Social geographer Ronald Snow and sociologist Orville Cunningham (1985) agree, suggesting that excessive drinking by young men is a way of proving their sexuality. They equate driving while drunk as bravery, a form of risk taking that validates their still-developing sense of male identity.

My own experience as a member of U.S. culture confirms these ideas. I, too, had to prove my masculinity by showing how much alcohol I could consume in an evening. I still recall the approval of my friends—as well as some of the retching that followed. If getting drunk were equated with femininity, we would have a lot more young women drinking to excess—and based on my observations of teenagers at parties, we well may be experiencing this process of cultural change at the moment. "Femininity" apparently is being redefined in more macho terms.

Drinking alcoholic beverages has both positive and negative consequences for health. Light drinking reduces the risk of heart attacks, and aids in recovering from them (Katzenstein 1994; Stipp 1994). Alcohol apparently stimulates the production of the "good" cholesterol (HDL) and of a substance that holds the body's blood-

Table 4-2 Drug Use by High School Seniors (in the last 30 days)

| | | Sex | | College Plans | |
	Total	M	F	None or Less Than 4 Years	4 Years
Marijuana	21.6%	24.7%	18.3%	26.0%	19.6%
Alcohol	50.0%	54.0%	46.0%	54.0%	48.0%
Been Drunk	32.3%	38.4%	26.1%	35.0%	30.6%
LSD	1.6%	2.1%	.9%	2.4%	1.2%
Powder Cocaine	2.1%	2.7%	1.6%	3.1%	1.8%
Crack Cocaine	1.1%	1.4%	.7%	2.1%	.7%
Heroin	.7%	.9%	.6%	1.0%	.6%
Barbiturates	3.0%	3.3%	2.6%	3.4%	2.8%
Cigarettes	31.4%	32.8%	29.7%	43.6%	27.3%
Marijuana Daily	6.0%	8.2%	3.5%	9.8%	4.4%
Alcohol Daily	2.9%	4.7%	1.1%	4.8%	2.2%

Source: Johnston et al. 2000; based on Table 4–7. Table 4–8 for daily use.

clotting system in check until injury occurs. These findings show that one or two drinks a day are good for people's health.

Heavy alcohol consumption increases the risk of heart attacks and of having problems with the endocrine, metabolic, immune, and reproductive systems. Heavy drinkers also run a higher risk than nondrinkers of developing cancer of the tongue, mouth, esophagus, larynx, stomach, liver, lung, colon, and rectum. People who both smoke and drink multiply their risk of developing cancer (*Seventh Special Report* 1990).

The Bill for Alcohol Abuse

Alcohol abuse is so extensive that each year 245,000 Americans are treated for this problem at substance abuse centers (*Statistical Abstract* 2001:Table 188). The bill for their treatment runs about $16 billion a year, which everyone, including abstainers, must pay (*Seventh Special Report* 1990). The total bill is much higher, if we consider lost employment, reduced productivity, and alcohol-related crime and social welfare. The total may run as high as $100 billion a year—making alcohol the most expensive of all drug abuse problems (Winslow 1995a). Then, too, there are its social costs, such as the greater likelihood of spouse and family abuse, disturbed children, and the breakup of marriages.

Pregnancy and Childbirth

Embedded in this social problem is another problem, the use of drugs by pregnant women. Like most drugs, alcohol affects an unborn child. A fetus, however, cannot metabolize alcohol, and drinking by a pregnant woman raises the fetus's blood alcohol level to about *ten times* the mother's. Approximately 1 in every 350 to 500 infants is born with some type of birth defect because the child's mother abused alcohol during pregnancy.

Fetal Alcohol Syndrome

The consequences are anything but pleasant. Children of drinking mothers may be born with a cluster of problems called **fetal alcohol syndrome,** the third most common cause of mental retardation in the Western world (Steacy et al. 1989).

| Parent's Education | | | | Region | | | |
High School Dropout	High School	Some College	College	North-east	North Central	South	West
20.9%	21.5%	21.4%	21.3%	26.0%	19.3%	17.4%	27.2%
50.0%	51.3%	48.1%	54.0%	58.0%	52.3%	44.9%	48.3%
33.1%	31.2%	31.9%	35.5%	39.3%	34.8%	26.5%	32.8%
1.7%	1.4%	1.4%	1.2%	1.4%	1.2%	1.4%	1.2%
2.0%	2.0%	2.1%	1.7%	2.1%	1.9%	2.2%	2.4%
1.1%	1.0%	.9%	.7%	.9%	1.2%	0.7%	1.6%
.8%	.5%	.8%	.6%	.4%	.7%	.8%	.9%
3.6%	2.6%	3.3%	2.3%	2.5%	2.5%	3.6%	3.0%
32.2%	32.8%	30.2%	27.4%	33.1%	35.6%	24.6%	28.1%
6.3%	5.9%	5.3%	4.1%	7.3%	5.9%	4.6%	7.4%
2.9%	3.0%	2.4%	2.9%	3.0%	3.1%	2.8%	2.9%

These children are born addicted to alcohol, and for a week to six months they go through painful withdrawal. They are irritable, their hearts beat irregularly, and some have convulsions. Complications follow them in life—joint deformities, heart problems, hyperactivity, brain damage, lower intelligence, and behavioral disorders (*Seventh Special Report* 1990; Steinmetz 1992; Dorozyaski 1993).

Each year about 5,000 U.S. children are born with fetal alcohol syndrome. This birth defect is not distributed evenly throughout the population, but is concentrated among groups that have the highest rate of alcoholism. Apparently the hardest hit are Native Americans, whose rate of fetal alcohol syndrome is two to three times the national average ("Congress" 1994).

As serious as it is, fetal alcohol syndrome must be put into perspective. We need to be aware of the problem, but not go into hysteria. In a study of 12,000 pregnancies, 204 women who were abusive drinkers delivered only five babies with fetal alcohol syndrome. In France and Italy, where most women drink moderately during pregnancy, fetal alcohol syndrome is no higher than in the United States (Chafetz 1990). As in so many other instances, we need more research.

Simply drinking alcohol, of course, does not lead to alcohol-related problems. Rather, social researchers have found that it is *how* one learns to drink that is significant. Studies of groups that have low rates of alcoholism, such as Spaniards, Italians, Orthodox Jews, Greeks, Chinese, and Lebanese, indicate five keys to low-problem drinking (Hanson 1995):

The Significance of How People Learn to Drink

- Drinking alcohol is a regular part of life.
- Alcohol is viewed as neutral—it is neither a poison nor a magic elixir.

After Prohibition ended, Americans celebrated their freedom to again drink openly. This particular celebration—an international beer drinking contest—took place in Los Angeles. To have the contestants lie on their backs while participating may have proved convenient—after a winner was declared, it is likely that some contestants remained in this position.

- Drinking is not viewed as a sign of adulthood or virility.
- There is no tolerance for abusive drinking.
- Learning to drink starts early, and in the home. Parents provide role models of moderate (light, social, non-abusive) drinking.

The opposite conditions lead to alcohol problems, especially within subcultures that view getting drunk as manly. Two more conditions have been identified as increasing the risk of problems with alcohol: learning to drink in situations that are emotionally charged and in which there is a good deal of ambivalence toward alcohol (Lolli 1958; Snyder 1958; Cahalan et al. 1969; Rockwell 1972; Glassner and Berg 1980).

Biological Causes

Some research supports a biological basis for alcoholism (Buck 1998). Sons of alcoholic fathers run a higher risk than normal of becoming alcoholics. But perhaps this is social, for the father is an alcoholic role model. The finding holds true, however, even for sons adopted at birth and reared by nonalcoholic parents. The biological key may be a difference in how the body's cells react to alcohol (Bishop 1988b). The evidence that links alcoholism to genes, however, is mixed, with some studies refuting other studies (Bishop 1990; Nazario 1990).

Nicotine

Nicotine is the second most popular recreational drug in the United States. The Surgeon General has identified smoking as "the chief, single, avoidable cause of death in our society, and the most important health issue of our time" (Smith 1986). Tobacco is so harmful that "a nonsmoker has a better chance of reaching the age of 75 than a smoker has of reaching the age of 65" (Goode 1989)! The dollar cost is also high, about $28 billion a year in health care and another $43 billion in lost productivity. Yet the tobacco industry spends more than $2 billion a year on cigarette ads, most of which are geared to convince young people that smoking is sexy, and the fast road to growing up. (For bizarre honesty in advertising, see the Global Glimpse box on the next page.)

Honesty in Advertising: A Cigarette Called Death

The Enlightened Tobacco Company of England manufactures a cigarette called Death. This brand is sold in a black package emblazoned with a skull-and-crossbones. Near the filter of each cigarette appears the death logo. The ads for the cigarette are bordered in black, resembling funeral announcements ("Enlightenment" 1994).

The company says that consumers have the right to smoke—and should be informed as to what they are doing to their bodies. They say this is better than half-truths, deceptions, and weasely health warnings. In the United States, we know that the Surgeon General's warning, written on each package of cigarettes, cannot really be true. After all, the smiling, happy, carefree young people smoking cigarettes in those thousands of ads wouldn't be so happy and smiling if the product were lethal.

By the way, as part of its marketing strategy, the Enlightened Tobacco Company donates 10 percent of its pretax profits to cancer charities. If there is a request, the company will also fund programs to get people to stop smoking.

The company says that it is taking the ethical high ground in selling cigarettes. Do you agree?

These objective conditions provoked extensive subjective concerns. They began with hesitant anti-cigarette sentiment, which, as it grew, unleashed a strident, powerful antismoking campaign. This has led to the creation of no-smoking sections in restaurants and other public facilities, and to a ban on smoking in offices, on domestic flights, and in government buildings. Table 4-3 shows how effective this campaign has been. As you can see, at the height of addiction, *most* men smoked, as did

Table 4-3   Cigarette Smoking by Sex and Age

	1965	1975*	1985	1995	1999
By Sex					
Male	52%	43%	33%	27%	25.2%
Female	34%	32%	28%	23%	21.6%
By Sex and Age					
Males					
18–24 years	54%	42%	28%	28%	29.5%
25–34 years	61%	51%	38%	31%	29.1%
35–44 years	58%	51%	38%	33%	30.0%
45–64 years	52%	43%	33%	27%	25.8%
65 and over	29%	25%	20%	14%	10.5%
Females					
18–24 years	38%	34%	30%	22%	26.3%
25–34 years	44%	39%	32%	29%	23.5%
35–44 years	44%	40%	32%	27%	26.5%
45–64 years	32%	33%	30%	24%	21.0%
65 and over	10%	12%	14%	12%	10.7%

Source: Statistical Abstract 1994:Table 212; 1997:Tables 220, 228; 1998:Table 238. Table 60: National Center for Health Statistics (2001) *Health.*
*Data are from the closest year available, 1974.

one of three women. Unfortunately, the people who have the lowest rate of smoking—those age 65 and over—do not represent positive results that have come out of the antismoking campaign; rather, by this age so many smokers have died prematurely that there aren't that many smokers left alive.

Figure 4-2 also depicts the decrease in smoking since its height of popularity in the 1960s. In a strange twist of logic, the tobacco industry—which denies that cigarettes cause cancer—claims credit for this decline. They say it is evidence of their efforts "to deter youths from smoking" ("Frequent Tobacco Use" 1992)! (For another view, see the Issues box on targeting kids and minorities, on the next page.)

Because the government, through Medicaid, pays much of the health costs of cigarette smoking, in the 1990s the states sued the tobacco companies. In 1998, the states were awarded $245 billion dollars from the cigarette manufacturers, with the money to be paid over 25 years. Some states are planning on spending a small percentage on antismoking initiatives, but others are thinking in terms of repairing their sidewalks (Meier 1999). This huge settlement did not put a single cigarette company out of business. To cover their costs, cigarette manufacturers merely raised prices for their captive addicts.

Marijuana

The third most popular recreational drug in the United States is marijuana. During the 1960s, marijuana was an underground drug smoked furtively by a few

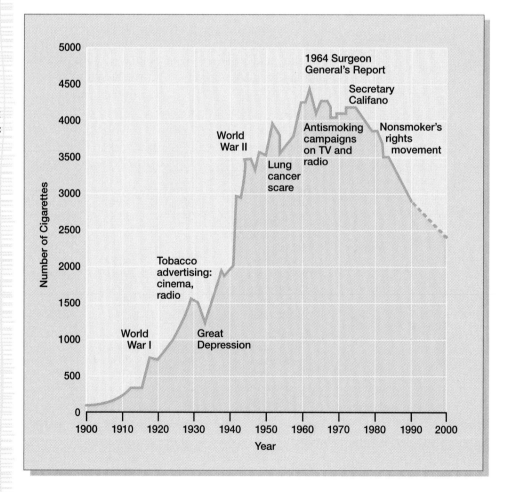

FIGURE 4-2
Number of Cigarettes Consumed Annually per Adult (Ages 18 and Older): United States, 1900–2000
(*Source*: Economic Research Service, U.S. Department of Agriculture; projection by the author.)

Targeting Kids and Minorities

Let's listen in on a conversation between Harry Reynolds, the CEO of a major tobacco company, and John Phillips, director of sales.

"John, I want to show you something. My daughter brought this social problems book home from college. Look at this table on page 109."

"Yeah, that confirms our own studies. Our customer base is eroding. Too many people are believing those lies the (expletive deleted) antismokers are telling—cancer and all that. We've got to get them started earlier."

"What've you got in mind?"

"Well, if we could get the kids hooked—oops, I mean started . . . I was thinking about adding some flavor they like."

"Good idea. They've already added cherry to Skoal Long Cut. That's getting a lot of kids started. And they've been smart about it—keeping the nicotine down so the kids gradually get into it. Then, of course, they move on to Copenhagen after they're hooked—I mean, used to the taste. No one's done butterscotch yet. That might work."

"Chocolate might be even better. If you okay it, we can test-market Chocolate Smokeless Tobacco. And, of course, chocolate-flavored cigarettes. We could even make them low-nicotine and low-tar."

"What about the minorities?"

"We're already loading *Ebony* with ads. My research department reported last week that one of eight pages of *Ebony*'s color ads go to cigarettes."

"Great. How about sponsoring cultural events, like a jazz festival?"

"Kool's already got that covered."

"Come to think of it, Parliament's already got that World Beat Concert Series, too."

"Yeah, but we're underwriting the Harlem Week Festival in New York City."

"And don't forget all the money we're using to buy—I mean, contribute—to the National Black Caucus of State Legislatures."

"And the United Negro College Fund and the National Urban League are already in our budget."

"Sometimes I wonder if all this money is paying off."

"Is it ever! You never see any of that antismoking propaganda in *Ebony*—and that's no coincidence."

"I've never read it, never even seen a copy. But I depend on you to know these things, John."

"But the real payoff is that African Americans are smoking more than the whites."

"Right. I remember those figures you showed me last week that blacks are about a third more likely to smoke. But what I hate is that they blame us for blacks having higher rates of lung cancer and heart disease and stuff like that!"

"It's the food they eat, Harry."

"Do you think we could target Latinos?"

"Marlboro's already got that pretty well covered. Remember those rodeos for Mexican Americans they sponsor in California?"

"That's right."

"And we're already buying off—I mean, contributing—all that money to the Hispanic Congressional Caucus and the National Association of Hispanic Journalists."

"I was just thinking about the Native Americans. Maybe we're missing them."

"I think you've got something there. And the Chinese Americans, too. And then there's the Abyssinian Americans and the . . ."

"But the perfect answer would be to bypass all that race and gender stuff and just target 3-year-olds of every background."

"Good idea. I'll get to work on it right away. Our competitors have already done a good job. Ninety percent of six-year-olds can match Joe Camel with Camel cigarettes. Too bad they can't use Joe anymore (laughs). But we can build on this. Maybe we could hand out cute cutouts of our cigarette packs to the preschools—and maybe coloring books, too."

That night both Harry and John enjoy peaceful sleep, dreaming of chocolate-flavored cigarettes, and butterscotch, and raspberry, and. . . .

Based on Johnson 1992; Freedman 1994;
Pollay 1997.

Although the popularity of marijuana has declined, it remains a major drug of choice of young Americans. Because of legal bans on research, we know little of the health consequences of marijuana use, either positive or negative.

FIGURE 4-3
Who Smokes Marijuana?
Note: Data are for 1998, using a national sample.
(*Source:* Johnston et al. 2000: Table 4–7.)

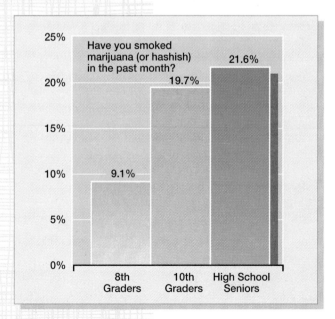

Have you smoked marijuana (or hashish) in the past month?

adventurous souls. By the 1970s, it was smoked by millions, especially at weekend parties. Based on personal experience, I can add that this drug became so popular and semi- "out in the open" at this time that many professors smoked marijuana with their students. By 1979, one of three Americans (36 percent) age 18 to 25 smoked marijuana at least once a month (*Statistical Abstract* 1998:Table 237). Today, that total has dropped in half (16 percent) (*Statistical Abstract* 2001:Table 189).

The states' reaction to marijuana's unexpected popularity was schizophrenic. Alaska legalized possession of marijuana for personal consumption, but Nevada made a "first-offense possession of even a minuscule quantity of marijuana a felony, punishable by up to six years in prison" (Goode 1989:30). Alaskans decided they had erred, and revoked their law (Egan 1991). Nevada kept its law.

Although marijuana has declined in overall popularity over the past two decades, it remains a drug of choice for high school students. As Figure 4-3 shows, during the past month more than 1 of 5 of all U.S. high school seniors smoked marijuana. Even 1 of 11 of all U.S. eighth graders did.

How does marijuana affect its users' health? At this point, we have little hard evidence that it harms or helps people's health. Many assertions have been made—that marijuana impairs the body's immune response, reduces the male sex hormone testosterone, lowers fertility, damages chromosomes, and causes brain damage. Although widely heralded in the mass media when the studies first appeared, such consequences have not been substantiated by later

Health Implications: Positive or Negative

research. This does not mean, of course, that such charges are false, but at this point, unlike with alcohol and nicotine, there is no firm basis to conclude that marijuana harms health.

Smoking marijuana does affect psychomotor performance, however, making it risky to smoke and run machinery, drive a vehicle, or fly a plane. THC, the primary psychoactive agent in marijuana, remains in the body several days after smoking, though its lingering effects are not perceptible to the smoker. In one study, pilots who were tested twenty-four hours after they had smoked marijuana, when they no longer felt "high," showed deterioration in performing a landing maneuver. Perhaps most telling is this finding: In a posthumous sample of more than 400 male drivers in California killed in auto accidents, 37 percent had THC in their blood (Goode 1989:147). Obviously, it is not prudent to ride or fly with someone who smokes marijuana.

Medical Uses of Marijuana

Research findings also show positive aspects of marijuana. Marijuana relieves glaucoma and helps to reduce the side effects of nausea and vomiting in patients undergoing chemotherapy (Baum 1993). It also relieves migraine headaches (Russo 1998). To discover marijuana's positive and negative effects, we need further research, but in our growing conservative climate such research is discouraged because of the social reputation of marijuana. Even physicians who used to be able to prescribe marijuana for patients with glaucoma and patients undergoing chemotherapy have been prohibited from doing so (Bishop 1992; Treaster 1991a, 1991b).

The Amotivational Syndrome

Marijuana is associated with an **amotivational syndrome,** meaning that people who smoke marijuana extensively may become lethargic, lose their concentration, stop carrying out long-range plans, and drift through life. Researchers have found that marijuana smokers tend to receive poorer grades and are more likely to drop out of high school (Kleinman et al. 1987). That this is not just a correlation and that marijuana is the cause, however, has not been proven. The evidence for an amotivational syndrome consists mainly of impressions and anecdotes: "Before she smoked grass, Shirley had so many plans, but look at her now." Research on Rhesus monkeys is intriguing: Monkeys that smoke are less motivated than nonsmoking monkeys to work for bananas. When researchers stop giving the monkeys marijuana, their motivation returns to normal after about nine months (Slikker 1992). Obviously, we need some solid research on humans.

As we have seen in other instances, we must approach "facts" with caution, for a look below the surface is likely to yield a different view. A deeper look here shows that, compared with their classmates, heavy marijuana smokers are more likely to come from broken homes, to drink more alcohol, to commit more delinquent acts, and to be involved in a subculture that places little value on academic achievement. In other words, marijuana is not the cause of the behavior but is just "one element in a large and complex picture of interrelated problems and behaviors" (Kleinman et al. 1987; White 1991).

Contrasting Reactions

Marijuana certainly is an excellent example of the subjective nature of social problems. As stated, physicians used to be able to prescribe marijuana as a medicine for a variety of conditions, but they no longer can do so. Marijuana possession used to be legal for anyone, but now it is subject to some type of penalty in every state. In Alabama, a man was *sentenced to death* for selling marijuana (*New York Times* 1991). With reactions to marijuana ranging from seeing it as a threat to society to viewing it as a treatment for medical problems, and with millions of users paying to smoke it and thousands of enforcement officers being paid to oppose it, marijuana amply demonstrates the subjective nature of social problems.

The Social History of Cocaine

Cocaine, a fourth drug that is used for recreational purposes, helps us understand how a drug can be transformed into a social problem. Lavishly praised by physicians in the late 1800s (including Freud, who enjoyed its effects), cocaine was used throughout the United States, especially in patent medicines. Yet by the end of the first decade of the twentieth century, cocaine had been transformed from a medicine and "pick-me-up" into a dangerous drug—much as Dr. Jekyll became Mr. Hyde (a story, by the way, that was written in three days by Robert Louis Stevenson while he was high on cocaine [Ashley 1975]). What caused this transformation?

We should note first that cocaine was never without controversy (Ashley 1975). When the Spaniards invaded Peru in the 1500s, they conquered a people who chewed coca leaves. The Spaniards attributed the drug's effects (especially the reduction of fatigue) to the devil and rejected the use of cocaine as evil. During the 1800s, a turnaround occurred when Angelo Mariana, a French chemist, introduced a wine that contained the coca leaf extract. This wine was considered so excellent that the pope presented Mariana with a medal of appreciation (Ray 1998).

As cocaine was becoming associated with respectable people, it was on its way to becoming a standard drug in the United States. Cocaine became so popular that hundreds of thousands of Americans sipped cocaine as a "pick-me-up," for it had become one of the main ingredients of a popular drink that took its name from the leaf, Coca-Cola.

In the late 1800s, however, cocaine's reputation began to suffer. Newspapers began to link cocaine with the poor and with criminals—especially gunmen—who were depicted as taking cocaine to stimulate their courage. Repeated publicity about "cocaine-crazed blacks" also led whites to believe that "blacks plus cocaine equals raped white women" (Ashley 1975).

Such news stories led to a public outcry, and in 1903 the Coca-Cola company found it expedient to eliminate cocaine from its drink. Even today, however, Coca-Cola contains an extract from the coca leaf (Miller 1994a). It was still legal to use cocaine in products, and in 1906 the Pure Food and Drug Act required that cocaine be listed if it was an ingredient in a product. But in 1914, the Harrison Act classified cocaine as a narcotic (an error, since cocaine is a stimulant), and provided penalties for selling cocaine. The Harrison Act paved the way to a black market in cocaine.

Today, about 10% of Americans admit to having used cocaine (*Statistical Abstract* 2001:Table 189). As Table 4-2 shows, in just the past month, about 3 percent of all U.S. high school seniors took cocaine in the form of powder or crack. Cocaine has become big business: At $30 billion to $50 billion a year, it rivals the largest U.S. corporations.

Popular and Medical Uses

Cocaine has two distinct uses, one popular and one medical. It usually is taken for its euphoric effects—feelings of well-being, optimism, confidence, competence, and energy. Cocaine also has a reputation as an aphrodisiac, for it is thought "to create sexual desire, to heighten it, to increase sexual endurance, and to cure frigidity and impotence" (Inciardi 1986:78–79). Physicians apply cocaine as a local anesthetic and a vasoconstrictor (a substance that reduces blood to the area to which it is applied). Cocaine is the medical profession's anesthetic of choice for surgery involving the nose, throat, larynx, and lower respiratory passages.

Risks of Cocaine Use

Cocaine use carries the risk of addiction. The euphoria that cocaine brings is followed by a letdown. When chronic users try to stop using cocaine, they typically plunge into a depression and look to cocaine to lift them out of it (Inciardi and McBride 1990). Those who become addicted report "a craving so intense they will

Chapter 4   Alcohol and Other Drugs

give up many of the things they value—money, possessions, relationships, jobs, and careers—in order to continue taking the drug" (Goode 1989:198–199). I'll never forget the homeless man I interviewed in Chicago. He was bright, educated, and articulate. While the manager of a Radio Shack in California, he became addicted to coke, stole from his employer, and ended up on Chicago's skid row.

Repeated use of cocaine can cause physical damage, especially ulceration of the mucous membranes in the nose. Several hundred deaths a year are attributed to cocaine (Kozel 1995, 1996). For reasons still unknown, cocaine is more dangerous on hot days (Lannin 1998). Though snorting is the preferred method of use, smoking cocaine base, called *freebasing*, is also popular.

Crack Cocaine

The potent form of cocaine that has drawn national attention is *crack*. Crack gives a pleasure so intense it is akin to orgasm. The high, which lasts from 5 to 12 minutes, is followed by a "crash" that leaves its users irritable, depressed, nervous, or paranoid. Although crack is inexpensive, because its effects are short-lived it is costly for users to remain high. The desire for the intense pleasure is so great that women sell their bodies in exchange for crack, and a new form of prostitute, the "crack whore," has emerged.

Among the dysfunctions of crack are birth defects, and each year thousands of babies are born addicted to crack. The cost of caring for just one year's crack babies during their preschool years is estimated in the billions of dollars (Humphries et al. 1992). Figuring out how to prevent this form of child abuse has proved frustrating to authorities, and has led to a controversial social policy, which is discussed in the Thinking Critically box below.

Crack can be produced easily in a home kitchen. With huge profits at stake, illegal drug entrepreneurs ("corner crack dealers") fight for territory ("turf") and customers. As a result, violence surrounds crack—stemming from those who will do

THINKING CRITICALLY ABOUT SOCIAL PROBLEMS

On Pregnancy, Drugs, and Jail

Consider the following court cases.

A pregnant woman in Washington, D.C., was charged with check forgery. The ususal sentence for first-time offenders is probation. When the woman tested positive for cocaine, the judge sentenced her to prison, saying; "I'm going to keep her locked up until the baby's born."

A California woman who had taken street drugs was charged with child abuse after she delievered a brain-damaged baby who died soon after birth.

An Illinois woman was charged with manslaughter when her two-day-old infant died due to her cocaine use during pregnancy.

In Florida, a woman was convicted of two counts of delivering drugs to a minor. The prosecution alleged that the woman had passed cocaine to her newborn child through the umbilical cord after the baby was delivered but before the cord was cut.

FOR YOUR CONSIDERATION

Should judges jail a pregnant woman because she uses drugs such as cocaine that can harm her developing child? If so, since it is known that alcohol and nicotine can harm a fetus, should judges be permitted to jail pregnant women who smoke cigarettes or drink alcohol?

Based on Broff 1989; Humphries et al. 1992; Pagelow 1992.

anything for the drug and from those who will do anything to be able to deal this highly profitable substance.

Following on the heels of intense publicity over the violence associated with crack, in 1986 the U.S. Congress made crack dealing a federal offense, and began meting out higher penalties for crack than for powder cocaine. Because powder cocaine is more likely to be used by whites and crack by African Americans (Lewis 1996; Riley 1998), blacks charged racial discrimination. After eight years of prison sentences that were handed down primarily to African-American users, in *U.S.* v. *Ricky Davis* (1994) the U.S. District court in Georgia declared that crack and cocaine are one and the same drug, and sentences imposed for the use of crack can be no heavier than those imposed for the use of powder cocaine.

From this brief social history of cocaine, we can see that several principles are involved in determining a drug's social reputation:

Principles Underlying a Drug's Social Reputation

1. A drug's reputation is not based on objective conditions. It does not, for instance, derive from tests that reveal that drug A causes serious problems, drug B does not, and therefore drug A is banned and drug B permitted. If such a scientific approach characterized a drug's social history, alcohol would be banned and marijuana would probably be available in grocery stores (Ashley 1975).

2. Like humans, drugs gain their reputation through the people and events with which they are associated.

3. Drugs that are associated with people or events generally considered respectable are likely to be defined as good and desirable; drugs associated with people or events generally considered disreputable are likely to be defined as bad and undesirable.

4. The reputation or social acceptability of drugs is not fixed but is subject to change.

THE HALLUCINOGENS

LSD

Perhaps the most famous of the hallucinogens is LSD (lysergic acid diethylamide). This drug was first synthesized by the Swiss chemist Albert Hoffman in 1938. Its psychoactive property was not discovered until 1943, when Hoffman accidentally inhaled a minute dose. He reported what happened to him:

> Last Friday, April 16, 1943, I was forced to stop my work in the laboratory in the middle of the afternoon and to go home, as I was seized by a peculiar restlessness associated with a sensation of mild dizziness. Having reached home, I lay down and sank in a kind of drunkenness which was not unpleasant and which was characterized by extreme activity of imagination. As I lay in a dazed condition with my eyes closed (I experienced daylight as disagreeably bright) there surged upon me an uninterrupted stream of fantastic images of extraordinary plasticity and vividness and accompanied by an intense, kaleidoscope-like play of colors. This condition gradually passed off after about two hours. (Hoffman 1968:184–185)

At first, LSD was thought to produce psychoses, and people avoided it. Then, in 1960, Harvard professor Timothy Leary began experimenting with LSD. Leary was fired for violating experimental guidelines and became a guru of the 1960s youth counterculture. He preached a message about how great LSD was, saying that everyone should experience changed consciousness and become nonconformist. Leary's

Attitudes toward a drug depend partially on the drug's social history. While some drugs are rejected, others become socially acceptable and are adapted into a group's culture. Such is the case with the use of mescaline (from peyote buttons) and psilocybin (from mushrooms) among some Native-American Mexicans. Shown here is a *huichol* (yarn painting), a standard art form among these groups. *Huicholes* reflect visions induced by these drugs.

slogan, "turn on, tune in, and drop out," struck a responsive chord with the youth of the time, and LSD use spread. This tasteless, odorless substance, an ounce of which contains 300,000 adult doses, reached its height of media attention in about 1967 and its peak of usage in about 1979 (Goode 1989:178–179). Although LSD use is not as widespread as it used to be, neither is it rare. Table 4-2 (pages 104–105) shows that about 3 percent of all high school seniors have used LSD within the past 30 days.

Peyote and Mescaline

The use of peyote is an old custom on this continent, as Native Americans were using this cactus when Cortez arrived in the 1500s. It is now used legally in the United States only in a sacramental manner by members of the Native American church. Some states, such as Oregon, however, prohibit any use (Neuhaus 1990; Lawson and Morris 1991). Mescaline, which was synthesized from peyote in 1919, produces similar visual effects. Both peyote and mescaline have had famous proponents: Havelock Ellis (1897, 1902) was enthusiastic about peyote, and Aldous Huxley (1954) sang the praises of mescaline. In the 1960s and 1970s, anthropologist Carlos Castaneda (1968, 1971, 1974) popularized the use of peyote among a cult-like following. The drug always has a die-hard group of users, with occasional recruits.

Psilocybin

The magic mushrooms of Mexico (*Psilocybe mexicana*) were also being used when Cortez arrived on these shores. Because they were associated with pagan rituals, Cortez launched a campaign against the mushrooms (as he had against peyote), driving their use underground. Not until the 1930s was it discovered that natives of southern Mexico were still using them. Their active ingredient is psilocybin, which was isolated by Albert Hoffman in 1958 and later synthesized. As with peyote, reports about this drug often contain a spiritual or religious emphasis (Ray 1998).

PCP

PCP (phencyclidine hydrochloride), called *angel dust*, was synthesized in 1957 by Parke-Davis and sold as a painkiller. As people found out, it also produced hallucinations. Because it requires a minimum of equipment, PCP is often manufactured in home laboratories. Affecting the central nervous system, PCP makes it difficult to speak and usually brings on altered body image and feelings of unreality. Some users report euphoria and feelings of power, loneliness, or isolation; others, numbness and feelings of dying (which is why PCP is also called "embalming fluid"). Higher dosages may result in loss of inhibition, disorientation, rage, convulsions, or coma (Crider 1986; Ray 1998).

THE AMPHETAMINES AND BARBITURATES

The Amphetamines

The amphetamines—Benzedrine, Dexedrine, Methedrine, Desoxyn, Biphetamine, and Desamyl—go by such street names as "cat," "goob," "speed," "ups," "crank," "splash," "pep pills," and "meth" (Goode 1989:188; Kozel 1996). Discovered in 1887, Benzedrine became popular in the 1920s in over-the-counter inhalers intended to dilate the bronchial tubes. Later Benzedrine was available by prescription in tablet form for hyperkinesis and, in 1939, as an appetite suppressant. During World War II, amphetamine was used to help soldiers stay awake. Also at this time, people began to soak the amphetamine from Benzedrine inhalers, and amphetamine abuse began. In the 1960s, "speed" (methamphetamine dissolved in liquid) began to be used by "speed freaks," who injected the drug, sometimes every two or three hours, for "runs" of three or four days. Each injection of this kind produces a "rush," a sudden feeling of intense pleasure, followed by moderate feelings of euphoria. In some areas users prefer "hot rolling," liquifying methamphetamine in an eye dropper and then inhaling it (Kozel 1996).

Some users hallucinate, while others develop feelings of paranoia, or become hostile and aggressive—symptoms that have been called the *amphetamine psychosis* (Ray 1998). Heavy amphetamine use is sometimes accompanied by behavioral fixations—in which activities are repeated over and over, such as counting the corn flakes in a box of cereal. Amphetamine withdrawal may bring depression, fatigue, anxiety, sleeplessness, feelings of terror, and thoughts of suicide (Goode 1989:192).

The Barbiturates

In 1862, Dr. A. Bayer of Munich, Germany (the Bayer of aspirin fame), successfully combined urea with malonic acid and made a new compound, barbituric acid, from which over 2,500 derivations have been synthesized. Of these, phenobarbital (Luminal), amobarbital (Amytal), pentobarbital (Nembutal), and secobarbital (Seconal) are the best known. Medically, the barbiturates are used as an anesthetic and to treat anxiety, insomnia, and epilepsy. Used for nonmedical purposes, they provide an experience similar to alcohol. Regular barbiturate use leads to physical dependence. Withdrawal causes nausea, anxiety, sweating, dizziness, trembling, muscular twitching, and sometimes convulsions, coma, and death. Because the risk of death is higher for those who stop "cold turkey" (abruptly), physicians usually substitute a long-lasting barbiturate and then slowly withdraw it (Ray 1998).

The Illegal Flower

Of the many flowers admired by Americans, one flower has a unique reputation. In 1901 it became illegal to import this flower or its products, and in 1942 Americans could not even grow it without a license from the Secretary of the Treasury. This flower is so loathed by officials that in 1956 a federal law went into effect that (except for first convictions for possession) prohibited judges from suspending sentences, giving probation, or granting parole for flower-related offenses. This law also made execution possible for someone selling certain derivatives of this flower to a person under age 18 (Ray 1998).

What flower is this? It is the opium poppy. The derivative so feared and hated by some (and desired by others) is heroin. Figure 4-4 illustrates the process by which opium yields morphine and heroin.

Challenging Traditional Views: How Addictive Is Heroin?

The common view is that heroin is so addictive and the withdrawal pains so severe that addicts will do anything to avoid withdrawal. Note how the writer William Burroughs (1975:135) described his own addiction:

> Junk (heroin) yields a basic formula of . . . total need. . . . Beyond a certain frequency need knows absolutely no limit or control. In the words of total need: "Wouldn't you?" Yes you would. You would lie, cheat, inform on your friends, steal, do *anything* to satisfy total need. Because you would be in a state of total sickness, total possession, and not in a position to act in any other way. . . . A rabid dog can't choose but bite.

FIGURE 4-4
Conversion of Opium into Heroin
(*Source:* From *The Heroin Trail* by the Staff and Editors of *Newsday* [New York: New American Library, 1974.] Originally in *Newsday* [February 1–March 4, 1973]. Copyright © 1973, 1974 by *Newsday* Inc. Used by permission of Dutton Signet, a division of Penguin Putnam, Inc. and *Newsday,* Inc.)

A team of sociologists headed by Bruce Johnson (1985) challenged such conventional views of heroin addiction. These researchers rented a storefront in a neighborhood in Harlem that had "the highest number of street-level heroin abusers in the country." They also rented another storefront in a similar area. These neighborhoods were so well known for heroin dealing that they drew customers from around the region. Some dealers even used brand names to build repeat business: Tragic Magic, Black Death, and Dynamite. For two years, a research staff of former heroin users built rapport with 201 heroin users. Collecting day-to-day reports on these addicts, the researchers found that many heroin users are *not* physically addicted; for a period of time they use heroin once or twice a day, and then—without suffering withdrawal symptoms—go for several days without the drug.

Use of heroin in Vietnam also supports these findings. About 14 percent of U.S. soldiers used heroin in doses far stronger than any available back home. After they left the stress of the war and were reintegrated with family, friends, and work, the vast majority ceased using the drug. They had few, if any, noticeable physical problems. As the Assistant Secretary of Defense for Health and Environment said:

> Everything that I learned in medical school—that anyone who ever tried heroin was instantly, totally, and perpetually hooked—failed to prepare me for dealing with this situation. (Peele 1987:211)

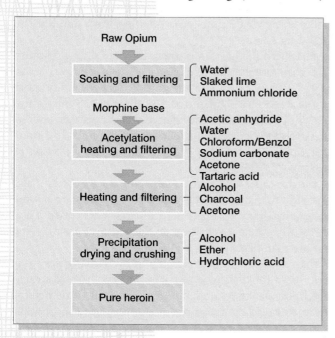

Reconciling the Evidence

How can we reconcile such contradictory conclusions? Certainly William Burroughs' description of his own addiction to heroin (and similar reports by others) is accurate. He did not make it up. At the same time, Johnson and his associates are also accurate. They did not make up their findings either. And other researchers have noted that some people use heroin on an irregular basis, such as at weekend parties, without becoming addicted. Where does this leave us? From these mixed reports, it seems reasonable to conclude that heroin is addicting to some people, but not to others. Some people do become addicts and match the stereotypical profile. Others use heroin on a recreational basis.

Both, then, may be right. With the evidence we have at this point, it would be inappropriate to side with either extreme. That is, it would not match research findings if we concluded that anyone can use heroin without getting addicted or that anyone who uses heroin gets addicted. We must await further research to find the key to the addiction.

The Dangers of Street Heroin

The primary danger of street heroin is that its users never know what their money is buying. No federal drug agency protects the consumer, and street heroin may be cut with substances that kill, or it may not be cut enough and thereby be potent enough to kill. Users may develop allergies to the quinine commonly used to cut heroin, or even to the heroin itself, and die from acute congestion and edema of the lungs. Some die so rapidly that the needle is still in their arm when they are found.

Fetal Narcotic Syndrome

As with alcohol and cocaine, pregnant women who use narcotics deliver babies that are addicted. Suffering from **fetal narcotic syndrome,** these newborns are pitiful. They have tremors, they are underweight and can't sleep right, and they vomit, sneeze, and frantically suck their tiny fists (*Drug Dependence in Pregnancy* 1979).

Do Narcotics Cause Crime?

Almost everyone knows that narcotics cause crime, prevent people from working, and destroy health. Crack cocaine is a notorious example. Sociologists James Inciardi and Anne Pottieger (1994), who studied Miami crack users, found that the average crack user had committed 6,000 crimes in just the past three months! This astronomical number comes into somewhat better focus when we learn that 98 percent of their crimes were illegal drug sales.

It is common knowledge that heroin addicts rob, steal, burglarize, or prostitute themselves in order to support their drug habit. Sociologists Bruce Johnson, Kevin Anderson, and Eric Wish (1988) interviewed 105 drug addicts. They found that during just the past 24 hours these men had committed 46 robberies, 18 burglaries, and 41 thefts. Seventy-five percent of the $7,771 they netted went for drugs, and 25 percent for other items such as food. The average street addict commits 150 nondrug crimes a year and inflicts thousands of dollars of losses on victims (Johnson et al. 1985:185).

Narcotics, however, are *not* the cause of these crimes. Nor do narcotics make people unproductive citizens, or destroy their health. These three beliefs are myths. To see how this can be, consider physicians who become addicted to narcotics. They do *not* rob, burglarize, or prostitute themselves. Nor do they stop working. Nor does their health deteriorate more than usual (Winick 1961).

Why not? The answer is that physician addicts are able to divert narcotics from legal sources in order to obtain them for their own use. They do not have to scramble for money to purchase narcotics, and they can continue to work at their medical practice. With pure drugs cheap and readily obtainable, there is no need to prey on others.

As functionalists stress, whenever laws are passed against a drug that is in high demand, a symbiotic black market springs up to meet that demand. Although it is illegal, cocaine is in high demand; the intricate black market that serves the demand stretches across continents. Shown here are 2,400 pounds of cocaine that were shipped from Colombia to the United States. The cocaine was seized in Baltimore, Maryland. The armed guard is a member of the Federal Drug Enforcement Agency.

In and of themselves, then, the narcotics do not drive people to crime, make people stop working, or destroy their health. Although such conditions are common among street addicts, they are not the consequence of narcotics. Jerome Jaffe (1965:292), a physician who studied physician addicts, concluded:

> The addict who is able to obtain an adequate supply of the drug through legitimate channels and has adequate funds, usually dresses properly, maintains his nutrition, and is able to discharge his social and occupational obligations with reasonable efficiency. He usually remains in good health, suffers little inconvenience, and is, in general, difficult to distinguish from other persons.

Crime as a Consequence of Laws, Addiction, and a Black Market

This point must be underscored. Narcotics do *not* cause the things we commonly associate with them. Rather, *the laws* that make these drugs illegal create a black market, handing over a monopoly to organized crime. The criminal underworld then commands the highest price possible, and *poor* addicts, who are dependent on this market as their source, turn to crime to buy drugs. Physician addicts, in contrast, who are not dependent on this black market, are able to function in a comparatively normal fashion.

This is one of the ironies of life. Those least able to afford high-priced drugs, the poor addicts, must pay the exorbitant prices demanded by the black market and have their health suffer as a consequence of the impurity of their drugs. In contrast, physician addicts, who could afford the high prices, are able to obtain their drugs cheaply and be assured that they are pure. Contemporary life is not without an abundance of such ironies.

As we noted in the preceding chapter, making a product or service illegal will not stop it from being sold. The law simply drives the transaction underground and makes a black market profitable. If tough laws are not the answer (remember mutilation and the death penalty for tobacco users), then what is? Let's look at some alternatives.

✦ Social Policy ✦

Difficulties in Agreeing on Social Policy

Of all the social problems, developing adequate policies for drug use is one of the most difficult. Like abortion, this problem is surrounded by irreconcilable differences of opinion, strong emotions, prejudices, fear, and befuddled thinking. It is also enveloped in contrasting moralities, subcultural values, and vested financial and personal interests. For just one example of the difficulty, perhaps impossibility, of any social policy being "adequate," see the Issues box on the next page.

Even a basic starting point, analyzing the health consequences of drugs, presents us with a dilemma. As Oakley Ray (1998) put it:

> From a medical point of view *no drug is safe*. With some doses, modes of administration, and frequency of use, all drugs cause toxic effects and even death. It is equally true that at some doses, modes of administration, and frequency of use *all drugs are safe*. The concern here is whether a drug, used the way most people use it today, is physically harmful. From this position, alcohol and marijuana are relatively safe drugs the way most people use them. Nicotine, in contrast, is a very harmful drug, since the usual amount of cigarette smoking does increase the mortality rate. (Italics added.)

From a medical standpoint, then, no drug is safe and all drugs are safe.

The matter becomes even more complicated when we add the *social* dimension. That is, under what circumstances do drugs cause social harm? To answer this, a symbolic interactionist would want to know from whose point of view we are defining social harm. For example, the dispossessed of the inner city and the middle classes are bound to see things differently. Functionalists would want to know when drugs interfere with people reaching their goals or with the welfare of society—and that is difficult to determine. And conflict sociologists might want to know whether the so-called social harm were not actually a prelude to wide-scale social change.

The "Get-Tough" Policy

Get tough appears to be the dominant sentiment in the United States. To solve this problem, let's pass stricter laws and enforce them vigorously. People who hold this view are convinced that this policy will help make our streets safe once again. What is wrong with this visceral response? Remember the discussion at the beginning of this chapter about other societies in history? The ones that slit noses and cut off heads? Even draconian measures don't work.

A War on Drugs

Back in the 1980s, President George Bush declared a "war on drugs." He ordered the Coast Guard, the Customs Service, the Border Patrol, the Immigration and Naturalization Service, and the Drug Enforcement Agency to stop illegal drugs from coming into the United States. The Pentagon even attempted to build a "'fence' of radar-equipped balloons" at the Mexican border (Fialka 1988). The result? Before this policy, a huge supply of drugs flowed into the United States. After this policy, the flow increased. The price of heroin then dropped, while its purity increased. So much for that war.

Why Can't We Just Lock Them All Up?

Some just shake their heads and say that if we can't stop the drugs from coming in, we at least can lock up the dealers and users. There are so many dealers and

ISSUES ᴉɴ SOCIAL PROBLEMS

The Larry Mahoney Case

"Larry Mahoney," said his friend, "wouldn't hurt anybody for the world." Another said that "since he was a little baby, he hasn't any meanness in him." Those are apt descriptions of this 34-year-old father from Kentucky. He is an all-around, pleasant, easygoing guy. How, then, could he have killed 24 teenagers and 3 adults?

It happened on a Saturday night in May. All Larry wanted was a good time, so he did what most of the "good old boys" of his town did: After a hard week at work at the chemical company, Larry headed for his favorite watering hole. There he met his friends, and he drank, and laughed, and drank some more. The time passed quickly, and Larry had to get home to his wife and children.

He climbed into his pickup truck and took off down the road. Things looked a little blurry, but they always did after his drinking sprees. This time, though, he didn't notice that he was going the wrong way on the interstate.

As if from nowhere, he saw a school bus headed toward him, and then he heard the sounds that he still can't shake—the loud crash of metal searing against metal, followed by piercing screams of agony as the bus with 27 passengers was engulfed in flames.

After he was charged with 27 counts of murder, Larry's friends came to his defense. Bobby Simmons, a gas station attendant, said, "It's a terrible mistake he made. But that boy ain't no murderer." Some families held bake sales and yard sales to raise money for his bail. Lillian Keef O'Banion, a widow in her eighties, put up the deed to her farm.

Chris Rogers, a farm worker, pinpointed the attitude in Carrolton, Kentucky, where Larry grew up and lived all his life, when he said, "Let's tell the truth about it. That could be you or me sitting in that jail. What he done ain't no different than what a lot of people in this town or anywhere else have done. To hear people on TV talk, you'd think Larry don't even feel bad about this. Let me tell you, he feels himself like he ought to be killed."

The national president of MADD (Mothers Against Drunk Driving), sickened at this support of Larry, said, "This was no accident. People intentionally drink, and they intentionally drive. I'm sick and tired of people sugar-coating murder."

A few miles south, on Interstate 70, where Larry Mahoney killed the 24 children and 3 adults, someone erected a white wooden cross and planted roses in the grassy median. Forty of the passengers on that church outing from Radcliff, Kentucky, escaped with their lives, but they wonder why their friends had to die just because Larry Mahoney wanted a good time.

What do you think? What is just? Should Larry Mahoney be fined and have his driver's license suspended? Or should he be given the death sentence, as some prosecutors have demanded? Or something in between? If so, what would ever be appropriate in this case?

Based on D. Johnson 1988

users, however, that we don't have enough jails and prisons to lock them up. Nor could we afford it. Consider the matter for a moment. Several million Americans use cocaine each year, while other millions use heroin, hallucinogens, barbiturates, and inhalants. Consider just marijuana. About 10 million Americans smoked marijuana during the past month. Certainly we can't lock all of them up. How many dealers does it take to supply those smokers? If each dealer has 25 customers, there are 400,000 dealers. These totals make it impossible to deal with users and dealers in this fashion.

Or consider this: To build one prison cell costs about $100,000. To keep one inmate locked up for one year costs a minimum of $25,000. If we were going to lock up all these drug offenders, where would we get the money? If we put two people in a cell, a half million new cells would run $50 billion. It would then cost another $25 billion a year to keep those million people in prison.

I haven't even mentioned the fact that there are people waiting in line to take the place of dealers who are arrested. Get rid of one dealer, and two fight to take his or her place.

I think you get the idea.

Consider also that get-tough policies fuel black markets. They provide a rich source of finances for independent entrepreneurs and organized crime. The criminalization of drugs—whether the prohibition of alcohol or of heroin, cocaine, or marijuana—forces people who want the drug to deal with an underground network, creates a lack of quality control in street drugs, and, in the case of addictive drugs, motivates the poor to prey on others. The latent dysfunctions—bankrolling organized crime, more muggings, burglaries, theft, prostitution, and premature deaths—are worse than the original problem that the laws address.

With illegal drugs so popular and attitudes so varied, how, then, can we develop a reasonable social policy?

Developing Reasonable Social Policy

Banning Advertising and Raising Taxes

An adequate social policy could begin by banning advertising for drugs known to be harmful. Nicotine is certainly a case in point, and we can begin by banning all advertising for cigarettes and tobacco products. We can also increase taxes, say, by $2 more a pack. Based on the Canadian experience, cigarette smoking would decline sharply (Kaiserman and Rogers 1991). Unfortunately, we also could expect heavy traffic in contraband cigarettes from Mexico.

Drug Education

An adequate social policy also must include drug education. Lack of a formal program means young people learn about drugs through an informal program—one directed from the streets. The informal communication network among youths operates quite effectively, but it is filled with misinformation, some of it dangerous.

The first requisite of a sound education program is accurate information. For this, we must have scientific studies to determine the beneficial and harmful effects of drugs. We then need to communicate that information, even though it may differ from our own ideology or views of what "good" drug use is. For example, perhaps marijuana has few harmful effects and is much safer than, say, tobacco. If so, that information needs to be communicated. On the other hand, any harmful effects also need to be communicated. The same is true of other drugs. Accurate information needs to be obtained and communicated, whether or not that information reflects our opinion of the drug.

This information must be *connected to the realities of the users*. Nonusers' ideas about morality and physical and psychological risks are not the same as those of users. For example, emphasizing violence as a consequence of PCP is ineffective if the users do not see violence as a problem. In the same way, stressing a milder consequence—that PCP produces a foggy, forgetful condition—can be effective if that is what the users experience and fear (Feldman 1985:5). To try to impose an outside reality onto users is to ensure failure.

Unintended Consequences of Drug Education

Drug education is a two-edged sword. On the one hand, students who are given information about drugs use drugs in greater moderation. On the other hand, this information piques curiosity, and more students are likely to use drugs (Blum et al. 1976; Levine 1986). More drug use, but in greater moderation, is what we can expect from formal drug education programs. The alternative, no formal drug education, produces two extremes: abstention by more, but heavier use of drugs by others. In sum, although drug education stimulates interest in drugs, it also cuts down on their abuse. If, then, the purpose of drug education is to decrease drug *use,* it is missing the mark; if its purpose is to decrease drug *abuse,* it is on target.

Dealing with Drug Addiction

We also need a social policy to deal successfully with drug addiction. We know that locking up addicts fails, for upon release most addicts go back to their drugs. A successful program cannot focus on addiction as though it exists in a social vacuum. The program must recognize that drug abuse is a consequence of background aspects of an addict's life, that it is often part of subcultural orientations and deprivations. These may include poverty, unemployment, dropping out of school, hopelessness, despair, and a bleak future. To reflect such life realities of drug abusers, multiple approaches must be developed.

Those who become drug dependent, whether their dependence is physical, psychological, or a combination of the two, have strong motivations to continue their drug use. Nicotine addicts have no difficulty obtaining their drug. Cigarettes are legal, openly available, and comparatively inexpensive. Tobacco crops are even subsidized by the Department of Agriculture. With the average cost of supporting a nicotine habit running about $1,000 a year, cigarette addicts do not mug, steal, or kill to obtain their drug. Heroin, in contrast, is illegal, its cost considerably higher, and many of its users are involved in criminal activities.

Addicts as Patients

A successful drug addiction program, then, would include free or very cheap drugs. For example, heroin addicts could be prescribed heroin by physicians who would treat them as patients. As Arnold Trebach (1987:369) put it:

> The availability of prescribed heroin would mean that multitudes of addicts would be able to function as decent law-abiding citizens for the first time in years. Their health should be much improved because their drugs would be clean and measured in labeled dosages. The number of crimes they commit should drop dramatically. By implication, addicts to other narcotics, such as morphine and codeine, would also reap the same benefits. They would be eligible to receive maintenance doses of the drugs on which they are dependent. Hordes of potential crime victims would, accordingly, be denied the pleasure.

Such a policy would break the addicts' dependence on the black market, remove a major source of profit for organized crime, and eliminate the need for addicts to prey on others. If the program provided only such benefits, it would be a night-and-day improvement over the present situation, but it still would not break the social cycle on which addiction is based. To make a dent in addiction would require a three-pronged attack: counseling for personal problems, practical help in seeking and maintaining employment, and clinical services for those who want to end their addiction.

Methadone Maintenance

Methadone maintenance helps us to understand some of the problems of developing rational social policies for dealing with drug addiction. Methadone, a synthetic narcotic that is in itself addicting, was developed by the Germans during World War II as a painkiller for casualties (Wren 1998). It is given orally in medically supervised clinics to 115,000 heroin addicts nationwide with the objective of breaking their addiction to heroin (Kleinfield 1999). Through this practice their addiction is transferred from an illegal drug, heroin, to a legal drug, methadone.

What sense does it make to transfer someone's addiction from one narcotic to another? If we are going to supply drugs to addicts, why not simply give them the narcotic to which they already are addicted? Obviously, the answer goes back to the social reputation of drugs with which this chapter opened. The social equation is: The narcotic heroin is evil; the narcotic methadone is good.

Methadone maintenance is a controversial treatment for heroin addiction. At least, it passes for treatment. Actually, methadone maintenance is the replacement of an illegal narcotic by a legal one. "Treatment" consists of merely transferring addiction from one drug to another.

As conceived, the methadone maintenance program called for extensive support services from counseling agencies and from employers. For budgetary reasons, however, at most locations these elements were deemed inessential and were cut. Of the original plan, all that is left is its "bare bones" function—the dispensing of methadone. This alerts us to a major danger of social policy: Bureaucrats may see a program differently from the way the professionals who designed it see it. If they scuttle essentials in order to cut costs, they dismantle the original program in all but name.

Basic Principles for Developing Successful Social Policy: The Example of Alcoholics Anonymous

Alcoholics Anonymous (AA) exemplifies principles that can be applied to other drug problems. The main principle is that the program should be directed and staffed by people who have experienced the addiction themselves—and have overcome it. They know firsthand what the abusers are going through, and they know how to talk their language on a "gut level."

Begun in 1935 in Akron, Ohio, by two alcoholics, AA is now a worldwide organization of 100,000 local groups, numbering about 2 million members in 160 countries ("AA Fact File," 1998). The essentials of Alcoholics Anonymous are summarized in what it calls The Twelve Steps. To overcome addiction to alcohol you must

1. Admit that you are powerless over alcohol and your life has become unmanageable.

2. Believe that a Power greater than yourself can help restore you to sanity.

3. Make a decision to turn your will and life over to God, as you understand Him.

4. Make a moral inventory of yourself.

5. Admit to God, yourself, and another human being the exact nature of your wrongs.

6. Be ready to have God remove your defects of character.

7. Ask God to remove your shortcomings.

8. Make a list of all persons you have harmed and be willing to make amends.

9. Make such amends wherever possible, except where it will injure others.

10. Continue to take personal inventory and promptly admit wrongs.

11. Seek through prayer and meditation to improve your conscious contact with God, as you understand Him, praying for knowledge of His will for yourself and the power to carry it out.

12. Have a spiritual awakening as a result of these steps and try to carry this message to alcoholics and to practice these principles in all your affairs.

(*Source*: The Twelve Steps are adapted with permission of Alcoholic Anonymous World Services, Inc. (A.A.W.S.) Permission to adapt the Twelve Steps does not mean that A.A. has reviewed or approved the contents of this publication, or that A.A.W.S. necessarily agrees with the views herein. A.A. is a program of recovery from alcoholism *only*—use of the Twelve Steps in connection with programs and activities which are patterned after A.A., but which address other problems, or in any other non-A.A. context, does not imply otherwise.)

To put these steps into practice, members meet weekly with others who have had alcohol problems or who are struggling to overcome them. From them they draw encouragement to continue their abstinence. They also carry the telephone number of "someone who has been through it," whom they can call at any hour for personal support in handling a crisis without turning to alcohol.

Matching the Subculture

Social policies must match the subculture of the audience. They must be geared to its age, racial, ethnic, sexual, and social class composition, and to its values, lifestyle, and problems (Crisp 1980). This means that programs for different groups need to have different emphases. For example, a program that is successful with middle-class youth will fail if it is transferred without modification to inner-city youth.

Rewarding Conventional Behavior

As sociologists Charles Faupel and Carl Klockars (1987) stress, a rehabilitation program should offer an alternative lifestyle and reward conventional behavior. For this, the addict needs to be integrated into a community of people where "straight" values are dominant, including social networks that value employment and nonexploitive relationships.

A Controversy: Teaching Drug Use

A social policy designed to teach the "evil" of drug use is doomed to failure. As we have seen, ours is a drug-using society. It seems, then, that a rational goal would be to teach people to *use* drugs sensibly and thus to decrease the amount of drug *abuse*. This principle would apply to all drugs—not just to those that match *our* ideas of "good" drugs.

Matching Cultural Values

Social policies also need to match general cultural values. A primary value in our culture is that people work productively. One reason that some drug use for pleasure is viewed negatively is the fear that individuals will drop out, live off the efforts of others, and not take care of themselves or contribute to society. Rehabilitation programs should address these concerns and encourage active participation in our economic system.

Another mainstream cultural value is individual rights. Ultimately, this value may include the right of a person to abuse his or her own body (Bayer 1978). Regardless of how others feel about the abuse, it seems that an individual has the right to consume substances that you and I may choose not to.

All Policies Are Controversial

As I said, developing adequate social policy for drug abuse is difficult. We all have strong opinions on some aspect of this problem, as well as other biases, due to our backgrounds. Because we see the world from different perspectives, no social policy will satisfy everyone, and all social policies are bound to displease many. I hold no illusions: The ones I suggest can meet no other fate.

◆ The Future of the Problem ◆

Broad Patterns of Drug Use

In light of the prodrug orientation of Americans, we can expect drug use to remain high. Because drugs are subject to fads, however, as some drugs decrease in popularity, others will become more popular. As a young clientele rushes to the latest high, we can expect moral entrepreneurs to alarm the public, who will perceive use of the drug as a threat to dominant values, with some even seeing it as a threat to society itself. Alarms over different drugs, then, will be sounded from time to time.

New Drugs

With advancements in chemistry, a new generation of drugs will appear. Designed to work only on particular receptors of the brain, these drugs will be much more precise in their effects. The public will increase its demand for them in order to ease the "psychological burden" of coping with the rigors of modern life. This will stimulate the demand for drugs, broaden drug markets, and put even greater pressure on physicians to become "drug dispensers." For an example, see the Technology box below.

TECHNOLOGY AND SOCIAL PROBLEMS

Viagra on the Internet

When Viagra made its appearance on the drug scene in 1998, it quickly became the butt of jokes throughout the world. Designed to help men with erectile problems, Viagra is a marvel of technology. Viagra has also quickly become an abused drug. It gained a reputation as a recreational aphrodisiac for men who had no penile dysfunctions, one that would enable them to prolong lovemaking. And for reasons I fail to understand, women, too, became abusers.

Obtaining Viagra legally requires a prescription from a physician. This has made Viagra a gold mine for doctors, who "sell" prescriptions for $35 to $50, the price of an office visit. Some even offer online services so you can bypass the formality of visiting a doctor (Rich 1998). On the Internet, just type in "Viagra," and sites will appear that offer this legal drug. After answering yes or no to just four questions, you pay $75 for the doctor's "consulting" fee (this keeps it legal), plus a subscription fee, and you can pick your dosage and the number of pills that you want. You might have to lie and say that you have erectile dysfunction, but as long as you have a valid credit card, for another $37.50 to $427.50 (plus delivery fee), UPS will deliver Viagra right to your door.

Who knows, the online physician may even read what you put down on your questionnaire. (Right.) But this is a bona fide doctor, one of the venturesome who use the new technology to multiply their pill pushing and still stay within the law.

If you don't want to fill out the questionnaire, you might try your local junior high school. At some, the girls are selling Viagra to each other. Such a fun drug!

Keep in mind a central point of this chapter, the significance of a drug's social reputation for determining how the users of that drug are treated. This drug is in good hands. With Bob Dole, a former vice president and presidential candidate, appearing in Viagra ads, it has a pusher of inestimable reputation.

Drugs in the Workplace

Workers—blue-collar workers, office employees, and executives—will continue to use drugs on the job. Easier to conceal than a bottle of vodka, marijuana has become a favorite recreational drug used at work. More and more, perhaps, marijuana and alcohol are likely to be combined at work, as well as during leisure. One consequence will be continued controversy over blood tests and urinalysis by both workers and employers (Verespej 1992; Drug Use Forecasting 1996).

The Unholy Alliance

The social reputations of drugs will continue to affect people's lives. Some drugs will remain in disrepute, their users castigated, disgraced, and stigmatized. From the standpoint of functionalism, we can expect drug enforcement agents, working with legislators and feeding the general public's fears through the news media, to keep many substances illegal. This will keep the black market profitable and will continue to produce large-scale drug crimes. The outcome will be a self-fulfilling prophecy, for the resulting crimes, especially the headline-producing violence, will continue to make the drug enforcement establishment vital for society. *Organized crime and drug enforcement agents*, then, will remain reluctant symbiotic partners, sharing a mutual interest in keeping drugs illegal.

The Easier Course

The social policies I have suggested are not likely to be part of our future. It is much easier not to figure out solutions, not to work with the disreputable who have become drug dependent, but simply to follow a knee-jerk, gut reaction of banning everything that is disliked. To join the "war on drugs" is politically expedient—and it means action, not a frustrating search for viable alternatives to our long history of failed get-tough policies.

The Hidden Threat in Social Policy

One final note. If we view ourselves as the "good" people and "them" as "evil strangers" in our midst (people who don't really belong in our society), then addicts and other drug abusers will continue to be treated harshly. We good people can turn a blind eye to what happens to them, for such views sever mutual identity, ultimately denying them even basic humanity. This approach, however, is dangerous for the development of social policy, not only for drug abusers but also for the mentally ill and others who violate middle-class standards of behavior. From such attitudes flow totalitarianism, the elimination of people's rights, and the treatment of others as subhumans, all for the sake of maintaining a middle-class view of the world. Lurking in the shadows of social policy, this threat needs to be brought into the light where it can be examined thoroughly.

◆Summary

1. What constitutes *drug abuse* is a matter of social definition. What is considered drug abuse at one time or in one society may be considered drug use at another time or in another society. From the historical record, we know that drug use and abuse are ancient.

2. Americans have a strong prodrug orientation, although they consider some drugs to be disreputable, and those who use them to be part of a social problem. People generally consider the particular drugs that they use to be outside the realm of a social problem.

3. A major problem in drug abuse is *addiction*—that is, becoming dependent on a drug so that in its absence one feels the stress of withdrawal. One of the most highly addicting drugs is nicotine. Heroin appears to be less addicting than previously thought.

4. Symbolic interactionists emphasize the social meanings of drugs. Prohibition, for example, has been viewed as a symbolic crusade: By associating abstinence with moral behavior, and alcohol use with unwelcome newcomers to society (who threatened the established political order),

the old order attempted to dominate society morally in lieu of politically.

5. Functionalists see legal drugs as functional for the medical profession, their patients, and those who manufacture and sell them. They see illegal drugs as functional for their users, manufacturers (or growers), and distributors. The dysfunctions of drugs include misprescribing, problems with the law, and abuse that harms people physically and socially. A major latent function of illegal drugs is to support agents of social control.

6. Conflict theorists look at the criminalization of drug use in terms of maintaining the powers that be. Opium, for example, was made illegal in an attempt to overcome the economic threat that cheap Chinese labor posed to white workers. Similarly, marijuana legislation was a tool directed against the Mexican working class in the United States. Some see the heroin trade as a means of defusing revolutionary potential.

7. Americans tend to turn to drugs as a solution to the stresses of modern life. Pharmaceutical companies, with the cooperation of the medical profession, play a central role in this orientation—and in the drug abuse to which it leads. Valium and Prozac are cases in point. Primarily pitched at women, their advertising encourages physicians to redefine problems of living as problems to be solved with drugs. This *medicalization of human problems* includes defining unruly children as sick and in need of medication.

8. Drugs do not have a single, consistent effect on everyone, because they act on different parts of the brain and vary with dosage as well as with the physiological and psychological characteristics of the user. Social factors also help determine a drug's effects, especially the setting and the user's expectations.

9. Of all the drugs Americans use, nicotine apparently causes the most harm. Alcohol abuse destroys vital body organs and causes *fetal alcohol syndrome*. The general social setting in which people learn to drink influences their chances of becoming a problem drinker. The evidence to determine whether marijuana harms it users' health, or to what extent it harms them, is not yet in. Cocaine's social history illustrates how a drug's status depends on the people with whom it is associated.

10. The narcotics are addicting but in and of themselves do not cause crime or destroy people's work incentive or health. Street addicts deal with a black market that demands exorbitant prices and motivates them to commit predatory crimes. Street addicts buy drugs whose purity is far from guaranteed—and suffer the consequences. Physician narcotic addicts, in contrast, maintain normal lives because they need not deal with a black market and are able to obtain pure drugs.

11. Developing an adequate social policy is difficult because drugs arouse strong emotions and prejudices. At a minimum, an adequate social policy would involve drug education that presents scientific findings honestly, whether they are favorable or unfavorable to any particular drug. It would also break the addicts' dependence on a black market and provide help for their multiple problems. Alcoholics Anonymous appears to be a model program.

12. We can anticipate that the future will bring more use of drugs in the workplace, more effective products from pharmaceutical companies (which will further increase the demand for drugs), and social policies similar to those we now have: illegal status for drugs that are out of favor, stigmas for their users, and overflowing coffers for members of organized crime.

◆ Key Terms

Addiction   See *Drug addiction.*

Alcoholic   Someone who has severe alcohol-related problems.

Amotivational syndrome   The tendency for people who smoke marijuana extensively to become apathetic, lose their concentration, and become unable to carry out long-range plans.

Craving   An intense desire for a drug.

Drug   A substance taken to change bodily functions, behavior, emotions, thinking, or consciousness.

Drug abuse   Using drugs in such a way that they harm one's health, impair one's physical or mental functioning, or interfere with one's social life.

Drug addiction   Depending on the regular consumption of a drug in order to make it through the day.

Drug dependence   See *Drug addiction.*

Fetal alcohol syndrome   A cluster of congenital problems caused by the alcohol consumption of the newborn's mother.

Fetal narcotic syndrome   A cluster of congenital problems caused by narcotic use of the newborn's mother.

Hyperkinesis   A term used to refer to a supposed medical condition that causes children not to pay attention and to disrupt classroom activities. Also known as hyperactivity, attention deficit disorder, and attention deficit-hyperactivity disorder (ADHD). See also *Medicalization of human problems.*

Medical addiction   Becoming addicted to a drug prescribed by a physician in the course of medical treatment.

Medicalization of human problems   To define the problems normally encountered in daily life as a matter of sickness, and therefore properly handled by the medical profession.

Methadone maintenance A program for heroin addicts in which the narcotic methadone is substituted for the narcotic heroin.

Moral entrepreneur A crusading reformer who wages battle to enforce his or her ideas of morality.

Psychological dependence The craving for a drug even though there no longer is a physical dependence on that drug.

Skid row The urban area inhabited by panhandling derelicts and alcoholics.

Withdrawal The distress that accompanies abstention from a drug to which one is addicted.

◆Critical Thinking Questions

1. Which perspective—symbolic interactionism, functionalism, or conflict theory—do you think best explains drug policies in the United States? Why?

2. What, if anything, is wrong with targeting cigarette or alcohol advertisements to minorities? How is it different from targeting advertisements of other products, like soft drinks, beer, or music?

3. If women can be prosecuted for child abuse for taking drugs during pregnancy, does it follow that they should be prosecuted for failure to attend prenatal classes or for not eating properly during pregnancy? Why or why not?

4. If you had the power to categorize which drugs should be legal and which should not, what criteria would you use for making your determinations?

Violence in Society
Rape and Murder

There wasn't much for teenagers to do in Littleton, Colorado. Not much happened in this quiet town of 35,000, a middle-class suburb southwest of Denver. Some of the high school kids liked to draw attention to themselves by wearing black trench coats and black shirts with swastikas. They called themselves the Trenchcoat Mafia and threw around a few phrases in German.

"Just kids. They'll grow out of it," was the adults' typical response. "We all went through something ourselves."

The Trenchcoat Mafia had their own table in the cafeteria and a group picture in the yearbook. The caption: "Who says we're different? Insanity's healthy.... Stay alive, stay different, stay crazy! Oh, and stay away from CREAM SODA!!"

Just another high school group: jocks, Goths, stoners, deadbeats, geeks, preppies. Every school has some.

The jocks despised the Trenchcoat Mafia. They threw them into lockers and called them scumbags, faggots, and inbreeds. They threw rocks and bottles at them from moving cars.

Two seniors, Eric Harris and Dylan Klebold, honors students and members of the Trenchcoat Mafia, talked and dreamed about killing their classmates, especially the jocks. Eric even had his own Web page, where he described whom he wanted to kill and how he wanted to do it. As a class project, Eric and Dylan made a video in which they pretended to kill the classmates they didn't like. Just talk. But as the imaginary killings they committed on Doom, the video game they loved, no longer satisfied, the boys hatched a plan for real killing. It was risky. Maybe they would survive, maybe not. But if not, they would go out in a blaze of glory. April 20, Hitler's birthday, would be perfect.

The carnage left Columbine High School seared into the national memory. TV viewers switched on their sets and found that a quiet Tuesday afternoon had been interrupted by stunning events. The drama was high as SWAT teams moved in and cautiously began to assess the situation. Bodies lay strewn on sidewalks. No one knew how many were dead inside the school. The nation watched transfixed as events unfolded.

As bombs went off and shots rang out, students ran in terror, cowering in closets and under tables. Harris and Klebold went from room to room in search of victims. In the library, they found several students hiding under a table. "Do you believe in God?" asked one of the shooters. "Yes," replied Cassie Bernall. "There is no God," the gunman retorted, as he placed a gun against her head and squeezed the trigger.

The boys killed twelve of their fellow students and one teacher before they turned their guns on themselves. They wounded twenty-three students.

Once again, the nation shook its head in collective disbelief.

Based on Bai 1999; Gibbs 1999.

◆ The Problem in Sociological Perspective ◆

The Sociological Perspective on Violence

Violence, the use of force to injure people or to destroy their property, goes far beyond individual tendencies or "violent personalities." Violence involves society itself. Some societies encourage violence, while others discourage it. As a result, some societies have high rates of violence, and others have low rates. **The sociological question of violence** *centers on what in a society increases or decreases the likelihood of violence.* Throughout this chapter, we grapple with this question.

Types of Violence

Sociologists divide violence into two major types: individual violence and group violence. **Individual** (or **personal**) **violence** consists of one person physically attacking others or destroying their property. **Group** (or **collective**) **violence** consists of two or more people doing these things to others. Sociologists divide group violence into three types.

1. **Situational group violence** is unplanned and spontaneous, for example, a brawl among hockey players. Something in the group situation stimulates or triggers violent action.
2. **Organized group violence** is planned, but it is unauthorized, such as terrorist acts committed by the Ku Klux Klan or the school shooting in our opening vignette.
3. **Institutionalized group violence** is carried out by agents of the government, for example, an army at war or the SWAT team responding to the crisis at Littleton.

Rape and murder, the focus of this chapter, can take the form of either individual or group violence, depending on whether the victim is attacked by an individual or a group.

◆ The Scope of the Problem ◆

What makes violence a social problem?

Is Violence a Personal Problem or a Social Problem?

If two people quarrel and fight, that is their *personal* problem. The same is true if a woman, enraged at discovering her husband with a lover, kills one and hospitalizes the other. And the same is true if a man rapes a woman. Although these three examples involve severe, bitter violence, they portray only objective conditions. To be a *social* problem, violence must also arouse widespread subjective concern. Many people must see the violence as reducing their quality of life, and want something to be done about it.

The Subjective Dimension of Violence

Violence has become a social problem in the United States, but it is important to note that it is not the amount of violence (an objective condition) that makes it a social problem. Rather, *subjective concern* about violence has become widespread. Parents worry about their kids at school. People talk about feeling vulnerable as they

With our high rate of violence, feelings of vulnerability and fear among members of the general population are common. Fear is not distributed evenly throughout society, however, but is related to income, age, gender, and race-ethnicity. The reasons for these variables are discussed in the text.

walk to their cars at night. Drivers lock their doors when driving through certain neighborhoods. This fear is not spread evenly throughout our society. As Table 5-1 shows, women are much more afraid of crime than men. As you can see from Table

Table 5-1	Are You Afraid to Walk Alone at Night in Your Own Neighborhood?*					
	2000		**1977**		**1967**	
	Yes	No	Yes	No	Yes	No
Sex						
Male	23	76	23	76	17	83
Female	52	47	63	37	55	44
Race						
White	36	61	43	57	36	63
Black/other	45	54	59	40	50	50
Age						
18 to 20 years	40	58	45	55	38	62
21 to 29 years	41	58	39	60	40	59
30 to 49 years	36	63	41	59	34	66
50 years and older	41	58	51	48	43	56
Education[a]						
College	38	61	41	58	38	62
High school graduate	38	61	46	53	39	61
Less than high school graduate	44	54	47	52	30	59
Income						
$50,000 and over	28	71	NA	NA	NA	NA
$30,000 to $49,999	34	66	NA	NA	NA	NA
$20,000 to $29,999	42	58	NA	NA	NA	NA
Under $20,000	50	48	NA	NA	NA	NA
Occupation						
Professional/business	34	65	40	60	37	63
Clerical/support	54	45	60	39	47	53
Manual/service	37	62	41	59	36	63
Farming/agriculture	31	69	17	83	18	82
Region						
Northeast	37	62	53	47	34	66
Midwest	34	64	36	63	37	63
South	42	57	47	52	42	58
West	42	57	46	54	40	60
Religion						
Protestant	39	59	45	55	37	63
Catholic	41	58	45	54	43	56
Jewish	36	64	60	40	47	53
None	35	64	40	59	36	64
Politics						
Republican	33	66	44	56	35	65
Democrat	43	56	48	52	40	60
Independent	39	59	41	58	39	60

*The question asked of a nationally representative sample of Americans was: How do you feel when you are out alone at night walking in your own neighborhood? The numbers may not total 100 percent because the "don't knows" and the refusals are not listed here.
[a]Beginning in 1996, education categories were revised slightly and therefore are not directly comparable to data presented for prior years.
Source: Sourcebook of Criminal Justice Statistics 2000:Table 2–41; National Opinion Research Center, "General Social Surveys, 1972–2000. Storrs, CT: The Roper Center for Public Opinion Research, University of Connecticut. (Machine-readable data files.) Table constructed by SOURCEBOOK staff.

FIGURE 5-1
The Clock of Violence

These figures are U.S. national averages. Crimes do not occur with this regularity. As the text indicates, crimes vary by time of the day and seasons. The FBI also counts armed robbery as a violent crime, whether or not anyone is hurt during the crime. Armed robberies, occurring on average every 46 seconds, are included in the total.
(*Source: FBI Uniform Crime Reports 2000: Figure 2.1.*)

The Objective Dimension of Violence

One violent crime every 22.1 seconds

One murder every 34 minutes

One forcible rape every 6 minutes

One aggravated assault every 34.6 seconds

5-1, fear recedes with higher income—largely because people with higher incomes live in "better" (read, more affluent and less violent) neighborhoods.

What about the *objective conditions* of violence? Are there rational grounds for fear, or are Americans overreacting to a small amount of violence that has been blown out of proportion by the media? As Figure 5-1 shows, a rape occurs on average every 6 minutes; every 35 seconds one person tries to injure someone else (aggravated assault); and every 34 minutes an American dies from such an attack

	Murder		Rape	
Country	Rank	Rate*	Rank	Rate*
Uganda	1	25.08	7	13.56
Bermuda	2	11.54	9	9.62
Luxembourg	3	11.18	3	29.71
Mexico	4	11.05	16	4.10
France	5	9.93	20	0.32
United States	6	9.07	6	23.72
Jamaica	7	8.24	4	29.72
Kuwait	8	5.84	5	24.65
Hungary	9	4.46	14	5.39
Hong Kong	10	2.64	18	1.54
Sweden	11	2.43	11	7.63
Austria	12	1.38	10	8.38
Korea	13	1.33	13	6.04
West Germany	14	1.26	8	11.35
Finland	15	1.20	12	6.93
Tunisia	16	1.01	1	46.03
Ireland	17	0.96	19	1.38
England and Wales	18	0.93	17	1.82
Denmark	19	0.65	15	4.83
Spain	20	0.47	21	0.18
Monaco	21	0.00	2	37.50

Table 5-2 How Countries Compare in Murder and Rape

*Rates reported per 100,000 people.

Source: Based on Archer and Gartner 1984.

(homicide or murder). In short, we are not talking about a fistfight here and there, an occasional rape, or isolated incidents of spouses turning on one another.

In this chapter, I will explain why the objective conditions of violence do not affect all groups the same way. For example, the murder rate of African Americans has grown so high that 1 of every 30 African-American males can expect to be murdered. For white males, the corresponding ratio is 1 of every 179 (Zawitz 1988). Murder is now the leading cause of death of African-American males between the ages of 15 and 34, and each year more African-American males are murdered than were killed in the entire nine years of the Vietnam War (Palley and Robinson 1988). In Harlem, the rate is so high that African-American men there have a lower life expectancy than men in Bangladesh (Winslow 1990).

Different Groups Have Different Rates of Violence

Rates of Violence Also Vary by Country

Although the United States certainly has a lot of violence, as Table 5-2 on the prior page shows, our rates of violence are not the highest in the world. From this table, you can see that countries with a high murder rate do not necessarily have a high rape rate, and vice versa. Monaco provides the best example: no killings, but one of the highest rape rates. The United States, unfortunately, is consistently high in both areas.

A word of caution, however. The totals in these tables are not "facts." Much reporting error goes into them, and at best they merely *indicate* how much violence a country has. From what I have seen personally in some of these countries, much of their violence never gets officially recorded—and that includes the United States.

Rates versus Amounts

Since the 1960s, not only has the amount of violence in the United States increased, but so has the **rate of violence,** the number of violent crimes for each 100,000 Americans. If over a ten-year period our population increased 20 percent and acts of violence increased 20 percent, the rate would remain unchanged; there would be more violence, but the increase would merely have kept pace with the larger numbers of people.

The Growth of Violence

Unfortunately, the growth in violence has far outpaced the growth of the U.S. population. To see how the *rate* of violence has changed, look at Figure 5-2. During twelve remarkable years, between 1968 and 1980, the rate of violent crime *doubled*. This means that if the population had not increased by a single person, there still would have been twice as many violent crimes in 1980 than there were in 1968. The rate then declined, and in 1984 it reached its low for the 1980s. It then turned upward again, reaching its peak in 1990. Then it dropped again, just as it did in the 1980s. Today's rate of murder, rape, robbery, and aggravated assault remains much higher than it was in 1968. The common perception of Americans that the United States has become more dangerous is true. Equally true, as you can see from Figure 5-2, the United States is becoming safer.

Our Current Decline Means More Violence Now than in the Past

Let's look at the theories that social scientists have developed to explain violence.

◆ Looking at the Problem Theoretically ◆

Before we look at violence from the perspective that sociology offers, let's briefly examine some of the theories developed in other academic disciplines.

NONSOCIOLOGICAL THEORIES

Theories Centering on Biological Factors

In the 1800s, Cesare Lombroso (1835–1909), an Italian physician, examined thousands of prisoners. Lombroso (1911) concluded that violent people (and other criminals) are

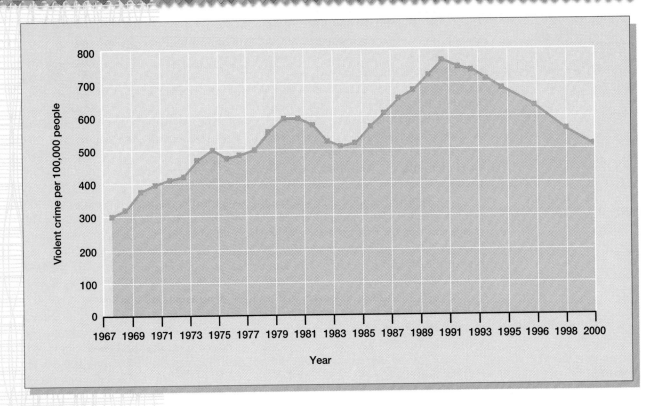

FIGURE 5-2
The Rate of Violence

(*Source:* Various editions of *FBI Uniform Crime Reports,* and 1997 and 2001.)

atavistic; that is, they are biological throwbacks to a more violent, primitive evolutionary state. With lower foreheads, larger ears, and receding chins, these people even look different. Enrico Ferri (1856–1929), a student of Lombroso's, added other reasons for their violent tendencies: insanity, learning, circumstances, and passion (Ferri 1913).

Other theorists have suggested different biological factors as causes of violence—from the shape of the skull (phrenology) to hormonal imbalance (endocrinology). Anthropologist Earnest Hooton (1939) concluded that the key is body type: Tall, thin men tend to be the killers, while short, heavy men are prone to sexual crimes. One famous biological explanation of violence is the XYY chromosome theory: Men normally have an X and a Y chromosome; some men, however, have an extra Y chromosome, and it supposedly propels them to violence.

Some theorize that brain damage, such as from a tumor, can cause outbursts of violence (Bylinsky 1973). Because between 10 and 20 million Americans suffer from brain damage, some biologists estimate that perhaps 200,000 of us are potential presidential assassins. Others base their explanations on human evolution. Those humans that survived were the violent ones, and they then passed their genes to their offspring. Consequently, we are violent by nature.

Psychologist John Dollard (1939), who also stressed that violence is built into our nature, proposed the **frustration-aggression** theory of violence. People become frustrated when they are unable to reach their goals. They then tend to strike out at others, whether that be through tongue-lashing or through physical violence.

Anthropologist Konrad Lorenz (1966) found a different key. Humans, he pointed out, don't have great strength, claws, or slashing teeth. Biologically ill-equipped for lethal behavior, we did not develop an inhibitory mechanism—as did dogs, wolves, and baboons—that stops violence automatically when an enemy becomes submissive. Because we have a powerful intellect, however, we learned to make weapons. Thus, with no blocking mechanism, when we are angry or wish to dominate, we destroy one another by using the powerful weapons that are at our disposal. As Lionel Tiger and Robin Fox (1971:210) remarked, if baboons had hand grenades, few baboons would be left in Africa.

Such theories of violence do not impress most sociologists. True to their calling, they look to *social* factors, not to chromosomes, inhibitory mechanisms, and so forth for an explanation. For example, not all men with XYY chromosomes are violent. *If* biological factors are involved, they are mediated through social factors.

Psychological Theories

Some psychologists point to learning as the cause of violence. Following the lead of B. F. Skinner (1948, 1953, 1971), they stress that if people's violence (the original reason for it is not relevant) is rewarded (or "reinforced"), they tend to be violent again. The reward can be any gain—consumables such as candy or food; social symbols such as money, status, or even a smile; or, in the case of rape—sex and power. The murderer's reward can include revenge, a sense of power, or satisfaction at exterminating an enemy. Other psychologists emphasize that violence is learned through **modeling,** copying another person's behavior. In a classic study, psychologists Albert Bandura and R. H. Walters (1963) found that children who see others hitting dolls or pounding on furniture tend to do the same things themselves. Children who have not seen this sort of behavior are less likely to perform it.

The Sociological Approach

In their explanations, sociologists look to an even broader social context. Rather than looking for violence-inducing characteristics *within* individuals, they focus on matters *outside* the individual. They examine how *social* life shapes and encourages—or discourages—violence. For example, in one society, violence may be channeled into approved forms, such as the social roles of warrior, boxer, or football player. Other societies may downplay violence and develop mechanisms to ensure that it rarely occurs.

Let's apply our three sociological perspectives to violence. In doing so, let's try to understand why males are more likely than females to be violent and why violence is higher in the working or lower classes.

SYMBOLIC INTERACTIONISM

Why do people kill? Consider what a detective on the Dallas police force said back in the 1960s:

> Murders result from little ol' arguments over nothing at all. . . . Tempers flare. A fight starts, and somebody gets stabbed or shot. I've worked on cases where the principals had been arguing over a 10 cent record on a juke box, or over a dollar gambling debt from a dice game. (Mulvihill et al. 1969:230)

Edwin Sutherland: Differential Association

People still kill over "little" things. Two theories developed by symbolic interactionists help us to understand why. In the first, sociologist Edwin Sutherland (1947) stressed that people learn criminal behavior by interacting with others. In its simplest form it goes this way: People who associate with lawbreakers are more likely to learn to break the law than people who associate with those who follow the law. To refer to this basic principle, Sutherland used the term **differential association.**

Although Sutherland developed his theory to explain lawbreaking, we can apply it to violence as follows:

1. People learn violence by interacting with others, primarily in intimate personal groups.

2. People learn not only techniques for being violent but also attitudes, motives, drives, and rationalizations about violence.

3. People use violence because they learn more attitudes (an "excess of definitions") favorable to using violence than they learn definitions unfavorable to using violence.

4. The most significant interactions for learning violence are those that are the most frequent, endure the longest, take place earliest in life, and are the most emotional or meaningful.

5. The mechanisms for learning violent behavior are the same as those for learning anything else.

Marvin Wolfgang: Subcultures of Violence

A second theory, **subcultural theory,** complements differential association. In a nutshell, this theory says that people who grow up in a subculture that approves of violent behavior have a high chance of learning to be violent. Sociologist Marvin Wolfgang wanted to know why the homicide rate was high among lower-class African-American males. In a classic study (1958), he examined homicide cases in Philadelphia from 1948 through 1952. He also observed police interrogations.

Wolfgang found that the young, lower-class African-American men he studied connected honor and manliness with the willingness to be violent. They saw insults as challenges to their manliness, and violence as the appropriate response. Situations that others might perceive as trivial were not trivial to them. Anyone who backed down from a confrontation was seen less than a real man—as "chicken" or feminine. Because their social interactions were a proving ground for their masculinity, violence became common. It also set off a self-fulfilling prophecy: The young men felt they had to carry weapons for protection and as a symbol of their manliness—which increased the likelihood that they needed to use them. Wolfgang concluded that to solve interpersonal problems the middle and upper social classes often turn to the legal system, which transcends personal confrontation. The lower classes, in contrast, are more likely to take matters in their own hands—and this breeds violence.

Fitting the Theories Together

Differential association and subcultural theory fit together well. According to subcultural theory, violence is woven into the life of some groups. According to differential association, people in these groups learn that violence is a suitable response to many of the problems of life. Thus, to be insulted by something, such as the price of a record on a jukebox, is not a trivial matter. The insult puts their self-concept and reputation at stake, and violence or the threat of violence is necessary to answer such a challenge. This equation continues. In the 1980s, sociologist Ruth Horowitz (1983) did participant observation of Chicano gangs. She found a similar connection between manliness, honor, and violence.

Michael Franzese, a college-educated member of the Mafia, learned similar ideas of manliness. He said:

> If somebody were to dishonor my wife or my child, I would view it as something that I had to take into my own hands. I don't see why I have to go to the police. As a man, I would feel that it was an obligation that I had to take care of. And I would have to be prepared in my own mind to kill this guy. This is a basic principle. (Barnes and Shebar 1987)

According to symbolic interactionism, then, because violence is considered more appropriate to the male sex role, we would expect to find more violence among males than females. We should also expect a social class difference, for the working class incorporates more violence into its definitions of appropriate male behavior than do the middle and upper classes. And such expectations are borne out:

Consistently, year after year, across racial lines and in every region of the United States, violence is more prevalent among males than females and among working-class males than males from higher social classes.

FUNCTIONALISM

Violence was one of the first social problems that sociologists studied. In the late 1800s, Emile Durkheim, the first university professor to be formally identified as a sociologist, examined the murder rates in Paris and the suicide rates in European countries (1897, 1904). He was struck by the remarkable regularity of the figures. Year after year, the countries with high rates of violence continued to have high rates, while those with low rates continued to have low rates. He found that a country's rate of violence is so regular that one can use it to predict its future rate. Durkheim called this **normal violence,** the violence that is normally present in a group.

Durkheim found this regularity to be a sociological puzzle. If murder or suicide rates represent the number of *individual* acts of killing, why is the rate in each society so consistent? Instead of being consistently high or consistently low, why doesn't the rate fluctuate—high one year and low another? To solve this puzzle, Durkheim developed the *sociological* perspective and concluded that the characteristics of a society regulate individual impulses and desires.

To appreciate Durkheim's conclusion, consider an agrarian society. Children follow in their parents' footsteps and remain in the village in which they were reared, where everyone knows one another. Their close bonds restrain individual impulses, for how they follow the norms affects their social standing—and they need the community to survive. The village's high social integration keeps the rate of violence low.

Now imagine that the society is undergoing rapid social change. It is industrializing, and these villagers are leaving for low-paying, unskilled jobs in cities where they know few people. There, husbands and wives work outside the home. They live surrounded by strangers, accumulate debts, and face the threat of unemployment. Their children go to schools where they are taught by teachers whom the family doesn't know. So unlike the factors that promote cohesion in farming communities, these characteristics loosen social bonds. People become strangers and begin to feel normless. They no longer know what rules to apply to their problems. Durkheim gave the name **anomie** to such feelings of being unconnected and uprooted. Under these circumstances, impulses to violence no longer have the constraints they did in the village. The city then becomes a more dangerous place.

Emile Durkheim: Asking the Sociological Question

Why Are a Group's Rates Similar from Year to Year?

Example of High Social Integration

Example of Weakened Bonds

An upsetting aspect of life in today's society is that you never know when you will become the victim of sudden, unexpected violence. Two phrases have entered our language that express this unwelcome aspect of our lives: "going postal" (referring to the frequency with which postal employees at work have killed one another) and "road rage" (referring to the anger and violence some drivers exhibit).

Another functionalist, Robert Merton (1968), used anomie to explain crime in U.S. society. He developed what is called **strain theory.** Merton said that success—especially in the form of money—is a **cultural goal,** a goal held out for all Americans. The approved (or legitimate) ways of reaching this goal, such as education

Robert Merton: Strain Theory

and high-paying jobs, are called **cultural means.** Almost all Americans learn to want success, but only some have access to the approved means to pursue it. Those whose way is blocked are more likely to turn to illegitimate means, such as robbery and theft. The *strain* (or frustration and anxiety) that comes from blocked goals also motivates people to commit crimes of violence. Just as strain theory would predict, we find higher rates of violence among groups that experience higher blockage to financial success—the poor, African Americans, and Latinos.

Walter Reckless: Control Theory

Strain theory does not explain why some people with blocked goals are violent and others are not. We all face blocked goals, but most of us are not violent. To answer this question, sociologist Walter Reckless (1973) developed **control theory** (also called **containment theory**). Other sociologists have expanded on these ideas (Gottfredson and Hirschi 1990; Burton et al 1998). Reckless assumed that people have a natural tendency toward violence. He then asked what forms of social control overcome our natural inclinations. He theorized that two systems control our "pushes and pulls" toward violence. The first, *inner* containment, refers to a person's capacity to withstand pressures to be violent. The second, *outer* containment, refers to groups in society, such as family, friends, and the state, that divert people away from violence. The likelihood that a person will be violent depends on the strength of these two control systems relative to the pushes and pulls toward violence. If the control systems are too weak, violence ensues. If they are strong enough, violence is avoided.

As you can see, this theory is so vague that it explains everything—and nothing. It accounts for differences in groups: If women are less violent, it must be because their systems of control are stronger. If some ethnic group is more violent, it must be because that group has weaker systems of control. It also accounts for differences in individuals: If John is violent and Mary is not, then John must have weaker controls and Mary stronger ones. When everything is vaguely answered, then nothing is answered.

CONFLICT THEORY

Violence Is Inherent in Society

Conflict theorists see violence as inherent in society. Because groups compete for limited resources, violence is to be expected. Although it may be hidden beneath surface cooperation and even goodwill, the true nature of human relationships is adversarial. When this basic nature emerges, violence often is the consequence.

Class Oppression Leads to Violence

The major division among people in our society is social class. Despite appearances to the contrary, say conflict theorists, the social classes have opposing vital interests. The essential division is between those who own the means of production—the factories, the machines, and the capital (investment money)—and those who work for the owners. The owners, or capitalists, profit from the labor of those who work for them (Marx and Engels 1848, 1906). The workers, who must struggle to put food on the table, pay rent, and buy clothing, are subject to the owners, who make decisions on the basis of profit, not people's welfare. For example, the owners can decide to lay off workers and move the plant to Mexico. Oppressed by such tension, the working class, both male and female, is the most likely to strike out violently at others.

The situation is particularly tense for working-class males. Traditionally, men of all social classes assumed the role of breadwinner. In capitalism's recurring cycles of unemployment and tight money, however, working-class men became expendable pawns. And today they also face competition from women for their jobs. Because their position in the family is threatened and their economic security flimsy, working-class men commit more violent crimes than do either working-class women or men from higher social classes. And the most exploited, those confined to the ghettos, have the highest rates of desperate, violent striking out against others.

Conflict theorists also point out that if we look beneath the surface reality of violence we will see that the controlling class is more violent than the working class. Just as the wealthy own the means to produce wealth, so they own the police powers of the state, which they use to suppress riots and strikes at home and to send armies abroad to protect their markets and resources (Vietnam, Grenada, Panama, Kuwait, Haiti, Serbia, and so on). Thus, it is not violence but the *form* of violence that differentiates the exploited from the exploiters. The rich may not kill with their own hands, but they account for vastly more deaths.

IN SUM

Because violence is a universal characteristic of human societies, sociologists are interested in its causes. True to their calling, they look for *social* causes. They want to know why some societies are more violent than others, as well as why some groups in the same society are more violent than others.

Symbolic interactionists stress that each group's culture specifies ways to handle problems. In some subcultures, violence is considered an appropriate response to many situations; other groups prefer more indirect ways of handling disagreements. Depending on the groups with which one associates (differential association), then, some people have a greater or lesser chance of learning to be violent.

Functionalists emphasize that social conditions that strengthen social bonds decrease violence, and social conditions that produce anomie increase violence. Violence tends to be highest among groups whose access to culturally approved goals is blocked. The pushes and pulls toward violence that people experience, however, do not necessarily result in violence. The outcome depends on inner and outer controls.

Conflict theorists stress that class exploitation underlies individual violence. Members of the working class have higher rates of violence because they face more tensions. Seldom is their violence directed against their oppressors, however, for the oppressors control the powers of the state and use them to protect their privileged positions. Misdirected, the violence of workers is aimed primarily against one another. The wars directed by the powerful kill more people than does the violence of the working class.

◆ Research Findings ◆

In reviewing the research on violence, we will focus on rape and murder, the two most serious forms of violence. Because rape only recently emerged as a social problem, we pay particular attention to its natural history, especially to the role of feminists in changing our ideas about rape. (Most state laws label consensual intercourse between someone above the age of consent and someone below the age of consent **statutory rape.** Our topic is **forcible rape,** an entirely different matter, as no consent is involved.) We then take a look at murder in the United States, examining the who, what, when, where, and why of the real-life "whodunits."

✦Rape✦

THE NATURAL HISTORY OF RAPE AS A SOCIAL PROBLEM

From a Personal to a Social Problem

When I say that rape emerged only recently as a social problem, I do not mean that rape is new to the social scene. On the contrary, accounts of rape go back thousands of years to the Old Testament and Greek mythology. What is new is the perception of rape as a *social* rather than a personal problem, and understanding rape as violence rather than passion. Let's see how this change took place.

As discussed in Chapter 1, objective conditions of society are not sufficient to constitute a social problem. A social problem requires subjective concerns—a significant number of people (or a number of significant people) being upset by those conditions. These subjective concerns are now so great that U.S. women age 35 and under fear rape more than any other crime, and women of all ages restrict their activities because of the possibility of rape (Warr 1985).

The Feminist Reconceptualization of Rape: From Passion to Power

The natural history of rape as a social problem began during the 1960s and 1970s, when Western women began to question their social roles (Friedan 1963; Millett 1970). Many women began to see themselves less as individuals who were facing unique circumstances and more as members of a social group that faced similar situations. Feminists analyzed how society makes men dominant and women subordinate. They stressed how females are taught to be supportive of males and to have lower educational and career aspirations.

As they analyzed their situation, feminists began to perceive rape as a social rather than a personal problem. In the traditional view, rape is considered a personal problem, a crime of individual passion. Men are thought to have an overwhelming sex drive, and when aroused they can lose control and take women by force. Women must be careful not to arouse men's passions.

Feminists attacked this view as blaming the woman for being raped. She must have acted provocatively or somehow stimulated the man, or he would not have lost control. If women would stop giving off the sexual cues that stimulate rape, the problem would go away. In reply to such a view, Dorothy Hicks, a physician who treated rape victims in Miami, Florida, asked if an 80-year-old woman or a 4-month-old baby is particularly sexy (Luy 1977).

The root of the problem, said feminists, is the basic relationships between males and females. Rape is a violent social statement, not an act of passion. It is a means of controlling women. Through rape and the fear of rape, men make women docile and ensure their own dominance.

This new view did not suggest that men deliberately use rape to frighten women into subservient positions. The process is much subtler. Men are taught "to associate power, dominance, strength, virility and superiority with masculinity, and submissiveness, passivity, weakness, and inferiority with femininity" (Scully 1990; Scully and Marolla 1999). To equate virility with strength teaches men that aggression is part of their sex role. By nature larger, taller, and stronger, and thus born for domination, no "real" man takes no for an answer. Besides, women say no when they don't really mean it, and, as many movies show, a woman's initial unwillingness may change as she is dazzled by a man's sexual advances (Reynolds 1976; Finkelhor and Yllo 1985, 1989).

To see violence and domination as the essence of rape helps make sense of previously incomprehensible findings. Some rapists, for example, beat their victims, even those who submit or those they already have raped. Other rapists threaten their

Chapter 5   Violence in Society: Rape and Murder

victims with death and insert dirt, sticks, stones, and even shoes into their victims' vaginas. This new view is now part of our legal system, and many states have renamed rape **criminal sexual assault.**

THE SOCIAL PATTERNS OF RAPE

Rape follows predictable social patterns. These patterns show that rape is not the act of a few sick men from the lunatic fringe of society, but that is intimately linked with our culture (Schwendinger and Schwendinger 1983; Scully 1990; Scully and Marolla 1999). Rape is so common in U.S. society that each year 63 of every 100,000 females in the entire country are forcibly raped (*FBI Uniform Crime Reports* 2000:27). The cumulative total is overwhelming: During their lifetime, 1 of every 7 American women is raped (*Sourcebook* 1998:Table 3.0004).

Rape follows patterns of acquaintanceship, time, season, geography, sex, age, and race. A woman is less likely to be raped by a stranger than by someone she knows. Night is more dangerous than day, for two of three rapes occur between 6 P.M. and 6 A.M. The most dangerous hours are 8 P.M. to 2 A.M.; the safest, from 2 P.M. to 8 P.M. As Figure 5-3 shows, July and August are the peak months for rape, while the fewest rapes occur in November and December. Another pattern is that between half and two thirds of rapists use no weapon, depending instead on surprise, threats, and physical strength. About a third use a knife or gun to subdue their victims.

The states also vary tremendously in their individual rates, and where a woman lives vitally affects her chances of being raped. A woman in Alaska, for example, runs over three times the risk of rape than a woman in West Virginia. From the Social Map on the next page, you can see which states are the safest, average, and most dangerous.

Rapists are not randomly scattered throughout society. Although women can rape men or other women, it is rare. Rape is almost exclusively a male crime. Young men rape at a disproportionate rate. Although only about 14 percent of U.S. males are ages 15 to 24, they account for about 40 percent of those arrested for rape (*Sourcebook of Criminal Justice Statistics* 2000:Table 47; *Statistical Abstract*

The Incredible U.S. Rape Rate

Rape Is Not Random: It Follows Social Patterns

Reasons for These Patterns

FIGURE 5-3

Forcible Rape by Month (Variation from the Annual Average)

(*Source: FBI Uniform Crime Reports 2000:27*)

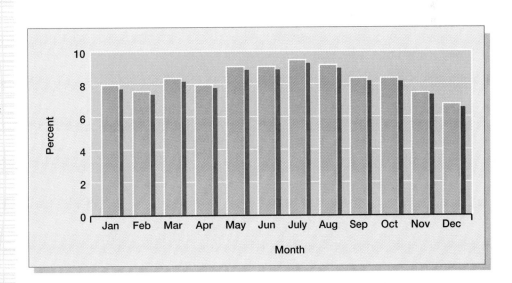

1998:Table 16). Similar findings hold true for race/ethnicity—only about 13 percent of the U.S. male population is African American, but they account for about 34 percent of arrested rapists (*Sourcebook of Criminal Justice Statistics* 2000:Table 4.10; *Statistical Abstract* 1998:Table 24).

Why are African-American men overrepresented in rape statistics? First of all, some bias is built into these figures. As we shall see, white women are less likely than black women to report rape. Because the rape of white women usually involves white men, their underreporting lowers the white figure. This, however, accounts for only a small part of the discrepancy. How do we account for the rest?

For this, our three theories prove helpful. First, according to conflict theory, the lower classes are oppressed—and one reaction to oppression is violence. Lower-class men commit forcible rape more frequently. Because African Americans are overrepresented in the lower social classes, they would be disproportionately involved. A second possibility centers on symbolic interaction and a subculture of violence. Among some groups of men, domination is a central theme, and many of their interactions contain overtones of aggression. Among them, rape can be a vehicle for **machismo,** symbolizing the strong, conquering, dominant male (Brownmiller 1975; Schwendinger and Schwendinger 1983:63). Certainly some groups consider rape legitimate, as Hunter Thompson documented in his account of the Hell's Angels (1967). Finally, the strain theory of functionalists may add a third explanation. Because African-American men often are blocked from legitimate avenues of attaining social status, their frustrations may lead them to turn against women inappropriately. Rape could be a way of establishing power in the face of socially imposed powerlessness (McNeely and Pope 1981).

Does Resistance Help Avoid Rape?

Is a woman more likely to be raped if she resists or if she gives up without a struggle? Sociologists Pauline Bart and Patricia O'Brien (1984, 1985) compared

Applying Our Three Theories

FIGURE 5-4

Social Map: Rape

(*Source: FBI Uniform Crime Reports* 2000:Table 5.)

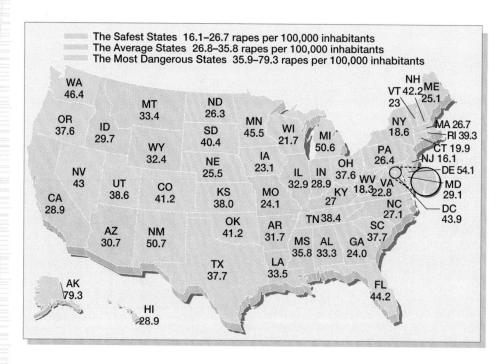

The Safest States 16.1–26.7 rapes per 100,000 inhabitants
The Average States 26.8–35.8 rapes per 100,000 inhabitants
The Most Dangerous States 35.9–79.3 rapes per 100,000 inhabitants

WA 46.4
OR 37.6
ID 29.7
MT 33.4
ND 26.3
MN 45.5
WI 21.7
MI 50.6
NH
VT 23
ME 25.1
NY 18.6
MA 26.7
RI 39.3
CT 19.9
NJ 16.1
DE 54.1
NV 43
UT 38.6
WY 32.4
SD 40.4
NE 25.5
IA 23.1
IL 32.9
IN 28.9
OH 37.6
PA 26.4
WV 18.3
VA 22.8
MD 29.1
DC 43.9
CA 28.9
CO 41.2
KS 38.0
MO 24.1
KY 27
NC 27.1
SC 37.7
AZ 30.7
NM 50.7
OK 41.2
AR 31.7
TN 38.4
MS 35.8
AL 33.3
GA 24.0
TX 37.7
LA 33.5
FL 44.2
AK 79.3
HI 28.9

Chapter 5 Violence in Society: Rape and Murder

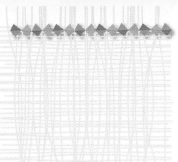

women who had been attacked. They found that the women who were raped generally tried to plead with their attackers, whereas those who had been able to avoid it had resisted—they yelled, fled, or fought off their attackers. In general, the avoiders had focused on not being raped, while the raped women had focused on not being killed. Other studies support the finding that women who resist are less likely to be raped (Kleck and Sayles 1990; Ullman 1998). Apparently the more strategies a woman uses (scratching, biting, kicking, screaming, and so on), the greater her chances of avoiding rape (McIntyre, Myint, and Curtis 1979; Block and Skogan 1982).

Does Resistance Help Avoid Injury?

Although a woman who resists her attacker is less likely to be raped, she apparently is more likely to be injured. Sociologist Sarah Ullman (1998) found this to be the case in a study of Chicago rape victims. This finding is supported by an earlier government study of a million rape victims (*Sourcebook* 1991:Table 3-20). It is likely that the women who successfully fight off their attackers make a better adjustment to their physical injuries than rape victims do to their rape. This, however, is a hypothesis, one for which we need research.

Profiling the Rapist

Ten Types of Rapists

The following summaries, worked out with Linda Henslin and based on studies of rapists who have been caught, profile ten "types" of rapists (Cohen et al. 1969; Hotchkiss 1978; Athens 1980; Hills 1980; Scully and Marolla 1999). These profiles show that many motivations underlie rape, but we do not know the proportion of rapists within each type or what other types may exist.

The Woman Hater

At some point in his life, the *woman hater* was severely hurt by a woman important to him. This hurt inflicted an emotional wound and created a hatred of women. By sexually assaulting women, he gains personal power. By degrading his victim and sometimes brutally assaulting her sexual organs, he retaliates for his unhealed hurt.

The Sadist

Although he has no particular negative feelings toward women, the *sadist* also beats his victim. He has learned to receive pleasure by hurting others, and women are merely handy outlets for him. By raping women, he combines the pleasure he receives from inflicting pain with the pleasure from sex. Enjoying the fear his victims show, he is likely to increase his sexual excitement by beating his victim before sexual penetration. He sometimes prolongs the pleasure by beating her during and after the rape.

The Generally Violence-Prone

For the *generally violence-prone* man, rape is just another act of violence. He sees the world as a violent affair. If one is going to get anything, one must wrest it from others using violent means—and that includes sex. This man will use whatever violence he considers necessary, even if it means severely injuring or killing his victim. Unlike the previous two types, his pleasure in rape is rooted in the sex rather than in the violence, and he uses only enough violence to make the woman submit. Even though she may be a total stranger picked at random, a woman who resists deserves violent treatment because she is "holding out" on him.

The Revenge Rapist

The *revenge* rapist uses rape to get even with someone. His victim may be the person he is angry at, or she may be a substitute. An example is a man who went to collect money that another man owed him. He thought, "I'm going to get it one way or another." When he found the man was not home:

I grabbed her and started beating the hell out of her. Then I committed the act. I knew what I was doing. I was mad. I could have stopped but I didn't. I did it to get even with her and her husband. (Scully and Marolla 1999:50)

The Political Rapist

The *political* rapist chooses his victim as a substitute for his enemy and uses the rape to make a political statement. In *Soul on Ice* (1968), for example, Eldridge Cleaver recounts how he raped white women to "strike against the white establishment." Much of the raping done by soldiers during war is of this type. The soldiers are not motivated by sexual satisfaction, a hatred of women, or sadism but by hatred of the enemy. By raping "the enemy's women," they show contempt for the enemy and declare their own superiority. An extreme example of political rape occurred in 1971 during the Bangladesh war for independence from Pakistan: The Pakistani army raped 200,000 Bangladeshi women (Russell 1979; Schwendinger and Schwendinger 1983).

The Walter Mitty

Generally passive and submissive, the *Walter Mitty* rapist has an unrealistic image of masculinity. He uses rape to bridge the gap between the way he perceives men ought to be and the way he perceives himself. He fantasizes that his victims enjoy being raped—for he is an excellent sex partner. Carrying his fantasy one step farther, he sometimes calls his victim the next day, asking her how she enjoyed it and trying to make a date with her. He is unlikely to beat his victim, but he will use as much force as necessary to make her submit.

The Opportunist

Unlike the first six types of rapists, the *opportunist* does not set out to rape. Rather, he grabs an unexpected opportunity, which often occurs during a robbery or burglary. For example, one man drove to a local supermarket to find someone to rob. The first person to come along was a pregnant woman. When he threatened her with a knife, she said she would do anything if he didn't harm her. At that point, he decided to force her to drive to a deserted area, where he raped her. He explained:

I wasn't thinking about sex. But when she said she would do anything not to get hurt, probably because she was pregnant, I thought, "why not." (Scully and Marolla 1999:52)

After feminists publicized their views about sexual violence, date rape became recognized as a special problem within the social problem of rape. Alcohol is often used by date rapists to lower the defenses of their victims. (This is not a photo of date rapists, but such "fun" activities involving alcohol often precede rape.)

Chapter 5 Violence in Society: Rape and Murder

The Date Rapist

Date rapists, also called *acquaintance rapists*, are the eighth type. Some of these rapists, called "collectors," feel that they deserve sex because they have invested time and money in a date or sexual seduction; they are collecting a sexual "payoff" from their investment. They prefer to avoid violence. As the Issues box below shows, date rape involves many motivations other than "collecting" and consists of much more than a man being more insistent than he should. In a study of students at Texas A&M University, psychologists Charlene Muehlenhard and Melaney Linton (1987) found that date rape most commonly occurs not between couples who are on their first date, but between couples who have known each other about a year. This study is summarized in Table 5-3.

The Recreational Rapist

A ninth type is the *recreational* rapist. For him, rape engenders male camaraderie, for he joins friends to participate collectively in a dangerous activity. As

ISSUES IN SOCIAL PROBLEMS

Date Rape

Carol had just turned 18, and it looked like her dreams had come true. It was only the beginning of her freshman year, and yet she had met Tom, the all-state quarterback. At Wiggins Watering Hole, the college bar, he had walked over to her table and made some crack about the English Comp professor. She had laughed, and the two had spent most of the evening talking.

When Tom asked to take her back to the dorm, Carol didn't hesitate. This was the man all the girls wanted to date! At the dorm, he said he would like to talk some more, so she signed him in. Once in the room, he began to kiss her. At first, the kisses felt good. But Tom was not about to stop with kissing;. He forced her to the bed, and, despite her protests, began to remove her clothing.

With his 240 pounds, and her 117, there was not much of a contest. She always wondered why she didn't cry out; she was asked this at the trial. This brutal end to her virginity also marked the end of her college career. Depressed and distrustful, she went back to live with her parents. After a hearing, the university suspended Tom for a few games. He then resumed his life as before. He still goes to Wiggins Watering Hole.

For Colleen, 27, the evening started out friendly enough. After a cozy dinner at her apartment, her boyfriend suggested that she lie down while he did the dishes. As she lay in bed, he walked in with a butcher knife. Her formerly tender lover bound and raped her. When it was over, he fell asleep.

The public has little understanding of date rape. Most seem to think it involves a reluctant woman who needs a "push" to go along with what she really wants. A study at UCLA found that 54 percent of the men and 42 percent of the women believe forced sexual intercourse can be permissible. At Auburn University, 61 percent of the men said they had touched a woman sexually against her will.

Convictions for date rape are hard to get, and some prosecutors discourage women from bringing such charges. A social worker at a rape treatment center says, "Most people are very understanding if a stranger breaks into your house with a gun and rapes you, but if you say you made a date with the rapist, they always wonder how far you went before you said no."

Obviously, most people don't know Carol and Colleen.

What can be done? Campus antirape groups offer one remedy. Through lectures and workshops, incoming freshmen can be introduced to the perils of date rape. Well-publicized prosecutions can cut the risk, and these groups can promote such prosecution. Student groups, composed of concerned students, both women and men, can pressure the college administration to react strongly to date rape. After all, "if there were a pattern of assaults on quarterbacks, universities would respond very quickly."

Based on Engelmayer 1983; Seligmann 1984.

Table 5-3 — Date Rape and Other Unwanted Sexual Activities Experienced by Undergraduates

These are the results of a survey of 380 women and 368 men enrolled in introductory psychology courses at Texas A&M University.

Percentages add up to more than 100 because often more than one unwanted sexual activity occurred on one date.

Unwanted Sexual Activity	Women Who Reported This Had Happened to Them (%)	Men Who Reported They Had Done This (%)
He kissed without tongue contact	3.7	2.2
He kissed with tongue contact	12.3	0.7
He touched/kissed her breasts through her clothes	24.7	7.3
He touched/kissed her breasts under her clothes	22.6	13.1
He touched her genitals through her clothes	28.8	15.3
He touched her genitals under her clothes	28.4	13.9
He performed oral sex on her	9.9	8.8
He forced her to touch his genitals through his clothes	2.9	0.7
He forced her to touch his genitals under his clothes	5.8	2.2
He forced her to perform oral sex on him	2.5	4.4
He forced her to have sexual intercourse	20.6	15.3

Source: Muehlenhard and Linton 1987:190.

sociologists Diana Scully and Joseph Marolla (1999) discovered in their interviews of imprisoned rapists, one man may make a date with a victim and then drive her to a predetermined location, where he and his friends rape her. One man said that this practice was so much a part of his group's weekend routine that they rented a house just for it.

The Husband Rapist

The last type is the *husband* rapist. Contrary to common opinion, marital rape is real rape. It is not an innocuous event involving a husband who is simply too insistent about having sex. After interviewing wives who had been raped, sociologists David Finkelhor and Kersti Yllo (1985, 1989) concluded that such an idea is a "sanitary stereotype." Marital rape can involve violence and sadism as horrible as any that we have discussed. Some wives are forced to flee in terror for their lives and sanity.

UNREPORTED RAPES

How Many Rapes Are Reported?

A question that has plagued researchers is the number of women who are raped but do not report it. As with other crimes, only some victims report rape to the police, but shame, guilt, and fears associated with rape may make the number of unreported rapes exceptionally high.

Solving the Question by Victimization Surveys

The two major sources of data on rape are police statistics and victimization surveys. The most comprehensive of the police statistics is the annual *FBI Uniform Crime Reports*. Because police statistics deal with reported offenses, unreported crimes leave huge gaps in our information. To overcome this problem of "dark numbers," social researchers conduct national surveys to determine the extent to which people have been victimized and whether they reported it to the police. In the most comprehensive of these surveys, *The National Crime Victimization Survey*, researchers interview a random, nationally representative sample of about 100,000 Americans.

The National Crime Victimization Survey reveals that the real rape totals are probably twice as high as the official figures (Schmalleger 1999:68). Because this victimization survey does not gather data on crimes against children under the age of 12, the actual rape total is even higher than this.

Four factors influence whether a woman reports her rape: the age of the victim, whether it was an attempted or completed rape, her race, and whether she knows the rapist. Females below 20 are the least likely to report rape; women between the ages of 35 and 49 are the most likely. Women are more likely to report completed rapes than attempted rapes (Hindelang and Davis 1977).

Table 5-4 shows differences in race/ethnicity and acquaintanceship. When African-American women are raped by strangers, half of them report the attack. When they know their attacker, the reporting rises to 61 percent. White women show a contrasting pattern: When they are raped by strangers, 62 percent report the attack; if they are raped by someone they know, only 1 in 3 does. The reasons for these racial differences are unknown.

REACTIONS TO RAPE

Let's look at what happens to the rape victim after her attack. We focus first on her personal reactions and then on what some pinpoint as a social problem itself, how the criminal justice system treats rape victims.

Disbelief and Shock

Disbelief is the first reaction of a woman who finds herself confronted by a rapist (McIntyre et al. 1979). The event is so frightening and alien that most victims report they could not believe it was happening. Shock quickly follows.

Styles of Dealing with the Trauma

The trauma of rape does not end with the physical attack. The woman typically finds her self-concept shattered, her emotions wounded, her whole life disrupted. About half of rape victims deal with their trauma in an *expressive* style, venting their fear, anger, rage, and anxiety by crying and sobbing, or by restlessness and tenseness. The other half reacts in a *controlled* style, carefully masking their feelings behind calm and composure (Burgess and Holmstrom 1974).

Many victims suffer from self-blame—feeling guilty for having been alone in that place at that time, for not having screamed or fought back. Many become afraid of the dark, of being alone, of walking on the street, and of doing such ordinary

Table 5-4	Percentage of Rapes Reported to the Police		
		The Victim Is	
		Black	**White**
The rapist is	A stranger	50	62
	Known by the victim	61	34

Source: Based on Shim and DeBerry 1988:82.

activities as shopping or driving. The victim's personal relationships may deteriorate, for husbands or male friends often wonder what "really" happened (Russell 1979).

The Trauma of Dealing with the Legal System

Although many police departments have grown sensitive to the plight of rape victims and have changed their procedures, the criminal justice system often adds to a victim's suffering (Madigan and Gamble 1991). Many police officers have little experience in dealing with rape victims. As they ask detailed questions of a sexual nature, some interrogators are insensitive or embarrassed, others disbelieving. Some suspect the victim is trying to use the police to "get even" with a boyfriend. Others think that the woman "asked for it." Some don't believe it was rape if a woman does not have visible physical injuries. Hostility, suspicion, and embarrassment from the police engender hostility and embarrassment in the victim.

One victim gave this account of her experience with police interrogators:

> They rushed me down to the housing cops who asked me questions like, "Was he your boyfriend?" "Did you know him?" Here I am, hysterical. I'm 12 years old, and I don't know these things even happen to people. Anyway, they took me to the precinct after that, and there about four detectives got me in the room and asked me how long was his penis—like I was supposed to measure it. Actually, they said, "How long was the instrument?" I thought they were referring to the knife—how was I supposed to know? That I could have told them 'cause I was sure enough lookin' at the knife. (Brownmiller 1975:365)

The "Legal Rape"

To be interrogated more as a suspect than a victim is only the beginning of some victims' assault by the criminal justice system (Frohmann 1991). In about half of the reported rapes, the assailant is arrested (*FBI Uniform Crime Reports* 2000). The victim then faces a dilemma. If she fails to press charges, the rapist goes free. But if she prosecutes, she must recount her rape in detail—to her attorney, in court, and to a defense attorney who may try to blacken her character. In some states, her prior sex life can be examined on the witness stand. In the courtroom, the accuser can become the accused. As one rape victim said of her experience:

Many rapes are never reported, and many that are reported are not prosecuted. As explained in the text, one reason women fear reporting that they have been sexually assaulted is "legal rape." Due to the efforts of feminists, criminal investigation procedures have changed, and more women officers are now assigned these cases.

> I had heard other women say that the trial is the rape. It's no exaggeration. My trial was one of the dirtiest transcripts you could read. Even though I

One of the steps in establishing a social problem is agitation by concerned people which arouses concern in many others. It was through this process that rape became defined as a social problem. To increase the visibility of the problem, many campuses feature posters placed in prominent spots to alert students to potential danger.

A lot of campus rapes start here.

Whenever there's drinking or drugs, things can get out of hand.
So it's no surprise that many campus rapes involve alcohol.
But you should know that under any circumstances, sex without
the other person's consent is considered rape. A felony, punishable
by prison. And drinking is no excuse.
That's why, when you party, it's good to know what your limits are.
You see, a little sobering thought now can save you from a big
problem later.

© 1990 Rape Treatment Center, Santa Monica Hospital

had been warned about the defense attorney you wouldn't believe the things he asked me to describe. It was very humiliating. I don't understand it. It was like I was the defendant and he was the plaintiff. I wasn't on trial. I don't see where I did anything wrong. I screamed, I struggled. (Brownmiller 1975:36)

Many reasons underlie this second victimization, which some call "legal rape." A primary reason is that, like our other institutions, the judicial system is under male domination and reflects traditional male views: that women going out alone at night or hitchhiking or going into bars are "asking for it"; that men's strong sex drive is hard to control; that women provoke men sexually and then change their minds just before sex—or even after it—and then cry rape.

The changed view of rape has led to a change in the treatment of rape victims within the judicial system. In many jurisdictions, women's groups work with hospital staffs to ensure that victims are examined privately and in accordance with the requirements for legal evidence. Many departments now use women officers trained both to investigate rapes and deal compassionately with rape victims.

Homosexual Rape

To be complete, I need to mention homosexual rape. Although we have concentrated on the social problem of men raping women, men also rape other men. As noted in Chapter 3, this form of rape (and forced prostitution) is common in our prisons, with young, slender prisoners often being marked as victims. At the moment, however, people prefer to ignore the objective conditions. Until there is an outcry from the public or from authorities, by definition we do not have a social problem.

✦ Murder ✦

If a Martian were to study the earth, he or she might find our fascination with murder bizarre. The Martian might report that murder has become a major form of U.S. entertainment, that every night Americans watch beatings, bombings, shootings, slashings, stabbings, strangulations, and other mayhem on television—with gruesome close-ups in living color.

Real-Life "Whodunits"

THE WHO

As any mystery reader knows, we must explore the who, what, when, where, and why of murder. Let's first examine the statistics so we can uncover the social patterns of murder. Then we can try to figure out the sociological "why" of those patterns.

Although most people's fears of murder center around strangers, of all major crimes in the United States, murder is the *least* likely to be committed by a stranger. It also is the most likely to be solved. Look at Figure 5-5 for a comparison of arrest rates by type of crime. Then look at Table 5-5, which shows that strangers account for only about 13 percent of U.S. killings. In cases where the relationship between the victim and killer is known, 87 percent of murder victims are killed by their husbands, wives, lovers, children, friends, acquaintances, or neighbors. (In 43 percent of killings, the relationship between murderer and victim is not known.)

The "who" of U.S. murder follows the patterns of social class, sex, age, and race that we found apply to rape. The poor are more likely to kill. So are younger people. Although only about 14 percent of the population is between ages 15 and 24, from this group come about half of the killers (*FBI Uniform Crime Reports* 2000:36; *Statistical Abstract* 1998:Table 16). Figure 5-6 illustrates how much more likely males are to kill than females. As you can see, males kill 89 to 90 percent of everyone who is murdered in the United States. Females, although they make up about 51 percent of the population, commit only 11 percent of the murders. As you can see from Table 5-5, spouse murders also follow this pattern; husbands are more than three times as likely to kill their wives than wives are to kill their husbands.

Similar startling differences mark African Americans and whites. Although African Americans make up only about 12 percent of the U.S. population, in 51 percent of the cases where the race of the killer is known, the murderer is an African American (*FBI Uniform Crime Reports* 2000:15). The murder rate of 15- to 24-year-old African Americans is several times higher than that of whites of the same

FIGURE 5-5
Crimes Cleared by Arrest
Note: The percentages are based on crimes known to the police. If cases not reported were included, the figures would change drastically.
(*Source: Sourcebook of Criminal Justice Statistics* 2000:Figure 3.1.)

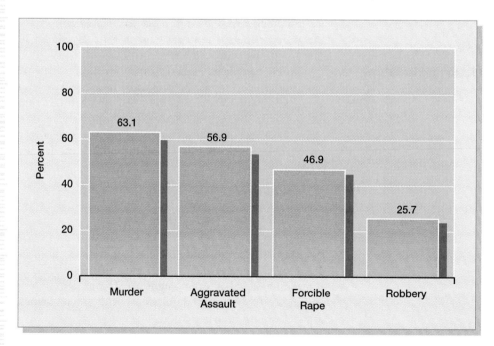

Table 5-5   Relationships of Victims to Their Killers

Relationship	Percent	Relationship	Percent
Family		Acquaintances	
Wife	4.6	Friend	2.2
Husband	1.3	Girlfriend	3.2
Son	1.8	Boyfriend	1.1
Daughter	1.3	Neighbor	.8
Brother	.6	Other acquaintances	24.0
Father	.9	Total	31.3
Mother	.7	Stranger	13.0
Sister	.1	Relationship unknown	42.6
Other Family	1.8	Total	100
Total	13.1		

Source: FBI Uniform Crime Reports 2000:20.

THE WHAT

THE WHEN

FIGURE 5-6
**Comparing Men
and Women Killers**
(*Source: FBI Uniform Crime Reports* 2000:18.)

age. From Table 5-6 you can see that murder is overwhelmingly *intraracial;* 85 percent of white victims are killed by whites, and 93 percent of blacks are killed by blacks.

Although people use various weapons to commit murder, every year the number-one choice of Americans is the gun. As you can see from Figure 5-7, all other types of weapons take a distant second place.

Like rape, murder is not evenly distributed across the seasons. July, August, and December are the highest months, and March and April the lowest (*FBI Uniform Crime Reports* 1997:14). Consistently, more murders occur during the last six months of the year. Nights are also more dangerous than days, and weekends more dangerous than weekdays. The most dangerous time of the week continues to be Saturday night, which, as sociologist Alex Thio (1978) observed back in the 1970s, may be why cheap handguns are called "Saturday night specials."

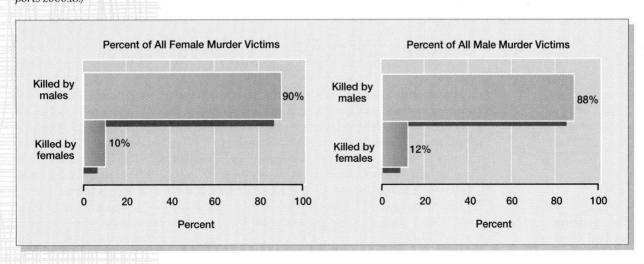

Table 5-6	Race/Ethnicity of Killers and Their Victims		
		Killers	
		White	**Black**
Victims	White	85%	15%
	Black	7%	93%

Note: Does not include victims or killers whose race is unknown.

Source: FBI Uniform Crime Reports 2000:18.

The good news is that between 1991 and 2000 the U.S. murder rate dropped 30 percent, plunging from 9.8 per 100,000 Americans to just 5.5 (*FBI, Uniform Crime Reports* 2000:14). Although this rate is the United States' lowest since 1967, when it was 6.2, it remains one of the highest in the world. As with rape, the states vary tremendously in their individual rates, and where you live vitally affects your chances of being murdered. A Louisianan, for example, runs more than fifteen times the risk of being murdered than does a South Dakotan. Figure 5-8 on page 155 ranks the states as the safest, average, and most dangerous.

THE WHERE

Most people think that large cities pose a higher risk of murder—and they are right. Each year, 3.8 of every 100,000 people living in rural areas are killed, but in our large cities (250,000 and over) this number jumps to 5.9 (*FBI Uniform Crime Reports* 2000:Table 2). Table 5-7 (on page 156) shows how uneven the murder rate is among cities.

SOCIAL BASES OF THE SOCIAL PATTERNS

THE WHY

Why do these patterns exist? As we will see, they reflect our society. We do not know all the answers, and some are complicated, but let's begin with the simpler reasons.

Acquaintanceship

Most murder victims are killed by someone they know, because most murders are crimes of passion spurred by heated arguments. As many analysts have pointed out, we are much more likely to argue with people we know than with strangers. It is with people we know that we share money, property, and love—the things that fuel quarrels and lead to violent death.

Poverty

Why are murderers so likely to come from the most deprived groups of Americans? The three sociological perspectives help us understand this pattern. Conflict theorists, who view the poor as oppressed people, see their high murder rates as the result of their poverty. As sociologist Elliott Currie (1985:160) put it:

> Brutal conditions breed brutal behavior. To believe otherwise requires us to argue that the experience of being confined to the mean and precarious depths of the American economy has *no* serious consequences for personal character or social behavior.

Because the murder victims of killers who come from poverty are also usually poor, conflict theorists conclude that they are striking out at one another instead of at their oppressors.

Functionalists who work within strain theory stress that being denied access to the approved means for attaining material success produces tension. Functionalists who emphasize control theory point out that the poor have fewer internal and external controls to inhibit the propensity to strike out at others that this strain produces. For example, the poor have less to lose if they become involved with the police. Compared with people from higher social classes, they risk less because they have less money saved, their jobs pay relatively little, and they are unlikely to own their homes or to belong to voluntary organizations such as churches or the Junior Chamber of Commerce.

The Meaning Behind Murder

To this, symbolic interactionists add that in some subcultures of the poor, police trouble can enhance one's reputation; one becomes more of a "man" for confronting the police or for going to prison. Symbolic interactionists also stress that

Chapter 5 Violence in Society: Rape and Murder

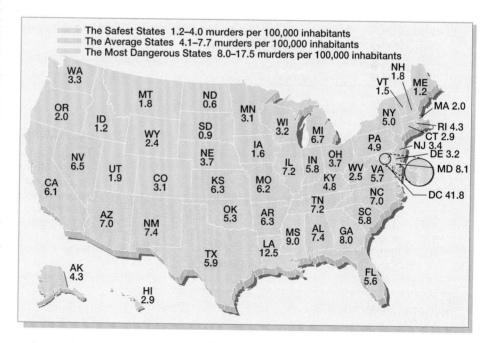

FIGURE 5-7
America's Choice of Murder Weapons, as Percent of All Killings
(*Source: FBI Uniform Crime Reports 2000:19.*)

FIGURE 5-8
Social Map: Murder
(*Source: FBI Uniform Crime Reports 2000:Table 5.*)

More Americans are killed by guns than by any other weapon. Liberals blame the easy availability of guns, and they campaign to have the sale of guns banned. To this, conservatives reply, "Guns don't kill people; people do." The debate continues, as do efforts to ban or limit the sale of guns.

the social classes have distinct ways to resolve disputes. A middle-class person with a grievance is more likely than a poor person is to use legal recourse, such as lawsuits. The poor, who place less trust in the judicial system and are unable to afford lawyers, are likely to settle disagreements outside the law, which can lead to heated words, physical assault, and death.

Some symbolic interactionists stress subcultural theory and differential association. In a subculture of poverty, using personal methods to settle scores with antagonists may be admired. People growing up in this subculture are likely to learn to react violently to life's problems. To trace the path by which people become involved

Table 5-7 Murder: The Ten Safest and Most Dangerous U.S. Cities (cities over 250,000)

	Safest			Most Dangerous	
Rank	City	Murder Rate per 100,000 People	Rank	City	Murder Rate per 100,000 People
1	El Paso, TX	2.2	1	Washington, D.C.	46.4
2	Mesa, AZ	2.4	2	Detroit, MI	42.6
3	Virginia Beach, VA	2.7	3	St. Louis, MO	38.1
4	San Jose, CA	2.9	4	Atlanta, GA	34.8
5	Honolulu, HI	3.4	5	New Orleans, LA	33.9
6	Arlington, TX	3.5	6	Birmingham, AL	30.7
7	Aurora, CO	4.3	7	Kansas City, MO	26.4
8	San Diego, CA	4.6	8	Newark, NJ	25.7
9	Santa Ana, CA	4.8 (tied)	9	Chicago, IL	22.8
10	Toledo, OH	4.8	10	Milwaukee, WI	21.3

Source: Statistical Abstract 2000:Table 3.130.

in murder, Lonnie Athens, a symbolic interactionist, interviewed 58 prisoners. He found a general pattern: The killer defined the victim's actions as intolerable—a spouse or lover refused sex or threatened to leave, a stranger or friend spewed insults. The killer interpreted the situation as calling for violence, often because the killer's self-image or social standing among friends was threatened. Faced with this interpretation of the situation—by which intolerable conduct and violence are appropriate responses—the individual killed.

A woman prisoner whom Athens (1980:36–37) interviewed said that a stranger at a party had accused her of cheating him of $20. The man kept insulting her and laughing at her:

> Then I told myself, "This man has got to go one way or another; I've just had enough of this (man) messing with me; I'm going to cut his dirty . . . throat." I went into my bedroom, got a $20 bill and my razor. I said to myself, . . . "now he's hung himself," and I walked out of the bedroom. I went up to him with a big smile on my face. I held the $20 bill in my hand out in front of me and hid the razor in the other hand. Then I sat on his lap and said, "O.K., you're a fast dude; here's your $20 back." He said, "I'm glad that you are finally admitting it." I looked at him with a smile and said, "Let me seal it with a kiss" . . . and then I bent over like I was going to kiss him and started slicing up his throat.

Killing as a Manly Act

This last example notwithstanding, why do men kill more often than women? As we have seen, men are more likely to value violence. Men in poverty especially are likely to believe that a real man is tough—and toughness includes the willingness to be violent. One's standing in the group may depend on being known as "the kind of guy who can't be pushed around." Not to fight when insulted is cowardice, the worst quality a young man can show in certain subcultures.

Among some groups, even killing is associated with manliness, and spilling blood brings honor. In the Mafia killing an enemy is the equivalent of courage, the measure of one's *capacity as a man*. There, "the more awesome and potent the victim, the more worthy and meritorious the killer" (Arlacchi 1980:113).

Symbolic interactionists stress that females are socialized not to be violent. Because males learn to associate bravado and violence with their role, while females learn less violent ways of handling loss of face, *around the world* men kill at a rate several times that of women (Daly and Wilson 1988).

Guns are also identified as masculine, and cultural stereotypes reinforce this image. For example, our culture romanticizes cowboys and hunters and bandits, who personify the union of guns, violence, and masculinity. The U.S. male is much more likely to reach for a gun to settle a quarrel than, say, a kitchen knife or a bottle of poison.

Why the Racial/Ethnic Differences?

Let's apply some of these social patterns to explain why African Americans kill at a higher rate than would be expected given their proportion of the population. African Americans are more likely to be poor, and the subculture to which lower-class African Americans belong identifies masculinity with the willingness to defend oneself aggressively. Functionalists would add that African Americans are socialized to strive for the cultural goal of material success, but racial discrimination blocks many of them from reaching that goal through legitimate means. This increases their strain, leading to a higher rate of violent crime, most of which is directed against people nearby. A pattern of racially segregated housing helps account for the intraracial pattern of murder, the black-on-black violence.

What about violence that crosses racial lines? To explain interracial patterns, functionalists stress the connection between race and money. If a burglary, robbery, or mugging results in a killing across racial lines, it is more likely to involve poor

African Americans robbing whites than poor whites robbing African Americans. Conflict theorists add that the oppression of African Americans by whites produces racial hatred that has many negative consequences, including deadly incidents of striking out against the dominant group.

To understand race and violence, we need to focus on another aspect of social class. In *The Declining Significance of Race,* William Julius Wilson (1978) analyzed the major class division that developed among African Americans. As racial barriers dropped, many African Americans got more education and better jobs and became middle class. Taking their opportunity, they moved out of the ghetto and into better areas of the city and into the suburbs. Left behind was an *underclass,* a group of people who were desperately poor and were plagued with social problems—unemployment, unwed motherhood, drug addiction, murder, and rape. As Wilson put it, this group "is increasingly isolated from mainstream patterns and norms of behavior." It is here that U.S. violence is concentrated.

Why the Temporal Patterns?

The timing of U.S. murder also reflects broader social patterns. During weekdays, when murders are least frequent, people are working and meeting personal and familial responsibilities. On weekends, when murders are more frequent, people are more likely to socialize in public and to drink more than usual. This increases the likelihood of quarrels, with the peak coming on the traditional "Saturday night out."

Why the Geographic Patterns?

Finally, the geography of murder intrigues sociologists. For more than a century, the South's murder rate has been higher than that in the rest of the country, leading some researchers to conclude that there is a "southern subculture of violence" (Huff-Corzine et al. 1991). Southerners supposedly learn more violent ways of resolving their disagreements than do people raised in other regions. They take violence more for granted, and more violent themes run through their music, literature, and even jokes. Apparently, southerners are more likely to own guns, to know how to shoot, and to use guns during quarrels. Sociologists find these explanations suggestive, but not totally satisfactory (Doerner 1978; Messner 1983; Huff-Corzine et al. 1986).

Before concluding this section, let's look at two patterns of murder that have gripped the public's attention: mass murder and serial murder.

Mass Murder

Mass murder is "the killing of four or more victims at one location, within one event" (Zawitz 1988). Examples are Richard Speck's murder of 8 nursing students in Chicago one July night in 1966; Charles Whitman's killing of 16 people in a sniper attack from a tower at the University of Texas that same year; James Huberty's shooting of 21 people at a McDonald's in 1984; the arson deaths of 87 people at the Happy Land social club in the Bronx in 1991; George Hennard's shooting of 22 people at a Luby's Cafeteria in Killeen, Texas, in 1991; Colin Ferguson's shooting spree as he walked through a New York commuter train and methodically fired forty shots, in 1993, an incident that left 6 people dead; and the rash of school shootings that has so alarmed the public, such as the one described in our opening vignette. To my knowledge, only one woman has joined the list of mass murderers, Priscilla Ford, who, during a 1981 Thanksgiving parade in Reno, Nevada, deliberately drove her car onto a crowded sidewalk, killing 6 people and injuring 23.

Serial Murder

Serial murder is "the killing of several victims in three or more separate events. These may occur over several days, weeks, or years" (Zawitz 1988). The elapsed time between murders distinguishes serial murder from mass murder. Between 1962 and 1964, Albert De Salvo ("the Boston Strangler") raped and killed 13 women; during the 1960s and 1970s, Theodore "Ted" Bundy killed dozens of women in four states, bludgeoning, strangling, and sexually molesting them; in the late 1970s, John Wayne Gacy sexually molested and killed 33 young men in Chicago; during 1976 and 1977,

David Berkowitz ("Son of Sam") murdered 6 people in the Queens, Bronx, and Brooklyn burroughs of New York City; and between 1979 and 1981, Wayne Williams killed 28 boys and young men in Atlanta (Levin and Fox 1985). Henry Lee Lucas drew national attention when, after his arrest for killing an elderly woman in Texas in 1983, he admitted to a killing rampage that lasted a dozen years and left hundreds of victims strewn across the nation. In fact, Lucas may have killed only 5 or 10 people (Ressler and Shachtman 1992). The rest may be lies that Lucas made up in an attempt to garner attention or at the urging of police, who sought to clear their books of unsolved murders. But the killer whose bizarre acts most riveted the nation was Jeffrey Dahmer of Milwaukee, who not only killed young men but had sex with their dead bodies. He also dismembered and ate parts of some of his victims.

Almost all serial killers are men, but an occasional woman joins this list of infamy. In North Carolina in 1986, the husband of Blanche Taylor Moore was taken to the hospital with arsenic poisoning; he survived, but the ensuing investigation led to the exhumation of 6 bodies, including her father, her first husband, and a boyfriend; arsenic was found in all of them. In 1987 and 1988, Dorothea Montalvo Puente, who operated a boarding house for senior citizens in Sacramento, killed 7 boarders. Her motive was to collect their Social Security checks. In Missouri, from 1986 to 1989, Faye Copeland and her husband killed 5 transient men. Aileen Wuornos hitchhiked along Florida's freeways and killed 5 middle-aged men after having sex with them. Moore, Copeland, and Wuornos are on death row.

I researched one of the first serial killings to attract the attention of the U.S. public. Fascinated by television reports, I went to Houston, where Dean Corll, with the aid of two teenage accomplices, had killed 27 boys. The 33-year-old had befriended Elmer Wayne Henley and David Brooks, two teenagers from broken homes. From 1971 to 1973, the boys picked up young hitchhikers—sometimes even their own neighbors and high school classmates—and delivered them to Corll to rape and kill.

My interviews confirmed what has become common knowledge about serial killers: that they successfully lead double lives that catch their friends and family unaware. Henley's mother swore to me that her son was a good boy and couldn't possibly be guilty. Some of his high school friends told me the same thing. They stressed that he was interested only in girls. I conducted my interviews in Henley's bedroom, and for proof Henley's friends pointed to a pair of girl's panties that were hanging in the room.

Mass murder is usually committed by men who relieve pressure by exploding in an outburst of murder. Serial murderers, in contrast, usually gain intense, personal satisfaction from killing. Many are motivated by lust, by sexual satisfaction that accompanies the killing. The FBI even uses the term "lust murder." Others, however, are more "garden variety," motivated by greed, like Dorothea Puente, who killed for money.

Many assume that mass and serial murders are more common than they used to be, but we do not know this. We may have more efficient investigative techniques, which allow the police to conclude that a serial killer is operating in an area, rather than to assume that a series of killings is unrelated. Part of the perception that such killings have increased is due to ignorance of our history; in our frontier past, serial killers went from ranch to ranch, and mass murderers wiped out entire villages of Native Americans.

◆ Social Policy ◆

Social policy on violence has three aspects: how to deal with violent offenders, how to deal with their victims, and how to prevent violence. Let's look at each.

DEALING WITH OFFENDERS

Two Extreme Positions:

Dealing with offenders brings us face to face with irreconcilable reactions on the part of the public and incompatible social policies on the part of officials. The extreme positions are held by the retributionist and the reformist.

The Retributionist

The **retributionist** focuses on the victims of violence. Seeing their suffering, retributionists argue that those who are violent deserve violence in return, that those who have caused suffering should suffer. Retributionists believe in an "eye for an eye and a tooth for a tooth." Matching violence with violence, they would castrate rapists and kill murderers.

The Reformist

The **reformist,** in contrast, directs our attention to the offenders. Reformists see violent offenders as the victims of an oppressive society. Emotionally wounded through dysfunctional families, social inequality, and discrimination, assailants vent their frustration and anger by blindly striking out at others. Reformists want policies to help families function better and to provide offenders with psychiatric, social, and medical services. They see the ultimate solution as prevention—helping families to function better and changing the social structure to eliminate social inequality and discrimination.

The retributionist and reformist views are so far apart emotionally and intellectually that their proponents can hardly communicate with one another. With their eyes on the offenders, the reformists plead for understanding and help in order to change people and social circumstances. With their eyes on the victims, the retributionists reply, "How would you feel if your daughter were raped and tortured?" The two groups are not talking about the same thing.

Between the Extremes

Somewhere between these extremes are people who do not care why people are violent (so they aren't concerned about social change), nor do they have a desire to repay offenders in kind. They simply want to get violent people off the streets and remove their threat to society. Their position is simple: Lock them up and throw away the key.

Steps That Can Be Taken:

These strong emotional reactions and extreme positions make it difficult to develop sound social policy for dealing with rapists and murderers. In addition, much is unknown about the causes of violence, and precious little is known about how to

prevent it. Realizing that there is no easy path and no simple truth, let's examine some steps that can be taken.

Letting Victims Determine the Penalty

First, why not let the victims of violent crimes determine the prison term of the offender? No law would need to be changed, because victims would choose within the sentencing limits already established by law. This approach, which would provide the victim with a sense of satisfaction and justice, has already been tried by a judge in Minneapolis who allowed a 65-year-old great-grandmother to determine the prison sentence of the 26-year-old man who raped her ("Minneapolis Judge" 1989).

Reducing the Penalty for Rape

Second, a legal change that might decrease rape would be, paradoxically, to *reduce* the penalty for it. Because current penalties are so severe, many juries are more inclined to acquit a man than to subject him to what they consider an unreasonable penalty, such as life imprisonment. Reducing penalties might lead to *more* convictions, and because convicted rapists tend to have committed other rapes, this could reduce the number of rapes in our society.

Establishing Degrees of Rape

If we were to adopt this policy, we might establish degrees of rape similar to the degrees of murder. Degrees of rape would reflect the reality that some rapes cause more serious injuries than others. Laws might include sexual assault in the following categories:

First degree—abduction that involves transporting the victim to another location and causing severe bodily injury

Second degree—abduction with less bodily injury

Third degree—no abduction but serious bodily injury

Fourth degree—no abduction and little bodily injury

Fifth degree—no abduction and no bodily injury

This suggestion can be improved upon. For example, some will feel that abduction is less important than serious bodily injury and may want to reverse the second and third degrees. In any event, I suggest that prison be mandatory for anyone convicted of rape, and that sentences be meted out according to injury. I also suggest that prosecutors enforce our current, severe kidnapping laws in all rape cases that involve abduction.

DEALING WITH VICTIMS

The second major issue is social policy for the victims of violence. For murder, there would seem to be no issue to deal with, for the victim is dead. The family of the deceased, however, has also been victimized—deprived for life of a loved one, a father, a mother, a child, a breadwinner, a homemaker. Besides being emotionally traumatized, sometimes for years, victims of rape must also bear medical expenses and deal with the loss of income from missed work. Their families, too, suffer anguish, frustration, anger, even shame.

Victim Compensation

A basic responsibility of government is to protect its citizens from violent crime. If it fails to provide basic safety, should its citizens have the right to be compensated for that failure? Although some might consider such an idea too utopian, it was first suggested by Hammurabi 4,000 years ago. For all the publicity they receive, one might think such policies are state secrets, but 44 states have programs to compensate victims of violent crime. Most compensate victims for both medical costs and lost earnings (Zawitz 1988).

Training Personnel

The treatment of rape victims in the criminal justice system is improving. More law enforcement personnel are being trained to deal with sexual assault. Some police departments assign special investigators and full-time prosecutors to sexual assault cases. As the skills of these professionals improve, more rapists will be convicted. Given the gender-sensitive nature of these investigations, some hospitals are training women—physicians and other hospital staff—to deal with female rape victims. Such steps should be encouraged. (See the Issues box on a bill of rights for rape victims below.)

Support Groups

For many victims, the trauma of violence lingers for years. They need long-term counseling services, especially support groups that are run by victims of violent crime. Such people have experienced the problems and can reach out to others (Gilmartin-Zena 1985; Chesler et al. 1990; Gardner 1992).

PREVENTING VIOLENCE

Four Social Policies:

1. Long Prison Terms for Repeat Offenders

2. Gun Control: Fewer Guns or More Guns?

Social policy also needs to center on preventing violence. I suggest four social policies. First, some men commit a large number of rapes. Some rape several times a month until they are apprehended—which can take years. Long sentences for these repeat offenders ("career rapists")—with little chance of parole—could protect many potential victims.

Second, we need some form of gun control. As we saw in Figure 5-7, most murder victims die from gunshot wounds. Proponents of gun control argue that because most murders are crimes of passion, emotional outbursts would be less lethal if people had restricted access to guns. Some propose that we could reduce the U.S. murder rate by registering firearms and licensing gun owners. Opponents argue that gun ownership is a constitutional right that should not be removed because some people abuse guns.

The two extremes of gun control are the most interesting. On the one side are those who want to abolish gun ownership altogether. On the other are those who argue that Americans need *more* guns. They argue that if all law-abiding citizens had guns, few rapists and killers would break into our homes—and even fewer would survive if they did. These two extremes show why it is difficult to establish social policy.

ISSUES ɪɴ SOCIAL PROBLEMS

A Bill of Rights for Rape Victims

You have the right to be afraid. It is a healthy, normal reaction to a life-threatening situation.

You have the right to be angry. But try not to show it; it can cost you physical injury, perhaps your life.

You have the right to do whatever will save your life.

You have the right to expect sympathetic and compassionate treatment from police and other authorities. You are the injured party, and they need you for any criminal investigation.

You have the right to know the status of your case and the whereabouts of the perpetrator if he is caught.

You have the right to know the progress of the police investigation if the offender has not been caught.

You have the right to expect support, not blame, from the rest of society.

You have the right to expect your government to protect you from violent crime. When it fails, you have the right to be compensated for the physical, emotional, and economic losses you have suffered.

Based on Hanson, October 5, 1977.

Third, policymakers should support research to determine how our culture creates a climate for violence. Remember the sociological question that was posed at the beginning of this chapter: What in a society increases or decreases the likelihood of violence? Because sociologists do not assume that Americans are genetically more violent than most people in the world, the answer lies in our culture. Once we determine what those aspects of the culture are, we can change them. I suggest that researchers

1. Examine less violent cultures to determine what factors minimize violence.
2. Determine how to help Americans channel aggression constructively.
3. Find ways to minimize antagonisms between the sexes.
4. Identify effective ways to teach males that females are not appropriate outlets for frustration, aggression, or violence.
5. To the degree that individual violence is based on economic inequality, develop programs to provide more opportunities for the disadvantaged.

We also can apply a fundamental point stressed throughout this book, that social problems do not consist only of objective conditions but also depend on subjective concerns. As sociologists Lynda Holmstrom and Ann Burgess (1989) emphasized, issues sometimes leap into prominence and then fade from sight. This could certainly happen with sexual violence. If we are to work toward effective solutions, we must keep this social problem before the public.

◆ The Future of the Problem ◆

Given our history and current situation, our rate of violence is destined to remain higher than that of most nations. From time to time, the murder and rape rates will decline, offering some hope, but these occurrences will be followed by rate increases. Changing our overall rate of violence would require major structural changes in our society. Without these changes, violence will be with us until our society ends—and that ending may well be a violent one.

Viewing the future through the lens of our three theoretical perspectives supports this view. Conflict theory indicates continuing tensions in society. Short of revolution (which has proven no panacea for any society), the wealthy will remain in control, and discrimination will continue. Thus, the poor and minorities will continue to show up disproportionately in the statistics on violence. The functionalist lens shows that violence works, not always, but often enough for it to be perpetuated—for people do get revenge and other satisfactions from killing their enemies. Some gain dominance and sexual satisfaction through forcible rape. The symbolic interactionist lens focuses on violence as a cultural symbol that is held out as a legitimate means of resolving conflict. This is a powerful symbol, for it combines violence, *machismo,* manliness, power, strength, and dominance. Violence will continue, as men try to live up to this cultural image.

The *sociological* perspective of violence is essential to understanding our present and our future. Our high rate of violence is not caused by an abnormal number of violent psychopaths. This social pattern is a product of our social structure, and of relationships between our social groups. Into whatever future we project ourselves, without major structural change violence will remain part of our way of life. This understanding of the *social* basis of violence can become the key to changing basic relationships, and to focusing that change in a direction that decreases violence.

1. Sociologists analyze how violence is rooted in society. How a society is organized—its social structure—increases or decreases the amount of violence in it.

2. Each society has a rate of violence that, without major social change, is fairly constant over time. Sociologists call this a society's *normal violence*.

3. Biologists, anthropologists, and psychologists have theories to account for violence. The sociological response is that whatever predispositions humans have toward violence are encouraged or inhibited by the society in which they live.

4. Symbolic interactionists use two theories to explain violence. The first, *differential association,* stresses that violence is learned in association with others. The second, *subcultural theory,* emphasizes that some groups are more approving of violence than others. People who grow up or associate with these groups are more likely to learn violence.

5. Functionalists stress that some people become dissociated from cultural norms. Durkheim used the term *anomie* to describe this uprooting and estrangement. Anomic individuals are more likely to rape and kill. Merton's *strain theory* suggests that people for whom the *cultural means* (such as education and well-paying jobs) to *cultural goals* (such as financial success) are blocked are likely to choose alternative paths—and violence is one

of them. *Control or containment theory* suggests that rapists and murderers have weak inner and outer control systems.

6. Conflict theorists emphasize that the members of a society compete for scarce resources. The major division is between those who own the means of production and those who do not. Those at the mercy of the owners have few resources, and they lash out violently—misdirecting their violence onto one another.

7. Feminists challenged the traditional view of rape as a personal problem, a crime of passion. Researchers, the public, and legal authorities now consider rape a social problem, a crime of violence rooted in the structure of relationships between men and women.

8. Rape and murder are not random, unpredictable acts. They are related to the larger social and economic patterns of society, reflecting social patterns of class, gender, age, race, timing, location, and acquaintanceship.

9. To prevent violence requires restructuring those aspects of society that foster violence. Without such restructuring, high rates of violence will continue. To determine a rational basis for social policy on these emotionally charged issues requires research on the causes of violence.

10. Rape may fade from the public's mind as a social problem. To find workable solutions, we must keep the issue alive.

♦Key Terms

Anomie Feeling estranged, uprooted, unanchored, normless—not knowing what rules to apply to the situations one faces.

Collective violence See *Group violence.*

Containment theory A functionalist theory that focuses on the pushes and pulls thought to cause people to commit criminal acts. Whether one commits a violent act depends on the relative strength of inner containment (controls within the individual) and on outer containment (controls outside the individual).

Control theory See *Containment theory.*

Criminal sexual assault A legal term that refers to forcible rape.

Cultural goal A goal held out as legitimate for the members of a society. See also *Cultural means.*

Cultural means The general, approved ways of reaching cultural goals. See also *Cultural goal.*

Differential association A symbolic interactionist theory that stresses how criminal behavior is learned. Applied to violence, it assumes that one learns violence the same way that one learns nonviolence. See also *Subcultural theory.*

Forcible rape Nonconsensual or forced sexual relations. See *Statutory rape.*

Frustration-aggression A psychological theory that stresses that aggression is likely when a goal is blocked.

Group violence A number of people directing injurious force against others or against their property.

Individual violence Injurious force by one person against another.

Institutionalized group violence Planned group violence carried out under the direction of legally constituted officials.

Machismo Masculinity symbolized by dominance and strength.

Mass murder Killing four or more persons at one time in one location.

Modeling Copying another's behavior.

Normal violence A group's usual level of violence.

Organized group violence Planned but unauthorized group violence.

Personal violence See *Individual violence*.

Rape See *Forcible rape*.

Rate of violence The number of violent acts per some constant number, usually per 100,000 people.

Reformist A social policy perspective oriented to helping offenders by changing either them or their environment. See *Retributionist*.

Retributionist A social policy perspective oriented to punishing offenders. See also *Reformist*.

Serial murder Killing several victims in three or more separate events.

Situational group violence Unplanned, spontaneous group violence, such as a brawl among hockey players.

(The) sociological question of violence What is it about a society that increases or decreases the likelihood of violence?

Statutory rape Consensual sexual relations in which one person is under the legal age of consent. See also *Forcible rape*.

Strain theory A functionalist theory that stresses the adaptations that people make when they feel strain from a disjuncture between cultural goals and cultural means.

Subcultural theory A symbolic interactionist theory that stresses the learning that occurs in a subculture due to its distinctive norms, attitudes, values, beliefs, and behaviors. Applied to violence, some groups place a higher value on violence than do others, making it likely that people growing up in those groups will learn violence. See also *Differential association*.

Violence The use of physical force to injure people or destroy their property.

◆ Critical Thinking Questions

1. Which of the profiles or types of rapists discussed in this chapter (pp. 145–148) are the most common? List what you believe the five most common types are and explain your choices.

2. Do you think that retribution or reform is the most appropriate way of dealing with violent crimes? Explain.

3. What responsibility do you believe that the public has to provide compensation to victims of crime? Should it be the responsibility of the government to guarantee the safety of its citizens? Why or why not?

Crime and Criminal Justice

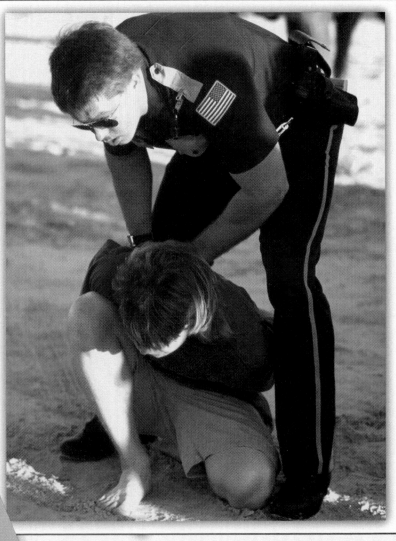

I was recently released from solitary confinement after being held therein for 37 months (months!). A silent system was imposed upon me and to even whisper to the man in the next cell resulted in being beaten by guards, sprayed with chemical mace, blackjacked, stomped and thrown into a strip-cell naked to sleep on a concrete floor without bedding, covering, wash basin or even toilet. The floor served as toilet and bed, and even there the silent system was enforced.... I have filed every writ possible against the administrative acts of brutality. The courts have all denied the petitions. Because of my refusal to let the thing die down ... I am the most hated prisoner in (this) penitentiary, and called a "hard-core incorrigible."

Maybe I am an incorrigible.... I know that thieves must be punished and I don't justify stealing, even though I am a thief myself. But now I don't think I will be a thief when I am released. No, I'm not that rehabilitated. It's just that I no longer think of becoming wealthy by stealing. I now think of killing—killing those who have beaten me and treated me as if I were a dog. I hope and pray for the sake of my own soul and future life of freedom that I am able to overcome the bitterness and hatred which eats daily at my soul.

—A letter from a prisoner in a state prison, as quoted in Zimbardo (1972).

✦ The Problem in Sociological Perspective ✦

What Is Crime?

What is crime? To help us understand its nature, let's look at the way one crime unfolded (Harlan 1988):

> On a Sunday morning in July, an undercover police officer entered a supermarket on Cape Cod. He purchased two cans of Del Monte whole-kernel corn and two cans of baby carrots.
>
> Corn and carrots were just the beginning of the crime wave.
>
> The following Sunday morning, undercover officers purchased Campbell's pork and beans and Progresso chicken-noodle soup. Then it was green beans. And more carrots.

What does selling vegetables have to do with crime? When he stood before the judge, unrepentant, and admitted that he had sold the canned goods, the owner of the store became a convicted criminal. He had violated Massachusetts "blue laws" that make it a crime to sell nonessential items on Sundays.

The Cultural Relativity of Crime

Your state may not have blue laws, but it does have merchandising laws. Consider, for example, the sale of alcohol as it relates to "closing hours." To sell whiskey, wine, or beer one minute before closing hour is legal; to sell them two minutes later is a crime.

These examples illustrate the essential nature of crime. **Crime** *is the violation of law*. Where there is no law, there is no crime. No activity is criminal in and of itself. Although we may agree that stealing, kidnapping, and rape are harmful and immoral, only law defines them as crimes.

This principle that law makes crime has many implications. One is that *crime is culturally relative;* that is, law and crime vary from one society to another. Acts that are criminal in one place and time may even be encouraged in other places and times. For example, in the early 1900s Margaret Sanger sent birth control information through the U.S. mail. Doing so was illegal, because such information was thought to injure the family and state. Sanger was indicted for mailing "obscene, lewd, and lascivious" materials. Today, in contrast, we consider the same act to be a service to an overpopulated world.

Travelers are sometimes surprised to find that an act taken for granted at home is a crime abroad, or that what is suppressed at home is taken for granted elsewhere. The cultural relativity of crime generates examples from the sublime to the ridiculous. Pork and alcohol are illegal in the Muslim Middle East, but a man may take several wives as long as he can support them. How puzzling our pork-chop-eating, monogamous society must seem to a Muslim!

Recall the material on abortion in Chapter 1. Before 1973, abortion was a criminal act. After 1973, it was not. If the antiabortion groups amend the Constitution or the U.S. Supreme Court reverses its 1973 ruling, abortion will again become a crime. In short, determining which acts are criminal is a **political process**—a struggle among groups with different interests and ideologies. As a result, different political systems make different determinations of what is illegal.

Because law defines crime, a sociological analysis raises such questions as: Which groups in a society have the power to get their views written into the law? Why do they pass laws against some acts but not against others? Why do some societies punish an act, while others ignore—or even encourage—it?

◆ The Scope of the Problem ◆

In considering crime as a social problem, we must also look at the **criminal justice system**—the agencies that respond to crime, including the police, courts, jails, and prisons. On the one hand, crime is a social problem when large numbers of people are upset about it, when they feel that crime threatens their security, peace, and quality of life. On the other hand, the criminal justice system is a social problem if people are upset about how it fails to prevent crime, or fails to rehabilitate offenders, or when it discriminates against certain groups of citizens. In this chapter, we will discuss these two intertwined parts of this social problem: crime and the criminal justice system.

CRIME AS A SOCIAL PROBLEM

How extensive is crime in the United States? We use two measures to assess it. The first is the number of crimes. Each year Americans are the victims of about 15,500 murders, 90,000 forcible rapes, 400,000 robberies, 910,000 aggravated assaults, 1.2 million automobile thefts, 2 million burglaries, and 7 million larcenies (*FBI Uniform Crime Reports* 2000). The second measure is the **crime rate**—the number of crimes per some unit of the population, usually per 100,000 people. Figure 6-1 shows how the U.S. crime rate climbed during the 1960s and the 1970s. It peaked in 1980 and then declined until 1984, when it again turned upward. In 1991, it again began to decline.

This drop in crime that began in 1991 has been heralded by the media. While the decline is good news, we should not be deceived. Crime remains so high that each year 3 of every 100 Americans are violently victimized and 18 of 100 have their property stolen (*Bureau of Justice Statistics* 2001:Table 1).

Although many societies have lower crime rates than ours, no society is without crime. As Durkheim (1897) pointed out, the very nature of crime makes it universal.

The Political/Power Dimension of Crime

Two Parts to This Social Problem:

1. Crime

2. The Criminal Justice System

How Extensive Is Crime?

Are There Societies Without Crime?

Each society passes laws against acts that it considers threatening to its well-being. The behavior already exists. Passing a law does not eliminate the behavior; it just makes it illegal. When there are laws (or rules), there will always be criminals (or rule breakers). Thus a society or nation can never be exempt from crime.

Subjective Concerns

As emphasized in previous chapters, an objective condition alone does not constitute a social problem. There must also be subjective concerns. People have to be upset about the condition—and Americans are very upset about crime. They fear for their personal safety and feel that their streets and cities are dangerous. Americans rank crime as the number one social problem facing the nation (*Sourcebook* 1998:Table 2.1).

THE CRIMINAL JUSTICE SYSTEM AS A SOCIAL PROBLEM

Example: Buddy, Gary, and Clyde

We cannot understand crime as a social problem without examining the system that deals with it. To see why, let's follow the case of Buddy Hudson, Gary Carson, and Clyde Johnson.

On a Saturday night, Buddy, a 19-year-old African American, teamed up with two whites, Gary, 34, and Clyde, 21, to rob a liquor store. The robbery netted them $1,590. A week later they tried their luck again, but this time it ran out. A witness called the police. The three fled, but the police had a description of the men, and they were arrested.

To ensure that the courts could not throw the case out for violation of procedure, the arresting officers read the men the 1966 Miranda warning:

1. You have the right to remain silent.
2. If you do not remain silent, what you say can be used against you.
3. You have the right to be represented by a lawyer during questioning and thereafter.
4. If you cannot afford an attorney, the state will provide one at its expense.

FIGURE 6-1

The U.S. Crime Rate

(*Source:* Based on the crimes of murder-manslaughter, forcible rape, robbery, aggravated assault, burglary, larceny-theft, and automobile theft as contained in various editions of the *FBI Uniform Crime Reports.*)

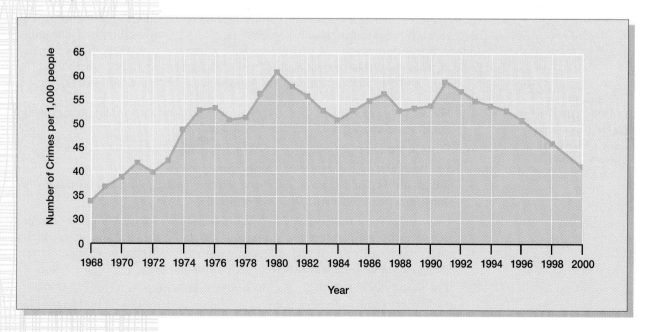

The state did provide an attorney. His advice was to say nothing—to let him talk to the prosecuting attorney, who determines what crimes suspects will be charged with. After meeting with the prosecuting attorney, he reported back that the evidence was solid, and they would be charged with armed robbery, resisting arrest, and assault with a deadly weapon. They could go to prison for up to 60 years. He added that he was able to "cut a deal." He could get the charges of assault and resisting arrest dropped in return for a guilty plea to armed robbery. The prosecuting attorney would agree to a 3-to-5 (a minimum of three years and a maximum of five years in state prison).

Buddy, Gary, and Clyde figured that if they held out their attorney could do better. Clyde's mother put up $5,000 to secure her son's release on bond, but, unable to raise bond money, Buddy and Gary remained in jail during the nine months it took for their case to come to trial (see the box on being poor and going to jail, on the next page.) Just before the trial, Clyde pled guilty. Both the prosecuting and defense attorneys appeared surprised when the judge suspended Clyde's sentence and placed him on probation for five years. Buddy and Gary were found guilty of armed robbery. (The other charges were thrown out for insufficient evidence.) The judge gave Gary a 6-to-10 and sentenced Buddy to a minimum of 15 years in prison.

> Social control is necessary if society is to survive. Without social control, we would have anarchy, and we all would be victims of the strongest and most ruthless; we would face constant extortion, injury, or death. The problem is how to make the state subject to the will of the people, to prevent it from being the agent that extorts, injures, and kills.

A reporter asked about the differences in the sentences. The judge replied, "I have to show consideration for the defendant who cops a plea. It saves the court the expense of a trial" (Gaylin 1974:188–189). He added that Clyde had a job and that to send him to prison would serve no purpose. Keeping him at his job, however, would maximize his chances of being rehabilitated. When asked if he gave the longer sentence to Buddy because he was black, the judge, who was white, denied any racial bias. "That," he said, "is insulting. Race has nothing to do with this case. These are the facts: Although Gary Carson is older, he has fewer 'priors' (previous arrests). He doesn't need as stiff a sentence to teach him a lesson. Buddy's 'priors' tell me he's more dangerous." The judge added, "For people like you, I wish Buddy were white and Gary black." The reporter nodded, thinking that at this point, Buddy might have the same wish.

This case shows why our criminal justice system can be "more criminal than just."

Is the Criminal Justice System More Criminal Than Just?

1. Many of the poor spend months (even years) behind bars awaiting trial, while those with money buy their release with bonds.

2. Defense attorneys encourage **plea bargaining,** pleading guilty (whether or not one is guilty) in return for a lesser charge.

3. Judges dislike "unnecessary trials" and impose harsher sentences on those who insist on a trial (Newman 1966; Gaylin 1974).

4. Factors that have nothing to do with an offense affect sentencing, such as age, employment, and the number of previous arrests. Even when the offense is the same, more lenient sentences are given to older defendants, those with higher-status jobs, and those with a better employment history.

5. The *number of adult arrests,* not the seriousness of previous charges, influences a sentence. Judges discount the type of charge because they know that in plea bargaining official charges often have little to do with the actual offense.

You Don't Have to Be Poor to Go to Jail—But It Helps

It isn't a crime to be poor, but it sure doesn't help when you're in trouble with the law. If you can't pay a fine, you go to jail.

"It's the only practical alternative," declares Woodrow Wilson, the judge in Bastrop, Louisiana. "Otherwise, some people would never be punished."

Every week people are ushered from Judge Wilson's courtroom to the city jail to pay their debts with days rather than dollars—or at least to wait until someone bails them out. Those with ready cash pay and leave.

This town isn't alone in how it handles indigent defendants. In rural areas especially, authorities routinely jail defendants unable to pay fines for nonviolent crimes such as public drunkenness, writing bad checks, and speeding. They do it even though it appears to violate U.S. Supreme Court rulings. Legal aid lawyers charge that the practice also damages the justice system, because defendants with money get a better shake than those without. Still, indigent defendants keep winding up in jail.

Legal aid attorneys can't patrol all the courts, and most abuses occur in small, outlying communities. Usually the attorneys try to help people already in jail; but even that can be too late. Roger Baruch, a prisoners-aid lawyer, recalls a man who spent six months in a Georgia jail because he couldn't pay traffic fines. By the time Mr. Baruch's group had filed the necessary papers, the man had been released.

Many judges and prosecutors claim not to know that such defendants are poor. "If they raised the issue, they wouldn't be put in jail," asserts an Aurora, Colorado, city attorney, "but I don't see that it's the responsibility of the court or the prosecutor to check out their ability to pay fines."

Officials in Monroe, Louisiana, about 20 miles south of Bastrop, hired a priest to evaluate defendants' finances. But he was let go because he sided with the poor too often.

Few believe that the problem ever will be solved. Mr. Baruch is one. He thinks that the practice is too deeply ingrained in Georgia's legal system.

"The so-called administration of justice is arbitrary and somewhat capricious," says Jackie Yeldell, a Bastrop attorney. "One thing is certain, though. You can be sure there aren't any wealthy persons in jail."

Based on Schmitt 1982.

The Recidivism Rate

If the criminal justice system seeks to rehabilitate people, its **recidivism rate**—the percentage of people released from prison who are rearrested—shows how inadequate it is. As Table 6-1 shows, within six years of their release about *half* end up back in prison (Zawitz 1998). If we include arrests and convictions beyond six years, the recidivism rate runs 85 to 90 percent (Blumstein and Cohen 1987). Despite repeated prison stays, about 50 percent of inmates answer yes when asked, "Do you think you could do the same crime again without getting caught?" (Zawitz 1998).

The crime rate of former prisoners is much higher than their recidivism rate. Few are apprehended when they commit their first crime after being released from prison. Most commit many crimes before being caught. Recall from Chapter 4, for example, that street addicts commit thousands of crimes in a single year (Inciardi and Pottieger 1994).

Prisons not only fail to rehabilitate; they may, it seems, have turned into crime schools. *The more often that someone has been put in prison, the greater that person's chances of going back to prison.* Why is our judicial system such a failure? Remember what was illustrated by the opening vignette: a penal system that produces contempt and hatred, not law-abiding behavior.

Table 6-1   Recidivism of American Prisoners

	Percentage of Young Parolees Who Within Six Years of Release from Prison Were		
	Rearrested	Reconvicted	Reincarcerated
All parolees	69%	53%	49%
Sex			
Men	70%	54%	50%
Women	52%	40%	36%
Race/Ethnicity			
White	64%	49%	45%
African American	76%	60%	56%
Latino	71%	50%	44%
Other	75%	65%	63%
Education			
Less than 12 years	71%	55%	51%
High school graduate	61%	46%	43%
Some college	48%	44%	31%
Crime Committed While on Parole			
Violent offenses	64%	43%	39%
Murder	70%	25%	22%
Robbery	64%	45%	40%
Assault	72%	51%	47%
Property offenses	73%	60%	56%
Burglary	73%	60%	56%
Forgery/fraud	74%	59%	56%
Larceny	71%	61%	55%
Drug crimes	49%	30%	25%

Source: Zawitz 1998a.

There is more to it than this, of course, and we will examine crime and criminal justice as aspects of the same social problem.

◆ Looking at the Problem Theoretically ◆

As we saw in Chapter 5, each of the three theoretical perspectives provides valuable insight into the problem of criminal violence. We will now use these perspectives to look at property crime and the criminal justice system. We will use symbolic interactionism to examine the social class bias of police enforcement and to learn why we must view crime statistics with caution. Then, through a functionalist perspective, we will see how crime is an adaptation to a society's core values. Finally, using conflict theory, we will examine why the law comes down hardest on the poor who have stolen little, while it often is lenient toward the wealthy who have stolen much.

The "Saints" and the "Roughnecks"

For two years, sociologist William Chambliss (1995) observed two groups of adolescent lawbreakers in "Hanibal High School." He called one group the "saints." These were "promising young men, children of good, stable, white, upper-middle-class families, active in school affairs, good precollege students." Despite their background, however, the saints were some of the most delinquent boys in the school, "constantly occupied with truancy, drinking, wild driving, petty theft, and vandalism." Yet their teachers and families considered the boys "saints headed for success." Not one saint was ever arrested.

Chambliss also observed a second group of boys, whom he called the "roughnecks." Of the same age and race as the saints, and from the same high school, these boys also were delinquent, although they committed somewhat fewer criminal acts than the saints. Their teachers saw them as "roughnecks headed for serious trouble," and the police often dealt with them.

How Social Class Worked: Applying Symbolic Interactionism
1. Expectations and Perceptions

Why did the community perceive these boys so differently? Chambliss found that this was due to *social class*. As symbolic interactionists emphasize, social class vitally affects our perception and behavior. The saints came from respectable, middle-class families, the roughnecks from less respectable, working-class families. These backgrounds led teachers and the authorities to expect good behavior from the saints but trouble from the roughnecks. And, like the rest of us, teachers and police saw what they expected to see.

2. Mobility and Visibility

The boys' social class also affected their *visibility*. The saints had automobiles, and they did their drinking and vandalism out of town. Without a car, the roughnecks hung around their own street corners, where their boisterous behavior drew the attention of police, confirming the idea that the community already had of them.

3. Interaction Styles

The boys' social class also equipped them with distinct *styles of interaction*. When police or teachers questioned the saints, they were apologetic. They showed respect for authority, a behavior that is perhaps the most important factor in winning authorities' favor (Westley 1953; Piliavin and Briar 1964). Showing respect elicited a positive reaction from teachers and police, allowing the boys to escape school and legal problems. The roughnecks, in contrast, were "almost the polar opposite." When questioned, they were hostile. Even when they put on a veneer of respect, everyone could see through it. Consequently, teachers came down hard on the roughnecks, and the police were quick to interrogate them and to arrest them rather than to warn them.

Differential Association and Subcultures

The saints and the roughnecks illustrate the differential association and subcultural theories introduced in Chapter 5. Unlike nondelinquent groups, both the saints and the roughnecks were immersed in vandalism and theft. Despite their similarities in delinquent behavior, however, the saints and the roughnecks were reared in subcultures that have different orientations to life. The saints learned that college was their birthright; the roughnecks did not. The saints wanted good grades; the roughnecks didn't care. The saints learned middle-class politeness, which showed in their choice of words, tone of voice, and body language; the roughnecks did not. The reactions by authorities to these subcultural differences deeply affected the boys' lives.

The Significance of Labeling

Chambliss' research illustrates what sociologists call *labeling*, a practice that can set people on different courses in life. The labels "saint" and "roughneck," for example, carry different expectations. They affect people's perceptions and channel behavior in different directions. All but one of the saints went to college. One became a doctor, one a lawyer, one earned a Ph.D., and the others went into management. Two of the roughnecks won athletic scholarships and went to college. They became coaches. One roughneck became a bookie. Two dropped out of high school, became involved in separate killings, and were sentenced to prison. No one knows the whereabouts of the other. Although such distinctive events in life have many "causes," the boys lived up to the labels the community gave them.

Another Example of the Power of Symbols

Sociologists Irving Piliavin and Scott Briar (1964) also found how interaction affects outcomes with the police. Doing participant observation of the police at work, they observed these two cases:

> An 18-year-old white male was accused of statutory rape. The girl's father was prominent in local politics, and he insisted that the police take severe action. During questioning, the youth was polite and cooperative. He addressed the officers as "sir" and answered all questions. He also said that he wanted to marry the girl. The sergeant became sympathetic and decided to try to get the charges against the youth reduced or dropped.

> A 17-year-old white male was caught having sexual relations with a 15-year-old girl. When he was questioned, he answered with obvious disregard. The officers became irritated and angry. One officer accused the boy of being a "stud," interested only in sex, eating, and sleeping. He added that the young man "probably had knocked up half a dozen girls." The boy just gave back an impassive stare. The officers made out an arrest report and took him to juvenile hall.

Both young men had solid evidence against them, and the police faced political pressure to prosecute the 18-year-old. His politeness and cooperation, however, changed the officer's perception. His deference—his respect and regard for police authority—sent a powerful message that put the police on his side. The 17-year-old's demeanor sent a negative message and elicited a negative reaction from the police.

Police Discretion

Symbolic interactionists emphasize how the police operate within a symbolic system as they administer the law. Their ideas of "typical" people—for example, of who is "safe" and who is "dangerous"—come alive during their work. The more a suspect matches their idea of a "typical" criminal, the more likely they are to arrest that person. **Police discretion,** deciding whether to arrest someone or to ignore a particular offense, is routine in police work.

Official Statistics Must Be Viewed with Caution

These examples show why sociologists approach official crime statistics with caution. As noted in Chapter 2, the "facts" of a social problem are not objective: A social "fact" is produced within a specific social context for a particular purpose. According to official statistics, working-class boys are much more delinquent than middle-class boys. Yet, as we have just seen, social class influences the reactions of the police, directly affecting *who gets arrested for what*. Similarly, as with Buddy, Gary, and Clyde, many factors affect how judges hand out sentences. Official statistics do not simply represent the "facts" of a society; they are biased social products.

FUNCTIONALISM

Crime Is Natural and May Represent the Core Values of Society

Functionalists consider crime a natural part of society, not an aberration. They also view many crimes as a reaction to the core values of a society. Let's see how *conformity* to cultural values can generate crime. Specifically, why did sociologist Albert Cohen (1955) say that conformity to the "American way" creates crime?

To see why, let's look at what sociologists Richard Cloward and Lloyd Ohlin (1960) identified as the crucial problem of the industrial societies: locating and training the most talented persons of every generation—whether born wealthy or poor—

to fill the technical positions of society. These positions require ability and diligence. At birth, however, we cannot tell who has these traits. Therefore, society tries to motivate *everyone* to strive for success. Intense competition allows only the talented to emerge as victors. "Regardless of race, creed, or social class, success can be yours" becomes the motto—a cry that arouses discontent and motivates people to compete intensely. Thus, by making success a universal goal—one that is not limited to the privileged, as in more highly stratified societies—industrial and postindustrial societies ensure their survival.

**Merton: Five
Adaptations
to Social Goals**

In doing so, however, they produce a lot of strain among their citizens. Although almost everyone learns the goal of material success, the approved means to reach that goal are limited. Only so many high-paying positions exist, for example. To illustrate the ways that people react to this strain, sociologist Robert Merton developed the model that is illustrated in Table 6-2. (The *conformists* don't experience strain. They have access to approved ways to strive after success. People who experience strain make the other four adaptations.) The *ritualists* give up on the goal but still keep active in culturally approved ways. An example is workers who no longer hope to get ahead, but who fulfill just enough requirements of the job to not get fired. The *retreatists* reject both the goal and the means; they may retreat into drugs, or perhaps into a monastery or convent. *Rebels* are convinced that society is corrupt and reject both the legitimate means and the goals. They also seek to destroy the social order and usher in a new one.

Innovation is the adaptation that interests us. This is where crime comes in. Finding the legitimate means to the cultural goal of success blocked, and yet wanting that goal, innovators turn to *illegitimate* means. Buddy, Gary, and Clyde are examples. Thus, a high proportion of crime is a response to accepting the cultural goal, or, as Cohen said, "conformity to the American way."

**An Explanation
for the Property
Crimes of the Poor:**

Why do the poor commit so much property crime: burglary, theft, and robbery? Functionalists stress how the poor are bombarded with messages that urge them to want material success. Television portrays vivid images of middle-class lives,

Table 6-2	**Merton's Typology of Individual Adaptation to Anomie**

Modes of Adaptation	Culture Goals	Institutionalized Means
0. Conformity	+*	+
1. Innovation	+	-
2. Ritualism	-	+
3. Retreatism	-	-
4. Rebellion	±	±

A + indicates acceptance, a - rejection, and a ± rejection of prevailing values and substitution of new values.
Source: Merton 1968: 194.

1. Closed Access

suggesting that full-fledged Americans can afford the goods and services portrayed in commercials and programs (Silberman 1978). Education is one of the main approved ways of reaching the goal of success, but the middle class runs the school system. There, the children of the poor are ill prepared for the bewildering world they confront, which conflicts so sharply with their background. Their grammar and swear words, their ideas of punctuality and neatness, their lack of paper-and-pencil skills—all differ from those of middle-class students. In addition, the schools that most poor children attend are inferior to the schools that educate children from higher social classes (Yeakey and Bennett 1990; Kozol 1999). These barriers create higher dropout rates among working-class students, blocking them from many legitimate avenues of financial success.

2. Open Access

Often, however, a different door opens to them, one that sociologists Richard Cloward and Lloyd Ohlin (1960) call **illegitimate opportunity structures.** These are opportunities woven into the texture of life in urban slums: robbery, burglary, selling drugs, prostitution, pimping, gambling, and other income-producing crimes or "hustles." The "hustler" or "player" becomes a model for others—glamorously successful, one of the few people around whose material success approximates the mainstream cultural stereotype. Some of the poor find such illegal income-producing crimes to be functional—and the poor are drawn into them in disproportionate numbers.

And Crime in Other Classes

Functionalists know that the middle and upper classes are not free of crime, of course. They point out that a different illegitimate opportunity structure opens to them, one that makes *different forms* of crime functional. For example, instead of engaging in pimping and burglary, members of the middle and upper classes turn to white-collar crime—tax evasion, bribery of public officials, securities violations, advertising fraud, and price fixing.

In Sum

In sum, conclude functionalists, a high crime rate is *inherent* in societies that socialize people of all social classes to desire material success, while limiting the legitimate means to success. Although society expands people's desires by holding out limitless opportunities, many poor people find the legitimate avenues to success blocked. Many of them turn to illegitimate means.

But Why Doesn't Everyone Become a Criminal?

If many do, you might note, this also means that many do not. Why not? With the success motif so prevalent in society, and with the legitimate means to success limited, why doesn't everyone who finds his or her way blocked become a criminal?

In a humorous fashion, this cartoon indicates an essential principle highlighted by functionalist theorists—that crime is functional for individuals and society. (By permission of Johnny Hart & Creators Syndicate, Inc.)

To answer this, sociologists have developed control theory, focusing on controls that inhibit crime. *Inner* controls are what most of us mean by self-control. They include internalized morality, such as our ideas of right and wrong and our religious principles. They also include fears of punishment, feelings of integrity, the desire to be a "good" person, and the ability to defer gratification (Hirschi 1969; Rogers 1977; Heckathorn 1990; Oyserman and Markus 1990; Brownfield and Sorenson 1993). *Outer* controls include authorities such as the police, courts, and teachers, the potential damage to one's social standing and reputation, and the reactions of one's family.

The combination of inner and outer controls keeps most of us in line most of the time. Most of us use approved means to try to fulfill our culturally engendered desire for success. We will return to control theory in the section on juvenile delinquency.

CONFLICT THEORY

According to the Federal Trade Commission (FTC), Chrysler Corporation misled car buyers and auto parts makers about which replacement oil filters to install in its 1971–1980 Japanese-made cars. The result was damaged engines that cost customers $500 or more to repair. The FTC did not require Chrysler to pay for the damage, only to notify car owners and auto parts makers of the need to use different oil filters.

In the 1980s, Chrysler let its executives drive cars with disconnected odometers, then sold them as new. Chrysler was ordered to give a $16 million rebate to customers. No one went to jail for fraud. (Bryant 1990)

Have you ever wondered about such cases? Top-level executives defraud the public of millions of dollars but receive nothing more than a fine, while a young man who steals a $5,000 automobile is sentenced to prison.

How can a legal system that is supposed to provide "law, liberty, and justice for all" be so inconsistent? Conflict theorists, who ask such questions about crime and criminal justice, stress that every society is marked by power and inequality. The most fundamental division of industrial society, they say, is between those who control the means of production and those who do not. Most people must sell their labor; a few can buy it. Those who buy labor are *the ruling class* and those who sell their labor *the working class*. The working class has three major divisions: the upper-level managers and professionals, the stable working class (mostly white-collar and blue-collar workers), and the unstable or marginal working class (those with shaky jobs, whose labor is in low demand). This last group includes most of the unemployed and people on welfare (Carter and Clelland 1979).

Members of the working class compete for a limited number of jobs. Positions in management and the professions are reserved for those who show high loyalty to the ruling class. In return, these workers get fairly secure, comfortable positions. The rewards for the stable working class are fewer, but they are adequate for survival. The marginal working class (also called the "reserve army" of the unemployed), however, receives little. Most burglars, muggers, armed robbers, and car thieves come from the marginal working class. In their desperate struggle for survival, they commit crimes against persons and property that threaten the social order, and they are punished severely.

Conflict theorists emphasize that the law is not an impartial social institution that administers a code shared by all. Rather, the law is controlled by the ruling class, which uses it to oppress the marginal working class and maintain their own privileges of power (Spitzer 1975; Jacobs 1978; Beirne and Quinney 1982). Because of this, the criminal justice system does not focus on the owners of corporations and the harm they do to the public through pollution, price manipulation, or unsafe products (Coleman 1989). Instead, the police and courts monitor the working class. Its violators are arrested, tried, and imprisoned, for they hold the potential of upsetting the social order.

Why Slaps on the Wrists for Crimes of the Powerful?

Violations by owners—the ruling class that controls the social order—cannot be totally ignored, however, for if their violations become too oppressive, they might provoke revolution. To prevent this, an occasional flagrant violation by the powerful is prosecuted. This stabilizes society by demonstrating that the system applies to all. It was to be expected, then, that Chrysler would be assigned only small penalties, and it was not surprising that its executives were not sentenced to jail or even fined. The ruling class comes down hard on the property crimes of the working class but ensures that lesser penalties are applied to its own versions of property crime.

The Chrysler case also illustrates how the powerful usually bypass the criminal justice system entirely. Instead of coming to court, they go before a state or federal agency (such as the Federal Trade Commission) that has no power to imprison. The FTC, run by equally privileged people, levies token fines. Most cases of illegal sales of stocks and bonds, price fixing, illegal restraint of trade, and so on are handled by "gentlemen overseeing gentlemen." In contrast, the property crimes of the working-class are channeled into a court system that does imprison. Burglary, armed robbery, petty theft, and stealing automobiles not only threaten the sanctity of private property but, ultimately, the positions of the powerful.

In Sum

Conflict theorists stress this unique perspective for viewing the criminal justice system: The powerful use the legal system to mask injustice, control workers, and stabilize the social system. Law enforcement is not a system of justice, but a cultural device used by the powerful to carry out their policies.

◆ Research Findings ◆

To understand crime as a social problem, we'll first examine five types of crime: juvenile delinquency, white-collar crime, professional crime, organized crime, and political crime. Then we'll look at the criminal justice system.

JUVENILE DELINQUENCY

The Origin of Juvenile Delinquency

When society industrialized in the 1800s, children worked full-time in factories and mines. Some operated machines 14 hours a day under miserable conditions for low pay. A few were even chained to their beds at night to ensure that they would be available for work in the morning, and then chained to their machines during the day to keep them from running away. Juveniles who broke the law were treated the same as adults. Earlier, in the 1700s, girls as young as 13 were burned to death for their crimes and 8- and 10-year-old boys hanged for theirs (Blackstone 1899). In the 1800s, society softened a bit, but age afforded neither an excuse for lawbreaking nor a protection from harsh penalties.

International trade unions, founded in the 1800s, ushered in labor laws designed to protect children (Phelps 1939; Kuczynski 1946). Formal schooling also came to be seen as necessary for children. The child labor laws and the new attitude toward schooling led to an important perceptual shift: Teenagers came to be seen as a separate class of people, not as oldish children or youngish adults. One consequence was new laws that classified juveniles as a separate category in the criminal justice system (Platt 1969). This change in the law produced a new category of crime—**juvenile delinquency.** The first juvenile court in the United States was established in Illinois in 1899, which means that juvenile delinquency has been around for about 100 years.

Extent of Juvenile Involvement in Crime

Some delinquency consists of **status crimes,** activities that are crimes if juveniles commit them, but not if adults do, such as curfew violations, underage drinking, and running away from home. These are not the primary social problem, for people are less concerned about them. It is the predatory crimes of violence that have most upset people and have captured headlines.

Although 13- to 17-year-old boys make up only 3.7 percent of the U.S. population, they commit about 17 percent of the nation's **crimes against the person**—murder, forcible rape, robbery, and aggravated assault. This is about *five times* the number of violent crimes as would be proportionate to their segment of the population. This group also commits about a third of the nation's **property crimes**—burglary, larceny, motor vehicle theft, and arson (*FBI Uniform Crime Reports* 2000:Table 38; *Statistical Abstract* 1998:Table 16). This is about *eight times* the number of property crimes that would be proportionate to their segment of the population.

Girls commit far fewer crimes than boys, but they are closing the gap, which also alarms people. As Table 6-3 shows, *fewer* boys are arrested for property crimes now than 20 years ago, but 8 percent more girls are arrested. For violent crimes, more boys *and* girls are arrested now; the girls rate of increase of arrests, however, is three times as high as that of boys. The change is startling: A generation ago, the primary offenses of girls were the status crimes of underage sex and running away from home. Today many are involved in gang violence, drugs, burglaries, armed robberies, and aggravated assaults.

The Delinquent Career

Sociologist Howard Snyder (1988) studied the court records of 69,000 juvenile delinquents in Phoenix, Arizona. He discovered these patterns in the "delinquent career":

Table 6-3 Arrests of Persons Under 18

	Number of Arrests				Percentage of Arrests		
	1981	1996	2000	Percent Change	1981	1996	2000
Property Crimes*							
Boys	398,924	387,295	241,820	−39%	81%	73%	70%
Girls	95,010	143,236	103,911	+8%	19%	27%	30%
					100%	100%	100%
Violent Crimes**							
Boys	47,415	86,721	53,813	+12%	89%	85%	82%
Girls	5,825	15,510	12,067	+52%	11%	15%	18%
					100%	100%	100%

*Property crimes are burglary, larceny-theft, motor vehicle theft, and arson.
**Violent crimes are murder, forcible rape, robbery, and aggravated assault

Source: Sourcebook 1993:Table 35; *FBI Uniform Crime Reports* 1992:Table 33; 1997:Table 40; 2000:Table 39 & 40.

1. After their first arrest, most youths (59 percent) never return to juvenile court.

2. The juveniles most likely to continue their delinquent behavior are those who are arrested a second time before age 16.

3. Juveniles who are charged with a violent crime (murder, rape, robbery, or aggravated assault) are likely to have committed many crimes.

4. The younger juveniles are when they are first charged with a violent crime, the greater the likelihood that they will be charged later with a violent crime. (Those first charged at age 13 are *twice* as likely to be arrested for a later violent offense than those first charged at age 16.)

5. The juveniles *most* likely to be rearrested are those originally charged with burglary, truancy, motor vehicle theft, or robbery (see Figure 6-2).

6. The juveniles *least* likely to be rearrested are those originally charged with underage drinking, running away, or shoplifting.

7. Girls are much less likely to be rearrested than boys (29 percent versus 46 percent).

The Significance of Graduating from High School

You may have heard the parents of a boy who has gotten in trouble with the law say, "If only we can keep him in school, he'll have a chance. If he drops out, he's lost." This common observation is supported by sociological research. A team of sociologists headed by Lawrence Rosen (Rosen et al. 1991) compared delinquents who completed high school with delinquents who dropped out. When they were

FIGURE 6-2

Based on Their First Crime, the Percentage of Youths Who Are Rearrested and Returned to Juvenile Court

(*Source: Juvenile Justice Bulletin*, August 1988.)

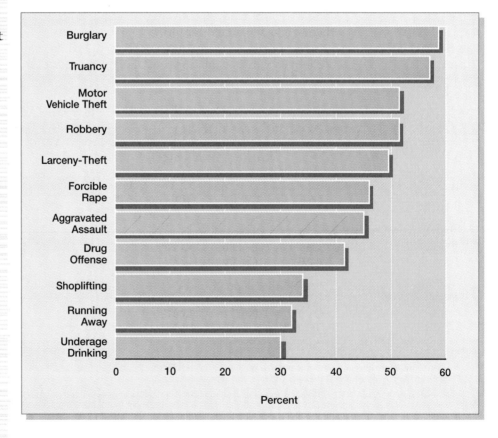

Chapter 6 Crime and Criminal Justice

Table 6-4	High School Graduation, Delinquency, and Adult Arrests		
	Percentage Arrested as Adults		
	African American	**White**	
Delinquent in high school			
Dropped out	47%	33%	
Completed high school	24%	18%	
Not delinquent in high school			
Dropped out	30%	22%	
Completed high school	16%	6%	

Note: Based on a longitudinal study of male Philadelphia high school students; no data for girls.

Source: Rosen et al. 1991:Tables 2, 5.

adults, the delinquents who completed high school were about *half* as likely to be arrested as those who dropped out. Other researchers compared delinquents who graduated with dropouts who were not delinquent. As you can see from Table 6-4, if delinquents graduate from high school, they are *less* likely to be arrested as adults than dropouts who were not delinquent.

Five Techniques of Neutralization

Juvenile delinquents know that their crimes are condemned by society, yet they don't go around moaning, burdened by guilt. How do they avoid blaming themselves? In a classic study, symbolic interactionists Gresham Sykes and David Matza (1957) uncovered five **techniques of neutralization** that delinquents use:

1. *Denial of responsibility.* Delinquents see themselves as propelled by social forces out of their control. They break laws because of unloving parents, bad companions, or their bad neighborhood. By denying responsibility, they break the

Sociologists have studied urban gangs since the 1920s. They have found that some of these gangs function as substitute families. They provide security and identity, and are always disproportionately made up of the poor. Shown here are the police searching members of the "Crazy Street" gang of Los Angeles.

link between themselves and their acts. ("I'm just a billiard ball on the pool table of life.")

2. *Denial of injury.* Delinquents admit their acts are illegal, but they deny they hurt anyone. They call their vandalism "mischief" or "pranks." This breaks the link between themselves and the consequences of their acts.

3. *Denial of a victim.* If delinquents admit they have done harm, they claim that the injury was not wrong "under the circumstances." The person they hurt was not a victim. What they did was "rightful retaliation." Vandalizing a school, for example, was revenge on unfair teachers; theft was a retaliation against dishonest storekeepers. With no victims, they transform themselves from wrongdoers into avengers.

4. *Condemnation of the condemners.* Delinquents also take the offensive, calling those who condemn them hypocrites and accusing the police of corruption and brutality. By attacking others, they deflect attention from their own behavior.

5. *Appeal to higher loyalties.* Some delinquents see themselves as torn between two incompatible expectations. The law pulls them one way, loyalty to friends another. The friends win out. If a rival gang hurts a friend, for example, retaliation is "more moral" than ignoring the injury.

These techniques allow delinquents to neutralize society's norms. Even if they internalized mainstream values—and not all have—these rationalizations let them commit crimes with a minimum of guilt or shame.

Some delinquents have little to neutralize. They grow up in **delinquent subcultures,** where people are oriented toward criminal activities. In these subcultures, they learn norms that support crime, as well as techniques for committing them. In some of these subcultures, youths even learn to rape, kill, and terrorize. For an example of such a subculture, see the box on the next page. As this box illustrates, some youths confront an illegitimate opportunity structure that offers a law-violating approach to the problems of life. Yet only some become delinquent. Why?

For answers, let's first consider social control and then labeling theory. According to social control theory, three factors are involved: inner controls, outer controls, and the desire to commit a crime. Because both those who do and do not become delinquent grow up in the same neighborhood, the outer controls look similar. But as sociologist Joan Moore (1978) found in her classic study of three Chicano barrios (neighborhoods) in Los Angeles, there are major differences, and they affect the youths' inner controls and their desire to commit criminal acts.

Moore used a variety of research techniques. She did participant observation of everyday barrio life, interviewed residents, and also hung out with former convicts. She found that the difference begins in the family. Despite their outward similarities, families in poor neighborhoods, like families everywhere, differ in their values and approaches to life. Some are more oriented toward work and education. Teaching these values increases their children's inner controls and reduces their desire to commit crimes. These children strive to do better in school, and as teachers reward their efforts, they receive further incentive to conform. Other children come from families where these values are minimal, and for them the criminally oriented peer group becomes more attractive. Because they are not oriented to work roles, for them gangs and crime are enticing.

Researchers have also found differences in outer controls. To make these stand out, let's look at the extremes among families. Everyone knows that some families

The Delinquent Subculture

Why Do Only Some Youths from the Same Background Become Delinquent?

Social Control Theory

Inner Controls: Differences in Families

Outer Controls: Differences in Families

THINKING CRITICALLY ABOUT SOCIAL PROBLEMS

Lords of the Slums

The Black Gangster Disciples rule this part of Chicago. Their insignia, a six-pointed star, marks the buildings. They prey on the single women who occupy more than 70 percent of the units in the Robert Taylor Homes and the Stateway Gardens. They store their drugs and guns in their apartments and turn them into prisoners. Calling the police is not an option here.

Always tenuous, the balance of power has shifted. As the police drive by in unmarked cars, the warning whistles of young boys precede them. Other boys wait for the police to pass, then resume selling their drugs.

To be a good drug dealer you have to be hard. One resident tells how the leader of the Black Disciples came to her door looking for her son, who owed $300 for drugs. A Disciple member put a gun to her son's head. She paid.

He meant business. He killed a 66-year-old man for only $17.

One father told his 15-year-old son to leave the gang. The Disciples broke the man's arm.

At Rockwell Gardens, members of another gang, the Vice Lords, beat a 32-year-old man to death in full view of the tenants. When the police arrived, the leader of the Vice Lords sat on a kitchen chair in the basketball court, his soldiers at his side. His boys followed the police from door to door, staring at each tenant who dared to answer the knock.

Confident in their power, some gangs engage in public relations. One gang lieutenant hands out dollar bills to children. Another has distributed more than a thousand pairs of sneakers. And some of the city's top drug dealers and gang leaders sponsor an annual "Players Picnic." They hire a band, give away hot dogs and ribs, and distribute flyers.

The management and staff of the housing projects deny any knowledge of the Disciples. And not everyone thinks things are so bad. The Disciples guard their buildings at night, and some residents say the buildings are safer now than when the police controlled them.

What principles discussed in this text could change this situation?

Based on Kotlowitz 1988.

are rotten (in sociological jargon, dysfunctional). Some parents abuse their kids, and the children run away. "On the run" they get in trouble, much more so than youths who come from families with loving parents and who remain home. To survive, many steal or sell their bodies. This common knowledge is supported by sociological research. Bill McCarthy and John Hagan (1992), for example, compared homeless adolescents in Toronto with youths who were still at home. They found more neglect and physical and sexual abuse by the parents of the homeless youths, and greater delinquency among those on the streets.

Labeling Theory: Consequence for Life

Labeling theorists stress the significance of being labeled a delinquent. This can be a matter of sheer luck. I know a teenager who did the same things that his buddies did, but he happened to go home early one night, so while everyone else "got busted" and became labeled a "delinquent," he did not. Also recall Chambliss' study of the "saints" and the "roughnecks," which illustrates how labels affect lower- and middle-class adolescents differently. Being labeled a troublemaker can set a youth apart and cause him to continue on the path to more trouble. In some instances, labels create a cloud of suspicion that cuts an adolescent off from conforming people and activities, thus pushing the individual to commit more violations.

In Sum

Social control theory shows why only some youths become involved in criminal acts. It sensitizes us to differences in the family and in the school, and to the significance of peer groups. Labeling theory helps explain why some adolescents graduate from delinquency into adult crime. Social control and labeling theory also, of course, apply to crimes committed by adults.

WHITE-COLLAR CRIME

Sociologist Edwin Sutherland (1949) coined the term **white-collar crime** for crimes "committed by a person of respectable and high social status in the course of his [or her] occupation." The two major types of white-collar crime are those committed by employees *on behalf of* a corporation and those committed *against* a corporation.

In crimes committed *on behalf of* a corporation, employees break the law in order to benefit a business organization. Examples include car manufacturers knowingly selling dangerous automobiles; drug companies faking test data so they can keep their drugs on the market; and corporations engaging in price fixing and tax dodging.

White-collar crime costs between $200 billion and $400 billion a year (Wells 1998), more than the cost of all street crime. Most white-collar crime never comes to the surface, but that which does is enlightening. In just one case, Exxon Corporation was found guilty of overcharging $895 million for oil; with interest, Exxon's fine came to more than $2 billion (Wermiel 1986b). Bank robbers may risk their lives for $10,000; executives manipulate computers and documents to make millions of illegal dollars for their corporations.

It is not uncommon for corporations listed on the major stock exchanges to produce a "criminogenic (crime-causing) culture." The corporate culture revolves around corporate profits and around personal success and recognition. Pressures to increase profits and climb the corporate ladder, combined with the way executives are insulated from the consequences of their decisions, often lead to an "ethical numbness" or insensitivity (Hills 1987).

The corporate culture so dominates its members that it can even influence decent people to calculate the cold-blooded deaths of others for profit. This is illustrated by the infamous "Pinto case." The Pinto was a car manufactured by Ford in the 1970s. After three young women in Indiana were burned to death when their Pinto burst into flames following a rear-end crash, the Ford Motor Company was charged with reckless homicide (Strobel 1980; Fisse and Braithwaite 1987). No executives were charged, just Ford itself. It was alleged that Ford knew that the Pinto's gas tank could rupture in a rear-end collision, spew gas, and burn passengers to death (Dowie 1977, 1979).

Disclosed at the trial was heart-wrenching evidence that supported this allegation and revealed the cold-blooded malice of Ford's executives. Installing a simple piece of plastic would have corrected the problem, at a cost of just $11 per car. The Ford executives faced a difficult decision—whether to pay the $11 or sentence drivers and passengers to a horrifying death. The following memo shows their cost-benefit analysis—a comparison of what it would cost the company to make the change ("Costs") or to pay for the deaths ("Benefits," meaning the amount of benefits that would have to be paid). As you can see, the cost of installing the plastic was high ($137 million) compared to the amount of money that would have to be paid if they simply allowed people to die ($49.5 million). Their estimates turned out to be too low: Several hundred people burned to death, and many others were disfigured.

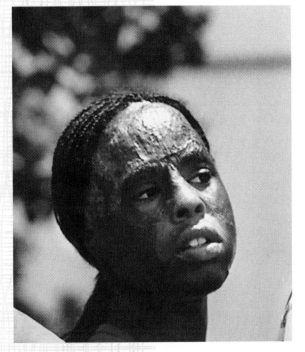

Sociologists compute the costs of white-collar crime in dollar terms, but their analyses generally make it sound as though white-collar crime were a harmless nuisance. Perhaps most is. But some white-collar crime has horrible costs. Shown here is Alisha Parker, who, with three siblings, was burned when the gas tank of her 1979 Chevrolet Malibu exploded after a rear-end collision. Outraged at the callousness of GM's conduct, the jury awarded these victims the staggering sum of $4.9 billion.

2. Crimes Committed Against a Corporation

The Example of Embezzlement: Cressey's Model

Ford's Internal Memo on the Pinto, "Benefits and Costs Relating to Fuel Leakage Associated with the Static Rollover Test Portion of FMVSS 208"

BENEFITS.

Savings: 180 burn deaths, 180 serious burn injuries, 2,100 burned vehicles.

Unit cost: $200,000 per death, $67,000 per injury, $700 per vehicle.

Total benefit: $180 \times (\$200,000) + 180 \times (\$67,000) + 2,100 \times (\$700) = \$49.5$ million.

COSTS.

Sales: 11 million cars, 1.5 million light trucks.

Unit cost: $11 per car, $11 per truck.

Total cost: $11,000,000 \times (\$11) + 1,500,000 \times (\$11) = \$137$ million.

Sources: Dowie 1977; Strobel 1980:286.

Ford was acquitted. The company recalled its 1971–1976 Pintos for fuel tank modification and launched a publicity campaign. Ford executives claimed that the internal memo was misunderstood; it "related to a proposed federal safety standard, and not to the design of the Pinto" (Fisse and Braithwaite 1987:253). Despite causing hundreds of deaths, Ford executives were never arrested or tried in court. They remained free, wealthy, and respected in their communities.

In 1998, a 13-year-old boy was burned to death when the gas tank of an Oldsmobile Cutlass station wagon ruptured. When GM was sued, a memo was discovered in which GM calculated the cost to fix the problem at $4.50 per vehicle but the cost of lawsuits at $2.40 per car. GM did not fix the problem (Boot 1998). The Pinto and Cutlass cases confirm the perspective of the conflict theorists. (For another example, see the photo on this page.) The powerful can manipulate our legal system and escape punishment for their crimes, including serial murder. It is inconceivable to imagine similar judicial results if poor persons plotted to kill automobile executives.

The main crime *against* the corporation is employee theft, ranging from snitching company supplies to embezzling company funds. It also includes sabotage by disgruntled employees. To avoid tarnishing their public images with the disgrace of internal crime, most corporations deal privately with these offenses.

Stealing company secrets, such as formulas, manufacturing processes, or even marketing plans—and selling them to a competitor is a form of theft. A gray area emerges when one company hires a key employee of a competitor, who steals nothing but brings with him such vital knowledge. The employee is hired specifically because of this knowledge, and commands a higher salary and often bonuses because of it. Because the knowledge is inside the individual's head, and no documents are stolen, this crime is very difficult to prove.

Sociologist Donald Cressey, who produced a classic study of embezzlers, found (1953) that employees embezzle because they have an "unsharable financial problem"—overdue taxes, children's college costs, sometimes gambling losses. He also found that, like juvenile delinquents, they rationalize their crime. A common neutralization technique is to equate embezzling with borrowing. Many view their theft as an unauthorized loan intended to tide them over in their financial emergency. Some think of themselves as having been cheated by their employers or taken advantage of. Such techniques let people violate the trust that their company placed in them and still consider themselves to be respectable, law-abiding citizens.

Exceptions to Cressey's Model

Cressey's findings are limited. Later research shows that not all embezzlers neutralize their crimes (Green 1993). Some just do it, without justifications (Benson 1985). Embezzlers also have many motivations, not just an unsharable financial problem. Some are impulsive, others greedy (Nettler 1974). Some embezzle just to help with ordinary family bills. Motivations can even change over the course of a long-term embezzlement. I knew an embezzler who headed a remote branch of a Spanish bank. After he embezzled a few thousand dollars for personal reasons, he saw it was so easy that he kept doing it even after he didn't need the money. When caught, his theft had amounted to millions.

Example: The Case of the Disappearing Billions

The most notorious crime against the corporation was the plundering of the U.S. savings and loan industry in the 1980s. Corporate officers, who had the trust of their depositors, systematically looted their banks of billions of dollars. The total cost ran about $500 billion—$2,000 for every man, woman, and child in the country (Kettl 1991; Newdorf 1991). Perhaps the most infamous culprit was Neil Bush, son of the president of the United States and an officer of Silverado, a Colorado savings and loan. Bush helped bankrupt Silverado by approving $100 million in loans to a company in which he held secret interests (Tolchin 1991a).

Future generations will suffer from this looting. The interest alone is exorbitant. At 5 percent, a year's interest on an increase of $500 billion in the national debt would run $25 billion, at 10 percent, $50 billion. Since the government does not pay its debt but merely borrows more to keep up with the compounding interest, the $500 billion will double in a few years. As the late Senator Everett Dirkson once said, "A billion here and a billion there, and pretty soon you're talking about real money."

Changes in White-Collar Crime

As more women have joined the corporate world, they, too, have been enticed by its opportunities for crime. As Table 6-5 shows, women's increase in white-collar crime parallels the rise in crime by female juveniles that we noted earlier. The largest increase is in embezzlement, where women are now as likely as men to be the perpetrators.

A second change is theft by computer. Employees insert fictitious information into their company's computer program and steal company funds. They may instruct the computer to issue checks made out to accomplices, for example.

Social Class Bias and White-Collar Crime

White-collar crime has a privileged position within the criminal justice system. Because of their social position and ability to manipulate the law, few corporate criminals are punished. (They can even get away with murder, as we saw with the Ford executives in the Pinto case.) When arrested, which is seldom, white-collar criminals usually receive lenient sentences. Federal records (Carlson and Chaiken 1987) show that compared with street criminals they are

1. More likely to have their cases dismissed by the prosecutor (40 percent versus 26 percent)
2. Less likely to have to put up bail (13 percent versus 37 percent)
3. More likely to get probation rather than jail (54 percent versus 40 percent)
4. More likely to get shorter sentences (29 months versus 50 months)

Table 6-5 Arrests for White-Collar Crimes, by Sex

	1981		2000	
	Male	**Female**	**Male**	**Female**
Embezzlement	70%	30%	50%	50%
Fraud	58%	42%	55%	45%
Forgery and counterfeiting	68%	32%	61%	39%
Fencing stolen property	88%	12%	83%	17%
Totals	71%	29%	62%	38%

Source: FBI Uniform Crime Reports 2000:Table 42.

It seems fair to conclude that this is another example of the social class bias that operates in the criminal justice system. This bias also operates *among* white-collar criminals. Even though they have committed the same crime, those at the top of the hierarchy generally are charged with lesser crimes and given shorter sentences (Coleman 1989).

How rarely executives are convicted for their crimes and, if convicted, how unusual it is for them to serve even one day in prison is revealed by a study of the 582 largest U.S. corporations. Sociologist Marshall Clinard (1990; Clinard et al. 1979) found that criminal charges had been filed against 1,553 executives. Only 56 were convicted, giving them a better than 96 percent chance of avoiding conviction if arrested. Of this small number, 40 served no time in prison, and the 16 who did served a total of 597 days. Their average stay of 37 days was about what the poor serve for disorderly conduct. Similarly, Neil Bush, the president's son who looted people's savings, had to pay a $50,000 fine—after friends of the president paid his legal fees (Tolchin 1991b; "Suit Settled" 1992). As sociologist Daniel Glaser (1978) observed, in a classic understatement, the criminal law has difficulty dealing with white-collar crime.

PROFESSIONAL CRIME

Crime as Work

Professional criminals make their livelihood from crime. They include not only the highly romanticized jewel thieves, safecrackers, and counterfeiters but also professional shoplifters, pickpockets, and fences—those who buy stolen goods for resale. Their activities, although illegal, are a form of work, and they pride themselves on their skills and successes.

The Criminal Subculture

In a classic study, Edwin Sutherland (1937) found that professional criminals organize their lives around their "work," much as people who work at legal jobs do. Professional thieves plan their work and may steal most every day of the year. They share values that emphasize loyalty, mutual aid, and scorn for the "straight world." They also associate with one another and try to avoid noncriminals ("Square Johns"). They teach one another technical skills for committing crimes and avoiding detection.

Some of the criminal activities Sutherland studied have declined. As people switched from cash to credit cards, pickpocketing faded, as did safecracking. As some forms of professional crime dwindle, however, others, such as computer fraud, increase. Thieves can now use computers at one location to hack into computers that may be thousands of miles away. As you can see from the box on page 189, crime is keeping up with changing technology.

"Chop Shop"

Maintaining Solidarity

Self-Definitions

Independent Professional Crime vs. Organized Crime

Although its forms change, professional crime continues to be characterized by in-group loyalty, scorn for the values of the straight world, and pride in specialized skills. One of my students found these traits to be evident among the car thieves he studied for my undergraduate course in deviance. Based on the demand for parts, the owner of the "chop shop" ordered specific cars, paying set prices according to the make and model he wanted. He and his workers used acetylene torches and other tools to disassemble the cars. They sold the fenders, motors, transmissions, seats, doors, and so on at standard rates to dealers in used auto parts. The small amount of metal that was left over was hauled away by an older man who sold it for scrap. Like small business owners across the country, the owner-manager of the chop shop carried a great deal of responsibility. He made the decisions, paid the rent on the shop, and had to meet the weekly payroll. Unlike "straight" employers, however, he paid wages in cash, and had to arrange for a surreptitious supply of oxygen for the acetylene torches.

Solidarity among team members helps them work together to perform their specialized functions. The men who worked in the "chop shop" socialized with one another when they were not working. They drank together at the same tavern (which was frequented by other professional criminals) and visited one another at home. By integrating their working and social lives, they minimized the intrusion of straight values, kept close tabs on one another, and reinforced ideas about the rightness and desirability of how they made their living.

Unlike amateurs, few professional criminals are troubled by their criminality. Crime is simply a way to make a buck. They see themselves as businesspeople, no different from clerks who sell shoddy merchandise or surgeons who perform unnecessary operations. Theirs is just another form of "making it" in U.S. society.

ORGANIZED CRIME

The professional criminals we have discussed are independent operators. By contrast, participants in **organized crime** work in a local organization, which, in turn, is part of a national network. Not only do they make their living from crime, but they also belong to interconnected criminal organizations.

TECHNOLOGY AND SOCIAL PROBLEMS

Using Technology to Commit Crime

The mathematics courses at the University of St. Petersburg were grueling, but, like his classmates, Vladimir Levin hoped they would pay off. Russia was crumbling, and jobs weren't easy to get. As Vladimir gained insight into how computer programs operate, he figured he had discovered a way to make his courses pay off handsomely.

Vladimir sat transfixed as he watched the numbers flash across his computer screen. He had gained access to a computer terminal at AO Saturn in St. Petersburg, and with his programming know-how he directed computers at Citibank in New Jersey to send money to bank accounts he had opened in San Francisco, Holland, Finland, and Israel.

It had been a tense week for Levin. As the time drew near, he had worried about all the things that could go wrong. But now he knew the scheme was going to work. It was like hitting the jackpot at a casino and watching the coins keep tumbling—only much better. When Levin saw the total hit $1 million, he smiled and started to relax. The numbers kept growing, and he called it quits at $12 million.

"Not a bad day's work," he thought. "The wonders of modern technology."

At their computers on the other end, Citibank officers didn't smile. They had spent vast amounts to make their computers impenetrable—the most protected in the nation, they were assured—and now some hacker had invaded them. Having their bank looted was bad enough, but they also didn't relish becoming a laughingstock: People began to joke about their full-page ads: "Call Citibank today and start using our PC banking service for free." It took a while to track down Levin and his accomplices, but with Citibank's determination and the cooperation of international police organizations, the culprits were apprehended.

Levin no longer needs his extensive mathematics background. In grade school he learned all the math he needs—how to subtract one day at a time from his prison sentence.

Based on "Citibank Thieves,"
St. Petersburg Press, 1995.

Origin of the Mafia

In one sense, the Mafia is a myth. The myth is that a criminal organization developed in Sicily, moved to the United States, and now controls organized crime here. The Mafia does exist, and it did originate in Sicily. The Sicilian government was weak, and local strongmen united to protect their families and communities from bandits. Establishing a private government, they also protected their communities from other strongmen in return for regular tribute (Anderson 1965; Blok 1974; Catanzaro 1992). As the formal government grew stronger, these men resisted and maintained their control over areas of Sicily. After the 1860s, they became known as the **Mafia.**

Maintaining Soildarity

The twin foundations of these private governments are the family and *omertá*, a law of secrecy. Violators of *omertá* pay with their lives. These twin foundations assure secrecy, solidarity, and separation from outsiders. To maintain these characteristics, the Mafia forges bonds through *village endogamy* (marriage between people from the same village) and *fictive kinship* (assigning obligations associated with close blood relatives to people who are not related; a godfather, for example, unites two families).

Non-Mafia Organized Crime

According to the Mafia myth, Sicilians began organized crime in the United States. New York City, however, has had organized crime for more than 150 years. It has been dominated by successive waves of ethnic immigrants—first the Irish, then the Jews, and only after that the Italians (Bell 1960). Today, organized crime in New York City is not dominated by any single ethnic group. It includes Sicilians and Italians, but also African Americans and Puerto Ricans. Miami has Cuban-organized crime, and San

Francisco and Los Angeles Japanese-organized crime (Wagman 1981). A new ethnic contender is Russian organized crime, which just recently arrived on the U.S. crime scene (Finckenauer and Waring 1999). Some organized crime has no ethnic basis at all, such as outlaw motorcycle gangs whose primary activity is dope dealing.

The Mafia myth, however, is valid in pinpointing an organization dominated by Americans of Sicilian-Italian descent, with connections across the United States and

Transplantation of the Mafia to the United States

abroad. Transplanted to the United States, the various Mafias—and I emphasize the plural—continued their illegal activities among their own ethnic group. Prohibition provided the stimulus for these tightly knit organizations to expand. By the time Prohibition was repealed in 1933, the Mafias had become a power structure in major cities, especially Chicago and New York (Sykes 1978). The Mafia developed a **bureaucracy,** a hierarchy with specialized personnel (gunmen, runners, executives, and others), departmentalization (narcotics, prostitution, loan sharking, and gambling), and an enforcement arm to keep profits flowing upward.

The Mafia as a Bureaucracy

Unlike most bureaucracies, the Mafia does not make public its organizational structure, but each major city appears to have the equivalent of a board of directors, a president and vice president, district managers with executive assistants, and, at the lowest level, soldiers who carry out the orders (Anderson 1965). About 5,000 members belong to about 24 "families" of 200 to 700 members each. These families are linked to each other by understandings and "treaties." The leaders of the most powerful families form a "commission" or "combine" to which weaker families pay deference (Cressey 1969; Riesel 1982a). The East Coast members call this structure the Mafia, or **cosa nostra** ("our thing").

Crime as Business

Crime is the Mafia's business, and they are successful. In spite of the U.S. government's "war" against the Mafia, it flourishes. The Mafia is the major importer and wholesaler of narcotics and runs the main U.S. loan-sharking operations {making illegal loans at high rates of interest). The Mafia controls some labor unions and in some areas the construction trade (Penn 1982; Riesel 1982b; Trust 1986). It has also infiltrated many legitimate businesses, such as the garment industry of New York City. Violence remains the way the Mafia does business—despite its public relations claim to the contrary.

Why the Mafia Has Been So Successful

Why has the Mafia been so successful, despite efforts of the U.S. government? We can cite the following reasons (*Organized Crime* 1976):

1. It is highly *organized*—a bureaucracy with full-time specialists in many criminal pursuits.

2. It provides illegal *services in high demand* (prostitution, gambling, and loan sharking)—"victimless crimes" in which no one complains to the police.

3. It wields influence through *political corruption*.

4. It uses *violence and intimidation* against victims and its own members.

The Mafia and the U.S. Ruling Class

Conflict theorists add a *fifth* reason—that the Mafia serves the goals of the U.S. ruling class. According to sociologist David Simon (1981), the ruling class has used organized crime to keep labor from getting too organized or becoming too "radical." Between the 1920s and the 1940s, periods of huge labor unrest, corporations hired gangsters to be strikebreakers and union infiltrators, especially among auto workers and longshoremen. Simon notes that during World War II, U.S. Navy Intelligence asked Mafia boss Lucky Luciano to detect German agents in the New York docks. Luciano cooperated.

The allegations of Judith Campbell Exner add another dimension to the connection between the ruling class and the Mafia. Exner claimed to be a lover of President John F. Kennedy and of Sam Giancana, the head of the Chicago Mafia. She also claimed to have carried messages between them (Kelley 1988). Supposedly, Giancana delivered votes to Kennedy in key states and, at Kennedy's request, plotted the assassination of Fidel Castro. This has led to one of the many theories about Kennedy's assassination, that the mob assassinated Kennedy when he turned on them and directed his brother, Robert, head of the Justice Department, to pursue organized crime. These are only allegations, and there may be no substance to them (DiEugenio 1997).

Organized Crime as a Threat to the United States

Many sociologists emphasize that organized crime threatens the well-being of the United States. The most serious problem is not gambling, prostitution, loan sharking, and so on, but the corruption of our social institutions. With their many millions of untaxed dollars, the Mafia bribes police, judges, and politicians, subverting the institutions and organizations that deal with crime. Thus violence, bribery, and other forms of corruption work their way into the social system (Cressey 1969; Teresa 1973; Gosch and Hammer 1975; Ianni and Reuss-Ianni 1976; Gudkov 1980; Schwidrowski 1980), leaving us with the frightening possibility that, as is the case in Russia today, much of our society could one day be controlled by organized crime.

While it's certain that crime will continue, and along with it various versions of organized crime, the role of the Mafia is uncertain. In recent years, the Mafia has faced more competition from other groups, *omertá* has been weakened, and the FBI has been more successful in infiltrating this organization. With the police using more powerful electronic surveillance techniques and more members being willing to talk to avoid jail or to have their sentences reduced, the police have been successful in indicting and convicting some top Mafia bosses. Perhaps the most famous was John Gotti, who, in spite of his crimes, which include murder, was romanticized and became a darling of the media. The power of the Mafia appears to be in decline, but it is far too soon to sound its death knell. We will have to see how the Mafia adapts to these changes.

POLITICAL CRIME

Two Types of Political Crime: to Change or to Maintain the Social Order

Some conflict theorists view almost every crime as political—an act by the ruling class to repress the working class, or an act of the working class to resist that repression. I use the term **political crime** in a narrower sense—to describe crimes designed either to change or maintain the social order. Crimes to *change the social order* include treason (the betrayal of one's country), sedition (rebellion, an attempt to

overthrow the government), and such activities as resistance to the draft. The blowing up of a federal building in Oklahoma City by Timothy McVeigh and his conspirators is another example.

Crimes designed to *maintain the social order* include the CIA's assassinations, manipulation of foreign governments, and domestic surveillance. In the same category are the illegal activities of the FBI, such as the thousands of burglaries it committed from the 1940s into the 1970s and the tens of thousands of letters it opened and photographed (Coleman 1995). Political crime also includes the illegal activities of President Richard Nixon and his aides during Watergate, and probably the activities of President Ronald Reagan and Lt. Col. Oliver North to support the contras of Nicaragua as well as the alleged financing of President Bill Clinton's campaign through drug money (Reed and Cummings 1994).

Political crimes are intended to either support or undermine (protest, bring about change) the social order. A dramatic political crime was the 1995 bombing of the federal building in Oklahoma City, Oklahoma.

In summary, political crime clearly illustrates that social problems are a matter of definition rather than a collection of objective facts. Some people see the illegal activities of those who want to change the social order as a major social problem, but they excuse the political crimes of government officials as necessary for securing the domestic order. Others view the illegal acts of government officials as an extreme social problem, because they subvert the constitutional system that the officials are sworn to uphold. For still others, all political crime, whether designed to maintain or to change the status quo, is a social problem because it is illegal.

THE CRIMINAL JUSTICE SYSTEM

Types of Crime and the Sting of the Criminal Justice System

Certain types of crime are easier to get away with than others. Least likely to be arrested are those who commit political crimes in order to maintain the status quo, for they are protected by the system they are supporting. Also running less risk are white-collar criminals who commit crimes in the name of a corporation, and those who comprise the top levels of organized crime. Respectability, wealth, power, and underlings insulate them. Probably the next safest are those who commit crimes against a corporation, and professional criminals. Those in the first group are insulated by the corporation's desire to avoid negative publicity; those in the other group are protected by skill, by a criminal subculture, and by having minimal contact with the "straight" world. Those who run the highest risk of arrest are "soldiers" at the lowest level of organized crime, who are considered expendable, and juvenile delinquents and others who commit street crime. Because political crimes designed to change the system threaten the power elite, the state probably is the most efficient in dealing with this type of crime.

Plea Bargaining as Subversion of the Criminal Justice System

Keeping in mind, then, that the sting of the criminal justice system is not an equal threat to all, let's examine how this system operates. Buddy, Gary, and Clyde, whose defense attorney suggested they plead guilty, represent in microcosm our criminal justice system. Prosecutors charge people with the most serious crimes possible, and then offer to accept a guilty plea to a lesser offense. Despite their constitutional obligation to *defend* their clients, public defense attorneys usually suggest that their clients plead guilty (Blumberg 1967; Maynard 1984). What is supposed to be a trial becomes the perfunctory validation of pretrial agreements.

Plea bargaining has become so prevalent that *most people accused of a crime do not receive a trial.* On average, juries hear only about 5 percent of criminal cases (Zawitz 1988a:84). Back in the 1960s, sociologist Abraham Blumberg explained that public defenders develop "implicit understandings" about what their job really is— to be team players who produce "assembly-line justice" for the poor (Blumberg 1967). The situation remains unchanged. Urging his client to accept a jail sentence, one public defender said, "Even if you're innocent, it's a good deal" (Penn 1985).

The criminal justice system is also slow and inefficient. Courtrooms are jammed and their hours in session short. Bureaucratic procedures wreck schedules. Police officers and other witnesses wait hours, even days, for cases to be called. Lawyers are expensive, and those assigned the poor are overburdened. Rules for presenting evidence are complex. The result is that cases advance at a snail's pace. For those who plead guilty, the average time between arrest and sentencing is 6 months (190 days). For those who choose a jury trial, it is 10 months (302 days) (*Sourcebook* 1998:Table 5.63). During this time, some innocent people remain behind bars, while some guilty people are released to commit more crimes while awaiting a distant trial.

The Public Defender as Team Player

Plea bargaining and the inefficiencies of the court system subvert the Sixth Amendment to the Constitution, which declares that "the accused shall enjoy the right to a speedy and public trial, by an impartial jury of the State and district wherein the crime shall have been committed." The poor do not receive a speedy trial. Indeed, most do not even receive a trial.

Is the Criminal Justice System Guilty of Racial Discrimination?

Let's discuss racial discrimination in the criminal justice system. As you will recall, Buddy, the only African American in the trio, received the most severe sentence. The judge claimed that this was only because of Buddy's "priors." What is the answer?

Perhaps: The Prison Population

The issue is complicated, and sociologists differ. Our system certainly seems to discriminate along racial lines. Although African Americans make up only 12 percent of the U.S. population, they constitute 42 percent of jail inmates and 47 percent of inmates in state prisons. Latinos, who also make up 12 percent of the population, constitute 16 percent of jail inmates. (*Sourcebook* 2000:Table 623). (The source does not provide these data on other minorities or on Latinos in state prisons.) As Table 6-6 shows, the pattern for those assigned to death row is similar. Perhaps no

Table 6-6 Prisoners on Death Row, by Race/Ethnicity

Race/Ethnicity	Number on Death Row	Percentage of Death Row Inmates	Percentage of U.S. Population	More or Less Than the Group's Percentage of the U.S. Population[*]
White	1,691	45.6%	70.7%	−36%
African American	1,598	43.0	12.3	+250
Latino	337	9.1	12.5	−27
Native American	42	1.1	.9	+22
Asian American	40	1.1	3.6	−69
Not reported	1	0.0	0	
Totals	3,709	99.8	100	

[*]This figure is computed by dividing the difference between the group's percentage of the U.S. population and its percentage of death row inmates by its percentage of the U.S. population.

Source: US Census 2000: PHC-T-9 Table 1:Table 19; Sourcebook of Criminal Justice Statistics 2000:Table 680.

statement illustrates the impact of the criminal justice system on African Americans better than this one: "On any given day, almost one in three black men between the ages of 20–29 are in prison or jail, on probation or parole" (American Civil Liberties Union 1996).

No: "Priors" and Victimization Surveys

Yes: Police-Civilian Encounters

Yes: Two More Studies

Bias Works in Both Directions

These data do not let us draw conclusions about bias, however, because they do not account for differences in crime among ethnic groups. Sociologists have compared victimization studies (which contain no police bias) with the arrest rates of African Americans and white Americans for rape, robbery, and assault. They find that the racial makeup that victims report closely matches arrest rates (Hindelang 1978; Langan 1985; Shim and DeBerry 1988).

Many sociologists, however, are convinced that the criminal justice system is biased against minorities (Sellin 1928; Green 1961; Bullock 1961; Keil and Vito 1989). Sociologists Douglas Smith and Christy Visher (1981) trained civilians to ride with the police in Missouri, New York, and Florida. After observing almost 6,000 encounters between police and citizens, they concluded that the police are more likely to arrest African-American suspects. An examination of felony convictions in Florida showed that whites were more likely to have their cases dropped or to receive probation, African Americans more likely to be convicted and to go to prison (Hale 1980). Sociologist Gary LaFree (1980), who examined court records in a midwestern community, found that African Americans who raped white women received more severe sentences than whites who raped white women.

Other studies show that bias works in *both* directions. Data released by the Bureau of Justice Statistics reveal that blacks are given longer prison terms for rape and drugs, but whites receive longer sentences for murder (Butterfield 1999). In a study of sentencing in Fresno, California, sociologist John Tinker (1981) compared Latino and Anglo defendants charged with felonies. In general, they received the same sentences. But Tinker also found this pattern: Latinos were more likely to have their charges dismissed, but, if tried, they were more likely to go to prison. Using a computerized system to track the processing of California offenders from arrest to sentencing, sociologist Joan Petersilia (1983) found a similar pattern. Minority suspects are more likely than whites to be released after arrest, but, if convicted of a felony, they are also more likely to be given longer

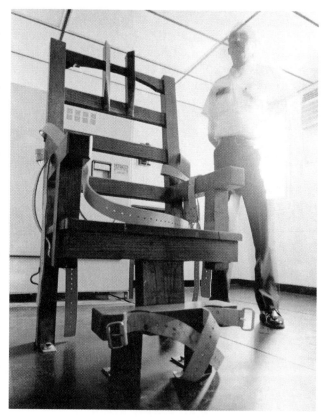

Throughout history, many methods have been used to execute prisoners. Death by electrocution was supposedly an improvement over earlier methods. Shown here is the electric chair at Starke, Florida. After foot-long flames shot from the head of a prisoner being executed, the courts ordered this chair not to be used.

sentences and to be sent to prison instead of jail. Petersilia, along with sociologists Stephen Klein and Susan Turner (1990), found that race did not make a difference in sentences for assault, robbery, burglary, theft, and forgery. For drug offenses, however, Latinos were more likely to be sent to prison.

Even Reverse Racism?

Sociologists Martha Myers and Susette Talarico (1986:246) found something even more surprising in Georgia—that blacks are favored in sentencing:

> Where blacks are a substantial minority (24–49 percent), black and white offenders bear the brunt of greater punitiveness equally. Once blacks become a numerical majority, white offenders are at a distinct disadvantage. Put concretely, they are more likely than blacks to be imprisoned.

Data from juvenile delinquents is similarly mixed. On the one hand, blacks are more likely to have their cases dismissed, and less likely to be determined to be delinquent. On the other hand, whites are less likely to be tried as adults, and more likely to receive probation. In addition, while they wait for a court hearing, blacks are more likely to be kept in juvenile hall, and whites to be sent home (*Sourcebook* 1998:Table 5.77).

At this point, then, we cannot conclude that the courts are biased for or against minorities or for or against whites. The evidence goes both ways.

Racial Bias in Capital Punishment

A look at **capital punishment** (the death penalty), however, shows overwhelming evidence of racial bias. Between 1930 and 1967, 455 U.S. prisoners were executed for rape. Forty-eight were white, 455 African Americans. No one has been executed for rape since 1967. Donald Partington (1965), a lawyer, examined all executions for rape and attempted rape in Virginia between 1908 and 1963. Convicted of these crimes were 2,798 men (56 percent whites and 44 percent blacks). Forty-one were executed for rape and 13 for attempted rape. *All* were black. *Not one* of the whites was executed.

Race was also critical in deciding who was given the death penalty for rape, but in this case it was the race of the attacker *and* the victim that was important. Sociologists Marvin Wolfgang and Marc Reidel (1975) studied rape convictions in Georgia. They found that the best predictor of whether a defendant would be sentenced to death was knowing that the victim was white and the accused black.

The death penalty was so biased that in 1972 the Supreme Court ruled in *Furman v. Georgia* that it was unconstitutionally applied. As Table 6-7 shows, 3,896 prisoners had been executed up to then. Fifty-three percent were black, 46 percent white, and 1 percent Native American or Asian American. States rewrote their laws and in 1977 again began executing prisoners. As Table 6-7 shows, since then 62 percent of those put to death have been white and 35 percent African American. Of the 3,064 prisoners on death row, 46 percent are white, 43 percent African American, 9 percent Latino, 1.1 percent Native American, and 1.1 percent Asian American (*Sourcebook of Criminal Justice Statistics* 2000:Table 6.80).

Gender Bias in Capital Punishment

The death penalty apparently shows a strong gender bias, for only 35 women have been executed since 1930, a mere 0.8 percent (*Sourcebook* 1991:Table 6.139; Word 1998). Since the death penalty was restored in 1976, 683 men have been executed, but only 5 women. At present, 1.5 percent of prisoners on death row are women (*Bureau of Justice Statistics* 2001 C.P. 2000 D.C.). Instead of bias in favor of women, however, these totals may reflect the relative frequency and severity of their crimes.

Geographic Bias in Capital Punishment

Whether the charge is rape or murder, geography vitally affects one's chances of being executed. As the Social Map on the next page shows, 13 states do not have the death penalty. And, of the 37 states that have it, some are much more willing to use it

Table 6-7   Prisoners Executed, by Race

Year	White Number	White Percentage	African American Number	African American Percentage	Native American/ Asian American Number	Native American/ Asian American Percentage	Total
1930–34	371	48%	395	51%	10	1%	772
1935–39	456	51%	421	47%	14	2%	891
1940–44	276	43%	362	56%	7	1%	645
1945–49	214	33%	419	66%	6	1%	639
1950–54	201	49%	209	50%	3	1%	413
1955–59	135	44%	167	55%	2	1%	304
1960–64	90	50%	91	50%	0	0%	181
1965–69	8	80%	2	20%	0	0%	10
Totals before the death penalty was abolished							
	1774	46%	2080	53%	42	1%	3896
1970–74	0	0%	0	0%	0	0%	0
1975–79	3	100%	0	0%	0	0%	3
1980–84	19	66%	10	34%	0	0%	29
1985–89	49	56%	39	44%	0	0%	88
1990–94	85	62%	50	36%	2	2%	137
1995–97	109	62%	63	36%	n/a	n/a	n/a
Totals since the death penalty was reinstated							
	265	62%	162	35%	n/a	n/a	n/a

Note: Because Table 6-8 includes the year 1996, its total is higher. For executions, Latinos are not listed separately in the source. They are included in the totals for whites. Table 6.79 of the source, however, lists 230 Latinos on death row. Because this table does not include prisoners executed by the federal government, the total does not agree with that in Table 6-8. n/a—not available

Source: Sourcebook of Criminal Justice Statistics 2000:Table 6.92; 1998:Table 6.88.

FIGURE 6-3
Social Map: Which States Have the Death Penalty?
(Source: Bureau of Justice Statistics (2001) C.P. 2000 D.C.)

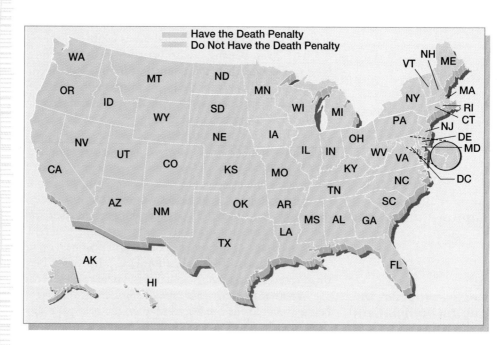

Chapter 6   Crime and Criminal Justice

The Prison
Experience:
Internal Structure

The Social
Production
of Brutality

The Zimbardo
Experiment

In Sum

than others. As Table 6-8 shows, this tendency is far more prevalent in the South. Of the 683 prisoners executed since 1977, three of every four (497) were executed in 11 southern states. Texas held the record before the death penalty was abolished, and does so once again. One of every three executions since 1977 has taken place in Texas.

Finally, let's look at the prison experience. Unlike Clyde, Buddy and Gary had to serve time. Prison turned out to be horrible. As with the prisoner whose letter opens this chapter, they were offered no rehabilitation program. They and their fellow prisoners were locked away, forgotten by society—except when a riot riveted public attention. The warden was a political appointee, awarded his supposedly easy job for party loyalty. As long as the prison remained "quiet," his job was secure. Buddy and Gary soon discovered that in return for the prisoners' cooperation in keeping the prison quiet, guards overlooked gambling, alcohol, drugs, and homosexual behavior. To supplement their low salaries, guards smuggled in alcohol and drugs.

Buddy and Gary were herded about like animals, forbidden to make even simple decisions. They were told when to work, what TV programs to watch, and when to sleep. Their letters were censored, their packages rifled, and their telephone conversations recorded. They expected these things, because they were prisoners.

They did not expect the brutality and violence of the guards, however. As the prisoner in the opening vignette observed, violence could result from breaking a rule or even the suspicion of having done it. Buddy and Gary concluded that the prison recruited sadists, for that is how they saw the guards. If they had studied sociology, however, they might have gained insight into this brutal fact of prison life.

Philip Zimbardo, a social psychologist, conducted a fascinating experiment. Using paid volunteers, Zimbardo (1995) matched 24 college students on the basis of their education, race, and parents' social class. He randomly assigned one group as guards and the other as prisoners. Without warning, one night real police cars arrived at the homes of those who had been designated prisoners. They were "arrested," fingerprinted, and taken to the basement of the psychology building at Stanford University, which had been turned into a prison. Both "guards" and "prisoners" were given appropriate uniforms.

Subject to the arbitrary control of their captors, the prisoners felt a loss of personal identity. The guards, in contrast, felt an increase in social power and status. They also developed strong in-group loyalty. After several days, rumors of a prison rebellion spread. The guards reacted brutally, with about a third treating the prisoners as though they were subhuman. Things started to get out of hand, and after six days Zimbardo stopped the experiment.

Zimbardo's experiment suggests a fundamental sociological principle, that the group vitally affects our orientations and how we act toward others. How a prison is organized is more important in determining how guards and prisoners act than are their individual personalities. As guards work in a prison, they discard the ideas they learned on "the outside." Their position leads them to see themselves as representatives of morality, and the prisoners as enemies that need to be subdued, rather than people who need to be helped. Their goal becomes upholding authority at all costs, even if this requires "justifiable" brutality. Eventually the guards come to see prisoners as "animals" who understand nothing but violence.

Zimbardo's study created controversy in the scientific community. It led to accusations of cruelty and irresponsibility in doing research. The federal government responded with strict guidelines for research with human subjects, and it is not likely that similar experiments will be conducted again. Zimbardo's research, however, provides insight into what is wrong with our prisons and why, despite a cost of about

Table 6-8 Number of Prisoners Executed, by Jurisdiction, 1930–2000

State	Number Executed Sentence of Death	
	Since 1930	Since 1977
U.S. total	4,542	683
Texas	536	239
Georgia	389	23
New York	329	0
California	300	8
North Carolina	279	16
Florida	220	50
South Carolina	187	25
Ohio	173	1
Virginia	173	81
Louisiana	159	26
Alabama	158	23
Mississippi	158	4
Pennsylvania	155	3
Arkansas	141	23
Kentucky	105	2
Missouri	108	46
Illinois	102	12
Tennessee	94	1
Oklahoma	90	30
New Jersey	74	0
Maryland	71	3
Arizona	60	22
Washington	50	3
Indiana	48	7
Colorado	48	1
District of Columbia	40	0
West Virginia	40	0
Nevada	37	8
Federal system	33	0
Massachusetts	27	0
Delaware	23	11
Oregon	21	2
Connecticut	21	0
Utah	19	6
Iowa	18	0
Kansas	15	0
Montana	8	2
Wyoming	8	1
New Mexico	8	0
Nebraska	7	3
Idaho	4	1
Vermont	4	0
New Hampshire	1	0
South Dakota	1	0

Source: Bureau of Justice Statistics 2001 C.P. 2000. D.C. Table 10.

$30,000 per year per prisoner (Dority 1993)—enough to send each prisoner to Harvard!—prisons fail to reduce crime.

If prisons are not the answer, what is?

◆ Social Policy ◆

Prevention

What is being done to solve these twin social problems of crime and the criminal justice system? We cannot eliminate crime, but to the extent that we can prevent people from breaking the law, we can reduce the problem. Because street crime bothers Americans the most, and poverty is closely associated with it, the best policy would be to reduce poverty. (Poverty is analyzed in Chapter 7.) As we saw, there is a direct relationship between adult crime and dropping out of high school, so programs that keep students in school also prevent crime.

THINKING CRITICALLY ABOUT SOCIAL PROBLEMS

Public Shaming as Social Policy

"Shame on you!"

Do you remember those horrifying words from your childhood? If your childhood was like mine, you do. The words were accompanied by an index finger that pointed directly at me, while another index finger rubbed on top of it, seeming to send shame in my direction.

It was effective. I always felt bad when this happened. Even worse when I saw the looks of disgust on the faces of my parents or grandparents in response to my childish offense, whatever it may have been.

If you ever read Nathaniel Hawthorne's *The Scarlet Letter*, you know about shaming. Hester Prynne, who committed adultery, a serious offense at the time, had to wear a red A on her clothing. For life, wherever she went, she was marked as a shameful adulteress.

Now judges are bringing back this old-fashioned device. Not the scarlet A, but its equivalent.

Thieves have been ordered to wear sandwich boards saying, "I stole from this store" and to walk outside the stores they stole from.

A Texas judge ordered a piano teacher who pleaded guilty to molesting his young students to give away his prized $12,000 piano, not to play for 20 years, and to post a sign on the door of his home declaring himself a child molester.

Drunk drivers have been ordered to put bright orange bumper stickers on their cars that say, "I am a convicted drunk driver. Report any erratic driving to the police."

The Minneapolis police department has organized "shaming details" for prostitutes. Prostitutes and their johns stand handcuffed in front of citizens who let loose with "verbal stones," shouting things like, "You're the reason our children aren't safe in this neighborhood!"

Kansas City broadcasts a popular television program, "John TV." Shown are the mug shots of men who have been arrested for trying to buy sex, and the women who have been arrested for selling it. Their names, birth dates, and home towns are displayed prominently.

Does shaming work? No one knows if it reduces lawbreaking. But shaming certainly is powerful. A woman convicted of welfare fraud was ordered to wear a sign that said, "I stole food from poor people." She chose to go to jail instead.

Even if shaming doesn't work, it does satisfy a strong urge to punish, to get even. In today's eager-to-punish climate, perhaps this is enough. And perhaps it does help to restore a moral balance.

Examples are based on Gerlin 1994
and Belluck 1998.

For treating convicted criminals, there are four basic approaches: retribution, deterrence, rehabilitation, and incapacitation. Let's look at each.

Retribution is punishing criminals to uphold collective values and demonstrate that criminal behavior will not be tolerated. Proponents of retribution see offenders as morally responsible people whose violations of social norms have created a moral imbalance. To help restore the moral order, their punishment should fit the crime (Cohen 1940). An interesting form of retribution is *shaming*, which is discussed in the box on page 201.

Restitution, making offenders compensate their victims, is another form of retribution. If people have stolen, for example, they need to pay the money back. Restitution is practical for property crimes, when the offender can repay the victim. It is less practical for unemployed offenders, although some judges require the unemployed to "work their debt off" in public projects.

Attempts to restore the "moral balance" are evident in the following examples of "making the punishment fit the crime":

A Memphis judge invited victims to visit the thief's house and "steal" something back (Stevens 1992).

A Florida judge sentenced a white man convicted of harassing an interracial couple to weekends working in an African-American church.

A Texas judge ordered a deadbeat who had fathered 13 children to attend Planned Parenthood meetings (Gerlin 1994).

A California judge ordered a man who hit a woman to donate his car to the local battered woman's shelter (Farah 1995).

Critics emphasize how difficult it is to decide that a crime merits a particular punishment, and how inconsistent judges are in making those decisions. They also note that for crimes of violence, retribution might require unusual measures, such as castration for rapists—acts that courts may rule are unconstitutional. A California judge, for example, wanted to withhold AIDS treatment from a man who raped two teen-age

Federal prisons are known as the country clubs of the U.S. prison system. Alabama, in contrast, has some of the toughest prisons. As shown in this photo shot at Huntsville, to be sentenced to serve "hard labor" means exactly that.

Halfway houses refer to a supervised environment, in which residents live "half way" between freedom and being locked up in an institution. Residents set their rules and enforce them, and they also have limited freedom to come and go. To allow more in-depth interaction and supervision, halfway houses are designed to be small. This one in Ogden, Utah, however has 154 residents and is a substitute for prison.

2. Deterrence

When Good Intentions Go Awry: The Failure of "Scared Straight"

girls after he was released from prison for a previous sexual assault (Farah 1995). Proponents reply that if retribution is the goal of punishment, the Constitution needs to be brought into line with the goal.

Deterrence aims to create fear by letting potential offenders know they will be punished. Proponents view offenders as rational people who weigh the possible consequences of their actions; if they see punishment as likely, they will avoid the crime. Starting in the 1970s, criminologist Ernest van den Haag (1975, 1983) proposed that we treat juveniles who commit violent crimes like adults ("adult crime, adult time"), abolish parole boards, and operate work programs for prisoners. With citizens demanding strong action, these attempts at deterrence have become popular.

Apparently, the longer the interval between a crime and its punishment, the less the deterrent value of the punishment. This underscores the need for swift punishment. Similarly, the more uncertain the penalty, the less its deterrent value. The solution: **uniform sentencing,** the same sentence for everyone convicted of the same crime. Critics point out that many offenders do not weigh the consequences of their acts. In the 1700s when England hanged pickpockets, for example, pickpockets worked the crowd during hangings because the spectators, their attention riveted on the gallows, made easy victims (Hibbert 1963).

One effort at deterrence that attracted the mass media was "Scared Straight." In this program, delinquents were sent on prison tours, where inmates gave them a close-up view of prison life. Leering and shouting obscenities, they said they could hardly wait for the youths to be sent to prison so they could rape them. Those who operated the program reported that it kept 80 to 90 percent of the youths from further trouble with the law. Sociological studies, however, showed that the program had backfired. Criminologist James Finckenauer (1982) matched delinquents on the basis of their sex, race, age, and delinquent behavior. He then compared those who had been exposed to the scared-straight program (the experimental group) with delinquents who were not exposed to it (the control group). Within six months, 41 percent of the experimental group but only 11 percent of the control group were again in trouble with the law.

Why did this program backfire? Finckenauer suggests that the boys were impressed by the macho performance of authoritarian, in-charge men—the type of powerful men they themselves wanted to be. Committing crimes showed their peers that they were not frightened and demonstrated that they, too, were macho.

The failure of "scared straight" does not mean that programs of deterrence cannot work. It does, however, point up the need for sociological research. We cannot assume that a program is successful just because it looks good, appeals to our common sense, or because its operators say that it works. We need solid research so we can evaluate programs and develop sound social policy. As described in the box on below, "prison boot camps" are operated by many states. They need just this kind of research so we can evaluate them.

3. Rehabilitation

The focus of **rehabilitation** is resocializing offenders, to help them become conforming citizens. Programs of rehabilitation include *probation*, returning offenders to the community under the supervision of a probation officer; *imprisonment* with the goal of teaching prisoners a trade or useful skills through high school or college courses; *parole*, releasing prisoners before they serve their full sentence, both as a reward for good behavior and as a threat (for, as in probation, if the court's rules are violated the convict goes back to prison to serve out the sentence); *furloughs*, freedom for a set time, such as a weekend, toward the end of the sentence, to let convicts adjust gradually to nonprison life; *halfway houses*, residences in which ex-convicts report to the authorities but supervise much of their own lives, such as

THINKING CRITICALLY ABOUT SOCIAL PROBLEMS

Squeeze You Like a Grape

As they step out of the police cars into the Georgia countryside, a guard shouts into their faces, "You're nothing! You're nobody! You're fools! You're maggots! You're motherf———s!"

The youths look dumbfounded. Another guard shouts, "I don't like ya. I got no use for ya, and I don't care who ya are on the streets. This is hell's half acre, and I don't give a damn if ya get tossed outta here into prison. I promise ya, ya won't last five minutes before you're somebody's wife. Do ya know what that means, tough guys?"

The offenders are ages 17 to 25. Convicted of nonviolent crimes, they have chosen 90 days of prison boot camp, followed by probation, rather than one to five years in prison.

"You have to hit a mule between the eyes with a two-by-four to get his attention," explains an official. "And that's what we do here." Within an hour of arriving, inmates are stripped of every sign of their previous life. Guards take their cigarettes and personal possessions. Their heads are shaved, and a white prison uniform with wide blue stripes replaces their jeans and T-shirts.

Inmates may not speak without permission. All responses must begin and end with "Sir." The lights go out at 10. Television watching is limited to one hour a day—only the news and PBS—all in black and white. No visitors are allowed for the first 45 days.

Inmates do hard physical labor. Up at 5 A.M., they cut grass with scythes and dig up tree trunks with shovels and pickaxes. If an inmate talks on the work crew without permission, he must do push-ups—or take the "chair position," unsupported, of course. Repeated violations mean being handcuffed and placed in a police car. Other inmates are made to watch as the violator is taken away to prison to serve the longer sentence.

Mississippi opened the first boot camp in 1985. Now 32 states operate them. Seven states have camps for women.

The warden of this Georgia camp says, "They're not going to leave here any smarter, but we can provide some structure and discipline that they've never gotten. We can't fix the sociological problems that led to crime in the first place, but we can influence what they do next."

The sociologist, of course, replies, "Let's see the statistics. We need matched groups (offenders of the same background convicted of the same crimes). When we compare the percentage of each group that is rearrested, we'll know if boot camps work."

To many, boot camps for prisoners make sense at a "gut level," and they have become popular. Americans think they are effective. The studies, however, have not yet been done. We still don't know if they work.

Sources: Lamar 1986; Gest 1987; *Life,* July 1988:82–83; Morash and Rucker 1990; Mackenzie and Parent 1991; *Sourcebook* 1998:Tables 1.76, 2.54.

FIGURE 6-4
The Failure of
Probation
(*Source*: Bureau of Justice.)

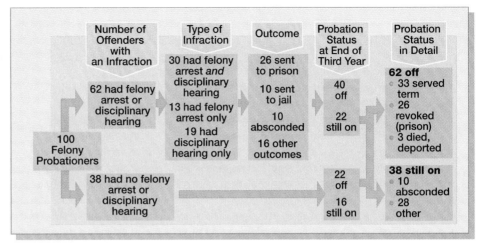

Number of Offenders with an Infraction	Type of Infraction	Outcome	Probation Status at End of Third Year	Probation Status in Detail
100 Felony Probationers → 62 had felony arrest or disciplinary hearing	30 had felony arrest *and* disciplinary hearing	26 sent to prison	40 off	**62 off** • 33 served term • 26 revoked (prison) • 3 died, deported
	13 had felony arrest only	10 sent to jail	22 still on	
	19 had disciplinary hearing only	10 absconded		
		16 other outcomes		
38 had no felony arrest or disciplinary hearing			22 off	**38 still on** • 10 absconded • 28 other
			16 still on	

The Failure of Probation

household tasks, drinking, drugs, and curfews; and *honor farms* for prisoners who have shown good behavior, where supervision is less stringent and convicts can learn cooperative, responsible roles (Morash and Anderson 1978).

The public is fed up with failed attempts at rehabilitation. Probation is especially offensive; the public perceives it as an opportunity for felons to commit more crime. The public's perception is accurate; probation has failed. Figure 6-4 summarizes what happened to 79,000 felons who were given probation. Within three years, 43 percent were rearrested for a violent crime (murder, rape, robbery, or aggravated assault) or a drug offense (Langan and Cunniff 1992). Another 19 percent had violated conditions of their probation.

The concept of probation is not unsound, however, although our implementation of it is. If probation were given to felons with the most promise, if they were provided with follow-up counseling, and if trained probation officers had small case loads, it might work. To find out, however, we need sociological research, ideally with experimental and control groups.

Another approach is **diversion,** diverting offenders *away from* courts and jails. The goal is to keep them out of the criminal justice system—to shift them to community organizations or funnel them into administrative hearings rather than criminal trials. Diversionary programs aim to avoid stigmatizing offenders and keep them out of the crime schools that jails and prisons have become.

If rehabilitation programs were successful, almost everyone would favor them. The cost of rehabilitation would certainly be less than the price criminals now exact from society—from the harm they cause their victims to the cost of supporting them in prison. The problem is that we do not know which rehabilitation programs work. The studies show conflicting results and do not inspire confidence.

4. Incapacitation

Consequently, the public clamors for **incapacitation,** removing offenders from circulation. The view of those proposing this solution is direct and to the point: Everything else has failed. We cannot change people who don't want to change, so let's get them off the street so they can no longer hurt people. Some offenders commit crime after crime ("career criminals"), so let's free ourselves of recidivists (DiIulio 1992). For a new form of incapacitation, see the Technology box on the next page.

TECHNOLOGY AND SOCIAL PROBLEMS

Using Technology to Stop Crime

The idea arose a couple of decades ago. "It's expensive to keep people in prison, and not everyone who is convicted of a crime should go to prison. Yet we need to keep tabs on these people. How can we use technology to do this?"

Technology soon provided an effective device, an ankle bracelet that transmits a signal to a central monitor. A transmitter is strapped around the offender's ankle, and a receiver is attached to a telephone in his or her home. If the offender leaves home, it breaks the signal and sets off an alarm at the monitoring station.

Able to transmit the location of an offender's whereabouts 24 hours a day, the device not only is effective, but it also lowers costs. To keep a juvenile in custody runs about $100 a day, but the cost for home monitoring is just $10 a day. To keep an adult in prison runs about $75 a day; it's only $12 a day to use the ankle device. The costs include equipment and staff.

Some jurisdictions have even developed a pay-as-you go plan. Judges give adult clients a choice—go to jail or pay $12 a day for electronic monitoring. Not eligible are drug dealers, those who committed a violent crime, and those who used guns to commit their crime.

Recent versions of the electronic device make it suitable for probation and parole. Software can be programmed with the offenders' work schedules and locations. Probation officers can park outside a workplace to pick up a signal, but, better yet, failure to appear at work also sets off a signal. Probation officers check to make certain the signal isn't false, then alert the police.

Hidden within this new technology is another benefit. Because electronic monitoring frees up prison cells, it allows courts to keep violent offenders in prison longer.

Special benefits go to victims of stalking. The software can be programmed to sound an alarm if an offender comes within a specified distance of a victim's home or workplace. Workers at the monitoring station warn the victim, who can leave the area.

Early versions of the ankle bracelet had a fatal defect. Some offenders managed to remove the bracelet and leave home while the signal kept transmitting to their telephone. Current versions are tamper proof.

The future of technology will soon make this tool seem primitive. Signaling devices will be implanted in felons' bodies. The electronic implant will be connected electronically to the Global Positioning System, satellites that can track the precise location of any object. Software will be programmed with the offender's schedule—times and location of work or rehabilitation classes, even routes to and from work and restricted places in the community. If the individual deviates from the schedule, a computer will notify the police to make an arrest.

This, of course, leads to the question of potential abuse by the government. Once authorities gain such power over felons, how do we keep them from turning it against us? Implants and the marvels of the Global Positioning System—what more could Big Brother ask to control its citizens?

Based on Campbell 1995, McGarigle 1997, "GPS Creates Global Jail" 1998, Knights 1999.

Criminologist James Wilson (1975) of Harvard University views incapacitation as the *only* solution that makes sense, and he advocates it in both the scholarly and popular media. Ernest van den Haag has proposed "added incapacitation," increasing the sentence each time someone is convicted. Some estimate that if everyone convicted of a serious offense were imprisoned for three years, our rate of serious crime would drop two thirds (Shinnar and Shinnar 1975). Others estimate that such sentencing would reduce crime by only 3 or 4 percent (Greenberg 1975; Cohen 1978).

"Weed and Seed"

An innovative program is "weed and seed"—"weeding out" crime from targeted inner-city neighborhoods and then "seeding" them with economic and social programs (Eastland 1992). "Weed and seed" assumes that programs cannot be effective without public safety. The police patrol on foot to build rapport with the community and file federal charges against drug dealers and violent gang members (federal pretrial detention and mandatory sentences are stiffer). Public schools, designated as safe havens, are kept open evenings and on Saturdays so adults can supervise homework and learn job skills themselves. In principle, "weed and seed" is sound, but we need research.

The Issue of Capital Punishment

The proponents of capital punishment argue that it is an appropriate retribution for heinous crimes, that it deters, and, of course, that it is an effective incapacitator. Its critics argue that killing is never justified. They add that if it did deter, then states with the death penalty would have a lower homicide rate than those without it—but they don't. In fact, the states without the death penalty average a lower homicide rate (*Sociological Abstract* 1997:Tables 315, 363). Opponents also argue that the death penalty is capricious: Jurors deliberate in secrecy and indulge their prejudices in recommending death, and judges are irrational—merciful to some but not to others. They also stress that innocent people have been executed.

FIGURE 6-5

Americans' Changing Attitudes Toward Capital Punishment

Question: "Are you in favor of the death penalty for persons convicted of murder?"

(*Source: Sourcebook of Criminal Justice Statistics* 2000:Table 2.61.)

Neither side convinces the other, and the data on whether the death penalty is effective are inconclusive (Bailey 1990; Peterson and Bailey 1991). Nevertheless, fear of crime is high, the public demands that "something be done," and, as Figure 6-5 shows, about two-thirds of Americans favor the death penalty. Figures 6-6 and 6-7 show the current increase in the number of prisoners sentenced to death and executed.

In sum, the United States has tried a variety of approaches to solve its crime problem. With little agreement on the basic purpose of the social response to crime

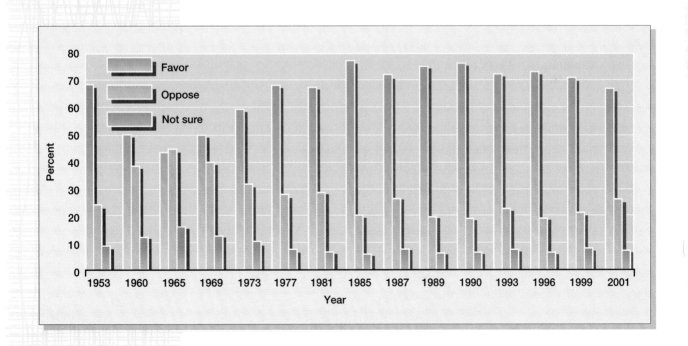

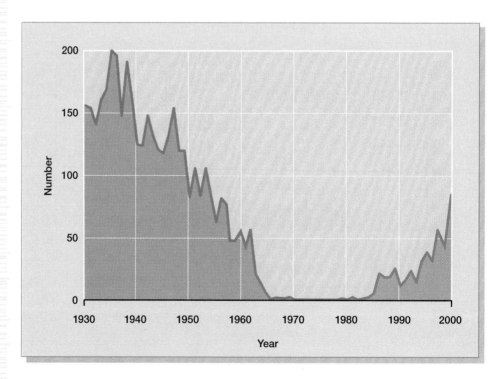

FIGURE 6-7
Persons Executed, 1930–2000
(*Source: Sourcebook of Criminal Justice Statistics* 1997: Tables 6–86, 6–88; Bureau of Justice Statistics 2001 CP, 2000 D.C.)

(prevention, retribution, deterrence, rehabilitation, or incapacitation), our solutions are piecemeal and in disarray. To have a social policy that operates on a rational basis, we need to reform the criminal justice system. I suggest the following goals and guiding principles:

1. Clear laws based on the broadest possible consensus, rather than on the interests or moral concerns of small groups.

2. Swift, sure justice based on legal evidence presented in adversarial proceedings. (This would require eliminating plea bargaining and lengthy delays based on legal technicalities; it would guarantee a speedy trial for all who plead not guilty and require more courts, more judges, and longer working hours for judges.)

3. More rehabilitation programs, including diversion for most first offenders (except for violent crimes) to try to incorporate them into the community.

4. Harsh penalties for repeat offenders, with the penalty becoming harsher each time a person is convicted ("added incapacitation").

5. Task forces to investigate organized crime and white-collar crime (with the provision that, for a specified time such as five years, members of the task forces cannot accept employment from the corporations they investigated).

6. Harsh penalties for those convicted of crime in the name of a corporation, including jail for executives, the forced sale of any division found guilty of crime, and huge fines to reduce the corporate profit motive (Liazos 1981).

7. Prison reform, including making the position of prison warden a civil service job, rigorously training prison guards and paying them well, allowing prisoners to have conjugal visits, and giving *to the nonviolent* the right to visit friends and family on the outside.

8. Unbiased studies of the criminal justice system.

◆ The Future of the Problem ◆

Will crime increase or decrease? The answer depends on the type of crime. Crime by women, for example, will probably increase as women continue to leave traditional roles and enter domains that used to be occupied by men.

We will be unable to tell whether white-collar crime is increasing or decreasing. If more of these cases are handled by the judicial system, it will *appear* to increase. Because we lack a base line of actual crimes from which to draw accurate comparisons, however, official statistics could show a doubling or even more in any given year, and we would still not know if this represented an increase or just more use of the judicial system.

The incidence of political crime will depend in part on political events. If we wage another unpopular war, or if the Supreme Court overturns key legislation designed to aid minorities, we could relive the political protests of the 1960s and 1970s. If we do have substantial illegal acts designed to change the political system, government officials may find the legal procedures too cumbersome and may, in turn, engage in illegal acts to protect a crumbling political system.

The Mafia will remain. If enforcement efforts succeed, the Mafia will turn increasingly to legitimate businesses. The Mafia will not forsake crime, however; illegal activities are the heart of its existence.

The Judicial System

The judicial system changes slowly. I anticipate that the criminal justice system will continue to focus on street crime, and that the crimes of the powerful will be largely overlooked or will be handled by civil agencies. I also anticipate an increase in a recent innovation in prisons—the hiring by states of private businesses to build and operate prisons. Private firms now operate about 150 prisons with over 100,000 inmates (*Sourcebook* 2000:Table 1.92, 1.93). Such changes, however, do not affect the basic system.

The Need to Cut Crime at the Root

To stop the poor from being recruited to street crime, we must open access to legitimate means of success. This means providing access to quality education and comprehensive job training, along with creating jobs that pay a living wage. People who have a high investment in the social system commit fewer crimes of violence. The greater their investment, the more they reject criminal norms. But to change the social system is a radical proposal, and, unfortunately, crime will remain a serious social problem.

◆ Summary

1. Whether an act is a *crime* depends on the law, which, in turn, depends on power relationships in society.
2. Crime is universal, because all societies have rules against acts they consider undesirable. Laws turn these acts into crimes. Since laws differ, crime differs from one society to another and in the same society over time.
3. The social problem of crime has two parts: the crimes committed and the criminal justice system. Crime is a problem because people are upset about the threat to their lives, property, and well-being; the *criminal justice system* is a problem because people are upset about its failures.
4. The "saints" and the "roughnecks' illustrate how social class affects the perception and reactions of authorities, as well as how crime statistics are distorted.
5. Functionalists note that property crimes represent conformity to the goal of success but rejection of the approved means of achieving it. Just as some have more access to legitimate means of success, others have more access to *illegitimate opportunities.*
6. Conflict theorists regard the criminal justice system as a tool that the ruling class uses to mask injustice, control workers, and stabilize the social system. Law enforcement is a means the elite use to maintain its dominance.
7. *Juvenile delinquents* use five major *neutralization techniques* to deflect society's norms: denial of responsibility, denial of injury, denial of a victim, condemning the condemners, and an appeal to higher loyalty.
8. *White-collar crime* is extensive but underreported. Corporations usually insulate white-collar criminals from the law, especially when the crimes benefit the corporation.
9. *Professional criminals* make their livelihood from crime. They have high in-group loyalty, scorn the "straight" world, and take pride in their specialized skills.
10. *Organized crime* is best represented by the Mafia, whose use of violence within a highly developed bureaucracy lies at the heart of its success.
11. *Political crime,* illegal activities intended to change the political system or to maintain it, ebbs and flows as political conditions change.
12. The criminal justice system fails to deliver justice because of overcrowded courts, *plea bargaining,* a team-player system that subverts public defense attorneys, possible racial bias, and prisons that foster hostility and hatred.
13. Because our criminal justice system has no underlying philosophy with which to establish and evaluate social response to crime, our policies of social control are in disarray.
14. Crime in the future will depend on social change, including the role of women, social policies toward crime, and economic and political events.
15. To get at the root of this problem requires reform of the criminal justice system and a basic overhaul of our social institutions, especially changes that open more opportunities to the poor.

Bureaucracy A highly structured hierarchy with specialized personnel.

Capital punishment The death penalty.

Corporate crime See *White-collar crime*.

Cosa nostra The term by which East Coast mobsters refer to the Mafia. See *Mafia*.

Crime Any act prohibited by law. What constitutes crime varies from one era to another and from one social group to another.

Crime against the person An illegal act that results in physical harm, such as assault, murder, and rape.

Crime rates The number of crimes per given unit of population, most commonly the number of crimes per 100,000 people.

Criminal justice system The agencies that respond to crime, including the police, courts, jails, and prisons.

Delinquent subculture A subculture whose members are oriented toward illegal acts.

Deterrence The attempt to prevent crime by producing fear.

Diversion Diverting offenders away from courts and jails to keep them out of the criminal justice system.

Illegitimate opportunity structure The opportunity, built into one's environment, to learn and participate in illegal activities.

Incapacitation A response to crime that focuses on removing offenders from circulation.

Juvenile delinquency Illegal acts committed by minors.

Mafia An organized and effective crime group; bureaucratized with specialized personnel and departmentalization. About 5,000 members belong to about 24 tightly knit "families."

Neutralization see *Techniques of neutralization*.

Organized crime Organizations devoted to criminal activities.

Plea bargaining Pleading guilty to a lesser crime in exchange for a reduced sentence.

Police discretion The decisions the police make about whether to overlook or enforce a law.

Political crime Illegal acts intended to alter or maintain a political system.

Political process A power struggle between interest groups and ideologies.

Professional criminals People who earn their living from crime.

Property crime Obtaining or destroying property illegally; burglary, theft, robbery, vandalism, and arson.

Recidivism rate The percentage of those released from prison who are rearrested.

Rehabilitation A response to crime designed to resocialize or reform offenders, so that they can become law-abiding citizens.

Restitution A form of retribution by which offenders compensate their victims.

Retribution A response to crime based on upholding moral values and restoring the balance upset by the criminal act. Making a thief repay what he or she stole is an example.

Status crimes Acts such as curfew violations or running away from home that are crimes when committed by persons of a designated status (for example, juveniles) but not when committed by others (for example, adults).

Techniques of neutralization How people justify their norm-breaking activities, making them more acceptable to themselves and others.

Uniform sentencing Giving the same sentence to everyone convicted of the same crime.

White-collar crime Crime committed either against a business, agency, or corporation (such as embezzlement and fraud) or on behalf of the corporation (such as price fixing, fraudulent advertising, antitrust violations, and corporate tax evasion).

◆ **Critical Thinking Questions**

1. What are the implications of the notion that there is no such thing as crime without law? How does that concept affect the way you think about our criminal justice system?

2. Which of the three perspectives (symbolic interactionism, functionalism, or conflict theory) do you think does the best job of explaining the nature of crime? Why?

3. Which of the three perspectives (symbolic interactionism, functionalism, or conflict theory) do you think does the best job of explaining why white-collar criminals are treated differently from street criminals? Is your

answer to this question different than your answer to Question #2? Explain.

4. Do you think that violent criminals should be treated differently from nonviolent criminals in terms of punishment? Why or why not? Consider the case of the criminally negligent manufacturer whose product kills people but who has no actual contact with victims versus the street criminal who commits murder in the commission of a robbery.

5. Which of the four basic approaches for treating criminals (retribution, deterrence, rehabilitation, and incapacitation) do you think is the most appropriate? Why?

Economic Problems

Wealth and Poverty

7

I AM HOMELES AND HUNGRY Anything will Help PlEA

At age 17, Julie Treadman faced more than her share of problems. Her boyfriend—her "first love"—had deserted her when she told him that she was pregnant. Exhausted and depressed, Julie had dropped out of high school. Now five months' pregnant, she wondered about her child's future.

When Julie had severe stomach pains, a neighbor called an ambulance and she was rushed to Lutheran Hospital. When hospital administrators' discovered that neither Julie nor her mother had money or credit, they refused her admission. Before they could transfer her to a public hospital for the poor, however, Julie gave birth to a stillborn baby.

This perplexed hospital administrators. They didn't want anyone around who could not pay their bills, but what could they do now? They quickly hit upon a Machiavellian solution: They ordered the ambulance driver to take Julie—dead baby, umbilical cord, and all—to the public hospital.

Based on an event in St. Louis, Missouri.

◆ The Problem in Sociological Perspective ◆

In this chapter, we examine economic problems facing our nation. Our primary focus will be on the unequal distribution of society's resources, especially as this produces the twin problems of wealth and poverty.

ECONOMIC SYSTEMS AND CHANGES

The Extremes of Social Class

The United States, where "all 'men' are created equal," has always had **social classes**—groups of people who occupy the same rung on the economic ladder. Where you are located on that ladder makes a vital difference for what life is like. We have the "working poor," full-time workers who have to depend on food stamps to survive, and we also have Bill Gates, the richest man in the world, who spent $75 million dollars for a house and $30 million for a Winslow Homer painting to decorate his living room. Most of us fall somewhere in between, of course. In this chapter, we shall look at the extremes, the rich and the poor, the powerful and the powerless. Let's start by considering how the economy affects all our lives.

The **economy** is not only money and jobs; it is the entire social institution that produces and distributes goods and services. How the economy functions affects the welfare of every individual, group, and community in the entire nation. At any given time, the U.S. economy is in a "boom," when everything seems to be percolating, or a "bust," when nothing seems to be going right. These "boom-bust" cycles plague **capitalist economies,** which are based on the private ownership of property and the investment of capital for the purpose of making a profit. Some students taking this course will graduate during a "boom" and will have their choice of jobs. Others, unfortunately, will graduate during a "bust," and even though they have earned bachelor's degrees, they will end up driving cabs, working in fast food restaurants, or spending time in unemployment lines.

Capitalist Economies

Socialist Economies

Previously, many nations, primarily eastern European countries under the domination of Russia, had **socialist economies;** the government owned the property, profit was illegal, and government committees decided what items—from cars to toilet paper—would be produced, and where they would be distributed. The government also set the price for the items—taking into consideration neither the quality of

Now that capitalism has won the economic war with socialism, the victor is consolidating its gains, moving us into a global economy. Foreign investment in Asia made its economies boom, as shown by the new Petronas Twin Towers in Kuala Lumpur, Malaysia. At 452 meters, the Towers are the world's tallest buildings. Foreign investors are fickle, however. At the hint of trouble they withdraw their capital, plunging an economy into paralysis.

G-7 and Global Stratification

The "Boom–Bust" Cycle

Why Did Capitalism Triumph?

Capitalist and Socialist Confrontations

the goods nor the demand for them. Everyone was guaranteed a job, and everyone worked for the government, which owned everything. Not only was everyone guaranteed a job, but to miss work when you weren't sick was a crime.

The socialist and capitalist economies were almost mirror images of one anther. Capitalists believed that socialism was immoral, that it denied people freedom of choice—including where to live, where to work, even candidates to represent them. Socialists believed that capitalism was immoral, that profit came before the welfare of people, and the poor were left to suffer. In what was known as the "Cold War," proponents of each ideology viewed the other as a mortal enemy and threatened one another with nuclear destruction.

The Triumph of Capitalism

Production in the socialist countries was inefficient. Workers could not be fired (they could be jailed for not showing up for work, however), and committees in each country's capital decided what would be produced and how it would be distributed. As workers in the capitalist countries enjoyed a growing standard of living, workers in the socialist countries fought a losing battle to maintain their already low standard. Living conditions, already minimal, worsened in Russia, and in 1989 its leaders, under Mikhail Gorbachev, abandoned socialism and reluctantly turned to capitalism. The Soviet Union broke up into fifteen independent states, which followed Russia into the seductive pursuit of capitalism. China and Cuba have clung to socialism, but they have begun the journey to capitalism by allowing limited private property and some pursuit of profit.

At this stage in world history, then, capitalism has triumphed. The newly independent states that are traveling the road to capitalism, however, have encountered torturous economic problems. Russia has been thrown into such economic and political disarray that its central authority is threatened, and, as discussed in Chapter 6, a mafia controls a large part of its economy. Consequently, the security of its nuclear weapons is in jeopardy, a matter to which we shall return in Chapter 15.

As capitalism has come to dominate the globe, the leaders of the major capitalist countries have divided the nations into three primary trading blocs: North and South America, dominated by the United States; Europe, dominated by Germany; and Asia, dominated by Japan. To try to control capitalism's troublesome cycle of "booms" and "busts," the most powerful seven nations, known as G-7 (the Group of 7) hold an annual summit. There they decide ways to control the global markets (Goad 1999).

One of the characteristics of capitalism is the certainty of the "boom-bust" cycle, along with the uncertainty of knowing when the economy will switch from "boom" to "bust" and back again. To try to control this cycle, G-7 uses the *International Monetary Fund*, a world bank that lends to nations in economic trouble. Yet the "boom-bust" cycle continues, and entire regions experience prosperity or poverty. In the 1990s, when the region dominated by Japan went into the "bust" part of the cycle and formerly booming factories in Thailand, Indonesia, and South Korea closed their doors, the value of these countries' currencies shrank, and capitalist leaders feared a global "bust." Now that we have global capitalism, the danger is that most of the world will be engulfed in these cycles.

A primary advantage of socialist economies was the more even distribution of a country's resources. This resulted in guaranteed jobs (although they paid little), an improved medical delivery system that reached almost everyone, and the elimination of hunger. Why did capitalism win the war? The simple answer is that capitalism is more efficient at producing wealth. In the socialist nations, there certainly was greater equality—almost everyone was poor. In the capitalist countries, although there is tremendous **social inequality**—the unequal distribution of wealth, income, power, and other opportunities—most people live at a high level. The wealth of capitalism, and the individual freedoms that it brings, are so attractive that millions of people beat down the door to enter the United States, whether legally or illegally.

For some individuals, however, such as Julie Treadman in our opening vignette, social inequality has dire consequences. Because we are examining social problems, social inequality is our focus.

FOUR ECONOMIC PROBLEMS FACING THE UNITED STATES

Four Problems:

Capitalism provides the setting for understanding problems of social inequality in the United States. Within this broad context of wealth and poverty are more specific issues that affect the future direction of the U.S. economy. Let's look at four of the problems that spell future trouble.

1. A Decline in Purchasing Power

The first is a decline in people's **real income** (income in constant dollars, that is, adjusted for inflation). For 25 years, from the end of World War II until 1970, the real income of U.S. workers rose steadily. For the past 30 years, however, real income has declined. The situation is deceptive, for workers have more dollars in their paychecks than they used to. But as Figure 7-1 shows, those dollars don't go as far as

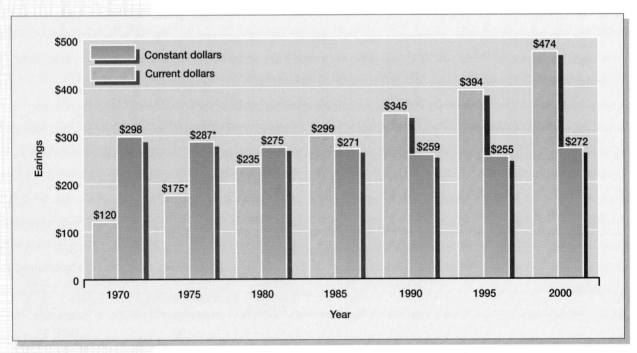

FIGURE 7-1
Average Weekly Earnings, in Current and Constant Dollars
*Note: Current dollars are the number of dollars earned that year. Constant dollars are those dollars adjusted for inflation and pegged to 1982. As 1975 is not given in the source, listed here is the mean of 1970 and 1980. Earnings include overtime.
(*Source: Statistical Abstract* 1993:Table 667; 2001:Table 616.)

they used to. Despite fat raises, you can see that U.S. workers have less purchsing power today than they did in 1970. Workers don't just *feel* poorer—they *are*.

What has softened the blow for the average family is that more family members are working. In 1940, only 16 percent of wives worked for wages. Today about 62 percent do (Davis and Robinson 1988; *Statistical Abstract* 2001:Table 577). Despite two incomes, however, the average family has barely kept up with inflation. Even with so many more wives now employed, after income is adjusted for inflation the average household today brings in just $2,000 more a year than it did in 1970 ($35,000 versus $33,000) (*Statistical Abstract* 1998:Table 739). After thiry years in which 15 million wives entered the labor force, the net gain in a family's income is only about 6 percent.

2. Taxes

The second major problem is taxes. Someone coined the term *Tax Freedom Day* to refer to the day when the average American has earned enough to pay his or her annual taxes. Politicians keep promising tax cuts, but because they never deliver on that promise Tax Freedom Day has been pushed forward relentlessly. It now falls on May 6 (Keating 1998). On average, each of us must work for the government for more than four months before we have a cent for our own needs!

3. Savings

The third major problem is illustrated by Figure 7-2. The U.S. savings rate has dropped to a low not seen even during the Great Depression of the 1930s. Americans save less than people in all other industrialized nations—just one-sixth of what the Japanese save. The significance of our drop in savings is that we have less money to invest in new plants and equipment, which may undermine our ability to compete in international trade or to increase our living standard.

4. The National Debt

Fourth, we import foreign goods at such a frenzied pace that the United States has become the largest debtor nation in the world. Each year, the amount that we spend on products we buy from other nations amounts to almost $436 billion more than the amount that we get from selling to them (*Statistical Abstract* 2001:Table 1297). These mountains of debt cannot keep piling up indefinitely. Just as

FIGURE 7-2

The Savings Slump, 1930–1997: How Much Americans Save of Their After-Tax Income

(*Source:* American Savings Education Council, 1999. *Statistical Abstract* 2001:Table 649.)

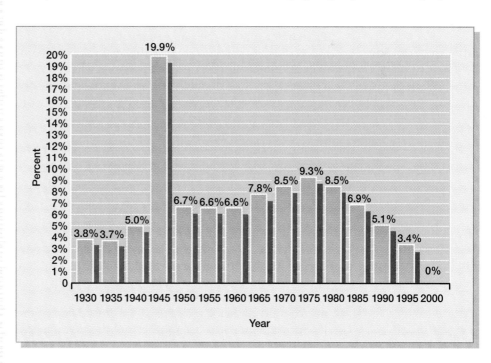

individuals must repay what they borrow or else get into financial trouble, so it is with nations. To finance the **national debt** (the total amount the U.S. government owes), we must pay over $200 billion a year in interest (*Statistical Abstract* 2001:Table 458). This is money that we cannot use to build schools and colleges, hire teachers, rebuild our cities, pay for medical services for the poor, operate Head Start programs, or pay for any other services to help improve our quality of life.

THE NATURE OF POVERTY

Three Types of Poverty:

1. Biological Poverty

2. Relative Poverty

3. Official Poverty

With this broad background, let's analyze poverty. You might think that poverty would be easy to define, but its definition is neither simple nor obvious. There are three types of poverty. **Biological poverty** refers to starvation and malnutrition—to the starving children in Bangladesh and the Sudan whose pictures you see on TV. It also refers to housing and clothing so inadequate that people suffer from exposure. Our homeless endure biological poverty.

More common is **relative poverty.** This refers to people living below the standards of their society or group. Some relative poverty is serious, such as the Americans who try to get by on only half or even one quarter of the average national income. On another level are members of country clubs who feel "poor" because they are among the few who don't have new Jaguars or Porsches. Relative poverty also exists on a world scale: What is poverty in the United States would mean comfortable living in India, where most families have little clothing, little food, and live in just a room or two.

The United States and most other countries also have a third type of poverty. **Official poverty** refers to the income level at which people are eligible for welfare benefits. People below this **poverty line** are poor; those above it are not. The United States developed its definition of official poverty in 1962. The poor spent about one third of their income on food, so the Social Security administration determined the poverty line by multiplying a low-level food budget by 3 (Fisher 1998). The U.S. government has kept this rough figure, adjusting it annually to match the Consumer Price Index, the official gauge of inflation.

The Poverty Line Is Stuck in a Time Warp

Sociologists point out that this definition is stuck in a time warp. Sociologist William Julius Wilson (1992) and policy analyst Patricia Ruggles (1990, 1992) stress how food preferences and cooking patterns have changed since the 1960s, but not the government's definition of poverty. Sociologist Michael Katz (1989) also notes how unrealistic this definition is; it assumes that everyone is a careful shopper who cooks all the family meals at home and never has guests. Who lives like this? Nevertheless, this is how the magical line is drawn to separate the poor from the nonpoor. Using this rock-bottom definition, let's look at official poverty in the United States.

◆ The Scope of the Problem ◆

Changes in the Number Below the Poverty Line

When the official definition of poverty was developed, about 40 million people—more than a fifth of the population—fell below the poverty line. In the early 1960s, President Johnson launched what he called the "war on poverty." With new welfare benefits and other programs, in just ten years the number of Americans below the official poverty line dropped to 13 percent, or about 25 million people. This dramatic reduction made it clear that poverty could be solved. Since then, however, little or no progress has been made, and the percentage has hovered between 12 and 15 percent. Currently, it is 11.8 percent (*Statistical Abstract* 2001:Table 684). With our larger population, that 11.8 percent represents 33 million people, about the same number who were poor before the "war on poverty."

Most people who fall below the poverty line are not permanently poor. Most are poor only for short periods, such as when they are injured or sick, or during layoffs or slow seasons (such as in winter, when there are few construction jobs). Although the U.S. total of poor people remains fairly constant from year to year, there is much change within it; each year millions of people rise above the poverty line, while millions of others fall below it.

The poverty line, of course, is arbitrary in the first place, and the number of "poor" people can be reduced or raised at will by changing the official definition. While some argue that the real number of poor is higher than the official measure, others claim it is less. They point out that many benefits of antipoverty programs are not counted when we figure a recipient's income. Medicare, Medicaid, food stamps, and HUD vouchers (the amount the government pays in rent for poor families) are not counted, but they reduce the poor's need for cash income.

Although experts may disagree about how many poor people there are, three facts stand out: Millions of Americans live in poverty; how poverty is defined has serious consequences, for the definition determines who will receive help and who will not; and poverty lies at the root of many of our other social problems. We have seen the connection between poverty and prostitution, rape, murder, and alcoholism and other forms of drug addiction. In coming chapters, we shall see how poverty is related to other social problems such as racism, illness, and family breakdown.

SOCIAL INEQUALITY

Social inequality contradicts our ideals. A common way Americans cope with this contradiction is to deny it. For example, when researchers ask people what class they belong to, most Americans—whether rich or poor—say that they are "middle class." Even Ann Getty, a former saleswoman who married the heir to the Getty oil fortune, told an interviewer, "I lead a very ordinary life" (*New York Times,* Sept. 7, 1980). Her "ordinary life" included living in a San Francisco mansion and taking along her personal chef whenever she flew to Paris.

We know that all Americans are not equal, of course, and that the life chances of a waitress's daughter differ immensely from those of a son born to wealthy parents. We all know that the rich and politically connected pass their advantages to their children. Because of this, we have legislation to help level the playing field. Social programs such as affirmative action, as well as college scholarships, and community colleges, are attempts to provide more equal opportunity.

Such programs, however, run up against **structural inequality,** the inequality that is built into our economic and social institutions. Differences in wages are an example. If a society has 100 million jobs and 30 million of them pay low wages, the job market has inequality built into it. Unemployment is another example. If a society has 107 million workers but only 100 million jobs, then 7 million workers will be unemployed, regardless of how hard they look for work. Job training programs will not solve this structural problem. The solution requires more jobs.

DISTRIBUTION OF INCOME AND WEALTH

A major consequence of structural inequality is a vast inequality in the income of Americans. Look at Figure 7-3. The poorest fifth of Americans receives only 4.3 percent of the nation's income, while 47.2 percent of the country's entire income goes

Most Poverty Is Temporary

Disagreements Over How Many People Are Poor

Poverty as a Root of Other Social Problems

The Tendency to Deny Social Inequality

Structural Inequality

How Income Inequality Has Increased

FIGURE 7-3
Distribution of the Income of the United States
(*Source: Statistical Abstract of the United States* 2001:Table 670.)

Percentage of the U.S. Population	Percentage of the Nation's Income Received
20%	47.2%
20%	23%
20%	15.6%
20%	9.9%
20%	4.3%

to the richest fifth. Despite numerous antipoverty programs, *income inequality today is greater than it was in the 1940s.* The poorest fifth of Americans now receive less of the nation's income than they did in the 1940s (a drop from 5.4 percent to 4.3 percent). The richest fifth receive more than ever (an increase from about 41 percent to 47.2 percent).

The Distribution of Wealth

Another way to view financial inequality is to look at the distribution of **wealth,** what people own—their property, savings, investments, and other economic assets. Americans are worth about $42 trillion, mostly in the form of real estate, corporate stock, and business assets (*Statistical Abstract* 2001:Table 689). As Figure 7-4 shows, one tenth of our families own nearly two-thirds of this wealth. They own half of the value of all real estate in the country, as well as 90 percent of all corporate stocks and business assets. At the top of this group, wealth is incredibly concentrated. The richest 400,000 households (about one half of 1 percent of all Americans) virtually control corporate America (Stafford et al. 1986–87; *Wall Street Journal,* July 28, 1986:38).

With $51 billion, the richest person in the United States—and the world—is Bill Gates, who dropped out of Harvard to cofound Microsoft Corp., the world's largest software company. Gates developed MS-DOS and Windows, two computer operat-

FIGURE 7-4
Distribution of the Wealth of the United States

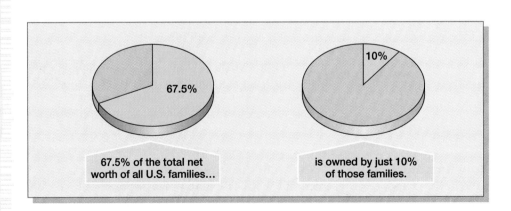

67.5%

10%

67.5% of the total net worth of all U.S. families…

is owned by just 10% of those families.

Chapter 7 Economic Problems: Wealth and Poverty

How Much Is a Billion Dollars?

ing systems, and gets a licensing fee each time a computer using these systems is sold. He has now expanded into global communications.

How much is a billion dollars? Since neither you nor I is likely to have a bank account this size, an illustration can help us grasp the enormity of a billion dollars—*one thousand million dollars:*

> Suppose you were born on the day Christ was born, that you are still alive today, and that you have been able to save money at the fantastic rate of one cent for every second that you lived—that is, $.60 for every minute, $36 for every hour, or $864 for every day of your life during these past two thousand years. At that rate, it would take you another thousand years to save one billion dollars. (Shaffer 1986)

The Problem with the Concentration of Wealth

As research scientist James Smith said, "Wealth is a good thing, and everyone ought to have some" (Stafford et al. 1986–87:3). Then what is the problem? Part of the problem is that vast wealth brings vast power. Because owning 10 or 20 percent of a company's stock is enough to control it, the 400,000 or so households who own nearly half of all corporate stock wield immense power over the economy. In their pursuit of even more wealth, this elite can move production to Mexico, Ireland, Portugal, or Taiwan, where labor is cheaper, closing down factories here and throwing thousands of people out of work. Most designer jeans, for example, are made in Korea or Hong Kong. The people in the United States who stand to lose their jobs—the workers—don't make these decisions, but they must live with the consequences.

Finally, because the rich can hire Washington lobbyists and pay for top financial advice, they perpetuate their advantages. They live in a world in which they are protected from unemployment, not being able to pay the rent, having the utilities cut off, the breakdown of the family car, injustice in the courts, and an unresponsive political system. Let's turn our attention to those who must cope with such things as part of their everyday lives.

Poverty is much more than having little money. Poverty means the reduction of life's chances—including the greater likelihood of disease, death, and divorce. This photo was taken in Appalachia, a region where poverty persists generation after generation.

The national debt has become a national concern. The taxes that go to pay its interest are money lost for other programs that could improve the quality of life of most citizens, such as building parks and libraries, and of poor citizens in particular, such as programs to help them overcome poverty. Shown here is the national debt clock on Sixth Avenue in New York City.

How Subjective Concerns Have Changed the Social Problem of Poverty

The War on Poverty

The Impact of Poverty:

THE EXTENT AND IMPACT OF POVERTY

As with other social problems, poverty does not depend solely on objective conditions. Subjective concerns are central. Consider the extremes: If poverty is extensive but few are concerned about it, it is *not* a social problem. If there is little poverty and many people want to do something about it, poverty *is* a social problem. Let's look at examples.

During the early years of the United States, most people were poor. Yet poverty was not considered to be a social problem. Life had always been like this, so people assumed that poverty was part of the natural order. As industrialization progressed, the nineteenth century produced an abundance of jobs and wealth. Poverty declined. But a mass migration to U.S. cities and the rapid growth of those cities made the smaller amount of poverty more visible, and public leaders declared it a social problem. As the immigrants were absorbed into the expanding work force, once again poverty was lost from sight. Then came the Great Depression of the 1930s. As people were thrown out of work, the ranks of the poor swelled. Poverty was proclaimed the greatest problem facing the nation, and the government established emergency programs to reduce it. World War II and postwar prosperity then diverted attention from poverty. Even though the objective conditions still existed, subjective concerns dropped. Tucked away in out-of-the-way rural areas and urban slums, the poor remained invisible to most.

In 1960, President Kennedy tried to make poverty a campaign issue, but subjective concerns were not really aroused until Michael Harrington wrote *The Other America* in 1962. Rarely has a single volume of social science transformed people's consciousness as did this one. Harrington passionately argued that in the midst of "the affluent society," one quarter of the nation lived in squalor. Policymakers read it, the media discussed it, and sociologists assigned it to their students. Within two years of the book's publication, President Johnson declared a "war on poverty." A raft of programs for the poor was begun: child-care services, Head Start, legal services, medical services, job training programs, subsidized housing, and community health centers. During the 1980s, politicians declared big government, budget deficits, and the national debt to be even greater social problems, and these programs were cut back.

The "war on poverty" was effective. As Figure 7-5 shows, 22 percent of Americans had incomes below the official poverty line in 1960, but in just ten years this total dropped to 13 percent. After holding steady for about 20 years, the national average has dropped again. It now is just 11.3 percent. Now look at the white, Latino, and African-American rates of poverty. As you can see, national averages cover up significant differences.

We'll return to these differences shortly, but first let's consider the impact of poverty. Being poor does not simply mean having less money and therefore going to fewer movies, buying fewer video games, having two pairs of slacks instead of a

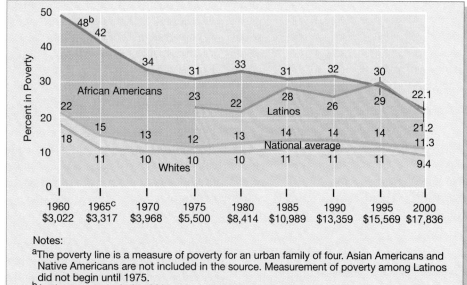

FIGURE 7-5

Trends in U.S. Poverty: Percent below the Poverty Line, by Race/Ethnicity[a]

(*Source:* U.S. Census 2000:Table A-4 Poverty in the U.S.)

Notes:

[a]The poverty line is a measure of poverty for an urban family of four. Asian Americans and Native Americans are not included in the source. Measurement of poverty among Latinos did not begin until 1975.

[b]As the source excludes African Americans for 1960, data from 1959 are used for African Americans.

[c]As the source excludes 1965 data, 1966 data are used.

dozen, and eating steak less often. Rather, people's economic circumstances envelop them, profoundly affecting every aspect of life, including housing, education, jobs, stress and well-being, health, and justice.

Housing

Most of the poor live in substandard housing. Many rent from landlords who neglect their buildings. The plumbing may not work. The heating system may break down in winter. Roaches and rats may run riot. And, unlike having a mortgage, paying rent does not build up equity in a home.

Education

Although public schools are supposed to give everyone an equal opportunity to succeed, the poor are at a disadvantage. Because our schools are supported by property taxes, and property in poorer areas produces less taxes, the schools the poor attend have smaller budgets, and usually outdated textbooks and inexperienced teachers who are paid less (Kozol 1999).

Poverty directly affects people's chances of getting an education. If you rank families from the richest to the poorest, as you go down the income ladder the likelihood that children will go to college drops (Manski 1992–93). Most poor children who do go to college attend community colleges where they are funneled into vocational programs. In contrast, the children of the middle classes attend state universities and private colleges. At the high school level, the exclusive boarding schools are reserved for children of the elite, whose learning environment includes small classes and well-paid teachers (Persell et al. 1992). These students inherit a cozy social network: Their schools' college advisers are connected with the admissions officers of the nation's most elite colleges. These networks are so efficient that half of a private school's graduating class may be admitted to just Harvard, Yale, and Princeton (Persell and Cookson 1985).

Employment

Unlike the career paths open to the children of the middle class and the rich, the low-paying jobs of the working poor lead nowhere. Because they are often laid off from their dead-end jobs, their low incomes are erratic. During unemployment, they have to cope with the complex bureaucracies of unemployment insurance, welfare, and other social programs designed to carry them along. Such experiences add to the stress of lives that are already filled with anxiety.

The poor are also given a different walk through the halls of justice. As discussed in Chapter 6, their life experiences make them more likely to commit robberies and assaults, crimes that are especially visible and for which offenders are severely punished. White-collar crime may be more pervasive and costly to society, but it is less visible and carries a milder punishment. As mentioned earlier, when the poor are arrested they lack the resources to hire good lawyers to defend themselves, and often cannot even post bail.

In short, wealth and income represent privileges—received or denied. The net result is a quality of life that goes right to the core of one's being. Job insecurity brings nightmares to the poor. Their jobs offer no pension plans and often no medical benefits. They live one paycheck away from eviction. If they get sick, they are laid off, and their job may not be there when they return to work. Among the stark repercussions: Those at the lower end of the income scale don't eat as well, they are more likely to have accidents at work and at home, and their children are more likely to die in infancy. And, like Julie Treadman in the opening vignette, they have less access to good medical care, which further jeopardizes their well being.

◆ Looking at the Problem Theoretically ◆

As we saw in previous chapters, each of the theoretical perspectives gives a different view of a social problem. Let's look at poverty through these lenses.

SYMBOLIC INTERACTIONISM

Andy, Sharon, and their two children live in a small house in a rural area. Andy farms sixty-five acres and works part-time in the local grocery store. Sharon works part-time as a cook at the Dew Drop Inn. Between their jobs and the farm, they make about $14,000 a year. They grow their own vegetables, and they fish in a nearby pond. Integrated into the community and with their basic needs satisfied, they don't think of themselves as poor. Neither do their friends and neighbors.

Leslie attends a private college. Her parents pay her tuition, rent, insurance, medical bills, and give her $600 a month "for extras." Unlike many of her friends, she has no car, and she complains about how hard it is to be poor. Her affluent friends feel sorry for her.

Keith, a struggling young actor, auditions often and works part-time as a waiter. He earns about $1,300 a month, which has to cover his rent, food, and all other expenses. "It's difficult to make it," he says, "but one day you'll see my name in lights." Keith sees himself as "struggling"—not poor. Nor do his actor friends think of him as poor.

Maria and her two children live in a housing project. Her rent is subsidized and cheap—$97 a month. Her welfare, Medicaid, and food stamps amount to $13,287 tax-free a year. Her two children attend school during the day, and she takes classes in English at the settlement house. Maria considers herself poor, and so do the government and her neighbors.

By the government's standards, all but Leslie are poor, and yet it is Leslie (and Maria) who *feel* poor. Why?

The Relativity of Poverty

Symbolic interactionists stress that to understand poverty we must focus on what poverty *means* to people. To evaluate their position in life, people *compare* themselves with others. Simple marginal living is often the norm in rural areas, but in Leslie's cosmopolitan circle people feel deprived if they cannot afford designer clothing. The meaning of poverty, then, is *relative* and differs from group to group within the same society, as well as from culture to culture and from one era to the next.

To understand poverty, we must focus also on how the non-poor view the poor. The dominant view may be that the poor are good people who are down on their luck and need a helping hand. Or the poor may be viewed as "no-goods" who refuse to work and are a drain on society's resources. Such differences in meaning are significant, for they have a direct impact on social policy. Let's look at how these views have changed.

Historical Changes in the Meaning of Poverty and Its Relationship to Social Action

The view of poverty in the early 1700s stands in marked contrast to today's perspective. Americans viewed poverty as God's will, and clergy preached that the poor were put on earth to provide an opportunity for the rest of us to express Christian charity (Rothman and Rothman 1972). Poverty was not seen as a social problem, but as a personal one, an ordinary part of life that required compassion on the part of others.

The poor had been scattered among hundreds of villages along country roads. By the time of the American Revolution, however, they started to be concentrated in colonial cities such as Boston, Philadelphia, and New York City. Welfare committees were set up, and they distinguished between the deserving and undeserving poor. The deserving poor were the blind, the handicapped, and the deserted mothers. The undeserving poor were the beggars, peddlers, idlers, and prostitutes. At this point, the meaning of poverty changed. It was no longer considered God's will, but was something that happened to people who had character flaws.

Sweeping reforms under President Jackson (1829–1837) again transformed the meaning of poverty. The reformers saw poverty as the product of corrupt cities. Urban temptations—alcohol, crime, and debauchery—held people in the bondage of poverty (Rothman and Rothman 1972).

Although we no longer believe that poverty is God's will, the idea that poverty ought not to exist—and the suspicion that it is due to the character of the poor—remain part of our symbolic heritage. We have vacillated since the Jacksonian era between viewing the poor as worthy people who deserve our help and as worthless people who deserve nothing but a kick in the pants. Symbolic interactionists make us aware that the meanings of poverty change as social conditions change.

FUNCTIONALISM

The Functionalist View of Social Inequality

In a classic essay in 1945, sociologists Kingsley Davis and Wilbert Moore developed the functionalist perspective on social inequality. Their argument is simple. Some tasks in society are more important than others. Because these demanding positions require talented people who are willing to make a sacrifice to prepare for them, they must offer high income and prestige. Finding oil, for example, is vital to keeping industry going, but it takes years of training in geology. Consequently, geologists must be offered both a substantial salary and the respect of others. Anyone can wash dishes, so unskilled workers earn poverty wages doing it. Thus, disparities in income help society function.

The Social Functions of

Functionalists go beyond this by saying that poverty itself is functional for society. Sociologist Herbert Gans (1973/1999), a proponent of this perspective, points out how the poor make significant contributions to society's well-being. For a summary of this view, see the Thinking Critically box on the next page. Functional theorists also analyze the dysfunctions of poverty, including alienation and despair, drug abuse, street crime, suicide, and mental illness.

CONFLICT THEORY

The Conflict View of Social Inequality

Conflict theorists view the functionalist argument as absolutely wrong. To say that inequality comes from the need to offer higher rewards for more responsible, demanding positions justifies the power of the wealthy and the deprivation of the poor. Social inequality, argue conflict theorists, comes from the struggle over limited resources. At any point in history, some group has gained control of society's resources, and that group uses its power to secure its gains and exploit the others. The result is a social class system in which the wealthy pass their advantages to their children, while the poor pass disadvantages on to theirs.

Marx's General Theory of Social Class Relations

Karl Marx (1818–1883) was the first sociologist to develop a general theory of social class and class relations. He argued that social class depends on a single factor, the *means of production*—the tools, factories, land, and capital used to produce wealth (Marx 1867/1967; Marx and Engels 1848/1964). People either own the means of production (the capitalists, or *bourgeoisie*) or they work for those who do (the workers, or *proletariat*).

Marx developed a radical view of society's institutions, such as its legal and political systems. They exist in a capitalist society, he said, to promote the interests of the owners and to control the workers. The history of a society is best understood as the conflict between owners and workers, the wealthy and the poor.

The day will come when the workers will revolt. They will lose their *false class consciousness* (their mistaken idea that they are capitalists) and gain *class consciousness*, a realization that they are all workers no matter what their status or occupation,

Functionalists argue that the highest salaries go to the positions that perform the most important functions for society. Critics respond that if this were true then garbage collectors would be among the most highly paid members of society. Shown here are two garbage collectors in Marietta, Georgia—who, needless to say, do not receive the salaries and stock options awarded CEOs.

THINKING CRITICALLY ABOUT SOCIAL PROBLEMS

Why We Need the Poor: How Poverty Helps Society

Most of us think of poverty in only negative terms: It is undesirable, and we should get rid of it. Functionalists, in contrast, identify the functions of poverty, that is, its positive consequences for society. Consider these twelve functions:

1. The poor ensure that society's dirty work gets done at low cost. If there weren't poor people, who would be willing to do these dirty jobs at low wages? Many industries, restaurants, farms, and hospitals could not survive in their present state without this underpaid work force.

2. The poor create jobs for others. Think of the social workers and welfare agencies that serve the poor and, not incidentally, shield the rest of us from them. Most police officers probably would be without jobs if it weren't for the poor.

3. The poor serve as guinea pigs in medical experiments. The rest of us benefit from these advances in medicine.

4. The poor make the economy more efficient. They spend welfare money on leftover goods such as day-old bread and the many "seconds" produced by our industry. They also buy the furniture and cars that the rest of us discard. Where else would these undesirable items go if it weren't for the poor?

5. The poor make others wealthy. Think of the many slum landlords who would have to get jobs if it weren't for the poor.

6. The poor help some people become upwardly mobile. Just above those on welfare are people who are striving to reach the fringes of the middle class. A good example is those who run the many small stores in the inner cities. Without the poor, they would have to close their doors.

7. The poor provide the front line soldiers for war, the dispensable ones who can be sacrificed during battle. (The Germans used to call them "cannon fodder.")

8. The poor stabilize our political system. Most vote for Democrats, so to the degree that this party helps the U.S. political system, the poor contribute to that effort.

9. The poor provide entertainment. Their lives of despair are the grist for countless stories, especially television news. The revelation of their murder and mayhem shock and frighten us. Some may disagree with this depiction, but to be transported out of our ordinary lives by dramatic accounts of the lives of others is certainly one definition of entertainment.

10. The poor enrich our music. They have given us the blues, Negro spirituals, country music (from the Southern poor), and rock (the Beatles came from the slums of Liverpool). Without their devastating experiences, the rest of us would have fewer tunes to hum.

11. The poor help our motivation. That there are "the projects," skid row, and soup lines keeps us on our toes. We know that we had better get an education and work hard or else we could end up there. The poor have replaced the "bogeyman" of past years.

12. The poor also help our self-concept. They make us all feel superior.

By the time functionalists get through with their analysis, one wonders how society could exist without the poor.

Based on Gans 1973/1999.

whether it be garbage collector or college professor. With their eyes finally opened and with a common identity, they will seize the means of production and use them for the good of all. Thus poverty will be eliminated.

Modificatons in Conflict Theory

Most sociologists acknowledge that Marx provided valuable insight into relationships between the powerful and the poor, but they find his class division, with only owners and workers, inadequate for today's society. Erik Wright (1979, 1985) points out that many managers of corporations have little in common with office and factory workers. In fact, some managers now have more power than the stockholders they work for (Cohen 1990). Ralf Dahrendorf (1959, 1973) points to authority, not ownership, as the key dimension of social class.

No matter what specific form it takes, conflict theory always stresses the relationship between those who have power and those who do not. The problems of the poor are due to their deprived position in a system of stratification, to their relative powerlessness and oppression.

In Sum

The Contributions of Each Theory

Each of the three theoretical lenses provides us a unique understanding of wealth, poverty, and inequality. Focusing on the individual level, symbolic interactionists make us more sensitive to how social class works in our everyday lives. They explain, for example, why the amount of income that people have (objective measures) differs from how people see themselves (relative poverty). Functionalists and conflict theorists look at the bigger picture. Where functionalists see inequality as originating from a broad social need to reward important positions, however, conflict theorists point to its origin in the means of production.

◆ Research Findings ◆

Who Are the Poor?

A striking characteristic of poverty is how it is distributed. The poor are concentrated in urban ghettos and in rural areas such as Appalachia. The Social Map on the next page shows the differences in poverty among the states. As you can see, the regional differences are striking.

Race/Ethnicity

As we saw in Figure 7-5 (page 221), poverty also follows lines of race-ethnicity: African Americans and Latinos are more than twice as likely as whites to be poor. This figure shows that the poverty rate of Latinos is about the same as that of African Americans and that the poverty rate for both groups has dropped in recent years. They are now about where the national average was in 1960. The drop in poverty among African Americans is especially striking. As Figure 7-5 shows, their poverty rate is now less than half of what it used to be.

Age

Poverty is also related to age. The poverty rate of children is 40 percent *higher* than that of adults; overall, 11.3 percent of U.S. adults are poor, but 16.2 percent of children live in poverty (Census Bureau 2001; Poverty in the U.S., 2000:Table A-4). Figure 7-7 shows how poverty among children mirrors the nation's racial-ethnic pattern: About one of eight white children lives in poverty, but for African-American and Latino children it is about one of three. For any child to have to live in poverty is unfortunate, but the extent of this poverty has severe implications for an entire generation of Latinos and African Americans.

Single-Parent Families

Why is poverty higher among children than adults, and why has it increased? There is no single answer, but part of the explanation is due to changes in family

FIGURE 7-6
Social Map: The Geography of U.S. Poverty
(*Source*: U.S. Census Bureau, Current Population Survey, March 1999, 2000, and 2001.)

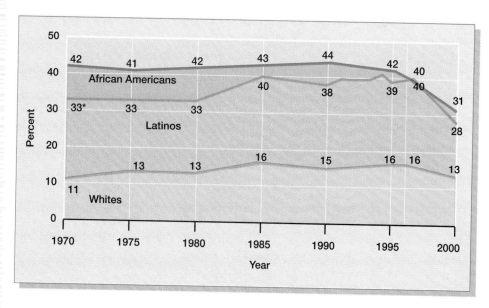

Least Poverty 5–10%
Average Poverty 11–14%
Most Poverty 15–25%

composition (see Figure 7-8 on page 228). Most poor children live in single-parent families, which are almost invariably female-headed. We have more female-headed families because of more births to single women and more divorce. A young unmarried mother has a hard time supporting both herself and a baby: She is not likely to receive much help from the father, she has a baby to care for, and if she is unskilled and undereducated, how can she compete in the labor market? Similarly, a wife's income usually takes a nose-dive after divorce: Child support is often unpaid, and if a woman has been out of the work force, her skills may be rusty. Consequently, compared with men, women and children are much more likely to be poor. Sociologists

FIGURE 7-7
U.S. Children in Poverty
(*Source*: U.S. Census Bureau (2000) Poverty in the U.S., 2000:Table A-2.)

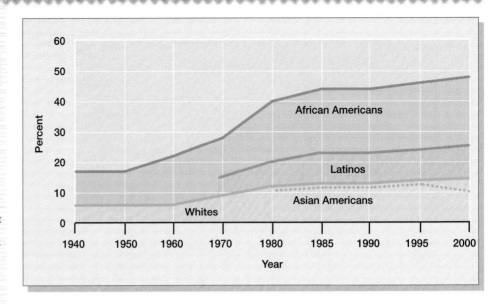

FIGURE 7-8
Growth in Families Headed by Women 1940–2000

Note: Asian Americans include Pacific Islanders.
(*Sources:* For 1940, 1950, and 1960, U.S. Bureau of the Census, *Current Population Reports*, Series P-20, various numbers; for 1970, *Statistical Abstract* 1994:Table 71; for later years, *Statistical Abstract* 2001:Tables 53, 54, 57.)

call this the **feminization of poverty.** (If you want to avoid poverty, see the Thinking Critically box below.)

The Elderly

Poverty also used to plague the elderly, but, as mentioned in Chapter 2, their economic situation has improved. At 10 percent, the poverty rate of Americans over age 65 is now *lower* than that of the nation as a whole (*Statistical Abstract* 2001:Table 683). Social Security is the primary reason for the reduction in poverty among the elderly. This improvement shows that social legislation can work and that we can allow a group to stay in poverty or not. We shall consider social policy later.

An Underclass to Do Society's Dirty Work?

Finally, there is the obvious pattern of low wages. People who are paid the minimum wage are likely to be poor. I am not referring to college students who take

THINKING CRITICALLY ABOUT SOCIAL PROBLEMS

Rules for Avoiding Poverty

If you want to avoid poverty, follow these three rules:

1. Finish high school.
2. Get married before having your first child.
3. Don't have a child before you reach the age of 20.

This message is being delivered to the black community by African-American leaders. Hugh Price, president of the National Urban League, and retired General Colin Powell say that 80 percent of African Americans who ignore these principles end up poor, but only 8 percent of those who follow them are poor. Although their statistics may not be exact, the rules are sound—and they apply to all racial-ethnic groups. To these "rules," one can add three more:

4. Go to college.
5. Stay married.
6. Avoid alcoholism.

Poverty among people who follow these six rules is practically nonexistent.

Based on Herbert 1998.

Poverty in the United States has become concentrated among women and children, a phenomenon that sociologists call the feminization of poverty. Poverty is especially high among teenage mothers, such as this young woman and her son.

such jobs while they are on the way to careers that pay well. Rather, we have an *underclass,* people who are locked into society's low-paying dirty work. Legal and illegal immigrants do "stoop labor" on farms and fill the sweatshops of our cities. Many work in the clothing industry's small factories or even at home, where they get paid a small amount for each piece of work they complete. Although there are no accurate counts, this underclass appears to number several million.

In Sum

The patterns sociologists uncover illustrate that poverty is not a matter of an individual here or there being lazy or stupid. Instead, it is a *structural* matter; that is, poverty is built into the social system and follows lines of age, gender, and race-ethnicity. Consequently, sociologists examine features of the social system: discrimination, marriage and reproductive patterns, how welfare programs function, a changing economy, and the creation of an underclass. We discuss some of these patterns in later chapters when we examine race-ethnic relations, gender discrimination, the changing family, and urban problems.

IS THERE A CULTURE OF POVERTY?

We boast of vast achievement and of power,
Of human progress knowing no defeat,
Of strange new marvels every day and hour—
And here's the bread line in the wintry street!

BERTON BRALEY, "THE BREAD LINE"

Poverty in the Midst of Plenty

How things have changed! We used to associate bread lines and soup kitchens with the Great Depression, or perhaps with Charles Dickens' description of nineteenth-century London. But the homeless are now part of every major city across this rich land. Some are tucked out of sight. The blatant presence of others on our cities' sidewalks, dressed in rags and ravaged by hunger, reveals the contrast between the American dream and its stark reality—between "us" and "them." Who are they, and how did they get that way? Some answers are provided on page 232 in the Thinking Critically box on the homeless.

The homeless are only one segment of the "hard-core" poor. Where the urban hard-core poor live is easy to spot. Every major city has sections with filthy streets and neglected buildings, some boarded up, others burned out. Children and adults loiter on sidewalks and stoops, and the air may be filled with an unpleasant odor of garbage or urine. Where the rural hard-core poor live is not so easy to spot. They are not as clustered together, and most are tucked away in tiny pockets.

A Culture of Poverty

Based on participant observation and life histories, anthropologist Oscar Lewis (1959, 1966) concluded that the hard-core poor develop a distinct way of life that traps them in poverty. He called this the **culture of poverty**—ways of coping with the despair and hopelessness that accompany poor people's realization of the overwhelming odds against their achieving success in mainstream society (Wilson 1987). They become passive, fatalistic, and think primarily of the present. They develop low aspirations and feel inferior, insecure, and desperate, as though they do not belong. They also become self-destructive, with high rates of alcoholism, physical violence, and severe family problems—broken marriages, desertion, wife beating, and single-parent households. The way of life they develop makes it almost impossible for them to break out of poverty.

This is an interesting concept, but is it true? To find out, economist Patricia Ruggles examined national statistics. Her findings both challenge and support a culture of poverty. Contrary to popular belief, few people pass poverty on to the next generation: *Most children of the poor do not grow up to be poor.* Only about one in five persons who are poor as children are still poor when they are adults (Corcoran et al. 1985; Sawhill 1988; Ruggles 1989, 1990). But in support of a culture of poverty, Ruggles also found that about 1 percent of the U.S. population remains poor year in and year out. They were poor 20 years ago, and they are poor today. This group has three primary characteristics: Most are African American, unemployed, and live in female-headed households. About half are unmarried mothers with children.

How do we reconcile Ruggles' findings? The fairest conclusion seems to be this: Some people may have a culture of poverty that perpetuates itself; they have behaviors that keep them poor for generations. Because most people who are poor today will not be poor in just a few years, however, we can conclude that most poor people do not have such a culture.

Is there a culture of poverty, one that locks its members into poverty and deprivation and is transmitted across generations? Sociologists dislike this theory and do their best to deny it, but it is no more unreasonable than the view that there is a culture of wealth. See the photo on the facing page.

The Basic Question: Who Has the Power?

Difficult to Answer in a Large, Modern, Complex Society

The Power Elite/Ruling Class

The Circulation of Elites

Is there a culture of wealth, one that locks its members into wealth and privilege and is transmitted across generations? Sociologists have no difficulty in agreeing that such a culture (or, more accurately phrased, subculture) exists, and in identifying it at such events as the Blandwood Ball in Greenwood, North Carolina (shown here). We sociologists, like the rest of society, perceive through colored lenses, and a culture of wealth matches our bias in favor of the oppressed of society. As symbolic interactionists point out, it is impossible to perceive events except from some perspective. We use the research methods described in Chapter 1 to overcome our biases.

Conflict theorists stress that to understand society we must understand who controls its scarce resources. Power, like wealth, is a scarce resource, and some people have much of it, while others have little or none. The possession of power is especially significant, because it determines how the other resources of society are divided. Let's ask, then, who makes the big decisions in the United States?

This is not easy to answer. In the past, societies had a simpler organization. In feudal societies, the serfs formed a working class and the feudal lords an ownership class. The feudal lords controlled both the means of production and the political system. Today, in contrast, the owners of the means of production do not directly run the political system. In today's political state, connections with business are complex, with numerous, indirect lines running from one to the other. Let's see what answers sociologists have come up with.

Sociologist C. Wright Mills (1959a) argued that a **power elite** rules the United States. With access to the center of political power, a tiny group makes the decisions that direct the country—and shake the world. As Figure 7-9 on page 233 illustrates, the power elite consists of the top leaders of the largest corporations, the top commanders of the armed forces, and a few elite politicians—the president, his cabinet, and members of Congress who chair the major committees.

Mills stressed that the power elite is not a formal group. It meets neither in secret nor in public. In fact, some members may not think that they belong to it. But, structurally, it exists. It consists of a group of people whose interests have coalesced. As people move from top posts in business to government and back again, or from the military to the defense industry, the power elite gains cohesion. White House aides join powerful law firms. A law partner joins the president's cabinet or is appointed secretary of the treasury. The head of the treasury becomes president of a leading bank or corporation. An air force colonel retires and heads the sales division of Lockheed or Boeing.

THINKING CRITICALLY ABOUT SOCIAL PROBLEMS

America's Homeless

When I met Larry Rice, who runs a shelter for the homeless in St. Louis, Missouri, he said that as a sociologist interested in social problems I needed to know firsthand what was happening on our city streets. I resisted, reluctant to leave my comfortable home and office to see who knows what. Larry offered to take me to Washington, D.C., where he promised that I would see people sleeping on grates within view of the White House. Intrigued, I agreed to accept his invitation, not knowing that it would change my own life.

It was a December night, and I saw what he promised: people dressed in rags and huddled over the exhaust grates of federal buildings. Not all of them survived that first night I was there. Freddie, a homeless, disabled man, froze to death as he sought refuge from the cold in a telephone booth. I vividly recall looking at the telephone booth where his stiff body was found, still upright, futilely covered by a tattered piece of canvas. I went to his funeral and talked with his friends.

It was too much to ignore. I had to find out more. I visited a dozen skid rows in the United States and Canada, sleeping in shelters and interviewing the homeless—in back alleys and street corners, parks and dumpsters. I became so troubled by what I found that for three months after I returned home I couldn't get through an entire night without waking up with disturbed dreams.

Here are the types of homeless I found:

1. *'Push-outs'*: People pushed out of their home, from teenagers kicked out by parents to adults evicted by landlords.

2. *Victims of environmental catastrophe*: From floods and fires to dioxin.

3. *The mentally ill*: Discharged from mental hospitals without support and unable to care for themselves.

4. *The new poor*: Unemployed workers whose work skills have become outmoded due to technological change.

5. *The technologically unqualified*: The unemployed who never possessed technological qualifications.

6. *The elderly*: Old, unemployable, and poor.

7. *Runaways*: Fleeing intolerable situations, they wander our streets.

8. *The demoralized*: After personal tragedy (often a divorce), they have given up in despair.

9. *Alcoholics*: The old-fashioned skid-row wino.

10. *Ease addicts*: They choose to be homeless, taking an "early retirement" (sometimes in their twenties).

11. *Travel addicts* ("road dogs" by their own term): They also choose to be homeless; addicted to a wanderlust, they continually travel.

12. *Excitement addicts*: They enjoy the thrill of danger, of "living on the edge."

As you can see, homelessness is not one-dimensional. It has many "causes." People get there by many "routes." Note how different the last three types (a minority of the homeless) are from the first nine types, people who do not want to be homeless. To solve this problem, we need multifaceted programs that are based on the various "routes" traveled to this dead-end destination called homelessness.

Shared Backgrounds and Interests

Their shared interests and interlocking experiences in business and politics are sufficient to assure that members of the power elite think alike on major issues. But, in addition, they come from similar backgrounds. Most are white Anglo-Saxon Protestants who have attended exclusive prep schools and Ivy League colleges. They share ideologies and values. Many belong to the same private clubs and vacation at the same exclusive resorts. Some even hire the same bands for their daughters'

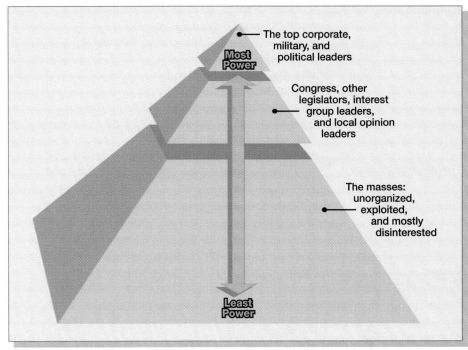

The top corporate, military, and political leaders

Most Power

Congress, other legislators, interest group leaders, and local opinion leaders

The masses: unorganized, exploited, and mostly disinterested

Least Power

FIGURE 7-9
How Power is Distributed in the United States; The Model Proposed by C. Wright Mills
(*Source:* Based on Mills 1959a.)

Three Segments of the Power Elite

The Ruling Class

An Informal Coalition

debutante balls. They are united, then, by shared backgrounds, contacts, ideologies, values, and interests (Domhoff 1974, 1990, 1998).

Mills said that the three groups that make up the power elite—the top political, military, and corporate leaders—are not equal in power. In identifying who was dominant, he did not point to the president, however, or even to the generals and admirals, but, rather, to the corporate heads. Because all three segments of the power elite view capitalism as essential to the welfare of the country, national policy centers around businesses interests. Making decisions that promote capitalism works to their mutual benefit.

Sociologist William Domhoff (1990, 1998) prefers the term "ruling class" instead of power elite. He studies the 1 percent of Americans who belong to the superrich, those so wealthy that *they are worth more than the entire bottom 90 percent of the nation* (Nasar 1992). This 1 percent controls the nation's top corporations and foundations, even the boards that oversee our major universities. It also owns the major newspapers and magazines and radio and television stations. Members of this powerful group attempt, and quite successfully, to shape the consciousness of the nation. It is no accident, says Domhoff, that from this group come most of the president's cabinet and top ambassadors.

Conflict theorists stress that we should not think of the power elite or ruling class as a group that meets and makes specific decisions. Rather, with their interlocking economic and political interests and similar worldview, their behavior stems not from a grand conspiracy to control the country but from a mutual interest in solving the problems that face large businesses (Useem 1984). Able to ensure that the country adopts the social policies it deems desirable—from fixing interest rates to sending troops abroad—this powerful group sets the economic and political conditions under which the rest of the country operates (Domhoff 1990).

The Pluralistic View

Not all sociologists agree with this view of a power elite that pulls the strings behind the scenes. Pluralists argue that social, economic, and political power is dispersed among many competing **interest groups,** such as unions, industries, professional associations, ecologists, hawks, doves, and the like. *No one group is in control,* they say. Sociologist David Riesman and his colleagues (1951) maintained that the interests of the country's diverse groups frequently conflict, making a united policy or action impossible. While Mills argued that members of the power elite settle important questions and differences among themselves, the pluralists maintain that the country's many groups are divided by essential differences. Thus power is distributed among many competing interest groups (Kornhauser 1961; Marger 1987).

Who Really Rules?

The Dahl Study

The controversy between the pluralists and the sociologists who support the view of the power elite is longstanding and unresolved. In 1961, sociologist Robert Dahl published an influential study on power in New Haven, Connecticut, the home of Yale University, which he felt proved the power elite did not exist. Dahl found little overlap between the university's and town's social elites, and little influence by either of them on the city's policies. Dahl's work became a classic supporting the pluralistic view of U.S. power.

The Domhoff Study

Sociologist William Domhoff (1978), who, as you have seen, supports the power elite view, decided to reanalyze Dahl's data and to collect more data for the same period. He found that Yale University, New Haven's businesses, and its other social institutions were interlocked extensively. Domhoff concluded that a power elite of corporate heads, bankers, social elites, and politicians shaped New Haven's economy. He documented not only how the New Haven elite shaped local decisions but also how they were connected to a national social and economic elite. He believes that each city in the United States has such a power center, and that lines run from these cities to the upper power structure.

The Useem Study

To see how interlocking the corporate elite is, sociologist Michael Useem (1979) examined the nation's 797 largest corporations. They had 8,623 directors. Of these, 1,570 were directors in two or more of the firms. Of those who did not hold multiple positions in these largest corporations, most held directorships in smaller firms. In another study, sociologist Gwen Moore (1979) found that those who held the 545 top positions in key U.S. institutions were clustered into 32 issue-oriented cliques (see Table 7-1). One core circle of 272 people was linked to almost all the smaller cliques. Moore (1979:689) concluded:

The Moore Study

> the evidence examined here indicates that considerable integration exists among elites in all major sections of American society. . . . The existence of a central elite circle facilitates communication and interaction both within that large, diverse group and between its members and those in more specialized elite circles and cliques.

Useem and Moore concluded that there is a national interlocking power elite. Yet, because they were unable to study how actual decisions are made (for example, policy on the Middle East), their studies do not demonstrate that U.S. elites form a cohesive ruling group.

Is There a Culture of Wealth?

Although the question of a cohesive ruling group must remain open until we have more evidence, this brings us to another significant question: Does the culture of the elite—its set of institutions, habits, family ties, and connections—allow the rich and powerful to perpetuate their privileges? In other words, is there a **culture of wealth** that keeps people from falling down the social class structure, just as some claim that a culture of poverty makes it difficult for poor people to pull themselves up? Of course there is. The elite of any city, region, or nation—indeed of any

Table 7-1 Members of the National Elite*

Sector	Position
Congress	Senators: members of House of Representatives in the following categories: chairperson and ranking minority members of all House committees; all members of the Rules, Appropriations, and Ways and Means Committees.
Federal administration—political appointees	Secretaries, assistant secretaries, and general counsel of cabinet departments; heads and deputy heads of independent agencies.
Civil service	Two highest civil service grades from all cabinet departments and independent agencies.
Industrial corporation	Fortune 500 largest industrial corporations.
Nonindustrial corporation	Fortune 300 largest nonindustrial corporations.
Holders of large fortunes	Holders of fortunes worth at least $100 million.
Labor union	Presidents of unions with at least 50,000 members; officials of the AFL-CIO.
Political party	Members of Democratic and Republican National Committees; state and city chairpersons of these parties.
Voluntary organization	Elected head and full-time director of various public affairs organizations including professional societies, farmers' organizations, women's groups, religious organizations, civil rights organizations, and business groups.
Media	Editors of the largest circulation newspapers and public affairs periodicals; syndicated columnists and news executives; broadcasters and commentators of national networks.

*This table lists the politicians, civil servants, and industrialists who, according to one study, make up the national elite of the United States.

Source: From Gwen Moore, "The Structure of a National Elite Network," *American Sociological Review* 44 (October 1979):673–691. Copyright © 1979 by the American Sociological Association. Reprinted with the permission of the author and the American Sociological Association.

group—tend to develop common sentiments and share similar values and goals. The sociological problem is not to determine whether this occurs but to discover how it operates.

Is the Concentration of Power a Problem?

That a culture of wealth exists, however, does not mean that the elite work together to rule the country. That is another matter entirely. Power and wealth do go together: Few poor people are powerful, and few powerful people are poor. Is the concentration of power and wealth a problem? The danger that many sociologists see is that it violates the democratic processes on which our country is premised and leads to oppression. Interlocking interests by wealthy people in powerful positions can result in a few nonelected individuals wielding immense control over the country. One of the major needs in the social problems area is more studies on the relationship of wealth and power.

Why Are Some Nations Poor Year After Year?

Three Explanations:

1. Economic Colonialism

Just as the United States is stratified into social classes, so the world's nations are stratified into rich and poor nations. The Most Industrialized Nations, which are wealthy, have **residual poverty,** or pockets of low income and deprivation. Most of the Least Industrialized Nations, in contrast, have **mass poverty**—most of their citizens live on less than $1,000 a year and are malnourished, chronically ill, and likely to die young. The Global Glimpse box below reports on the abysmal conditions of some children in nations that experience mass poverty.

Why are some nations poor year after year? Three answers have been proposed. The first is that the rich nations exploit the poor nations (Harrington 1977; Lipton 1979; Benson and Lloyd 1983; LaDou 1991). To obtain their raw materials, the more powerful nations used to invade and conquer weaker nations ("political

A GLOBAL GLIMPSE

Children of the Least Industrialized Nations

What is childhood like in the Least Industrialized Nations? As in the United States, the answer depends primarily on who your parents are. If you are the child of a rich person, childhood can be pleasant. If you are born into poverty but live where there is plenty to eat, life can still be good—although you will lack books, television, and education. If you live in a slum, however, life can be horrible, worse than in the slums of the Most Industrialized Nations. Let's look at the slums of Brazil.

You can take not having enough food, broken homes, alcoholism, drug abuse, and a high crime rate for granted. Even in the ghettos of the Most Industrialized Nations, you would expect these things.

You might not expect the brutal conditions in which Brazilian slum (*favela*) children live. Sociologist Martha Huggins (1993) reports that poverty is so deep that children and adults swarm over garbage dumps to find enough decaying food to keep them alive. The owners of these dumps hire armed guards to keep the poor out—so they can sell the garbage for pig food. The Brazilian police and death squads murder about 2,000 of these children each year. Some associations of shop owners even put assassination teams on retainer and auction victims off to the lowest bidder! The going rate is a half month's salary—figured at the low Brazilian minimum wage.

Life is cheap in the Least Industrialized Nations—but death squads for children? To understand why,

note that Brazil is politically unstable with a long history of violence. With high poverty and a small middle class, mob violence and revolution always lurk just around the corner. The "dangerous classes," as they are known, threaten the status quo. Homeless children, with no schools or jobs, roam the streets, washing windshields, shining shoes, begging, and stealing to survive.

These children annoy the "respectable" classes, who see them as trouble. Sometimes they break into stores. They hurt business, for customers feel intimidated when they see poorly dressed adolescents clustered in front of a store. Some children even sell items that compete with the stores. Without social institutions to care for them, one solution is to kill them. As Huggins notes, murder sends a clear warning, especially if it is accompanied by ritual torture—pulling out the eyes, ripping open the chest, cutting off the genitals, raping the girls, and burning the victim's body.

FOR YOUR CONSIDERATION

Can the Most Industrialized Nations do anything about this situation? Or is it none of our business? Is it, though unfortunate, an internal affair for the Brazilians to handle?

colonialism"). Now they use **economic colonialism.** The Most Industrialized Nations import raw materials from the poor nations and give them industrial products in return. The Most Industrialized Nations control the market for food and raw materials, determining what price they will pay. The poor nations must sell their food and natural resources—from bananas and coffee to tin and manganese—at prices so low that they are lucky to keep up with their expanding populations, much less develop their own industrial capacity. As a result, these nations remain poor.

In this context, we might ask what would happen if one of the small, oil-rich nations were to gain control over the area's resources. By being able to set oil prices, that nation could lead the Most Industrialized Nations by the nose. Would the Most Industrialized Nations allow this? The answer should be obvious: no. When such an attempt was made, the result was the Gulf War. At the time of that brief war, few Americans took the government's statements about "protecting Kuwait" at face value. Even the person on the street cynically talked about the bottom line being lower oil prices. As I write this, the United States continues military excursions against Saddam Hussein's Iraq—for the same reason.

2. Interlocking Elites and Overlapping Circles of Power

A second answer as to why some nations remain poor is that their own power elite exploits them. Although these nations are dirt poor, each has a wealthy elite that lives a sophisticated, upper-class lifestyle in the major cities of its home country, and even sends its children to Oxford, the Sorbonne, or Harvard. The multinational corporations channel their investments through this local circle of power, which profits from exploiting its own country's resources. This local elite emulates the Most Industrialized Nations and builds laboratories and computer centers in the capital city. Such projects, however, do not help the majority of their people, who live in poverty in remote villages (Lipton 1979).

3. National Cultures of Poverty

A culture of poverty provides a third answer to the continuing poverty of the Least Industrialized Nations (Landes 1998). (Oscar Lewis meant for this concept to apply to Latin American countries as well as to Watts or Harlem.) As ambassador to India, John Kenneth Galbraith (1979), a social economist, observed what he described as a culture of fatalistic resignation, reinforced by religion. He pointed out that most of the world's poor eke out a living from the land. With barely enough to live on, they are reluctant to experiment with a different way to farm, because it might fail and lead to hunger or death. Their religion also teaches them to accept conditions on earth and look to the afterlife for greater rewards. Galbraith emphasized that the poor countries do not lack resources. Most have many untapped natural resources—most much greater than resource-starved Japan. But their weakness in world markets, combined with their fatalistic culture, makes it unlikely that they will rise from poverty.

These three reasons—economic colonialism, an exploiting local elite, and a culture of poverty—remain a matter of debate among social scientists. Perhaps each holds part of the truth. Rather than being exclusive, these three explanations may be complementary.

✦ Social Policy ✦

HISTORICAL CHANGES IN SOCIAL POLICY

Social Policies Depend on Assumptions of Cause

What we think causes a social problem influences the social policies we favor. We reviewed how people's ideas about poverty changed: It first was considered God's will, then was thought to result from character flaws, and then was attributed to the evils of the city. As these views changed, so did social policies. In colonial times, when

Historical Shifts in Views About Causes of Poverty and Matching Social Policy

poverty was thought to be God's will, it was a person's religious duty to shelter, feed, and clothe the poor. The poor were cared for on a private, individual basis.

During the American Revolution, when the poor were considered lazy and wayward people who needed discipline, Boston opened a workhouse. There the poor had to do menial labor until they showed that they had acquired self-discipline and appreciated hard work. Philadelphia Quakers took a gentler view and built almshouses that took in poor women and children. These social policies marked a departure from providing relief on an individual basis; instead, the government established institutionalized care of the poor (Nash 1979).

In the 1830s, when people believed that the squalor of cities caused poverty, they developed a matching policy. The logical solution was to take the poor away from the corrupting influence of the city, to country institutions that would reawaken their sense of decency and order (Rothman 1971). This attempt failed because the institutions filled up and budgets were cut. They became human warehouses of the worst sort.

To appreciate the attitudes of the time, consider this statement from Henry Ward Beecher, the most prominent clergyman of his day:

> It is said that a dollar a day is not enough for a wife and five or six children. No, not if the man smokes and drinks beer. . . . But is not a dollar a day enough to buy bread with? Water costs nothing, and a man who cannot live on bread and water is not fit to live. A family may live on good bread and water in the morning, water and bread at midday, and good water and bread at night. (quoted in Thayer 1997)

A dollar went a lot further in those days, to be sure, and people did pump water freely from back yard wells. But to live on only bread and water?

During the Great Depression of the 1930s, the focus shifted to the masses of poor people whose problem was unemployment. At his 1937 Inaugural Address, President Franklin D. Roosevelt said:

> Millions of families are trying to live on incomes so meager that the pall of family disaster hangs over them day by day. . . . I see one-third of a nation ill-housed, ill-clad, ill-nourished. (quoted in Fisher 1998)

The Roosevelt administration created large-scale welfare for the unemployed, established massive work projects, and tried to revive the economy to create jobs. During World War II, the economy picked up and poverty declined sharply.

The less visible and permanent kinds of poverty remained. As described, the rediscovery of poverty in the 1960s led to new social policies based on the idea that the poor had been left behind during the country's rise to prosperity. Some programs provided education and training so the poor could get jobs. Others acknowledged that some of the poor, such as single mothers, children, and the elderly, needed to be subsidized.

The Essential Assumptions: Internal or External Causes

Views have shifted from attributing the problem to forces within the person (laziness, stupidity, evil) to attributing it to forces outside the person (God, evil cities, the economy). Our cycles of social reform still reflect this duality of internal and external forces. On the one hand, explanations based on genetic and biological causes lead to such policies as doing nothing (because no social policy will help), or even to sterilization. On the other hand, explanations based on social causes spur programs of education, aid, social reform, job retraining, and stimulating the economy.

Chapter 7   Economic Problems: Wealth and Poverty

Although different generations define poverty differently, in each era the core issues remain: Who is responsible? and What shall we do about it?

THE FEMINIZATION OF POVERTY

The Poverty of Women and Children

The poverty that clusters around women and children is a special problem. To alleviate it, we can provide job training for women whose job skills are rusty or nonexistent. For many of them, to work requires child care facilities, and policies that promote child care will help. In addition, the amount of child support that is awarded to divorced mothers can better reflect the father's earnings, and courts can better enforce those payments from fathers. It also seems reasonable that absent fathers, whether or not they were married to their children's mother, should support the children they have helped bring into the world, rather than letting them become the government's responsibility. Unfortunately, some unemployed fathers can pay little or nothing. Their own poverty is a related problem that must be solved.

PROGRESSIVE TAXATION

Taxation as Social Policy to Redistribute Wealth

A broader policy to help reduce inequality is **progressive taxation,** tax rates that progress (increase) with income. The federal and state governments tax wealthier people at higher rates and redistribute some of this money to the poor through welfare, Medicaid, housing subsidies, and food stamps. Table 7-2 shows the taxes that Americans pay according to their income.

Few wealthy people approve of the government taking their money in order to distribute it to the poor, and to retain more of their incomes they hire legal experts to find loopholes in the tax laws. A few wealthy individuals and profitable corporations are so successful at this that in some years they manage to pay no taxes. These are exceptional cases, however, and most of the taxes collected by the government comes from corporations and the wealthy.

Table 7-2   Income Taxes Paid by Americans

Adjusted Gross Income	Number of Returns	Tax Paid as a Percentage of Adjusted Gross Income	Approximate Tax Paid	Total Amount Paid
Less than $5,000	15,590,000	2.0	$100	$1,861,000,000
$5,000–$10,999	16,645,000	2.2	$300	$6,151,000,000
$11,000–$18,999	20,138,000	4.7	$1,000	$20,297,000,000
$19,000–$29,000	19,965,000	7.6	$1,900	$39,255,000,000
$30,000–$39,999	12,380,000	9.9	$3,500	$43,330,000,000
$40,000–$49,999	9,099,000	10.7	$4,800	$43,675,000,000
$50,000–$74,999	13,679,000	12.1	$8,200	$112,168,000,000
$75,000–$99,999	5,374,000	14.8	$16,000	$85,984,000,000
$100,000–$199,999	4,075,000	18.3	$31,300	$127,548,000,000
$200,000–$499,999	1,007,000	25.6	$95,000	$95,665,000,000
$500,000–$999,999	178,000	30.2	$258,000	$45,960,000,000
$1,000,000 or more	87,000	31.4	$1,077,000	$93,699,000,000

Source: Statistical Abstract 1998: Table 553.

To keep people from starving and to stimulate the dormant economy during the Great Depression of the 1930s, the federal government began the Works Progress Administration. Men were put to work constructing public buildings, parks, and roads; women were put to work canning food. Even artists were put to work. Shown here is a mural painted by WPA artists in the public school in Wilton, Connecticut. (By the way, every child in the United States sat at a desk like those shown here. The little hole in the upper right corner of the desks is an inkwell. Each student inserted a bottle of ink in which to dip his or her pen.)

1. Social Insurance Programs

2. Teaching Job Skills

3. Welfare

4. Workfare

FOUR TYPES OF PUBLIC ASSISTANCE PROGRAMS

We can divide public assistance programs into four types. The first, social insurance programs such as unemployment compensation and Social Security, is designed to help those who help themselves. Money is deducted from paychecks, and workers draw on this pool when they need it. Few argue that workers who are laid off when an entire industry, such as steel or automobiles, is hit by recession don't deserve help.

The second type of program attempts to make the poor self-supporting so that they are no longer in need of social welfare. Most center around teaching job skills. This includes formal courses and on-the-job-training such as the Job Corps. Some programs even teach personal grooming, punctuality, and politeness so that prospective workers will meet employer expectations.

A third type of program is *welfare*—money, food, housing, and medical care that are given to anyone with a low enough income. Here the distinction between the deserving and the undeserving is replaced by a humanitarian notion that people in need should be helped regardless of who is responsible. These programs, such as Aid to Families with Dependent Children (AFDC), food stamps, and public housing, generate controversy because people think they encourage laziness and unwed motherhood, and are given to people who could work and take care of themselves. One consequence is a disparaging of people on welfare, the topic of the Issues box on the next page.

A fourth type of program is *workfare*. Critics of welfare claim that it reduces people's incentive to work. They say, "Why will people work if they can get it free?" As U.S. welfare rolls swelled to 14 million people in the early 1990s, despite it being a period of prosperity, criticisms grew. Stories abounded about "welfare queens," "welfare Cadillacs," teenaged girls getting pregnant so they could get away from

ISSUES in SOCIAL PROBLEMS

Welfare: How to Ravage the Self-Concept

My husband left me shortly after I was diagnosed with multiple sclerosis. At the time, I had five children. My oldest child was 14, and my youngest was 7. My physician, believing I would be seriously disabled, helped get me on Social Security disability. The process took several months, and so it became necessary for me to go on public aid and food stamps.

By the time I needed to depend on my family in the face of a crisis, there weren't any resources left to draw on. My father had passed away and my mother was retired, living on a modest income based on Social Security and my father's pension. Isn't it funny how there is no social stigma attached to Social Security benefits for the elderly? People look at this money as an entitlement—"We worked for it." But people who have to depend on public aid for existence are looked at like vermin and accused of being lazy.

I can tell you from my own experience that a great deal of the lethargy that comes from long periods on welfare is due primarily to the attitudes of the people you have to come into contact with in these programs. I've been through the gamut: from rude, surly caseworkers at Public Aid, to patronizing nurses at the WIC [Women, Infants, and Children] clinic ("You have *how* many children?"), to the accusing tone of the food pantry workers when you have to go begging for a handout before the thirty-day time span has expired. After a while your dignity is gone, and you start to believe that you really are the disgusting human trash they all make you out to be.

Christine Hoffman, a student in the
author's introductory sociology class.

their parents, and women having many babies in order to get bigger welfare checks. As criticisms mounted, the states adopted workfare, which required that anyone who applied for welfare take job training classes and submit evidence of trying to find work.

Workfare was met with severe criticism ("It's just a way of throwing the poor into the streets"), but national welfare rolls plummeted. Overall, the number of Americans on welfare was cut in half (Bernstein 2000). This reduction occurred during the longest "boom" period in U.S. history, however, and we don't know how many of these people will return to welfare when the next "bust" period comes and welfare rules are eased. In the meantime, millions fear losing their low-paying jobs that barely keep them from starvation.

PRIVATE AGENCIES AND VOLUNTEER ORGANIZATIONS

Non-Government Programs

We generally think in terms of government aid for the poor, but the United States also has thousands of volunteer organizations and private groups working on their behalf. Because they work mainly with the desperate poor, who are tucked in out-of-the-way corners of our urban centers, their activities are largely invisible to most Americans. The soup kitchens of the inner city are run by volunteer organizations, most of them religious. The most well-known of these organizations is the Salvation Army. In addition to its well-known soup kitchens and shelters for the homeless, its efforts on behalf of the poor also include alcohol counseling and job training.

The efforts of these groups are well-intentioned, and without them the social problem of poverty would be much worse. But the quality of what they do varies widely, as my experiences in the homeless shelters drove home. See the Thinking Critically box on page 232.

REGULATING THE POOR

Critics of welfare point to the grudging, humiliating way in which it is administered. Our eligibility rules are among the most complex in the world, with the result that many poor people fail to receive benefits. Welfare agents probe the private corners of poor people's lives. The rules and benefits are not uniform, and some states pay much less than others. After a set period of time, despite their continuing need or debilitating situation, people are kicked off welfare. Many end up on the streets.

Social Welfare Viewed from the Conflict Perspective: A Way to Control the Poor

To analyze social welfare, sociologists Frances Piven and Richard Cloward use conflict theory. They (1971, 1982, 1989, 1997) argue that capitalism needs a pool of low-skilled, temporary workers that it can draw on when the economy is booming and lay off when it slows. Welfare maintains this pool of workers at a minimal cost, keeping the poor alive until the next business expansion. Piven and Cloward support their assertion by documenting the changing rules of welfare—in times of high unemployment, when political disorder looms, the rules grow lax. In "boom" times those workers are needed and welfare rules are tightened. The purpose of welfare, they conclude, is to control the unemployed, maintain social order, and provide capitalists a pool of cheap labor.

More recent events support Piven's and Cloward's analysis. It is not an accident that during the longest "boom" in U.S. history, states tightened their rules for welfare eligibility (instituting fingerprinting and home visits) and started to emphasize job training. New York City even changed the name of its locations from "welfare centers" to "job centers" (Giuliani 1999). According to this conflict theory analysis,

CENSUS 2000

As the value of the dollar and the cost of living change each year, so does the government's poverty thresholds. Here is a selection of thresholds used to classify families in poverty for the 2000 Census:

Size of family unit	Without related children under 18	1 related child under 18	2 related children under 18
One person	$8,794	NA	NA
Two persons	$11,239	$11,869	NA
Three persons	$13,738	$13,861	$13,874
Four persons	$17,603	$18,052	$17,463

Now consider that according to the 2000 Census, 46 percent of poor families have one member who is working full-time. How can that be? To illustrate, imagine a mother with two small children who works 40 hours a week for 49 weeks out of the year at $7 an hour (just over the minimum wage). She would make $13,720 annually. This would make her family "officially poor," despite having a member holding down a full-time job. For all intents and purposes, a family of this size would be poor even if the mother got a raise to $7.25 an hour, which would take this family just above the official poverty line. The arbitrary nature of poverty thresholds illustrates the fluidity of poverty and how people experience it.

then, we can expect eligibility rules to loosen during the next recession so that the pool of marginal workers can survive until capitalists need them again.

GIVING THE POOR MORE MONEY

The Income Maintenance Experiments

Eliminate poverty by giving enough money to poor people so they are no longer poor. Who hasn't thought of this solution? It is so obvious. But what would happen if we did this?

This is exactly what some social scientists wanted to know, and they convinced the government to go along with their plans. They developed what are known as the income maintenance experiments. Between 1975 and 1979, millions of dollars were given to thousands of poor people in order to find out what they would spend it on—liquor or food for the kids? Would they work less? How would the free money affect relations between husbands and wives?

The study was well done. Random samples of low-income people in Denver and Seattle were selected. Different subsamples were given different amounts of money. If people got jobs or earned more money, the amount they received was cut slowly. This was to help avoid the **welfare wall**—the disincentive to work when the amount from working is not much more than the amount from welfare. The families were guaranteed this money for either three or five years, so they could change their living habits without worrying that the program might suddenly end.

What were the results? Some people did work less or drop out of the labor market. The reduction in work averaged 9 percent for husbands, 23 percent for wives, and 15 percent for female heads of households (West and Steiger 1980). Those who quit their jobs enjoyed the extra money and were glad to get away from poorly paying, unpleasant jobs. Most people, however, continued working as much as before.

Compared with control groups, these people spent more on durable goods (cars, refrigerators, TVs) than they did on nondurable goods (food, entertainment) (Pozdena and Johnson 1979). They also bought more housewares and clothing (Johnson et al. 1979). In households headed by women, most of the new spending went for better housing. With the security that came from a regular income over several years, they also saved less and went into debt more—just like many families who are not poor.

One of the interesting consequences of this experiment was that it broke up marriages (a finding that has been challenged by some sociologists [Cain and Wissoker 1990]). Women who had been putting up with unhappy marriages found that this new source of income made it possible for them to leave their husbands. Congress was upset to learn of this and canceled the program because it did not want to encourage families to break up. Thus, the income maintenance experiments had some major and controversial effects on the lives of the poor. How you regard those effects depends on whether you think people should work regardless of the nature of the job, and whether you think they should keep their family together regardless of the nature of the marriage.

EDUCATION ACCOUNTS

How Could We Lose on This Proposal?

A promising proposal is *education accounts*. The government would establish a credit of, say, $25,000 for everyone at age 18 who graduates from high school (Haveman and Scholz 1994–95; Oliver and Shapiro 1995). This money (which would be

adjusted annually for inflation) could be used only for education. Based on their background, abilities, and preferences, youths could choose from approved colleges and technical and vocational schools. They could spend the money on direct educational costs, such as tuition, books, and living expenses. Each youth would receive an annual statement of the value of the account. An attractive aspect of this proposal, besides allowing individual choice, is that ultimately it would cost little or nothing: It would reduce welfare and increase people's earning power *for their entire lives.* The additional taxes from those larger earnings could pay for the program. If any proposal is a "no brainer," this one is.

PROVIDING JOBS

Philosophical Disagreement About How to Provide Jobs

Perhaps the most direct way to deal with poverty and to avoid the criticisms of those who don't want to give anything away is to provide jobs. President Roosevelt lifted millions out of poverty during the Great Depression by providing jobs building bridges, roads, and parks. Thus, two paths—stimulating the economy and providing government-created jobs—lead to the same destination. On the basis of their ideology, people disagree violently about how jobs should be created. One group says it is the government's responsibility to create jobs; the other insists that this is the role of private business.

Applying This Policy to the Urban Poor and to Women

This debate never will be resolved. Rather than becoming embroiled in it, let's note that regardless of the path we choose to get there, the important factor is that the jobs be available. Also important is that the jobs either provide a wage that lifts people out of poverty or else serve as a stepping stone to jobs that will. Dead-end jobs that keep people in poverty do not meet the goal. And because good jobs are often in the suburbs, where they are inaccessible to the inner-city poor, we need to buttress this social policy by providing transportation that helps move the poor to the jobs. We also need to recognize that poverty clusters around women with children, so quality child care facilities also need to be made available.

✦ The Future of the Problem ✦

Poverty begs for a solution. The homeless, the rural poor, and those trapped in the inner cities can't be wished away. But no solution comes without a high price tag.

Two Voices

Some want vast programs that spend immense sums on the poor. They say, "Let's just do it, because it's right, and we can worry about the bill some other time." "Besides," they add, "if we can afford all those new weapons for the military, we can afford any programs needed to help the poor." Others, in contrast, argue that we should establish effective programs to help the poor, but that it is not right to saddle future generations with our spending. "If we can't pay for programs now, we can't afford them." Most Americans seem to find themselves between these positions—feeling that it is not right to have homeless people huddled over heating grates, or children's futures blocked because of their parents' poverty—but not knowing what to do about the situation. With the politicians and the public not seeing any clear solutions, and with the poor remaining disorganized and having little

The Middle

Muddling Along

political clout, I anticipate that we shall continue to muddle along with our present programs. From time to time, there will be modifications, of course, a little tinkering that gives the appearance of progress. Limits have been placed on how long people can receive welfare, and some modest job training programs have been initiated.

The Coming Conflict

It would be much more satisfying for you—and for me—if I were to see Utopia ahead: The government decides to eliminate poverty. Their solutions work, and everyone gets a guaranteed annual income. There are no more poor people. Everyone is prosperous and happy. But such a future does not match reality.

As conflict theorists stress, we will give the poor as little as is necessary to prevent revolution. When hundreds of thousands across the land reach the new time limits of welfare and are cut off from benefits, protests may become violent. If the inner cities start to explode like a series of powder kegs across the United States, or even in the face of such a threat, the choice will be to call out the National Guard to stop the burning and looting or to change the eligibility rules of welfare. Is there any question of the choice that would be made?

◆Summary

1. There are several types of *poverty*. *Biological poverty* refers to starvation and malnutrition. *Official poverty* refers to falling below arbitrary standards set by the government. *Relative poverty* is feeling poor by comparison with others, although the individual may be objectively well off. Poverty follows lines of age, gender, and race-ethnicity.

2. Symbolic interactionists show how the meaning of income (i.e., whether people see themselves as being rich or poor) differs from its objective measures. Functionalists emphasize that inequality helps allocate talented people to demanding tasks and less talented people to less demanding tasks. Functionalists point out that although poverty may be dysfunctional for individuals, it is functional for society. Conflict theorists stress that those who win the struggle for society's scarce resources oppress those who lose. They also stress that a *power elite* of top politicians and corporate and military leaders make society's big decisions. Pluralists disagree. They see society as made up of many groups that compete with one another in a marketplace of power and ideas.

3. Why do some people remain in poverty year after year?

Some suggest that the reason is a *culture of poverty*, self-defeating behaviors that parents pass on to their children. Most sociologists, however, view what is called the culture of poverty not as the *cause* of poverty, but, instead, as an adjustment to the problems of life with few resources. Why do some countries remain in poverty year after year? Some suggest that this is due to a national culture of poverty. Others look to *economic colonialism* and exploitation by national elites.

4. Policies for dealing with poverty have been as diverse as beliefs about its causes. In the seventeenth century, poverty was considered God's will, and it was a person's religious duty to help the poor. During the Great Depression, the poor were considered victims of economic conditions and were helped on a mass basis. Today, our welfare programs cause bitter debate. Rules have been tightened to make fewer people eligible for welfare and to "encourage" the poor to look for work.

5. The future is likely to bring a continuation of our piecemeal welfare programs, with Americans continuing to be divided on the matter of the "deserving" and "undeserving" poor and to what extent they should be helped.

◆Key Terms

Biological poverty Material deprivation so severe that it affects biological functioning.

Culture of poverty Characteristics of the poor that help the poor stay poor. They include low income, weak families, alcoholism, and low self-esteem.

Culture of wealth Characteristics of the wealthy that help keep them from falling down the social class ladder.

Economic colonialism One nation exploiting another nation's resources.

Economy A society's system of producing and distributing goods and services.

False consciousness Karl Marx's term for the illusion held by the oppressed that they are not oppressed—workers thinking of themselves as entrepreneurs or investors, for example.

Feminization of poverty The growth of poverty among women and children.

Chapter 7 Economic Problems: Wealth and Poverty

Interest groups Groups organized around different interests (from the environment to animal rights).

Official poverty The level of income recognized by a government as constituting poverty.

Power elite A small group of wealthy, powerful people said to make the major economic and political decisions in the United States.

Progressive tax Tax rates that increase with income.

Real income Income in constant dollars, that is, with inflation removed.

Relative poverty Deprivation as measured by the standards of one's society and culture. On a personal level, it is self-measurement based on one's reference groups.

Residual poverty Pockets of poverty in an otherwise affluent society.

Social class A group of people who occupy the same rung on the economic ladder.

Social inequality The unequal distribution of wealth, income, power, and other opportunities.

Structural inequality Inequality that is built into economic and social institutions.

Wealth Savings, property, investments, income, and other economic assets.

Welfare wall The disincentive to work when the income from working is not much more than the income from welfare.

◆ Critical Thinking Questions

1. One of the concerns of Federal Reserve Chair Alan Greenspan is increased employment. Whenever the unemployment rate gets "too low" there is pressure to increase interest rates to slow down the economy. What does this say about the capitalist system of the United States in connection to welfare and other policies designed to reduce unemployment and poverty?
   • Which one of the perspectives (symbolic interactionism, functionalism, or conflict theory) does Greenspan's practice tend to validate? Explain.

2. What is your reaction to Gans' observations reported in the Thinking Critically About Social Problems Box (p. 225) on how poverty helps society?
   • Do you think Gans is serious?
   • Do you think these benefits outweigh the costs of poverty to society? Explain.

3. Review the different rates of poverty by age, sex, geography, and race–ethnicity. Now explain them. (To answer this question sociologically, you might wish to first ask, "Why don't all groups have the same rate of poverty?")

Race and Ethnic Relations

William Potter Gale, a former colonel who served under General Douglas MacArthur in the Philippines in World War II:

Damn right I'm teaching violence! It's about time somebody is telling you to get violent, whitey. You better start making dossiers, names, addresses, phone numbers, car license numbers on every damn Jew rabbi in this land.

Thomas Robb, publishers of "The Torch," a Klan newsletter:

Today we see the evil is coming out of government. To go out and shoot a Negro is foolish. It's not the Negro in the alley who's responsible for what's wrong with this country. It's the traitors in Washington.

Keith Gilbert, who started his own church, Restored Church of Jesus Christ, in Post Falls, Idaho:

Hitler is the reincarnation of the prophet Elijah. *Mein Kampf* is part of the Bible. The "terrible day of destruction" is coming.

Bill McGlocklin, the Grand Kaliff of an organization in Denham Springs, Louisiana, called the Invisible Empire, Knights of the Ku Klux Klan, told reporters that the Klan had called on the mother of a white teenage girl who had been seen with black companions and warned her that "if she can't do anything about it, the Klan can, and will."

Outside Hayden Lake, Idaho, is a neatly lettered sign marking the entry to the Church of Jesus Christ Christian. It says, "Whites Only." Members of the congregation carry rifles and wear Nazi swastikas. Richard Butler, the church's leader, argues that Jesus Christ was an Aryan, not a Jew, and Jews should be destroyed as the children of Satan. He keeps a photo of Adolf Hitler on a table in his living room.

Based on King 1979; Starr 1985b; Murphy 1999.

◆ The Problem in Sociological Perspective ◆

Prejudice, discrimination, and racial violence are facts of life in the United States. Hostilities and tensions among racial and ethnic groups surface in street riots, disturbances in our schools, and the media-captivating activities of extremist groups such as those profiled in the opening vignette.

Discrimination as a Worldwide Problem

Prejudice and discrimination are common around the world. In northern Ireland, Protestants discriminate against Roman Catholics; in Israel, wealthier Jews, primarily of European descent, discriminate against poorer Jews of Asian and African backgrounds; in Japan, the Japanese discriminate against just about anyone who isn't Japanese, especially the Koreans and Ainu, who live there (Spivak 1980; Fields 1986; "Law Enacted . . ." 1997). The disintegration of the former Soviet Union exposed the uneasy alliances among numerous race-ethnic groups, and in every society around the world men discriminate against women.

Prejudice or Discrimination?

The difference between prejudice and discrimination is simple. **Prejudice** is an attitude—a prejudging of some sort. Usually the prejudging is negative, but it can be positive. **Discrimination,** in contrast, is an action. It refers to singling out a person or persons for unfair treatment. The unfair treatment can be based on almost anything. Often it is based on appearance—age, race, sex, height, weight, or disability. Income and religious or political beliefs are other common bases of discrimination.

Minority Group Defined

When people are discriminated against because they belong to a group, they are called a minority. **Minorities,** as sociologist Louis Wirth (1945) defined them, are groups of people who are singled out for unequal treatment on the basis of their physical or cultural characteristics and who regard themselves as objects of collective discrimination. Discrimination denies minorities full participation in their society.

"Minority" in this sense does not necessarily mean a *numerical* minority in a society. In colonial India, for example, a handful of British discriminated against millions, and in South Africa the black majority was relatively powerless, negatively stereotyped, and discriminated against. Universally, men discriminate against women, although there are more women than men in each society. Accordingly, in this chapter I refer to those who do the discriminating as the **dominant group;** this group has more power and privileges, and higher social status.

The Origin of Minority Groups

What is the origin of minority groups? Some come into being when a government expands its political boundaries. As anthropologists Charles Wagley and Marvin Harris (1958) pointed out, small tribal societies have no minority groups (except for females, whom we discuss in Chapter 9.) In tribal societies everyone is "related," speaks the same language, practices the same customs, shares similar values, and belongs to the same physical stock. Another way minority groups originate is through migration—when people with different characteristics move into a political unit. The migration can be involuntary, as with Africans who were forcibly brought to the United States, or voluntary, as with Turks who chose to move to Germany for work.

Minorities come into existence, then, when, due to expanded political boundaries or migration, people with different customs, languages, values, or physical characteristics come under control of the same state organization. There, some groups who share physical and cultural traits discriminate against those with different traits. The losers in this power struggle are forced into minority group status; the winners enjoy the higher status and greater privileges that their dominance brings.

Wagley and Harris noted that all minorities share these five characteristics:

Five Characteristics of Minority Groups

1. They are treated unequally by the dominant group.
2. Their physical or cultural traits are held in low esteem by the dominant group.
3. They tend to feel strong group solidarity because of their physical or cultural traits—and the disabilities these traits bring.
4. Their membership in a minority group is not voluntary but comes through birth.
5. They tend to marry within their group.

Sharing cultural or physical traits, having similar experiences of discrimination, and marrying within their own group create a shared identity—sometimes even a sense of common destiny. These shared experiences, however, do not mean that all minority groups have the same goals. Wirth (1945) identified four objectives of every minority group:

Four Objectives of Minority Groups

1. **Pluralism:** The group wants to live peacefully with the dominant group, but yet maintain its distinctive culture, the differences that set it apart.
2. **Assimilation:** Focusing on the culture they share with the dominant group, members of the minority group want to be absorbed into the larger society and be treated as individuals rather than as members of a special group.

3. **Secession:** Wanting cultural and political independence, the minority seeks to separate itself nationally.

4. **Militancy:** Convinced of its superiority, the minority wants a reversal in status and seeks to dominate the society.

Dominant groups also differ in their goals and attitudes toward minorities. As Figure 8-1 illustrates, sociologists George Simpson and J. Milton Yinger identified six policies that dominant groups adopt. As you can see, these can parallel or oppose the aims of minorities. We will begin with the most humane.

1. Pluralism. Pluralism means that a dominant group permits or even encourages cultural differences. The United States' "hands-off" policy toward immigrant associations and foreign-language newspapers is an example of pluralism. Freedom of religion in the United States has been so extensive that Simpson and Yinger (1972) noted that "religious pluralism is now nearly fully the fact as well as the ideal." Switzerland provides an outstanding example of successful pluralism; although the French, Italian, and German Swiss have retained their separate languages and other customs, they live peacefully together in a political and economic unit. None of these groups is a minority.

2. Assimilation. Assimilation is an attempt to "eliminate" the minority by absorbing it into the mainstream culture. In its more severe form, *forced* assimilation, the dominant group bans the minority's religion, language, and other distinctive customs. In the former Soviet Union, the Russians treated Armenians this way. *Permissible* assimilation, in contrast, permits the minority to adopt the dominant group's patterns at its own speed. In Brazil, for example, an ideology supports the intermarriage of its racial and ethnic groups and favors an eventual blending of its racial-ethnic groups into a "Brazilian stock." In the United States, cultural minorities have been expected to give up their differences, but racial minorities have been expected to maintain their physical differences by marrying within their own groups.

3. Segregation. Also known as *continued subjugation*, segregation is an attempt by the dominant group to keep a minority "in its place," that is, subservient and exploitable. When whites were in control of South Africa, they despised the blacks and

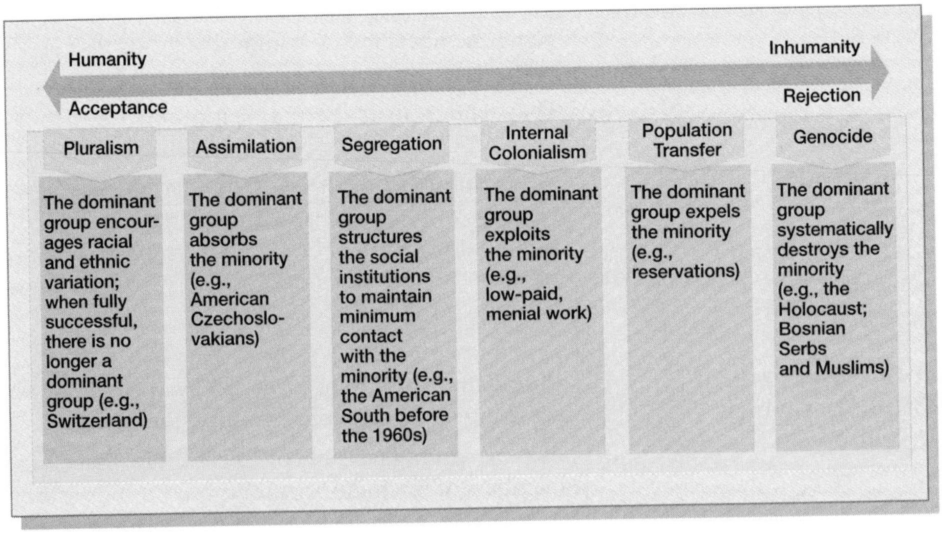

Six Policies of Dominant Groups

FIGURE 8-1
Policies of Dominant Groups Toward Minorities
(*Source:* Henslin 2000; based on Simpson and Yinger 1972.)

Pluralism	**Assimilation**	**Segregation**	**Internal Colonialism**	**Population Transfer**	**Genocide**
The dominant group encourages racial and ethnic variation; when fully successful, there is no longer a dominant group (e.g., Switzerland)	The dominant group absorbs the minority (e.g., American Czechoslovakians)	The dominant group structures the social institutions to maintain minimum contact with the minority (e.g., the American South before the 1960s)	The dominant group exploits the minority (e.g., low-paid, menial work)	The dominant group expels the minority (e.g., reservations)	The dominant group systematically destroys the minority (e.g., the Holocaust; Bosnian Serbs and Muslims)

Humanity / Acceptance ← → Inhumanity / Rejection

their customs, but they found their presence necessary. As Simpson and Yinger (1972) put it, who else would do the hard work? To subjugate the black majority, this small, dominant group of whites used **apartheid,** the forced segregation of blacks and whites in almost all spheres of life. Because of international sanctions, apartheid was dismantled.

4. Internal colonialism. This policy refers to an exploitation of the minority group by the dominant group. It accompanies segregation, and precedes the next two policies, population transfer and genocide.

5. Population transfer. In *direct* **population transfer,** the minority is forced to leave. This is what happened when King Ferdinand and Queen Isabella (who financed Columbus' voyage to North America) drove the Jews and Moors out of Spain, and when the U.S. government forced Japanese Americans into camps during World War II. *Indirect population transfer* means making life so miserable for a minority that its members "choose" to leave. Facing the bitter conditions of czarist Russia, for example, millions of Jews made this "choice."

6. Genocide. Hatred and greed can lead the dominant group to turn to a policy of extermination, or **genocide.** The most infamous example is the Holocaust, when death camps were set up by the Nazis to allow them to systematically exterminate minorities. Between 1933 and 1945 the Nazis slaughtered about 6 million Jews, a quarter of a million Gypsies, hundreds of thousands of Slavs, and unknown numbers of homosexuals, communists, physically disabled, and mentally ill people whom Hitler did not consider "pure" enough to be part of his mythical Aryan race.

Hitler was convinced that **race**—the inherited physical characteristics that identify a group of people—was reality. He believed that a race called the Aryans were responsible for the cultural achievements of Europe. These tall, fair-skinned, mostly blond-haired people—a biologically superior "superrace"—had a destiny to establish a still higher culture, a new world order. This required forcing "inferior" races to perform tasks too lowly for the Aryans, avoiding the "racial contamination" that breeding with inferior races would engender, and isolating or destroying races that might endanger Aryan culture.

The Holocaust

One of the darkest periods in race relations in the world took place in Germany prior to and during World War II. Hitler, the chancellor of Germany, was determined to create hatred of Jews. He harnessed the propaganda machine of the state, including movies, radio, books, newspapers, magazines, and posters, such as the one shown here. This poster is an advertisement for the notorious anti-Semitic movie, *The Eternal Jew,* which in 1937 was shown daily from 10 a.m. to 9 p.m. at the Munich Museum.

DER EWIGE JUDE

GROSSE POLITISCHE SCHAU IM BIBLIOTHEKSBAU DES DEUTSCHEN MUSEUMS ZU MÜNCHEN · AB 8. NOVEMBER 1937 · TÄGLICH GEÖFFNET VON 10-21 UHR

CENSUS 2000

Sociologists look at race as a *social construct*. Having wrestled with how to most appropriately capture race as a meaningful category, the Census Bureau classified the U.S. population into five separate races for the 2000 Census. Here are the five categories along with the Census Bureau's operational definitions. (Note how the definitions rely on geography and cultural background, not biological or physiological distinctions.)

- "White" refers to people having origins in any of the original peoples of Europe, the Middle East, or North Africa.
- "Black or African American" refers to people having origins in any of the Black racial groups of Africa.
- "American Indian and Alaska Native" refers to people having origins in any of the original peoples of North and South America (including Central America) and who maintain tribal affiliation or community attachment.
- "Asian" refers to people having origins in any of the original peoples of the Far East, Southeast Asia, or the Indian subcontinent.
- "Native American and Other Pacific Islander" refers to people having origins in any of the original peoples of Hawaii, Guam, Samoa, or other Pacific Islands.
- The "some other race" category was added for those who felt they didn't fit any of the above categories.

Two other things are noteworthy about the way the Census Bureau handles race and ethnicity. First, the questionnaire allowed respondents to identify membership in more than one race. A small minority (about 6 million people) did so, but this does raise some question about how meaningful it would be to compare the U.S. population's racial composition over time, since previous censuses did not allow respondents to identify themselves as belonging to multiple racial groups. Finally, the Census Bureau considers race to be separate from Hispanic origin. In other words, anyone from the above races could also be Hispanic, which is defined as a person "from Cuban, Mexican, Puerto Rican, South or Central American, or other Spanish culture or origin regardless of race."

Source: U.S. Census Bureau (2001).
Overview of Race and Hispanic Origin.

Race as a Social Reality

vs.

Race as Historical Myth

While most people today find Hitler's ideas bizarre, in the 1930s both lay people and the scientific community took them seriously. Many biologists and anthropologists, for example, believed that some races were inherently superior to others. It is not surprising that these scientists always concluded that Caucasians were the superior race, for they themselves were Caucasian.

Ideas of racial superiority that justify one group's rule over another may be less popular today, but the idea of race remains a social reality. Almost everyone identifies with some "racial" group, classifies other people into "racial" groups, and treats them accordingly. Everyone has ideas, opinions, and attitudes on this topic, and these feelings and beliefs motivate their behavior. In this sense race remains very real.

In modern biology, however, pure race is a myth. People show so great a mixture of physical characteristics—skin color, hair texture, nose and head shapes, height, eye color, and so on—that no pure races can be substantiated. Instead, human characteristics flow endlessly into one another, and this melding makes any attempt to draw sharp lines arbitrary. Large groupings of humans, however, can be classified by blood type and gene frequencies. Depending on the criteria, biologists and anthropologists can develop arbitrary listings that contain any number of

Ethnicity

"races." Some scientists have classified humans into as few as two "races," others into as many as 2,000 (Montagu 1964).

Because the idea of race is so embedded in our culture, race is a social reality that social scientists must confront. As sociologists deal with this topic, they often prefer to avoid a term so imprecise and sometimes provocative as *race*. Many, as I will do in this chapter, use the term *ethnic* or *race-ethnic* group. Derived from the Greek *ethnos,* meaning "people" or "nation," an **ethnic group** refers to people who identify with one another on the basis of their ancestry and cultural heritage. Their sense of belonging may center around unique physical characteristics, foods, dress, names, language, music, and religion. As we just saw, collective discrimination and intermarriage also may be significant factors.

✦ The Scope of the Problem ✦

Many ethnic groups with different histories, customs, and identities populate the United States. The largest groups are listed in Figure 8-2.

Immigration and Anglo/Conformity

U.S. immigrants, whatever their background, confronted **Anglo-conformity;** that is, they were expected to maintain English institutions (as modified by the American Revolution), speak the English language, and adopt other Anglo-Saxon ways of life. The United States was supposedly destined to become a modified version of England. Many thought that the evolving society would become a **melting pot;** it would "melt" the European immigrants together into a new cultural and biological blend. As sociologist Milton Gordon (1964) put it, "the stocks and folkways of Europe [would be], figuratively speaking, indiscriminately mixed in the political pot of the emerging nation and melted together by the fires of American influence and interaction into a distinctly new type."

The Melting Pot

The melting pot became a reality for most European immigrants; most lost their specific ethnic identities and merged into a mainstream culture. Although individuals may identify themselves as "three-quarters German and one-quarter mixed Italian and Greek—with some English thrown in," they tend to think of themselves as "American." Some groups, however, have retained their unique cultures and ethnic identities. In recent years, large numbers of immigrants, especially those from Mexico, Cuba, Haiti, Vietnam, and India, have retained a strong ethnic identity.

Ideological Myth vs. Reality

The concept of a melting pot also conceals as much as it reveals, for it referred to specific groups of Americans only. Americans of Anglo background never intended for non-Anglos to become part of a "biological mix." On the contrary, they wanted to enforce "racial" purity; they even passed laws prohibiting blacks and whites from marrying.

Prejudice and Stereotypes

Each new group of immigrants confronted prejudice, and new arrivals still do. Helping to keep prejudice alive are **stereotypes,** generalizations of what people are like. For example, the English immigrants despised the Irish immigrants who followed them, viewing them as dirty, lazy, untrustworthy drunkards. The Irish survived this stereotyping, became "respectable," and joined mainstream society. Minorities also hold stereotypes of the dominant group, and today whites and minorities hold debasing stereotypes of one another (Leonard and Locke 1993). As the Technology box on the next page features, the Internet has become a means of perpetuating hatred.

When Does a Social Problem Exist?

Prejudice and stereotypes are not necessarily social problems. Even if people are prejudiced against one another, diverse groups can coexist peacefully. A social problem exists when people get upset because prejudice deprives minorities of the rights

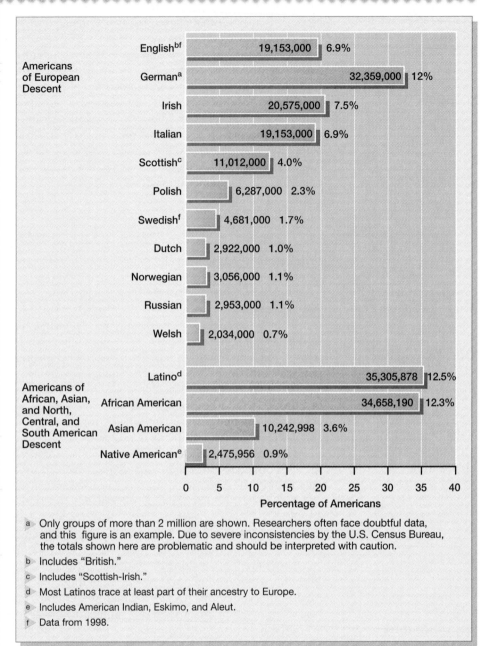

FIGURE 8-2
Racial and Ethnic Groups in the United States[a]
(*Source: Statistical Abstract* 1998: Tables 38, 58. U.S. Census Bureau 2001. Detailed Data Table PCT024. U.S. Census Bureau 2001: Table 1-7 C2KBR/01-1. Overview of Race and Hispanic Origin.).

Americans of European Descent

English[bf]	19,153,000	6.9%
German[a]	32,359,000	12%
Irish	20,575,000	7.5%
Italian	19,153,000	6.9%
Scottish[c]	11,012,000	4.0%
Polish	6,287,000	2.3%
Swedish[f]	4,681,000	1.7%
Dutch	2,922,000	1.0%
Norwegian	3,056,000	1.1%
Russian	2,953,000	1.1%
Welsh	2,034,000	0.7%

Americans of African, Asian, and North, Central, and South American Descent

Latino[d]	35,305,878	12.5%
African American	34,658,190	12.3%
Asian American	10,242,998	3.6%
Native American[e]	2,475,956	0.9%

Percentage of Americans

a Only groups of more than 2 million are shown. Researchers often face doubtful data, and this figure is an example. Due to severe inconsistencies by the U.S. Census Bureau, the totals shown here are problematic and should be interpreted with caution.
b Includes "British."
c Includes "Scottish-Irish."
d Most Latinos trace at least part of their ancestry to Europe.
e Includes American Indian, Eskimo, and Aleut.
f Data from 1998.

to which their citizenship entitles them. And if prejudice turns into hatred, discrimination, or conflict, ethnic relations are severely troubled.

As with other social problems, however, exactly what is problematic about ethnic relations depends on one's vantage point. As the chapter's opening vignette indicates, for members of the Ku Klux Klan and its sympathizers, minorities are the source of the social problem. These people think that minority group members who mix with the mainstream and prosper do so at the expense of whites.

Others are upset that prejudice and discrimination have thwarted the American ideal of equality of "life, liberty, and the pursuit of happiness." They see this failure

Underlying some aspects of U.S. race relations was the ideal that the United States would become a melting pot of the nations of the world. Sifted together, immigrants would become a new people. As discussed in the text, this ideal was more ideology than reality, and did not apply to everyone.

Numbers Fail to Show the Significance of Discrimination

Measures of Discrimination

Income

of principles that the Constitution guarantees, along with the harm and tensions it engenders, as the social problem of ethnic relations. This is how we shall look at the social problem of race and ethnic relations—as discrimination that hurts people.

The significance of discrimination goes far beyond any statistics about how many people are denied some particular benefit of society. Too often, we end up focusing on such cold numbers. Although numbers are important, what we often miss is how discrimination can touch all areas of its victims' lives. Because of discrimination, people often see themselves through the very lens that the dominant group uses to view them. They can come to deprecate ("put down") their own abilities, to think of themselves as less capable, less worthy, and, ultimately, as less human. Discrimination, in short, can detract from people's sense of being, the sense of their own humanity.

We don't have adequate measures of this vital aspect of discrimination, however, so we will have to concentrate on its surface manifestations. As we do so, keep in mind that for millions of Americans, discrimination is the central fact of their lives.

Discrimination is most readily visible in the area of economic well-being. As Table 8-1 shows, family incomes of African Americans, Latinos, and Native Americans are substantially less than those of whites. The average family income of Native-American families is only 42 percent of the average income of white families, Latinos and African-Americans only 62 percent.

As this table also shows, the average family income of Asian Americans is higher than that of white families. This leads to the question of whether the lower family incomes of the other groups are due to discrimination or to a lack of preparation to compete in the U.S. economic system. As you can see from this table, a much larger percentage of Asian Americans than any other group—including whites—have completed college and are equipped for the better jobs. The issue is much more complicated than this, however, for

TECHNOLOGY AND SOCIAL PROBLEMS

What Should We Do About Hate Speech?

The Internet has proven a marvelous source of information. I personally am extremely pleased that the Internet developed, as I am now able to live and travel in other countries and still do sociological research. Libraries and other sources lie at my fingertips—waiting to be accessed through a telephone line.

The Internet is also proving to be a remarkable source of misinformation. Anyone can put up a Web site and fill it with distortions of truth or with outright lies. People can nurse grudges, seek revenge for perceived wrongs, and fan hatred.

Such negative communications are upsetting, especially the hatred. Consider these statements:

Civil Rights come out of the barrel of a gun, and we mean to give the niggers and Jews all the civil rights they can handle.... Our security team will see that no live targets escape from the range. Any who refuse to run or can't for any reason will be fed to the dogs. The dogs appreciate a good feed as much as we do.

—An invitation to a summer conference held by the Aryan Nations at Hayden Lake, Idaho. The group's founder, Richard Butler, is a former Lockheed executive. (Statements quoted in Murphy 1999)

Who's pimping the world? The hairy hands of the Zionist.... The so-called Jew claims that there were six million in Nazi Germany. I am here today to tell you that there is absolutely no ... evidence to substantiate, to prove that six million so-called Jews lost their lives in Nazi Germany.... Don't let no hooked-nose, bagel-eating, lox-eating, perpetrating-a-fraud so-called Jew who just crawled out of the ghettoes of Europe just a few days ago ...

—Statements of Khalid Abdul Muhammad, as quoted in Herbert 1998.

Hatred knows no race-ethnic boundaries; the first statement is by a white, the second by an African American.

Should we ban such statements—and punish their authors as lawbreakers? Should we allow such statements to be circulated as part of free speech, regardless of their inflammatory rhetoric, twisting of fact, prejudice, or hatred?

Canada has taken steps to ban hate speech. Ingrid Rimland of San Diego runs a Web site on which she sells anti-Semitic literature and publicizes the views of Ernst Zundel. Zundel, an immigrant from Germany who has lived in Canada 40 years, denies the Holocaust took place and preaches anti-Semitism. Canadian authorities accuse Zundel of controlling the Web site and have charged him under laws that prohibit the use of telephone lines to spread hate messages based on race, religion, or ethnic origin ("Canada Tries to ..." 1998).

The technological solution may be at hand, a "hate filter" developed by a human rights group (Mendels 1998). When installed on a computer, this software blocks access to Web sites designed by those espousing intolerance: the Ku Klux Klan, skinheads, and neo-Nazis, as well as those that spew hatred for homosexuals or other groups.

Some say that in order to make bad ideas look silly, we should let them be viewed in the cold, hard light of day. Others take the position that censorship or even hatred is wrong; it is an attack on free speech and threatens us all. Still others say that hatred needs to be fought in any way it can, including through the passage of laws and by using filters.

What do you think?

The Significance of Income

we also must ask how lack of preparation is related to discrimination. That is, what factors of discrimination lead to some groups attaining so much less education?

Poverty, unemployment, and income produce cold statistics. Behind these abstract measures of economic well-being, however, are people whose lives are affected adversely. At issue is whether they can afford health care, education, or nourishing food—not whether they can afford a boat or a new car, or whether they can afford to vacation out of state—economic decisions that middle-class people might make.

Table 8-1 Indicators of Relative Economic Well-Being

	Family Income	
	Median Family Income	Percentage of White Income
White	$51,244	
Asian American	$56,316	110%
Latino	$31,663	62%
African American	$31,778	62%
Native American	$21,614	42%

	Poverty	
	Percentage Below Poverty	Percentage of White Poverty
White	9.8%	
Asian American	10.7%	109%
Latino	22.8%	233%
African American	23.6%	241%
Native American	31.2%	318%

	Education	
	Percentage Who Have Completed College	Percentage of White College Completion
White	26.1%	
Asian American	43.9%	168%
Latino	10.6%	41%
African American	16.5%	63%
Native American	9.4%	36%

NA = Not Available
Source: Statistical Abstract 1998:Tables 51, 52, 54, 55; 2001:Table 37.

A Matter of Life and Death

Table 8-2 reflects how race-ethnicity can translate into matters of life and death. As you can see, an African American baby has *more than twice* the chance of dying as does a white baby; the chances of a mother dying during childbirth are *five* times higher for African American women. On average, African American women die about five years younger than white women, African American men seven and one-half years younger than white men. As measured by number of days sick, African Americans are not as healthy as whites. (Unfortunately, the data are not available for other race-ethnic groups.) In short, higher income provides better nutrition, housing, and medical care—and a longer life.

Internal vs. External Causes

Prejudiced people think that minority groups are to blame for their own conditions. Extremists ascribe the blame to inborn racial or ethnic inferiority. Others, somewhat less extreme, perceive the groups as having negative characteristics, such as laziness, but consider these traits to have been acquired. Regardless of whether racists consider a minority group's position to be due to innate (genetic) traits or to

Table 8-2　Race and Health

	Infant Mortality*	Maternal Deaths*	Life Expectancy
White	6.0	5.8	77.5
Black	14.3	20.8	72.2

*The rate is the number per 1000. Infant mortality refers to the number of deaths per year of infants under 1 year old per 1000 live births. Data are not given in the source for other race/ethnic groups.

Source: Statistical Abstract 2001.

be due to acquired (cultural) traits, they turn matters upside down: They blame the group that is discriminated against instead of the discrimination.

Individual Discrimination

To understand the effects of discrimination, we need to move beyond thinking in terms of **individual discrimination,** one person treating another badly on the basis of race or ethnicity. While this certainly creates problems, it primarily is a matter for the individuals to resolve. The law, however, may become involved if one person illegally withholds, say, employment or housing from someone on the basis of race-ethnicity.

Institutional Discrimination

Sociologists, however, encourage us to move beyond individual situations and to think in broader terms. They point to **institutional discrimination** as the essence of the social problem. This is discrimination that is built into the social system to oppress whole groups. For example, for generations whites denied African Americans the right to vote, join labor unions, work at higher-paying and more prestigious jobs, attend good schools, or receive care at decent hospitals. The group that controls most real estate sales in the United States, the National Association of Real Estate Boards (NAR), used to support racial discrimination as a *moral* principle. Its 1924 code of ethics stated:

Example of Real Estate

> A Realtor should never be instrumental in introducing into a neighborhood . . . members of any race or nationality, or individuals whose presence will clearly be detrimental to property values in that neighborhood. (Newman et al. 1978:149)

The federal government had the same policy. To obtain loans from the Federal Housing Authority (FHA), developers of subdivisions had to exclude nonwhites (Valocchi 1994; Oliver and Shapiro 1995). Even after World War II, the FHA denied loans to anyone who would "unsettle a neighborhood." The FHA manual stated:

> If a neighborhood is to retain stability, it is necessary that properties shall continue to be occupied by the same social and racial classes. (Duster 1988:288)

Example of Mortgages

Times changed, and so did the federal government and the NAR. In 1950, under pressure, the NAR deleted the reference to race or nationality. The NAR continued to discriminate, however, and it was not until 1972 that the NAR adopted a pro-fair-housing position.

But where is institutional discrimination today? Laws and practices have so changed that it seems this must be a thing of the past. A study of 9,000 U.S. financial institutions, however, shows that institutional discrimination is alive and well. Summarized in Figure 8-3, this study shows how discrimination is built into the social system. When bankers were shown these findings, they denied that they discrimi-

FIGURE 8-3
Race/Ethnicity and Mortgages: An Example of Institutional Discrimination

The figures refer to applicants for conventional mortgages. Although applicants for government-backed mortgages had lower overall rates of rejection, the identical pattern showed up for all income groups. Median income is the income of each bank's local area.

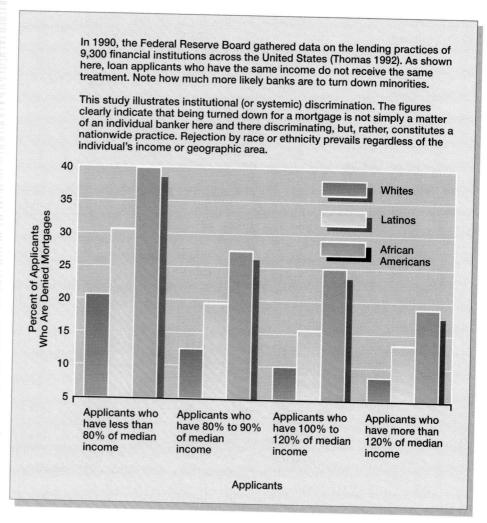

In 1990, the Federal Reserve Board gathered data on the lending practices of 9,300 financial institutions across the United States (Thomas 1992). As shown here, loan applicants who have the same income do not receive the same treatment. Note how much more likely banks are to turn down minorities.

This study illustrates institutional (or systemic) discrimination. The figures clearly indicate that being turned down for a mortgage is not simply a matter of an individual banker here and there discriminating, but, rather, constitutes a nationwide practice. Rejection by race or ethnicity prevails regardless of the individual's income or geographic area.

Whites

Latinos

African Americans

Percent of Applicants Who Are Denied Mortgages

Applicants who have less than 80% of median income

Applicants who have 80% to 90% of median income

Applicants who have 100% to 120% of median income

Applicants who have more than 120% of median income

Applicants

nated against anyone. They claimed that they gave whites more loans because they had better credit histories. To find out, the researchers went back to their data. They compared the late payments of applicants, even the loan size to their incomes. The results? When two applicants for a mortgage are identical in terms of debts, loan size relative to income, and even characteristics of the property they want to buy, African Americans and Latinos are 60 percent more likely to be rejected than whites (Thomas 1992; Passell 1996).

A fascinating aspect of institutional discrimination is that it can take place without racist intentions. *Discrimination can occur even when those doing the discriminating and those who are its objects are unaware of it.* An example is coronary bypass surgery. Two physicians, Mark Wenneker and Arnold Epstein (1989), studied all patients admitted to Massachusetts hospitals for circulatory diseases or chest pain. After comparing age, sex, payer (insurance, individual, and so on), and income, they found substantial racial inequalities: Whites were 89 percent more likely to be given coronary bypass surgery. The particular interracial dynamics that underlie medical decisions being made on the basis of race are unknown.

Discrimination Without Awareness: The Example of Heart Surgery

Cultural Bias in I.Q. Testing

Another example is IQ testing. Some questions asked on these tests favor children from certain backgrounds (Knowles and Prewitt 1969). The following is a sample question from a standardized IQ test:

A symphony is to a composer as a book is to a(n) _____:
_____paper
_____sculptor
_____musician
_____author
_____man

What is discriminatory about this question? At first glance, it seems like an objective question that applies equally to everyone. Children from certain ethnic backgrounds, however, are more familiar with the concepts of symphonies, composers, sculptors, and musicians than are other children. This tilts the test in their favor (Turner 1972). Those who make up the test do not intend to discriminate and are unaware that they are doing so.

If we turn matters around, perhaps the discriminatory nature may become more apparent. Suppose that you were asked to take an IQ test that contained these questions:

If you throw the dice and "7" is showing on the top, what is facing down?
_____seven _____snake eyes _____box cars _____little Joes _____eleven

Which word is out of place here?
_____splib _____blood _____gray _____spook _____black

These questions, suggested by Adrian Dove (n.d.), a social worker in Watts, are slanted toward a nonwhite, lower-class experience. With these *particular* cultural biases, is it not obvious that children from some social backgrounds will perform better than others?

In Sum

Institutional discrimination is built into our social system. It operates throughout society—often with those involved unaware of it.

♦ Looking at the Problem Theoretically ♦

Prejudice, discrimination, hostility, and tensions characterize many relations between ethnic groups in the United States. To account for them, social scientists have developed contrasting theoretical views. Although separately each of our three theoretical perspectives presents a limited perspective, taken together they bring more of the picture into focus.

SYMBOLIC INTERACTIONISM

"What's in a name?" asked Juliet. "That which we call a rose, by any other name would smell as sweet."

This may be true of roses, but in human relations words are not meaningless labels. The labels we learn color the way we see the world and influence what we experience.

The Role of Labels in Prejudicial Perception

Selective Perception

Symbolic interactionists stress that labels (such as stereotypes) affect prejudice by causing **selective perception.** Stereotypes lead us to see certain things and make us blind to others. They shape our perception, and we tend to look at the members of a group as though they all were alike. As Simpson and Yinger (1972) said: We fit new experiences into old categories by selecting only those cues that harmonize with our prejudgment or stereotype.

Emotionally Charged Ethnic Labels

Racial and ethnic labels have special power over people. They are shorthand for emotionally laden stereotypes. "Nigger," for example, has numerous connotations. By no means is it neutral. It is so loaded with negative emotions that television commentators won't quote it, using the phrase, "the N word," instead. Nor are "honky," "spic," "mick," "limey," "kraut," "dago," or the many other words that people use to refer to members of ethnic groups neutral. The emotional impact of such words overpowers us, blocking out other kinds of realities about people (Allport 1954).

Socialization into Prejudice

Symbolic interactionists examine how we are socialized into prejudice and discrimination. No one is born with prejudice or the desire to discriminate. Indeed, we are born without standards, values, or beliefs. But all children are born into particular families and ethnic groups where they learn values, beliefs, and ways to perceive the world. If their group is prejudiced against another group, children learn to dislike that group and to perceive its members negatively. Similarly, if discrimination is common, children learn to practice it routinely.

Stereotypes and the Self-Fulfilling Prophecy

Stereotypes are powerful. They justify prejudice and discrimination. The negative stereotypes used to characterize ethnic group X legitimate the withholding of opportunities from its members and justify placing them into positions considered appropriate for people with such characteristics. Stereotypes create a **self-fulfilling prophecy.** For example, if a stereotype defines members of ethnic group X as lazy, then it legitimizes keeping them out of jobs that require dedication, industry, and energy. If "permissible" jobs are not available, members of ethnic group X are liable to be seen standing around street corners while members of ethnic groups Y and Z are working. Seeing them idle reinforces the original stereotype of laziness, while the basic discrimination that created the "laziness" passes unnoticed.

Like Hitler's Nazis, the Ku Klux Klan wants to create and fan hatred. Their original targets were blacks, Jews, and Roman Catholics. In recent years, they have given up on Roman Catholics, diminished their efforts against Jews, and now focus on African Americans. During the 1920s, the KKK was a potent political force in some states, especially Indiana. Although the Klan today is but a shell of its former self, groups that promulgate hatred, even though small, are dangerous to the health of a nation.

Labeling, Compartmentalization and Genocide

Some ethnic labels are so powerful that they block out the morality that people learn early in life. In the 1960s and 1970s, for example, young American men were sent to a small Asian nation where they were required to kill, an act that most found repugnant. They were given labels to help them overcome their deeply rooted taboo against killing. Calling the Vietnamese "the enemy," "slopes," and "gooks," for example, helped U.S. soldiers to perceive them not as individuals but as members of a group—an inferior group. The army bureaucracy adopted a similar strategy: Weekly it would release reports, not of *people* killed, but of "body counts" and "kill ratios." Such labels help people **compartmentalize,** that is, to separate their acts from the feelings or attitudes they engender, which would be incompatible with their self-respect.

If an ethnic group is targeted for slaughter, the dominant group uses dehumanizing labels to relegate that group to a subhuman status. In this way, those assigned to kill are not killing "real" people. This helps them commit acts that are incompatible with their moral training and self-concept. Just as terms that dehumanized the Vietnamese helped U.S. soldiers commit acts that otherwise would have challenged their identities as moral beings, so in the 1700s and 1800s white settlers called Native Americans "savages," something less than human. Troops and settlers destroyed about 90 percent of the Native American population (Garbarino 1976). The Boers, Dutch settlers in South Africa, characterized the native Hottentots as animals of the jungle and wiped them out. Viewing the local population as less than human, British settlers in Tasmania hunted them for sport and even for dog food. Today, much as in earlier U.S. history, Indian tribes in Brazil are being wiped out as miners, ranchers, and loggers seize their lands (Linden 1991; "Guardian of Brazil Indians . . ." 1997).

In Sum

Symbolic interactionists examine how labels (or symbols) affect our relationships: how we learn ethnic labels, how we use labels to classify one another, how our classifications affect our perceptions and sort people out for different kinds of life experiences, how symbols of ethnicity change, and how symbols are used to justify discrimination and violence.

FUNCTIONALISM

Why does ethnic discrimination persist in the United States? As you will recall, functionalists argue that the benefits of a social pattern (a characteristic of society) must be greater than its costs, or else that pattern would disappear. The benefits (or functions) of discrimination, then, must outweigh its costs (or dysfunctions). Let's see how this could be.

Functions of Past Ethnic Discriminations

It is easy to see the functions of past race-ethnic discrimination, how it directly benefitted the dominant group. Whites gained free land by killing Native Americans or driving them west. Whites benefitted from owning slaves. They procured the labor free of charge, sold the cotton the slaves produced, and sold their labor as masons, carpenters, or factory workers. Slave labor allowed many owners to live a "genteel" life of leisure or to pursue art, education, and other "refinements."

A Legacy of Dysfunction

And today? The legacy of hatred that slavery bequeathed is a dysfunctional one. Our urban riots, for example, exact a high cost—in property, lives, and heightened tension, hostility, hatred, and fear. It would appear that the high costs of discrimination would lead to its elimination. Because ethnic discrimination remains a fact of life in the United States, however, functionalists search for its benefits, or functions. Since ethnic discrimination was functional for the dominant group in the past, functionalists look for how today's dominant group still benefits.

Functions of Present Ethnic Discrimination

1. The "Dirty Work" of Society

Ethnic stratification, the unequal distribution of a society's resources based on race or ethnicity, has three major functions. The first is to ensure that society's **dirty work** gets done. Sociologist Herbert Gans (1999) defines dirty work as society's "physically dirty or dangerous, temporary, dead-end and underpaid, undignified and menial jobs." Sociologist Emile Durkheim (1964, 1965) stressed that society needs a **division of labor,** people performing specialized tasks. Dirty work, such as garbage collection, is a necessary but disagreeable task within this division of labor.

Society can fill these jobs either by paying high wages to compensate for the work's unpleasantness and degradation, or by forcing people to do them for low wages. To get society's dirty work done, then, it is functional to bar an ethnic group from higher positions. This ensures that the jobs will get done and get done cheaply.

When an ethnic group climbs the social class ladder, it leaves the dirty work behind. Since the dirty work remains, other ethnic groups are recruited to perform those tasks. For example, many African Americans have moved into the middle class, and illegal aliens are doing much of the work they used to do. Mexicans who have entered the United States illegally, for example, have little control over their working conditions. They take jobs that practically no one else will do, often working long hours in crowded, dirty, sometimes dangerous conditions. And they work cheaply, for employers don't have to pay unemployment compensation, Social Security, hospitalization, overtime pay, disability compensation, or vacations.

Apart from what one could say about the inherent injustice of this situation, it is functional. The dirty work gets done, and *most* Americans benefit; they eat the produce that illegal aliens pick and wear the clothing they make. The illegal aliens also benefit; they earn far more than they would in Mexico. Their families, left in Mexico in desperate conditions, also benefit; they are sent part of the earnings. Even the government of Mexico benefits, for the illegal immigration siphons off its more ambitious and dissatisfied citizens—who otherwise might direct their energies toward overthrowing an oppressive Mexican elite.

Boxing is another example of ethnic succession in dirty work. It entertains sports fans and produces advertising revenues, but because of the harsh discipline it requires and the danger it entails, few are willing to box. Accordingly, most fighters come from ethnic groups that are largely blocked from more socially approved avenues of success. The result is an "ethnic succession" in boxing (Weinberg and Arond 1952). That is, as an ethnic group climbs the social class ladder, fewer of its members are willing to seek fame and fortune by boxing. New fighters, in turn, come from another ethnic group that is struggling up the ladder. In general, Irish boxers gave way to Germans, then to Italians, then to African Americans, who now are being rivaled by Latinos.

2. Ethnocentrism in the Dominant Group

Another major function of ethnic inequality is **ethnocentrism,** a sense of group identity so strong that members of other groups are viewed as inferior. Ethnocentrism helps the dominant group justify its higher social positions and greater share of society's material rewards. They don't have to question or feel guilty about getting more, for aren't they superior? And aren't they performing the more responsible tasks that society requires? Ethnocentrism also fosters cooperation and camaraderie, helping the dominant group attain common goals, such as directing the country's politics and economics.

3. Ethnocentrism in the Minority Group

Ethnic stratification also produces ethnocentrism among minority groups. Their visible differences and the discrimination they face because of their distinctiveness creates cohesion, a sense of identity with one another. Seeing that other ethnic groups have "made it" nourishes the hope that they, too, will succeed. This hope for the future strengthens the social system: It encourages minority groups to work hard, minimizes rebellion, and makes them willing to put up with demeaning circumstances for the time being.

Dysfunctions: Disrupting Society and Denying Individual Potential

Ethnic discrimination is also dysfunctional; that is, it interferes with people's welfare and even the functioning of society. If an ethnic group becomes too alienated, it may disrupt society through strikes and riots. Another dysfunction is the destruction of human potential. Prejudice and discrimination can lower children's self-esteem, decreasing their capacity to compete in school and work. Because they confront discrimination, many minority children drop out of school and waste their potential in low-level jobs or street crime. Society is the loser, for it is denied the contributions these youngsters could have made.

To Analyze Functions Is Not to Promote Those Functions

Functionalists do not promote the social phenomena they analyze. They argue that social characteristics persist only because they are functional. By analyzing the functions and dysfunctions of ethnic stratification, they uncover some of the hidden consequences of institutional arrangements.

CONFLICT THEORY

What had seemed a personal hatred of me, an inexplicable refusal of southern whites to confront their own emotions, and a stubborn willingness of blacks to acquiesce, became the inevitable consequence of a ruthless system which kept itself alive and well by encouraging spite, competition, and the oppression of one group by another. Profit was the word: the cold and constant motive for the behavior, the contempt and despair I had seen. (Davis 1974)

With these words, Angela Davis, an African-American Marxist, recounted her new understanding of U.S. race and ethnic relations. What does she mean by this statement?

According to Marxist conflict theory, ethnic groups are pitted against one another in order to exploit workers and increase profit. It works this way:

Extracting the Surplus Value of Labor

The United States is a **capitalist** society; that is, our economic system is based on investing capital with the goal of making a profit. Profit depends on selling items for more than they cost to produce. In conflict theory, this is called extracting the **surplus value of labor.** For example, if each item a factory produces costs the owner of the factory $1 for materials, $1 for rent, utilities, and transportation, $1 for advertising, transportation, insurance, and the cost of borrowing money, and $1 for a worker to run a machine, the total cost of the item is $4. If the owner sells it for $5, he or she makes $1 profit. Conflict theorists say the profit represents the surplus value of the labor used to produce the item.

A Split-Labor Market Lowers Wages

Lower wages help investors and owners increase their profit. To keep wages low, capitalists use a *split-labor market;* that is, they weaken the bargaining power of workers by splitting them along racial, ethnic, or gender lines (Reich 1972, 1981; Shafir 1995; Bernstein 1996; Shafir and Peled 1998). If they can keep workers fearful and distrustful of one another, employers can prevent them from uniting to demand a higher wage.

The Reserve Labor Force

Capitalists also use the unemployed, or the **reserve labor force,** in the same way. If all workers were employed, the high demand for labor would let workers insist on pay increases and better working conditions. The unemployed form a pool from which owners can draw when they expand production or want to break a strike. When the economy contracts or when the strike is settled, these workers are laid off to rejoin the unemployed, with no unsettling effects on society. Minority workers are ideal for the reserve labor force, because employers rely primarily

Distorted Perception of the Self: False Class Consciousness

on the more numerous white workers. In addition, white workers seldom object to what happens to minorities, especially to the unemployed (Willhelm 1980).

Another technique used to control workers is to nourish **false class consciousness,** getting workers to identify with employers. For example, if white workers believe that their living standards will fall if minorities make economic gains, they have a stake in discrimination. False consciousness prevents workers from seeing that their welfare is bound up with that of all workers, regardless of ethnicity or color. Thus workers are "duped" into identifying with the property interests of capitalists instead of with their true working-class interests (Willhelm 1980).

Distorted Perception of Others: The Enemy

The consequences are devastating, say conflict theorists. A minority may see its group as able to make gains only at the expense of whites or other ethnic groups. Whites may come to think of themselves as moral, hardworking taxpayers—and the competing minority as lazy, sexually promiscuous people who swell the welfare rolls, and who are supported by confiscatory taxes placed on their own hard labor. The minority, in turn, may portray whites as ruthless, untrustworthy, hate-mongering hypocrites.

Pitting one ethnic group against another leads to outbursts of violence, and our urban ghettos occasionally erupt in flames. The attempt to strike out at their oppressors, however, usually is misdirected at their neighbors. The present system so distorts reality that it leads minorities and whites to see one another as enemies. They fail to see that the other is an essential part of their own class interests. The reality is that they both have a common enemy, the wealthy, who, to line their own purses, use ethnic divisions and hatred to oppress both.

Concessions Made in Order to Defuse

Riots and other violence that result from this situation sometimes put pressure on the social system. When the elite feel threatened, they try to defuse the bomb that might disrupt their power. They often use concessions, giving a little here and there, whatever seems necessary to quiet the workers. They may increase welfare benefits, assign token representation on decision-making committees, offer government aid to reconstruct the inner cities—or build swimming pools and gyms or even offer "night basketball." From the conflict perspective, these acts are not intended to change anything, only to protect the privileged position of the powerful.

An End to Discrimination?

Racial and ethnic antagonisms, then, divide the working class and strengthen capitalists. A racist environment not only deflects working-class hostilities, but it also prevents working-class consensus, the solidarity that would allow workers to challenge the control of the United States by the wealthy who own the means of production. Ethnic discrimination will end only when white and minority workers see that they both are oppressed. Losing their false class consciousness, they will see the true source of their oppression, unite, and create a new social order in which they will receive the full value of their labor. With the new racial-ethnic harmony, society will no longer have minority and dominant groups.

In Sum

The Theories Working Together

None of the three theoretical perspectives has an exclusive claim to truth. Each presents a particular truth. Each focuses on selected aspects of ethnic relations, emphasizing those aspects above any other. Symbolic interactionists alert us to the powerful role of labels in defining human relations: Labels help determine how people see themselves and other ethnic groups, and help people discriminate with a clear conscience. Functionalists turn our attention not only to the dysfunctions of ethnic discrimination, but also to its benefits—its role in the division of labor, and the consequences of the ethnocentrism that it produces. Conflict theorists stress how prejudice and discrimination destroy worker solidarity, help hold down wages, and increase the profits of capitalists. Each theoretical lens, then, produces a unique understanding of race-ethnic relations. Combined, these perspectives provide greater understanding of ethnic discrimination than does any one of them alone.

◆ Research Findings ◆

Whites make up 71 percent of the overall U.S. population, minorities 29 percent (African Americans 12 percent, Latinos 12–13 percent, Asian Americans 3.6 percent, and Native Americans 1 percent). (See Figure 8-2 on page 254 for a review of these totals.) As the social map below shows, the states' distribution of dominant and minority groups seldom comes close to the national average. This is because minority groups tend to be clustered in regions. The extreme distributions are represented by Maine and Vermont, which have only 2 percent minority, and Hawaii, where minorities outnumber Anglos 76 percent to 24 percent.

What major problems do minority groups in the United States face? How do they differ from one another? How is their relationship to the dominant group changing? What are their strategies for bringing about social change? To answer these questions, we shall present an overview of the four largest minority groups in the United States: Native Americans, Latinos, African Americans, and Asian Americans.

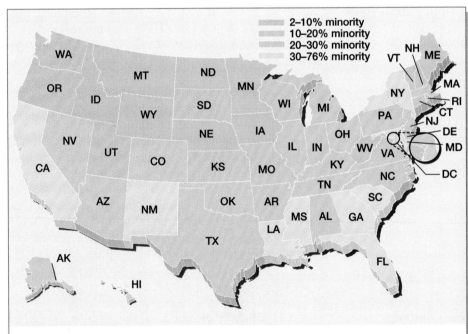

FIGURE 8-4
The Distribution of Dominant and Minority Groups in the United States
(*Source: Statistical Abstract* 1998:Table 38; U.S. Census PHC-T-6.)

Note: These totals are for the year 2000. Whites make up 71 percent of the U.S. population, minorities (African American, Asian American, Latino, and Native American) 29 percent. As this map shows, the states' distribution of dominant and minority groups seldom comes close to the average. Only 10 states will be within 5 points of the national average (North Carolina, Arizona, Nevada, Alabama, Illinois, Alaska, Florida, New Jersey, South Carolina, and Georgia). The extremes are represented by Maine and Vermont at 2 percent minority and Hawaii at 76 percent minority.

Chapter 8   Race and Ethnic Relations

When Columbus arrived on the shores of the "New World," the Native American population was about 5 million (Thornton 1987). Reaching a low of a quarter of a million around 1900, Native Americans now number about 2.5 million (*Statistical Abstract* 2001:Table 16). This includes Eskimos and Aleuts. Native Americans belong to more than 500 tribes (O'Hare 1992).

Early Relations

At first, relations between the European settlers and the Native Americans were peaceful. American (and Canadian) authorities even encouraged marriage between whites and Native Americans. In 1784, Patrick Henry introduced a bill in the Virginia House of Delegates to offer tax relief, free education, and cash bonuses to whites and Indians who intermarried (Kaplan 1990). As more Europeans arrived, they began a relentless push westward. The Native American population blocked this expansion, and the Europeans began a policy of genocide. As part of this policy (called "pacification"), the U.S. Cavalry slaughtered tens of thousands of Native Americans. When it butchered the huge herds of buffalo on which the Great Plains Indians depended, many thousands more died from malnutrition and disease. In fact, European diseases, especially smallpox, measles, and the flu, may have killed more Native Americans than bullets, for the Native Americans had no immunity to them (Kitano 1974; Schaefer 1979; Dobyns 1983).

From Genocide to Containment

In reading the accounts of this period, I am struck by the barbarity of the Anglos. One of the most grisly acts was the distribution of blankets contaminated with smallpox. The blankets were presented as a peace offering. Another was the Trail of Tears, which took place after the government changed its policy from genocide to population transfer and began to relocate Native Americans to specified areas called "reservations." The Trail of Tears was a forced march from the Carolinas and Georgia to Oklahoma, a journey of a thousand miles. Fifteen thousand Cherokees were forced to make this midwinter march in light clothing. Those who fell exhausted, mostly elderly and children, were left to die. Four thousand Cherokees perished.

Because each tribe was a nation, the U.S. government made treaties with the tribes. These treaties, ratified by the U.S. Senate, granted the Native Americans specified lands forever. The treaties often were broken when Anglo settlers demanded more Indian land and natural resources. In 1874, for instance, when gold was discovered in South Dakota's Black Hills, those reservation lands were flooded with Anglos. The cavalry supported the settlers, resulting in the well-known defeat of "General" (actually, Lt. Colonel) Custer at Little Big Horn in 1876 (Churchill and Wall 1990). The symbolic end to Native American resistance may have been the 1890 massacre at Wounded Knee, South Dakota, where the cavalry

With about half living on reservations, Native Americans are the "invisible minority" in the United States. With few exceptions, Native Americans have met oppression with silence, withdrawal, and legal claims. Shown here is one of the instances in which they have broken that silence, a protest that the Cleveland Indians use Native Americans as their mascot.

murdered 300 (out of 350) Native American men, women, and children (Kitano 1974; Olson et al. 1997).

Stereotypes to Justify Inhumane Acts

History Written by the Victors

As noted earlier, stereotypes and labels can justify inhumane acts, helping to keep the acts from conflicting with favorable definitions of the self. So it was with the U.S. Indian policy. Whites viewed Native Americans as stupid, lying, thieving, murdering, pagan "savages" (Simpson and Yinger 1972). Killing a dangerous savage was seen as making the world a safer place for civilized people. The victors who wrote our history texts labeled whites as "pioneers," not "invaders"; their military successes were "victories" but those of the Native Americans "massacres"; the seizure of Native American lands was called "settling the land," and the Native Americans' defense of their homelands against overwhelming numbers was not "courageous" but "treacherous" (Josephy 1970; Henslin 1999).

Continuing Effects

The government's attempt to destroy the Native Americans' way of life and relocate Native Americans on reservations still has negative effects today. As Table 8-1 on page 257 shows, Native Americans rank the lowest on indicators of economic well-being. Their income and education are the lowest of all ethnic groups, and one of three Native American families falls below the poverty line. Their life expectancy is also about eight to ten years less than that of the nation as a whole: One in four Native Americans dies before the age of 25, compared with the national average of one in seven. Their suicide rate is double the national average, and their rate of alcoholism runs perhaps five times that of the nation (Snipp and Sorkin 1986; O'Hare 1992). It seems fair to conclude that Native American life in the dominant Anglo society is not satisfying.

The Reservation and Education

Why do so few Native Americans finish college? As social scientists Murray and Rosalie Wax documented in the 1960s, a huge cultural gap separates the children's home and school life. Native American parents teach their children to be independent; at school they are rewarded for being dependent on their teachers. Native American parents teach their children not to embarrass their peers; their teachers expect them to correct one another in public. Geared to urban Anglo values, the schools prepare Native American children for a life that most will never lead. Because the school system, which is based on the values of the dominant group, denigrates Native American culture and teaches concepts that are largely irrelevant to reservation life, the parents are alienated from it and refuse to visit their children's schools. The teachers, alienated by the rejection of their efforts, avoid the homes of their students (Wax and Wax 1964, 1965, 1967, 1971).

Dead center in this conflict of values between the schools and the reservation are the children. Torn between home and school, their choice generally goes to the family and tribe. Lacking motivation to do well in school, they drop out. As the Waxes expressed it, the deck is so stacked against Native American children that they are, in effect, pushed out of school. Their continuing low rate of college graduation indicates little change in the conditions documented in the 1960s.

Changing Relations and Native American Activism

Native Americans can be called the invisible minority. With about half living in rural areas, a third on remote reservations, and half in just four states—Oklahoma, California, Arizona, and New Mexico—most Americans are hardly aware of their presence in U.S. society (O'Hare 1992). In addition, for the past 100 years or so, seldom have Native Americans made headlines by disrupting the Anglo-dominated society that they have refused to join. Today's conflicts are primarily legal and center on trying to enforce the rights granted by treaties. Minor legal skirmishes have centered on maintaining traditional fishing and hunting rights. Major legal skirmishes include demanding the water of the Arkansas, Colorado, San Juan, and Rio Grande rivers. What most upsets Anglos, however, are the Native Americans' demands to

The Treaties: Backed Up by the Full Faith and Honor of the U.S. Government

millions of acres of land ranging from New England to the Southwest. In New York, for example, the Oneida tribe is suing for 270,000 acres (Dao 1999).

The government's primary legal strategy has been to obstruct the justice system by postponement. In some instances, legal cases are never heard, for those who filed the motion die and others lose interest as proceedings drag on for years, sometimes for generations. Some tribes, however, have won their legal battles. Blue Lake of New Mexico, a heavily forested area sacred to the Taos tribe, has been returned to them. Alaskan Native Americans, primarily the Inuits and Aleuts, were awarded a cash settlement of nearly $1 billion and legal title to 40 million acres. The Penobscot and Passamaquoddy tribes of Maine were awarded $81 million, the Miccosukee tribe of the Seminoles $975,000 and a perpetual lease on 180,000 acres in Florida, and the Sioux $105 million (Goldberg 1981).

Such settlements sound impressive, but in order to receive their award the Penobscot and Passamaquoddy had to give up claim to 12.5 million acres, the Miccosukee had to drop their claim for 5 million acres, and after 58 years of litigation, the Sioux's $105 million came to just 15 cents an acre for the 703 million acres of the Black Hills that whites took from them in 1877.

Some whites have hit upon a legal strategy that goes straight to the jugular—trying to strip Native Americans of their legal status as separate nations and remove their immunity to lawsuits. So far, such attempts have been rebuffed (Anderson and Moller 1998).

Based on their status as separate nations, Native Americans in some states have the legal right to operate gambling casinos. One small tribe, the Mdewakanton Dakota in Minnesota, has struck it rich. Its casino near Minneapolis-St. Paul nets over $600,000 a year for each man, woman, and child of the 270-member tribe (Farney 1998). The Oneida tribe of New York, consisting of just a few hundred families, used to live in trailers on 32 acres. Now they employ 3,000 people in their casino, hotels, convention center, gasoline stations, and restaurants. Anglo neighbors have grown resentful of the tribe's new affluence (Dao 1999). Native Americans being wealthy, much less having an income higher than the national average, is an exception, of course, as is evident from the data we reviewed in Table 8-1.

The Right to Self-Determination

Native Americans insist on the right to self-determination—to remain unassimilated in Anglo culture and run their own affairs as separate peoples. Native Americans had no term for the many tribes that inhabited North and South America. The term *Indian* was given to them by Columbus, who mistakenly thought that he had landed in India. The name stuck, and many Native Americans still use it to refer to themselves (Shively 1999). The term *Native American* was also made up by Anglos. Thinking of the 500 culturally distinct tribes as "one people," then, is an Anglo way of viewing matters. The tribes see themselves as many nations, many peoples.

These separate identities have served the dominant Anglos well, for they have not had to face a united Native American population. Perhaps, then, the most significant change in this aspect of ethnic relations is the development of **pan-Indianism.** Moving beyond identification with only a particular tribe, some Native Americans emphasize common elements that run through their cultures. They are trying to utilize these themes to build a united self-identification and work toward the welfare of all Native Americans. If effective, national Native American organizations will develop. They can help force the courts to act on the many Native American lawsuits, initiate hundreds more, and develop self-help measures that center around Native American values. Pan-Indianism, however, is a controversial issue among Native Americans. Some reject it in favor of cultural diversity, preferring to stress the many Native American histories, languages, and even musical styles (Rolo n.d.).

LATINOS (HISPANICS)

Numbers and Countries of Origin

The largest ethnic group in the United States is the Latinos (or Hispanics), people who trace their origins to the Spanish-speaking countries of Latin America and to Spain. Like Native Americans, few Latinos think of themselves as a single people. They consider themselves Americans of Mexican origin, Americans of Cuban origin, and so on, and do not readily identify with the terms *Latino* or *Hispanic*. Most consider such a grouping to be artificial, and so it is. It is important to stress that *Latino* and *Hispanic* do not refer to a race, but to ethnic groups. Latinos may identify themselves racially as African American, white, or native American (Salas 1996; Diaz-Calderon 1996, 1997).

In addition to 21 million Chicanos (those whose country of origin is Mexico), Latinos include about 3.5 million Puerto Ricans, 1.2 million Cuban-Americans, and 4 million people from Central and South America (U.S. Census, 2001, The Hispanic Population, Table 1). While most Chicanos live in the Southwest, most Latinos from Puerto Rico live in New York City and those from Cuba in the Miami area of Florida.

Officially tallied at 35.3 million, the number of Latinos in the United States is probably several million higher. Although most Latinos are U.S. citizens, millions have entered the country illegally. Most illegal immigrants are from Mexico. Each year, over a million people are apprehended at the Mexican border or at points inland and returned to Mexico (*Statistical Abstract* 2001:Table 313). Most immigrate for temporary work and then return home. Many do not. In 1986, the federal government passed the Immigration Reform and Control Act, which permitted illegal immigrants to apply for U.S. citizenship. Over 3 million people applied, the vast majority from Mexico (Espenshade 1990). To understand better the reasons behind this vast subterranean immigration, see the Issues box on page 272.

Latinos are clustered in the states shown in Figure 8-4. Within those states, they are concentrated in certain areas and cities. There, immigrants establish a culture that is comfortable with their immigrant background, such as this Miami restaurant that serves Nicaraguan food. When Latinos who are assimilated into mainstream culture visit these areas, they do so like non-Latinos, as tourists.

Geographic Distribution

Although there are vast stretches of Middle America where no Latinos can be found, the United States has more Latinos than Canada has Canadians. As Figure 8-5 shows, 7 of 10 Latinos are concentrated in just four states—California, Texas, New York, and Florida. Latinos have recently become the largest minority group in the United States, and they are bringing seismic changes to some areas, such as Florida's Dade County, which contains Miami. With the prominent Latino presence, especially with regard to the amount of Spanish that is spoken, some Latinos call Miami "the capital of South America."

The Spanish Language

The factor that clearly distinguishes Latinos from other U.S. minorities is the Spanish language. Although not all Latinos speak Spanish, most do. About 17 million Latinos speak Spanish at home. About half cannot speak English or can do so only with difficulty (*Statistical Abstract* 2001:Table 47). Being fluent only in Spanish in a society where English is spoken almost exclusively is a severe obstacle to getting a good job.

Until recently, teachers discouraged Latinos from speaking Spanish, and some schools punished children who spoke Spanish at school. Despite the 1848 Treaty of Hidalgo, which ended the Mexican War and guarantees Mexicans the right to maintain their culture, from 1855 until 1968 California banned teaching in any language other than English. In a 1974 decision (*Lau v. Nichols*), the U.S. Supreme Court ruled that to use only English to teach students who cannot understand English violated their civil rights. This decision, which paved the way for bilingual instruction for Spanish-speaking children, resulted from a lawsuit by Chinese students who wanted to receive instruction in Chinese (Vidal 1977; Lopez 1980).

The growing use of Spanish has become a social issue. Senator S. I. Hayakawa of California initiated an "English-only" movement in 1981. Supporters of this movement have succeeded in getting about half the states to pass a law declaring English their official language (Amselle 1995).

Deprivation

Latinos fare poorly on the indicators of quality of life shown in Table 8-1 on page 257. They are more than twice as likely as Anglos to be poor. Their median income is only three fifths that of Anglos, their unemployment rate is double that of Anglos, and only one of ten is a college graduate. At *every* level of education, whether it be a high school diploma or a doctorate, whites earn more (*Statistical Abstract* 1996:Table 244; 2001: Table 218). In response to this, some Latinos have begun a movement that rejects assimilation and emphasizes the maintenance of Latino culture.

The best-known Chicano leader was César Chávez (1927–1993), who organized migrant farm workers. His grape boycott of 1965 carried the labor struggle into U.S. kitchens. After five years of conflict, grape growers signed a contract with the Chávez group. Migrant farm workers, primarily Chicanos, later affiliated with the largest U.S. labor organization, the AFL-CIO.

Despite their numbers, Latinos hold only a tiny fraction of

FIGURE 8-5
Geographic Distribution of the Latino Population
(Source: *Statistical Abstract* 1998:Table 38; U.S. Census Bureau (2001) *The Hispanic Population* Table 2.)

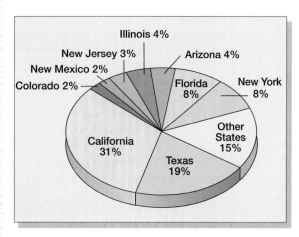

Illinois 4%
New Jersey 3%
Arizona 4%
New Mexico 2%
New York 8%
Colorado 2%
Florida 8%
Other States 15%
California 31%
Texas 19%

Political Power

The Illegal Travel Guide

Manuel was a drinking buddy of Jose's, a man I had met in Mexico. At 45, Manuel was friendly, outgoing, and enterprising.

Manuel had lived in the United States for seven years and spoke fluent English. Preferring his home town in Colima, Mexico, where he palled around with his childhood friends, Manuel always seemed to have money and free time.

When Manuel invited me to go on a business trip with him, I accepted. I never could figure out how he made his living and how he could afford a car, a luxury that none of his friends had. As we traveled from one remote village to another, Manuel would sell used clothing that he had heaped in the back of his older-model Ford station wagon.

While chickens ran in and out of the dirt-floored, thatched-roof hut, Manuel whispered to a slender man of about 23. The poverty was overwhelming. Juan, as his name turned out to be, had a partial grade school education. He also had a wife, four hungry children under the age of 5, and two pigs—his main food supply. Although eager to work, he had no job, for there was simply no work available.

As we were drinking a Coke, the national beverage of Mexico's poor, Manuel explained to me that he was not only selling clothing, he was also lining up migrants to the United States. For $200 he would take a

man to the border and introduce him to a "wolf," who, for another $200 would surreptitiously make a night crossing into the promised land.

When I saw the hope in Juan's face, I knew nothing would stop him. He was borrowing every cent he could from every relative to scrape the $400 together. He would make the trip, although he risked losing everything if apprehended, for wealth beckoned on the other side. He knew people who had been there and spoke glowingly of its opportunities.

Looking up from the children playing on the dirt floor with the chickens pecking about them, I saw a man who loved his family. In order to make the desperate bid for a better life, he would suffer their enforced absence, as well as the uncertainties of a foreign culture whose language he did not know.

Juan handed me something from his billfold, and I looked at it curiously. I felt tears as I saw the tenderness with which he handled this piece of paper—his passport to opportunity—a Social Security card made out in his name, sent by a friend who had already made the trip and who was waiting for Juan.

It was then that I realized that the thousands of Manuels scurrying about Mexico and the millions of Juans they were transporting could never be stopped, for the United States held their only dream of a better life.

elected offices. Of the 100 U.S. senators, none are Latino. Of the 435 representatives, 17 are Latino. Overall, of the 495,000 elected public officials in the United States, only 5,200 are Latino (*Statistical Abstract* 2001:Tables 390, 400). While Latinos make up about 12 or 13 percent of the population, they hold only about 1 percent of the elected offices. Yet, compared with the past, this small amount represents substantial gains in the political system.

It is likely that Latinos soon will play a larger role in U.S. politics, perhaps one day even beyond their overall numbers. This is because they are concentrated in four states that hold one fourth of the 538 electoral votes: California (47), New York (36), Texas (29), and Florida (21). Already, a president has seen the political wisdom of appointing a Latino, Federico Peña, as U.S. Secretary of Transportation and later as U.S. Secretary of Energy, and another Latino, Henry Cisneros, as Secretary of Health, Education, and Welfare. In addition to their ritual kissing of babies, presidential candidates now ritually utter a few Spanish phrases.

Internal Divisions   The potential political power of Latinos has not been realized because of severe divisions of national origin and social class. These distinctions nourish disunity and

create disagreements about social and economic policy. As mentioned, Latinos do not think of themselves as a single people, and national origin is highly significant. People from Puerto Rico, for example, feel little sense of unity with people from Mexico. It is similarly the case with those from Venezuela, Colombia, or El Salvador. Latinos from rural and urban areas also have different cultural traditions and political views.

Social class divisions also obstruct united action. Like people of other ethnic backgrounds, Latinos are divided by education and income. Most of the half million who fled Cuba after Fidel Castro came to power in 1959 were well-educated, financially comfortable professionals or businesspeople. The 100,000 "boat people" who arrived in 1980, however, were mainly lower-class refugees to whom the earlier arrivals would hardly have spoken in Cuba. The earlier arrivals, having prospered in Florida and in control of many businesses and financial institutions, feel vast divisions between themselves and other more recent immigrants.

AFRICAN AMERICANS

American Apartheid

It was 1955, in Montgomery, Alabama. As specified by law, whites took the front seats of the bus, while blacks went to the back. As the bus filled up, blacks had to give up their seats to whites.

When Rosa Parks, a 42-year-old African-American woman and secretary of the Montgomery NAACP, was told she would have to stand so white folks could sit, she refused. She stubbornly sat there while the bus driver raged, whites felt insulted, and blacks, observing from the back of the bus, also wondered what she was doing.

Mrs. Parks was arrested. Instead of passing as an incident of little importance, her arrest touched off mass demonstrations, led 50,000 blacks to boycott the city's buses for a year, and thrust an otherwise unknown preacher who had majored in sociology at Morehouse College in Atlanta, Georgia, onto the stage of history.

Dr. Martin Luther King, Jr., who was later murdered in Memphis, Tennessee, organized car pools and preached nonviolence. Incensed at this radical organizer and at the stirrings in the normally compliant black community, the segregationists also put their beliefs into practice—by bombing homes and dynamiting churches.

The segregation of whites and African Americans (then called Negroes or colored) was not limited to the Deep South. This 1939 photo was taken in Oklahoma City, Oklahoma. Memories of such conditions are still vivid in the minds of many Americans.

In the 1950s, the South was still practicing apartheid. African Americans, then called Negroes, were not allowed to stay at hotels or to eat in restaurants that whites pa-

tronized. They even had to use separate toilets and water fountains. It was only a few years earlier, in 1944, that the U.S. Supreme Court had decided that African Americans could vote in the southern primaries. Just one year earlier, in 1954, the Court had ruled that African Americans had the legal right to attend public schools with whites (Carroll and Noble 1977; Polenberg 1980). Not until 1967 would the Court strike down the last of the laws (in Virginia and South Carolina) prohibiting marriage between blacks and whites (O'Hare 1992).

King led African Americans in a strategy called **civil disobedience,** deliberately but peacefully disobeying laws that are considered unjust, in order to break down institutional barriers. Inspired by Mahatma Gandhi, who had played a critical role in winning India's independence from Great Britain, King (1958) based his strategy on these principles:

The King Strategy

1. Active, nonviolent resistance to evil
2. Not seeking to defeat or humiliate opponents, but seeking instead to win their friendship and understanding
3. Attacking the forces of evil rather than the people who are doing the evil
4. Being willing to accept suffering without retaliating
5. Refusing to hate the opponent
6. Acting with the conviction that the universe is on the side of justice

There was no overnight success, but the barriers did come down. In 1964 Congress passed the Civil Rights Act, making it illegal to discriminate in hotels, theaters, and other public places. Then, in 1965, the Voting Rights Act banned the literacy and other discriminatory tests that had been used to keep African Americans from voting.

Rising Expectations and Violence

Encouraged by such gains, African Americans experienced **rising expectations;** that is, they expected better conditions to follow right away. The lives of poor African Americans, however, changed little, if at all. Frustrations built, finally exploding in Watts in 1965, when residents of this central Los Angeles ghetto took to the streets in the first of the "urban revolts." The violence, which occurred despite the protests of Dr. King, precipitated a white backlash that threatened the interracial coalition that King had spearheaded. Congress refused to enact civil rights legislation in both 1967 and 1968. When King was assassinated on April 4, 1968, ghettos across the nation erupted in fiery violence. Under threat of the destruction of the nation's cities, Congress reluctantly passed the sweeping Civil Rights Act of 1968.

Leadership Following King's Assassination

After King's death, black militants filled the leadership void. Like King, they emphasized black unity and pride in black identity. But, unlike King, some of them saw violent confrontation as necessary for gaining equality. The Black Panthers stirred up fear and hatred among whites as they paraded in military-style dress and brandished rifles. The militants lost their most forceful leaders, however. Assassinations and police bullets killed some; others were bought off with official job titles and a government paycheck.

The leadership fragmented. It even disagreed about basic purposes, some arguing for secession from the United States, others for total integration. Leaders also disagreed about methods, some wanting violent confrontation, others peaceful protest. Integration and political action won. A more moderate approach replaced militancy, and even the Black Panthers switched to community organizing, providing breakfasts for schoolchildren, and running for political office. Lacking a charismatic leader, the momentum that had propelled the struggle for equality faded.

Political Gains

Changes in political representation show mixed results. On the positive side, the mayors of many large U.S. cities are African American, and of 435 representatives, 39 are African American. But of 100 senators, none is African American, when we would expect about 12 based on population. Of the 495,000 elected officials in the United States, only about 9,000 are African American (*Statistical Abstract* 2001:Table 399). African Americans, who number 34.6 million, make up about 12 percent of the population, but they hold only about 2 percent of the elected offices. Yet, compared with the past, this small amount represents substantial gains in the U.S. political system.

Educational Integration and "White Flight"

An elusive goal is an integrated public school system. After the pathbreaking 1954 Supreme Court decision to integrate public schools, whites fled the cities and relocated in all-white suburbs. Others remained in the city but opened all-white private schools. In one of the ironies of race relations, the 1954 Supreme Court decision led to U.S. schools becoming even more segregated. In Atlanta, Georgia, for example, "white flight" changed the school system from 55 percent white to 90 percent black (Stevens 1980). White flight continued, and now the schools of the major U.S. cities are primarily African American. Baltimore, for example, has just 13 percent whites in its public schools; in some of its high schools, only 1 percent of students are white (Olesker 1997).

Strong gains, however, have been made in education. The percentage of African American high school graduates who attend college has increased from 42 percent in 1980 to 59 percent today (*Statistical Abstract* 2001:Table 262). And it is the college graduates who are making inroads in the better-paying positions and are joining the middle class. Because African Americans are more likely than whites to drop out of high school and less likely to graduate from college, a smaller proportion of African Americans will be prepared to compete for the better jobs.

The changes are stunning when one realizes that in the 1950s whites were still forcing African Americans into "black-only" areas—and the law stood on their side. With the progress that African Americans have made in education, employment, and legislation, the question has been raised whether race still underlies their relations with whites. Some sociologists have suggested that, rather than race, the significant factor has become social class.

"Reverse Segregation"

This view is supported by an event in Westland, Michigan, where African Americans banded together to keep out whites as neighbors. Annapolis Park is a subdivision of expensive homes inhabited by African Americans. The city council voted to allow the construction of a trailer park near the neighborhood. Objections to the trailer park, in which whites would live, were based on social class, not race. As one Annapolis Park homeowner said: "Let's face it. These are going to be lower-class whites. You wouldn't want a $15,000 home next to your place, would you?" (Associated Press, February 5, 1981).

The Issue of Race vs. Social Class

Sociologist William Wilson (1978) put the matter this way: "Race relations in America have undergone fundamental changes in recent years, so much so that the life chances of individual blacks have more to do with their economic class position than with their day-to-day encounters with whites." Wilson uses the term **social class** to refer to "any group of people who have more or less similar goods, services, or skills to offer for income in a given economic order and who therefore receive similar financial remuneration in the market-place." He says that social class is so significant today that it, not race, most determines African Americans' **life chances**—their quality of life and experiences. Neither Wilson nor any other sociologists denies that race is significant in life, just that social class is more significant.

Two Worlds of Experience

Wilson (1978, 1987) also points out that social class now separates African Americans into two groups—those with money and those without. Official statistics support this. On the one hand, the African-American middle class has expanded, and it now holds three times the proportion of African Americans than it did in 1940. One of every four African-American families makes more than $50,000 a year. On the other hand, one of every seven African-American families makes less than $10,000 a year (*Statistical Abstract* 2001:Table 37). These figures indicate a division of African Americans into the "haves" and the "have-nots," and with it, two contrasting worlds.

One world consists of the middle class. They work at jobs that offer advancement, earn good incomes and benefits, and live in middle-class suburbs or in exclusive areas of the city. They face little crime, and their children, who go to better schools, are motivated to go to college and prepare for good jobs. Not sociologically surprising, their orientations follow their middle-class experiences and middle-class lifestyles. They represent and believe in the "American dream." The second world consists of those who are stuck in the ghetto. They live in poverty; confront violent crime daily; attend terrible schools; face dead-end jobs or welfare; and feel despair, as well as either apathy or hostility. The aspirations and values of these two groups have little in common.

Many sociologists take hearty exception to the idea that we have changed from racial oppression to economic class subordination. They say it misses the vital element—ethnic discrimination—that still underlies the relative impoverishment of African Americans. They emphasize that at *all* levels, whether among factory workers, managers, or supervisors, income gaps separate African Americans and whites—and whites are *always* on top. Just as with Latinos, at every level of education, whether it be a high school diploma or a doctorate, whites earn more (*Statistical Abstract* 1996:Table 244; 2001:Table 218). Both Wilson and his critics agree that an African-American child's chance of growing up poor is much greater than that of a white child. It is Wilson's view, however, that social class, not race, is mainly responsible for perpetuating this situation.

Toward an Integration of the Issue

It seems fair to conclude that each position is partly correct, that each pinpoints part of today's ethnic reality. It is likely that both ethnic discrimination and a disadvantaged social class position make their relative contributions: Those who are poor face far fewer opportunities and much greater discrimination; those who enjoy an advantaged class position face much greater opportunities and considerably less discrimination.

ASIAN AMERICANS

World War II

> It was a quiet Sunday morning, the seventh of December, 1941, a day destined to live in infamy, as President Roosevelt was later to say.
>
> At dawn, waves of Japanese bombers began an attack on Pearl Harbor, a U.S. naval station in Oahu, Hawaii. To their surprise, Japanese pilots found the U.S. Pacific Fleet securely anchored and unprepared for battle. The Americans were sitting ducks.

The attack on Pearl Harbor forced the United States into World War II and left no American untouched. Some left home to battle overseas; others left their farms to work in factories that supported the war effort. All lived with the rationing of food, gasoline, sugar, coffee, and other essentials.

This event touched Americans of Japanese descent in a special way. Just as waves of planes had rolled over Pearl Harbor, so waves of suspicion and hostility rolled over the 110,000 Japanese Americans who called the United States "home." Overnight, they became the most detested ethnic group in the country (Daniels 1975). Many Americans feared that Japan would invade the United States and that Japanese Americans would sabotage military installations on the West Coast. Although not a single Japanese American committed even one act of sabotage, on February 1, 1942, President Franklin Roosevelt signed Executive Order 9066, authorizing the removal of any people considered threats to military areas. All people on the West Coast who were *one-eighth* Japanese or more were jailed in detention centers called "relocation camps." They were charged with no crime, neither indicted nor tried. Having some Japanese ancestry was sufficient reason to be imprisoned.

This was not the first time that Asian Americans had met discrimination. For years, differences in appearance and lifestyle had prompted Americans of European background to discriminate against Americans of Asian ancestry. Lured by gold strikes in the West and ready jobs for unskilled labor, about 200,000 Chinese immigrated between 1850 and 1880. There was a rush to unite the West with the East, and the Chinese were put to work building the East-West railroad. Although 90 per-

cent of Central Pacific's labor force was Chinese, when the famous golden spike was driven at Promontory, Utah, in 1869 to mark the joining of the Union Pacific and the Central Pacific railroads, white workers prevented the Chinese from being present (Hsu 1971). After the railroad was finished, many Chinese settled in the West. To intimidate this new competition, white workers formed mobs and vigilante groups.

Fears of "alien genes and germs" grew, and legislators passed anti-Chinese laws (Schrieke 1936). In 1850, the California legislature passed the Foreign Miner's Act, levying a special tax on Chinese (and Latinos) of $20 a month—at a time when wages were a dollar a day. The Chief Justice of the California Supreme Court ruled that Chinese could not testify against whites in court (Carlson and Colburn 1972). In 1882 Congress passed the Chinese Exclusion Act, suspending all Chinese immigration for 10 years. Four years later, the Statue of Liberty was dedicated. The tired, the poor, and the huddled masses it was to welcome obviously did not include the Chinese.

Exclusionary Policies

These exclusionary practices led Chinese immigrants to form segregated communities called "Chinatowns." Four stages were involved in their development (Yuan 1963). The first was *involuntary segregation:* Discrimination forced the immigrants into separate living areas. The second was *defensive insulation:* The immigrants banded together for mutual help. The third was *voluntary segregation:* They chose to remain in the segregated community because that was where their friends and relatives lived, it avoided language difficulties, and it allowed them to follow their customs and religion (Buddhism), which were strange to the dominant group. The final stage, now in process, is *gradual assimilation:* As they become acculturated, individuals move out of Chinatown and adopt even more mainstream customs.

Four Stages in the Development of "Chinatowns"

"Spillover Bigotry"

When the Japanese began to immigrate, they met spillover bigotry that had been directed against the Chinese. They also confronted discriminatory laws. Even the U.S. Constitution became a tool that was used against them. Initially a document that allowed only whites to be citizens, it was amended in the 1860s to include African Americans (Amott and Matthaei 1991). Because Asians had not been named in the amendments, the Supreme Court ruled that this prohibited them from becoming citizens (Schaefer 1979). Seeing its opportunity, California passed the 1913 Alien Land Act, prohibiting anyone ineligible for citizenship from owning land. (Most Native Americans were not granted citizenship in their own land until 1924; the Chinese gained citizenship in 1943, but for those born in Japan the exclusion remained until 1952.)

Contrary to stereotypes that prevail in our society, the 10.2 million Asian Americans are diverse peoples divided by many cultural heritages, including different languages and religions. Compared with the rest of the population, Asian Americans are more likely to be foreign-born and to live in urban areas. Most Asian Americans live in the western states, one of three in California, one in ten in New York. With 7 percent, Hawaii comes a close third (*Statistical Abstract* 2001:Table 24). The two largest groups of Asian Americans, those of Chinese and Filipino descent, are concentrated in Los Angeles, San Francisco, Honolulu, and New York City. The third largest group, those of Asian Indian descent, is the most geographically dispersed. Figure 8-6 shows the ethnic background of Asian Americans.

With their individual cultures and histories, each Asian American group faces its own problems and makes its own adjustments. Many of the Chinese living in the urban settlements known as "Chinatowns," for example, face the usual problems of ghetto poverty: poor health, high suicide, poor working conditions, and bad housing. Poverty among Asian Americans differs according to their country of origin, being greatest among the Cambodians, Hmong, and Laotians, and least among Japanese Americans (Lee 1998). Most Asian Americans, however, live comfortably. As Table 8-1 on page 257 shows, Asian Americans have been remarkably successful. Their median family income outstrips that of whites, Latinos, and African Americans.

The general economic success of Asian Americans is due to three main factors: family life, educational achievement, and assimilation into the mainstream culture.

Of all ethnic groups, including whites, Asian American children are the most likely to grow up with two parents and the least likely to be born to a single mother (Lee 1998). Most grow up in closely knit families where they are socialized into values that stimulate cohesiveness and high motivation to succeed (Bell 1991). Within a framework of strict limits and constraints, they are taught self-discipline, thrift, and industry (Suzuki 1985). This early socialization provides strong impetus for the next two factors.

The second factor is educational achievement. Most Asian Americans get better grades in school than other groups, and they go farther in school than the rest of the population (Lee 1998). This open doors to economic success.

Assimilation, the third factor, is indicated by several measures. With about two of five marrying someone of another racial-ethnic group, Asian Americans have the highest intermarriage rate of any minority. They also are the most likely to live in integrated neighborhoods (Lee 1998). Japanese Americans, the financially most successful of Asian Americans, are the most assimilated (Bell 1991). About 75 percent say that their best friend is not a Japanese American.

Asian Americans are becoming more prominent in politics. With 60 percent of its citizens being Asian-American,

Divisions Among Asian Americans

Why Have Asian Americans Been So Successful?

1. Family Life

2. Educational Achievement

3. Assimilation

FIGURE 8-6
The Ethnic Background of Asian Americans
(*Source: U.S. Census Bureau Statistical Abstract 2001:Table 22.*)

And Politics

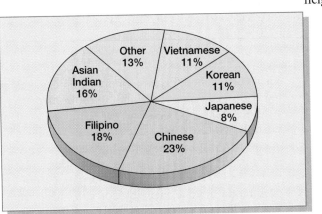

Chapter 8   Race and Ethnic Relations

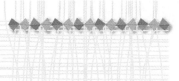

Hawaii has elected Asian-American governors and sent several Asian-American senators to Washington (*Statistical Abstract* 1998:Table 38; Lee 1998). The first Asian-American governor outside of Hawaii is Gary Locke, who in 1996 was elected governor of Washington, a state in which Asian Americans make up less than 6 percent of the population.

◆ Social Policy ◆

Although the goal of a unified society is laudable, the attempt to use our social institutions to reshape everyone into an Anglo mold does not work. Accordingly, it seems reasonable for social policy to center around the twin goals of encouraging cultural pluralism and preventing ethnic discrimination.

ENCOURAGING CULTURAL PLURALISM

Four Suggestions

The first goal of social policy, encouraging cultural pluralism, would focus on "cultural integrity"; that is, it would encourage pride and appreciation of ethnic cultures. Here are possible specifics:

1. Establishing national, state, and local "cultural centers" that feature a group's heritage
2. Holding "ethnic appreciation days" in the public schools, where ethnic customs, dress, dances, history, and food would be featured
3. Teaching history (and all courses with an historical emphasis) in ways that recognize the contributions of the many groups that make up the United States
4. Teaching foreign languages in our public schools, from grade school through high school. Starting so early, all students could learn two foreign languages

The first two suggestions are easy to implement, and they can go a long way toward encouraging appreciation of cultural differences and pride in one's own heritage. The last two, which are more extensive, could accomplish the same purposes. Note the emphasis on the public school system. It is here that our young people, the most malleable of our citizens, receive extensive training and are most likely to come into close contact with different ethnic groups.

Appreciation, but Not Retreat

Cultural pluralism does *not* mean a retreat by minority groups into their ethnic culture. Like members of the dominant group, members of minority groups need to be prepared to compete within the dominant Anglo institutions. Although they should be encouraged to retain and to take pride in their rich heritage, children of minority groups, like the children of the dominant group, need to become proficient at English and other basic skills. The school system is uniquely situated to provide these tools. Without them, members of minority groups are at a severe disadvantage in meeting their number-one need—competing with Anglos for jobs, especially well-paying positions that offer advancement.

PREVENTING ETHNIC DISCRIMINATION

Legal Enforcement

The second social policy, preventing ethnic discrimination, involves using the law to ensure that ethnic minorities are not discriminated against in jobs, housing, education, or any other areas of life that pertain to all citizens. This requires that our local, state, and federal governments be watchdogs. The Civil Rights Act of 1964, which forbids discrimination by race, color, creed, national origin, and sex, must be enforced. This law covers unions, employment agencies, and, as amended in 1972, all businesses with 15 or more employees. It also prohibits discrimination in voting, public accommodations, all federally supported programs such as road construction, and federally supported institutions such as colleges and hospitals. Preventing ethnic discrimination also means funding the Equal Employment Opportunity Commission (EEOC), the organization empowered to investigate complaints and recommend action to the Department of Justice.

Tuition Vouchers

As noted, "white flight" was a common reaction to the forced integration of the public school system. U.S. parents have the right to send their children to any schools they can afford, and this right needs to be protected. Although controversial, there is an effective solution to white flight. If education vouchers in the amount of the average cost per student in a district's schools were given to each student, their parents could choose any school they wished, private or public. All schools, of course, must be open to students of any race-ethnic background.

THE DILEMMA OF AFFIRMATIVE ACTION

The *Bakke* Case

The Civil Rights Act of 1964 created a dilemma, how to make up for past discrimination without creating new discrimination. The first dispute to catch the public's attention was the precedent-setting *Bakke* case (Sindler 1978). In 1972 and 1973, Allen Bakke was denied admission to the medical school of the University of California at Davis. He sued when he learned that the school had admitted African Americans, Asian Americans, and Chicanos who had lower grade point averages than he and had scored lower on the entrance exam. Bakke argued that had he been a member of a minority group he would have been admitted—in other words, that he had been discriminated against because he was white. The U.S. Supreme Court ruled 5 to 4 that the Davis medical school had to admit Bakke because it was illegal to use quotas for minorities.

Inconsistency and Controversy

Following the *Bakke* case, the Supreme Court handed down a series of inconsistent rulings. It ruled that colleges cannot use quotas in determining whom they admit, but they can use race as a factor in order to create a diverse student body (Walsh 1996). Then in a 1989 precedent-setting *City of Richmond* decision, the Court ruled that state and local governments "must almost always avoid racial quotas" in awarding construction contracts. "Almost always" means that it might be okay, but then again it might not, which left everyone confused about where and when and in what ways preferential treatment is or is not constitutional.

The national debate continued, with few fond of affirmative action, but no one seeing alternatives to erase the consequences of past discrimination. Then during the 1990s, the tide turned against affirmative action. In 1995, the Supreme Court ruled that the Federal Communications Commission's policy of giving preference to minorities and women in awarding broadcast licenses was unconstitutional. In 1996, in *Texas v. Hopwood*, a Circuit Court of Appeals ruled that the University of Texas Law School's special admissions program to increase the number of African American and Latino students was illegal. The Supreme Court refused to consider an appeal, letting this ruling stand (Walsh 1996). Perhaps the most significant law was Proposition 209, a 1996 amendment to the California state constitution that banned race and gender preferences in hiring and in college admissions. Despite appeals by a coalition of civil rights groups, the U.S. Supreme court upheld the California law in 1997.

The Basic Dilemma

These legal rulings highlight a major dilemma in the pursuit of ethnic equality: How can we correct past discrimination against minorities without discriminating against individual members of the dominant group? Affirmative action helped correct the institutional discrimination that was built into our society, but if we no longer can use it, what corrective mechanisms will take its place? Although affirmative action creates resentment and its own injustices, we live in a world in which we have no perfect alternatives. No one has been able to develop an alternative social policy to correct institutional discrimination in such a way that no one is hurt.

PRINCIPLES FOR IMPROVING ETHNIC RELATIONS

Four Sound Principles

Social policies should follow sound sociological principles. Those developed by social psychologist Gordon Allport (Pettigrew 1976) can provide a basic map for us:

1. Ethnic groups should possess equal status in the situation (interethnic housing, for example, should involve occupants from the same social class background).

2. Seeking common goals provides the best context for interethnic contact (for example, parents from different ethnic backgrounds working to improve their children's school).

3. Cooperative dependence is desirable; that is, to attain their goals, the groups must pull together (for example, to improve an integrated school system, in which case voters from the various ethnic groups would be needed to vote for a bond proposal).

4. Authority, law, and custom should support interaction between the groups (for example, for authorities to stand behind school integration makes positive interaction between the ethnic groups more likely).

◆ The Future of the Problem ◆

Ethnic relations are constantly changing. Most Americans today reject many patterns of discrimination that were once taken for granted. While huge gaps still remain between our ideals of equality and the reality of ethnic relations, the United States is moving toward greater equality.

From Apartheid to Integration

Before World War II, the U.S. government supported apartheid. The war caused the dislocation of various ethnic groups, and U.S. society was never the same. One such dislocation was the migration of hundreds of thousands of African Americans to the north to work in the war industries. After the war, the federal government moved gradually from apartheid to a policy of integration and social equality. This broke many of the institutional barriers directed against minorities. I can see no way that those barriers will ever be reestablished.

Controversy Over Affirmative Action

Stubborn barriers to equality remain, however, and ethnic relations are haunted by them, as well as by consequences of past discrimination. Affirmative action was designed to overcome these barriers, but it has come under heavy attack. Court rulings are destined to be controversial, and, judging from what we have seen, likely inconsistent, leaving people confused. Of necessity, they will disappoint one side or the other when two sides hold incompatible philosophical positions. With effective mechanisms to remedy the inequality yet to be developed, the proper role of affirmative action in a multicultural society is likely to remain a hot issue for quite some time.

Jobs

The major battlefield for ethnic equality will be jobs. The outcome is of fundamental importance since access to good jobs determines so much of people's quality of life. Two issues will be central to the outcome, the removal of remaining structural barriers and the preparation of workers. The dismantling of barriers is likely to be a very slow process. Preparation of workers depends on education.

Education

For most Americans, education holds the key to the future. Those with the best education will get the better jobs and enjoy the more satisfying lifestyles. Any group that receives less schooling than the national average is disadvantaged in our technological society. Granted this principle, then, as Table 8-1 on page 257 shows, the future looks brightest for Asian Americans and whites, but much less bright for African Americans and Latinos. It looks the worst for Native Americans. Obviously, policies that foster educational achievement among these minority groups need to be developed.

A Permanent Underclass?

A disturbing possibility is that we have developed a permanent **underclass** (Wilson 1978, 1987), an alienated group, primarily in the inner cities, that has little education, lives in single-parent families, has high rates of violent crime, drug abuse, disease, births to single mothers, and death by murder. Its norms are self-defeating, if the goal is to succeed in mainstream society.

A Tragic Cycle

This group, which was left behind as neighbors moved into middle-class jobs and middle-class neighborhoods, becomes more disadvantaged with each passing year. Unless ways are found to reach its members, the tragic cycle will perpetuate itself, with the children now being born in those conditions fated to repeat their parents' lives. A primary structural factor that makes this sorry possibility likely is that most jobs are located in the suburbs. Those who inhabit our urban ghettos lack the means of transportation to reach those jobs and the financial ability to move closer to them.

Collective Violence

These conditions, significant for justice, also carry severe implications for society as a whole. If large groups of people are kept out of mainstream society, limited to a meager education, denied jobs and justice, and banned from decent neighborhoods—a spark could ignite collective violence. More riots, then, are likely, such as the one in Los Angeles in 1992 that took 60 lives, left 2,300 people injured, burned down thousands of businesses, and destroyed $1 billion of property (Rose 1992; Stevens and Lubman 1992).

Bitter Divisions?

Militants, whether from a minority group or the dominant group, are an unpredictable factor in future ethnic relations. While ethnic pride is laudable, any group, of any race or ethnicity, that preaches hatred creates divisions between race-ethnic groups. The resurgence of the Ku Klux Klan, though involving only a handful of people, shows an alarming potential of violence. I anticipate that the occasional outbursts of such groups, though dramatic, will be limited mainly to headline-grabbing, and will pose no serious threat to the future.

Social Action and the Great Divide

In 1944, Gunnar Myrdal (1898–1987), a sociologist from Sweden, wrote that the United States was caught between two major forces. In his classic *An American Dilemma*, Myrdal contrasted the "American creed," as expressed in Christian ethics and the Declaration of Independence, with the un-Christian and undemocratic behavior he observed. He expressed his conviction that Americans would resolve the dilemma in favor of the higher values of the American creed, rather than the lower ones of discrimination and prejudice. Conditions are much better today than they were in the 1940s—but the dilemma he identified continues.

In U.S. race-ethnic relations, valleys of hatred and despair follow peaks of goodwill and high hopes. The future will bring more of the same. Although as individuals we have little power or influence, our actions, collectively, are significant. Ultimately, they form society and give shape to race-ethnic relations. None of us can overcome structural barriers, yet, together, we can play a part in dismantling them. I do not mean to sound Pollyannish, but, as C. Wright Mills realized, we can ask how we can help create a more positive future.

◆Summary

1. Ethnic *discrimination* occurs worldwide, as *ethnic groups* living in the same society struggle for dominance. *Dominant groups* develop *ideologies* and *stereotypes* to support their dominance.

2. *Minority groups* share five characteristics: unequal treatment, distinctive traits, solidarity, membership by birth, and marriage within their own group. They have four objectives: *pluralism, assimilation, secession,* and *militancy.* Five objectives of dominant groups are assimilation, pluralism, *population transfer,* continued subjugation, and *genocide.*

3. Although the idea of *race* greatly affects human behavior, biologically speaking, no human group represents a "pure race."

4. Ethnic discrimination is a life-and-death matter, affecting both the quality of life and mortality rates.

5. *Individual discrimination* consists of overt acts by individuals. *Institutional discrimination* is built into the social system.

6. Symbolic interactionists focus on how symbols of race and ethnicity divide people and affect their behavior, particularly how they affect perception, sort people into different life experiences, and justify discrimination and violence. Functionalists analyze functions of discrimination, such as ensuring that society's *dirty work* gets done and fostering *ethnocentrism,* as well as its dysfunctions, such

as destroying human potential. Marxist conflict theorists stress how capitalists increase their profits through the ethnic divisions of workers.

7. Ethnic discrimination in the United States is especially severe for Native Americans, Latinos, and African Americans. They have less education, higher unemployment, lower incomes, and higher rates of poverty than Anglos. The pressures these groups have placed on white-controlled social institutions have forced social change. Asian Americans have made the most social and economic gains—primarily through assimilation and family values that stress hard work, thrift, and education.

8. Major cleavages along social class lines divide U.S. ethnic groups. Some sociologists argue that *social class* has become more significant than ethnicity in determining an individual's *life chances.*

9. Efforts to encourage cultural pluralism and prevent ethnic discrimination are part of contemporary social policies. Ethnic groups that attain the most education have the brightest future. The major battlefield is jobs. Dilemmas over affirmative action continue.

10. With the creation of an *underclass,* we can expect urban riots. In no foreseeable future will *prejudice* and discrimination be eliminated. The storm cloud on the horizon is the resurgence of groups that preach division and hatred.

◆Key Terms

Anglo-conformity Requiring or expecting everyone in the United States to adopt the English culture (as modified by the American Revolution).

Apartheid The enforced segregation of people on the basis of race or ethnicity.

Assimilation The absorption of a minority into the mainstream culture.

Capitalism An economic system based on investing capital to make a profit.

Civil disobedience Deliberately but peacefully disobeying laws that are considered unjust.

Compartmentalize To keep separate in one's mind feelings, attitudes, and behaviors that are incompatible with one another.

Dirty work The tasks in society that few people want.

Discrimination The act of singling out a person or persons for unfair treatment.

Division of labor People performing different sets of specialized tasks.

Dominant group The group with more power, privilege, and social status that discriminates against a minority group.

Ethnic group A group of people who identify with one another on the basis of their ancestry and cultural heritage.

Ethnic stratification Society divided along ethnic lines; the unequal distribution of resources on the basis of race or ethnicity.

Ethnocentrism A strong identity with one's own group, causing one to deem other groups inferior.

False class consciousness Workers identifying with the wealthy (employers, owners, investors) instead of with other workers.

Genocide Killing an entire people.

Ideology A set of values and beliefs, often used to defend a social arrangement or to advocate change in it.

Individual discrimination Discrimination by one person against another.

Institutional discrimination Discrimination that is built into the social system.

Life chances What one may expect to get out of life (due to the conditions of the group into which one is born).

Melting pot The expectation that the European immigrants to the United States would "melt" or blend together, that is, interact, intermarry, and form a cultural and biological blend.

Militancy Seeking to dominate society (in Wirth's terminology).

Minority group A group of people who, on the basis of physical or cultural characteristics, are singled out for unequal treatment and who regard themselves as objects of collective discrimination.

Pan-Indianism Moving beyond tribal identification and working for the welfare of all Native Americans.

Pluralism Different ethnic groups living peacefully with one another, while maintaining their distinctiveness and tolerating differences in others.

Population transfer A minority relocating within a society or leaving the society altogether. In direct transfer, the minority is forcibly moved; in indirect transfer, the

dominant group makes life so miserable for the minority that they "choose" to leave.

Prejudice An attitude toward someone or something whereby one prejudges the other, usually negatively.

Race Inherited physical characteristics that visibly identify a group of people.

Reserve labor force The unemployed, who can be called to work during periods of labor strife or economic expansion. Also called reserve labor army.

Riot Violent crowd behavior aimed against people and property.

Rising expectations The belief that better conditions will come soon. Rising expectations develop when institutionalized barriers begin to fall; if conditions do not immediately change, frustration builds, sometimes resulting in group violence.

Secession A minority withdrawing from a society in order to establish its own nation.

Selective perception Seeing only certain things, while being blind to others.

Self-fulfilling prophecy A prediction or expectation about how things will be that brings about the

situation that was predicted or expected.

Social class A group of people who find themselves at about the same point on the economic ladder; they have similar education, types of work, and income.

Split-labor market Workers split along lines of race, ethnicity, or gender.

Stereotype An exaggerated belief consisting of unfounded generalizations of what people are like.

Surplus value of labor If an item sells for more than it cost to produce, that profit (or extra amount, or surplus value) is said to be due to the value of the labor that went into producing the item.

Underclass An alienated group of people living primarily in the inner cities that has little education, high rates of unemployment, female-headed families, welfare dependency, violent crimes, drug abuse, disease, births to single women, and death by murder.

◆Critical Thinking Questions

1. On page 249 is a list of five characteristics shared by all minority groups. Pick any minority group in the United States and give examples of each of these five characteristics.

2. On pages 249–250 is a list of four objectives of minority groups. Explain how each objective applies to:
   • African Americans
   • Asian Americans
   • Native Americans
   If you identified differences between the groups, what do you believe the bases of those differences are?

3. Which of the six policies that Simpson and Yinger identify (pp. 250–251) as those adopted by dominant

groups do you believe are currently being applied by Anglos toward
   • African Americans?
   • Native Americans?
   • Asian Americans?

4. Do you think that laws against hate speech should be eliminated (on the basis that they violate the constitutional guarantee of the right of free speech)—or that they should be strengthened and enforced? Explain.

5. Which of the three sociological perspectives (symbolic interactionism, functionalism, or conflict theory) do you find best explains why prejudice and discrimination exist in the United States? Explain.

Sex Discrimination

O utside the delivery room of a Delhi hospital, the expectant mother's family keeps vigil, her husband smoking and playing cards with the menfolk, the women knitting and recalling their own deliveries.

When the nurse brings the news, everyone falls silent. Faces drop—the newborn is a girl. Some relatives console the father; others curse the mother.

This scene is familiar in India. The birth of a son is seen as a gift from God; the birth of a daughter, at best, a disappointment.

This attitude persists, especially in India's tradition-locked villages. As a result, many girls face hardships and even early death.

Female infanticide is not uncommon, although specific instances are seldom documented. Authorities leave such sensitive family matters alone.

"Strangling baby girls at birth might be a thing of the past," says Promilla Kapur, a sociologist specializing in the problems of Indian women. "However, what was done in a fairly crude manner is still often achieved indirectly."

A female infant can be deprived of milk or ignored if she falls sick. The male child gets the most nourishing food and preferential treatment from his mother.

The Indian girl stands little chance of earning money for her family. In Hindu society almost all women are expected to remain at home with their family. Jobs for women, especially uneducated women, are few . . . and most Indian women are uneducated.

Based on Chacko 1977.

◆ The Problem in Sociological Perspective ◆

You can see how important the sex of a child is in India. Parents on the edge of survival despair at the birth of a girl, for she must be fed and clothed but can contribute little to the family's income. They rejoice at the birth of a boy, for his birth signals the arrival of a child who can help sustain them in their old age.

Women as a Minority Group

While the Indian situation is extreme, *sex is* the *major sorting device in every society in the world*. In our own society, men are paid more for the same work, and they dominate politics and public life. As noted in the last chapter, a minority is a group that experiences discrimination. Even though women make up 51.3 percent of the U.S. population (*Statistical Abstract* 2001:Table 11), sociologists consider them a minority group because of their position relative to males, the dominant group.

The Development of Sexism as a Social Problem

Sociologists have not always referred to women as a minority group. This came about only gradually, as they began to note parallels between the social positions of women and men and those of African Americans and whites. In 1944 Gunnar Myrdal, a Swedish sociologist who studied U.S. race relations, mentioned the parallels in *An American Dilemma*. He also noted the historical connection: The legal status of African-American slaves was derived from the legal status accorded to women and children in the seventeenth century, whose lives were controlled by the male heads of family. In 1951 an American sociologist, Helen Hacker, was the first to apply the term *minority* to women. Noting that discrimination against women "takes the form of being barred from certain activities or, if admitted, being treated unequally," Hacker said that women were marginal to a masculine society.

Just as the perception of sociologists was changing, so was that of women, who began to challenge traditional relations between the sexes. Many came to see themselves not as *individuals* with less status than males, but as a *group* of people who

Each society assigns positions to its members on the basis of their sex. Anthropologists have found that the prestige of an occupation does not depend on the actual occupation, but on the sex associated with it. Around the world, the activities assigned to men are given higher prestige than those assigned to women. When men occupy the positions normally assigned to women, however, the prestige increases. An example is women as cooks and men as chefs. Why are the "great" chefs of the world men (with few exceptions, such as Julia Child)? Shown here is Emeril LaGassie, an eminent television chef. Does his food taste better because it has been cooked by a man?

were discriminated against. During the 1960s and 1970s, women discussed and publicized their dissatisfactions with being second-class citizens in a male-dominated society. When large numbers of women in the United States and around the world concluded that something needed to be done, the matter changed from an objective condition of society to a social problem. This further stimulated sociological interest, and sociologists began to investigate **sexism,** the belief that one sex is innately superior to the other, and the discrimination that results from that belief.

Let's see how extensive this problem is today.

♦ The Scope of the Problem ♦

As we saw in the chapter's opening vignette, sexism is not limited to the Western world. How long has it been common? Some social scientists, such as anthropologist Marvin Harris (1977:46), claim that male domination of society "has been in continuous existence throughout virtually the entire globe from the earliest times to the present." After reviewing the evidence, historian and feminist Gerda Lerner (1986:31) agreed, saying that "there is not a single society known where women-as-a-group have decision-making power over men (as a group)." She also concluded that there was less gender discrimination in horticultural and hunting-and-gathering societies, where women contributed about 60 percent of the group's total food.

Is Male Dominance Universal?

Conclusions of universal domination by men make some social analysts apprehensive: If people think that men always have dominated, they may conclude that this behavior is innate. They might then use this conclusion to justify women's subjugation today. This nature-nurture controversy is summarized in the Issues box on pages 290–291. There you will also see that some researchers question the universality of male dominance.

Don't women presidents, prime ministers, and monarchs disprove the universal domination of society by men? Sociologists point out that these are *individual* women in positions of power, not examples of women-as-a-group controlling a society. Those societies, too, are male-dominated, for men hold almost all the key positions. Sweden comes closest to exhibiting political equality between the sexes: Half of its cabinet ministers and 43 percent of its parliament are women ("Women in the Riksdag" 1998).

The Sexual Stratification of Work

Every society stratifies its members by sex; that is, they single out males and females for different activities. Around the world, for example, most work is **sex-typed,** associated with one sex or the other. Does this mean that anatomy requires that men and women be assigned particular work? In 1937, anthropologist George Murdock reviewed information on 324 societies. He found that what is considered "male" or "female" work differs from one society to another. For example, in some societies the care of cattle is women's work; in others, it is men's work. The only exception was metalworking, which was universally men's work. Three pursuits—making weapons, pursuing sea mammals, and hunting—were almost always men's work, but there were exceptions. No specific work was universally assigned to women. Making clothing, cooking, carrying water, and grinding grain were commonly allocated to women, but not always. Biology, then, is not occupational destiny.

What does this have to do with sexism? That one society assigns an activity to men while another assigns it to women could be taken as a type of equality. Social scientists, however, discovered this: *Universally, men's activities are always given greater prestige.* Whenever men are assigned a type of work, that work is considered superior (Linton 1936; Rosaldo 1974). If taking care of cattle is men's work, then cattle care is thought to be important and carries high prestige. If taking care of cattle is women's work, however, it is considered less important and carries less prestige. To cite an example closer to home, when delivering babies was "women's work," the responsibility of midwives, it was given low prestige. But when men took over this job (despite opposition from women), its prestige shot up (Ehrenreich and English 1973). *It is the sex associated with the work that provides its prestige, not the work itself.*

Sexism pervades every society in the world, and it touches almost every aspect of our social life. In her classic 1951 article, Helen Hacker listed these areas of discrimination against U.S. women:

1. *Economic.* Women are usually relegated to monotonous work that falls under the supervision of men, for which they get unequal pay, promotion, and responsibility.

2. *Education.* Professional schools, such as architecture and medicine, apply quotas for women; there, women's participation is limited.

3. *Political.* Women are often barred from jury duty and public office.

4. *Social.* Women are permitted less freedom of movement, fewer deviations in dress, speech, and manners, and a narrower range of personality expression.

Hacker also described how the three major roles of a female—sister-daughter, wife, and mother—fit this pattern of discrimination. She said that a sister does more housework than her brother, a wife is expected to subordinate her interests to those of her husband, and a mother bears the stigma for an illegitimate child. While some of the specifics of sex discrimination have changed since Hacker did her analysis—women are no longer barred from jury duty nor do they face quotas from professional schools—her summary remains remarkably current. Feminists still struggle against unequal treatment in informal social life, education, jobs, and politics.

◆ Looking at the Problem Theoretically ◆

Why are societies sexist? Let's apply our three theoretical lenses to see what contrasting perspectives emerge.

SYMBOLIC INTERACTIONISM

We must distinguish between two terms. When we consider how males and females differ, we usually think first of **sex,** the different *biological* equipment of males and females. Then we might think about **gender,** how we express our "maleness" or "femaleness." Symbolic interactionists stress that sex is biological, and gender is learned, or social.

Symbolic interactionists study how we are socialized into **sex roles,** the attitudes and behaviors expected of males and females. Each society has ideas that some activities are "male" and others "female." To teach that a specific activity applies to a

Major Areas of Sex Discrimination

Sex and Gender

Socialization into Sex Roles

Chapter 9 Sex Discrimination

specific sex requires that a society's institutions work together. The result is so effective that people feel shame if mismatching occurs in their own behavior, and insulted and angry if they see it in others. In the short space we have, I can indicate only a few of the elements involved in this orchestration of a society's institutions.

The process begins *before* birth (Henslin 1999). The expectant parents mentally project their child's participation into activities that are sex-typed. The father may see himself teaching his son how to play baseball; the mother may imagine dressing her daughter in frilly dresses and hearing people say how cute she looks.

Sex as a Master Trait

When their child is born, the parents announce its sex to the world. Through cards, cigars, and telephone calls, they proclaim: "It's a girl!" or "It's a boy!" Even the newspapers report this momentous event. And momentous it is, for *in every society of the world the announcement launches people into their single most significant life-shaping circumstance*. Sex is a **master trait,** cutting across all other identities in life. Whatever else we may be, we always are a male or a female.

Cast onto the stage of life with an assigned role to play, we spend much of our childhood and young adulthood learning what our role requires. Throughout the world, parents are the first "significant others" to teach children this role. The specifics vary from one society to another, but in our society parents begin by using pink and blue, colors that have been imbued with sex-role significance. Parents continue to coach us in our expected roles for longer than most of us want their help.

Subconscious Socialization

A classic study indicates that parents also teach sex roles subconsciously, that is, without being aware of it. In a classic study, psychologists Susan Goldberg and Michael Lewis (1969) recruited mothers of six-month-olds to come into their laboratory so they could observe the development of their children. Unknown to the mothers, the researchers also carefully observed the mothers. They found that the mothers kept their girls closer to them, and they touched and spoke more to them than to their sons. By the time the children were 13 months old, the girls were more reluctant than the boys to leave their mothers. During play, they remained closer to their mothers, and returned to them sooner and more often than the boys did.

Goldberg and Lewis then surrounded each mother with colorful toys and placed her child on the other side of a small barrier. The girls cried and motioned for help more than the boys did; the boys tried to climb over or go around the barrier more than the girls did. The researchers concluded that without knowing it, the mothers had rewarded their daughters for being passive and dependent and their sons for being active and independent.

The Goldberg-Lewis study is difficult to interpret. Were these differences brought about by the mother's behavior, as the researchers suggest? Or did the researchers observe biological differences that were showing up at the age of 13 months? In short, were the mothers responding to differences in their children (the boys wanting to get down and play more, and the girls wanting to be hugged more), or were the mothers creating those differences? We don't yet have enough evidence to draw a firm conclusion.

In childhood, boys are generally allowed to be more active and to express more independence. Preschool boys, for example, are given more freedom to roam farther from home than their preschool sisters. They are also allowed to participate in more rough-and-tumble play—even to get dirtier and to be more defiant (Henslin 1999). Again, we face the same problem. Are the parents and teachers creating these differences in behavior? Or are the children responding to biological predispositions?

Stereotypes Become Reality

Most symbolic interactionists assume that the differences are learned. They emphasize that stereotypes tend to become reality. If males are considered to be aggres-

ISSUES IN SOCIAL PROBLEMS
The Nature/Nurture Controversy: Biology versus Culture

The causes of the differences between men and women intrigue people. Proposed answers are roughly either biological or cultural. Most but not all sociologists favor the cultural side. Here are the basic arguments among them.

BIOLOGY IS THE ANSWER

Sociologist Steven Goldberg (1974, 1986, 1989) finds it astonishing that anyone should doubt "the presence of core-deep differences between men and women, differences of temperament and emotion we call masculinity and femininity." He argues that inborn differences, not the environment, "give masculine and feminine direction to the emotions and behavior of men and women." Here is his argument:

1. The anthropological record shows that all societies for which evidence exists are (or were) **patriarchies** (societies in which men dominate women). Stories about **matriarchies** (societies in which women dominate men) are myths.

2. In all societies, past and present, the highest statuses are associated with males. All of them are ruled "by hierarchies overwhelming dominated by men."

3. The reason for this one-way dominance of societies is that males "have a lower threshold for the elicitation of dominance behavior...a greater tendency to exhibit whatever behavior is necessary in any environment to attain dominance in hierarchies and male-female en-

CULTURE IS THE ANSWER

For sociologist Cynthia Fuchs Epstein (1986, 1988, 1989), the answer lies solely in social factors, especially socialization and social control. Here is her argument:

1. The anthropological record shows more equality between the sexes in the past than we had thought. In earlier societies, women, as well as men, hunted small game, devised tools for hunting, and gathered food. Studies of today's hunting and gathering societies show that "both women's and men's roles have been broader and less rigid than those created by stereotypes. For example, the Agta and Mbuti are clearly egalitarian..." This proves that "societies exist in which women are not subordinate to men. Anthropologists who study them claim that there is a separate but equal status of women at this level of development."

2. Not biology but rigidly enforced social arrangements determine the types of work that women and men do in each society. Few people can escape these arrangements to perform work outside their allotted range. Informal customs and formal systems of laws enforce this gender inequality of work, which serves

sive and dominant and a person knows he is male, he tends to fulfill those expectations by being aggressive and dominant. If females are considered to be passive and submissive and a person knows she is female, she tends to fulfill those expectations. Not everyone follows the script, but so many do that most members of a society see "clearly" why *their particular stereotypes* represent reality.

In Sum
  Symbolic interactionists emphasize that each of us is born into a society in which, from childhood, the symbols of male and female sort us into separate groups. Thus males and females acquire different ideas of themselves and of one another. Starting within the family and reinforced by other social institutions, the newcomer learns the meanings that society associates with the sexes. These symbols then be-

counters and relationships." Males are more willing "to sacrifice the rewards of other motivations—the desire for affection, health, family life, safety, relaxation, vacation and the like—in order to attain dominance and status."

4. Just as a six-foot woman does not prove the social basis of height, so exceptional individuals, such as a highly achieving and dominant woman, do not refute "the physiological roots of behavior."

In short, only one interpretation of why every society, from the Pygmies to Sweden, associates dominance and attainment with males is valid. Male dominance of society is "an inevitable resolution of the psychophysiological reality." Socialization and social institutions merely *reflect*—and sometimes exaggerate—inborn tendencies. Any interpretation other than inborn differences is "wrongheaded, ignorant, tendentious, internally illogical, discordant with the evidence, and implausible in the extreme." The argument that males are more aggressive because they have been socialized that way is equivalent to claiming that men can grow moustaches because boys have been socialized that way.

To acknowledge this reality is *not* to condone or defend discrimination against women. Whether one approves what societies have done with these biological differences is not the point. The point is that biology leads males and females to different behaviors and attitudes—regardless of how we feel about this or wish it were different.

the interests of males. Once these socially constructed barriers are removed, women can and do exhibit the same work habits as males.

3. The human behaviors that biology "causes" are only those involving reproduction or differences in body structure. These differences are relevant for only a few activities, "such as playing basketball or crawling through a small space."

4. Female crime rates, which are rising, indicate that the aggressiveness that often is considered a biologically dictated male behavior is related to social not biological factors. When social conditions permit, such as with women attorneys, females also exhibit "adversarial, assertive, and dominant behavior." Not incidentally, their "dominant behavior" also shows up in their challenging the biased views about human nature that men scholars have proposed.

In short, not "women's incompetence or inability to read a legal brief, to perform brain surgery, [or] to predict a bull market," but social factors—socialization, gender discrimination, and other forms of social control—are responsible for gender differences in behavior. Arguments that assign "an evolutionary and genetic basis" to explain gender differences in sex status "rest on a dubious structure of inappropriate, highly selective, and poor data, oversimplification in logic and inappropriate inferences by use of analogy."

come an essential part of how we picture life—a picture that forces an interpretation of the world into "proper" activities for males and females.

Two Functionalist Theories of the Origin of Male Dominance:

1. Strength, Bravery, Warriors, and Rewards

FUNCTIONALISM

If male dominance is universal, or even nearly universal, how did it come about? Although the origins of sexism are lost in history, functionalists have two theories to account for it.

The first theory was proposed by anthropologist Marvin Harris (1977). He said that male dominance is universal because it is based on two universal conditions: (1) social—the necessity to survive warfare, and (2) biological—differences in the physical strength of males and females. Harris' controversial explanation goes like this: In prehistoric times, humans lived in small groups. Because each group was threatened by others, it had to recruit people who would fight in hand-to-hand combat. People feared injury and death, so the recruiting wasn't easy. To coax people into bravery, there had to be rewards and punishments. Because an average woman is only 85 percent the size of an average man and has only two thirds his strength (Gallese 1980), males were better at hand-to-hand combat. They were selected to be the warriors—and females became their reward. Men who did not live up to their group's expectations of bravery were killed or banished; those who did were rewarded with women, for both their sex and labor. Some groups allowed only men who had faced an enemy in combat to marry.

Because some women were stronger than some men, to exclude all women from combat might seem irrational. But if women were to be the chief inducement to get men to fight, such separation was necessary. To make the system work, men had to be trained from birth for combat, and women had to be trained from birth to give in to male demands.

According to this explanation, the reward for male bravery came at the direct expense of females. In almost all band and village societies, men assigned the "drudge work" to women—weeding, seed grinding, fetching water and firewood, doing the routine cooking, and even carrying household possessions during moves. Because men preferred to avoid these onerous tasks—and could if they had one or more wives—women were an excellent bait to induce men to bravery.

The second theory is based on human reproduction (Lerner 1986; Hope and Stover 1987; Friedl 1990). It also goes back to early human history, when life was short and women gave birth to many children. Because only women get pregnant, carry a child for nine months, give birth, and nurse, their activities were limited for a considerable part of their lives. To survive, an infant needed a nursing mother. With a child at her breast or in her womb and one on her hip or her back, a woman was physically encumbered. Thus women everywhere took on the tasks associated with the home and child care, while men took over hunting large animals and other tasks that required more speed and longer absence from the base camp (Huber 1990).

The result was that men grew dominant. They left camp to hunt animals, made contact with other tribes, and accumulated possessions in trade. Men also made and controlled the weapons used for hunting and warfare, and gained prestige by returning triumphantly with prey from hunting or with prisoners from warfare. In contrast, little prestige was given to the routine activities of women, who were not seen as risking their lives for the group.

Eventually, men took over society. Their weapons, items of trade, and the knowledge they gained from other groups became sources of power. As women became subject to their decisions, men justified their discrimination by developing ideas of inherent differences between the sexes. They also shrouded many of their activities in secrecy and formed elaborate rules and rituals to avoid "contamination" by females. When tribal societies developed into larger groups and hand-to-hand combat ceased to be routine, men, enjoying what they had, held on to their privilege and power.

In Sum

If either of these theories is true, the *origin* of male dominance is rooted in both social and biological factors. The *maintenance* of male dominance, however, is purely social, a perpetuation of a millennia-old pattern. With their dominance rooted in ancient custom, and reluctant to abandon their privileged position, men use cultural devices to keep women subservient. For an example, see the Global Glimpse box on the next page on female circumcision.

2. Pregnancy, Childbirth, and Infancy

Chapter 9 Sex Discrimination

A GLOBAL GLIMPSE

Female Circumcision

Female circumcision is common in parts of Africa, Malaysia, and Indonesia. This custom, often called female genital mutilation by Westerners, is also known as clitoral excision, clitoridectomy, infibulation, and labiadectomy, depending on how much of the vagina is removed. Worldwide, between 100 million and 200 million women have been circumcised.

In some cultures only the girl's clitoris is cut off, in others the clitoris, the labia majora, and the labia minora. The Nubia in the Sudan cut away most of the girl's genitalia, then sew together the remaining outer edges with silk or catgut, so that as the wound heals the vagina fuses together. They leave a small opening—the size of a matchstick or a pinhole—for urine and menstrual fluids. In East Africa the vaginal opening is not sutured shut, but the clitoris and both sets of labia are cut off.

Among most groups, the surgery takes place between the ages of 4 and 8. In some cultures it occurs seven to ten days after birth; in others, not until girls reach adolescence. Often done without anesthesia, the pain is so excruciating that adults hold the girl down. In urban areas, the operation may be performed by physicians; in rural areas, a neighborhood woman usually does it.

Female circumcision can cause shock, extensive bleeding, infection, infertility, and death. Ongoing complications include vaginal spasms, painful intercourse, and lack of orgasms. The tiny opening makes urination and menstruation difficult. Frequent urinary tract infections result because urine and menstrual flow build up behind the opening.

When the woman marries, the opening is surgically enlarged to permit sexual intercourse. In some groups, this is the husband's responsibility. Before a woman gives birth, the opening is enlarged further. After birth, the vagina is again sutured shut, a cycle of surgically closing and opening that begins anew with each birth.

One woman, circumcised at 12, described it this way:

"Lie down there," the excisor suddenly said to me, pointing to a mat stretched out on the ground. No sooner had I laid down than I felt my frail thin legs tightly grasped by heavy hands and pulled wide apart. I lifted my head. Two women on each side of me pinned me to the ground. My arms were also immobilized. Suddenly I felt some strange substance being spread over my genital area.... I would have given anything at that moment to be a thousand miles away; then a shooting pain brought me back to reality.... I underwent the ablation of the labia minor and then of the clitoris. The operation seemed to go on forever.... I was in the throes of agony, torn apart both physically and psychologically. It was the rule that girls of my age did not weep in this situation. I broke the rule. I reacted immediately with tears and screams of pain.... Never have I felt such excruciating pain!

[After the operation] they forced me, not only to walk back to join the other girls who had already been excised, but to dance with them...I was doing my best... then I fainted....It was a month before I was completely healed....When I was better, everyone mocked me, as I hadn't been brave, they said. (Walker and Parmar 1993:107–108)

Why does this custom exist? Some groups believe that it enhances female fertility. Others hold that it reduces female sexual desire and makes it less likely that a wife will betray her husband. The more extensive forms guarantee that a woman will be a virgin when she marries. Feminists, who call female circumcision ritual torture to control female sexuality, point out that every society that practices it is male-dominated.

What do you think?

Based on Mahran 1978, 1981; Ebomoyi 1987;
Lightfoot-Klein 1989; Denney and Quadagno 1992;
Edgerton 1992; van der Kwaak 1992; Merwine 1993;
Walker and Parmar 1993.

CONFLICT THEORY

Power, Privilege, and Resources

Conflict theorists provide a contrasting view of sexism. For background, consider these principles: Power yields privilege. In every society, the powerful enjoy the best resources available. Their privileged lifestyles encourage them to feel that they are superior beings. Consequently, the powerful clothe themselves with ideologies that justify their position, cling tenaciously to their privilege, and utilize the social institutions to maintain their power.

As a group, men are no exception to these principles. They, too, cling to their positions, cultivate images of female inferiority to justify their greater privilege, and use economic and legal weapons against women. As Helen Hacker (1951) put it:

> In the wake of the Industrial Revolution, as women acquired industrial, business, and professional skills, they increasingly sought employment in competition with men. Men were quick to perceive them as a rival group and made use of economic, legal, and ideological weapons to eliminate or reduce their competition. They excluded women from the trade unions, made contracts with employers to prevent their hiring women, passed laws restricting the employment of married women, caricatured the working woman, and carried on ceaseless propaganda to return women to the home or keep them there.

The Struggle for Equality

Now that greater sexual equality is a part of U.S. life, it is easy to lose sight of the prolonged and bitter struggle by which women gained their rights. In the 1800s, females were under the legal control of a man, either a father or a husband, and possessed no legal or social right to self-determination. Women could not vote, make legal contracts, testify in court, hold property in their own name, or even spend their own wages (which by law belonged to the husband). To secure these rights, women had to confront men and the social institutions that they dominated. Men first denied women the right to speak in public, spat upon those who did, slapped their faces, tripped them, pelted them with burning cigar stubs, and hurled obscenities at them. Leaders of the women's movement persisted. They chained themselves to posts or to the iron grillwork of public buildings and went on talking while the police sawed them loose. If arrested, these women would go on hunger strikes in jail.

In 1916, feminists (then called *suffragists*) formed the National Women's Party. They formed a picket line around the White House in January 1917. After picketing for six months, the women began to be arrested. They refused to pay their fines, and judges sent hundreds to prison, including Lucy Burns and Alice Paul. How seriously these women threatened male prerogatives is demonstrated by their treatment in prison:

> The guards from the male prison fell upon us. I saw Miss Lincoln, a slight young girl, thrown to the floor. Mrs. Nolan, a delicate old lady of seventy-three, was mastered by two men. . . . Whittaker (the Superintendent) in the center of the room directed the whole attack, inciting the guards to every brutality. Two men brought in Dorothy Day, twisting her arms above her head. Suddenly they lifted her and brought her body down twice over the back of an iron bench. . . . The bed broke Mrs. Nolan's fall, but Mrs. Cosu hit the wall. They had been there a few minutes when Mrs. Lewis, all doubled over like a sack of flour, was thrown in. Her head struck the iron bed and she fell to the floor senseless. As for Lucy Burns, they handcuffed her wrists and fastened the handcuffs over her head to the cell door. (Cowley 1969:13)

Chapter 9 Sex Discrimination

Today it is difficult to imagine U.S. women being treated this way for trying to gain rights men already possess. The early suffragists were persistent and outspoken, however, and they used bold tactics to force a historical shift in the balance of power.

Since those days, there has been no overt conflict between men and women as a group (Hacker 1951). Today women face more subtle discrimination, including hidden quotas, jokes, glass ceilings, and the "purely personal preference" that men occupy the more responsible positions. Women still press for a greater share of society's power, but the struggle has changed. Women today pressure lawmakers, compete for positions in good colleges and graduate schools, and fight obstacles that inhibit advancement at work, including sexual harassment.

In Sum

From the conflict perspective, social equality is gained only by forcing men to yield—for men as a class do not willingly cede their control of society's institutions. Let's examine that struggle, pausing first to consider again the question of natural differences between the sexes.

◆ Research Findings ◆

THE QUESTION OF NATURAL DIFFERENCES BETWEEN THE SEXES

Are There Natural Differences?

Apart from obvious physical differences between males and females, what are the natural differences between the sexes? Has nature made one sex more intelligent? More aggressive? Dominant? Protective? Nurturing? Tender? Loving? Passive?

The difficulty of separating culture from biology has plagued researchers in their attempt to answer such intriguing questions. Because each society places males and females on different roads in life, the society in which they are reared shapes any innate differences that may exist. As sociologist Carol Whitehurst (1977:36) observed, we do not know if males and females are innately endowed with differences in intelligence, aggression, or nurturance because "there is presently no way to separate the effects of the inherent characteristics from those which are learned and culturally molded."

Four Approaches in Studying this Question:

1. Studies of Children

To untangle this knotty problem, researchers have taken four approaches. The first focuses on children. If girls and boys show consistent differences at early ages, biology may be at work. In testing for differences, researchers have found that girls generally score higher than boys on verbal skills (Goleman 1987). Most girls begin to speak earlier than boys and are quicker to talk in short sentences and then to use longer sentences. They read earlier, and do better in grammar, spelling, and word fluency. Boys, in contrast, tend to do better on spatial tasks (Bardwick 1971).

Test results in mathematics have provided a puzzle for researchers. When boys and girls are compared nationally, boys always outperform girls. This holds true if we compare their overall scores, or if we compare the scores of those who have taken specific courses: general math, algebra, geometry, or calculus (*Digest of Education Statistics* 2001:Table 126). Year after year, boys also average 35 to 40 points higher in math on the S.A.T.'s (college entrance tests). In 1967, boys scored 40 points higher; in 2001, it was 35 points higher (*Digest of Education Statistics* 2001:Table 135).

Do such differences reflect innate abilities? Some researchers think so. For fifteen years, psychologist and feminist Camillia Benbow searched for an environmental explanation. Gradually, she ruled out all possibilities and reluctantly concluded that these results are due to "a basic biological difference between the sexes in brain functions" (Goleman 1987).

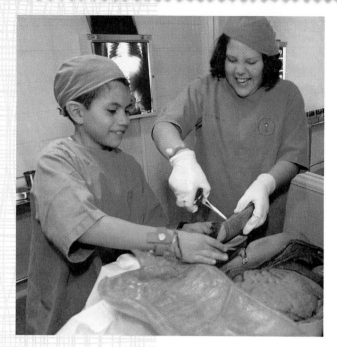

Universally, children imitate the adults around them. This process of modeling or role playing helps children prepare for roles they will later play. Here, school children pretend to be doctors at the Kids' City mall in Mexico City.

Other social scientists insist that cultural factors explain such differences. To explain girls' higher verbal performance, they point to three social causes: (1) girls identify more with their mothers (who are themselves more verbal), (2) both mothers and fathers hold and speak to their daughters more than to their sons, and (3) little girls' games are more linguistic than boys' games (Bardwick 1971). As Carole White-hurst (1977:36) put it: "All *apparent sex* differences in intelligence *may* be explained by early learning and continual reinforcement."

This likely is true of verbal differences. In 1967 girls outscored boys on the verbal portion of the S.A.T.'s, but in 1972 boys outscored girls, and boys have held the lead ever since (*Digest of Education Statistics* 2001:Table 135). The explanation must be environmental, for certainly there was no switch in male-female brain functions during this time. What that environmental explanation is, however, eludes us. During this same time, in no year have girls outperformed boys in mathematics, and biological explanations are excellent candidates for this consistent difference. If girls suddenly take the lead in mathematics, as boys did in verbal scores, this would be strong evidence of environmental causes.

Differences in aggression also show up in children. As Judith Bardwick (1971) pointed out, from early childhood to adulthood males tend to be more active and extraverted, females more passive and introverted. Again, the question is: Does this mean that males are innately more "aggressive" than females? Some researchers point to cultural factors. Parents may subtly (or less subtly) encourage their sons to be aggressive, believing that "sticking up for your rights," "showing you're not a sissy," and so on, are signs of masculinity. Parents may also express pleasure when their daughters are less demanding and more compliant—traits considered feminine. From infancy on, then, parents mold their children into cultural stereotypes of masculinity and femininity.

2. Cross-Cultural Studies

A second approach researchers have taken is to compare men and women cross-culturally. We essentially covered this approach in the box on the nature-nurture controversy (pages 290–291), where we saw that researchers fail to agree on the meaning of anthropological findings.

3. Studies of Animals

The third approach researchers have taken to separate innate biological factors from cultural molding has been to observe animals. The findings about aggression are noteworthy, for differences show up early and consistently: "Within a month after birth, male rhesus monkeys are wrestling, pushing, biting, and tugging, while the female monkeys are beginning to act shy, turning their heads away when challenged to a fight by young males" (Bardwick 1971:91). Bardwick adds:

> The males quickly surpass the females in the rate of achieving independence from their mothers (helped by the way the mothers punish them more, pay less attention to them, and hold and carry them less). The males had higher general

activity levels, did more biting, pushing, shoving, yanking, grabbing, and jerking. They also did more thumbsucking and more manipulation of their genitals.

4. The Vietnam Veterans' Study

We must always be cautious when drawing conclusions about humans from animal research, of course. To understate the matter, humans are not monkeys. Aggression, however, is related to the level of male hormones (Bardwick 1971; LeVay 1993), a matter that we shall now consider.

The fourth and most recent approach is intriguing. In 1985, the U.S. government began a health study of Vietnam veterans. To be certain the study was representative, the researchers chose a random sample of 4,462 men. Among the data they collected was a measurement of testosterone for each veteran. Until this time, research on testosterone and human behavior was based on very small samples. Now, unexpectedly, sociologists had a large random sample, one that is turning out to hold surprising clues about human behavior.

When the veterans with higher levels of testosterone were boys, they were more likely to get in trouble with parents and teachers and to become delinquents. As adults, they are more likely to use hard drugs, to get into fights, to end up in lower-status jobs, and to have more sexual partners. Not surprisingly, this history makes them less appealing candidates for marriage, and they are less likely to marry. Those who do marry are less likely to share problems with their wives. They also are more likely to have affairs, to hit their wives, and to get divorced (Dabbs and Morris 1990; Booth and Dabbs 1993).

The Vietnam veterans study does *not* leave us with biology as the sole basis for behavior, however. Not all men with high testosterone levels get in trouble with the law, do poorly in school, or mistreat their wives. A chief difference, in fact, is social class. High-testosterone men from higher social classes are less likely to be involved in antisocial behaviors than are high-testosterone men from lower social classes (Dabbs and Morris 1990). Social factors (socialization, life goals, self-definitions), then, also must play a part. Uncovering the social factors and discovering how they work in combination with biological factors such as testosterone will be of high sociological interest.

Perhaps a Combination of Biology and Culture

From our current evidence, we can conclude that *if* biology provides males and females differences in temperament, personality, or predispositions in behavior, culture overrides those differences. It shapes people into the types of men and women that predominate in a particular society. Because people wear cultural blinders that mask the workings of their culture, each considers the characteristics implanted into their males and females to be overwhelming evidence of the "natural" differences between the sexes.

Initial findings from the Vietnam veterans study indicate that some behaviors that we sociologists usually assume to be due entirely to socialization are also influenced by biology. In the years to come, this should prove to be an exciting—and controversial—area of sociological research. One level of research will be to determine if there are behaviors that are due only to biology. The second will be to discover how social factors modify biology. The third will be, in sociologist Janet Chafetz's (1990:30) phrase, to determine how "different" becomes translated into "unequal."

No Final Answer

At this point, we have no final answer to the question of natural differences between the sexes in aggression, nurturing, forms of intelligence, and so on. Some researchers are convinced they are innate, others that they are learned. Like other areas of science, we must examine the data with an open mind, not try to make the evidence fit ideologies that favor either biology or culture. Unfortunately, the research has become emotionally charged, and to draw conclusions on one side or the other indicates to some that one is "faithful" or "unfaithful" to an ideology. This, of course, is not science. One would hope that data, not ideology, will one day answer this question once and for all.

Let's examine inequality between the sexes, with a focus on U.S. society.

DISCRIMINATION IN EVERYDAY LIFE

Routine Sexism

> Leaning against the water cooler, two men—both minor executives—are nursing cups of coffee, discussing last Sunday's Giants game, postponing the moment when they have to go back to work.
>
> A vice president hears them talking about sports. Does he send them back to their desks? Probably not. Being a man, he is likely to join in the conversation and prove that he is "one of the boys," feigning an interest in football that he may not share at all. These men—all men in the office—are his troops, his comrades-in-arms.
>
> Now, assume that two women are standing by the water cooler discussing whatever you please: women's liberation, clothes, work, any subject except football, of course. The same vice president sees them and wonders whether it is worth the trouble to complain about all those bitches standing around gabbing when they should be working. "Don't they know," he will ask, in the words of a million men, "that this is an office?" (Korda 1973:20–21, paraphrased)

Feminine Terms as Insults

In everyday life, women routinely encounter antagonistic attitudes from men. They find their capacities, characteristics, interests, attitudes, and contributions devalued. Masculinity is highly valued, representing success and strength; femininity is devalued, perceived as failure and weakness. During World War II, for example, a team of researchers headed by sociologist Samuel Stouffer studied the motivation of combat soldiers. Out of this research came a sociological classic, *The American Soldier*. Stouffer and his colleagues reported (1949:132) that officers used feminine terms as insults to motivate soldiers:

> To fail to measure up as a soldier in courage and endurance was to risk the charge of not being a man. ("Whatsa matter, bud—got lace on your drawers?")

A generation later, in the Vietnam war, similar accusations of femininity were used to motivate soldiers. Drill sergeants would mock their troops by saying, "Can't hack it, little girls?" (Eisenhart 1975). In the marines, the worst insult to male recruits is to compare their performance to a woman's (Gilham 1989).

Sociologists have observed this same behavior in sports. Douglas Foley (1999) heard ex-football players tell high school boys who had a bad game that they were "wearing skirts." Jean Stockard and Miriam Johnson (1980) heard boys playing basketball shout, "You play like a woman" to boys who missed a basket.

Most people dismiss such remarks as insignificant. Stockard and Johnson, however, point out that they represent a general devaluation of women, a derogatory attitude that underlies the discrimination that women face in everyday life. They say: "There is no comparable phenomenon among women, for young girls do not insult each other by calling each other 'man.'"

Inequality in Talk

Conversations between men and women also mirror their relative positions of power in society. Sociologists have observed that when men and women are talking, men are more likely to interrupt conversations and to control changes in topics (West and Garcia 1988; Smith-Lovin and Brody 1989; Tannen 1990). Even in college, men interrupt their instructors more often than women do. They do so even more often if their instructor is a woman (Brooks 1982).

Devaluation Underlies Discrimination

Sociologist Carol Whitehurst (1977:8–9) summarized the routine devaluation and discrimination that women face in everyday life:

Women often are made the butt of jokes and are ridiculed, particularly for their efforts in behalf of women and women's rights. Their complaints and reports of mistreatment often are dismissed, treated lightly or even derisively. A woman often is not treated as if her opinions carry equal weight to those of a man, even if she has equal professional status. . . . When [men] . . . respond to a woman's complaint with "you're so cute when you get mad," it should be perfectly obvious that women are not being taken seriously, but are being considered on a level with children or idiots.

Although we are seeing changes in male-female relationships, the devaluation of women continues to be a background feature of social life. As Whitehurst says, this devaluation is important because it underlies all other forms of oppression.

DISCRIMINATION IN EDUCATION

The Past: Wombs Dominate the Mind

Let's first take a glimpse at the past. About a century ago, leading educators claimed that women's mental life was dominated by their wombs. Dr. Edward Clarke, for example, a member of Harvard University's medical faculty, warned that education and study posed dangers for women. He wrote:

A girl upon whom Nature, for a limited period and for a definite purpose, imposes so great a physiological task, will not have as much power left for the tasks of school, as the boy of whom Nature requires less at the corresponding epoch. (Andersen 1988:35)

Clarke added that to preserve their fragile health, women should study only one third as much as men—and not study at all during menstruation.

The Present:

This quote reminds us of how far we have come. Yet, in many countries today, women are still discriminated against in education. Table 9-1 provides a glimpse of how education is disproportionately reserved for boys in Africa and Asia. Although times have changed tremendously, contemporary U.S. education still contains strong elements of sexism. School sports are part of it. Boys become the football players, and girls join the drill team, drum majorettes, and pep squads (Foley 1999). As Carol Whitehurst (1977) put it, "The boys perform, the girls cheer." It is difficult to imagine girls playing a rough sport, with boys sitting on the sidelines with bated breath, eagerly jumping to their feet and even into the air when a girl makes a great play.

Sports

Considered important for "masculine" development, boys' athletic programs are widely publicized and amply funded. Considered peripheral to "feminine" development, girls' sports are largely ignored and underfunded. Although Title IX of 1975 prohibits sexual discrimination in education, inequality in sports continues. Despite changes, many schools have not made their sports programs equally accessible to male and female students.

In the classroom, both women and men teachers tend to pay less attention to girls than to boys. They also ask boys more open-ended questions and girls more yes-no questions. By late adolescence, boys generally are more the focus of teacher-pupil interaction, girls more on the margins (Corson 1992).

Teachers expect girls and boys to be different, and they nurture those "natural" differences. Just as they did a century ago, their expectations perpetuate

Table 9-1	For Every 100 Boys, How Many Girls Are Enrolled in Secondary School?		
Africa		**Asia**	
Uganda	53	Bangladesh	50
Cameroon	68	India	52
Kenya	69	China	73
Ethiopia	76	South Korea	92
Sudan	77		
Egypt	79		

Source: Riley 1997:7.

Consequences for Vocational Choice

the existing social order. High school counselors and teachers foster sex-linked aspirations by encouraging girls to choose "feminine" occupations and boys to enter "masculine" ones.

By the time they enter college, the gender tracking is evident. Women earn 90 percent of bachelor's degrees in nursing, while men earn 84 percent of bachelor's degrees in military "science." Similarly, men earn 83 percent of bachelor's degrees in the "masculine" field of engineering, while women are awarded 77 percent of bachelor's degrees in the "feminine" field of library "science" (*Statistical Abstract* 1997:Tables 300, 303, 305; 2001:Table 287). It is socialization—rather than any presumed innate characteristics—that channels males and females into sex-linked educational paths.

The Masculinity of the College Experience

Another factor may affect students' aspirations. When they enter college, they face a man's world. Not only are most of their professors men, but they study mostly men authors in their literature courses, memorize the thinking of men in their philosophy courses, and read almost exclusively about famous men in their history courses. The social sciences, including sociology, also concentrate on the contributions of men (Acker 1973; Whitehurst 1977; Vetter and Babco 1986). How this affects the orientations of women and men students is unknown at the moment, but it has to be significant.

Example of the Sciences

The greatest change in education is revealed at the undergraduate level. The change is so great that some now think that men are discriminated against, and special programs should be put into place to help men. At the undergraduate level, women outnumber men and earn 55 percent of all bachelor's degrees. But between the bachelor's and the doctorate something happens. Look at Table 9-2, which gives us a snapshot of doctoral programs in the sciences. You can see how aspirations (enrollment) and accomplishments (doctorates conferred) are sex-linked. In all but one of the doctoral programs men outnumber women, and in all of them women are less likely to complete the doctorate. It is significant that the four programs women are least likely to complete are considered masculine endeavors. The reasons for this excess dropout rate are not precisely known, but among them is childbirth, with its

Table 9-2 Doctorates in Science, by Sex

Field	Students Enrolled in Doctoral Programs		Doctorates Conferred		Completion Ratio* (higher or lower than expected)	
	Women	Men	Women	Men	Women	Men
Agriculture	35%	65%	22%	78%	−37	+20
Mathematics	33%	67%	22%	78%	−33	+16
Engineering	17%	83%	12%	88%	−29	+6
Computer sciences	24%	76%	19%	81%	−21	+6
Social sciences	47%	53%	38%	62%	−19	+17
Biological sciences	48%	52%	41%	59%	−15	+13
Physical sciences	27%	73%	23%	77%	−15	+5
Psychology	69%	31%	64%	36%	−7	+16

*The difference between the proportion enrolled in a program and the proportion granted doctorates divided by the proportion enrolled in the program.

Source: *Statistical Abstract* 1997:Tables 977, 979.

greater responsibilities, demands on time, and, often, changed interests. Sociologists also suggest that a lack of women role models is significant (Etzkowitz et al. 1992).

THE MASS MEDIA

The mass media shape and reinforce sex-role expectations, which, in turn, affect our behavior. Let's look first at children's books, then at television, music, video games, and advertising.

Are children's books more than just entertainment? To see if they transmit stereotypes, a research team headed by sociologist Lenore Weitzman (1972) examined the books that had won the Caldecott Award of the American Library Association for the best illustrations. Libraries consider these books so prestigious that most order them for their shelves. Some even put them in special collections and hand out brochures about them.

Because women make up about 51 percent of the population, we can expect about half the characters in these books to be female. The researchers found hardly any females. Almost all the books featured boys, men, and male animals. (For every female animal, there were 95 male animals!) When pictured at all, girls were passive and doll-like, while boys were active and adventuresome. While the boys did things that required independence and self-confidence, most girls were shown trying to help their brothers and fathers.

Feminists recommended to the Caldecott committee books that they felt presented more positive images of females. They also formed companies to publish nonsexist books (Williams et al. 1987). Their goal was to have "Dick speak of his feelings of tenderness without embarrassment and Jane . . . reveal her career ambitions without shame or guilt."

Breaking stereotypes was not this simple, however. By the 1980s, almost as many girls as boys were the central characters in the Caldecott winners. In the illustrations, males still outnumbered females two to one, and traditional stereotypes dominated (Dougherty et al. 1987; Heintz 1987). Girls were more likely to be shown indoors and as dependent, submissive, and passive; boys were more likely to be portrayed outdoors in independent, competitive activities.

Television Children's television also reinforces stereotypes. A primary message is that "men are born with more ambition than women" (Morgan 1982, 1987). In the cartoons that so fascinate young children, for example, males outnumber females by four or five to one. As a result, children who watch more television do more sex-typing than children who spend less time in front of their electronic socializer (Rothschild 1984; Kimball 1986).

Perhaps the TV show *Teenage Mutant Ninja Turtles* captures the situation best. The original turtles are named Michelangelo, Leonardo, Raphael, and Donatello—after men artists whose accomplishments have been admired for centuries. A female turtle was added. Her name? Venus de Milo. The new turtle is

Children's Literature

Role models are important for what we aspire to, what we become, and how we evaluate ourselves. Shown here are young girls trying to dress like Britney Spears.

named not for a person, but for a statue world-famous for its curvacious and ample breasts. She never did anything. And, how could she—she has no head or arms. The kids get the message. ("Getting the Message" 1997).

Adult television reinforces the message of male dominance. On prime time, male characters outnumber female characters by two to one (Gerbner 1998). Males are more likely to be portrayed in higher-status positions (Vande Berg and Streckfuss 1992). Despite exceptions, most female characters are passive and indecisive. Commercials seldom feature women's voices as the voice-over. The message may be subtle—only obvious when researchers point it out—but viewers get it, for the more television that people watch, the more they tend to have restrictive ideas about women's role in society (Signorielli 1989, 1990).

Stereotypes of gender and age are reinforced on television (Gerbner 1998). About 9 out of 10 women on prime time are below the age of 46, and about 2 of every 5 are shown in some sort of sexual interaction. Women are depicted as losing their sexual attractiveness earlier than men, and starting at age 30, fewer and fewer women are shown. Older women practically disappear from television. While women characters decline after age 30, men just begin to peak. Men are portrayed as aging more gracefully, with their sexual attractiveness lasting longer.

Music   Music also perpetuates sexual stereotypes. Songs for teenagers often tell boys that they should dominate male-female relationships, that they have failed if a girl is not their subordinate partner. In contrast, these songs tell girls to be sexy, passive, and dependent, and that they can control boys by manipulating the boys' sexual impulses (Stockard and Johnson 1980). Images of the sexes are especially harsh in music videos. Often females are simply decorations or background ornaments for male action. Males are aggressive, even domineering, while females are affectionate, dependent, and nurturing (Seidman 1992). Some rap groups glorify male sexual aggression and revel in humiliating women.

Feminists have protested the degradation of women in many forms, one being the exposure of the female body to sell products. The resulting change, however, has not been a decrease in the number of such ads. Instead, we now have ads that explicitly display the male body to sell products. This is a form of equality, although not the one that was hoped for.

Video Games   Video games contain similar messages. Researchers examined 124 characters in video games, and found that male characters outnumber female characters thirteen to one. Thirty percent of the time, females were kidnapped or had to be rescued. Although men, too, sometimes needed to be rescued, they were never saved by women (Provenzo 1991).

Advertising   Advertising is another powerful mass medium. On average, we are exposed to 1,600 advertisements each day (Draper 1986), and their message of what "ought to be" between the sexes comes through loud and clear (Rakow 1992). The point that researcher Lucy Komisar (1971:304) made about advertising still applies, and describes other mass media as well:

> Advertising is an insidious propaganda machine for a male supremacist society. It spews out images of women as sex mates, housekeepers, mothers, and menial workers—images that perhaps reflect the true status of most women in society, but which also make it increasingly difficult for women to break out of the sexist stereotypes that imprison them.

Fighting Back

In Sum

Why Don't Women Dominate Politics?

Socialization

Professions, Perceptions, Positions, and Power

Changes

Feminists have fought back at the use of the female body to sell products. In one campaign, they spray-painted their own additional lines to billboards (Rakow 1992). For example, a billboard featuring a Fiat with a woman reclining on its roof saying, "It's so practical, Darling," was transformed by the spray-painted line, "When I'm not lying on cars, I'm a brain surgeon."

Such resistance has had no impact. The use of the female body—especially exposed breasts—to sell products continues unabated. In addition, the male body has become more prominent in advertising, and more than ever, parts of it, too, are selected for exposure and for irrelevant associations with products.

The essential point is that the mass media—children's books, television, music, video games, and advertising—influence us. They shape the images by which we see one another as men and women. Mostly subtle and beneath our level of awareness, these images then channel our behavior, becoming part of the means by which men maintain their dominance in social life. This includes politics, to which we now turn.

THE WORLD OF POLITICS

Politics provides an excellent illustration of the relative position of men and women in the United States. Without exception, men wield political power at all levels. This holds true whether one considers party leadership, elected office, appointed office, or the policy-making levels of the civil services.

About 8 million more women than men are of voting age, and more women than men vote in our national elections (*Statistical Abstract* 2001:Table 401). So why don't women take political control of the nation? As Figure 9-1 shows, women are vastly underrepresented in political decision making. In fact, the higher the office, the fewer the women. Only a handful of women have been governors or mayors of large cities. Despite the political gains women have made in recent elections, since 1789, over 1,800 men have served in the U.S. Senate, but only 24 women have served, including the 9 current senators. Not until 1992 was the first African-American woman (Carol Moseley-Braun) elected to the Senate.

Part of the reason for women's underrepresentation is due to socialization. As we have seen, our social institutions help to socialize females into dependency. This leads to the following syllogism: Politics is a form of dominance; dominance is masculine; therefore, politics is "unfeminine." This perception imposes severe restraints on women's recruitment, participation, and performance.

Other significant reasons center on sex roles and the relative positions of men and women. First, women are underrepresented in law and business, the careers from which most politicians come. Further, most women do not perceive themselves as a class of people who need political action to overcome domination. Most women also find the irregular hours that running for elective office requires incompatible with being a mother. Fathers, in contrast, whose ordinary roles are more likely to take them away from the home, do not feel this same conflict. Women are also less likely to have a supportive spouse who will play an unassuming background role while providing child care, encouragement, and voter appeal. Finally, men prefer to keep their power and have been reluctant to bring women into decision-making roles or to regard them as viable candidates.

Recent social change, however, means that we can expect more women to win political office. More women are going into law and business, where they are doing more traveling and making statewide and national contacts. Increasingly, child care has become the responsibility of both parents. A main concern of many party leaders

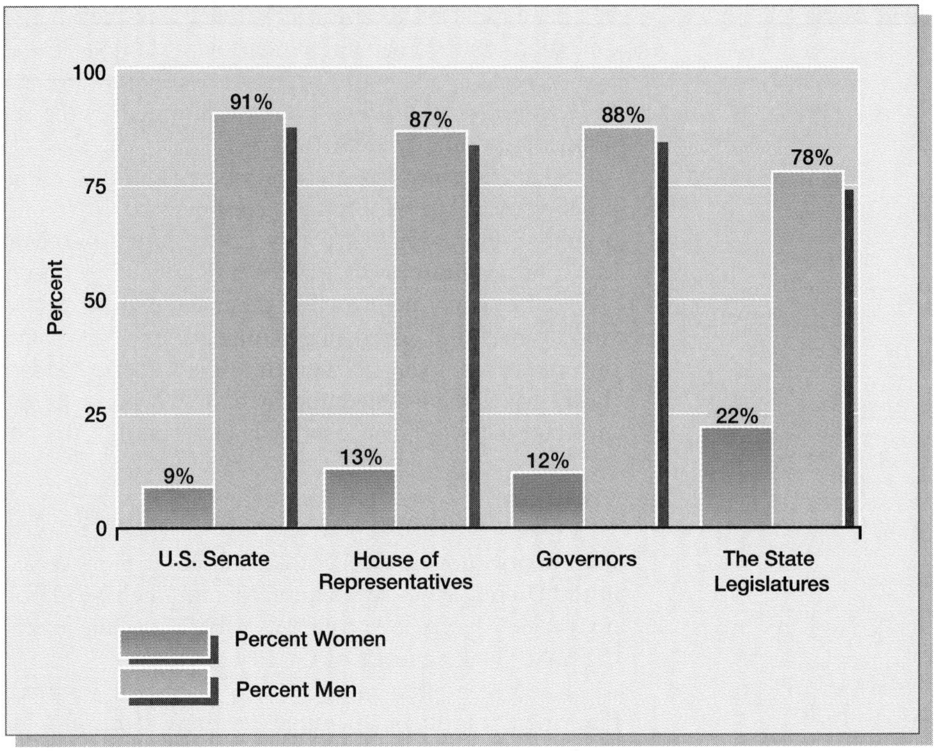

FIGURE 9-1
Who Controls U.S. Politics?

(*Source: Statistical Abstract 2001:*
Table 390; 1998:Tables 469, 475, 478;
National Women's Political Caucus
1998 and National Governors Association 2001 (nga.org))

today is not the sex but the "winnability" of a candidate. This generation, then, is likely to see a fundamental change in women's political participation. In time, a woman will occupy the Oval Office.

THE WORLD OF WORK

Trends in Women's Participation in the World of Work

Year after year, more women enter the world of paid employment. Table 9-3 documents this trend for the United States. We can see that, with one exception, for more than 100 years the number of U.S. women employed outside the home increased consistently. The exception is the period immediately following World War II, when many women left factories and offices to return to being full-time wives and mothers. Today, close to half of all U.S. workers are women.

As you can see from Table 9-3, one of the more significant changes is women's **labor force participation rate,** that is, the proportion of the population age 16 and older that is in the labor force. In 1900, about one of every five women was employed outside the home. By 1945, this rate had doubled. The watershed year was 1985, when for the first time in U.S. history, 50 percent of all women were employed, at least part-time, outside the home. As the Social Map on the next page shows, women's participation rates differ by state. The rate ranges from 51.3 in West Virginia to 69.0 in Nebraska.

The world of work is no exception to the general pattern of discrimination against women. Women constantly face an "old boy's network," social contacts that keep jobs, promotions, and opportunities circulating among men. To overcome this exclusion, some women professionals are developing a "new girls' network." They

Table 9-3   Women in the Civilian Labor Force

Year	Number	As a Percentage of all Workers	Percentage of Women in the Labor Force	Percentage of Women Not in the Labor Force
1890	3,704,000	17	18	82
1900	4,999,000	18	20	80
1920	8,229,000	20	23	77
1930	10,396,000	22	24	76
1940	13,783,000	25	29	71
1945	19,290,000	36	38	62
1950	18,389,000	30	34	66
1955	20,548,000	32	34	66
1960	23,240,000	33	36	64
1965	26,200,000	35	37	63
1970	31,543,000	37	41	59
1975	37,087,000	39	42	58
1980	45,487,000	42	48	52
1985	51,050,000	44	50	50
1990	56,829,000	45	54	46
1995	60,944,000	46	56	44
1997	63,036,000	46	57	43
2001	65,600,000	47	60	40

Note: Pre-1940 figures include women 14 and over; figures for 1940 and after are for women 16 and over.
'Indicates the author's estimate.

Source: 1969 Handbook on Women Workers, 1969:10; Manpower Report to the President, 1971:203, 205; Mills and Palumbo, 1980:6, 45; U.S. Bureau of the Census, various years; Statistical Abstract 2001:Table 568; 1989:Table 622; 1998:Table 647.

FIGURE 9-2
Social Map: How Likely Is a Woman to Work for Wages?
Note: Refers to women who are 16 years old and over who are in the civilian labor force; commonly called the *labor force participation rate.*
(*Source:* U.S. Bureau of Labor Statistics. *Statistical Abstract* 2001:Table 572.)

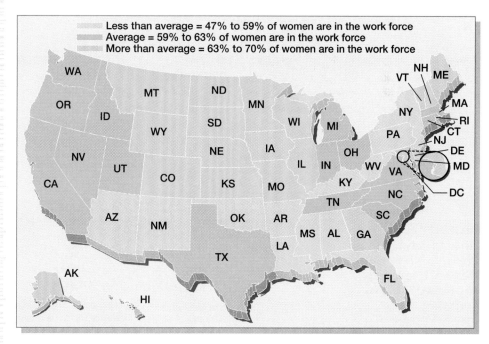

pass opportunities among one another, purposefully excluding men in order to help the careers of women.

But we need more than anecdotes to pinpoint discrimination at work. We need hard numbers, and the most precise figure is the *gender gap* in wages. At all ages and at all levels of education, the average man is paid more than the average woman. Considering all jobs in the nation, and looking at only full-time, year-round workers, women average only *67 percent* of what men earn (*Statistical Abstract* 2001:Table 218). Until the 1980s, women's earnings hovered between 58 and 60 percent of men's, which means that to be paid two thirds of what men make is an improvement! The gender gap in pay characterizes all industrialized nations, but only in Japan is the gap larger than in the United States (Blau and Kahn 1992).

Figure 9-3 gives us a snapshot of how powerfully gender affects earnings. If men and women have the same education, the average man earns much more than the average woman. This is true of all occupations and all levels of education. This gender gap in pay translates into an astounding lifetime total: *Between the ages of 25 and 65, the average man who graduates from college earns about a million dollars ($945,000) more than the average woman who graduates from college.* Remember, we are comparing only full-time workers, not part-time women workers with full-time men workers, or any such thing. This is the *average* difference.

But maybe the pay gap is deserved. As we saw with scientists (Table 9-2 on page 300), fewer women earn Ph.D.s. Women are also more likely to work at lower-paid jobs, such as clerical work. For example, women make up 98 percent of all secretaries, stenographers, and typists. And women professionals, such as physicians, often put in fewer hours than men (Steinhauer 1999). Researchers checked such factors, and found that they justify about half the pay gap (Kemp 1990). The balance, they conclude, is due to gender discrimination.

Economists Rex Fuller and Richard Schoenberger (1991) help us understand how gender discrimination creates this gender gap in pay. They examined the starting

The Gender Gap in Earnings

Explaining the Pay Gap

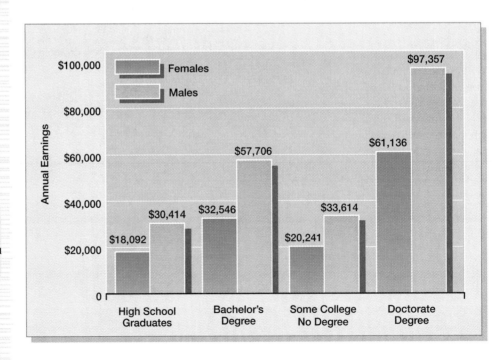

FIGURE 9-3
How Much Will You Earn? Cash Penalties and Rewards for Being Male or Female
(*Source: Statistical Abstract* 2001:Table 218.)

One of the major changes occurring in U.S. business is the ascent of women into positions of power, from which they had been excluded. Although we have nothing even close to a balance of men and women in positions of authority in business, we are experiencing a fundamental change.

salaries of 230 business majors at the University of Wisconsin, of whom 47 percent were women. They found that the women's starting salaries averaged 11 percent ($1,737) less than those of the men.

Were the women less qualified? Did they have lower grades? Or fewer internships? If so, they deserved lower salaries. To find out, Fuller and Schoenberger compared the men's and women's college records. What they uncovered can best be described as *deep* gender discrimination: The *women* had earned higher grades and done more internships. In other words, women had to have higher qualifications than men in order to be offered lower salaries!

What happened after these graduates were on the job? Did their bosses realize that the recruiters had made a mistake, so that after a while these initial salary differences were wiped out? On the contrary. The gender gap grew. In four years, the women were earning 14 percent ($3,615) less than the men.

Sociologically, it seems fair to conclude that "maleness" is so valued by employers that they pay hard cash for it—a conclusion that applies to other industrialized nations as well (Rosenfeld and Kalleberg 1990; Sorensen 1990; Shellenbarger 1995).

The "Mommy Track"

Wives are more likely to be the caretakers of their marriages—to take more responsibility for the children, to spend more time doing housework, and to do more of the "emotional work" that marriages require. Consequently, most employed wives face greater role conflict than do employed husbands (Hochschild and Machung 1995). To reduce this conflict, Felice Schwartz (1989), a feminist, suggested that corporations offer women a choice of two career paths. The first is well known. Executives on the "fast track" work 60 or 70 hours a week. Many travel extensively, and at night and on weekends they take home a briefcase jammed with work. Their family life often suffers. The second would be a "mommy track," which would stress career and family. Less would be expected of a woman on the "mommy track," for her commitment to the firm would be lower and her commitment to her family higher.

That, of course, say critics, is what is wrong with this proposal. A "mommy track" would relegate women to an inferior position in corporate life. It would encourage women to lower their aspirations and be satisfied with fewer promotions (Ehrlich 1989; Day 1990). To encourage women to withdraw from the hard-driving, competitive climb up the corporate ladder would confirm stereotypes of women executives and justify the executive pay gap. In order not to be sexist, such arrangements would have to provide an optional "daddy track" for men. The solution, suggest critics, is for husbands to carry their share of family responsibilities and for corporations to offer on-site day care, flexible work schedules, and parental leave without loss of benefits (Auerbach 1990; Galinsky and Stein 1990).

WHY IS OUR WORK FORCE SEGREGATED BY SEX?

**Two Explanations:
1. Conflict Theory:
A Dual Labor Market**

Two explanations compete for why our labor force is segregated by sex (Blau 1975; MacKinnon 1979). The first is based on conflict theory. As we saw in Chapter 7, Marxist conflict theory emphasizes how a pool of low-paid labor helps capitalists. They draw on those workers during periods of economic expansion, then lay them off when the economy slows down. The result is a **dual labor market**—better-paid workers who are employed regularly coupled with temporary, marginal, low-paid workers. Women are not singled out because they are women, nor are African Americans and Latinos singled out because of who they are. All are singled out because, as minorities, they are relatively powerless. Sticking them in the underpaid and underutilized pool of marginal labor works.

**2. Symbolic
Interactionism: The
Role of Stereotypes**

The second explanation is based on symbolic interaction (MacKinnon 1979). Because men *see* women as less profitable, they pay them less. A stereotype of women is that they are less capable, less productive, and less dedicated to employers. This stereotype is a lens through which employers perceive women. They then assign women more menial jobs and pay them less, while they assign men more responsible positions and pay them more.

Toward a Synthesis

Each explanation probably holds part of the answer. Women do confront structural barriers in the marketplace, and in some industries marginal pools of labor are profitable. The stereotype of women as less capable continues, affecting expectations and payoffs. Whatever the factors that created sex discrimination, it tends to be self-perpetuating. And, we might add, whatever their personal opinions, employers generally will pay the least they can.

SEXUAL HARASSMENT

Another form of sex discrimination that operates within the world of work is **sexual harassment,** using one's position to make unwanted sexual demands. If power is unequal, the less powerful person is relatively unable to ward off such demands. The most vulnerable women are those who lack job alternatives.

**The Individualistic
View**

The traditional view of sexual harassment makes it a *personal* matter of sexual *attraction.* A man gets interested in a woman and makes an advance; the woman accepts, rejects, or says "maybe." Perhaps she even uses body language to indicate that she *wants* to be approached sexually. There are always sexual attractions between men and women; some just happen to take place at work. These are events between individuals, and are not a *social* problem.

The Structural View

Catharine MacKinnon (1979), the attorney and professor who wrote the classic book on sexual harassment, changed our thinking. She rejected this traditional view. She argued that sexual harassment is a *structural* matter (built into the marketplace).

The most notorious case of sexual harassment at the end of the twentieth century was that between President Bill Clinton and Paula Jones. Jones accused Clinton of making crude advances to her when he was governor of Arkansas and she was a low-level state employee. The case was settled out of court for $850,000.

She noted that women generally occupy an inferior status in boss-worker relations. She also said that the emphasis on women as sex objects at work encourages sexual harassment. Often women are hired because of their sexual attributes, although this precondition usually is hidden under the requirement that the newly hired be young, "attractive" women who can make a "good appearance" to the public. In short, sexual harassment begins with hiring procedures that judge women on factors other than their job qualifications (Silverman 1981).

From Personal Problem to Social Problem

Although widely accepted now, MacKinnon's view was new and controversial at the time. Until 1976, in fact, sexual harassment was literally unspeakable—a "problem with no name." Until then, the traditional view dominated, and women considered unwanted sexual advances as something that happened to them as individuals. They did not draw a connection between those advances and their lower position in the marketplace. As women's liberation groups raised awareness of the *group* basis of these problems, women gradually concluded that the sexual advances by men in more powerful positions at work were part of a general problem. As more women came to the same conclusion—and became upset about it and demanded that something be done—sexual harassment as a *social* problem was born. To catch a glimpse of how this definitional process is occurring in Japan, see the Global Glimpse box on the next page.

Sexual Harrassment in Japan

The public relations department had come up with an eye-catcher: Each month the cover of the company magazine would show a woman taking off one more piece of clothing. The men were pleased. Never had they so looked forward to the company magazine.

Six months later, with the cover girl poised to take off her tank top, the objections of the female employees had grown too loud to ignore. "We told them it was a lousy idea," said Junko Takashima, assistant director of the company's woman's affairs division. The firm dropped the striptease act.

The Japanese men didn't get the point. "What's all the fuss about?" they asked. "Beauty is beauty. We're just admiring the ladies. It just adds a little spice to boring days at the office."

"It's degrading to us, and it must stop," responded women workers, who, encouraged by the U.S. feminist movement, broke their tradition of silence.

The Japanese (like Americans until the 1970s) have no word of their own to describe such situations. They have borrowed the English phrase "sexual harrassment" and are struggling to apply it to their own culture. This is difficult, because a pat on the bottom has long been taken for granted as a boss's way of getting his secretary's attention.

The cultural expectation that all Japanese workers are part of a team that works together harmoniously also makes it difficult to complain. But some women have begun to speak out, using their new vocabulary—and the changed perception that comes with it.

Based on Graven 1990.

As MacKinnon pointed out, sexual harassment refers to a continuum of severity and unwantedness. It may consist of a single encounter at work or a series of incidents. Sexual relations may be a condition for being hired, retained, or advanced. Sexual harassment may include:

> verbal sexual suggestions or jokes, constant leering or ogling, brushing against your body "accidentally," a friendly pat, squeeze, or pinch or arm against you, catching you alone for a quick kiss, the indecent proposition backed by the threat of losing your job, and forced sexual relations. (MacKinnon 1979:2)

MacKinnon (1979:29) added:

> Sexual harassment takes both verbal and physical forms. . . . Verbal sexual harassment can include anything from passing but persistent comments on a woman's body or body parts to the experience of an eighteen-year-old file clerk whose boss regularly called her in to his office "to tell me the intimate details of his marriage and to ask what I thought about different sexual positions." Pornography is sometimes used. Physical forms range from repeated collisions that leave the impression of "accident" to outright rape. One woman reported unmistakable sexual molestation which fell between these extremes: "My boss . . . runs his hand up my leg or blouse. He hugs me to him and then tells me he is 'just naturally affectionate.'"

Sexual Harassment and Power

The power element in sexual harassment becomes evident when we examine consequences of refusing. As MacKinnon (1979:35) explained:

> Retaliation comes in many forms. The woman may be threatened with demotions and salary cuts; unfavorable material may be solicited and put in her personal file; or she may be placed on disciplinary layoff. In one case, a sexually disappointed

foreman first cut back the woman's hours, then put her on a lower-paying machine. When she requested extra work to make up the difference, he put her to sweeping floors and cleaning bathrooms. He degraded and ridiculed her constantly, interfered with her work so it was impossible for her to maintain production, and fired her at two o'clock one morning.

Once a woman has been harassed, she has limited options (MacKinnon 1979:52). Objecting, submitting, or ignoring the act are all risky. If she objects, she may be hounded into quitting or get fired outright. If she submits, he may tire of her. If she ignores it, she gets drawn into a cat-and-mouse game with few exits: He may tire of the game and turn to someone else, or he may fire her to hire a more willing victim.

The Thomas Hearings

Although the term *sexual harassment* did not exist until 1976, it became a household word in 1991 when a national audience viewed the Senate hearings for Clarence Thomas' confirmation to the U.S. Supreme Court. Now sexual harassment is a top subject of executive education programs, and corporations try to specify in writing what behaviors are intolerable (Adler 1991; Lublin 1991). A credibility gap exists, however. Most men executives feel that offenders are punished adequately; most working women disagree and say that they fear losing their jobs if they file charges (Lublin 1992).

Changing Definitions

The Equal Employment Opportunity Commission has broadened the definition of sexual harassment to include all unwelcome sexual attention that affects an employee's job conditions or creates a "hostile" working environment (Adler 1991). The legal concept has become so fuzzy that a woman employee who was *not* asked for sexual favors—while all the other women were—was ruled a victim of sexual harassment (Hayes 1991).

The Mitsubishi Motors Case

Ordinarily, sexual harassment claims are settled privately. It is difficult to prove these charges, and women who make legal claims run the risk of frustration, embarrassment, and retaliation at work. As victims have taken these risks, however, they gradually have transformed the workplace, and today's work environment is much freer of sexual harassment. The landmark decision came in 1998. Three hundred women who worked at the Illinois plant of Mitsubishi Motors claimed that the company tolerated a hostile work environment. Some claimed they had been groped by fellow workers, others that they had been threatened with the loss of their jobs if they didn't agree to have sex, and that management had ignored their complaints. The women were awarded $34 million, an average of $113,000 each. The size of this decision caught employers' attention nationwide; to tolerate a hostile work environment affects the corporate bottom line.

Sexual Harassment and Race

When sexual harassment crosses racial lines, it puts women at a special disadvantage. If they protest, they can be seen as insensitive to cultural differences—they simply misunderstood what was a "normal" sexual invitation in another racial-ethnic group. Or they may be seen as prejudiced—that is, they are offended by the sexual offer because it was made by someone not of their own race—with the implication that they would have welcomed it if it had been made by someone of their own race-ethnicity.

Males as Victims

With more women managers, sexual harassment is no longer exclusively a female problem. Men also find themselves victims. One man claimed that his chief financial officer, a woman, made sexual overtures to him "almost daily." Another objected that his woman supervisor told him that she had dreamed about him naked. One victim reported that his complaints received little sympathy, that most men don't understand why a man would take offense at a woman's sexual advances (Carton 1994). Eventually, norms will change to account for women's growing power.

**Homosexuals/
Heterosexuals**

In 1998, the Supreme Court broadened sexual harassment law to include people of the same sex. The Court ruled that sexual harassment is not limited to behavior between men and women, and does not have to include sexual desire. The law now covers the harassment at work of homosexuals by heterosexuals (Felsenthal 1998). By extension, the law now also includes the sexual harassment of heterosexuals by homosexuals.

VIOLENCE AGAINST WOMEN

Rape and Murder

Rape and murder are twin fears that stalk women in this society. Women know that these acts of violence are more than a remote possibility, and that it is men whom they have to fear. They know that some women suddenly disappear when they are on their way to school, the grocery store, or their campsite at Yosemite. Some resurface raped and brutalized. Others are found dead, stuffed in the trunk of their own car. Rape and murder were reviewed in Chapter 5, and there is no need to go beyond the materials of that chapter. The bottom line, however, remains: Women tend to be the victims, men the victimizers.

Family Violence

Females also are disproportionately the victims of family violence, topics we shall review in Chapter 11. A particular form of violence against women, genital mutilation, was the focus of the box on page 293.

**A Feminist
Application of
Conflict Theory**

To explain these patterns, feminist sociologists often use conflict theory. They argue that violence against women is an expression of power, that men use violence to try to maintain their positions of privilege (Alder 1992). From this, it follows that if men lose status as gender relations change, we can expect high rates of violence by men against women to continue.

**A Feminist
Application of
Symbolic
Interaction Theory**

Feminist sociologists also use symbolic interactionism; they stress how U.S. culture encourages males to be violent. An example is video games in which barely clad young women are hunted down and killed. In one of these games by Nintendo, zombies suck the blood of scantily dressed sorority sisters (Pereira 1993). The point, say feminists, is that U.S. culture teaches men to "associate power, dominance, strength, virility, and superiority with masculinity" (Scully 1990). To associate strength and virility with violence, they add, is to produce violence.

**The Example of
Video Games**

Players of video games can often choose the characters they wish to play. The choice may include both men and women. As a sign of changing times, I see virile men players choosing to be women characters. Bob may choose to "be" "Melissa, the hot-tempered, evil, axe-wielding killer," so he can see how she compares with "Annie, the mean strumpet with the .45," or if she can bring down "Fred, the escaped loony with a chain saw." Even with this change, however, I note that the players both at home and at the arcades are almost exclusively boys and young men. Symbols of violence, though changing in form, maintain their dominance among young males.

◆ Social Policy ◆

AN AREA OF IRRECONCILABLE IDEOLOGIES

**Opposing Sides
with Incompatible
Ideologies**

With hundreds of organizations having grown up around issues of sex discrimination, it is easy to get lost in specific social policies and to miss the watershed differences between the two main opposing groups, the radical feminists and the conservative traditionalists. Each would like to speak for all women, and each wants its views to be dominant. Let's examine their fundamental distinctions.

Policy Implications of the Radical Feminists

Radical feminists insist that our society is so rotten at the core that it must be restructured (Bernard 1971). We cannot simply tinker with society, making sporadic changes here and there, such as demanding equal pay or busting a hole in the glass ceiling. Such policies, though correct in their intent, are superficial remedies for severe problems that threaten to destroy the basic humanity of women and men. Social policies must eradicate the social roots of sexism.

We must break the gender division of labor. To do this, the sexes cannot be socialized differently. If they are, despite any changes we might make, women will continue to "end up in service positions or servant roles, no matter what class of job they hold—factory work, technician, secretary, research assistant" (Bernard 1971:237). Women will still perform the supportive or stroking functions, continue to be "the restorers, the healers, the builder-up-ers," and be disqualified from the top positions because they are systematically forbidden to be aggressive (Bernard 1971:237).

To implement this radical ideology requires that we restructure society, for we must remove all sex distinctions in the socialization of boys and girls. Such a program might

1. Encourage females to be as aggressive as males

2. Socialize girls and boys identically (this might require removing all children from their homes and boarding them in government preschools in which all distinctions of gender are removed—where both sexes wear identical uniforms and hairstyles, teachers do not know the gender of their students, children have no sex-linked names, and children's books make no distinctions between males and females).

3. Require equal treatment of the sexes throughout education, including athletic training and sports.

4. Require that husbands and wives share housework equally and all children be placed in child-care facilities so that both parents are free to compete in the marketplace.

5. Require that all top and lower-level positions in government, industry, education, religion, science, medicine, the military, the media, and any other positions of leadership that influence ideas be held equally by women and men.

Anything less than such radical restructuring of society would perpetuate ideas about qualitative differences in the sexes. No such social policies are possible in our society, of course. Most of us would find them abhorrent, and only a dictatorship could enforce them. Consequently, the goals of the radical feminists will not be achieved.

Policy Implications of the Conservative Traditionalists

The conservative traditionalists, in contrast, believe that gender distinctions are natural and desirable and ought to be encouraged. They hold that a woman's proper role is to be a home-making wife and mother; a man's to be a bread-winning husband and father. This ideology, so abhorrent to that of the radical feminists, would require an antithetical set of social policies. Such a program might

1. Require parents to take full responsibility and care for their own preschool children (no publicly supported child care).

2. Encourage girls at home and at school to become full-time wives and mothers and boys to become providers and protectors of their wives and children (textbooks would present women and men in these roles).

3. Require that husbands provide the primary financial support of their wives and children.

4. Protect women from heavy work and unreasonable hours of employment and give job preference to a man who is supporting dependents.

5. Include tax breaks that favor full-time homemakers.

Like those of the radical feminists, these social policies, absent the endorsement of a dictator, will never become the law of the land. They, too, will continue to represent extreme views.

Between the Extremes

Innumerable positions fall between those of the conservative traditionalists and the radical feminists. It is likely that some of these reflect your own views and the causes you support: well run child-care facilities for working parents, policies that encourage fathers to enjoy closer relations with their children, the right for both mother and father to take an extended leave from work when a child is born, summer camps for all children, enforcement of child support awards, the end of economic discrimination at work, and, at home, a more equitable distribution of housework.

THE BATTLE LINES

Probably most of us would agree with the majority of these proposals. And most of us probably would also agree with the principle that we should have equality between the sexes. Few of us realize how radical the view of sexual equality is, however.

The ERA as an Example of Controversial Social Policy

To see why I say this, let's look at how the United States reacted to the proposal of an equal rights amendment (ERA). Between 1924 and 1971, Congress held 12 hearings on this amendment, and in 1972, the House and Senate passed this version:

Section 1 Equality of rights under the law shall not be denied or abridged by the United States or by any State on account of sex.

Section 2 The Congress shall have the power to enforce, by appropriate legislation, the provisions of this article.

Section 3 This amendment shall take effect two years after the date of ratification.

Within hours after the Senate passed this resolution, Hawaii ratified the amendment. Twenty-one additional states ratified in 1972, eight in 1973, three in 1974, one in 1975, none in 1976, and one, the thirty-fifth, in 1977. With only three states short of the necessary three fourths majority, the amendment hit a roadblock, and no further states ratified. When the seven-year limit for ratification expired in March 1979, Congress extended the time for ratification by three years and three months. Momentum and sentiment had swung the other way, however, and five states rescinded their ratification.

Why did this simple statement proposing equality of rights under the law for the sexes fail? Does it not simply match what any decent, fair-minded person would want? The problem is that no one knew the consequences if the ERA became law. Because its terms were so broad, its meaning could be determined only through court decisions in lawsuits. The interpretation process might have extended over centuries (Lee 1980). Consequently, no one knew for certain what they were fighting for or against.

Two Opposing Sides with Irreconcilable Differences

This, however, did not deter groups from lining up on either side of the ERA, each convinced that it understood the consequences of the amendment. Women were not on one side, opposed by men on the other. Rather, women were on both sides, as were men. In the forefront of the battle were two groups: mainstream feminists, largely represented by the National Organization for Women (NOW), and the conservative traditionalists, largely represented by the Eagle Forum. Most women, however, watched from the sidelines, passively silent and strangely acquiescent about the outcome that affected them so vitally.

The convictions of these two main groups of activists appear to have been based on hopes and fears. The feminists *hoped* that the amendment would bring equality of the sexes, help eliminate sexual stereotypes, and give women access to all areas of participation and leadership in society. The traditionalists, in contrast, *feared* that the amendment would lead to the elimination of protective work legislation (such as that preventing women from lifting weights in excess of designated amounts), to the drafting of women for combat, to unisex sleeping arrangements in military barracks, college dormitories, and prisons, and to unisex public rest rooms.

As these groups argued and fought on opposing sides of the ERA, they were blinded to what they had in common. For example, they agreed that pornography degrades women, encourages violence against women, and that it should be highly restricted, if not banned. Each group also desired the best for women. But because each viewed what is best from the lens of its own ideology, neither was able to see the point of view of the other. U.S. women were divided by this controversy.

The defeat of the ERA in 1982 did not end the matter. ERA is very much alive. Other forms of the ERA have been proposed by feminists—and just as strongly opposed by conservatives. When feminists feel that the political climate is more conducive to ERA, they will again propose it as an amendment to the U.S. constitution. And once again feminists and conservatives will battle its passage.

IDEOLOGY AND SOCIAL POLICY

Ideology colors all questions about relations between the sexes and the role of women and men in society. Within this ideological morass, no social policy is seen as neutral. With irreconcilable points of view abounding, every proposal seems subversive to someone. To be sound, social policy must consider these cleavages. It must also be based on the principle that both men and women deserve the right to make informed choices about their roles in life. For example, forcing a woman to be a homemaker is no more an example of freedom than is forcing her to be a paid worker. To move beyond ideological rhetoric, then, social policy ought to support an environment in which neither men nor women are forced into predetermined roles.

◆ The Future of the Problem ◆

Although sexism will remain a fact of life, the historical trend is toward greater equality between women and men, and I anticipate that this will continue. Previous generations of women fought hard to win rights that we now take for granted, such as the right to vote and to own property. Today's and tomorrow's struggle centers on removing stereotypes and gaining greater access to leadership, especially in business and politics.

The most significant social trend that will affect this social problem is the employment of women. As even larger numbers of women join the labor force, women will continue to reshape social relationships. They also will increase their stress-related health habits and problems. Employment will continue to alter power

Battles Harden Lines

Simmering Beneath the Surface

Going Beyond Ideology to a Supportive Environment

Centers of the Struggle:

Stereotypes and Leadership

Employment and Power Relationships at Home

CENSUS 2000

The Census Bureau collects data in a number of ways, but its most popular method—sending questionnaires to homes—overlooks an important group of people in society, the homeless. In an attempt to provide a demographic portrait of the homeless population in the United States, 2000 Census Bureau employees went out to the streets and collected data at soup kitchens, shelters for both adults and juvenile runaways, and hotels and motels used to provide emergency shelter for those without a home. While the results of the census indicate that men are more likely to be found at these places than women, a growing number of women are housed in these makeshift quarters as well. Additionally, as the table below indicates, women of color are disproportionately locked into homelessness.

Since African American women and men each comprise about 6 percent of the U.S. population, their presence in homeless shelters can be described as radically disproportionate. Latino men and women also each comprise about 6 percent of the U.S. population, and they too are disproportionately represented in homeless shelters, although not to the extent of African Americans. This is consistent with a pattern some sociologists have called "double victimization," which refers to the inequality that exists not only between men and women, but white women and women of color as well. Most available evidence shows that this holds true throughout the political and economic spheres: when gender inequality and discrimination are concerned, white, non-Hispanic women fare much better than their Latino and African American counterparts.

Source: Smith, Annetta and Denis Smith (2001). *Emergency and Transitional Shelter Population: 2000. Census Special Report.* Washington, D.C.

THE RACE-ETHNICITY OF THE U.S. HOMELESS

	RACE				HISPANIC ORIGIN	
	White	African American	Other		Hispanic	Non-Hispanic
Both Sexes	43%	42%	15%	Both Sexes	21%	79%
Male	45%	40%	15%	Male	20%	80%
Under 18	34%	47%	19%	Under 18	28%	72%
Female	39%	44%	17%	Female	22%	78%
Under 18	33%	48%	19%	Under 18	28%	72%

relationships between husbands and wives, because wives who work outside the home have more control over family decisions than wives who do not. As more wives work outside the home, husbands gradually will take on greater responsibilities for the housework and children. This will not mean equality in household responsibilities any time soon, however, for in dual-earner families, husbands do considerably less housework than their wives (Galinsky et al. 1993; Robinson and Godbey 1996).

Legal Pressures

Women are likely to make greater use of the Equal Pay Act of 1963 (forbidding discrimination in salaries), Title VII of the Civil Rights Act of 1964 (forbidding discrimination on the basis of sex), and the Fourteenth Amendment (forbidding a state to "deny any person within its jurisdiction the equal protection of the laws"). Such legal pressures will not eliminate the problem, but they will continue to undermine the structure of sexism.

Changed Roles Lead to Changed Images

Changes in our sexual stereotypes are imminent because of the increasing numbers of women in the work force. More children are growing up with the model of a mother who more fully participates in family decisions. Seeing both mothers and fathers bring home paychecks, these children take it for granted that a man is not the exclusive breadwinner and that a woman is more than a mother and a wife.

Changed Images Lead to Changed Roles

As women come to play a fuller role in the decision-making processes of our social institutions, our stereotypes—which lock men into activities considered masculine and push women into roles considered feminine—will be broken. As more endeavors become desexualized, both men and women will be free to do activities compatible with their desires or proclivities as *individuals*—not because the activity matches a stereotype. This will free more men to play more supportive roles and "get more in touch with their feelings," and more women to take leadership roles and become more assertive.

Will These Changes Create a "New Personality"?

As sociologist Janet Giele (1978) pointed out, the ultimate possibility for the future is a new conception of the human personality. Our stereotypes block us from certain experiences by casting us into gendered roles. Without meaning to and without realizing it, many of us simply follow activities dictated by our culture. As these stereotypes are abandoned, men and women will perceive themselves, and one another, differently. People will develop a new consciousness of who they are and of their potential. New paths will open to them, ones that allow feelings and expressions of needs that our cultural stereotypes deny. Women are likely to think of themselves as more active masters of their environment, men to feel and express more emotional sensitivity. Each will be free to explore these other dimensions of the self. As the future unfolds, it will reveal exactly what such "greater wholeness" of men and women looks like.

◆ Summary

1. Although females make up 51.1 percent of the U.S. population, men discriminate against them. Consequently, sociologists refer to men as a dominant group and women as a minority group.
2. Every society *sex-types* occupations. That is, some work is thought suitable for men and other work for women. There is no inherent biological connection between work and its assignment to a particular sex, for "women's work" of one society may be "men's work" in another. In all societies, however, "men's work" is given greater prestige than "women's work."
3. Symbolic interactionists examine *gender* (masculinity and femininity), looking at how each society socializes the sexes into its ideas of what men and women ought to be like. Socialization includes learning *sexism,* the belief that one sex is innately superior to the other and the discriminatory practices that result from that belief.
4. Functionalists theorize that sexual discrimination is based on the need of early human groups to engage in hand-to-hand combat. Men had the physical advantage but needed to be motivated to become warriors. Women, offered as inducements for men to fight, were assigned the drudge work of society. A second functionalist explanation is that because women were physically encumbered through childbearing and nursing, men became dominant as they took control of warfare and trade.
5. Conflict theorists emphasize that the rights that U.S. women enjoy resulted from a power struggle with men. The confrontations and violence between the sexes in the late 1800s and early 1900s have been replaced by legal pressure and economic and educational competition.
6. Given the inextricability of nature and nurture, we cannot prove the extent to which natural differences exist between the sexes. Both genetics and socialization can explain females' earlier proficiency in verbal skills and males' greater aggressiveness and abilities at mathematics. The door to biological explanations in sociology has been pried open a bit, however, by the studies of Vietnam veterans.
7. Women confront discrimination in most of life, including a generally belittling attitude from men. The educational system generally supports existing sex roles—as do the mass media. Although women outnumber men voters,

men dominate politics; women tend to see politics as incompatible with femininity and motherhood.

8. Women often are segregated into lower-paying positions that offer less advancement. They also confront *sexual harassment* at work.

9. All social policies to deal with sex discrimination have ideological implications. Different groups of women propose antithetical social policies.

10. In the future, even larger numbers of women will be employed outside the home. This will continue to change power relationships at home and fuel pressures for anti-discriminatory statutes and changes of gender images. The direction of the future is toward greater equality between the sexes.

◆ Key Terms

Dual labor market   A pool of employees divided into two main segments, regularly employed and better-paid workers and low-paid temporary workers.

Gender   The socially learned behaviors that are attached to the sexes. Refers to socialization or culture. Commonly called femininity or masculinity. See *Sex.*

Labor force participation rate   The proportion of the population 16 years and older that is in the labor force.

Master trait   A characteristic so important to one's identification that it overrides almost all others. One's sex is an example.

Matriarchy   A society in which women as a group dominate men as a group.

Patriarchy   A society in which men as a group dominate women as a group.

Sex   The physical identity of a person as male or female. Refers to biology. See *Gender.*

Sex roles   The behaviors and attitudes expected of males and females.

Sex-typing   Associating something with one sex or the other. "Men's work" and "women's work" are examples of sex-typing of occupations.

Sexism   The belief that one sex is innately superior to the other and the discrimination that supports such a belief.

Sexual harassment   The use of one's position to make unwanted sexual demands on someone.

◆ Critical Thinking Questions

1. List ten common examples of sexism in U.S. culture today.
   - In what ways would your list be different if you had written it ten years ago?
   - In what ways do you think it will be different if you were to write it ten years from now?

2. Which of the three perspectives (symbolic interactionism, functionalism, or conflict theory) do you think best explains sexism in the U.S.? Explain.

3. In what ways do you think that gender differences are accented or reduced in cyberspace?
   - What do you think the implications of cyberspace will be for the future of gender differences in society?

Medical Care
Problems of Physical and Mental Illness

To prepare for the birth of their first child, Kathie Persall and her husband, Hank, read books and articles about childbirth and took childbirth classes together. One morning, unexpectedly at 5 A.M., the protective "bag of waters" that surrounds the fetus broke.

By 10 A.M., Kathie was on the maternity ward, hooked up to an electronic fetal monitor (EFM) and an intravenous feeding tube. These restricted her movements, and she felt uncomfortable. Kathie was informed that the hospital had a rule that delivery must take place within 24 hours after the waters break for fear of infection. At 11 A.M. the resident physician (not her own doctor) said that Kathie's labor would be speeded up by Pitocin, a powerful drug.

Kathie's sister, Carol, knew that inducing labor can lead to caesarean section. She urged Hank to get Kathie off Pitocin. By evening, doctors noted that Kathie's cervix was not dilating rapidly enough. They increased the Pitocin. One nurse thought that the flow of Pitocin looked blocked. She wiggled the bottle, and a large dose sped through Kathie's veins. A massive contraction lasting between five and ten minutes ensued. The baby's heartbeat dropped from 160 to 40 beats per minute. The doctor rushed in, cut off the Pitocin, and substituted another drug to stop the contraction. He said the situation had turned into an emergency requiring a caesarean. Hank, who had been trying to comfort Kathie, protested. He insisted that Kathie and Hank sign a consent form in case a caesarean became necessary. On the form, Hank and Kathie read the long list of things that could go wrong. They did not want to sign it, but how were they to resist the hospital? Moreover, Kathie was in pain and exhausted.

At midnight, the doctor told Kathie that a caesarean was necessary because she had dilated only 5 centimeters in 13 hours of labor and would need another 13 to dilate enough for a normal birth. Kathie knew it was wrong to assume that just because the first 5 centimeters had taken 13 hours the next would take as long. Nevertheless, at 1:10 A.M., she went into surgery.

When the baby was born, Kathie could not even look at her new son because she was vomiting too severely from the anesthetic. A caesarean delivery is major surgery, and it took Kathie seven weeks to recover. She was left with a disfiguring scar—and anger at the doctors, the hospital, and the procedures that had created the need for surgery.

✦ The Problem in Sociological Perspective ✦

More Than Biology

In Chapter 6 we focused on the twin problems of crime and the criminal justice system that is set up to deal with crime. When considering the topic of medical care, we again need to focus on twin problems: illness and the medical care system that is set up to deal with illness. Unlike a medical approach to illness, which focuses on the origin and development of disease, the sociological approach examines how *social* factors affect health.

Table 10-1	The Ten Most Important Problems Facing the Nation	
Rank	**Problem**	**Percent Who Rank It Number One or Two**
1.	Terrorism	23
2.	The economy	16
3.	Health care	11
4.	Taxes	8
5.	Crime	5
6.	Social security	5
7.	National security	5
8.	Homeland security	4
9.	Foreign policy	4
10.	Environment	3

A random sample of Americans was asked: 'What do you think are the two most important issues for the government to address?'

Source: Sourcebook of Criminal Justice Statistics Online. Harris Interactive, Inc., The Harris Poll (Los Angeles: Creators Syndicate, Inc., Apr. 24, 2002), p. 8. Table adapted by SOURCEBOOK staff.

There is no doubt that subjective concern about this problem runs high. As Table 10-1 shows, the U.S. public sees health care as the third most pressing social problem facing the nation. Health care even outranks taxes and crime as problems for the government to address.

THE SOCIAL NATURE OF HEALTH AND ILLNESS

Most of us think of illness in biological terms, but much more is involved. What is considered health or illness depends on cultural ideas. This concept may seem strange. Isn't fever, for example, always a sign of illness? Not always. Many people dismiss a low-grade fever as "just a little temperature." Whether it is considered a sign of illness depends on how high the fever is and how long it lasts. Even then, interpretations of what fever means and how to treat it differ—even among medical authorities.

Ideas about health and illness are not fixed. Years ago, coal miners reluctantly accepted lung cancer as an almost inevitable consequence of their job. They knew that longtime workers became short of breath and coughed up blood, and they even wrote folk songs about "black lung." Eventually the

Changing Ideas About Disease: The Example of Black Lung Disease

workers concluded that their symptoms constituted a disease and that they did not have to put up with it. Their unions had to fight not only management, as you would expect, but also a medical profession that refused to acknowledge coal mining as the cause of this disease. The result was a new understanding, not just of black lung disease but also of how the environment can create disease (Smith 1987).

Effects of Industrialization

The social nature of disease is also apparent when we consider industrialization. When the United States industrialized and became more affluent, heart disease became our number-one killer. Eating richer foods and getting less exercise increased heart attacks. The pursuit of pleasure leads to many diseases, including gonorrhea, syphilis, AIDS, and, of course, a whole rack of diseases that come from smoking.

Iatrogenesis

Another example of the social nature of illness is **iatrogenesis,** injuries caused by medical care. This is what happened when the nurse jiggled Kathie's bottle of Pitocin and the baby's heartbeat plummeted. Iatrogenesis is not trivial. Each year, about 90,000 Americans die of infections that they acquire in hospitals (Stolberg 1998). The most common injuries are from drug complications and mistakes in diagnosis. About one fourth are due to negligence (Winslow 1991). The discussion on medical incompetence in the Thinking Critically box on page 323 focuses on another aspect of iatrogenesis.

Organizational Rules

The medical approach to pregnancy also highlights the *social* nature of health and illness. Physicians have defined a natural process (pregnancy and birth) as something that requires fetal monitors and powerful drugs. They also define a woman as "ill" if she does not deliver within 24 hours after her water breaks. This arbitrary definition of "illness" is imposed on a natural process in which some women deliver a baby in one hour, but others not for 48 hours or longer.

THE SOCIAL ORGANIZATION OF MEDICINE
AS A SOURCE OF PROBLEMS

This takes us to the second part of this social problem, the social organization of medicine. Let's consider costs, caesarean births, and quality of medical care.

Soaring Costs

As we all know, it is expensive to visit a doctor. It wasn't always so. To see how the cost of medical treatment has soared, look at Figure 10-1. In 1970, the nation's medical bill was $75 billion, but by 2000 it had exploded to $1.3 trillion, *18 times higher*. During this time, the U.S. population increased by only 30 percent. If medical costs had increased at the same rate as our population, the nation's health bill would run $100 billion, one thirteenth of what it is now. Or consider this: If our population had grown at the same rate since 1970 as our medical bill, more than *half* of the world's population would be crowded into the United States.

Reasons for Rising Costs

Why did the nation's medical bill explode? A major factor is the growing number of older people, who require more medical treatment than others. Three aspects of the social organization of medical care are also contributing factors: the development of expensive technology accompanied by a demand for the latest treatment on the part of patients; a preoccupation with last-minute heroic intervention rather than with prevention; and the view that medical care is a commodity to be sold for a profit.

"Fee-for-Service"

Medicine for profit is called a *fee-for-service system*. This means that physicians collect a fee for each service they perform. Patients used to pay for these services directly, but now they typically pay for them through insurance. Fee-for-service increases costs, for, just like mechanics, the more services that physicians sell, the

FIGURE 10-1
The Soaring Costs of Medical Care: **The Nation's Medical Bill**
(Source: Statistical Abstract of the United States, 1989:Table 136, 1998:Table 164; 2001:Table 119.)

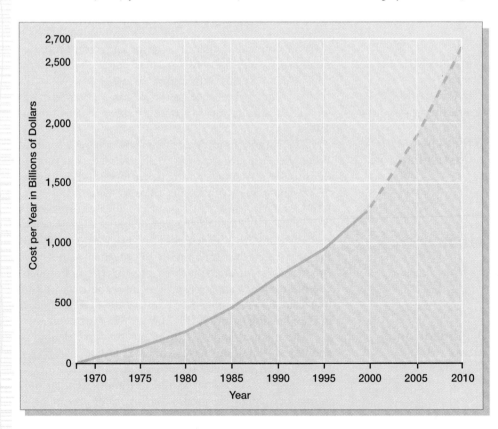

Chapter 10 Medical Care: Problems of Physical and Mental Illness

THINKING CRITICALLY ABOUT SOCIAL PROBLEMS

Medical Incompetence

Most physicians are competent, but all physicians make mistakes. Most of us could accept this statement. The following statement, however, may be more controversial: Some physicians are so incompetent that they should not practice medicine. And you may find this one even more controversial: Some of the most incompetent physicians are so admired by their medical colleagues that they are promoted to the leadership of their state medical associations.

I once would have thought that the last two statements could not possibly be true. Then I studied suicide in Missouri. Poring over the coroner's records, I was struck by one decision that a person who had been shot several times may have committed suicide. Then I read about a father in Warren, Ohio, who was convinced that his 20-year-old daughter, found dead in a field seven miles from her home, had not committed suicide. For 17 years, he kept the case alive. Finally her former boyfriend was charged with strangling her.

When it became apparent that the coroner had missed "obvious" clues to the cause of the woman's death—"suspicious marks" on her neck—the sheriff's department investigated the coroner. Among their findings were these rulings:

- Suicide—the man had been run over with a bulldozer and shot

- Suicide—an inmate was found hanged on his knees with toilet paper stuffed in his mouth

- Death by carbon monoxide from a lawn mower—the lawn mower didn't work

- Death by carbon monoxide—no carbon monoxide was found in the person's blood

This coroner had served as president of the Ohio State Medical Association three years before his exposure.

Makes you wonder, doesn't it?

There are other types of medical blunders. A man entered a Tampa hospital to have his right foot amputated. He awoke after surgery to find that the surgeon had removed his left foot. In another hospital, a woman awoke from surgery to find that her surgeon had removed the wrong breast. And after the case of the wrong foot, in the same Tampa hospital, a respiratory technician was supposed to disconnect a man from a ventilator. The technician forgot to check the patient's identification, and disconnected the wrong patient, who died an hour later.

I trust that these surgeons and the respiratory technician will not be promoted. But that coroner did become president of the state medical association....

What do you think?

Based on an AP release, February 12, 1995.

The Example of Caesarean Sections

higher their profit. Consider our opening vignette: Do you think Kathie's physician created a crisis situation so that a caesarean would be "required" and she could earn a larger fee? It is unlikely. But some physicians are that crass, and they are eager to perform unnecessary surgery in order to increase their profits. As shown in Figure 10-2, in 1970 about 1 of 18 babies was delivered by caesarean section. Now the total is 1 of every 4 or 5.

Are U.S. women less healthy than they used to be, and therefore less able to deliver naturally? As there is no reason to make such an assumption, we must draw the conclusion that the increase in caesarean deliveries can be attributed to the medical profession. This conclusion is supported by the finding that the percentage of caesarean sections in some hospitals is *five* times that in other hospitals—and most of those are unnecessary (Kilborn 1988).

Being able to charge more for caesarean deliveries is just part of the picture. Many doctors also desire them because they allow the physician to be *in control* of the delivery process—to decide when babies will be born so that it will be at a time convenient for them, and they won't be called at midnight or 3 A.M. Because these

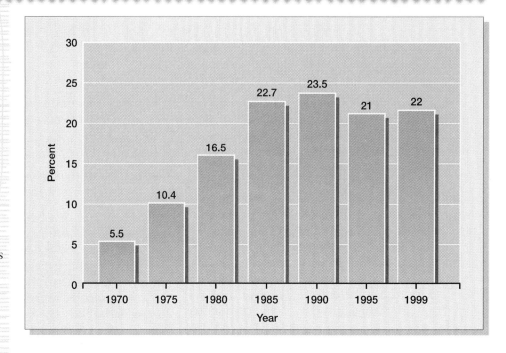

FIGURE 10-2
The Growth in Caesarean Births
These are caesarian births as a percentage of all births.
(*Source: Statistical Abstract* 1991: Table 91; 1998: Table 105; 2001: Table 81.)

births are designed to fit the physician's schedule, more births now occur on Tuesdays than any other day of the week.

You probably will not be surprised to learn that the income of obstetricians jumped as they performed more caesarean deliveries. You might be surprised, however, to learn that gynecologists (OB/GYN) see only slightly more patients per week than family doctors, internists, and pediatricians, but their income is higher than all of them. Their income has increased so much that it now almost ties that of surgeons (*Statistical Abstract* 2001:Table 157).

Today's medical care crisis has its roots in the rise of specialized medicine that occurred around 1900 (Stevens 1971; Rosenberg 1987). Specialization moved medical care from the home to the hospital, and encouraged a fascination with the latest medicines and techniques. Because specialized medicine is based on advanced training in research, it centers around medical schools. Because doctors prefer to practice

Part of our changing health consciousness includes changing attitudes toward the disabled—and the attitudes of the disabled toward themselves. Shown here is Franz Nietlispach of Switzerland as he breaks the finish line tape of the 102nd Boston Marathon, the men's wheelchair division.

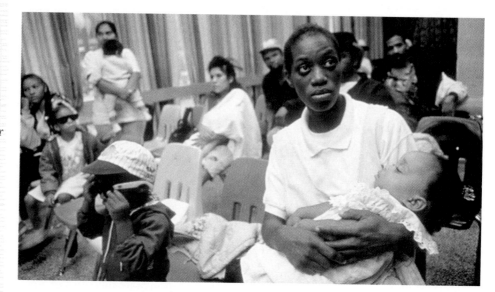

In the United States, medicine is a commodity to be sold. The result is a two-tier system of medical care—one for those who can pay, the other for those who cannot. Shown here is a waiting room for the poor. If the waiting room gets too crowded, these patients may have to return another day.

A Shifting Social Organization of Medicine

near these schools, physicians are clustered around cities with medical schools or research hospitals, while the inner cities and rural areas have a shortage of doctors.

With health care viewed as a commodity rather than a right, the United States has developed a **two-class system of medical care,** one kind for those who can pay and another for those who cannot. Julie Treadman, who was featured in the opening vignette of Chapter 7, was at the lower end of this two-tier system; she was refused admission to one hospital and transferred with her dead baby to another. Because we treat health care as a commodity to be sold to the highest bidder, our medical care ranges from the finest in the world at major universities to that provided by an underground network of unlicensed, foreign-trained physicians who can barely understand their patients and who have flunked their U.S. exams.

A Profound Consequence

◆ The Scope of the Problem ◆

ILLNESS AS A SOCIAL PROBLEM

The Nation's Health

How much illness is there in the United States? The answer depends on how we measure illness. One practical measure is the number of days that illness prevents people from carrying out their normal activities. For the average American, it is 15 days per year. As Table 10-2 shows, however, those days are not spread evenly throughout the population. They are higher for females and the elderly, and they are somewhat higher for African Americans. For the poor, they are almost *triple* those of higher-income Americans.

Measures of Health: 1. Life Expectancy

A key measure of a nation's health is life expectancy at birth. In the United States, this measure has been rising for a century and now stands at about 74 years for males and 80 years for females (*Statistical Abstract* 2001:Table 96). These are overall averages, but, as with so many other conditions in our society, life expectancy is related to income: Those with more money live longer. Men with a family income of $25,000 or more live six to seven years longer than men with family incomes under $10,000 (Pamuck 1998).

Table 10-2	Number of Days Americans Are So Sick That They Cut Down on Their Activities for More than Half a Day
Sex	
Males	12
Females	17
Age	
Under 65	12
65 and over	31
Ethnicity	
White	14
African American	16
Family Income	
Under $10,000	28
$10,000 to $20,000	21
$20,000 to $35,000	13
Over $35,000	10

Source: Statistical Abstract 2000:Table 211.

2. Infant Mortality

There is no question that women are the biologically stronger sex. From the beginning of life, more male fetuses than female fetuses are not healthy and naturally abort. At birth, girls have a better survival rate, and in every society of the world, women live longer than men. For every U.S. man who makes it to age 75, almost two U.S. women have survived. Yet U.S. women see doctors more often, averaging seven visits a year compared to five for men (*Statistical Abstract* 1998:Table 194; 2001:Table 159). Do women get sick more often than men? Or are men less likely to admit they are ill because illness does not fit some macho image? No one is sure.

While our life expectancy has been rising, our infant mortality rate has been falling. The *infant mortality rate* (of each thousand babies, the number who die before their first birthday) is one of the most accurate measures of a group's health conditions: It reflects the quality of nutrition, the health of mothers and babies, and the quality of health care. In 1960, the U.S. rate was 26 deaths per 1,000 babies. Now it is just 6.8 per 1,000 (*Statistical Abstract* 1990:Table 110; 2001:Table 104). As the Social Map below shows, however, infant deaths are not distributed evenly across the United States. Note how the states with the highest death rates cluster in the South, while those with the lowest rates cluster in the West. This, again, shows the *social* basis of health, illness, and even death.

FIGURE 10-3
Social Map: The Geography of Death: Infant Mortality Rates
(*Source: Statistical Abstract 2001:Table 104.*)

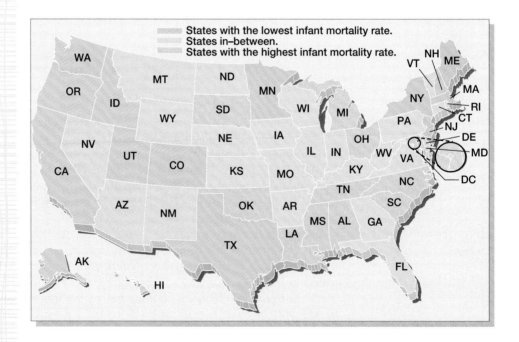

Considering that our life expectancy is increasing and our infant mortality decreasing, we can conclude that the United States has no *health* crisis. (It does have a *health care* crisis, however, which we shall discuss.) There are health problems, to be sure, and some are severe—cancer, drug abuse, AIDS, and suicide. Tremendous battles have been won against most infectious diseases, and many people survive cancer and AIDS. Overall, the nation's health has been improving.

All of the Least Industrialized Nations have a worse infant mortality rate and a shorter life expectancy than we do (*Statistical Abstract* 2001:Table 1330). Life expectancy in some of these nations is less than 50 years, and infant mortality rates run 15 to 20 times higher than ours. That life expectancy and infant mortality improve with industrialization is another example of how *social* conditions affect the *biology* of health.

So why is our infant mortality rate cause for concern? The reason becomes obvious when we compare our rates with those of other nations. Figure 10-4 shows that fifteen nations have a *better* record of saving babies than we do. The cold numbers in this figure translate into needless deaths. If our rate were the same as Sweden's, for example, 4 of every 10 of the 28,000 U.S. infants who die each year would live (*Statistical Abstract* 2001:Table 102). Our overall life expectancy (males and females combined) of 77.3 years is also less than in these fifteen nations (with the exception of Czech Republic and Portugal). Japan, with a life expectancy of 80.8 years, holds the world record.

Why are infant mortality and life expectancy rates better in other industrialized nations? The usual explanation is poverty, the many Americans who live on the edge

**FIGURE 10-4
Infant Mortality
Rates**
Infant deaths (babies who
die before one year of age)
per 1,000 live births in 12 industrialized countries.
(*Source: Statistical Abstract*
1998:Table 1345; 2001:Table 1330.)

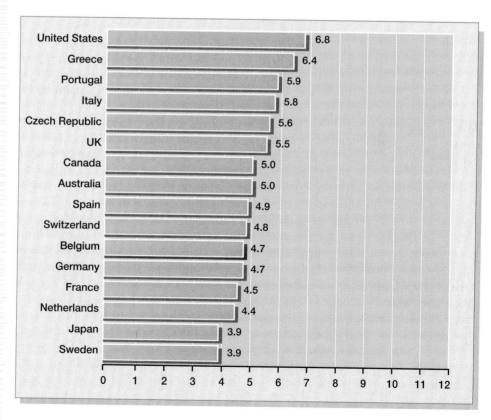

of survival. As we saw in Table 10-2, poor people are sick more often. They also experience more stress, have more emotional problems, suffer more accidents and violence, and don't eat as well. Poverty lies at the root of many health problems, and our advances in medical care are not reaching the poor to the same extent that they are reaching those who are better off.

Poverty vs. Lifestyle?

1. Refugees

While poverty is important, lifestyle is even more significant. Sociologist Ruben Rumbaut and geographer John Weeks (1994) were puzzled to find that poor immigrant women in California had a lower infant mortality rate than U.S.-born California women. Vietnamese and Cambodian refugees, for example, despite their much higher rates of poverty, unemployment, and welfare, had the lowest infant mortality rates. Rumbaut and Weeks found the *social* basis for these differences. The U.S.-born women gained more weight during pregnancy and were more likely to have abused drugs, including alcohol. Another major reason was that these women were more likely to have a "surgically scarred uterus" from abortion. The immigrant women had fewer abortions.

2. Utah and Nevada

No matter what one's social class is, lifestyle is a key factor in health. Let's look at Utah and Nevada, two adjacent states with similar socioeconomic profiles. Although these states have similar levels of income, education, medical care, urbanization, and even climate, Nevadans have higher rates of cancer and heart disease. They also are about twice as likely to die from lung diseases and suicide, and almost three times as likely to die from AIDS and murder (Centers for Disease Control 1994; *Statistical Abstract* 2001:Table 109). Nevadans even have more car wrecks. Lifestyle underlies these dramatic differences. The large Mormon population in Utah believes that it is sinful to use tobacco, alcohol, and even caffeine, or to have sex outside of marriage. The results show up in their health.

It is difficult to overstate the importance of lifestyle in determining health and illness, for *social and personal habits are the major causes of illness and death in our society.* To mention the most obvious offenses: Overeating and lack of exercise lead to heart disease and stroke. So does smoking, which also causes cancer. Prolonged, heavy consumption of alcohol scars the liver and harms other body organs. It also takes a toll on the nation's general health by being a factor in many violent crimes.

The Examples of Gonorrhea, Syphilis, and AIDS

Sexually transmitted diseases (STDs) are another obvious example of how lifestyle is related to health. Citizens of Utah, for example, have a low incidence of these diseases. To state the obvious: Singles who practice abstinence run zero risk of STDs, as do couples who have sex exclusively with one another. All others are at risk, but the risk increases with the degree of promiscuity and with unprotected sex. As with catching a cold, chance is also an important factor—being in the wrong place at the wrong time. Although the greater the promiscuity and unprotected sex, the greater the chances of contracting an STD, some who have come down with gonorrhea, syphilis, and even AIDS contracted it from their first sexual intercourse. We shall examine the relationship of AIDS and lifestyle later.

Another Example: Occupational Environmental Diseases

Polluted environments, as you know, are also sources of disease. Each year, 50,000 to 70,000 Americans die from cancer, lung disease, and neurological disorders that originate from their occupations or from pollution of the environment (Landrigan and Baker 1991). Some claim that this is just the tip of the iceberg. For example, during and after World War II, millions of Americans worked with asbestos; many of them have died or will die of cancer caused by asbestos dust. Hundreds of other substances also cause cancer many years after exposure, and we have not even identified many of these substances. Ironically, some asbestos substitutes also produce cancer (Meier 1987b).

Nor have we reached the end of the asbestos death trail. The rehabilitation and demolition of older homes with asbestos in their flooring, pipe coverings, and other materials expose a new generation of workers to this carcinogen. The scrapping of naval ships is especially troubling, for the sloppy way it is being done releases clouds of asbestos dust (Englund and Cohn 1997; Cohn 1998).

The Social Basis of Mental Disorders

Some researchers conclude that the incidence of emotional problems are increasing. If so, this probably reflects the higher stress and fewer social supports of modern life. Although emotional problems are called "mental illnesses," researchers usually can find no organic illness (Szasz 1961). **Psychoses,** emotional disorders so severe that people lose contact with reality and "go crazy," do not appear to have increased, but the milder forms of emotional problems, such as depression and anxiety attacks, have. Some even claim that neuroses are seven times more common than they were at the end of World War II. Maybe so, but in 1945 the mental health establishment was in its infancy, and since then it has expanded its definition of mental illness. Today, more behaviors are now labeled "illnesses" (Dohrenwend 1975).

Suicide is one of the more dramatic behaviors that are often taken as a sign of mental illness. We explore suicide in the Issues box on the next page.

Problems with Mental Health Care Delivery

Standing among the police, I watched as the elderly nude man, looking confused, struggled to put on his clothing. The man had ripped the wires out of the homeless shelter's main electrical box and then, with the police in pursuit, had run from one darkened room to another.

I asked the officers where they were going to take the man, and they replied, "To Malcolm Bliss" (the state hospital). When I commented, "I guess he'll be there for quite a while," an officer replied, "Probably for just a day or two. We picked him up last week—he was crawling under cars at a traffic light—and they let him out in two days."

The homeless have become a common sight in our major cities. Sociologists have documented the major avenues to homelessness, one of which is mental illness. Almost all the homeless are in need of medical attention, but few of their physical and mental needs are being met.

Suicide: The Making and Unmaking of a Social Problem

Suicide—deliberately drawing a razor blade across one's arteries, putting a gun in one's mouth and pulling the trigger, or swallowing a lethal dose of pills—chills the imagination. As sociologist Emile Durkheim (1897/1951) documented more than 100 years ago, suicide is more than individual inclination or a sign of personal problems. Suicide, concluded Durkheim, is based on social conditions, for countries have different suicide rates, and year after year a country's rate remains about the same. Look at Figure 10-5. From one year to the next, these rates show little change. You can expect about 31,000 Americans to kill themselves this year, and the next year, and the year after that (*Statistical Abstract* 1994:Table 125; 2001:Table 107).

For each American who commits suicide, about ten attempt it. Although many more women than men attempt suicide, more men than women succeed at it. This is likely because the women's attempts are more a "cry for help," while the men are more serious about accomplishing the act. In addition, men tend to choose methods that allow less intervention, such as guns, while women are more likely to use pills. The one provides less time to change one's mind or to allow someone to intervene. Year after year, suicide is the third most common cause of death of 15-to-24-year-olds. It used to rank second (just after accidents),

but it has been pushed a notch lower due to the rise in homicide (*Statistical Abstract* 1989:Table 118; 2001: Table 107).

Suicide illustrates the making and unmaking of a social problem. Until 1958, mental health professionals showed little interest in it, even though they were treating suicidal patients. Then around 1960, mental health professionals began to publicize the idea that suicide was a national problem. The National Institute of Mental Health (NIMH) took this to heart and began to finance an innovative idea—suicide prevention centers. The idea of swift intervention when people contemplate or attempt suicide was appealing, and across the nation suicide prevention centers were established to conquer this social problem.

They failed. The suicide rate didn't budge. The problem was that the centers had no new techniques for reducing suicide.

The major problem is not detecting suicidal intent, but managing patients known to be suicidal (Stone and Stein 1968). This is difficult. Psychiatrists receive inadequate training in how to treat suicidal patients, and they sometimes even contribute to suicide through a pattern of engagement and abandonment. The therapist initially responds with sympathy and concern, and the suicidal person begins to depend on the therapist as a helper. As treatment continues, the

---

A Two-Tier System

The police explained that to be admitted as a long-term patient one must be a danger to others or to oneself. Visualizing this old man crawling under cars in traffic and risking electrocution by ripping out electrical wires with his bare hands, I marveled at the definition of "danger" that the psychiatrists must be using.

Here in front of me, the two-tier medical system was stripped of its coverings. A middle-class or wealthy person would have received different treatment. Of course, such a person would not be in a shelter for the homeless in the first place.

Deinstitutionalization

Back in the 1970s, state mental hospitals began to discharge tens of thousands of seriously disturbed patients. The idea behind **deinstitutionalization** was that they could lead more normal lives in the community than they could in institutions. The plan was to support them with medications and community mental health services. To save money, however, few of the planned community centers were ever built. Most patients were simply left to fend for themselves. They ended up on the streets, living in run-down hotels when they could afford it or, often, in bus stations or cardboard boxes in back alleys. Some were sent back to mental hospitals when they

patient becomes more vulnerable, dependent, and demanding. Disliking this pressure, the therapist pulls back, calls the intense dependency "infantile regression," and becomes less accessible just when the patient is most vulnerable. Feeling abandoned, the patient commits suicide (Light 1973).

These treatment failures and the lack of new techniques kept the suicide prevention centers from fulfilling their optimistic promise. Gradually, suicide as a social problem faded from the limelight. The government reduced its funding, and most of the suicide prevention centers closed. Some kept their doors open by broadening their focus to general crisis intervention.

Suicide illustrates how social problems are socially constructed. As Figure 10-5 shows, our suicide rate is not exceptional. Compared with other industrialized nations, our rate falls in the lower third. Today's suicide rate is also about the same as it was in the 1960s and 1970s. (It was 11.6 in 1970.) Yet back then there was tremendous publicity about suicide, public outcry about the "epidemic" of suicide, and the invention of suicide prevention centers. With the same rate today, we no longer consider suicide a pressing social problem. The objective conditions did not change, just the subjective concerns. Suicide became a social problem because of political activity: Mental health professionals and government officials used the mass media to arouse the public.

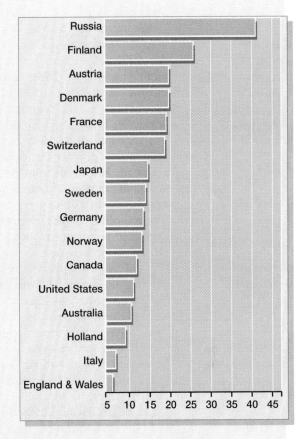

FIGURE 10-5
International Suicide Rates
(*Source: Statistical Abstract of the United States* 1998:Table 1348.)

lapsed into psychosis; others were left to wander the streets, no matter how bizarre their behavior.

The unfeeling, cruel way deinstitutionalization was carried out is illustrated by what occurred in Austin, Texas. Patients from the state mental hospital were loaded in a van and driven to Houston (so they wouldn't bother Austin residents). There they were dumped at the Greyhound bus station on skid row (Karlen and Burgower 1985).

Not everything about our mental health services is bad, of course, but the examples cited here represent part of a social problem.

A central problem is that we live in an age of *chronic* disorders (that is, they are lingering and ongoing), but our medical services are geared for *acute* illnesses (those that have a sudden onset, sharp rise, and short duration). Our approach to cancer, heart disease, and other chronic disorders is heroic, hospital-based, and expensive. Open-heart surgery is dramatic, but prevention is much more effective. We could save untold suffering and lives through public health measures against pollution, for

Problems with Physical Health Services

example, or by public campaigns against smoking. Such efforts, however, account for only a small fraction of what we spend on heroic measures to deal with health problems after people are stricken with them.

This emphasis on "heroic medicine" is expensive. Intervening at advanced stages of a disease requires technical equipment, rare drugs, medical teams, and highly trained specialists. Patients with serious illnesses want the best care, and the medical world has taught us that "the best" means complex, technical, and expensive. By promoting exotic "cures," companies that manufacture medical equipment and drugs feed this surge in cost.

Another problem is that this age of specialists and hospital care has led to a shortage of primary care doctors who treat routine problems. Consequently, for their basic medical needs some patients go to hospital emergency rooms, which stay open day and night and do not require an appointment. These services, however, are more expensive than office care; treating a fever or a splinter runs three to five times more. Insurance companies have rebelled at using hospital emergency rooms as doctors' offices and refuse to pay for such treatment. Patients now have to prove that their visit to an emergency room was an emergency.

Seizing the opportunity, our profit-oriented medical system made efficient marketing adjustments. Chains of "walk-in stations" appeared. Staffed by a rotating shift of private physicians, they are open at more convenient hours—in some instances day and night—and cost the same as a visit to a doctor's office. Their price and convenience have made them popular.

Health care remains a commodity to be purchased, not a citizen's right, however, and people without cash, a credit card, or a medical card are out of luck. Despite pretensions to the contrary, profits, not health care, are the engine that drives the U.S. health care system. One consequence is that the United States is the only industrialized nation without a national health insurance plan.

One final problem with the medical delivery system is the uneven distribution of medical services. In some areas, there is an abundance of physicians; in others it is difficult to find a doctor. At one extreme, Beverly Hills has one doctor for every 275 residents, while just down the road in Bell Gardens there is one doctor for every 27,000 residents, worse even than Haiti (Olivo 1999). The national distribution of physicians is shown on the Social Map on the next page.

◆ Looking at the Problem Theoretically ◆

SYMBOLIC INTERACTIONISM

Symbolic interactionists study how people use language and other symbols to define and alter social reality. As an example, we all self-diagnose; that is, we figure out what our symptoms mean. Should we go to bed, call a doctor, or just carry on? People from different social classes and subcultures make these decisions differently. For example, lower-class people are more likely to regard back pain as part of life, middle-class people to view it as a health problem that needs to be treated. Similarly, to many people cold or flu symptoms indicate a visit to the doctor, while to adherents of alternative medicine they indicate a need for drinking more water and taking more vitamin C and other antioxidants.

Just as social classes and subcultural groups perceive health and illness differently, so groups compete to get their view of health accepted. This, in turn, changes

The lowest third–145 to 197 doctors per 100,000 residents.
The middle third–198 to 226 doctors per 100,000 residents.
The highest third–227 to 686 doctors per 100,000 residents.

FIGURE 10-6
Social Map: Where the Doctors Are
(*Source: Statistical Abstract: 1998*)

the way we view "reality." For example, through the years the American Psychiatric Association listed homosexuality as a mental illness and had specialists who treated it. Homosexuals objected at being defined as ill, and through lobbying and other political pressure succeeded in getting the APA to drop homosexuality as a mental illness. Establishing definitions is a two-way street: Just as medicine and psychiatry can de-classify a behavior that had been considered an illness, so they can declare other be-haviors to be illnesses. Asserting that alcohol abuse is a disease (not "drunkenness") is an example, as is defining children's unruly behavior as a symptom of "attention deficit disorder" (see Chapter 4).

How Definitions Affect Perceptions

Definitions of health and illness have an impact on how we see the world and on our behavior. If alcohol abuse is defined as a disease, we perceive the sick person one way, but if it is defined as drunkenness, we perceive the drunkard another way entirely. The behavior that is thought appropriate in response to these definitions also changes—in the one instance, sympathy and help might be viewed as appropriate; in the other, condemnation or humor. As we saw with the example of homosexuality and the APA, symbols sometimes result from a political process. In short, definitions are not inherent in a behavior; they are, rather, symbols that affect how we view the behavior. They determine whether we view it as a problem or not, and what we think are appropriate ways to deal with it.

Why the Definitions of Physicians and Patients Clash

Symbolic interactionists analyze communications between doctors and patients. Eliot Friedson (1961) examined how patients and doctors use different frames of reference. Patients come from a **lay referral network,** a set of friends, relatives, neighbors, and coworkers with whom they have talked over their medical problems. This network helps them decide which doctor to see—or even whether to see a doctor at all. In this lay referral network, a physician's knowledge is considered important, but so is the physician's personality. People want someone who shows an interest in them; they don't want to be a faceless patient. Also important is the amount of confidence the doctor exhibits. People also want to be sure they won't come away empty-handed; getting a shot or a prescription is important, not just advice to get more rest or to go on a diet.

The physician, in contrast, uses a **professional referral network,** made up of other physicians and medical professionals. Here the meaning of "doing doctoring" is different, for medical schools put the emphasis on organs, symptoms, and diseases apart from the person. Sympathy for the patient and understanding an illness from the patient's point of view are less important than determining what and why some organ is malfunctioning and prescribing appropriate treatment (Haas and Shaffir 1993; Conrad 1995).

One consequence is that some doctors treat patients not as persons, but as objects with sick organs, a process referred to as **depersonalization.** Patients detest being depersonalized, for it strips away their humanity (Olivo 1999). To doctors who see patients as objects, the psychological and aesthetic costs of procedures are of little importance. This is what happened with Kathie Persall's caesarean, and it is one reason that midwifery has reemerged as an appealing alternative (Weitz and Sullivan 1986). Another consequence of depersonalization is a tendency to sue physicians, for it breaks a social bond between patient and physician. The threat of malpractice suits, in turn, has produced **defensive medicine;** that is, physicians order lab tests and consultations that may not be needed, in order to leave a "paper trail" that shows they did everything reasonable in case they are sued.

Problems in Communication

These different backgrounds and expectations of physicians and patients lead to problems in communication. In an age of specialized medicine characterized by brief encounters between people from different walks in life, doctors often fail to tend to the personal or emotional side of health problems. Their long, strange-sounding words often baffle patients:

> When Mrs. J., a 47-year-old Queens schoolteacher, was told in a routine examination that she had a "uterine fibroid" and needed a hysterectomy (removal of the uterus), the only thing she could think of was "tumor." She asked the doctor if it was cancerous, and he frightened her more by saying, "Sometimes when we go in we find them to be cancerous." Fearing cancer of the uterus, she consulted two other physicians and learned that the fibroid was small, common in middle-aged women, and soon likely to shrink as she went into menopause. (Larned 1977: 195–196)

On the lighter side, one patient was unhappy after being put on a low-salt diet. As if that weren't bad enough, when she was hospitalized she was further dismayed to find that she was also put on a low-sodium diet (Silver 1979:4).

FUNCTIONALISM

The Basic Question: Who Benefits?

Functionalists assume that customs or social institutions persist only if they fulfill important social needs. The functionalist perspective, then, raises some interesting questions. Whose needs are met by a health care system that is hospital-based and oriented toward acute illnesses? Who benefits from allowing occupational and environmental diseases to flourish? What are the benefits of depersonalizing patients such as Kathie Persall, of making childbirth a rigorous medical procedure?

How the Medical Profession Benefits

Let's start with the obvious: It is difficult for doctors to make money from healthy people. Patients who get well quickly also mean less profits. But an expensive, hospital-based system oriented toward acute illness—now that's a dream come

Chapter 10 Medical Care: Problems of Physical and Mental Illness

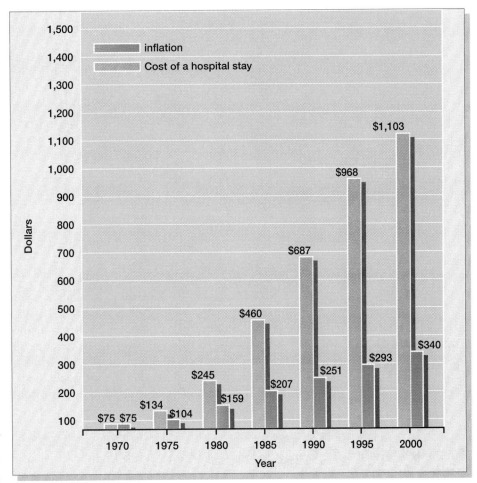

FIGURE 10-7
How Much Does It Cost to Stay in the Hospital? One Day's Cost Compared to Inflation

A comparison of the cost of all goods sold in the United States with an average per day cost of a hospital admission.
(*Source: Statistical Abstract of the United States* 1998:Table 137; 2001:Table 162.).

true. Everyone—physicians, medical suppliers, and drug companies—makes money from giving patients intensive care. Each year, about one of every eight Americans is admitted to a hospital and stays an average of six days. The average daily cost is shown in Figure 10-7. This figure also illustrates the skyrocketing cost of medical care better than words can say.

In our fee-for-service system, doctors sell their services. The more services they sell and the higher price they charge, the more they earn. One result is unnecessary surgery, such as the caesarean surgery mentioned earlier (see Figure 10-2 on page 324). Another example is hysterectomies, which we will review in the section on conflict theory.

How Patients Benefit

Physicians, nurses, and investors in the U.S. health care industry, then, benefit from our fee-for-service system. Patients benefit, too, however, for this system lets them shop around. They can choose which doctor to see and what service to purchase. That this system is functional for patients is indicated by our rising life expectancy and our decreasing infant mortality.

A Self-Correcting System

There are problems, of course, but functionalists point out that the system is self-correcting. For example, although the medical system is oriented to acute illnesses, after environmental health problems were recognized as serious, the government passed anti-pollution laws and formed the Environmental Protection Agency (EPA),

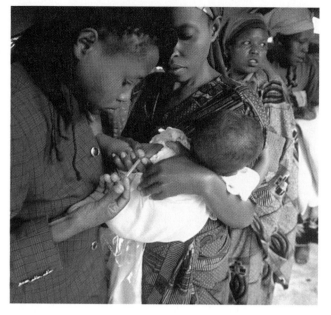

With the exportation of Western medicine to the Least Industrialized Nations, life expectancy there has increased dramatically. One reason for this change is a lower death rate of children. Shown here is a nurse in Rwanda, giving an injection to a baby.

and medical schools developed training programs in environmental medicine. Likewise, runaway costs have led to cost controls: HMOs (discussed later), new forms of medical care such as outpatient surgery, and limitations on the number of days Medicare and Medicaid pay for hospitalization. In short, functionalists regard health care as a system that responds to the shifting needs of the nation.

Global Functions and Dysfunctions

Functionalists also analyze functions and dysfunctions of medicine on a global level. Exporting modern Western medicine to the Least Industrialized Nations provides an excellent example. The vaccines, immunizations, and medicines were both functional and dysfunctional: They reduced those nations' death rates, but they also caused their populations to surge, outpacing their ability to grow food and leading to mass starvation and political upheaval.

CONFLICT THEORY

The Basic View of Conflict Theorists

Conflict theorists shake their heads in disbelief when they hear anyone refer to the U.S. medical system as self-correcting. They view our patterns of illness and health care as the outcome of clashes between interest groups—which the most powerful have won. They argue that the poor are sicker than others because they have lost the struggle for who will get the available income, wealth, education, food, housing, good jobs, and medical services.

How Conflict Theorists See Medicare and Medicaid

What about Medicaid, which benefits the poor? Conflict theorists see this program, too, as the result of conflict. A groundswell of resentment about the treatment of the poor forced politicians to do something. Sentiment toward socialized medicine had grown, and the American Medical Association (AMA) campaigned to preserve the fee-for-service system. Medicaid, then, was just a Band-Aid designed to prevent the profit system from being replaced with socialized medicine. To consider, as functionalists would, that Medicaid was passed because health providers saw that the poor needed free medical services is naive. It ignores the millions of dollars that the AMA spent lobbying to *prevent* this federally funded health insurance for the poor from becoming a reality.

Competing Interests of Doctors and Patients

Conflict theorists also take a different view of doctor-patient relationships. A Marxist perspective emphasizes how patients and doctors form two classes in regard to the means of production of medicine—those who control it and those who receive it. Physicians want to maximize their income, while patients want to get well with the least expense. To reach their goal, physicians try to maintain power by controlling their interactions with patients. Their common failure to explain procedures or diagnoses is no accident; it is a way of keeping the oppressed class of patients ignorant and dependent (Waitzkin and Waterman 1974). This is also why doctors often prolong a patient's uncertainty about a problem or its treatment. Alienation of patient and physician, like that of owner and worker, is an inevitable part of a system in which the interests of the one oppose those of the other.

The Exploitation of Women

Sociologists who have done participant observation of the practice of medicine report a bias *against* women's reproductive organs. Sociologist Sue Fisher (1986), for example, was surprised to hear surgeons recommend total hysterectomy (the removal of both the uterus and the ovaries) even when no cancer was present. She found that male doctors regard the uterus and ovaries as "potentially disease-producing" as well as unnecessary after the childbearing years, and that some surgeons routinely recommend this profitable operation for every woman who has finished bearing children. At a minimum, one third of all hysterectomies cannot be justified for medical reasons (Podolsky 1990). It is no wonder that feminists refer to hysterectomies as a "war on the womb" (Fisher 1986).

Many surgeons look at hysterectomies as a virtual money machine. To increase their profits, surgeons drum up business by "selling" the operation. Here is how one resident explained it to sociologist Diana Scully (1994):

> You have to look for your surgical procedures; you have to go after patients. Because no one is crazy enough to come and say, "Hey, here I am. I want you to operate on me." You have to sometimes convince the patient that she is really sick—if she is, of course [laughs], and that she is better off with a surgical procedure.

One way that surgeons convince a woman to "buy" the operation they are offering for sale is to say that her fibroids *might* turn into cancer. This statement is often sufficient, for it frightens the woman, who can picture herself lying in a casket, her tearful family inconsolable after the loss of their wife and mother. What the surgeon does *not* say is the rest of the truth—that the fibroids probably will not turn into cancer and that a variety of nonsurgical treatments are available.

The Larger Picture: The Exploitation of Illness

From a Marxist conflict perspective, the entire medical system is an industry whose goals are profit and power. To reach these goals, its practitioners exploit sick people (Reynolds 1973). Marxists argue that their perspective best explains why medical care for the rich is so much better than that for the poor: Health care is *not* the goal of the U.S. medical system; the goal is profit for those who practice it. Physicians are businesspeople, patients are customers, and health care is a commodity bought by those who can afford it. The government pays an increasing proportion of the nation's health care bill because government in a capitalist society perpetuates and underwrites the interests of capitalist industries—including medicine. Conflict theorists argue that health care should be a right of *all* citizens, and that illness should never be exploited for profit.

◆ Research Findings ◆

To help us understand these issues, we will concentrate on social inequalities of health and health care. After a brief look at physical health problems in the United States, we will discuss inequalities by age, race, and social class, highlight studies of occupational health problems, examine our two-class system of medicine, and consider how health insurance creates its own inequalities. Finally, we will discuss mental health problems.

Historical Changes in Health Problems

Figure 10-8 compares today's ten leading causes of death with those of 1900. As you can see, only five of the ten leading causes of death are the same. Most of today's top ten killers—heart attacks, cancer, lung diseases, accidents, and suicide—are caused by people's behavior or by environmental pollution. As a sign of changing times—and health—note that during the 1990s, murder edged into the top ten. It is still there, the tenth leading cause of death in the United States. These changes in leading causes of death over the past hundred years reinforce the point made earlier about how health and illness are related to lifestyle and the environment.

A Reduction of Infectious Diseases

Figure 10-8 also reveals how significant infectious diseases used to be. Pneumonia was the number one killer, with tuberculosis (TB) close behind. Every household also feared polio, whooping cough, German measles, smallpox, and diphtheria. Then, during the first half of the twentieth century, these diseases receded, death rates plummeted, and life expectancy rose from 47 years to over 70. What happened?

Why This Decline?

The usual answer is that modern medicine wiped out these diseases. I do not want to detract from the real accomplishments of modern medicine, for most of us know someone who would not be alive today if it weren't for bypass surgery. And drugs have played a significant role in treating some diseases, such as syphilis, bacterial pneumonia, and hypertension. And some vaccinations, such as the one for polio, have reduced deaths dramatically.

Most of the infectious killers of the nineteenth century, however, had been declining for decades *before* antibiotics, immunizations, or specific drugs had been developed (McKeown 1980). Although medical myth has it that new drugs and vaccinations conquered TB in the 1950s, as Figure 10-9 shows, TB had been declining since the 1800s. If modern medicine did not conquer the infectious diseases so feared by earlier generations of Americans, what did? The answer is not dramatic: cleaner public water supplies and improved social and economic conditions. Infectious killers declined as people became healthier and stronger from cleaner water, better and more food, and better housing.

The Return of TB

Infectious diseases, however, have a way of fighting back. They can go underground and develop new strains that are resistant to known drugs and vaccines. The Technology box on page 341 discusses worldwide implications of this problem. Even TB has resurfaced with deadly strains. More people around the world die of TB now than when the vaccine was discovered (Garrett 1999). Some strains have become resistant to *all* known treatment (Altman 1992a; Specter 1992). Health officials in New York City so fear the possibility of an outbreak of tuberculosis that they order the arrest of TB patients who refuse treatment or who terminate care before their course of treatment is completed. They lock these patients in hospital rooms where guards sit at their door every hour of every day (Specter 1992).

The most feared infectious disease today, however, is AIDS. Let's look at how AIDS is related to behavior.

HOW DISEASE IS RELATED TO BEHAVIOR AND ENVIRONMENT: THE CASE OF AIDS

The Social Basis of AIDS

AIDS is an excellent example of the relationship between behavior, environment, and disease. This disease was first noted in male homosexuals. One person, Gaetan Dugas, an airline steward from Canada, played a key role in its rapid transmission, for

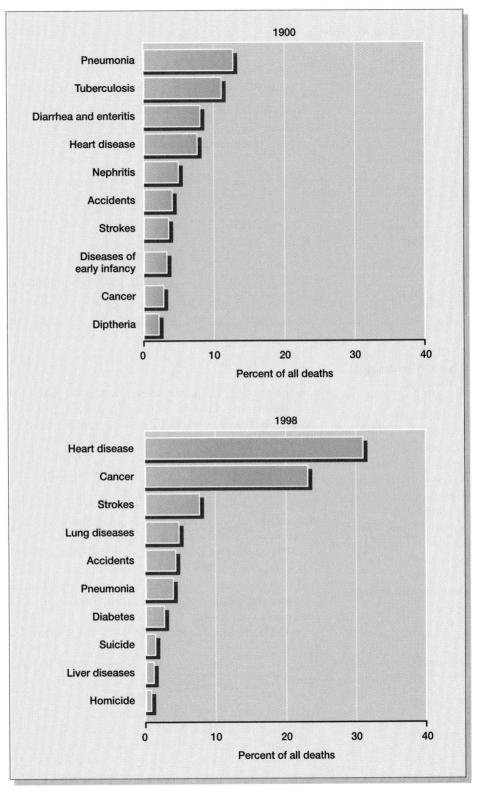

FIGURE 10-8
The Ten Leading
Causes of Death in
the United States
(*Source*: Rockett 1994; *Statistical
Abstract* 1998:Tables 138, 142;
2001:Table 107.)

Chapter 10 Medical Care: Problems of Physical and Mental Illness   **339**

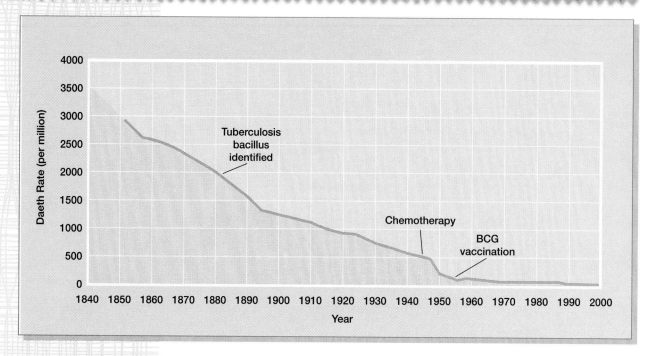

FIGURE 10-9

The "Conquest" of Tuberculosis

One of the greatest killers used to be tuberculosis, and many people believe that modern medicine "conquered" TB with the discovery of streptomycin in 1947 and a vaccine in 1954. In fact, the death rate for TB had been declining steadily for almost 100 years before these discoveries. Many other infectious diseases "conquered" by modern medicine follow a similar pattern. (*Source:* McKeown 1980; *Statistical Abstract of the United States* 1998:Table 139. Data from 2000 are the author's estimate.)

he or one of his sex partners had sex with 40 of the first 248 AIDS cases reported in the United States (Shilts 1987). The disease then hit another group whose lifestyle also encouraged its transmission—intravenous drug users who shared needles. The third of the groups that were the hardest hit represents an environmental risk: Hemophiliacs, who need regular blood transfusions, were exposed to the disease through contaminated blood. Lifestyle was also central to how the disease entered the general population; the bridge was prostitutes who had sex with intravenous drug users and with bisexual and heterosexual men. Lifestyle and environment continue to be significant: AIDS is more common among drug users who share needles and among people who have multiple sexual partners.

AIDS is a global epidemic, with millions of people around the world infected. Of all regions in the world, sub-Saharan Africa has been hit the worst. There, AIDS is the leading cause of death. In some African countries, AIDS is expected to wipe out half the teenagers (Nullis 2000). Hardest hit is Botswana, where about one of every three adults has AIDS (Will 2000).

The situation is quite different in the United States, where a combination of drugs, called protease inhibitors, has dropped AIDS deaths from a high of 50,000 in 1995 to under 16,000 now (Holmes 1998; *Statistical Abstract* 1998:Table 144; 2001:Table 105). The new drugs—at a cost of $20,000 per year per patient—prevent people who are infected with the HIV virus from developing full-blown AIDS and keep those who have the disease from succumbing to infections (such as the flu or pneumonia) that used to kill people with AIDS. The incidence of new infections has also dropped to half of what it was. But complacency seems to be growing among those groups most susceptible to AIDS. Researchers report an upsurge in unsafe sexual practices among gay men, for example (Holmes 1998; Maugh 1998).

TECHNOLOGY AND SOCIAL PROBLEMS

Superbugs in the Global Village

The retired detective came down with a fever, and he didn't want to eat, wash, or get dressed. His daughter took him to the hospital. He died a few hours later.

The outcome was not too unusual for a 79-year-old. But what happened next was. When a lab analyzed a vial of his blood, the doctor could hardly believe the results. Nothing would kill the staph infection in the deceased's blood, not even vancomycin, the antibiotic of last resort.

Japan reported another case, and others cropped up in France and England. Tests showed that the strains from these cases were not related to one another, and so far a worldwide outbreak of infections that are immune to every type of antibiotic has been avoided. Apparently the detective's strain of staph was buried with him.

But it is just a matter of time. At some spot in the world, someone else will come down with a germ that is resistant to every known antibiotic. With global travel, in just a matter of days that strain will spread throughout the global village.

The signs grow more ominous. A bacteria resistant to vancomycin has shown up in chicken feed. No one knows how this happened, but the fear is that it will be transmitted to chickens, then mutate to humans (Grady 1999).

Following the discovery of penicillin in the 1940s came a series of effective microbe killers. By the 1970s, more than 100 antibiotics sat on pharmacy shelves. The war against microbes had been won, or so the medical industry thought. Researchers relaxed, and stopped developing new antibiotics. Promising new drugs, already in development, were even canceled as superfluous.

In the presence of antibiotics, the weak germs die off, but strong ones can mutate, survive, and proliferate. This is especially likely to happen if people do not complete the full course of their medical treatment and stop taking a drug when they feel better. The more antibiotics are used and misused, the more drug-resistant bugs proliferate.

Are antibiotics misused? The Institute of Medicine reports that 20 to 50 percent of the 145 million prescriptions given to U.S. outpatients each year are unnecessary. The same goes for the 190 million doses of antibiotics given to hospital patients.

We all carry staphylococcus germs on our skin and nostrils. There they are harmless, but they wait for a chance to infect us through scrapes and cuts and surgical incisions. If our current, relatively mild staph are replaced by a mutant, virulent strain, simple cuts and scrapes could become mortal wounds. A sore throat could be fatal. Patients who go to hospitals for routine surgery might be carried out in coffins (Stolberg 1998).

This threat has broken through the apathy of the medical industry. Pharmaceutical firms are searching frantically for the next generation of antibiotics to fight the next generation of microbes. The race is close, and no one yet knows which will win.

If we win and are able to develop new antibiotics in time to prevent a global epidemic, will we then repeat this process—overprescribing, not completing the course of treatments—with the microbes again mutating and developing resistance to the new drugs?

Granted the notable folly of much of human behavior (and the institutional factors that promote it—especially a medical establishment eager for profits), I am certain that this is exactly what will happen. A sage once said that those who do not study history are doomed to repeat it. I would add that although we study history, and even know its lessons, in some instances we are still doomed to repeat it. This is one.

The HIV virus mutates rapidly, and medical researchers fear that the protease inhibitors may prove to be only a stopgap measure. Already some newly infected patients have contracted strains of HIV that are resistant to protease inhibitors (Kalb 1998). If drug-resistant strains become widespread, as is likely, the epidemic could surge again. Several new drugs, however, hold the promise of taking over where the protease inhibitors leave off.

Although African Americans make up just 12 percent of the U.S. population, they account for about 57 percent of all new HIV infections. A combination of reasons underlies this startling statistic. The first is cultural-behavioral: a disbelief that it can happen, a distrust of doctors, a reluctance to talk about it, lack of knowledge about its transmission, higher-than-average use of injected drugs, and reluctance to use condoms. The second is organizational: Most money for HIV prevention has bypassed African Americans, going instead to AIDS organizations with roots in the gay community (Stolberg 1998).

SOCIAL INEQUALITIES IN PHYSICAL ILLNESS

Poverty and Health

Let's look more closely at the social inequalities that underlie the U.S. health picture. From earlier chapters, especially Chapter 7 on wealth and poverty and Chapter 8 on racism, it should not surprise you to learn that economic factors largely determine who will be healthy and who will be sick. Poor children, for example, are more likely to be undernourished or to lack a balanced diet. As a result, they are more vulnerable to disease. As we saw in Table 10-2 (on page 326), the poorer people are, the sicker they are. Even their death rates are higher.

This takes us to the heart of the matter. *Social* inequality—the essential factor that underlies our patterns of disease and death—is seldom considered a problem for our health care system to deal with. Instead, our system focuses on acute health problems, patches people up, and sends them back to the same environment from which they came.

Occupational Health Problems

Occupational health hazards are also distributed unequally in society. For example, the workers in manufacturing plants, not the managers, are more likely to be exposed to dangerous working conditions and toxic chemicals. Some chemicals merely irritate the skin; others cause skin cancer or attack vital body organs. Carbon monoxide, mercury, and uranium destroy the kidneys; the ethers, chlorines, and the heavy metals invade the nervous system.

Machinery and equipment also can be harmful to health. The noise level of some factories causes hearing loss—for workers (bosses are usually sheltered behind protective partitions or in quieter buildings). Arc welding, lasers, and radar all produce radiation and damage the eyes. Increasingly considered a social problem, occupational illnesses will receive more attention in the future.

Paying the Bill: Inflation, Insurance, and Medicaid

Looking at who pays the medical bill helps to expose social inequalities of health care. Before today's patchwork insurance coverage, there were private facilities for those who could pay (considered "the worthy") and public hospitals and clinics for those who could not (considered "the unworthy") (Rosenberg 1987). Because medical students need patients to practice on and public hospitals provided them, some public facilities were affiliated with medical schools. The medical care at these facilities was often superior. On the whole, however, with the lowest salaries, the worst working conditions, and outdated equipment, public hospitals attracted the least qualified doctors and nurses. **Iatrogenesis,** injuries caused by medical care, was common, including death due to a low level of medical knowledge and incompetent physicians.

Before World War II, professional health care was still fairly primitive. Most health care took place at home, and doctors made house calls to supplement and direct home health care. Hospitals, which were considered a last resort, were feared places. They were known as "the place where people go to die."

After World War II, medical technology improved, and the costs of treating illness increased. Many middle-class people with serious health problems found that they could no longer afford hospital care. Coupled with the desire of physicians and hospital owners to have more income, this problem led to the creation of medical and hospitalization insurance. The idea spread, and such insurance eventually became a standard benefit for business and government employees. As a result, most working-class and middle-class people with steady jobs received medical care. The poor were still left out in the cold, with only charity facilities to draw on.

Unanticipated Consequences

Those who suffered the most health problems, the poor and the elderly, were passed over. In 1966, Congress tried to remedy this sorry situation by passing Medicaid for the poor and Medicare for the elderly. Neither is comprehensive or generous, but overnight these plans provided medical coverage for millions who needed it the worst. Because they did not control what health providers could charge, however, the cost of medical care rose rapidly. Soon people's out-of-pocket expenses were as much as they had been before these government programs.

As functionalists stress, human actions have unanticipated consequences. One of Medicaid's was that it undermined public hospitals. City and county officials figured that since the poor now had medical insurance, they no longer needed free facilities. Eager to save money, many cities and counties closed their public hospitals and clinics. This left many of the poor in the lurch; because Medicaid's rates were low, many doctors and private hospitals refused to accept Medicaid patients. The working poor have been especially hard hit—their income is so low that they cannot afford to buy insurance, but not so low that they qualify for Medicaid. 15.5 percent of the nation, or about 42 million people, have no health insurance (*Statistical Abstract* 2001:Table 144).

Race/Ethnicity and Insurance

Lack of medical insurance highlights the racial-ethnic inequalities that run throughout U.S. society. Since African Americans and Latinos have a larger proportion of working poor, they are more likely to lack medical insurance. While 14 percent of whites are not covered by insurance, the rate for African Americans is 21 percent, and for Latinos 33 percent (*Statistical Abstract* 2001:Table 144).

SOCIAL INEQUALITIES IN MENTAL ILLNESS

Social Class and Mental Health: Consistent Findings

Do some social classes have more emotional problems than others? This intriguing question has a consistent answer. Since 1939, sociologists have found that people's emotional well-being gets worse as you go down the social class ladder. Those in the lower social classes are more likely to be depressed, anxious, nervous, and to have phobias. (In sociological parlance, this is known as an "inverse correlation between mental problems and social class.") This finding has been confirmed in numerous studies (Faris and Dunham 1939; Hudson 1988; Ortega and Corzine 1990; Lundberg 1991; Miller 1994b; Lynch, Kaplan, and Shema 1997).

The Midtown Manhattan Project

The term *mental illness* is so imprecise, however, that we have to be suspicious of what is being measured. For example, experts disagree about when to apply labels such as "schizophrenic" or "depressive." One of the best studies was carried out by sociologist Leo Srole and his colleagues at Columbia University in 1978. In what is known as the Midtown Manhattan Project, the Srole team developed its own scale of symptoms, trained its own interviewers, and then interviewed a representative sample of New Yorkers. As shown in Figure 10-10, these researchers also found that the poor have more emotional problems.

Four Explanations of the Greater Emotional Problems of the Lower Classes

Why do the poor suffer more mental disorders than people in other classes? According to the *drift hypothesis,* people with emotional difficulties tend to be less successful in life, so they drift from higher-income families down into the lower classes (Fox 1990). According to the *genetic hypothesis,* genes cause schizophrenia, manic depression, and other severe disorders. Therefore, the poor have more of these genes. Why should this be? The answer is provided by the drift hypothesis: Even if these genes once were distributed evenly among the social classes, many of those with them would drift downward, leaving a disproportionate number of poor families with these traits.

According to a third explanation, the *socialization hypothesis,* children who are reared by disturbed parents are more likely to learn pathological ways of coping with the world. They are less equipped to deal with the challenges of education and career. Those in the higher classes who are reared in such homes drift to the lower classes, while lower-class children from such homes remain in the lower class.

The genetic explanation for the most severe disorders, such as schizophrenia and manic depression, is influential in the medical community. But since the family that rears the child is usually the biological family, it is difficult to separate the genetic influences from the effects of socialization. To try to do so, researchers have studied identical twins who have been reared in different families. They have found them to have more mental problems than fraternal twins who were reared in the same family. They conclude that their research validates the genetic hypothesis. Social psychologist Leon Kamin (1981), however, who reviewed the data that "prove" that a recessive gene causes schizophrenia, found so many methodological problems that he concluded the research is worthless.

Sociologists prefer an explanation called the *environmental hypothesis.* Here the focus is on how the environments of the social classes differ. Let's rephrase the basic finding that the lower classes have more "mental illnesses": Another way to say this is

FIGURE 10-10
Social Class and Mental Problems: The Impaired/ Well Ratio

In a study of mental health problems among adults between ages 20 and 59, the ratio of people seriously impaired by their symptoms to people with no symptoms increased sharply for those who grew up in the poorer classes. Number 1 is the wealthiest, number 6 the poorest.

(*Source:* From Leo Srole et al., *Mental Health in the Metropolis: The Midtown Manhattan Study.* Copyright © 1978 by Leo Srole. Reprinted with the permission of Esther Srole.)

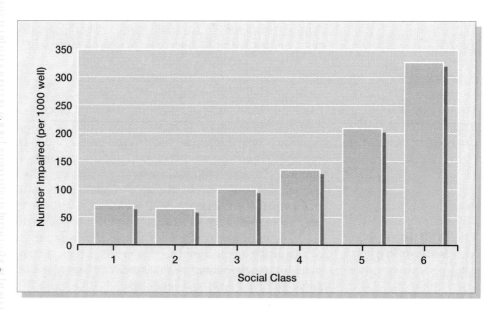

A form of Western medicine is talk therapy; that is, troubled individuals talk to a counselor or therapist about their problems. In spite of its cost, there is no evidence that talk therapy is any more effective than talking to a friend or neighbor.

that the social classes that are better off financially are happier, less depressed, less filled with anxiety, and less phobic (that is, they have fewer fears). In short, they are "mentally healthier." And why wouldn't they be? For them, life is better—less "nasty, brutal, and short." People who are in the middle classes and above have better job security, finances, physical health, and marriages. Not only do they have greater security at the present time (not absolute security, of course, but much greater security than the poor have), but they also have hope for the future. They realistically plan and look forward to a larger house, better cars, more exotic and longer vacations, their children's college, and a relaxing, enjoyable retirement. Of course, sociologists say, their mental health is better. Why would anyone expect anything less?

Compare this situation with the stress-filled package that comes with poverty: less job security, lower wages, more unpaid bills, trouble paying the rent and insistent bill collectors; more divorce, alcoholism, and violence; and even greater vulnerability to crime combined with worse physical health and less access to good medical care. Such conditions certainly deal severe blows to people's emotional well-being.

To be fair (and my bias as a cultural sociologist certainly shows up here), as with some of the materials we covered in the preceding chapter, environment versus heredity must remain an open question.

Therapies in Health Care

In order to understand how mental health services are related to social inequality, let's consider types of therapy and health care institutions. In **individual psychotherapy,** a therapist listens and guides the patient toward a resolution of emotional problems. A type of psychotherapy is **psychoanalysis,** which Sigmund Freud pioneered as a way to uncover the unconscious motives, fantasies, and fears that shape people's neurotic behavior. The patient meets an analyst several times a week and talks about whatever comes to mind, while the analyst listens for hidden patterns, particularly those that reveal crucial experiences in early childhood. More common is **short-term directive therapy,** in which a counselor focuses on current situations in order to help clients understand their problems. In **group therapy,** a group of patients, with the guidance of a therapist, help each other to cope with their problems.

Drug therapy, the use of tranquilizers, antidepressants, and antipsychotic drugs to relieve people's problems and help them cope with life, is another option. As with Prozac (discussed in Chapter 4), some of these drugs have serious side effects. Drug therapy is often criticized for being a way to treat the symptoms of troubled people without ever getting at their underlying problems.

In some cases, especially depression, **electroconvulsive therapy (ECT)** (also known as electroshock therapy) is used. Wires are attached to either side of a patient's skull, and low-voltage electric shocks are sent repeatedly through the brain. A side effect is memory loss. I used to be a student worker at Renard Hospital in St. Louis, an expensive, private mental hospital affiliated with Washington University Medical School. Occasionally, I held patients down during ECT treatment. I vividly recall how they convulsed wildly as the electricity coursed through their brains, and how disoriented they were afterward.

Again—the Ability to Pay

The type of therapy a troubled person is likely to receive does not depend on the person's problems, but on the ability to pay. Those who have money and good insurance are more likely to be guided through their problems with **talk therapy**—psychotherapy, group therapy, and so on. "Talk" therapy is expensive, and it would be a rare instance in which a poor and uninsured person receives it. The poor and uninsured are likely to receive no help at all. When they do receive help, they are likely to be given drug therapy, which has been called the new "pharmaceutical straitjacket." (The drugs given in mental hospitals make patients drowsy, lethargic, and easier to handle. They also often make them confused.)

A Surprising Statement

It is difficult, however, to say that these patterns of therapy and social class represent inequality: *We do not know which therapies work.* Costly psychoanalysis may be no more effective than drug therapy or even no therapy at all. It may even be less effective. Consequently, we cannot say whether the poor are receiving worse—or better—treatment for their emotional problems. The rigorous studies that demonstrate the effectiveness of therapy are yet to be done. An emerging type of therapy, described in the Technology box on the next page, is also likely to remain unexamined and unproven.

A Two-Tier System

Health care facilities for treating mental illness used to parallel the facilities for treating physical problems: public hospitals for the poor and private hospitals or office visits for the affluent. The state and county hospitals had so many patients and so little money that thousands of patients languished in back wards, where they were driven as crazy by the disturbed people around them and the stark rooms they called home as they were by their own inner turmoil. Few received anything that could be called treatment.

With deinstitutionalization, described earlier in this chapter, the population of state and county mental hospitals shriveled. Although such places now offer short-term treatment and outpatient services, they still warehouse chronic patients who cannot cope in other environments.

How Nursing Homes Replaced Mental Hospitals

As with physical illness, forms of payment shape what happens in the care of mental illness. Medicare allowed the states to transfer the cost of treating the poor to the federal government. Because many of these patients were elderly and qualified for nursing homes, a new dimension of health services came into being. As psychiatrists Fritz Redlich and Stephen Kellert (1978:24) put it:

> Nursing homes have been referred to (not incorrectly) as decentralized back wards, providing primarily custodial care to many former mental patients. The primary force behind the change was not an improvement in therapy . . . but Medicare legislation.

In Sum

In conclusion, social inequalities in the treatment of mental problems continue, but today far more services are available over a wide range of facilities. As with physical illness, the working poor are less likely to receive mental health services.

TECHNOLOGY AND SOCIAL PROBLEMS

Cyberbabble, Cybershrinks, and Cybershams

As the text makes clear, the effectiveness of therapy is questionable. Talking to a friend or clergy (or your mother-in-law, for that matter) may be as effective (or ineffective) as psychotherapy. Talking, in other words, may be helpful regardless of who the listener is. It is more pleasant to have a supportive, sympathetic, and understanding listener than someone who challenges what you say—but even that this kind of listener is more effective in helping with problems has not been demonstrated.

Email therapy has now made its appearance; patient and therapist send electronic messages (email) back and forth. Some therapists offer a one-shot deal for just $20. Others exchange email for $100 a month or more (Millar 1997). Some therapists and patients use chat rooms. Others add video links so they can see each other. Some sell their virtual couches for $2.50 a minute (Cohen 1997).

Cybertherapy offers an advantage that the telephone does not: Time zones make no difference. Patients traveling around the world can zap off an email whenever they like without waking the therapist in the middle of the night.

Presently, cyberbabble is unregulated. Anyone can claim to be a counselor and seek online patients. But not for long. Respectability and control are on their way. The American Psychological Association is setting up guidelines, and California requires that insurance companies pay for online therapy (Cohen 1997).

Does cyberbabble work? No one knows. But, then, no one knows if other forms of therapy work either. So the therapists might as well collect fees this way as any other. And they don't even have to leave home. Quite a deal.

◆ Social Policy ◆

Forces Pushing Up Costs

We have reviewed major conditions that have pushed up the cost of health care. The fee-for-service system encourages physicians to sell specialized services and to get patients to come back for visits. Doctors who are paid for every office visit, whether a visit is necessary or not, tend to encourage visits rather than dissuade them or practice preventive medicine. Focusing on acute problems is also profitable for hospitals, which get most of their added costs reimbursed. With depersonalization breaking bonds between physician and patient, and living in a litigious society, patients are more likely to look for reasons to sue. Expensive malpractice insurance further drives up costs. Overall, concentrating on disease intervention is more expensive and less effective than prevention. Let's look at policies that address these basic forces.

BEING PAID TO STAY HEALTHY

Some employers give their workers a rebate for staying healthy—or at least for staying away from doctors. In return for a higher insurance deductible, such as $1,000 a year, employees who spend less than the deductible are paid the difference. Workers who spend only $100 collect $900, which is a nice bonus. Where this program has been tried, employee health costs go down. As one teacher said, "Before, I kind of overdid it. Now I feel I have an investment in my own health."

HMOs

In the best-known type of prepaid medical care, the **health maintenance organization (HMO)**, a medical corporation (sometimes owned by physicians) bids to take care of the health needs of a business's employees. The firm pays a set fee for each employee. If an employee's health care costs amount to more than this fee in one year, the medical corporation loses money; if it costs less, it makes money. Because the corporation receives no more than this annual fee, its directors are motivated to reduce medical costs. Doctors, who are paid annual salaries, may receive bonuses for reducing patient cost. They try to strike a balance between ignoring trivial and self-limiting disorders and giving good health care. They especially want to treat medical problems before they become more serious and their remedy grows expensive. Where fee-for-service doctors are happy to charge $35 each time a patient runs to them with the sniffles, and will hold their hands for a few minutes and prescribe the same medication that is available over the counter, HMO doctors don't feel the same way about the matter.

To reduce costs, HMOs encourage preventive medicine. The doctors make more money if they can teach patients to stay well, to adopt a lifestyle that improves health—based on better diet, exercise, rest, and avoiding excessive usage of drugs, including alcohol. Unnecessary tests, surgery, and hospital admissions also represent a loss to the physicians and medical corporation, so they avoid them. For the same reason, they also minimize the length of hospital stays. The reduction in costs can be dramatic, as HMO patients have less surgery and hospitalization than fee-for-service patients (Robinson 1991; Ward 1991; Winslow 1995b).

A Conflict of Interest

The built-in conflict of interest should be obvious. The physician's dilemma: Profits or patient care? An unintended consequence of avoiding hospitalizing patients and conducting expensive tests or treatments is that some *necessary* treatments, tests, and hospitalizations are withheld. For example, a woman I know was sent home from the hospital even though she was still bleeding from her surgery. If she had remained longer, she would have used up more than her "share" of allotted costs and eaten too greatly into the corporation's profits. This would not have happened to a fee-for-service patient.

Limiting Doctors

Physicians are chafing at HMOs. Their two major concerns are loss of autonomy and reduced quality of health care. Doctors have to call their HMO for permission to give certain treatments. This puts the HMOs in the position of dictating to doctors what treatment they can give their patients (McGinley 1999). ("You can do that if you want, but we won't pay for it.") Some HMOs even determine how many patients the doctors are to see each day. One HMO, for example, insisted that its physicians see eight patients an hour, limiting them to $7\frac{1}{2}$ minutes per visit. This did not leave the doctors enough time for completing paperwork, analyzing lab results, and, of course, for calling HMO officials to get approval for treatments (Greenhouse 1999).

The problems are making the news. A mother tried to get her HMO doctor to refer her toddler to a specialist because of a persistent ear infection. She succeeded—after a year (Kilborn 1998). A physician recalls how he fought with his HMO for three hours to get permission to do a procedure. The HMO officials kept refusing, even though the woman was coughing up life-threatening amounts of blood (Steinhauer 1999). The doctor of the acquaintance I mentioned (the one who was sent home from the hospital still bleeding) may have wanted her to remain until she was well, but could not receive approval from the HMO he was working for.

PHYSICIAN EXTENDERS

Delegating Responsibility

Another strategy for controlling costs is **physician extenders,** doctor's assistants who perform primary care services. Half to three quarters of all problems dealt with in a typical doctor's office are medically trivial, and physician assistants and nurses can provide much of this medical care and educate patients with chronic disorders. To delegate routine and time-consuming responsibilities to assistants makes more sense than making sure everyone who has the sniffles is seen by a physician whose job requires twenty-three years of education and commands one of the highest salaries of any occupation.

Conflict with Doctors

The use of physician extenders has led to a rivalry, however, and the first volleys in a battle over turf have been fired. Physician extenders must work under the supervision of physicians, but they don't like doctors breathing down their necks. They want to be able to give more independent care, but their efforts at greater autonomy have been met with hostility from doctors (Aston and Foubister 1998). At this point, the attitude of the medical profession is, "If they want to do more, they can go to medical school."

TRAINING PHYSICIANS

Closing the Gender Gap

Medical schools graduate about 15,000 physicians a year, the same now as they did in 1980 (*Statistical Abstract* 2001:Table 289). As Figure 10-11 shows, a startling change has occurred in the gender makeup of those graduates: In 1960, only 6 percent of medical school graduates were women. Today about 43 percent are women.

FIGURE 10-11
Social Map: M.D. Degrees, by Sex
Asterisk indicates the author's estimate.
(*Source: Statistical Abstract of the United States* 1994: Table 295; 2001:Table 289.)

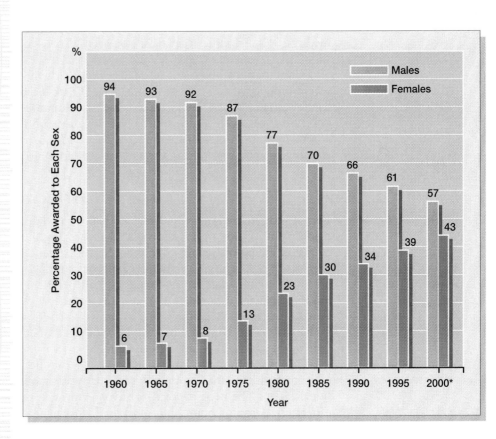

Will Gender Change Make a Difference?

It is doubtful that this change will have any significant affect on how medicine is practiced. The system is in place, the characteristics we reviewed are firm, and gender is mostly irrelevant. Women doctors are as likely as men doctors to be generous or greedy, patient- or profit-oriented, in favor of heroic medicine or preventive medicine, with a preference for fee-for-service or socialized medicine, and so on. Such orientations are consequences of core values in the general society and of those promulgated in medical schools. Gender does not make someone lean in one direction or the other.

Breaking a Monopoly and Getting Medical Care to the Poor by Purposefully Overproducing Doctors

A social policy that might reduce costs and help get doctors to the poor, where they are needed the most, would be to overproduce physicians. The government could encourage the opening of new medical schools (finance, approve, and even give tax breaks to investors) and subsidize more medical students. I suggest that we modify a system that Mexico has. Students could go to medical school free of charge (and even receive a small monthly stipend) in return for spending a specified amount of time in areas where there is a doctor shortage. I suggest the new physicians be required to give four years back for the eight that they spend in medical training. If they refused, they would not be given their final certification. During those four years, the government would fund their medical malpractice insurance and pay them a salary equal to the net average earnings of beginning general practitioners.

This would not only help solve the problem of getting doctors to the areas where the need is greatest, but it also would produce several other positive factors. As more doctors graduated, patients would have a greater choice of physicians. Competition among doctors would increase, and if market forces had their way, the rise in medical costs would slow. The waiting period in doctors' offices would lessen as overcrowding and overscheduling decrease. As word gets around and patients have more alternatives, the most incompetent physicians should be driven out of medicine. Communities that have not been able to lure a physician to their town should also be able to recruit resident physicians.

The outcry of physicians to such a proposal would be loud, for their income would drop as prices for their services fell. The physicians' labor union (or more accurately, their business organization), the American Medical Association, would mobilize to fight such a proposal. Currently, by controlling the nation's medical schools, the AMA limits the supply of physicians, guaranteeing high medical costs. An oversupply is not in the interest of this powerful monopoly.

OUTREACH SERVICES

Home Health Care

Because hospitalization is expensive and many hospital stays are unnecessary, they are being replaced with outreach services whenever possible. **Home health care,** for example, is less expensive and often more humane than care that is available in nursing homes and hospitals. Many elderly people are put in nursing homes not because they are ill but because they can no longer live independently at home. Home health care lets them remain at home, in the environment they are used to and that they prefer. On the negative side, home health care encourages profiteering. For instance, a home health care company may pay its workers $10 an hour to care for the homebound, yet charge Medicare $25 an hour and pocket the difference.

Community Health Care

Outreach programs for the mentally ill can be improved. We can provide ex-mental patients the community care that was supposed to accompany deinstitutionalization. The need is great, as anyone who takes time to talk to the homeless can attest. Group homes and supervised apartments can be established for the

mentally disturbed, the mentally handicapped, and the chronically ill who have difficulty living in the community on their own.

The "Worthy" versus the "Unworthy"

Such programs are costly, of course, but cost is not the primary obstacle. If we refer to a "worthy" group, such as wounded veterans, hardly anyone objects. But if we suggest establishing such services for the homeless, who are viewed as "unworthy," the objections are never-ending. Obviously, it is not the cost, but the beneficiaries, that are people's concern.

PRACTICING PREVENTIVE MEDICINE

The American Medical Association found that *most* deaths of Americans under the age of 65 are preventable (Dandoy 1990). Accordingly—and because it senses profit—the AMA has begun to stress preventive medicine.

Three Types of Prevention

Preventive medicine sounds ideal as a way to ensure good health and reduce medical costs, but how do you put it into practice? Health planners distinguish among three types of prevention. **Primary prevention,** such as improved nutrition and childhood vaccinations, keeps a disease from occurring in the first place. **Secondary prevention,** such as self-examination for breast cancer, involves detecting a disease before it comes to the attention of a physician. **Tertiary prevention** is not very different from medical care. It means to prevent further damage from an already existing disease. Examples are controlling pneumonia so that it does not lead to death, and maintaining a diabetic on insulin.

Lifestyle

Primary prevention is promising because proper nutrition, exercise, not smoking, and so on can prevent disease before it ever occurs. For example, only about 15 percent of people who get lung cancer are nonsmokers. A diet rich in beta carotene, raw fruits and vegetables, and vitamin E supplements reduces this risk of cancer. Wheat bran, canola oil, soy milk, cantaloupe, avocados, olive oil, and green vegetables such as cabbage also appear to reduce the risk (United Press International 1998). And those leafy green vegetables that are hardly anyone's favorite—broccoli, brussel sprouts, and spinach—also seem to fight cancer.

Bovine Growth Hormones

Milk, however, may increase the risk of cancer (Mayne et al. 1995). This may be due to the pesticides and herbicides in the cows' fodder. Milk from cows that have been given hormones to promote their growth has become a matter of international controversy. European researchers claim that bovine growth hormones pave the way for cancer by inhibiting the body's natural cancer fighters (Epstein 1999). Some researchers accuse Monsanto, a global corporate giant, of caring more about profits than people's health. To this some reply with a yawn, "Big surprise."

Immunizations

Childhood immunizations, too, are effective. Although they cost only pennies, they save human lives as well as vast sums that would have been spent on medical care. Yet about one of five U.S. children has not been immunized against measles, tetanus, diphtheria, hepatitis, and polio (*Statistical Abstract* 2001:Table 182). For many rural and poor areas, the figure is worse. In China, which is poor and which has a population of more than a billion people, 95 percent of children are immunized. As the Global Glimpse box on the next page makes clear, however, the Chinese medical system is woefully inadequate.

Drug Abuse and Homicide

Although not usually thought of in these terms, no program of preventive medicine would be complete unless it also tries to prevent drug abuse and homicide. From what we learned in Chapters 4 and 5, to reduce drug abuse is to prevent many serious health problems, and to prevent the untimely deaths of many inner-city youths. Drug abuse programs, then, are one way to improve the nation's health.

A GLOBAL GLIMPSE

Health Care in Sweden, Russia, and China

To understand our own social policy, it helps to examine health care in other nations. The following countries illustrate contrasting themes in health care around the world. Looking at health care in Sweden, Russia, and China helps us place the U.S. medical system in cultural perspective (Henslin 1999).

HEALTH CARE IN THE MOST INDUSTRIALIZED NATIONS: SWEDEN

Sweden has the most comprehensive health care system in the world. National health insurance financed by contributions from the state and employers covers all Swedish citizens and alien residents. The government pays most physicians a salary to treat patients, but 5 percent work full time in private practice (Swedish Institute 1990). Except for a small consultation fee, medical and dental treatment by these government-paid doctors is free. The state also pays most of the charges of private physicians. The government reimburses travel expenses for patients and for the parents of a hospitalized child. Only minimal fees are charged for prescriptions and hospitalization.

Medical treatment is just one component of Sweden's broad system of social welfare. For example, people who are sick or must stay home with sick children receive 90 percent of their salaries. Swedes are given parental leave at the birth of a child, and are guaranteed a pension.

Sweden's socialized medicine is also inefficient. Swedes have not solved the twin problems of getting rid of waiting lines and getting physicians to work. With salaries of medical personnel guaranteed, regardless how many patients they see, the system has poor productivity. When reporters visited Sweden's largest hospital on a weekday morning, when 80 of 120 surgeons were on duty, they found 19 of 24 operating rooms idle. Their photos of empty operating rooms—at a time when there was a one- to two-year waiting period for hip replacements and cataract operations—provoked a public outcry (Bergström 1992). Due to public pressure and an emphasis on accountability, efficiency is improving (Hakansson 1994).

HEALTH CARE IN THE INDUSTRIALIZING NATIONS: RUSSIA

As I write this in 1999, Russia is in disarray. Its economic-political system is on the verge of collapse. It can't pay its debts, and it barely is being kept afloat by emergency loans from the World Bank—and this only because the Most Industrialized Nations fear a nuclear holocaust should Russia step into the brink of anarchy.

Russia's health care system is similarly in tatters. Under the communists, Russia had established a system that made health care available to most. Like the rest of the nation's production, the health care system was centralized. The state owned the medical schools and determined how many doctors would be trained in what specialties. The state paid medical salaries, which it set, and determined where doctors would practice.

Under Russia's fitful, torturous transition to capitalism, its health care system has fallen apart, and the health of the population has declined. An example is Moscow's ambulance system. It used to be efficient—dial 03 and an ambulance would arrive within minutes. Now an ambulance sometimes takes eight to twelve hours to arrive because drivers are using the ambulances as free-lance cabs, and they keep emergency cases waiting (Field 1998).

The only hospitals comparable to those of the United States are reserved for the elite (Light 1992). In the rest, conditions are deplorable. Patients must bring their own linens, medicines, and syringes with them to the hospital. Doctors are paid about $35 a month, and may go unpaid for six months at a time (Paddock 1999). Surgical scalpels are resharpened until they break. Sometimes even razor blades are used for surgery (Donelson 1992). Some hospitals do not even have a doctor on staff. Outdated and broken equipment is not replaced. Some doctors face the choice of operating without anesthetic or not operating at all (Paddock 1999).

Perhaps no event more pinpoints the disarray than this:

Three patients lay unconscious in the intensive care unit, kept alive only by the Siberian hospital's life support system. Two were elderly; one was 39.

On Wednesday, the hospital received a telegram from the local power company: "You haven't paid your bill for five years. You owe us $94,931. Pay up, or we'll shut off your electricity." The next morning, at 6 A.M., the company shut off the power. Forty minutes later, all three patients were dead. (Paddock 1999)

The years of environmental degradation under the communists have also taken their toll. Serious birth defects have jumped to four times the U.S. rate. A likely culprit is radiation pollution from decades of nuclear irresponsibility (Spector 1995). Perhaps the single best indicator of the deterioration of health is the drop in life expectancy that began in the 1960s and continues today (Cockerham 1997). As shown in Table 10-3, the health of Russians is closer to that of China than to the Most Industrialized Nations.

HEALTH CARE IN THE LEAST INDUSTRIALIZED NATIONS: CHINA

Because this nation of 1.2 billion people has a vast shortage of trained physicians, hospitals, and medicine, most Chinese see "barefoot doctors," people who have only a rudimentary knowledge of medicine, are paid low wages, and travel from village to village. Physicians are employees of the government, and the government owns all the country's medical facilities. With its emphases on medicinal herbs and acpunc-

ture, Chinese medicine differs from that of the West. Although Westerners have scoffed at the Chinese approach, some have changed their minds, and on a limited basis, medicinal herbs and acupuncture are used in the United States.

Recent changes include payment for medical treatment. A hospital stay can now cost several hundred yuan, when the average monthly wage is 200 yuan. Private medical clinics are also arising. Some physicians take extra jobs because they cannot survive on their salaries, and bribery of medical personnel who are supposed to give free treatment has become routine. Some doctors demand bribery, as with the surgeons who, arms scrubbed and held high in the air, refused to enter the operating room until the patient's relatives had stuffed their pockets with cash (Sampson 1992).

FOR YOUR CONSIDERATION

No nation has discovered the perfect medical system, and every country faces a medical crisis of "too much demand at too great a cost" (Moore and Winslow 1993). How would you say the U.S. medical system is superior—and inferior—to each of these systems? Would you pick one over the U.S. system? Why? Short of socializing medicine, which goes against the values of Americans, how do you think the U.S. medical system can overcome the deficiencies reviewed in this chapter—and maintain its strengths?

Table 10-3   Indicators of Health

	Sweden	United States	Russia	China
Life expectancy	79.4	77.3	67.3	71.6
Infant mortality[a]	3.9	6.7	20.1	41.4
Birth rate[b]	NA	14.2	9.4	16.0
Death rate	NA	8.7	13.9	6.7
Health costs as a percent of gross domestic product	8.4	13.7	NA	NA

[a]Per 1,000 live births.
[b]Per 1,000 population.
NA = Not Available

Source: Field 1998; *Statistical Abstract of the United States* 1998:Tables 1345, 1348; 2001:Table 1330.

Taking a Back Seat to Heroic Intervention

Preventive medicine is quiet and unassuming, and is often obscured by the drama of open-heart surgery, screaming ambulances, and doctors and nurses rushing about in emergency rooms. If you take care of your body and manage to stay well, no one thinks much about it. Become seriously ill, however, and everyone is concerned. Preventing something from happening means that you never see it happen. In fact, this is what most people want—not to get sick. Yet few are willing to work for it. Although entire communities could reduce their risk of heart disease, unhealthy habits such as fast food, booze, and the boob tube are much more appealing to most of us than are vegetables, fruit juices, and aerobic exercise.

A Growing Medical Problem

Something disturbing is happening in the United States, and it does not bode well for our health:

> In Cape Canaveral, Florida, while waiting for a space shot, I struck up a conversation with an English couple in their twenties. As we chatted while awaiting the delayed launch, I asked them what they thought about the United States. They looked at each other in that knowing way that couples do, and asked if I really wanted to know. I said I did. They replied, hesitatingly, that they had never seen so many fat people in their lives.
>
> When a friend from Spain visited me, he commented on the things that struck him as different. He was surprised to see people living in metal houses (no mobile homes in Spain). He also asked why there were so many fat Americans.

Are these valid perceptions? Or are they perhaps highly ethnocentric observations by foreigners? I wish I could say the perceptions aren't true, but the statistics bear them out. Americans are getting fatter. In 1980, one of four Americans was overweight. Now it is one of three (*Statistical Abstract* 1998:Table 242). This increase in weight flies in the face of what we know about preventing medical problems. Our knowledge has gone one way, but our lifestyles another. For example, the average American drinks 50.8 gallons of soft drinks a year—more sugared, caffeinated, and carbonated water and chemicals than milk and fruit and vegetable juices combined (*Statistical Abstract* 2001: Table 704). Since this lifestyle is firmly ingrained, it is more difficult to implement preventive medicine than it is to continue the less effective but more dramatic medical

More Americans are overweight today than ever before in the history of the United States. In 1980, one fourth (25.4 percent) of Americans were overweight. Today, that total has jumped to one third (34.8 percent). The likely causes are a surplus of income, an abundance of food, less physically active occupations (a reduction in farming), more leisure, and more sedentary lifestyles (television watching), accompanied by more sugary foods and a custom called "snacking." The extra weight carried by this one third of Americans produces a variety of health problems, from weakened knee joints to heart attacks.

procedures. To put this in plain English, most people apparently prefer to go to a doctor to be treated for health problems than to exercise and start eating healthier.

HUMANIZING HEALTH CARE

What Is Depersonalization?

Depersonalization is a problem in medicine. What do people mean when they complain about it? People object that they are treated as things, not as people with feelings and personal needs. For Kathie Persall, depersonalization was based on a hospital policy concerning induced labor and caesarean sections—a policy that ignored her desires. When one psychiatrist says to another, "I have a paranoid schiz on Ward 5," or an OB/GYN doctor says to the nurse, "There is a pelvic in Room 3," she is depersonalizing the patient (Henslin and Biggs 1999). Without their knowledge or consent, some people are even used as guinea pigs to see if a new medicine works.

Examples of Depersonalization

Sociologists who have studied depersonalization in public clinics note how the poor not only have to wait for hours to be seen, but aren't even given normal eye contact. Nurses address them by number and don't look in their direction when they respond. If they aren't able to see a doctor that day, it's just one of those things. After all, what do they have to do that's important, anyway?

How to Repersonalize Medical Treatment

Sociologist Jan Howard and her assistants (1975), who made such observations, also make policy recommendations for repersonalizing health care. This must begin in medical training, she stresses. Medical students need to be taught the *inherent worth* of patients—the view that each individual is valuable and deserves personal attention. Physicians and nurses also need to learn *holism,* the view that a person's body, feelings, attitudes, and actions are intertwined and should not be segregated into discrete organ systems for the convenience of clinicians. Howard also notes how waiting rooms can be made more humane by having adequate lighting, comfortable seats, appropriate reading materials, warm decor, convenient bathrooms, and noninstitutional furniture arrangements.

SELF-CARE GROUPS

The Goals, Their Potential and Resistance

One reaction to high costs and depersonalization is the emergence of self-care groups. Some of these groups are in sharp conflict with the medical profession; others are begun, promoted, or even supervised by medical professionals. The goals of self-care groups are to maintain health, prevent disease, increase self-esteem, and do self-diagnosis, medication, and treatment. Diabetics, heart attack victims, cancer patients, people who have had breast surgery, smokers, alcoholics, and people who suffer from rheumatism, arthritis, AIDS, deformities, mental illnesses, and genetic problems have formed groups to help each other. They discuss new developments in their diseases or problems, encourage one another to take preventive measures, and support one another emotionally. Blind to the potential of such groups for treating many of the problems they see in their practices, few physicians encourage self-care groups. Almost all continue to focus on acute care. (From a conflict perspective, one could say that self-care groups threaten their profits and control, for many of their suggestions bypass physicians.)

In Sum

The policy ideas discussed here address two problems of health and medical care: high costs and the general lack of preventive medicine. They aim to move health care away from the hospital and back to changes in lifestyle. They offer low technology and inexpensive alternatives to highly technological and expensive hospital care.

✦ The Future of the Problem ✦

TECHNOLOGY

"Pushes for Technology"

As we look to the future, the first significant trend is more technology. Medical technology, and the heroic efforts that often accompany it, will continue to develop, and people will continue to demand the best technology available when their lives are threatened—regardless of the cost. Cost is a factor only when the emergency is over and the bills arrive.

Technology Has Led to Severe Ethical Dilemmas

Out of these technological advances have arisen ethical problems that plague medical professionals and lay people. If people can be kept alive artificially, must doctors keep them alive? Does "brain dead" really mean "dead"? If so, should physicians be allowed to remove "body parts" from people who (only because of machines) are still breathing? In some hospitals, they already do so. Should medical researchers be allowed to test dangerous drugs on these people, because, after all, they are "really" dead? They already do this in some hospitals. Another controversy, euthanasia, is discussed in the Thinking Critically box below.

THINKING CRITICALLY ABOUT SOCIAL PROBLEMS

Should Doctors Be Allowed to Kill Patients?

Euthanasia is a hot topic among both medical professionals and the lay public. Articles on euthanasia regularly appear in the print media and on television, designed, some say, to provide information, or, as others claim, to subtly condition the U.S. public to accept it.

Except for the name, this is a true story:

> Bill Simpson, in his seventies, had battled leukemia for years. After his spleen was removed, he developed an abdominal abscess. It took another operation to drain it. A week later, the abscess filled, and required more surgery. Again the abscess returned. Simpson began to go in and out of consciousness. His brother-in-law suggested euthanasia. The surgeon injected a lethal dose of morphine into Simpson's intravenous feeding tubes.

At a medical conference in which euthanasia was discussed, a cancer specialist (oncologist) who had treated thousands of later-stage patients, announced that he had kept count of the patients who had asked him to help them die. "There were 127 men and women," he said. Then he added, "And I saw to it that 25 of them got their wish." Thousands of other physicians have done the same (Nuland 1995).

When a doctor ends a patient's life, such as by injecting a lethal drug, it is called *active euthanasia*. To withhold life support (nutrients or liquids) is called *passive euthanasia*. To remove life support, such as disconnecting a patient from oxygen often falls somewhere in between. The result, of course, is the same.

Two images seem to dominate the public's ideas of euthanasia: One is of an individual devastated by chronic pain, and a doctor mercifully helping to end that pain through euthanasia. The second is of a brain-dead individual, a human vegetable with no future, being kept alive by machines. How accurate are these images?

In Holland euthanasia remains illegal, but it is practiced openly. In 1984, the Royal Dutch Medical Association set standards for euthanasia, and the government honors those standards. The results have been studied thoroughly (Shapiro 1997). Although physicians must report the deaths they assist, two of three go unreported (Keown and van der Wal 1999). In a study of 3,200 physician-assisted deaths, one fifth

How the Internet Is Affecting Medicine

The Internet is helping to give some control back to patients. People who have rare diseases, for example, can participate in discussion groups on the Net. In this new type of self-care group, although people don't meet personally, they share their experiences and knowledge with one another. Physicians are concerned. Not only do they feel threatened because they are no longer the sole possessors of esoteric knowledge on rare disease, but they also fear that misinformation may be circulated. Medical experiments may also be contaminated; by sharing information on the Internet, some patients are able to determine whether they are receiving an experimental drug or a *placebo,* a substance that is designed to look like a medicine but that has no medical value (Bulkeley 1995).

REDIRECTING MEDICINE

The Carlson Predictions

In the 1970s, Rick Carlson (1975) drew a bleak picture of the future. In the year 2000, he foresaw a more complex and stressful society, a larger aging population with incurable degenerative diseases, and more illnesses resulting from lifestyle and environmental deterioration. Carlson held out little hope that our medical system would turn to preventive medicine and work on overcoming the environmental and

took place without the patient's consent. Most of these patients were in a coma, but in one case a physician ended the life of a patient with breast cancer who said that she did not want euthanasia. In the doctor's words, "It could have taken another week before she died. I needed this bed" (Hendin, Rutenfrans, and Zylicz 1997).

Some Dutch, concerned that if they have a medical emergency they may be euthanized, carry "passports" that instruct medical personnel that they wish to live. Most Dutch support euthanasia, however, and more carry another "passport," one that instructs medical personnel to carry out euthanasia (Shapiro 1997).

In the United States, Oregon made assisted suicide legal in 1997. The next year, doctors helped only fifteen people commit suicide. Not one was suffering from intractable pain. Instead, these individuals felt that they would become dependent in the future, and they chose death rather than future dependence (Smith 1999).

Dr. Jack Kevorkian, a Michigan pathologist (he didn't treat patients—he studied diseased tissues) decided that regardless of laws, doctors had the right to help people commit suicide. He did, 120 times. He provided the poison, as well as a machine to administer it,

and watched while the patient pulled the lever. But he never touched that lever. He left bodies in motels, in vans, and dropped them off at hospitals.

Michigan prosecutors tried Kevorkian for murder several times but couldn't get a jury to convict him. Then, in 1998 Kevorkian played a videotape on national television, showing him giving a lethal injection to a man dying from Lou Gehrig's disease. Prosecutors impounded the tape and put Kevorkian on trial again. Kevorkian was convicted of second degree murder and sentenced to 10 to 25 years in prison.

FOR YOUR CONSIDERATION

If Kevorkian had lived in Oregon, he could have killed people any time they asked him to do so. But not in Michigan—or in any of the other states. Do you think Michigan or Oregon is right? Why? What do you think the future will hold? Will we go the way of Oregon or Michigan? Do the results of doctor-assisted deaths in Holland and Oregon justify assisted suicide?

Finally, as is evident in Holland, physician-assisted deaths have a way of expanding. In addition to what is reported above, Dutch doctors also kill newborn babies that have serious birth defects (Smith 1999). Their justification is "quality of life." What do you think?

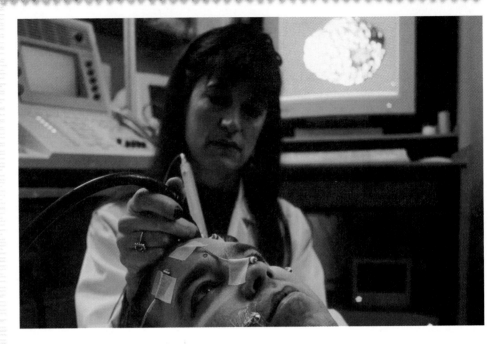

New technology has allowed medicine to make stunning advances. Many people now survive health problems that would have killed them if they had experienced those problems just a decade or so ago.

lifestyle causes of illness. He concluded that poverty would not be cured and that the poor would continue to have more illnesses than the affluent. He was right on all counts.

Carlson argued, however, that we can change our health care system, transforming it into a much better system for meeting our medical problems. His ideas are worth repeating. An effective system would include these elements.

The Potential

First, it would teach people *to demand better health rather than more medicine.* To do this, people must be aware that their health is largely their own responsibility. Such a program would require more research on self-health care and disease prevention. Some physicians would continue to provide acute and emergency care, but others would be retrained in preventive and environmental medicine. The infirm aged would be cared for in residential complexes that are humane, pleasant, and efficient, such as those in Denmark and Sweden. Funds saved from spending less on acute and emergency medicine should go to accident prevention, food safety, occupational safety, and programs focusing on nutrition and exercise. Efforts would be made to reduce the stresses of modern life by staggering work hours; designing more relaxing work environments in offices and schools; building hiking and bike paths, tennis courts, and parks in our communities; and reducing noise pollution.

Why the Potential Is Unlikely to Be Realized

The potential for improving the general health of our people is immense. A focus on preventive medicine, however, runs counter to the entrenched cultural orientation—the norm of heroic intervention in acute cases—of both the public and the medical profession. This makes it unlikely that we will redirect the focus to improving general health through prevention.

◆ Summary

1. What is considered health and illness varies with culture and social class. Thus, what people consider a health problem is not based solely on biological factors, but varies from one group and time to another.

2. Industrialization brought better health, but with it also came an increase in some health problems—cancer, heart disease, drug addiction, and other chronic illnesses caused by lifestyle, general aging, and environmental pollution. AIDS illustrates the relationship among behavior, environment, and disease. Physical and emotional problems are more common among the poor. To explain the relationship between social class and mental illness, sociologists prefer environmental explanations rather than genetic ones.

3. The U.S. medical system is centered on specialized, hospital-based, and heroic intervention. A fee-for-service system increases cost. In preventive medicine, the emphasis would be on changing people's lifestyles and environment.

4. Social inequalities in medical and mental health services stem largely from the way we pay medical bills. In our fee-for-service system, health care is not a right but a commodity sold to the highest bidder. The United States has a *two-class system of medical care*—public clinics and public hospitals for the poor, and private clinics and private hospitals for the more affluent.

5. Two policies designed to control medical costs are to pay patients to stay healthy and to pay doctors not to see patients unnecessarily. HMOs are a form of prepaid health practices that give successful bidders a fixed amount of money per year to attend to the health needs of a group of people. Medical services and tests come directly off the corporate bottom line, leading to a conflict of interest in treating patients. On the other hand, if they let their patients become too sick, it costs more than if they catch problems early.

6. The medical profession may respond to changing patterns of illness by adapting its approach so that the focus moves from acute problems to chronic problems and problems caused by lifestyle and environmental pollution. If so, the emphasis will be on preventive medicine—better health habits, a cleaner environment, and education designed to teach people how to take care of themselves and to manage their illnesses.

◆ Key Terms

Coinsurance Insurance requiring the policyholder to pay part of the cost.

Defensive medicine Medical practices performed by physicians out of fear of malpractice suits.

Deinstitutionalization A policy developed in the 1960s of discharging patients from the state and county mental hospitals into the community, where they were supposed to receive community-based services.

Depersonalization Treating patients as things, rather than as individuals.

Drug therapy The use of drugs such as tranquilizers and antidepressants to treat emotional problems.

Electroconvulsive therapy (ECT) A treatment for emotional problems in which a low-voltage electric current is passed repeatedly through the brain. Also known as electroshock therapy.

Euthanasia Mercy killing.

Group therapy A treatment for emotional problems in which members of the group talk about how they interact with others and help each other to cope with their problems.

Health maintenance organization (HMO) A comprehensive prepaid health care organization designed to reduce costs by minimizing unnecessary medical services.

Home health care Organized health services for people living at home with chronic or disabling diseases.

Iatrogenesis Illnesses or other health problems caused by medical care.

Individual psychotherapy Treatment for emotional problems. A therapist listens and tries to guide the client toward a resolution of those problems.

Lay referral network Friends and relatives from whom sick people get suggestions about what to do about their illnesses. See *Professional referral network*.

Neurosis Mild forms of emotional problems and personality disorders.

Physician extenders People who help physicians with their work, including nurses, physician assistants, nurse practitioners, and nurse's aides.

Primary prevention Measures that keep a disease from occurring, such as vaccinations. See *Secondary prevention, Tertiary prevention*.

Professional referral network The health providers that physicians use to evaluate themselves; also used in the sense of the health providers that direct patients toward treatment. See *Lay referral network*.

Psychoanalysis A treatment for emotional problems created by Sigmund Freud; the goal is to uncover unconscious motives, fantasies, and fears by having patients speak about whatever comes to mind.

Psychoses Serious emotional problems, characterized by loss of sense of reality and inability to carry out daily tasks.

Secondary prevention Early detection and precautions that keep a disease from getting worse.

Short-term directive therapy A treatment for emotional problems in which a therapist actively tries to solve the client's problems.

Talk therapy Treatments of emotional problems that are based on "talking" (psychotherapy, group therapy, etc.).

Tertiary prevention Medical care of an existing disease aimed at preventing further damage.

Two-class (or two-tier) system of medical care A system in which different medical institutions serve the poor and the affluent.

Uniform coinsurance An insurance policy that requires that the holder pay a fixed percentage of the costs.

◆ Critical Thinking Questions

1. If you were asked, "What do you think are the two most important issues for the government to address?" what would your answer be? How are your answers different from the ranking in Table 10-1 on page 321? Explain.

2. What do you think the government's role should be in dealing with healthcare issues? Why?

3. What political, economic, or other social factors do you think contribute to the United States being the only industrialized country that doesn't have a national health care system?

4. Why do you think women live longer than men?

5. Which of the perspectives (symbolic interactionism, functionalism, or conflict theory) do you think best explains health care problems in the U.S.? Explain.

The Changing Family

Nancy and Tom were pleased. Their four-year-old daughter, Melissa, had been accepted at Rainbow Gardens Preschool in Manhattan Beach, California, a prosperous suburb of Los Angeles. The preschool came highly recommended by their close friends, whose son was attending the school. With Nancy's promotion and Tom's new job, schedules had become more difficult, and Rainbow Gardens was able to handle the pressing need for more flexible hours.

At first Melissa loved preschool. She would happily leave Nancy or Tom, whoever drove her, for the pleasures of her little friends and the gentle care of loving teachers. Then, gradually, almost imperceptibly, a change came over her. At first, Melissa became reluctant to leave her parents. Then she began to whimper in the mornings when they were getting her ready. And lately she had begun to have nightmares, waking up crying and screaming several times a week, something she had never done. The counselor they took Melissa to said it was nothing to worry about; all kids go through things like this from time to time. Melissa was just going through a "developmental adjustment," and she would be just fine in a little while.

When allegations of sexual abuse of three-, four-, and five-year-olds at Rainbow Gardens made headlines, it was devastating to parents around the nation. The unthinkable had become real. Had it happened at their preschool, too—with their child? But for Nancy and Tom, it was more than a nagging question. Overnight, Melissa's nightmares, her crying, and her bed wetting took on new meaning. The gentle teachers, so affectionate with the children, child molesters? Melissa undressed, photographed, forced to commit sexual acts with adults, and threatened with the death of her puppy if she told?

Nancy and Tom don't know. It is either this or simply a "developmental adjustment." Now it is Nancy's and Tom's turn for nightmares.

◆ The Problem in Sociological Perspective ◆

"Nightmare at Day School" could be the title of a horror movie, a real-life one for some parents. Each year between 800 and 900 children are sexually abused at day-care centers (Finkelhor and Williams 1988). While this is a small number compared with the approximately 19,000 children who are sexually abused each year by family and household members, it is a frightening prospect for parents. How did we get into this situation? Why are 5 million U.S. children entrusted to the care of strangers in a new social institution called day care (*Statistical Abstract* 2001: Table 557)?

The Family Is Engulfed in Change

Day care—and its risks—are one aspect of vast changes that have swept our society, engulfing families and forcing them to adjust. For the family, change is nothing new. As the basic social institution (also called the basic building block of society), the family always feels changes that occur in other parts of society.

Effects of Industrialization on the Family:

The single most significant event to affect the family is the industrial revolution. Because its consequences were so severe and because they continue to affect family life today, let's explore its significance. To understand what happened, we must first note that before industrialization, almost everyone worked at home. Economic survival was perilous, and the entire family was involved: Both parents worked, and so did their children. When industrialization moved production to factories, however, it vitally affected family life:

1. Removing the Father from the Home

1. Men left home to work in factories, opening a major gap between the husband-father and other family members. For most of the day they now lived different lives, one at work and the others at home. Husband and wife no longer shared activities during their working hours. Separated from the household, the husband-father's orientation to life changed.

2. Children: From Economic Assets to Economic Liabilities

2. Industrialization turned children from an economic asset into an economic liability. When production was farm-based, children contributed to their family's survival—from milking the cows to working in the fields. In some of the first factories, children still worked alongside adults. As we saw in Chapter 6, however, the movement to "save" children ended their employment. Although children could no longer bring home a paycheck, they still consumed much of the family's limited resources. Children became nonproductive and expensive.

3. Increased Education

3. Industrialization brought a demand for more education. As children spent more years in school, they became dependent on their parents longer. Their education and longer dependency made children even more expensive.

4. A Lower Birth Rate

4. The discovery of vulcanized rubber during the 1840s made large-scale production of the condom possible. With further refinements in design and manufacture in the 1920s, the condom allowed couples to limit the number of their children (Convensky 1980; Davis 1980; Douvan 1980; Laslett 1980). As children became nonproductive and expensive, the birth rate plunged. Today, our birth rate is the lowest in our history, and it is expected to fall still further. (See Figure 11-1 on p. 364.)

5. From Rural to Urban

5. Industrialization changed people's settlement patterns. Until about one hundred years ago, almost everyone in the world lived in the country. As production moved to factories, workers moved where the work was. Housing in the city was expensive, and people reduced the size of their families even more.

6. Loss of Functions

6. As industrialization continued, other institutions grew stronger and stripped the family of many of its traditional functions, such as producing food, educating the young, providing recreation, and nursing the old and sick.

7. Change in Women's Roles

7. Industrialization changed women's family roles. The wife-mother had been responsible for basic food production (milk, butter, eggs, vegetables), preparation (baking and cooking), and storage (canning). She also made, washed, ironed, and mended the family's clothing, cleaned the house, and took care of the children, the sick, and the elderly. As her functions were reduced, she increasingly became an "emotional provider"; that is, the wife-mother was expected to be the stable counterpoint to the husband's pressures at work and to lavish attention on a diminishing number of children.

8. Greater Equality

8. Industrialization brought greater equality to the family. As traditional roles changed, so did feelings about how things "ought to be" between husband and wife and between parents and children. This gradual change did not happen without struggle, for men were reluctant to give up their more privileged positions. Indeed, the struggle over equality (or authority) is still a primary source of marital problems.

9. More Divorce

9. Industrialization increased divorce. Before industrialization, divorce was rare. But with the fundamental changes I have outlined, especially the stripping of functions from the family and the reduced birth rate, marriages became fragile.

10. Longer Lives and More Intergenerational Ties

10. Industrialization improved health, reduced mortality, and brought longer lives. One consequence is that today's grandparents are more likely to be alive and to participate in the lives of their grandchildren if they so wish than at any time in history (Bengtson et al. 1990). Now that we have four- and even five-generation families, some great-grandparents rear their grandchildren and even their great-grandchildren, especially when the mothers of those children are teenagers.

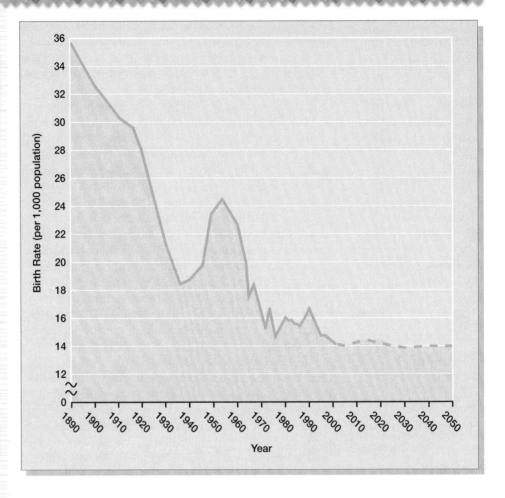

FIGURE 11-1
U.S. Birth Rate,
1890–2050
(*Source: Statistical Abstract,* various editions and 2001:Table 4. Dotted line indicates U.S. government projections.)

11. The "Quiet Revolution"

11. The changes continue. One of the most fundamental changes ever to affect the family—women leaving home to take paid employment—is having a major impact on this generation. This trend began with the industrial revolution. With but a single interruption—at the end of World War II, when millions of women left the jobs they had taken in the war industries—it has continued without letup. What is new is the extent of the change: In the 1980s, for the first time in history, more than half of married women worked for wages at least part time outside the home. Today about 61 percent do (*Statistical Abstract* 2001:Table 575).

That so many women work for wages reinforces most of the trends we have discussed, especially changes in husband-wife roles, divorce, and the birth rate. It also complicates rearing children, which some consider *the* social problem of today's family. After the shootings at Columbine High School in Colorado in 1999, many blamed the parents of the two boys. Because the movement of wives and mothers from the home is part of a gradual historical trend, and yet is so fundamental—forcing change in all family relationships—it sometimes is called the *quiet revolution*.

In Sum

The family is always in transition. Just as it adapted to large-scale social events that began centuries ago, so it adapts to today's current events of smaller magnitude. The family is not an independent unit, and to survive it must adapt continuously.

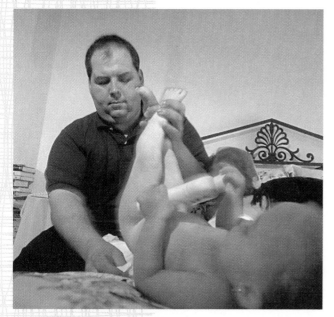

The family is always changing, for people adjust their relationships to the changes taking place in society. As ideas of masculinity change, for example, behaviors that once were not acceptable for men come to be thought of as legitimate. After those changes become standard, a current generation may have difficulty understanding why such behaviors were formerly off-limits, and how they ever threatened men's "masculinity."

Is Divorce a Sign of Weakness or Strength?

FIGURE 11-2

How Many Millions of Americans Are Divorced?

(Source: *Statistical Abstract of the United States* 1989:Table 50; 1998:Table 61; 2001:Table 49.)

Because the family provides for the economic well-being of its members, as with industrialization of years past and with computerization today, it is especially sensitive to changes in the economic sphere.

◆ The Scope of the Problem ◆

Troubles, or Social Problems? Since the family is always adapting to changes in society, what makes those adaptations a social problem? Sociologist C. Wright Mills (1959b) said that when an individual here and there gets divorced, we have a **personal trouble.** If divorce is widespread, however, it is a sign that there is a problem with the *structure* of marriage. In other words, Mills said that widespread personal troubles indicate a social problem. As we have seen throughout this text, however, such objective conditions are not adequate for making a social problem; we also need subjective concerns. We certainly have them when it comes to the contemporary family.

Indicators That the American Family Is in Trouble Let's consider indicators that the family is in trouble. If you mention this to someone, usually the first thing to pop into their minds is divorce. As Figure 11-2 shows, perceptions that divorce has become more common are true. Between 1980 and 2000, the number of divorced Americans doubled; the population, in contrast, increased only 24 percent. Another way to look at this is to compare the number of Americans getting married with the number getting divorced. As Figure 11-3 shows, for every two couples getting married, another couple is having their marriage declared null and void.

We can interpret divorce statistics in different ways, of course. Some even see them as a sign that families are becoming *stronger*—no longer willing to put up with miserable marriages, men and women terminate them and look for better ones. Even if that interpretation is not correct, Figure 11-3 does show something positive about divorce. After rising for about eighty years, U.S. divorces peaked in 1980, held steady for about fifteen years, and then began to decline. The ratio of one divorce for every two marriages has held steady. Although this statistic shows such regularity, divorce is not evenly distributed across the United States. As the Social Map on page 367 shows), the risk of divorce is considerably less—or greater—in some states than in others.

Divorce involves things that we can't put numbers on—the hopes

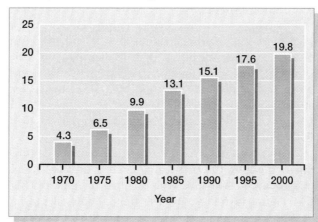

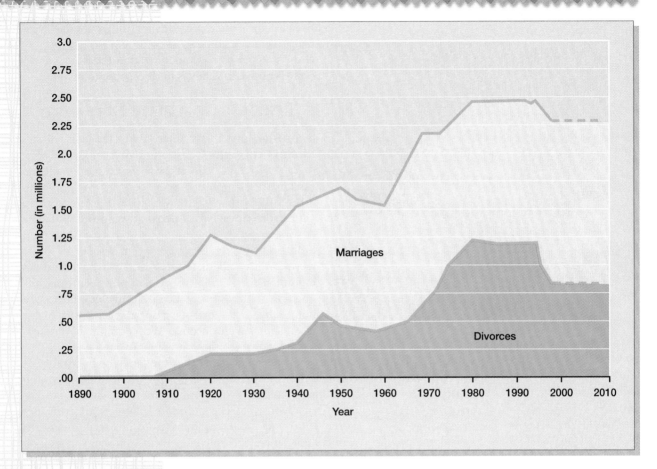

FIGURE 11-3

American Marriage, American Divorce

(*Source: Statistical Abstract*, various years, and 1998:Table 92.)

The Children of Divorce

The Slowing Rate of Remarriage

and dreams of millions of adults crushed, shattered, and transformed into bitterness and rancor. Although people are concerned about the couples involved, they see them as adults who make their choices—and their mistakes. What really concerns people are the *children* of divorcing parents. Each year, the lives of more than 1 million children are disrupted by divorce (*Statistical Abstract* 1998:Table 160). These children are filled with unsettling fears of the future as their parents break up. Divorce is so extensive that, as Figure 11-5D shows, only about 2 of 3 U.S. children live with both parents.

Few adults enter into divorce lightly. Divorce is usually a painful decision, preceded by dissatisfaction and unhappiness, sometimes misery and brutal conditions. Yet it is the children who suffer from their parents' actions. If quarreling parents remain together, their children are vulnerable to anxiety and depression (Jekielek 1998). If they divorce, they find themselves on an emotional roller coaster, filled with fears and anxiety about an uncertain future (Weissbourd 1996). For most children, divorce also means a reduced standard of living (Weitzman 1985; Grella 1990). For many, it means poverty.

People are taking longer to remarry. In the 1960s, a third of divorced women remarried during the *first* year after their divorce. Within two years, half had remarried. Today, it takes five years for half to remarry (*Statistical Abstract* 1998:Table 161). Figure 11-6 illustrates this trend. Some take this slower rate of remarriage as a negative sign, an indication that people distrust marriage more than they used to and

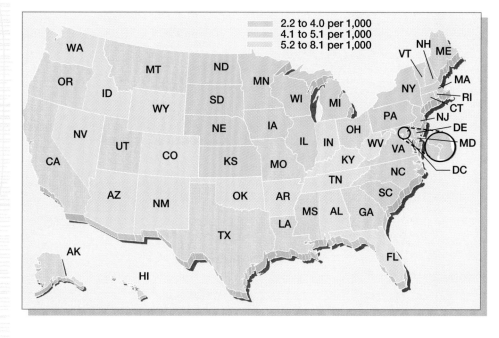

2.2 to 4.0 per 1,000
4.1 to 5.1 per 1,000
5.2 to 8.1 per 1,000

FIGURE 11-4
Social Map:
Variations
in Divorce
Divorce varies widely among the states. Massachusetts has the lowest rate, 2.2 per 1,000 population, and Nevada the highest at 8.1 per 1,000. The national average is 4.3. (*Source: Statistical Abstract of the United States* 2001, Table 118.).

are, therefore, more hesitant to marry. This could be, but it also could mean that people are more selective than they used to be. Perhaps they are even making wiser choices. No one knows for sure.

Figure 11-7 summarizes another indicator of trouble in U.S. families, one that has greatly upset people. Each year, more than 1 million babies are born to unmarried mothers. This is one third (33 percent) of all U.S. babies (*Statistical Abstract* 2001:Table 69). This rate differs sharply from our past; in 1940, the rate of unwed motherhood was about *one sixth* of what it is today.

Births to
Single Women

Despite the best efforts of single parents, their children are more likely to drop out of school, to get in trouble with the police, and to end up in poverty. A special subproblem is the relationship of children to absent fathers. In the typical case, the father maintains contact with his children for a short period after the divorce and then reduces his contact as his interests become focused on a new woman. Often, her children replace his own.

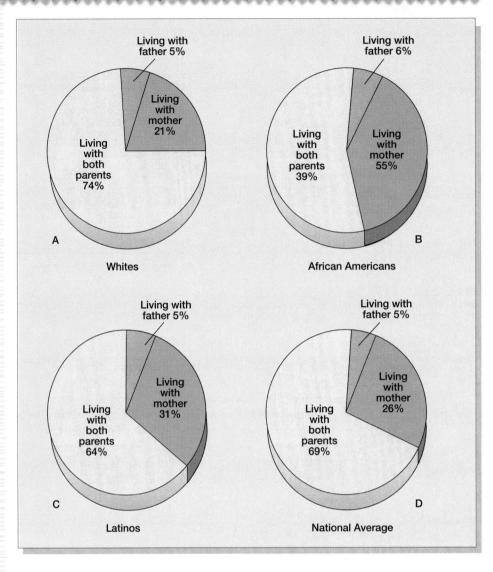

FIGURE 11-5
What Are the Living Arrangements of U.S. Chlildren?
(*Source: Statistical Abstract 2001:Table 57.*)

Whites

Living with father 5%
Living with mother 21%
Living with both parents 74%

A

African Americans

Living with father 6%
Living with mother 55%
Living with both parents 39%

B

Latinos

Living with father 5%
Living with mother 31%
Living with both parents 64%

C

National Average

Living with father 5%
Living with mother 26%
Living with both parents 69%

D

As we have seen throughout this text, social problems often follow lines of race and ethnicity. So it is with children's living arrangements. As you can see from Figure 11-5, 3 of 4 white children live with both parents, but for African-American children the figure is 2 of 5. The Latino configuration falls between the white and African-American patterns but is closer to the figures for whites. The source does not provide data for other racial-ethnic groups. As Figure 11-7 shows, the proportion of births to single women also follows racial-ethnic lines.

One-Parent Families: Births to single women, and divorce, can be looked at as individual matters, of course, and they are. When multiplied by millions, though, their consequences reverberate throughout society. The primary problem is that the children are denied benefits that children in two-parent families take for granted, especially the benefit of a male role model. Millions of boys and girls grow up without a father, compelled to learn the male role from mothers, boyfriends, television, and the streets. It is especially hard on boys to be denied the opportunity to model themselves after a responsible man. The

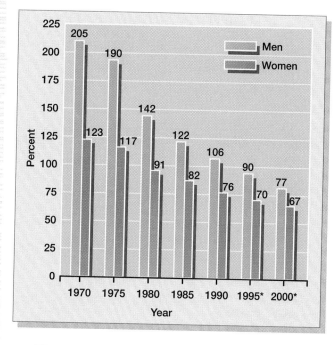

FIGURE 11-6

Of Every 1,000 People Who Divorce, How Many Remarry Each Year?

*Indicates the author's projections.

(*Source: Statistical Abstract* 1998: Table 159.)

substitute sources to which most turn are grossly inadequate for both their needs and those of society. With increases in both divorce and births to single women, *17 million* children live without fathers at home. Another *3 million* live without their mothers (*Statistical Abstract* 2000:Table 70). As always, overall statistics conceal individual variations. The Social Map on the next page shows how the states compare in the percentage of families that are headed by single parents.

Having only one parent at home has significant effects on children. The absence of the father is especially important. Sociologists may argue (as they do) about cause and effect, that this or that is not proven and could be due to something else, but every year of every decade children who come from mother-headed families are more likely to drop out of school and get in trouble with the law. This statistic applies to every region of the country and to every racial-ethnic group. There just are no exceptions. There is no other group in which children reared by both parents are more likely to drop out of school or get into trouble with the law.

FIGURE 11-7

Of All Births, What Percent Are to Single Women?

*Indicates the author's projection.

(*Source: Statistical Abstract* 1992: Table 87; 1998:Table 100; *Statistical Abstract* 2001: Table 69.)

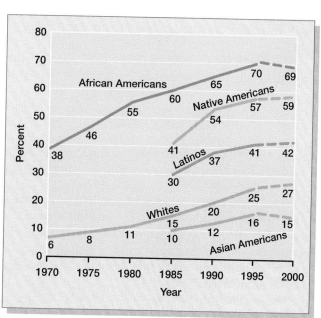

The absence of the father is proposed by some as the major explanation for some of the problems we analyzed in other chapters. The higher a group's rate of mother-headed families, for example, the higher is that group's rate of violent crimes. Such a statistic says nothing about the individual child, of course. A child reared by his or her mother may never get in trouble with the law. Similarly, just as children from mother-headed homes are more likely to drop out of

FIGURE 11-8

Social Map: Families Headed by Single Parents

These are percentages of families with children that are headed by single parents. Utah (at 14 percent) and the District of Columbia (at 62 percent) are so extreme that they fall into their own classifications. The states closest to these extremes are Idaho and North Dakota at 19 percent and Louisiana and Mississippi at 35 percent.

(*Source*: "Kids Count Data Sheet" 1999. Used by permission of the Annie E. Casey Foundation. www.aecf.org)

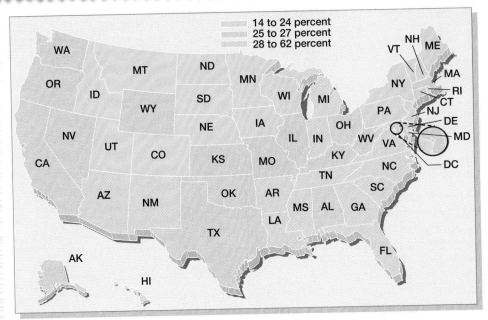

14 to 24 percent
25 to 27 percent
28 to 62 percent

school, any particular child may grow up to become an artist, an astronaut, or (and what can you expect of this author!) a sociologist. But, *on average*, which is what sociologists deal with, the absence of a father is more likely to lead to such problems.

We don't understand the mechanisms by which this occurs, and as much as we would like it to be otherwise, on average, a mother by herself does not do the same job in rearing children that a mother and father do. On a personal note, let me add that it was difficult for my wife and myself to guide a son through the turbulence of adolescence. To counteract the effects of peer groups required countless discussions, and even our combined experience was at times barely sufficient for this shared task. But for so many, the burden falls on just one parent, who finds it too much to cope with.

Sociologist Travis Hirschi (Pope 1988:117–118) says that, all else being equal, one parent is probably sufficient. The problem, he says, is that rarely is all else equal:

> The single parent (usually a woman) must devote a good deal to support and maintenance activities that are at least to some extent shared in the two parent family. Further, she must do so in the absence of psychological or social support. As a result, she is less able to devote time to monitoring and punishment, and is more likely to be involved in negative, abusive contacts with her children.

One-parent families are not limited to fatherless families, of course. Our 3 million motherless households also present tremendous obstacles to fathers who rear children alone. How should a single father teach female roles to his daughter? Whether man or woman, the single parent must try to be both mother and father, which, if not impossible, is certainly a formidable task. (We don't have enough studies on the consequences of father-headed families.)

The essential problem appears to be defective discipline—in either direction, excessive leniency or excessive control (Pope 1988). To find the proper balance is difficult for any family, but more difficult for one parent to achieve than for two.

Life for single mothers is usually filled with difficulties. In the typical case, these mothers are younger, have little education, and have an inadequate income. Although their resources are highly limited, their responsibilities are great.

As always, it is difficult to determine cause and effect, and sociologists are especially good at complicating explanations by adding more data. In this case, when we add cross-cultural data, we see that explanations based around father absence are not adequate. Look at Figure 11-9, which compares rates of unwed motherhood in ten Most Industrialized Nations. Four of them have a rate higher than ours. Yet in none of them is the rate of juvenile delinquency or violent crimes as high as ours. Therefore, something else also has to be at work. That "something else" is the culture within which one-parent families live—family support systems, subcultures of violence, access to guns, and views of life. Sociologists have *not* unravelled this thorny problem.

While some might disagree that divorce, a slowing rate of remarriage, and families headed by one parent indicate a social problem, no one disputes that runaway children offer dramatic evidence that something is drastically wrong with many U.S. families. No central agency keeps track of runaways, so we lack firm figures. The media often say that 1 million children run away from home each year, but that is simply a round number used to gain the public's attention. Whatever the total, each year about 100,000 children are arrested on charges of running away from home (*Sourcebook of Criminal Justice Statistics,* 2000:Table 4.6). Runaways certainly are not fleeing happy homes, but, instead, intolerable situations—incest, beatings, and other debilitating family conditions.

Runaways and "Pushouts"

The streets are tough, and survival is precarious. Runaways (and "pushouts," children who have been shoved out by parents who no longer want them) often fall into the hands of predators, making their already bruised lives even more complicated. As adults who work with runaway children observe: "Their alternative to starvation is to steal or to turn to the only thing they have—their bodies. Most get involved in prostitution and pornography when they tire of sleeping in doorways, have no money and no place to go."

Family Violence

Family violence is another indication that all is not well. Police and welfare workers know the scene well: the battered child, wife, husband, parent, or even grandparent. Physical abuse is not the rare manifestation of personal problems; family violence in some form occurs in more than half of all U.S. households and in

Equality is a theoretical goal with which most of us agree in principle. Because we all perceive reality from particular corners in life, however, putting "equality" into practice is more problematic: What some see as gaining equality, others view as a demand for privileges. For one group to gain equality, then, some other group must undergo a reduction in privileges. Shown here is one example of this problem.

every social class. About 50 million people are victimized every year by other family members. Sociologists Suzanne Steinmetz and Murray Straus (1974; Straus 1992) stress that it would be hard to find a group or institution in the United States in which violence is more of an everyday occurrence than the family. They add that we know only about the tip of the iceberg.

The Family Is Not Disintegrating

Problems of violence, divorce, runaways, and so on indicate severe problems in the U.S. family. They do *not* indicate, however, that the family is disintegrating. Although the contemporary family is in trouble, as a social institution it will endure its present crisis. In spite of its problems, humans have found no satisfactory substitute for the family, and millions of people report that their needs of intimacy and sense of identity and belonging are met within marriage and family. In this text, however, we examine *problems,* not the joys of marriage and family, and at this point we will turn our theoretical lenses on them.

◆ Looking at the Problem Theoretically ◆

For most of us, the family is our major support system. It nourishes and protects us when we are young. It gives us security and love and shapes our personality. Sociologists call it our **family of orientation** because it introduces us to the world and

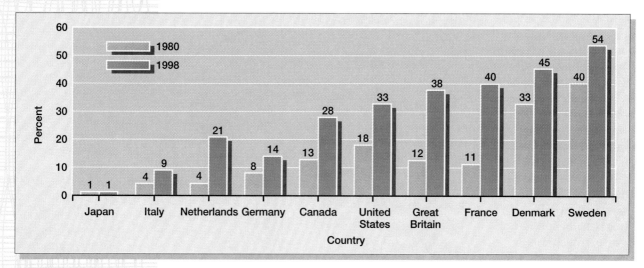

Figure 11-9
The Increase in Births to Single Women in the Most Industrialized Nations*
*Note: As a percentage of all births.
(Source: Statistical Abstract 2001:Table 1331.)

Why Has Divorce Increased?

Changing Ideas of Marital Satisfaction

An Overloaded Institution

Ideas of Love

teaches us ways to cope with life. As a result, most of us try to establish stability, identity, and intimacy by marrying and forming what is called a **family of procreation.**

In spite of how much we value marriage and family, however, divorce has become common. Why? Sociologists have used their three theoretical lenses to examine how divorce is related to changes in society. As always, each lens yields a different interpretation, but the theoretical contribution of each dovetails neatly with the others, as you will see.

SYMBOLIC INTERACTIONISM

To explain why our divorce rate is so high, symbolic interactionists examine what people expect out of marriage. In 1933, sociologist William Ogburn noted that personality was becoming more important as people chose a husband or wife. A few years later, in 1945, sociologists Ernest Burgess and Harvey Locke observed that affection, understanding, and compatibility were becoming more central to marriage. These sociologists had documented a major change: Society had become more complex and impersonal, and increasingly people were looking for marriage to satisfy their needs for intimacy.

These trends have escalated. Society has grown more impersonal, and today husbands and wives expect even greater emotional satisfaction from one another. We have come to see marriage as a solution to the tensions produced by our problem-ridden society (Lasch 1977), and we are likely to expect our spouse to meet all our personality and emotional needs. Because these expectations place a heavy burden on marriage, often more than it can carry, sociologists say that marriage and family have become an *overloaded institution*.

Our idea of love encourages us to expect marriage to deliver too much. To Americans, love carries ideas of total happiness. If we are "truly in love," we will be satisfied emotionally and, we hope, enjoy a continuous emotional high. For Americans, love has become *the* reason for marriage. In effect, we learn that we should base a lifelong relationship on a temporary emotional state. The idea of love motivates people to marry, but the unrealistic expectations associated with it set people up for disappointment. When dissatisfactions arise in marriage, as they inevitably do,

One of the traditional functions of marriage, although not mentioned in the text, was to maintain racial/ethnic and even religious lines. In Minnesota, for example, even though both were white, a marriage between a German Lutheran and a German Roman Catholic was frowned on. Lines were so severe that a marriage between a Swedish Lutheran and a German Lutheran upset the respective families. To cross what was called the "color line" was unthinkable, a violation of a more. Today's situation is vastly different, as illustrated in this photo.

Ideas About Children

Ideas About Parenting

Changing Marital Roles

spouses tend to blame one another, believing the other to have somehow failed them. Their engulfment in the symbol of love blinds them to the unreality of their expectations.

Ideas about children have also undergone a historical shift that has strongly affected the contemporary family (Henslin 1992). In medieval society, children were seen as miniature adults (Aries 1962). With no sharp separation between their worlds, adults and children freely mixed with one another. At about age 7, boys became apprentices in some occupation, while girls of this age learned the homemaking duties associated with their cultural role. Today's ideas of childhood are quite different, and we consider age 7 a tender phase of early childhood. In short, children are no longer seen as miniature adults. They have been culturally transformed into impressionable, vulnerable, and innocent beings.

As ideas about children changed, so did ideas about parenthood. Three generations ago, children "became adults" when they graduated from eighth grade and took a job. Since we now view children as more vulnerable and expect them to be dependent much longer, we also expect parents to provide more protection and nurturance. We even expect them to provide opportunities for "self-development," to help their children "reach their potential." As the tasks associated with child rearing have expanded, and as the expected emotional ties between parents and children have become more intense, the family has been thrust into even greater "emotional overload" (Lasch 1977).

The past is being wiped out as change sweeps away traditional ideas of the "right way" to be a wife or a husband. No longer can husbands assume that their wives will stay home, take care of the house and children, and attend to their personal needs. Nor can a wife assume that her husband will have the sole responsibility to support the family. Traditional roles—whatever their faults, and there were many—provided clear-cut guidelines for behavior. Newlyweds knew what to expect of one another—and neither they nor their friends and relatives questioned those basic expectations.

Today's newlyweds are expected to work out their own roles. While this gives them a great deal of freedom and flexibility, it also produces another source of disagreement. A couple's ideas may not mesh. They may disagree over whether the wife should be career-oriented, or to what extent, and over how to divide responsibilities for the home and children. Because guidelines are still unclear, couples face a role vacuum that can create much discontent. How can you adequately fulfill your marital role if you can't agree on what that role entails?

Collectively, then, these fundamental changes in the meaning of marriage—our ideas about love, children, and the roles of husband and wife—have put pressure on spouses and provided a strong push toward divorce. They created the "emotional overload" mentioned earlier. We expect marriage to provide unlimited emotional satisfaction, something that it cannot deliver.

Perception of Alternatives

While these fundamental changes were occurring, another change also affected marriage deeply. More women were taking jobs outside the home, which also changed people's ideas about marriage. As wives earned paychecks of their own, they began to see alternatives to putting up with unhappy marriages. Symbolic interactionists consider the *perception of alternatives* as an essential first step to making divorce possible.

Changed Attitudes Toward Divorce

It is difficult for us to grasp how seriously divorce was once taken. Divorce used to mean failure, irresponsibility, and immorality. Divorced people were social outcasts, suspected of all sorts of evil things. Then, as divorce became more common, its meaning was transformed; it changed from being a symbol of failure to one of self-fulfillment, of opportunity rather than shame. This symbolic change also helped to increase the rate of divorce. When divorce carried a stigma, it was held in check. As divorce became a sign of personal change and development, however, the stage was set for widespread divorce.

Legal Changes

The law also had held divorce in check, for divorce was granted only on rigorous grounds. In some states, such as New York, a divorce required that one spouse prove that the other had committed adultery; this required witnesses and a trial. The law was liberalized to reflect people's changing ideas about divorce, and in most states, "incompatibility" now suffices. In many states, couples can work out their own "no-fault" divorce, and judges "compatibly" divorce them. These legal changes have further reduced the stigma attached to divorce, which, in turn, has contributed to the divorce rate.

Are These Changes Good or Bad?

Are these changes good or bad? Symbolic interactionists take the position that nothing is good or bad in and of itself. They view "goodness" and "badness" as value judgments. Thus, depending on its assumptions, one group is alarmed at changes in divorce, sex roles, ideas of what children are, and so on, while another looks at these same changes and feels pleased that the family is evolving. Symbolic interactionists can't say which view, if either, is correct, for symbolic interactionism provides no framework to make value judgments about anything.

In Sum

To explain why divorce increased, symbolic interactionists analyze how the symbols associated with the family have changed. They stress that symbols both reflect and create reality. That is, symbols not only represent people's ideas, but they also influence their behaviors and ideas. Although symbolic interactionists can analyze social change, they cannot pass judgment on it.

FUNCTIONALISM

When functionalists examine social change, they look at how change in one part of a social system affects its other parts. In the section on "The Problem in Sociological Perspective" (pages 362–365), we examined how industrialization and urbanization affected the family. We saw, for example, how the birth rate fell as children became more expensive, dependent, and unproductive.

Let's see how the industrial revolution and urbanization also affected these seven traditional functions of the family and how this is related to divorce:

Seven Traditional Functions of the Family:

1. Economic production
2. Socialization of children
3. Care of the aged
4. Care of the sick and injured
5. Recreation
6. Sexual control of family members
7. Reproduction

1. Economic Production

Changes in how production was organized is the key to why these functions changed. Before industrialization, the family was an economic team, its members forced to cooperate for their survival. *Moving production from home to factory disrupted this team.* It isolated the husband-father from the daily activities of the family, separated the wife-mother from the production of income, and made older children, who could go to work for wages, less dependent on their parents and siblings.

2. Socialization of Children

While economic production was changing, the government grew larger, more centralized, and more powerful. As it did so, it also began to undermine family functions. For example, through public education the government took over much of the responsibility for socializing children. To make certain that families cooperated, the states required attendance at public schools, threatening parents with fines and jail sentences if they did not put their children in their care.

3 and 4. Care of the Aged and Sick

Care of the aged and the sick took a similar course. As the central government expanded and its agencies multiplied, care of the aged became a government obligation. Before this, there had been few trained physicians, and medicine had been a family matter. As medical schools developed, along with hospitals and drugs, medicine came under government control. Gradually medical care shifted from the family to medical specialists.

5. Recreation

As industrialization continued, the country became more affluent. The family's disposable income increased, and businesses sprang up to compete for that income. Entertainment and "fun" had been home-based—card games, parlor and barn dances, sleigh rides, and so on. As family-centered activities gave way to public-centered paid events, the family lost much of its recreational function.

6. Control of Sexuality

The family had also controlled sexuality, but this, too, changed. Sexual relations in marriage were the only ones viewed as legitimate; those outside marriage were considered immoral. Although this was only an ideal, and matrimony never enjoyed a monopoly on sexual relations, the "sexual revolution" opened many alternatives to marital sex. Consequently, marital control over sexuality is considerably weaker than it used to be.

7. Reproduction

At first glance, reproduction appears to remain solidly in the family's domain. Yet even this vital and seemingly inviolable function of the family is not going unchallenged. Recall Figures 11-7 and 11-9: about 1.3 million single women have children each year. This means that one third of reproduction has moved away from the traditional family unit of husband and wife. In addition, married women can get abortions without informing their husband, and teenagers can obtain birth control and abortions without parental consent. Buttressed by laws, rules, procedures, and

government funding, then, some control over reproduction has moved away from the family unit.

Can reproduction be moved even farther from the family? Some envision a future in which women, single or married, homosexual or heterosexual, order semen with the specifications they want: sex, race, intelligence, height, even personality traits and musical or sports ability (Bagne 1992). Childbirth may even be divorced from the family unit. Sociologist Judith Lorber (1980:527), for example, talks about a system of "professional breeders." She says:

> A system of completely professional breeders and child rearers could be conducted with the best of modern technology—fertility drugs for multiple births, sperm banks, embryo transfers, and uterine implants to expand the gene pool and so on. Professional breeders could be paid top salaries, like today's athletes, for the 15–20 years of their prime childbearing time. Those who were impregnated could live in well-run dormitories, with excellent physical care, food, and entertainment.

We are caught in the middle—between the past and the mind-boggling, technologically driven future. Although we can speculate, none of us knows the specifics of that future. Perhaps Lorber's vision may come about—although I hope never to live to see such a *1984*, Hitleresque *Lebensraum* future.

In Sum

The family, then, has lost many of its traditional functions, and others are under assault. From a functionalist perspective, such changes have weakened the family unit. The fewer functions that family members have in common, the fewer are their "ties that bind." With these bonds removed, or weakened, the family is more fragile. Divorce, then, is common—the inevitable consequence of eroded functions in a context of great social strain.

CONFLICT THEORY

Conflict theorists point us in a different direction. They stress that marriage and family reflect the inequality of men and women in society. In general, men control, dominate, and exploit women, and marriage is one of the means by which they do so.

Traditional Male-Female Relationships Represent Inequality and Exploitation

Historically, men decided who their daughters would marry. They often made this decision according to benefits they themselves would derive, such as gaining favor with more powerful men. A common example is kings making alliances with other kings. Custom and the law also allowed men to discipline not only their children, but also their wives. This included spanking or even beating them—if they "needed" it. Men were so dominant that they made women responsible for taking care of their personal needs. The home was a place where women served their fathers, husbands, and brothers.

Our own forms of marriage and family reflect these millennia-old patterns of power. One of the most striking examples is the traditional U.S. wedding ceremony. While the mother sits passively on the side, the father walks down the aisle with his daughter and "gives" her to her husband. This is certainly a pale reflection of the power men once wielded, when they were able to choose their daughters' husbands, but it is a reflection nonetheless.

Reflections Today

Although men's power has eroded severely, inequality remains, making marriage an arena for this struggle between the sexes—and the key to understanding our family problems. In individual marriages, however, historical causes drop out of sight. People do not see their personal experience as rooted in history or in terms of broad historical change. What happens to them in marriage does not occur in the abstract,

The 1950s marked a watershed era in U.S. middle-class families. As millions of soldiers returned home from World War II, their millions of wives and girlfriends, who had worked in the war industries during their absence, returned to the home. Freed from economic pursuits, the wife was expected to focus her efforts exclusively on the home. With more free time, she was expected to put more effort into nurturing the children, even to help them "develop their potential," a new concept in parenting. This historical period is bathed in images that characterized only a minority of families, but these images form a mythical lens through which we view that "ideal" period of family life.

Consciousness of Oppression

In Sum: Divorce as a Sign of Changing Power

Why you **need** a kitchen extension phone

First, it's a great help in running the house —near shopping lists and at your finger tips for calls to the plumber or other repairmen.

Next, it saves you trouble. Biscuits won't burn, or a pot boil over, because a telephone call took you out of the kitchen. And you can still keep a watchful eye on playing children.

It saves you lots of steps, too. Your husband,

like you, will find it one of the most useful phones in your house.

And when all your work is done, it's easy and fun to take a break and chat with a friend on your handy kitchen extension.

Fact is, extension phones in the places your family works, sleeps and plays help so much and cost so little.

SPRING-A-LING!
IT'S KITCHEN TELEPHONE TIME!
Drop in soon at your local Bell Telephone business office and see the colorful kitchen phones on display there. One of them will be just right for your kitchen!

BELL TELEPHONE SYSTEM

but is a pivotal struggle over rights, obligations, and privileges.

As women participate in social worlds beyond the home, they resent arrangements that they once took for granted. Sociologist Arlie Hochschild (1999) points out that in the *typical* case, after returning home from an eight-hour shift of work-for-wages, the wife puts in a "second shift" doing cooking, cleaning, and child care. In two-paycheck families, wives average fifteen hours more work each week than their husbands. The cumulative total is incredible: Over a year, wives work an *extra month of twenty-four-hour days.* Husbands resist attempts to reduce their power, and wives resent their reluctance to share. Within the intimacy of the family, then, this basic historical situation is played out. At times, this competition between the sexes breaks into open conflict, as spouse battering and child abuse.

This analysis may fly in the face of your experience. Many wives do not *feel* oppressed, and some husbands feel that they are oppressed. A woman who does not feel oppression, say conflict theorists, is blind to her real situation and may be suffering from false consciousness. A man who feels oppressed, however, may be expressing social reality, for the social system oppresses both males and females. The difference, however, is that although society may torment both sexes, it is the creation of men and reflects their reality (de Beauvoir 1953).

This unequal balance of power causes men and women to experience marriage, even dating, differently. For example, if being a wife and mother is a woman's main role in life, women look primarily for security in a husband and are more anxious than men about dating, finding a mate, and the outcome of marriage (Greer 1972). In contrast, if men find their basic security outside marriage at work, they are less concerned about the outcome of dating and their marital relationship. This is why most women invest more in the relationship and are more dependent on its outcome (Firestone 1970). As relationships between men and women change, as, for example, women become more career-oriented, so will their dating and marital relationships.

In short, conflict theorists stress that marriage and family reflect fundamental relationships between men and women. Divorce reveals the basic conflict inherent in family life, the inequalities that pit husband and wife against one another. Higher

divorce rates are not a sign that the family is weakening but, rather, that women are making headway in their historical struggle with men (Zinn and Eitzen 1990).

◆ Research Findings ◆

Let's look at major characteristics of marriage and family today: the age at first marriage, cohabitation, remaining single, childlessness, family violence, sexual abuse, and abandonment of the elderly. Then let's consider whether these characteristics indicate the death of the family.

COHABITATION AND THE CHANGING AGE AT FIRST MARRIAGE

Changes in Age at First Marriage

From 1890 to 1950, Americans married at younger and younger ages. By 1950, U.S. brides were younger than at any time in our history, and by 1970 so were the grooms. After plateauing for a few years, there was an abrupt reversal in the average age of first marriage. Today, for women it is the *highest* in our history, and for men, the highest in 100 years (U.S. Census, 2000).

Cohabitation

Why this reversal? Figure 11-10 holds the answer. More couples are **cohabiting,** living together in a sexual relationship. If cohabitation had not become common, the average age at first marriage might show little change.

Why has cohabitation become so common? As I have written elsewhere (1980:103–105):

> Many interrelated factors have come together to culminate in cohabitation. The single most important is that of our changed sex codes. Premarital sex is now much more acceptable among the young than ever before in the history of our country. It is not a long way from viewing sexual relations between unmarried persons as permissible to accepting the idea of unmarrieds living together. If a couple feels that premarital sex is right, engaging in sexual relations in a furtive or fleeting manner is not consistent. Such couples feel they ought to be able to live together so they can enjoy sexual relations in a relaxed setting, and also enjoy one another on many other dimensions over a longer period of time. . . .
>
> Most cohabitants are not opposed to marriage in principle. They are opposed, rather, to marriage for themselves at this time. For a variety of reasons they do not feel that they are yet ready to handle the commitments that marriage entails (Macklin 1974:59). . . . Often this attitude is due to feeling unable to handle the responsibilities of marriage. Financial dependence also leads to this attitude, as marriage often poses an economic threat. Many cohabiting college students avoid marriage in order to remain eligible for dependent benefits, sometimes that of Social Security, but more commonly that of parental subsidy for college.

The Increasing Number of Single Americans

So many Americans have postponed the date of their first wedding that the percentage of single young people has surged. In 1970, of women age 25 to 29, only 1 of 9 (11 percent) had never married. Today, 1 of 3 (30 percent) is single. In 1970, only 1 in 5 (19 percent) of men of this age was single; today it is 1 of 2 (52 percent) (*Statistical Abstract* 1993:Table 52; 1998:Table 62; 2001:Table 49 & 51).

Remaining Single

Few look at being single as a permanent alternative to marriage. Some do, however, and as sociologist Peter Stein (1992) found, they still feel a strong need for intimacy, sharing, and continuity. To attain these satisfactions, which marriage and family ordinarily provide, singles cultivate a network of like-minded people with whom they establish close and caring friendships.

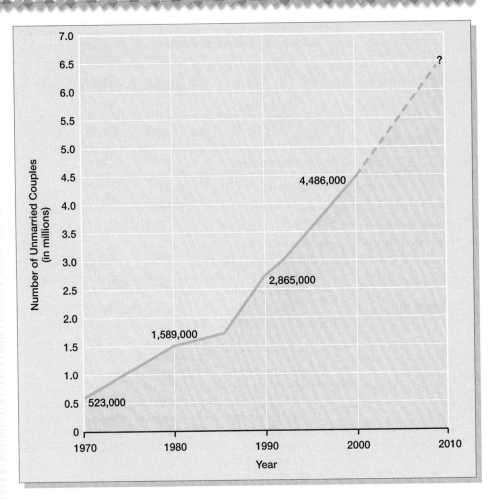

FIGURE 11-10
Cohabitation in the United States
(*Source: Statistical Abstract* 1985: Table 54; 2001:Table 51.)

CHILDLESSNESS

Pressures to Have Children

A small minority of married couples cannot have children. As sociologist Charlene Miall (1986) found, infertile couples feel stigmatized because our society strongly favors child rearing. Faced with cultural expectations to be fertile, they maneuver defensively, tiptoeing around topics in their conversations with friends, relatives, and fellow workers. They even select friends who are comfortable with childlessness.

The Process of Remaining Childless

Even fewer couples choose to remain childless. Sociologist Jean Veevers (1973, 1980) found that of 52 wives who had been married at least five years and had deliberately never borne a child, about a third had married with an explicit agreement with their husbands not to have children. In fact, they had sought husbands who would agree to this condition.

About two thirds of these wives, however, had planned to have children, but had kept postponing the decision to do so. These women had moved through four stages. At first, they postponed children for a definite time while they worked toward a specific goal, such as graduating from school or buying a house. They then shifted their postponement to a vague future, a "sometime" that never seemed to come. In the third stage, they decided they might want to remain childless, and, finally, in the fourth stage, they viewed childlessness as a permanent rather than a transitory state.

The Stigma

The "Mythical" Child

The wife is the usual victim of marital violence. Violence can begin over "nothing," simple disagreements that are part of all marriages. Some men, however, view violence as a legitimate way to express their frustrations in life. Husbands who are violent are likely to have been reared in homes in which their own fathers were violent, a process sociologists call the "cultural transmission of violence."

All the wives who decided to remain childless felt stigmatized. Friends and relatives put pressure on them to bear children, and made negative comments because they weren't pregnant. These pressures peaked during their third and fourth years of marriage, then decreased after they were married for five or six years. The couples talked about adopting a child "one day," what Veevers calls their "mythical child." Few couples, however, made an effort even to contact a child placement agency, and none of those who did followed up their initial contact.

The "mythical child" was significant in helping the couples adjust, for it made childlessness seem temporary. Talking about adoption also affirmed their normalcy—they were telling themselves and others that they were "normal" people who like children. Even after the wives became too old to bear children, adoption remained a symbol that held open the possibility of socially altering biological facts.

FAMILY VIOLENCE

The middle-aged man, an alcoholic, pushed the frail 70-year-old woman to the floor when she refused to give him money. She sprawled there, stunned and helpless, while he screamed insults. When the police arrived, the woman was concerned about protecting her attacker. She didn't want him to be arrested. He was her son.

This was not the first—or last—time that this woman would be victimized by her son. Parent abuse is but one form of family violence that researchers and the general public are discussing.

Murray Straus heads the Family Violence Research Program at the University of New Hampshire. He and fellow sociologists Susan Steinmetz and Richard Gelles have studied this cruel irony—that the social group we most often look to for warmth, intimacy, help, and love is sometimes characterized by cruelty and violence. To determine the amount and types of violence in U.S. homes, they interviewed nationally representative samples of couples. Their questions about acts of intentional physical injury ranged from slapping, pushing, kicking, biting, and beating to attacking with a knife or gun (Straus et al. 1980; Straus and Gelles 1988; Straus 1992).

These sociologists found that physical violence is more common among family members than any other group of people. It occurs so often that they did not report their data in incidents per 100,000 people, as does the FBI in its reports of violence, but in rates per 100. Each year, 16 of every 100 spouses physically attacks their husband or wife. This is 1 of 6! To my knowledge, no other violent crime even approaches this rate.

Because most couples (84 percent) were not violent during the past year and most violence is mild (such as slapping), some dismiss these figures. To this, Straus and Gelles (1988) reply (paraphrased):

> Let's suppose we are talking about a university. Would anyone say that there wasn't much of a problem because, after all, 84 percent of the faculty didn't hit a student last year? Or would anyone argue that this isn't significant because, after all, most episodes were just slapping, rather than punching or beating up?

The most violent family members are children. During the year preceding the interview, two thirds of them had attacked a brother or sister. Most had shoved or thrown things, but one third had kicked or bitten a sibling. In rare instances, the attack involved a knife or gun. Straus suggests that these totals are severe underestimates.

Equality Between the Sexes?

When it comes to violence, husbands and wives are about equally as likely to attack one another (Gelles 1980; Straus 1980, 1992). If we look at the *effects* of violence, however, sexual equality vanishes. As Straus points out, even though she may cast the first coffeepot, he usually casts the last and most damaging blow. Because most men are bigger and stronger than their wives, women are at a disadvantage in this literal battle of the sexes, and more women than men need medical attention. And when one spouse kills another, three times out of four the wife is the victim (*FBI Uniform Crime Report* 2001; *Criminal Justice Statistics* 1998:Table 3.129).

Violence and Social Class

Although marital violence occurs in all social classes, it is not distributed equally among the classes. Violence follows "social channels," which makes some spouses more likely to be abusers—or victims—than others. The highest rates (Gelles 1980) are found among

Families with low incomes

Blue-collar workers

People under 30

Families in which the husband is unemployed

Families with above-average numbers of children

Families living in large urban areas

Minority ethnic groups

Individuals who have no religious affiliation

People with low education

Poverty as a Key

Poverty is the key to understanding most of these findings. Poverty opens only some of the doors, however, for age and religion are also factors, and family violence occurs in all social classes. In general, however, blue-collar husbands are considerably more violent than white-collar husbands. The researchers suggest that this is because blue-collar husbands experience more stress than their white-collar counterparts. Another reason would be subcultural—a greater identification of "manliness" with violence among blue-collar men.

Alcohol as a Key

Sociologists Glenda Kantor and Murray Straus (1987) also found another key: alcohol. Based on a national probability sample, they found a direct relationship between alcohol consumption and wife battering; that is, the more a husband drinks, the more likely he is to beat his wife. The lowest rates of violence against wives are by husbands who do not drink, the highest among those who go on binges.

The Social Heredity of Violence

Straus, Gelles, and Steinmetz also discovered what they call the *social heredity of violence*—children learning from their parents that violence is a solution to problems, a lesson they apply after they marry. As Figure 11-11 shows, the more violence that children experience, the more likely they are to be violent after they marry. As these researchers (1980:113) explain: "Those with scores of zero are the people whose parents did not hit them and did not hit each other. At the other extreme are people with scores of 9. They are the people whose parents frequently hit them when they were teen-agers and whose parents were frequently violent with each other." They drive home this point by saying:

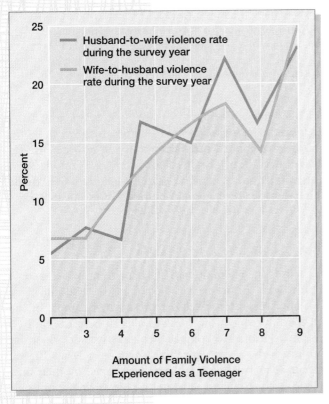

FIGURE 11-11
How Is Marital Violence Related to Amount of Family Violence Experienced as a Teenager?
(*Source:* From Murray A. Straus, Richard J. Gelles, and Suzanne K. Steinmetz. *Behind Closed Doors: Violence in the American Family* [Garden City, NY: Doubleday, 1980], p. 112. Copyright © 1980 by Murray A. Straus and Richard J. Gelles. Reprinted with permission.)

When one member of a couple had experienced the double whammy of being hit as a child and observing his or her parents hitting each other, there was a one in three chance that at least one act of violence had occurred during the year of the study!

Why does a woman remain with a husband who abuses her? Sociologists Kathleen Ferraro and John Johnson (1992), who interviewed battered women, found four primary reasons. Some women feel that they can change their husband, whom they view as basically "a good man." Many tend to rationalize away the violence—their husband was under a lot of stress, or even, it was their own fault for provoking him. Others see no way out, no option such as a job or another relationship. Finally, a few wives feel that marriage is sacred, divorce sinful, and no matter what happens they must remain married.

After putting up with abuse for years, however, some women abruptly leave their husbands. Why? Ferraro and Johnson found that one or more things had occurred: (1) the violence had escalated, (2) the woman's resources had changed (for example, she had a job), (3) the relationship had changed (such as the husband no longer expressing remorse after a beating, or the wife concluding that she no longer loved him), or (4) the abuse had become more visible (for example, taking place in public).

Some wives, of course, leave their husbands after the first blow, and never return. Others, after being brutalized for years, kill their husbands. Wife beating has become a controversial defense for wives who have killed their husbands. For example, Cindy Hudo, a 21-year-old mother of two in Charleston, South Carolina, was charged with the murder of her husband, Buba. Here is what she said:

I start in the car and I get down the road and I see Buba walking, and he's real mad. I just look at him. So, I pull over, you know, and I'm trying, you know—"I didn't know to pick you up. You know, I'm sorry." And he didn't even say nothing to me. He just started hitting on me. And that's all I wanted to do, was just get home, because I was just self-conscious. I don't want nobody to see him hitting me, because I didn't want him to look bad. I had to go to work in a half-hour, because I was working a double-shift. And he told me I had forty minutes to get all my furniture out of the house and get my clothes and be out or he was going to throw them out. And I was sitting there, because I could talk him down. You know, because I didn't want to leave him. I just talked to him. I said, "Buba, I don't want to leave." I said, "This is my house." And then he told me . . . (unclear) my kids. And I said, "No, you're not taking my kids from me. That's too much." And so I said, "Just let me leave. Just let me take the kids. And, you know I'll go, and you know, I won't keep the kids from you or nothing like that." And he said, "I'm going to take them and you're getting out."

[Buba then loaded a shotgun, pointed it at Cindy, and said:] "The only way you're going to get out of this is if you kill me and I'll—I'll kill you." [Buba then gave the shotgun to Cindy and] just turned around and walked right down the hall, because he knew I wouldn't do nothing. And I just sat there a minute. And I don't know what happened. I just, you know, I went to the bedroom and I seen him laying there and I just shot him. He moved. I shot him again because I thought he was going to get up again. . . .

I loved him too much. And I just wanted to help him. ("20/20," October 18, 1979)

Although Cindy had shot and killed her husband, who at the time was unarmed and unresisting, a jury acquitted her on the basis that she was a battered wife.

As with Cindy Hudo, in a few celebrated cases wife battering as a defense for homicide has worked, and wives have been acquitted for intentional murder. No matter how understandable the desire to kill may be under conditions of extreme duress, brutality, and fear, this defense raises nagging questions about justifying the killing of spouses.

SEXUAL ABUSE IN THE FAMILY

Marital Rape

How Common Is Marital Rape?

How common is marital rape? This is an area of human behavior about which people are secretive, making it difficult to gather information. Sociologists David Finkelhor and Kersti Yllo (1983, 1989), however, interviewed a representative sample of the Boston metropolitan area. Of the 330 women in their sample, 10 percent reported that their husbands had used physical force to compel them to have sex. Based on another sampling technique from which we can generalize, sociologist Diana Russell (1980) estimates that 12 percent of married women have been raped by their husbands. If 10 to 12 percent is even close to being accurate, we are talking about millions of married women who have suffered this form of sexual abuse.

Three Types of Marital Rape

From interviews with fifty women who had been raped by their husbands, Finkelhor and Yllo found three types of sexual assault in marriage:

1. *Nonbattering rape.* In about 40 percent of the cases, the husband sexually assaulted his wife without intending physical harm. This usually was preceded by a conflict over sex, such as the husband feeling insulted when his wife refused to have sex. These cases seem to express the husband's need to maintain power and domination over his wife.

2. *Battering rape.* In about 48 percent of the cases, the husband intentionally inflicted physical pain during the sexual assault. He was retaliating for some supposed wrongdoing on his wife's part.

3. *Perverted rape.* In these instances, about 6 percent, the husband seemed to be sexually aroused by the violent elements of rape. These husbands forced their wives to submit to unusual sexual acts. (The remaining 6 percent contain elements of more than one type.)

Effects of Marital Rape

How did the rapes affect the wives? The short-term effects were anger accompanied by grief, despair, shame, and a feeling of "dirtiness." The most common long-term effect was the woman's inability to trust intimate relationships or to function sexually.

The Timing of Marital Rape

Marital rape most often occurs during separation or when a marriage is breaking up. In rare instances, however, husbands rape their wives throughout marriage. One woman, for example, had endured marital rape for twenty-four years—her marriage only ended when her husband divorced her!

Chapter 11   The Changing Family

Marital rape is often viewed as a case of the husband being a little too insistent and the wife a little too reticent. Marital rape, however, can be every bit as violent as a rape by strangers. The victims of marital rape often feel locked into their situation. Seeing few alternatives and living in fear, they are often victimized for years.

Why Do Some Women Put Up with Marital Rape?

Although most women quickly leave a marriage after being raped by their husbands, some remain. Why? The answer appears to be similar to why women who are physically but *not* sexually abused remain with their husbands. They are afraid to leave. They fear they do not have the skills to make it on their own. Or, they have children, and with their low self-esteem, feel they cannot survive without their husbands.

Incest

Another area that sociologists have investigated is **incest**—forbidden sexual relations between relatives, such as brothers and sisters or parents and children. Sexual relations between siblings or with one's own children are condemned almost universally. If a culture allows these, it is for specific categories of people, and often under specific circumstances. Examples include Thonga lion hunters of East Africa, who may have sex with their daughters on the night before a big hunt, and brother-sister marriages among the Egyptian pharaohs and the Incas of Peru (La Barre 1954; Beals and Hoijer 1965). Apart from such rare exceptions, incest is viewed as abhorrent, sinful, or unnatural. Revelations of incest are met with repugnance, and incest is one issue on which most Americans strongly agree.

With such strong condemnation, incest should be rare, but sociologists have found that it is not (Lewin 1998). Diana Russell (1986) interviewed a probability sample (from which we can generalize) of 930 women in San Francisco and found that before they turned age 18, 16 percent had been victims of incest. Her definition included any relative, and she defined incest so broadly that it included not only sexual intercourse and rape but also unwanted kisses. In only 5 of 100 cases were the police informed. While this study does not adequately reflect common assumptions about incest, we can conclude that official figures underreport it.

Who Are the Offenders?

Who are the offenders? Russell found that uncles are in first place, followed by first cousins, then fathers (biological, adoptive, step, and foster), brothers, and finally other relatives from brothers-in-law to step-grandfathers. In Russell's sample, incest between mother and son was rare, a finding other researchers support (Lester 1972).

Effects on Victims

Incest creates enormous burdens for its victims (Bartoi and Kinder 1998; Lewin 1998). Finkelhor (1980) found that both male and female victims of incest have lower self-esteem, and boys victimized by older men are four times as likely as nonvictims to engage in homosexual behavior. Russell (n.d.) found that incest victims who experience the most difficulty are those who have been victimized most often, those whose incest took place over longer periods of time, and those whose incest was "more serious," such as sexual intercourse as opposed to sexual touching.

Susan Forward, a psychotherapist who was herself a victim of incest, reports:

> I understand incest not only as a psychotherapist but as a victim. When I was fifteen my father's playful seductiveness turned into highly sexualized fondling. This is a difficult admission for me to make, but even more painful is the fact that I enjoyed my father's attentions.
>
> I felt enormously guilty about my participation in the incest, as if I had been responsible. I know now I was not. It was my father's responsibility as an adult and as

a parent to prevent sexual contact between us, but I didn't understand that at the time.

I also felt guilty about competing with my mother—who was only thirty-three and very attractive.

I was flattered by my father's attraction to me, and his caresses felt good, but after several months my guilt became too great. I somehow found the courage to tell him to stop, and he did. The psychological damage, however, had already been done.

As my guilt feelings accumulated, my self-image deteriorated. I felt like a "bad girl." I began to punish myself unconsciously, most prominently by marrying an unloving man instead of pursuing the acting career I had dreamed of since I was five. Later, when my children were in school, I finally got a job on a television series. Good jobs followed and success was within my grasp. But my guilt still fought me on an unconscious level, telling me that I didn't deserve success. So I allowed myself—unconsciously, of course, to become overweight and matronly at twenty-eight. My acting career stagnated. My marriage was a mess. I was desperately unhappy. Yet I had absolutely no idea that there was any connection between what my father had done to me and the problems in my life. (Forward and Buck 1978:1)

The "Pro-incest Lobby"

A tiny minority take the position that incest is not a problem. The problem, they say, is the *attitude* toward incest. If the attitude were different and incest were allowed, no one would have a problem. This small "pro-incest lobby," sometimes called the "new permissivists," claims that the state should not pass laws against incest because they are based on outdated biblical ideas. They argue that prohibiting incest chills affectionate relationships of sexual love that can bind people to one another (De Mott 1980).

If the pro-incest lobby ever were to succeed in removing what has been called the "last taboo," the change certainly would affect family life—and, as most would say, devastatingly. The chances of this happening range from impossible to remote.

OLD AGE AND WIDOWHOOD

Problems of Adjustment

In contrast with our past, most Americans today survive to old age. Old age brings many problems of adjustment, especially health, the death of loved ones, and the knowledge of one's own impending death. When the elderly retire (or disengage from productive roles, as sociologists put it), their social worth can be challenged. They may even face subtle and less subtle accusations of being parasites—of robbing younger workers by bankrupting the Social Security system.

The Family as Buffer

The family stands as a buffer between the individual and negative evaluations that can destroy self-esteem. It provides a sense of belonging and personal worth. For most adults, the love and understanding of a spouse and children contribute welcome equilibrium. In sharp contrast to their general social devaluation, the elderly especially value acceptance within the family.

From Extended to Nuclear Family

Several generations ago, Americans lived in **extended families;** that is, other relatives, perhaps a grandmother or an uncle, lived with the parents and their children. During this agrarian period, the aged, who owned the land, could maintain positions of authority, gradually relinquishing control while easing younger family members into responsible roles. Although we cannot be sure, the transition to old age may have been smoother and perhaps less painful than today.

The **nuclear family,** consisting of only parents and children, has become our dominant family form. It excludes the "older generation" and unmarried relatives. Because they now live apart, the young are thought to be less able to console the old or provide as much direct social support. A common image is of people living in

The Myth of Family
Abandonment

Intimacy at a
Distance

The
Institutionalized
Elderly

Adjustment to
Widowhood

dispersed family units, with the elderly living alienated and isolated from the ungrateful children they reared. Eventually the elderly live out their last years in nursing homes, abandoned and embittered.

We noted in Chapter 2 that such imagery is far from the truth. A team of sociologists who studied the residents of Muncie, Indiana, found that older Muncie residents maintain contact with their children (Caplow et al. 1982). National studies show that 55 percent of Americans age 65 and over are still living with their spouse. Another 15 percent live with other people, and 30 percent live alone (*Statistical Abstract* 2001:Table 40).

Sociologist Elaine Brody (1978) reports that abandonment of the elderly is about as true as the illusion of a golden past in which the whole family lived idyllically on a farm, joyfully meeting each other's every need. She says that in the United States both the elderly and the young *prefer* to live apart. The elderly prefer to live near, but not with, their children—described as "intimacy at a distance."

Sociologist Suzanne Steinmetz (1988) reports that parents and their adult children who live together tend to get on one another's nerves. The elderly appear to be acting on a good "sixth sense," then, when they want to live near, but not with, their children. Far from abandoning their aged parents, children remain key figures in the support system of the elderly (Bengtson et al. 1990).

As discussed in Chapter 2, the 5 percent of the aged who are institutionalized are not typical of most older people. Nationwide, only 10 percent of nursing home residents are married, only about half have a surviving adult child, and most have severe illnesses that require professional care. And again contrary to myth, most nursing home residents who have families have not been "dumped." As Elaine Brody reported (1978:20–21):

> Prior to institutionalization, most families have endured severe personal, social, and economic stress in attempting to avoid admission [to a nursing home]; it is typically the last, not the first, resort; and the decision is made reluctantly. The "well" spouse usually is in advanced old age. The adult children are often approaching or engaged in the aging phase of life with attendant age-related stresses and often are subjected to competing demands from ill spouses or their own children.

Family warmth, affection, and understanding help people adjust to old age. But when death ends a marriage, it destroys an essential part of this vital support system. The survivor then faces life without the partner who had provided such solace and orientation to life. With the disruption of family relationships and the loss of social roles, the widowed face three main problems: loneliness, anxiety, and economic survival (Hiltz 1989).

Sociologist Robert Atchley (1975) studied retired school teachers and retired employees of a telephone company who were in their 70s. He found that the widowers generally did better than the widows. They were more likely to be active in organizations, to have more contact with friends, and to be less anxious. The key, Atchley found, was money. Widowers were more financially secure and therefore less anxious generally. Atchley also found a surprising variable—the ability to afford a car. Those with cars, whether widows or widowers, got out of the house more, participated in more group activities, and visited their friends more often. The mobility a car offered was *the* key factor in reducing social isolation, loneliness, and anxiety.

Atchley's findings can be summarized as a principle that runs through social life: In general, the more adequate their income, the better people adjust to whatever challenges they face.

"Money can't buy happiness" is an old saying that you're probably familiar with. This saying is false. Money does buy happiness. Compared with poor people, wealthier people are more satisfied with life—and more optimistic about the future. Their health is better, they live longer, and even their marriages last longer.

THE DEATH OF THE FAMILY?

A Picture of Decline?

Marriage is doomed. Our high divorce rate shows that it is no longer a viable social institution. Its many problems signal the end of the contemporary family unit. As Figure 11-10 (on page 380) shows, cohabitation is almost *nine times* higher than it was in the 1970s. If this trend continues, eventually most people will live together, not marry. Moreover, as Table 11-1 illustrates, the average household has been *shrinking*, indicating that there is little left of the family. And as more unmarried women bear children, marriage will become a quaint custom reserved for a few traditionals.

Are such proclamations of the death of the family true? Let's look at sociological research.

The Highest Marriage Rate in History

The truth is that marriage flourishes. A *larger* proportion of Americans marry today than ever before. As Figure 11-12 shows, about 95 percent of Americans marry—the *highest* percentage in our history.

The "Middletown" Research

Sociological research in Muncie, Indiana, also indicates that the U.S. family is not disintegrating. Muncie is one of the most thoroughly researched of U.S. cities. In the 1920s and 1930s, sociologists Robert and Helen Lynd (1929, 1937) analyzed life in this mid-American city, which they called "Middletown." In the 1980s, other sociologists updated this classic study to find out if the family had declined during those fifty years. If it had, they would find higher rates of suicide, mental breakdown, and domestic violence.

To their surprise, Theodore Caplow and his fellow researchers (1982) found these problems to be *less* frequent in Middletown than they had been two generations earlier. They found that people are not living in isolated nuclear families but are embedded in larger kin networks, where they find economic support and satisfying personal relationships. Most parents and their grown children keep in close touch. Perhaps their most surprising finding was that marriage had become more vibrant. Marriage in the 1920s was shallower, with less communication between husband and wife.

Table 11-1	Average Size of U.S. Households			
1960	**1970**	**1980**	**1990**	**2000**
3.3	3.1	2.8	2.6	2.6

Source: Statistical Abstract 1991:Table 61; 1994:Table 70; 2001:Table 54.

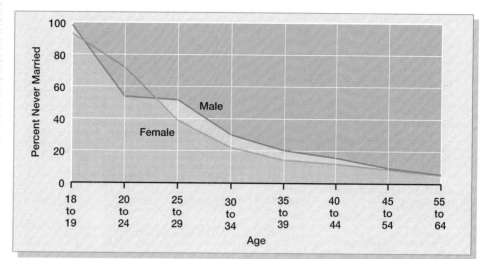

FIGURE 11-12

The Percentage of Americans Who Have Never Married, By Age

(*Source: Statistical Abstract 2001:Table 51.*)

Now that male and female roles are less segregated, husbands and wives talk things over more—and are *more satisfied* with marriage. Caplow concludes that "for most of their members most of the time, Middletown's composite families provide a safe and comfortable niche in a hazardous world." The idea that the family has declined is a "sociological myth."

Yes, but . . .

Despite such a rosy assessment, U.S. families are struggling to adjust to severe challenges. As noted previously, the family always has been in transition, but recent transitions are startling. Figure 11-13 shows that only a quarter of U.S. households consists of a married couple with their children, the same as the number of Americans who live alone. Only 53 percent of all U.S. households are made up of married couples, with or without children. Table 11-2 also indicates the vast change engulfing the family. Note especially the increase in the number of children who are living with only one parent.

Changes, but No Collapse

What shall we make of these contradictory findings? We can conclude that the changes and problems the family is experiencing are not signs of its collapse. Despite divorce, cohabitation, unwed motherhood, family violence, and forces that pull people apart and even make them flee, family life remains attractive: Americans are marrying at their highest rate in history, and most divorced people eventually remarry, although more slowly than before. Some sociological research even documents areas of family life that have improved over the years, especially more satisfying interaction between spouses.

◆ Social Policy ◆

The Family Besieged by Professionals

Social policy for the family is mired in controversy, for every policy steps on someone's toes. In *Haven in a Heartless World* (1977), social historian Christopher Lasch said that people are looking to the family as a refuge of love and decency in a cruel and heartless world. The family, however, generally cannot provide these comforts because it has been besieged by professionals—doctors, social workers, and teachers. They have attempted to enlarge their own professional domains at the expense of the family. Under the guise of helping, these practitioners have stripped the family of some of its functions, eroding its capacity to provide protective intimacy.

Table 11-2 How U.S. Families Are Changing

	1970	1980	1990	1998	Change since 1970
Marriages performed	2,159.0	2,390.0	2,448.0	1,840.0	Down 15%
Divorces granted	708.0	1,189.0	1,175.0	920.0	Up 30%
Married couples	47,500.0	52,300.0	56,300.0	56,490.0	Up 19%
Unmarried couples (cohabitants)	523.0	1,589.0	2,856.0	4,486.0	Up 758%
Persons living alone	10,851.0	18,296.0	23,000.0	26,727.0	Up 134%
Married couples with children at home	25,541.0	24,961.0	24,537.0	25,248.0	Up 1%
Children living with both parents	58,926.0	48,294.0	46,658.0	48,386.0	Down 18%
Children living with one parent	8,230.0	11,528.0	16,624.0	19,799.0	Up 141%
Average size of household	3.3	2.8	2.6	2.6	Down 21%
Married woman who are employed	18,000.0	24,000.0	30,000.0	34,6310.0	Up 92%

*2,159.0 represents 2,159,000

Source: U.S. Department of Commerce and *Statistical Abstract* 1992:Tables 49, 52, 56, 60, 62, 66, 67, 68, 69, 73, 127, 134, 619; 1999:Tables 61, 66, 71, 79, 85, 88, 92, 575, 576, 653.

What did Lasch mean? One example is professionals who claim to be experts in sexual adjustment. They write books and magazine articles about what sexual relations between husband and wife "ought" to be like. They appear on radio and television and proclaim their expertise. As a result, husbands and wives feel less able to work out their own sexual problems, for only "sexual experts" have the "real" answers. Another group of professionals stakes claim to child rearing. They profess to know the correct method for rearing children, making parents worry that, as mere laypersons, they may be damaging their children through improper parenting. Husbands and wives, then, look to "professionals," who intrude into these traditionally private areas of family life.

In short, Lasch says, we are on a road that leads to a "therapeutic society," where "experts" claim that all problems are their domain. "Public concern" by "experts" about the plight of the family—on television, radio, and in magazines and books—masks what is really happening. The family is being placed under control of outside influences. It is even worse than this, Lasch says, for contrary to popular opinion, "experts" have *not* benefited the family. Instead, they have marketed new services and products and established self-serving miniempires.

Professionals have reacted bitterly to this attack on their skills, accomplishments, and motives. They deny that they have self-serving motives and that they intrude into family life, undermine its authority, and cause it less "self-sufficiency" (Joffe 1978). The troubled family needs them, they reply.

The Dilemma of Family Policy: Taking Sides

Lasch's denunciations expose a core dilemma. Any social policy for the family finds itself on one side or the other of issues that divide fair-minded people who have the best interests of the family at heart. For example, consider what seems to be a neutral matter, making financial aid available to troubled families. One side suggests that such a policy would aid the family; another side, however, sees it as an attack on family self-sufficiency; it discourages families from looking out for themselves, making them further dependent on "Big Brother."

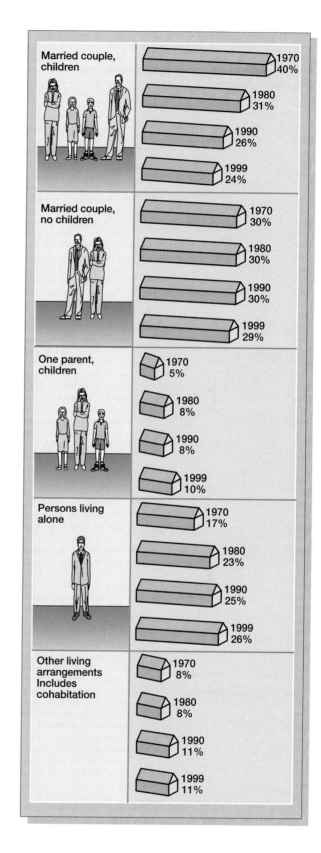

FIGURE 11-13
What Are Americans' Living Arrangements?
(*Source: Statistical Abstract 2000:Table 60.*)

The Battleground of Definitions: Intervention or Interference?

Another example is Hillary Rodham Clinton's book, *It Takes a Village: And Other Lessons Children Teach Us*. Its declared purpose was to make the public aware of the need of community involvement in child care. This seemed innocent enough, yet the book raised a storm of controversy, for some viewed it as a rallying cry for the state to intrude even further on the family, to eventually take child rearing away from parents.

Almost all policy falls on one side or the other of this explosive issue. Suppose a woman is undergoing counseling, and her therapist concludes that her problems are due to her husband being dominant. If the therapist encourages the woman to confront her husband, is this helping her to take steps toward rightful equality? Or is it yet another intrusion on private arrangements within the family, about which others should have no say?

Another example may make the underlying issue clearer. Suppose a 14-year-old girl is forbidden by her parents to have sex because they believe that premarital sex is wrong. The daughter faces a dilemma. She is afraid that if she does not have sex with her boyfriend he will date more cooperative girls. She also is "in love" and wants to please her boyfriend. The girl goes to a family planning clinic and tells them her plight. Counselors encourage her to assert herself against domineering and old-fashioned parents. They assure her that she can come to them for a free and confidential abortion if she becomes pregnant. They also offer her a Norplant.

How Values Underlie Policy

Who is "right" in these examples? As symbolic interactionists stress, our understanding of what "ought" to be ultimately depends on our values. As sociologist Carole Joffe (1978), who originated the above examples, said: "From a feminist perspective, the decision of a wife to confront her husband's sexism or a teenager to seek out adequate contraception is a step forward in 'liberation.'" From another standpoint, of course, the husband is carrying out his proper role, and to talk about "adequate" contraception is to have prejudged the issue. From this perspective, neither example represents a step toward "liberation," and both intrude on family privacy.

Each Family Member Has A Different Experience and View

We face divisive issues, then, when it comes to family social policy. We need to emphasize the symbolic interactionist position that different family members experience family life differently. Arrangements that some find comfortable and satisfying, others find oppressive (Joffe 1978). As the Thinking Critically box on children's rights on the next page shows, the issue of harming some by helping others pervades family policy. Government intervention to some is government interference to others. Both sides agree, however, that the young and defenseless need to be protected from physical and psychological brutality, as well as from anything that deprives them of their health and well-being. But even here a basic dilemma plagues social policy: the desire to allow or encourage families to be responsible and independent versus the need to protect individuals within the family (Chilman 1988). How do we guarantee such protection without a "Big Brother" to watch over every family's shoulder?

The Issue of Poverty

Apart from certain family problems, such as marital rape and child abuse, some sociologists see poverty as the root of family troubles. For them, the best solution is a robust economy with full employment. To this, we might add educational opportunities open to all. These would not solve all the family's problems, especially, say conflict theorists, those rooted in sexist-power orientations. They would, however, help to solve many of them.

Family policy in Sweden is the most extensive in the world. As you read the Global Glimpse box on Swedish family life (page 400), ask yourself which of Sweden's family policies would work in the United States.

THINKING CRITICALLY ABOUT SOCIAL PROBLEMS

Child Rights

In 1943, the U.S. Supreme Court determined that a cardinal principle of U.S. law is that "the custody, care, and nurture of the child reside in the parents." This decision usually has been interpreted to mean that parents have a total right to decide matters concerning the welfare of their children, with the state intervening only to stop abuse or neglect.

Americans, however, are divided over how many rights parents should have over their children. The central question is: At what point does the authority of the state supersede the authority of parents? When does the privacy of the family take precedence over the concern of well-intentioned outsiders? Let's look at the major arguments.

One group has lined up under the banner of child rights. In the journal *Human Rights*, Patricia Wald (1974) wrote that a "very young child" has the right "to be consulted and informed about critical decisions in his life, and (the) right to be represented in those decisions." To protect the child from the "consequences of unilateral parental actions…the child's interests deserve representation by an independent advocate before a neutral decision maker."

Wald also suggested that communities provide runaway shelters (or homes) to which children under 16 who do not want to return home can go. "Parents would have no right to forcibly take their children away from such homes," she proposed. A child ought to be able to seek legal advice to redress grievances against his or her family. Some say that children should be able to sue their parents for poor child rearing.

These proposals are designed to balance a system that favors the parents at the expense of children. For example, if parents want to take a better job out of town, they are involved in a "critical decision that would affect the child's life." Because this would mean that the child has to leave friends and attend a different school, the child should have the right to "an independent advocate to argue his or her case before a neutral decision maker." If the child does not want to go and the parents insist on moving, the independent advocate should be able to remove the child from the family.

The government has encroached on the family and eroded its rights to rear children without interference from "Big Brother." Parents' rights need to be strengthened. The law needs to enforce the supremacy of parents over their children and over schools. The Family Protection Act proposed by Phyllis Schlafly (1979) represents this position:

1. Parents must have the right to visit public school classrooms and school functions.

2. Parents must be able to review textbooks before their use in public schools and help select other materials taught their children.

3. No federal funding should be given for courses that encourage children to rethink the values their parents have taught them, courses commonly called "values clarificaiton" and "behavior modification."

4. A child needs parental consent to enroll in courses about religion or "ethics," and parents should have the right to keep their children out of such courses if they find them offensive.

5. Parents must give permission for unmarried minors to get contraceptives or an abortion and must be informed if they are treated for a venereal disease.

6. The legal presumption must favor the parents' rights. If a child's "right to self-expression" conflicts with the parents' "right to educate or discipline," in the absence of compelling evidence of parental unfitness or other grave reason, the courts must presume in favor of the parents' rights.

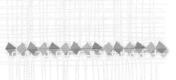

CENSUS 2000

The American family has changed significantly over the years, but there are a number of things that have remained the same. One of them is that for both married and unmarried couples, men tend to be older than their female counterparts, as the following data from the 2000 Census illustrate:

Percent

Age difference	Unmarried couples	Married couples
Male 6+ years older	25%	20%
Male 2–5 years older	29%	36%
About the same age	26%	32%
Female 2–5 years older	12%	9%
Female 6+ years older	9%	3%

As you can see, in about one-fourth of all couples the man is significantly older than his female partner. On the other hand, in only 9% of unmarried couples and 3% of married couples the woman is significantly older than her male partner.

Differences in earnings for couples are also gendered. Consider the following data:

Percent

Earnings difference	Unmarried couples	Married couples
Male earns $30,000 plus higher	14%	30%
Male earns $5,000–$29,999 higher	41%	29%
About the same	24%	26%
Female earns $5,000–$29,999 higher	18%	11%
Female earns $30,000 plus higher	4%	4%

This table shows that in over half of all couples, men earn at least $5,000 more than their female partner. On the other hand, in only 22% of unmarried couples and 15% of married couples does the woman earn $5,000 or more than the man.

Source: U.S. Census Bureau (2001). *America's Families and Living Arrangements.* P20-537. Table 8.

✦ The Future of the Problem ✦

The Sea of Social Change

Social change characterizes our society. Familiar landmarks are torn down and replaced, seemingly overnight, by a supermarket or another of an endless series of fast-food outlets. Computers recognize your speech, type your message, and check your grammar; cars announce your location, even guide you through traffic in a strange city. On the Internet, you can type something in English, and it is translated instantly into German or Spanish or any major language and transmitted to someone in a distant part of the world. Soon you'll be able to have one telephone number that will stay with you for life and will be valid throughout the world. Change is so rapid and extensive that parents and children live in different worlds—so much so that grown children visiting their parents after an absence of months or years often find that after the first hour or two they have little left to talk about.

Future Shock

The speed, extent, and intensity of today's social change are mind-boggling. We barely get used to one changed idea, object, or relationship when another overpow-

ISSUES in SOCIAL PROBLEMS

What Does Daycare Cost a Company?

Suppose that you are the president of Union Bank in Monterey, California. You have been asked to provide a day-care center for your employees. You would like to do so, but you can't spend stockholders' money on day care simply because you think it is a nice idea. You have to know the bottom line.

"Find out what it would cost us," the managers told Sandra Burud, a social science researcher. At first, it may sound fairly easy. You simply add the cost of the facilities and personnel, and you have the answer. But what you want to know is the net cost. After all, day care is supposed to benefit the company. Will the benefit be greater or less than the cost?

Now the problem becomes difficult. Some of the variables are easy to measure: out-of-pocket expenses, employee turnover, interview costs, hiring bonuses, and job advertisements. Some are impossible to measure, such as poor morale and loss of reputation if a lot of employees quit. In fact, Burud decided she couldn't put numbers on those variables and had to skip them. Other variables are in between: productive time lost while a current employee is on maternity leave or is job hunting, while the job is left open, and while a new employee is learning. Turnover costs are high: Merck

Pharmaceuticals has found that new employees cost it five months of work during their first fourteen months on the job, concluding that job turnover costs one to two times an employee's annual salary.

To determine the net costs of day care, Union Bank had to open a day-care center to see what happened. That cost the bank $105,000. Then Burud compared 87 users of the center with a control group of 105 employees. She found that turnover among the center's users was 2 percent; among the control group, 10 percent. Users of the center were also absent an average of two days a year less than the control group, and their maternity leaves were one week shorter.

The bottom line? After subtracting its costs of running the day-care center, the bank saved $232,000.

Should you, the president, have your bank open a day-care center? Now, that is an easy decision.

Such companies as Marriott Hotels have paid attention to the bottom-line results of corporate day care and have opened their own centers. Other companies, such as Levi Strauss and AT&T, subsidize their employees' child care.

Based on Solomon 1988; Shellenbarger 1994.

---

ers it—and us. Alvin Toffler (1971) called this dizzying barrage of change to which we have no leisure or opportunity to adjust future shock. **Future shock** is the vertigo, the confusion, the disorientation that we experience when our familiar world is transformed.

The U.S. family is experiencing future shock. It has already had to adapt to large-scale social change, for industrialization and urbanization left little untouched. Now computers are changing work habits, education, recreation, and entertainment. Parents and children e-mail messages to one another from office, school, home, and friends, giving updates on changing plans. Because the family is continuing to adapt to changing social conditions, its future is unclear. But let's venture into these unchartered waters.

The Direction of Change

The lofty goals of love and marriage are firmly established in our culture, and people will continue to marry at a rate close to what we now have. The age at first marriage will continue upward, then stabilize. Cohabitation will continue to increase for another decade, and then gradually level off. The proportion of married women employed outside the home will continue to increase, eventually plateauing at about 75 to 80 percent. Marriage will become even more oriented around companionship.

With this orientation and more wives working outside the home, husbands and wives will develop more equal relationships. Marriage will remain brittle; our high divorce rate will continue to drop for a while and then level off. Day care will become more common for children of working parents (see the Issues box on page 401). Whether you interpret such changes as good, bad, or indifferent depends, of course, on your values.

The Ideological Struggle

The struggle by ideologically committed groups to control the family will intensify. Family policy will mirror those contrasting ideologies. With their incompatible views of right, justice, and the good life, conflicting groups will continue to try to make family policy conform to their own vision of reality and propriety. Regardless of who wins in the short term, this competition of ideas and values will continue. The future looks exciting, the outcome uncertain. Much of your own family life hangs in the balance.

◆ Summary

1. The family is always adjusting to social change. One of the most significant effects of the industrial revolution was the removal of economic production from the household.

2. Whether change within the family is a social problem or merely a form of adaptation is a matter of values and views. Indicators that many see as evidence of a social problem include divorce, runaway children, births to single women, one-parent families, and violence and sexual abuse in the family.

3. In analyzing problems of the family, symbolic interactionists stress our changing ideas of sex roles and expectations of marriage; functionalists, the declining functions of the family; and conflict theorists, the unequal distribution of power in the family. All these underlie our high divorce rate.

4. After declining for sixty or seventy years, the median age at first marriage increased. The primary reason is *cohabitation*. As many people postpone marriage, a growing proportion of the young are single.

5. In our pro-parenthood society, childless couples face a stigma. Married couples remain childless because of infertility, the decision not to have children, or the continuous postponement of children until childlessness becomes inevitable.

6. Physical violence between family members is common. While wives initiate about as much violence as husbands, they are injured more often. People reared in violent homes are more likely to be violent to their own spouses and children. Violence is related to alcohol. Incest and marital rape are more frequent than commonly supposed.

7. That the elderly are abandoned by their families is a myth. Most keep in close touch. The elderly prefer to live near their children, but not with them, a preference called "intimacy at a distance." Widowhood appears to be easier for men than women; this is not due to gender—rather, those who are better off financially adjust better to the death of a spouse.

8. The family is far from doomed, and is much healthier than most imagine. More Americans are marrying today than ever. The "Middletown" studies indicate that husbands and wives are more satisfied with married life than they were fifty years ago.

9. Social policy on the family is controversial. Controversy also surrounds the intervention of "family professionals"; they claim to help families, but some accuse them of expanding their domain at the expense of the family.

10. These trends are likely to continue: increases in cohabitation, age at first marriage, two-paycheck families, day care, and marital equality. Groups concerned about the family differ in their ideas and values, and it remains to be seen which groups will be dominant in policy decisions.

◆ Key Terms

Cohabitation A couple living together in a sexual and emotional relationship outside marriage.

Extended family A family in which other relatives, such as the "older generation" or unmarried aunts and uncles, live with the parents and their children.

Family of orientation The family into which one is born and from which one receives one's basic orientations to life.

Family of procreation The family formed by one's marriage and that generally results in procreation, or the birth of children.

Future shock The confusion or disorientation that accompanies rapid social change.

Incest Forbidden sexual relations between relatives, such as brothers and sisters or parents and children.

Nuclear family A family consisting of a husband, wife, and their children.

Personal trouble A problem experienced by an individual that, were it widespread, would indicate the presence of a social problem. Examples are unemployment and divorce. They are personal troubles for those who experience them, but social problems if widespread, for then they indicate that something is wrong with the structure of the marketplace or of marriage.

◆ Critical Thinking Questions

1. List and explain what you consider to be the five greatest benefits and the five greatest downsides of the changes in the composition of U.S. families.
   - Do you think the positives outweigh the negatives, or vice-versa? Explain.
2. Which perspective (symbolic interactionism, functionalism, or conflict theory) do you believe does a better job of explaining the changes that are taking place in U.S. families? Explain.

3. Rank the seven traditional functions of the family according to how important you think they are in maintaining today's family. Explain your rankings.
4. With the huge increase in cohabitation, the high divorce rate, and the extent of abuse in families, do you think that the institution of marriage is doomed? Explain.

Urban Problems

12

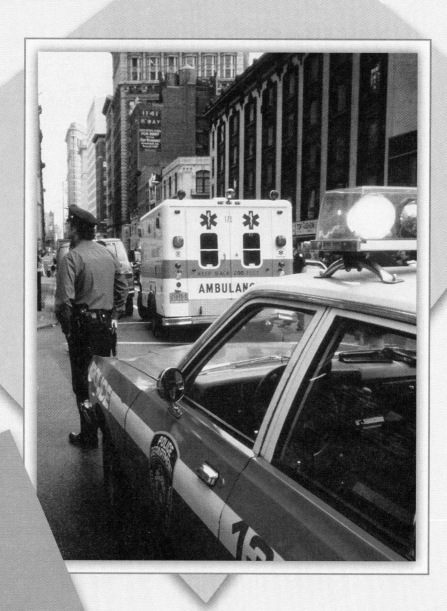

*K*ellie Moiser was a 17-year-old who worked part time at the corner ice-cream store. But mostly she dreamed of becoming a model. Knowing how attractive Kellie was, her mother encouraged her dream, saying it would be a way out of the ghetto.

But Kellie never got the chance.

Michael Hagan, 23, also lived in the slums of south-central Los Angeles. He likes Olde English "800" Malt Liquor, especially when he smokes PCP.

He also likes guns.

And a little blood doesn't bother him, either.

One Monday evening he was on a binge with other members of his gang, when they decided to go after a rival gang. They piled into a blue Buick and sped toward enemy turf. There they spotted four teenagers, two of them girls.

The teenagers were not gang members. They were just kids who had gone out for ice cream and were in the wrong place at the wrong time. They ran when they saw the gun. But Kellie didn't run fast enough. Hagan methodically pumped fifteen slugs into her, six into her back.

It took Kellie's mother, Irene, to solve her daughter's murder. Out of a fury born of grief, she stormed the streets in search of the killer, even barging into local dope houses. A sympathetic inmate in the county jail sent her a letter telling her who killed her girl.

Irene says, "I knew these gang members when they were just babies. Now look at them. They've turned into killers."

"Jail ain't bad," says Hagan. "To me, life is not much better on the streets than in jail. I can live here, no problem."

"The gang is your family," he explains. "If you're a Crip, I fight for you, no matter what the odds. If you're the enemy, it's do or die."

Hagan adds, "If I had a son, I'd give him a choice: either he can go to school and be a goody-goody, or he can hit the streets."

Hagan smiles broadly as he says, "I done did something, and I'm known. I consider myself public enemy No. 1."

Based on Hull 1987.

◆ The Problem in Sociological Perspective ◆

Hagan is part of the American nightmare—the unsafe streets, the drive-by shootings, the senseless killings, without conscience, that destroy those who are trying to build a future. Before we get to Hagan, however, let's look at the history of cities.

The Urban Movement

Two hundred years ago, almost everyone in the world lived in rural areas. Only 3 percent lived in towns of 5,000 or more (Hauser and Schnore 1965). By 1900, the total was up to 13 or 14 percent. Today, half of the entire world lives in cities.

In its early history, the United States, too, was almost exclusively rural. In 1800, only about 6 of 100 Americans lived in towns of 2,500 or more. As Figure 12-1 shows, cities became more and more popular, and around 1920 half of Americans lived in cities. Today about 4 of every 5 Americans do. The states differ in their degree of urbanization, of course, which is illustrated on the Social Map on page 401.

The Evolution of Cities

The speed and extent of today's urbanization are new to the world scene, but cities are not. Perhaps as early as 6000 to 8000 B.C., people built cities with massive walls, such as biblically famous Jericho (Homblin 1973). Some, however, think cities originated later, in conjunction with the invention of writing. In about 3500 B.C., cities developed in several parts of the world—first in Mesopotamia, then in the Nile,

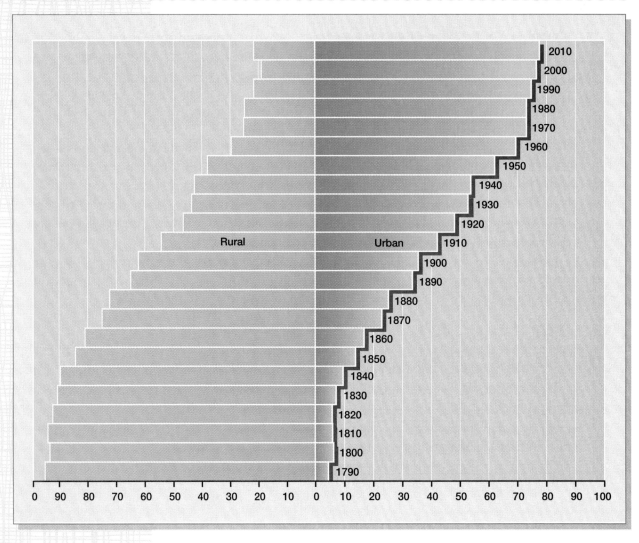

FIGURE 12-1
The Percentage of the U.S. Population That Is Rural or Urban
(Source: U.S. Bureau of the Census, Statistical Abstract, 2001:Table 30, with projection from 1990 to 2010 by the author.)

Indus, and Yellow River valleys, around the Mediterranean, in West Africa, Central America, and the Andes (Fischer 1976).

The evolution of cities depended on agriculture. Only when agriculture produced a surplus could some people stop producing food and gather in cities to pursue other occupations. A **city,** in fact, can be defined as a large number of people who live in one place and do not produce their own food. Thus, more efficient agricultural techniques spur urban development. The invention of the plow during the fourth millennium B.C. created an agricultural surplus that stimulated the development of towns and cities (Curwin and Hart 1961).

During the next five thousand years, the food surplus was only enough to allow a small minority of the world's population to live in urban areas. Then the industrial revolution of the 1700s and 1800s set off the urban revolution that we are still experiencing today. It stimulated the invention of mechanical means of transportation and communication, and allowed people, resources, and products to be moved efficiently—essential factors on which the modern city depends.

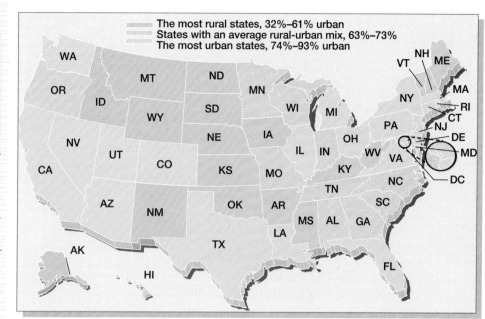

FIGURE 12-2
**Social Map:
How Urban Is
Your State?
The Urban-Rural
Makeup of the
United States**

The most rural state is Vermont, where two of three (68 percent) of residents live in rural areas. The most urban state is California, where only 7 percent live in rural areas. Washington, D.C., is 100 percent urban.

(*Source: Statistical Abstract* 2001:Table 30.)

The most rural states, 32%–61% urban
States with an average rural-urban mix, 63%–73%
The most urban states, 74%–93% urban

Cities as Solutions

In themselves, cities are not problems. On the contrary, they are designed to solve problems, to make life better by transcending the limitations of farm and village. Cities offer the hope of a better life, of gaining work, education, and other advantages. With these benefits, cities are growing around the world. As discussed in the Global Glimpse box on the next page, people in the Least Industrialized Nations are deserting their rural way of life and flocking to urban areas for just these reasons.

Table 12-1 lists the world's ten largest cities. Note that only four are in the Most Industrialized Nations, and that those in the Least Industrialized Nations are growing much more rapidly. In fifteen years, Tokyo is the only city from the Most

Table 12-1   The World's Ten Largest Cities

Rank	City	Country	Population 2000	Remarks
1	Tokyo	Japan	34,900,000	incl. Yokohama, Kawasaki
2	New York	USA	21,160,000	incl. Newark, Paterson
3	Seoul	South Korea	21,150,000	incl. Inchon, Songnam
4	Mexico City	Mexico	20,750,000	incl. Nezahualcóyotl, Ecatepec, Naucalpan
5	São Paulo	Brazil	20,250,000	incl. Guarulhos
6	Bombay	India	18,150,000	incl. Kalyan, Thane, Ulhasnagar
7	Osaka	Japan	18,000,000	incl. Kobe, Kyoto
8	Delhi	India	17,150,000	incl. Faridabad & Ghaziabad
9	Los Angeles	USA	16,800,000	incl. Riverside, Anaheim
10	Jakarta	Indonesia	15,850,000	incl. Bekasi, Bogor, Depok, Tangerang

Source: Th. Brinkhoff: The Principal Agglomerations of the World, http://www.citypopulation.de, 11.05.2002

A GLOBAL GLIMPSE

Why City Slums Are Better than the Country: The Rush to the Cities of the Least Industrialized Nations

Images of the Least Industrialized Nations that portray pastoral life distort reality. The rural poor of these countries are flocking to the cities at such a rate that, as we saw in Table 12-1, these countries now contain most of the world's largest cities. In the Most Industrialized Nations, industrialization generally preceded urbanization, but in the Least Industrialized Nations *urbanization is preceding industrialization.* The cities cannot support their swelling populations.

The settlement patterns are also different. When rural migrants and immigrants move to U.S. cities, they usually settle in deteriorating housing near the city's center. The wealthy reside in suburbs and luxurious city enclaves. Migrants to cites of the Least Industrialized Nations, in contrast, establish illegal squatter settlements outside the city. There they build shacks from scrap boards, cardboard, and bits of corrugated metal. Even flattened tin cans become valuable building material. The squatters enjoy no city facilities—roads, public transportation, water, sewers, or garbage pickup. After thousands of squatters have settled an area, the city acknowledges their right to live there and adds bus service and minimal water lines. Hundreds of people use a single spigot. About 5 *million* of Mexico City's residents live in such conditions, with hundreds of thousands more pouring in each year.

This story is repeated throughout South America, Africa, India, and the rest of the so-called undeveloped world. Why this vast rush to live in the city under such miserable conditions? At its core are "push" factors arising from a breakdown of traditional rural life. With the importation of modern medicine, a safer water supply, and better transportation and distribution of food, the death rate dropped, and the rural populations are multiplying. There is not enough land for everyone, and rural life can no longer satisfy many people. "Pull" factors also draw people to the cities—the hope of jobs, education, better housing, and even a more stimulating life.

> At the bottom of a ravine near Mexico City is a dismal bunch of shacks. Some of the families have 14 children.
>
> "We used to live up there," Señora Gonzalez gestured toward the mountain, "in those caves. Our only hope was one day to have a place to live. And now we do." She smiled with pride at the jerry-built shacks... each one had a collection of flowers planted in tin cans. "One day, we hope to extend the water pipes and drainage—perhaps even pave...."
>
> And what was the name of her community? Señora Gonzalez beamed. "Esperanza!" (McDowell 1984:172)

Esperanza is the Spanish word for hope. This is what lies behind the rush to these cities—the hope of a better life. And this is why the rush won't slow down. In 1930, only one Latin American city had over a million people—now fifty do! The world's cities are growing by one million people each week (Brockerhoff 1996).

Will the Least Industrialized Nations adjust to this vast, unwanted migration? They have no choice. Authorities in Brazil, Guatemala, Venezuela, and other countries have sent in the police and army to evict the settlers. It doesn't work. This just leads to violence, and the settlers keep streaming in. The adjustment will be painful. The infrastructure (roads, water, sewers, electricity, and so on) must be built, but these poor countries don't have the resources to do it. As the desperate flock to the cities, the problems will worsen.

Do you see any solutions?

Industrialized Nations expected to remain on this list of top ten. It will still be the world's largest city, followed by Bombay, Lagos, Shanghai, Jakarta, São Paulo, Karachi, Beijing, Dhaka, and Mexico City. New York City will drop to the 11th spot (*United Nations Demographic Yearbook* 1997).

Cities as Problems

Cities not only solve problems, they also create them. Cities especially have difficulty meeting people's needs of **community,** the feeling of belonging, the sense that

others care what happens to you and that you can depend on the people around you. Some people do find community in the city, but others find alienation and live in isolation and fear. Still others, like Hagan, band together to create fear and make the city a miserable place to live.

◆ The Scope of the Problem ◆

An Antiurban Bias

Americans have long had an antiurban bias (Smith 1996). In 1780, Thomas Jefferson said that cities were "pestilential to the morals, the health, and the liberties of man." He (1977) added that cities contribute to the good government of a nation about as much as sores contribute to the body's strength. Though attitudes have not always been this extreme, Americans often picture rural life as the serene source of virtue and the city as the corrupter of youth and the source of evil.

An Ambivalence

Many Americans carry an image of an agrarian paradise, where life is innocent, simpler, and happier (Hadden and Barton 1973). The cold brutality of contemporary urban life—the many Hagans wandering the streets in search of victims—makes people long for something better. This reaction shows people's deep ambivalence: While masses of people dream of fleeing the city to find safety and security, they remain fascinated with the city, for it offers work, cultural attractions, and diversions.

In light of this ambivalence—the city's threat and its allure—we will examine the major problems facing our urban centers.

What Is Urban About Urban Problems?

In one sense, almost all social problems are "urban." Because most Americans live in cities, poverty, crime, unemployment, divorce, drug addiction, violence, and so forth are concentrated in cities. None of these problems is simply urban, however, because these problems can—and do—occur everywhere. Aside from their greater frequency in cities, there is little that is specifically urban about such problems.

In two senses, however, there are *urban* problems. For one thing, city life *increases* social problems. The *rates* of burglary, robbery, suicide, alcoholism, and rape, for example, are higher in cities than in rural areas. Why should this be? Why do urban areas increase these activities and produce people like Hagan? Or, conversely, why do rural areas diminish them? We will return to this question.

Second, the United States is facing an *urban crisis*. U.S. cities have areas that almost everyone fears and avoids. There, amidst burned out and boarded-up buildings, addicts and the unemployed slouch on apartment steps. Drug dealers openly work their street corners, a lucrative turf that they defend by violence. People like Hagan prowl the streets. Anyone entering these areas is at peril—even the police. During economic downturns, some cities shorten the school year because they cannot meet the payroll; others slash library and garbage collection budgets and even reduce police and fire protection. Across the nation the middle class is rushing to the suburbs, leaving the inner city to the poor, a flight that further impoverishes the city. Another problem is **urban sprawl,** replacing farm land with asphalt and buildings as cities spread into the countryside. The term **urban crisis** refers to this cluster of interrelated urban problems.

◆ Looking at the Problem Theoretically ◆

As usual, our three theoretical perspectives yield contrasting insights. As we apply symbolic interactionism to the slums, we will glimpse their social organization, which ordinarily remains invisible to outsiders. Functionalism will explain the zones of activity that develop as a city expands. Finally, the conflict perspective will show us how class conflict creates urban problems.

SYMBOLIC INTERACTIONISM

If Americans are ambivalent about the city, they are not so when it comes to the slums. Most fear them; everyone avoids them. Most middle-class Americans shake their heads and say that they can't understand why anyone would live "like that."

Provides an Insider's View of Social Life, Including Slums

These are outsider's views. Symbolic interactionists try to see how life looks to the people who live it. They try to discover the meanings that people give to their experiences, how they feel about their situation, and how they cope with their problems. As they produce studies of the worlds of the urban poor, they try not to impose their own values or views on others. This approach to understanding urban life is called the **Chicago school of sociology,** because it represents the approach used by the sociology department of the University of Chicago in the 1920s and 1930s.

The Chicago School of Sociology

This department produced classic studies of urban life. In 1923 Nels Anderson wrote *The Hobo,* followed in 1927 by Frederic Thrasher's *The Gang.* In 1929 Harvey Zorbaugh's *The Gold Coast and the Slum* contrasted the poor and the rich in Chicago. Then, in 1932, Paul Cressey published *Taxi-Dance Hall,* about women who made their living by dancing with men. Making the city their sociological laboratory, these sociologists, as others have done since, focused on the lives of the poor.

The contrasts of the city—its many groups with dissimilar ways of life—fascinated sociologists at Chicago. They were especially impressed with how people of different backgrounds live in separate areas and develop unique subcultures. As Louis Wirth (1938) said, the city is made up of "a mosaic of social worlds." While fascinatingly different, their distinctive customs make it easy for people from different areas to misunderstand one another.

Whyte's Study

In this tradition, sociologist William Foote Whyte did participant observation in a slum for two or three years. In *Street Corner Society* (1943, 1995), Whyte explains that what may look to the outsider to be disorganized is, in fact, a tightly knit way of life. By participating in the residents' lives—hanging around the street corners, going to dances, playing baseball, and so on—Whyte uncovered rigid distinctions between people. For example, the young men were divided into two main groups, the college boys, who were upward bound, and the corner boys, who remained in their old neighborhood. Other major figures included racketeers and politicians. Each group had its own statuses, its own norms, and its own ways of controlling its members.

Suttles' Study

Thirty years later, when sociologist Gerald Suttles did participant observation of a Chicago slum, he found social statuses and forms of communication equally as complex. Although Italians, African Americans, Puerto Ricans, and Chicanos shared the same physical space, each had its own forms of communication—its own distinctive language, gestures, and clothing. Often, one group's customary ways of expressing itself were offensive to another (Suttles 1968:66–67):

> Whites say that Negroes will not look them in the eye. The Negroes counter by saying the whites are impolite and try to "cow" people by staring at them. . . . The most subtle accounts are those which describe almost entirely nonverbal encounters: "When I went over to the Negro nurse, she didn't even look up," "I'd go again (to an Italian restaurant) but they really stare you down," "I can understand why those guys (older Italian street group) can't half speak English, but why they gotta eyeball everybody walk past?"

Within each area of the city, different groups stake out a unique existence. They develop their own forms of self-expression, live by their own codes, and evaluate their members accordingly. Although these expectations unite a group's members, they hinder communication with others. This creates hostility among the diverse groups that compose the urban mosaic. As the quote shows, these differences lead to suspicion and misunderstanding. They sometimes lead even to death.

Anderson's Studies

In the 1970s, sociologist Elijah Anderson did participant observation in another Chicago slum. He, too, emphasizes how it is essential to see the world as others see it. Focusing on Jelly's, a bar and liquor store in an African-American area, Anderson (1978) explains the intricate boundaries between "us" and "them." He found three main groups at Jelly's:

The regulars. These men see and present themselves as hard-working. They subscribe to mainstream values, are proud of their involvement in families, and have aspirations of getting ahead. Their values can be summed up with the single word *decency*—working regularly and treating other people right.

The wineheads. These men neither value work, nor do they work regularly. Their main concern is getting enough money to buy wine. They beg from others and are given low status.

The hoodlums. These men pride themselves on "being tough" and having access to easy money. Few work regularly. They are involved in petty theft, stickups, burglaries, and fencing stolen property. The other men at Jelly's do not trust them, nor do they trust one another.

Anderson (1990, 1995) then took a job at the University of Pennsylvania and moved into what he calls the Village-Norton, a neighborhood in Philadelphia that was being "gentrified"; that is, more affluent people were moving into the area and rehabilitating its buildings. **Gentrification** creates tensions because it raises property values, taxes, and rents, forcing the poorer residents to move to lower-rent areas. Although the area begins to look prettier, the poor resent the invasion of their neighborhood and do not benefit from it.

The Village-Norton bordered a ghetto, and tension between residents of the two areas was acute. Both African-American and white residents viewed any unknown African American walking the streets of the Village-Norton suspiciously. Whites were afraid to look too long at African Americans they didn't know lest their look be interpreted as an invitation to interact. They pretended not to see other pedestrians or looked right through them without speaking. Used to more outgoing interaction, many African Americans found this behavior offensive. The truce was uneasy, and people had to live in the area for a while before they learned adequate street etiquette, that is, the norms that allowed the two groups to coexist.

In Sum

Within the larger, impersonal urban setting, people stake out territory, establish social boundaries between themselves and others, and work out a sense of identity and belonging. This is no less true of the slums. If you look beyond the run-down buildings, you find an intricate network of norms, associations, and friendships.

Symbolic interactionists also remind us that the poor do not experience urban problems in the abstract. They encounter specific problems. For example, they do not experience the concept of urban decay. Rather, they deal with cutbacks in city services; buses that run late or not at all; factories that move to Mexico and wipe out their jobs overnight; and, of course, killers like Hagan who stalk their neighborhood, hallways, and elevators. In short, symbolic interactionists focus on how people make sense of their experiences as they attempt to cope with urban life.

Burgess' Theory of Concentric Zones

The University of Chicago also produced urban studies that reflect the functionalist perspective. Sociologist Ernest Burgess studied how cities grow. As Figure 12-3 illustrates, he located five zones, each with distinct functions. Burgess visualized the city expanding outward from its center, the central business district (Zone I). Zone II, encircling the downtown area, contains the city's slums. To escape the slum, skilled and thrifty workers move to Zone III. Zone IV contains better apartments, residential hotels, single-family dwellings, and enclaves where the wealthy live. Still farther out, beyond the city limits, is Zone V, a commuter zone of suburbs or satellite cities.

Burgess intended his **concentric zone theory** to represent the "tendencies of any town or city to expand radially from its central business district." He noted, however, that no "city fits perfectly this ideal scheme." Some cities face physical obstacles such as lakes or rivers that make their expansion depart from this model. As Burgess also noted, businesses deviate from this model when they locate in outlying zones. Burgess could not anticipate today's suburban shopping malls, strung like beads around the city.

Mobility as an Essential Characteristic of Cities

This classic model of urban growth helps us understand urban problems. Burgess stressed that city dwellers are always on the move. In addition to commuting for work, school, shopping, and recreation, they move into better zones when they

FIGURE 12-3

Burgess' Concentric Zone Theory of the Growth of the City

On the right side of this figure are the concentric zones that flow from the central business district as a city expands. The left side shows the city of Chicago in 1925. The light vertical line represents the shore of Lake Erie.

(*Source:* From Ernest W. Burgess, 'The Growth of the City: An Introduction to a Research Project' in *The City,* edited by Robert E. Park, Ernest W. Burgess, and Roderick D. McKenzie (Chicago: University of Chicago Press, 1925), pp. 47–62 in 1967 ed. Reprinted with the permission of the University of Chicago Press.)

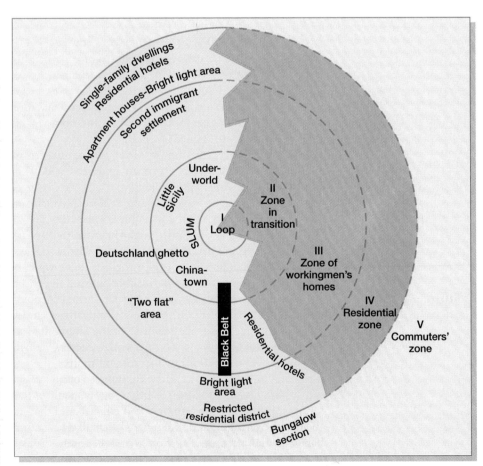

Chapter 12   Urban Problems

can afford to. This creates an **invasion-succession cycle,** with one group moving into an area that is already occupied by people with different characteristics. The invasion creates antagonisms between the groups: The one resents displacement; the other feels unwelcome. Although Burgess did his analysis about seventy-five years ago, the process continues. Today, however, people not only move outward, away from the city center, but, as in gentrification, also *toward* it.

Social Problems and the Zone in Transition

Burgess also noted that the most mobile areas have the most severe social problems. This is due to a lack of community, to fewer controls over people's behavior, to *anomie* or alienation. As Burgess put it, high mobility leads to demoralization, which is accompanied by promiscuity, vice, juvenile delinquency, urban gangs, crime, poverty, and the breakup of families. Mobility and problems are concentrated in Zone II. In this *zone in transition,* we find the city's "poverty, degradation, and disease," the "underworlds of crime and vice." In Burgess's colorful phrase, this zone is "the purgatory of lost souls."

This zone also contains the seeds of its own regeneration—social workers, preachers, artists, and political radicals—all, says Burgess, "obsessed with the vision of a new and better world." To this, we might add that in recent years financiers have seen value in this area and, in a process called *urban renewal,* have constructed office buildings, financial centers, stadiums, and luxury hotels. This is another movement *toward* the city center.

Many cities diverge from Burgess' concentric model, and his theory has many critics (Alihan 1938; Hoyt 1939; Harris and Ullman 1945; Palen and Schnore 1965; Berry and Kasarda 1977; La Gory 1980). All cities, however, have zones of functional specialties—areas of warehouses or those that specialize in selling and servicing automobiles or clusters of restaurants and shops. Cities also have zones that "specialize" in urban problems—skid rows, red light districts, and high-crime, delinquency, and graffiti-marked areas.

It is significant that the functionalist approach implies that a city's problems are transitory. Over time, a city will absorb its dispossessed and poor and equip them for a better life.

CONFLICT THEORY

How Class Conflicts Create Urban Problems

Conflict theorists reply that such a view overlooks the basic class conflict that underlies urban problems. Manuel Castells (1977, 1983, 1989) sees the problems facing our cities as the consequence of our capitalistic system. From mom and pop operations, businesses have expanded, merged, and grown powerful. Business leaders dictate government policy and tap the public treasury. By insuring home mortgages, for example, the government increases the profits of developers who build and market homes. By subsidizing interstate highways, the government finances a transportation system to move the goods that the wealthy manufacture.

These two policies also solved a major problem faced by the wealthy. In the early 1900s, they built factories that utilized multistory buildings. The newer assembly-line techniques made these buildings obsolete; moving raw materials and manufactured goods from one floor to another was inefficient. Expressways, built at taxpayer expense, allowed factory owners to relocate their production to the suburbs, where land prices and taxes were lower. Government-insured home mortgages subsidized a pool of workers to live nearby. The expressways also allowed the corporate elite to maintain access to the central business district, to use its marketing and financial institutions, and to continue to enjoy its cultural benefits (professional sports, theaters, and concerts).

This flight by corporate management and skilled workers led to the city's decline. By destroying the city's tax base, it crippled the city's ability to maintain services and help the many poor who were left behind. After they moved their power base from city to suburb, these corporate leaders also oppressed the city by supporting a coalition of rural and suburban districts that voted against proposals designed to aid cities. In effect, corporate leaders abandoned areas they no longer needed to the poor, about whom they did not care.

A downtown in ruins, however, did not fit into their plans. Redeveloping the downtown area attracts tourists, which means profits. To tourists—and indeed to a city's nearby comfortable suburbanites—the downtown area makes the city seem a phoenix, reborn from the ashes of destruction. The city, however, is the repository of the poor and powerless, and away from the resurrected downtown live the huddled masses—the destitute in a seemingly affluent society—oppressed by leaders who pursue their own political and economic interests (Teaford 1986). Because this underclass threatens the stability of society, and thus the privileged, they must be controlled, the topic of the Thinking Critically box on "gladiators" for the ruling class on the next page.

◆ Research Findings ◆

Is the city inherently alienating? Let's first consider this question, and then look in depth at the decline of the central city, urban violence, and the changes that are affecting U.S. cities and their welfare.

IS THE CITY INHERENTLY ALIENATING?

From early on, sociologists were fascinated by the sharp contrast between the intimacy and neighborliness of village life and the anonymity and self-centeredness of urban life. In the 1880s, Ferdinand Tönnies noted that agricultural people develop a sense of community because they share the same activities and values. Tönnies (1957) used the term **Gemeinschaft** to refer to such bonds of intimacy and shared tradition. He used the term **Gesellschaft** to refer to the impersonality and self-interest associated with urban areas. (In German, *Gemeinschaft* means "community"; *Gesellschaft*, "society.")

Impersonality and self-interest are ordinary characteristics of the city, but sometimes they are carried to extremes. When it occurred, the following event made national headlines and upset the entire country:

> Twenty-eight-year-old Catherine Genovese, who was known as Kitty in her Queens neighborhood, was returning home from work. After parking her car, a man grabbed her. Kitty screamed, "Oh my God! He stabbed me! Please help me!"
>
> For more than half an hour, thirty-eight respectable, law-abiding citizens watched the killer stalk and stab Kitty in three separate attacks. Twice the sudden glow from their bedroom lights frightened him off. Each time he returned, sought her out, and stabbed her again. Not one person telephoned the police during the assault.
>
> When interviewed by the police, the witnesses said: "I didn't want to get involved," "We thought it was a lovers' quarrel," "I don't know," and "I was tired. I went back to bed." (*New York Times*, March 26, 1964)

The Urban Renaissance and the New Underclass

Gemeinschaft versus Gesellschaft

Extremes of Impersonality and Self-Interest

The Kitty Genovese Case

CENSUS 2000

Every state grew in population during 1990–2000. Nevada experienced the highest growth (66%) while North Dakota grew the least (.5%). Notice how the counties that lost more than 10% of their population are mostly found in the country's midsection.

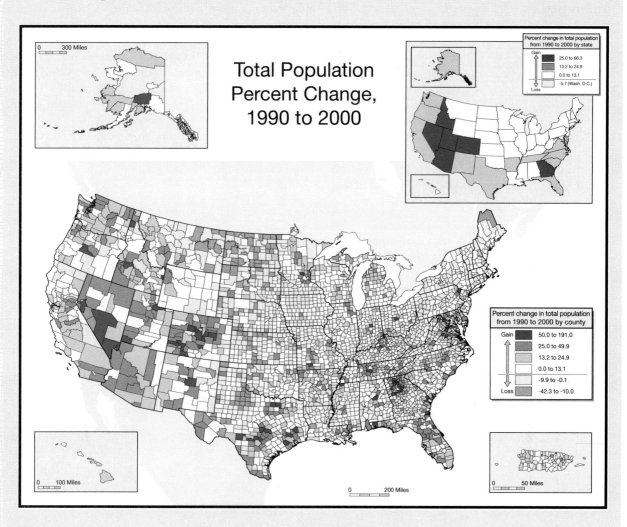

Total Population Percent Change, 1990 to 2000

Percent change in total population from 1990 to 2000 by state

Gain
25.0 to 66.3
13.2 to 24.9
0.0 to 13.1
Loss
-5.7 (Wash. D.C.)

Percent change in total population from 1990 to 2000 by county

Gain
50.0 to 191.0
25.0 to 49.9
13.2 to 24.9
0.0 to 13.1
-9.9 to -0.1
Loss
-42.3 to -10.0

Road Rage

Even traffic accidents now hold a new danger—angry people whose wrath explodes under pressure:

In 1995, in crowded traffic on a bridge going into Detroit, Deletha Word bumped the car ahead of her. The damage was minor, but the driver, Martell Welch, jumped out. Cursing, he pulled Deletha from her car, pushed her onto the hood, and began beating her. Martell's friends got out to watch. One of them held

Chapter 12 Urban Problems

Deletha down while Martell took a car jack and smashed Deletha's car. Scared for her life, Deletha broke away, fleeing to the bridge's railing. Martell and his friends taunted her, shouting, "Jump, bitch, jump!" Deletha plunged to her death. Whether she jumped or fell is unknown. (*Newsweek*, September 4, 1995)

How Cities Undermine Community

Alienation *and* Community

The Urban Villagers

Why should the city be alienating? In a classic essay, sociologist Louis Wirth (1938) said that urban dwellers live anonymous lives marked by segmented and superficial encounters. This undermines kinship and neighborhood, the traditional bases of social control and solidarity. Urbanites then grow aloof and indifferent to other people's problems—as happened with Kitty Genovese's neighbors. In short, the personal freedom that the city provides comes at the cost of alienation.

The city is certainly not inevitably alienating. Most drivers who witnessed the tragedy that befell Deletha Word did nothing. But after Deletha went over the railing, two motorists jumped in after her, risking injury and their own lives in a futile attempt to save her. Some urbanites, then, are far from alienated.

There are also enclaves of community within the city. Sociologist Herbert Gans, a symbolic interactionist, did participant observation in the West End in Boston. He was so impressed with the sense of community that he entitled his book *The Urban Villagers* (1962). He said:

> After a few weeks of living in the West End, my observations—and my perceptions of the area—changed drastically. The search for an apartment quickly indicated that the individual units were usually in much better condition than the outside or the hallways of the buildings. Subsequently, in wandering through the West End, and in using it as a resident, I developed a kind of selective perception, in which my eye focused only on those parts of the area that were actually being used by people. Vacant buildings and boarded-up stores were no longer so visible, and the totally deserted alleys or streets were outside the set of paths normally traversed, either by myself or by the West Enders. The dirt and spilled-over garbage remained, but,

Urban life is often alienating. To consistently feel anonymous in a crowd of strangers can make people grow aloof and indifferent to other people's problems.

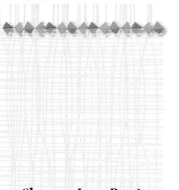

since they were concentrated in street gutters and empty lots, they were not really harmful to anyone and thus were not as noticeable as during my initial observations.

Since much of the area's life took place on the street, faces became familiar very quickly. I met my neighbors on the stairs and in front of my building. And, once a shopping pattern developed, I saw the same storekeepers frequently, as well as the area's "characters" who wandered through the streets everyday on a fairly regular route and schedule. In short, the exotic quality of the stores and the residents also wore off as I became used to seeing them.

Slum or Low-Rent District?

In short, Gans found a community, people who identified with the area and with one another. Its residents had extensive networks of friends and acquaintances. In spite of its substandard buildings, most West Enders had chosen to live there. *To them, this was a low-rent district, not a slum.*

Most West Enders had low-paying, insecure jobs. Some were elderly, living on small pensions. Unlike the middle class, they didn't care about their "address," and the area's inconveniences were something they put up with in exchange for cheap housing. In general, they were content with their neighborhood.

As we saw before, and now again in Gans' study, sociologists who have done participant observation document how the city provides community. They stress that the city is divided into little worlds that are knowable down to their smallest details (Lenz-Romeiss 1973; Karp and Yoels 1990; Keans 1991). Feeling that they fit in, they experience emotional security in a familiar world.

Types of Urban Dwellers

What, then, is the answer? Is Wirth right? Is urban life a struggle for safety and survival, providing more threat than security? Or are these other sociologists correct? Not everyone in the city faces the same situation, and the answer depends on whom one is discussing. Let's look at the five types of urban dwellers that Gans (1962, 1968, 1991) identified. The first three live in the city by choice and are not alienated, while the latter two are outcasts of industrial society who live in the city despairingly, without choice or hope.

1. *The cosmopolites.* These are the intellectuals, professionals, and artists who have been attracted to the city. They value its conveniences and cultural benefits.

2. *The singles.* Roughly between the ages of 20 and 30, the singles have not decided to settle in the city permanently. For them, urban life is a stage in their life course. Businesses and services, such as singles bars and apartment complexes, cater to their needs and desires. After they marry, many singles move to the suburbs.

3. *The ethnic villagers.* Banding together, working-class ethnics form tightly-knit neighborhoods that resemble villages and small towns. Family- and peer-oriented, they try to isolate themselves from the dangers and problems of urban life.

4. *The deprived.* Destitute, emotionally disturbed, and having little income, education, or work skills, the deprived live in neighborhoods more like urban jungles than urban villages. Like Hagan, some of them stalk those jungles in search of prey. Neither predator nor prey has much hope for anything better in life—for themselves or their children. See the Thinking Critically box on danger and alienation in the city on the next page for an example of the deprived. The box on "gladiators" for the ruling class (page 416) illustrates the contempt in which they are held.

THINKING CRITICALLY ABOUT SOCIAL PROBLEMS

Danger and Alienation in the City

It is a summer afternoon in the Robert Taylor Homes, no different from most other days in the nation's largest public housing complex except for the intense heat.

Shots crackle from pistols near a play area. Laughter turns to screams as children dart for cover behind buildings and in stairwells crowded with craps shooters and winos.

The gunfire is soon over. The angry men bent on shooting each other have run off. The dice games and wine drinking resume. The basketball hoops again rattle above the scorching asphalt, and the children return to the dilapidated play equipment.

Taylor Homes, 15 blocks long and one block wide, consists of 28 identical red and cream 16-story towers surrounded on all sides by other impoverished neighborhoods. Many residents view Taylor Homes as a separate city within Chicago, an island of poverty adrift in a city of plenty.

Mrs. Wallace has lived in Taylor Homes since it was built. "There are a lot of good people here," she says. "They go to work, come home, and close their doors. They take the attitude that if nobody bothers them, they won't bother anybody. They try to get their kids to do the right thing, which is hard when so many parents don't."

John Smith remembers better times at Robert Taylor Homes. He has reared his children here. "And I sent all 12 to college," he says proudly with a deep, resonant voice. "I worked two jobs to do it, but I did it. I was firm with them and demanded that they do the right thing. They never gave me any trouble."

"But things are different now," 68-year-old Mr. Smith says from the chair in which he sits each day. "Things are tense now. The young people have nothing to do. No jobs. No recreation programs. So they are rowdy. They don't go to school. They make trouble."

As he talks, a young man walks by several times wielding a metal pipe. Mr. Smith pauses and gives the youth a stern look. The youth leaves.

"You have to watch them or they will hurt you," he said. "If they think you have something, they will slash you or knock you over the head and take it."

Asked why he doesn't move, Mr. Smith says, "Son, things are bad all over. It's not just here."

One hundred fifty thousand people live in Chicago's public housing. Single mothers occupy 94 percent of the units. Many buildings are controlled by gangs. The police have given up enforcing laws against drugs and burglaries. The head of Chicago's public housing put it this way:

> As long as they don't go after and injure innocent people, it's fine. I can't stop them from using drugs. Everybody belongs to a gang. They are going to burglarize apartments to support their habits. You send a message. You don't say you can do these things, but over time they know that the only thing that's going to set me off is when they start hurting innocent people.

What do you think can be done to change this situation?

Based on Sheppard 1980; J. Anderson 1995.

---

5. *The trapped.* These people are not here by choice, either. Some could not afford to move when other ethnic groups "invaded" their neighborhood. Others are "downwardly mobile"; they drifted into the slums from a higher social class. Many are elderly and are not wanted elsewhere. Some are alcoholics and other drug addicts. Like the deprived, the trapped suffer from high rates of assault, mugging, and rape.

Skid Row   Some of the trapped and deprived live on **skid row,** an area of bars, flophouses, cheap restaurants, pawnshops, and rescue missions. This term may have originated in Seattle, from the "skid road" used by lumberjacks to transport logs (Bahr 1973).

Urban problems, including slums, are a worldwide problem. Shown here is a slum in Bangladesh. Note how its enterprising residents are preparing objects for sale.

In Sum

Suburbs Also Have Problems

Redlining and Disinvestment as Causes of Urban Decay

Populated almost exclusively by homeless men, skid row is marked by poverty and personal problems. Contrary to the stereotype, however, many people living on skid row do not drink. About a third are heavy drinkers, another third drinks moderately, and the other third either abstains from alcohol or drinks little. Skid row dwellers are marked by homelessness, acute personal problems, and poverty (Bogue 1963; Nieves 1998).

Gans' typology illustrates the complexity of urban life and its problems. The city is a mosaic of social diversity, and not all urban dwellers experience the city in the same way. Each group has its own lifestyle, and each experiences specific problems. Consequently, some find community, security, and welcome cultural diversity in the city. Others, trapped and deprived, find threats to their health and safety; theirs is a life of despair in an urban jungle.

THE DECLINE OF THE CENTRAL CITY

As people fled the central city for the suburbs, the city declined, losing population, financial resources, and political power. The suburbs, however, in which more than half of Americans now live (Rybczynski 1999), are not utopias. They have their own problems, especially the older ones, those built shortly after World War II. From traffic congestion to street crime, they have problems more commonly associated with the city (Winsberg 1991; Barbanel 1992). They even have **suburban sprawl,** the disappearance of open areas as the suburb expands into the countryside.

As we saw, conflict theorists trace the decline of the city to capitalists, whose policies damaged cities and encouraged suburbanization. Banks and savings and loan associations tightened this noose by **redlining,** refusing to lend money for mortgages in areas they considered undesirable (King 1994; Squires 1997). (Loan officers used to draw a "red line" around neighborhoods they considered bad risks.) These areas are usually either in the ghetto or in neighborhoods undergoing integration.

As sociologist John Palen (1981) noted, redlining creates a self-fulfilling prophecy. The area's residents can't get loans for home improvements, and banks refuse to finance the sale of homes there. Only people with cash or those who are eligible for government loans can purchase homes. Home sales decline, property values drop, and many homeowners stop improving their homes. As the neighborhood declines, it justifies the "wisdom" of the lending officials who avoided the area because it was a "bad risk."

Bankers insist that **disinvestment,** their withdrawal of investments from an area, is the *result* of deteriorating housing, not its cause (Ferguson 1991). Because redlining is now illegal, it is practiced covertly. A banker in southern Illinois told me that he would loan no money in a certain area. He then added, "If you tell anyone that I said this, I will deny that the conversation ever took place."

> "It just doesn't pay," groans Linda Kutz as she looked mournfully around her. "This used to be a good business," she continued. "I could get good rents and keep my building up. I knew my tenants, and they respected me. But now—nothing but animals!" Linda muttered as she looked despairingly at the shambles of what was a nice apartment just a few days before.

Like urban landlords across the country, Linda Kutz is abandoning her apartment building. She is caught between the cross-pressures of high taxes, the city insisting that she bring her buildings into conformity with the housing code, tenants who damage her property and refuse to pay their rents, and a costly and long eviction process.

When she went to the police, they asked, "Did you see them (the renters) do it?" She said, "No, I wasn't here." Pointing to holes in the wall and feces in the floor ducts, she said, "But you can see for yourself what they did." Their response: "If you didn't see them do it, we can't do anything about it." With three of her apartments vandalized during the past year, Kutz says she has no choice but to walk away and let the banks foreclose.

Abandonment. Each year, landlords abandon thousands of **housing units**— places of residence such as houses or apartments. Some of these buildings need only minor repairs. Why, then, are abandoned buildings part of the urban scene? As Kutz indicates, vandalism, high taxes, a slow eviction legal process, and housing codes that sometimes border on the quixotic all play a role. As another landlord told me:

> "Look at this building," he said, indicating the workers on the roof. "I don't know how long I can keep this up. I want to provide a nice place for my renters. Then comes the city inspector who says I have to add rain gutters. Every time someone moves in, an inspector examines my building. No one's ever said anything about gutters before. The building is over a hundred years old and has never had rain gutters. Why does it suddenly need them now?"

All these factors add up to higher risk, and, sometimes, financial loss. Unable to find a buyer, some landlords stop paying their property taxes or making repairs, collect as much rent as long as possible, and then walk away from their buildings. The abandoned

The Landlords'/-ladies' Dilemma

When financial institutions withdraw financing from an area, a process known as *redlining,* the neighborhood deteriorates. Formerly good buildings, even grand ones such as this building in the Woodlawn area of Chicago, fall into disrepair and are eventually abandoned. They become havens for drug addicts, prostitutes, and rapists.

Arson

buildings become a dangerous playground for children, a shelter for junkies, a target for looters, fun for vandals, and profit for arsonists.

Some owners of buildings and businesses who face huge losses see fire as the solution. Those afraid to set the fire themselves hire "torches" (professional arsonists), who are seldom apprehended because arson often destroys the evidence of the crime. Many insurance companies also prefer to pay off a blaze of "suspicious origin" and recover the cost in their general rates than fight a case in court and risk jeopardizing their reputation for paying claims. Some cynically call arson the "modern way of refinancing."

Even when a company does fight a claim, it can easily lose. As an insurance claims agent told me during an investigation:

> We won't have to pay on this one. The fire began in the basement on a pile of clothes. There was no source of fire [heating element or electricity] there. The insured was paid off on another fire just three years ago. The police have the case.
>
> I talked to the detective in charge of the case. The insured had lost his job, and the mortgage holder had begun foreclosure (the legal process of getting possession of the property), but the man stuck to his story. ("I don't know anything. I wasn't there.") The company paid.

Except when people are killed, urban arson receives little publicity or concern. The public shows little interest, and often neither do the police. Functionalists can well see the core truth in the phrase "the modern way of refinancing." Perhaps it is functional for society to let entrepreneurs refinance their losses by spreading the cost over tens of thousands of policyholders.

URBAN VIOLENCE

In addition to decline, our urban centers also face violence. We have already discussed this topic in Chapters 5 and 6. Here we will examine violence by youth gangs and in the schools, and the collective violence both urban dwellers and government officials fear—riots.

Values and Self-Identity: Why Lower-Class Boys Are Attracted to Gangs

Why do we have gangs? Gangs intrigue both the public and sociological researchers. In the 1920s, sociologist Frederic Thrasher studied 1,313 gangs in Chicago. Thrasher (1927) found that gangs start as innocent play groups that compete for space in crowded and deteriorating areas of the city. Boys band together because their participation in a group gives them a valued identity. The group then becomes the impetus for criminal activities.

The Thrasher Study

The Cohen Study

Why are lower-class boys so attracted to gangs? In another classic study, sociologist Albert Cohen (1955) found a key to this attraction; the boys are measured by middle-class standards, but lack the socially approved means to meet those standards. The boys don't feel comfortable in school, because it is run by middle-class people who constantly judge them by their standards of speech, behavior, and classroom performance. In self-defense, the boys reject those standards and form a subculture of like-minded adolescents in which different standards prevail, standards by which they can succeed. Doing well in school becomes equated with girls and sissies. The boys also reject the standards of other authority figures, and give approval to violating the law.

"Supergangs"

Some so-called gangs are actually groups of adolescents who do nothing worse than get drunk, use drugs, skip school, write graffiti, steal from parked cars, and vandalize property. I say "nothing worse" because we now face the rise of "supergangs" like the Crips and Bloods, with their hundreds of individual gangs and thousands of

Although urban violence is decreasing, it remains a matter of major concern. With guns the major weapon used in killings, gun ownership has become one of the most controversial topics in U.S. society.

members. These gangs, and others like them, are no innocent play groups; their members rape, rob, and kill. The Crips and Bloods have gone national, with affiliated gangs in most major cities, and even in many smaller ones.

Youth gangs are culturally diverse. They are not limited to any race or ethnic group. Los Angeles has white gangs, African-American gangs, Mexican-American gangs, even Colombian and San Salvadoran gangs (Hull 1987; Lamar 1988; Stanley 1990).

The Miller Study

Although middle-class gangs exist, almost all gang members are poor, urban youth. Gangs primarily draw lower-class males, says Miller (1958) in his classic analysis, because of the values that dominate their subculture: trouble, toughness, smartness, excitement, fate, and autonomy. These values replace the middle-class values that the boys reject, and are the means by which they attain status. Trouble provides excitement and relieves the monotony of their everyday lives. Trouble also lets them show they are smart and tough and allows them to exhibit their autonomy, or freedom from authority. Violence also fits in well, for it allows the boys to show how tough they are. Fate fits in because it helps explain their lot in life: If you get hurt, that is simply because your number came up. In short, gangs offer an arena in which lower-class boys construct an identity that corresponds with their own system of values.

Girl Gangs

Increasingly, these same values apply to lower-class girls. Female gang members, who come from backgrounds similar to the boys, associate with these gangs. They play supportive roles, hiding weapons and drugs and providing alibis and sex. Girl gangs also exist, some every bit as violent as male gangs. Some will kill a victim just to get her pair of earrings (Faison 1991).

Violence in Gang Life

Miller (1975) identified two forms of violence between gangs, the rumble and the hit. The **rumble** is an encounter between fairly large numbers of gang members. In the **hit,** known in the media as a "drive-by shooting," a small group, usually in cars, hunts members of rival gangs. Finding them, they blast away with shotguns, rifles, and pistols. Here is how Miller (1975:38) describes a hit:

A carful of gang members cruises the area of a rival gang, looking for rival gang members. If one is found, he will be attacked in one of several ways; gang members will remain in the car and shoot the victim, or will leave the car and beat or stab him. If the victim is wearing a gang sweater, this will be taken as a trophy and in fact this kind of coup-counting is often given as the reason for the "hit" expedition.

Not having known anything else, gang members take violence for granted. Since violence is a normal part of their social world, they believe that people will be violent toward them and that they ought to be violent toward others. Life is cheap, violence routine, and killing normal. For some, like Hagan in the opening vignette, a victim doesn't have to be a gang member. Life can be destroyed for little or no provocation.

As long as gangs limit their violence to their own area of the city, the public is seldom concerned. The common attitude is "let them kill each other off." When violence affects the lives of the general public, however, or when there is an outrageous killing (that is, something the public defines as not "normal" gang killing), youth gangs generate publicity and "become" a "problem." The killing of Ben Wilson is an example.

Ben Wilson, the 17-year-old star forward of the Illinois state champion basketball team, was walking with his girlfriend during a school lunch break. Suddenly, they were confronted by three teen-age gang members. As the 6-foot 8-inch Wilson tried to move past them, one youth turned to a companion and said, "This guy pushed me. Pop him." The teenager pulled out a .22-caliber pistol and fired two shots into Wilson's stomach. Wilson died a day later—on Thanksgiving eve. (Starr and Maier 1985)

School Violence

The idea that U.S. schools would need guards and metal detectors to protect their students used to be unimaginable. Yet what was nonexistent has become common. The worst kids in school used to carry a switchblade, but today those kids take guns to class. And others bring guns to defend themselves from classmates who carry guns! As a 15-year-old in a Baltimore junior high school said, "You gotta be prepared—people shoot you for your coat, your rings, chains, anything." He then proudly displayed his "defensive" .25-caliber Beretta (Hackett 1988).

And then, of course, there is Columbine—and all the other schools where students have gone on killing sprees. In their wake, they have left dead students and teachers—and fear on the part of students, parents, and entire communities.

Violence has become so bad that in some grade schools teachers practice "duck-and-cover" drills to protect children from neighborhood shootings (Mydens 1991). In some high schools and even junior highs, rape and assault go unreported. Guilt stops some teachers from reporting that they were attacked; they feel that the assault would not have occurred if they had somehow done a better job in the classroom. Some find it easier to forget the attack, because assault cases usually require at least three court appearances. Others don't report attacks because they are afraid they will be killed if they do. Often there are no witnesses, and it is the teacher's word against the student's. Except for incidents that cannot be hidden, such as shootings, school violence seldom comes to the attention of the police or public primarily because, like prison wardens—and I use the analogy with good reason—school administrators want to "run a nice, quiet school." The last thing they want is to rouse the community with stories about teachers versus students or to publicize unsafe conditions at school. They hush up and downplay incidents. This relieves pressure on them and protects their jobs, for one sign of their success or failure is the amount of violence in their schools.

Riots in U.S. History

The year was 1747. The place was the bustling port of Boston. The Royal Navy had been impressing (kidnapping legally) local men for forced service. Fed up,

Although riots are often thought of as a recent development in the United States, they are rooted in our history. Shown here is an engraving based on a newspaper account of the New York City Draft Riots of July 13–16, 1863. Until then, the Civil War's Union Army was made up of volunteers. Rioters violently protested the initiation of a draft. They also looted stores—another behavior that is not new.

THE RIOTS IN NEW YORK: CONFLICT BETWEEN THE MILITARY AND THE RIOTERS IN FIRST-AVENUE—SEE NEXT PAGE.

seamen and others armed themselves and rioted. For three days, they dominated the city, forcing the governor to flee. The mobs freed the impressed men, gaining another victory for the urban rioters of the time.

Urban riots, seemingly so modern, have been with us since the 1700s. According to historian Richard Brown (1969), rioting by the lower-class urban population even helped start the American Revolution.

Heavy urban rioting occurred in the 1830s through the 1850s. At least 35 major riots and numerous minor ones took place in Baltimore, Philadelphia, New York, and Boston. These cities had three labor riots, three anti-Catholic riots, and several riots by volunteer firemen. At the root of this rioting was the rise of the urban slum, the lack of effective police, and a flood of immigrants—chiefly Irish Catholics, who were involved heavily in this urban violence. Ethnic and religious hostilities motivated violence between the Irish and Protestants; prejudice and competition for jobs underlay violence of whites against blacks (Brown 1969).

Communal Riots

Until the 1960s, the most common twentieth-century U.S. race riot was the **communal riot.** In this type, also called a *contested area riot*, one group would contest another's control of an area of the city. According to sociologist Morris Janowitz (1970b), the cities in which communal riots occurred contained large numbers of migrants—both African American and white—who were living in segregated areas. The police had little capacity to deal with outbreaks of mass violence, and often conspired with white rioters against African Americans.

Background Factors and Precipitating Incidents

Sociologists have found that in the background of riots are rising tensions and minor outbursts of violence. Then comes a **precipitating incident** that triggers the riot. For example, between 1917 and 1919 whites bombed more than twenty-seven homes of Chicago blacks. None of these incidents led to riots. What did, however, was the death of a 17-year-old black youth who swam into an area of Lake Michigan used exclusively by whites. When other blacks challenged the whites' use of this part of the beach, crowds of blacks and whites began throwing stones at one another. The black youth, still in the water, drowned. Rumors abounded that he had been stoned to death, and a riot ensued. Thirty-eight people were killed, 537 injured, and about 1,000 left homeless.

Riots were sporadic through the years, but in the 1960s they erupted across the nation. Harlem, Brooklyn, Watts, Newark, and Detroit were hit. These riots were different. Because the rioters were not challenging the control of some area of the city, as in a communal riot, but, instead, looted stores, they are referred to as **commodity riots** (Janowitz 1970a). The 1960s riots were followed by a calm period, which was broken by the Miami riots of 1980 and 1989 and the Los Angeles riot of 1992.

Chief Background Factors in Commodity Riots

When Watts went up in flames in 1965, it aroused national concern. Rioting peaked in 1967, with 41 major riots and 123 less serious ones. The riots of 1967 so upset the nation that President Johnson appointed a National Advisory Commission on Civil Disorders to study them. The commission identified five significant background factors (Kerner 1968):

1. *Discrimination and segregation* in employment, education, and housing that excluded many blacks from economic benefits.

2. *Isolation*—due to black in-migration and white flight, poor blacks were concentrated in the city, with deteriorating facilities and services and unmet human needs.

3. *Destroyed opportunity* from segregation and poverty, which enforced failure on the young. Life in the ghetto often culminated in crime, drug addiction, welfare, and bitterness and resentment against society in general and white society in particular.

4. *Frustrated hopes*—stimulated by the judicial and legislative victories of the civil rights movement, unfulfilled hopes created frustration.

5. *Powerlessness,* combined with alienation and hostility to society, led to the conviction that only violence could change the "system."

These are *background* factors. By themselves, they do not cause riots. The poor and minorities often experience discrimination, segregation, isolation, poor services, little opportunity, frustrated hopes, and powerlessness. These make up the background of their everyday lives in our urban centers. Rioting, however, is infrequent; poor people live in quiet desperation in spite of their disadvantage and oppression. For a riot, anger must rise to fever pitch (Piven and Cloward 1977). There must be a *precipitating incident*, a spark that kindles the tinder.

Precipitating Incidents That Raise the Level of Anger

But there always are incidents. Why does one set off a riot, while others do not? Social psychologists Kurt and Gladys Lang (1968) identified two necessary conditions. For an incident to precipitate a riot, it must be perceived as a threat to the group's well-being and evoke moral outrage. The precipitating incident is often a confrontation between an African American and a white police officer. The incident escalates in people's minds as they talk excitedly about it and as rumors sweep the area. Violence then erupts, and the riot moves into full swing.

The Los Angeles riot of 1992 followed this scenario perfectly. Background conditions were the long-term poverty of African Americans and Latinos and their oppression by the police. The precipitating incident that inflamed passions was the acquittal of Los Angeles policemen who were accused of assaulting Rodney King, an African-American traffic violator. A passerby had videotaped the police beating King. The videotape clearly showed the officers savagely pounding a prostrate man with their nightsticks. Television stations repeatedly broadcast the pictures to stunned audiences. *Everyone* knew the men were guilty.

Within minutes of the verdict, angry crowds gathered. That night, mobs set fire to businesses in south-central Los Angeles, and looting and arson began in earnest. The rioting spread to other cities—Atlanta, Tampa, and even Madison, Wisconsin, and Las Vegas, Nevada. Whites and Koreans were favorite targets. The Los Angeles riot was spectacular—4,000 fires; dramatic footage of looting and beatings; the president appearing on television ordering the Seventh Infantry, SWAT teams, and the FBI into Los Angeles and federalizing the California National Guard; sixty dead, which made it the most deadly riot in the United States since the Civil War. It seemed different, but sociologically it was a "routine" riot. That is, it followed the patterns sociologists have identified.

What Are Results of Riots?

Beyond the obvious—the burning, looting, and killing—what are the results of riots? First, rioting can have positive consequences, such as stimulating the flow of federal funds to the inner city. Most positive consequences, however, are short-lived. Second, as sociologists George Simpson and Milton Yinger noted (1972), riots speed segregation, for whites flee to the suburbs. While rioters may gain a sense of having struck a blow for freedom, they have in fact only indicated their need for freedom—they have not shaken the basic institutions that support their oppression and enforce their poverty (Piven and Cloward 1977). Not one riot in the history of the United States has eliminated the underlying discrimination and poverty that are the background factors. The sad truth is that because these background conditions remain and precipitating events are bound to occur, we are destined to have more riots.

THE CITY IN CHANGE

In addition to violence and general decline, U.S. cities face extensive change. In this section we will examine the transition in power, changes in urban government, the emerging megalopolis, and the brightening of the sun belt.

Are U.S. Cities Obsolete?

"Are U.S. cities becoming obsolete?" John Teaford (1986), an urban historian, posed this question. He was referring to the problems we have reviewed here and in earlier chapters—ranging from rape and murder to pornography and drug addiction—that often make U.S. cities threatening, alienating places to live. Our inner cities have become so fearful that they are avoided by all except those who live there and those who must transact business there. Locked in these pockets of poverty, many inner city residents live short, brutal lives.

Challenges from the Suburbs

The suburbs may once have been bedrooms for the city, but no longer. Cities used to hold the jobs, but now the suburbs do. Nearly three quarters of suburbanites work in the suburbs, not in the nearby city. Just as suburbanites used to commute to the city for work (and many still do), now many urbanites commute to the suburbs for work (Rybczynski 1999).

A Reversal?

This change presents a major challenge to cities, but no one need erect a grave marker over our cities. Although the flight from central cities has shifted resources and power from city to suburb, decline does not mean death, and the cities' fortunes may reverse. An indication that this reversal may have begun is reviewed in the Thinking Critically box on the next page.

THINKING CRITICALLY ABOUT SOCIAL PROBLEMS

Reclaiming the City

The story is well known. The inner city is filled with crack, crime, and corruption. It stinks from foul, festering garbage strewn on the streets and piled up around burned-out buildings. Only those who have no other choice live in this desolate, abandoned area where danger seems to lurk around every corner.

What is not so known is that middle-class and wealthy African Americans are moving back into some of these areas, transforming them into affluent enclaves.

Howard Sanders was living the American Dream. He earned a degree from Harvard Business School, took a position with a Manhattan investment firm, and had an apartment on Central Park West. But he missed Harlem, where he had grown up, and he moved back, this time with his wife and daughter.

So have African-American lawyers, doctors, professors, and bankers.

What's the attraction? The first is the nostalgia factor, a cultural identification with the Harlem of legend and folklore. It was here that black writers and artists lived in the 1920s, here that the blues and jazz attracted young and accomplished musicians.

The second is practical. Harlem offers housing value. Five-bedroom homes with 6,000 square feet are available. Some come with Honduran mahogany. Some brownstones are only shells, and have to be rehabbed. Others are in perfect condition. With the influx of the new professionals, prices have risen. A shell sells for $80,000, a home in perfect condition for $450,000.

This is the rebuilding of community. People who "made" it want to be role models. They want children to see them going to and returning from work.

When the middle class moved out of Harlem, so did the amenities. Now that young professionals are moving back in, the amenities are following. There were no coffee shops, restaurants, jazz clubs, florists, copy centers, optometrist offices, art galleries—the types of things city residents take for granted. Now there are.

The same thing is happening on Chicago's West Side and in other U.S. cities.

The drive to find community—to connect with others—is strong, and it is the basic motivator for this reclamation. As one migrant, an investment banker, said, "It feeds my soul."

Based on Cose 1999; McCormick 1999.

Urban Government

Regardless of its problems, the city must be governed. To accomplish this herculean task, during the nineteenth century the **political machine** emerged—an organization that operated behind the scenes to circumvent the city's official procedures. In return for loyalty, the machine distributed government jobs and favors. The head of the machine, usually called the "boss," directed an organization whose members were put on the city payroll whenever possible (a practice called patronage). Their official job was a subterfuge; their real function was to obey the boss and his underlings.

Merton's Functional Analysis of the Political Machine

In a classic functional analysis, sociologist Robert Merton (1968) examined bigcity "machine politics." He wanted to know why, despite attempts at reform, the machine continued year after year. Merton applied two basic assumptions of functionalism: (1) Something does not exist in a society unless it contributes to that society, and (2) no part of society exists in isolation; each part is related to the other parts of the social system.

Merton found that the political machine helped the disadvantaged, businesspeople, and individuals who wanted to get ahead. The machine helped the disadvantaged obtain food, welfare, jobs, scholarships, and legal assistance when children ran afoul of the law or when bill collectors became too threatening. Those who received such favors knew without question whom to vote for in the next election.

Businesspeople also needed favors. They wanted to bypass building codes and the many bureaucratic regulations that impeded their efforts to expand. In return for under-the-table payoffs, the boss would pull strings at the appropriate government agency. The boss thus became a mediator between the sometimes irrational demands of bureaucrats and the needs of modern business.

The machine also helped people move up the social class ladder. The ambitious always confront obstacles in their path, and the ambitious poor are no exception. They don't have the money to start their own businesses, and many don't have the grades to attend professional schools. In return for their loyalty, the machine helped some get hired by local businesses. Others went to work for the boss. After demonstrating competence and loyalty—especially loyalty—they were rewarded with secure incomes in an entrenched political structure.

In short, Merton found that the political machine existed because the official channels of society failed to provide needed services; the machine stepped in to fill the void left by the more culturally approved structures of society.

Functions to Some Are Dysfunctions to Others

As functionalists also stress, something that is functional for some may be a source of problems for others. The political machine passed over minorities when it handed out political favors—systematically excluding them from the powerful positions in city hall. It also "contained" minorities to specified areas of the city, ordering real estate agents to keep designated areas "pure" (Royko 1971). Fire marshals and city inspectors enforced city and state codes strictly when property was scheduled to pass into the "wrong hands," but overlooked violations for buyers whose ethnicity was approved. The machine may also be dysfunctional to the general public if it sacks the city treasury or diverts tax monies while streets, sewers, bridges, lighting, and other public services deteriorate.

The Decline of the Political Machine

The machine, which had dominated politics during the first half of the twentieth century, gradually declined. With the death of Chicago's Mayor Daley in 1976, the last of the old-fashioned political machines began to pass into history. What remains today is but a shell of its former power. Six basic factors explain the machine's decline:

1. Immigration slowed to a trickle. This removed a major function of the machine (serving unmet needs in return for loyalty) and undermined one of its major bases of power.

2. Education increased. As many moved into the mainstream of society, they became less dependent on machine favors.

3. Suburbanization occurred. As whites and industry left the city, the machine lost the broad revenue base on which its power depended.

4. Civil service laws were passed. As city workers came under the protection of these laws, it became difficult for the machine to demand their loyalty.

5. Blacks migrated north. As African Americans moved from the South, the white power establishment held onto control until it was too late to pass to its political successors an intact, powerful machine.

6. New standards of city management came into vogue. The public wanted city agencies to be headed by professionals rather than given as rewards for political service.

The political machine may be down, but it isn't dead. After Richard Daley died, Richard Daley became mayor of Chicago. That is, the mayor's son, who was barely

able to pass the Illinois bar exam, was elected mayor. He has been reelected several times. The machine his father passed to him, though weakened, still functions.

The New City Management

The professionalization of city management, which weakened the political machine, has also contributed to urban problems. Mayors or city managers head a vast system of departments. Each is assigned a particular task and works fairly independently of the others. Communication breaks down, and with departments' chiefs and their workers being more loyal to their own department than they are to the city or the mayor, they perform their work without concern for how it fits into the larger picture (Lowi 1977). For example, in Granada, Spain, the government was concerned about the rundown appearance of the buildings along one of its main streets. The city spent hundreds of thousands of dollars fixing the fronts of these buildings, painting and repairing concrete, iron, and stonework. The results were impressive. The only problem was that another unit of the government had slated these same buildings for demolition (Arías 1993).

The Transition to Minority Leadership

Another major change in city governance comes from the "white flight" to the suburbs and the migration of African Americans to the cities. Statistics tell the story of this transition in city rule: In 1964, there were only 70 elected African-American officials at all levels of government in the United States. Today there are 9,000. From 70 to 9,000 in 35 years! Latinos have also increased their total, to more than 5,000 (Eisinger 1980; *Statistical Abstract* 2001:Tables 399, 400).

Sociologist Peter Eisinger studied this transition of power. To govern a city, its major groups must cooperate. If whites were to withdraw their cooperation from an elected minority mayor, winning control of the formal apparatus of government would be a hollow victory. To see what happened after African-American electoral victories, Eisinger interviewed the economic, political, and social leaders in Detroit and Atlanta. He found that in neither city did the white elites engage in confrontational politics, despite ample opportunity. Instead, the transition to the new leadership led to coalition building and cooperation between the groups.

This transition of power, Eisinger says, is like what happened in Boston almost a century ago. At that time the Yankees, or white settlers from England, were in control. When thousands of poor Irish immigrated to Boston in the 1880s, they threatened the Yankees' entrenched power. By 1900, however, the Irish had displaced Boston's historical elite. Eisinger concludes that we are involved in a similar process today. Although the players have changed, the game is the same—and the results will be similar.

THE EMERGING MEGALOPOLIS

Separate Cities Are Merging Into a Single Unit

Another major change is the development of the supermetropolitan unit called the **megalopolis.** The term refers to the "overspill" of urban areas into one another (Gottmann 1964). The megalopolis is an area that was once made up of small towns and cities, but now has interconnected metropolitan centers. The first U.S. megalopolis was the area between New York, Boston, and Washington, D.C.—covering ten states, the District of Columbia, and hundreds of local governments. The areas between Chicago and Cleveland and between San Francisco and San Diego are becoming megalopolises.

These metropolitan areas are merging into a single unit. They are so intertwined that some people work in one and live in another, using air shuttles to taxi back and forth. Washington, D.C., New York City, and Boston are tied together by such air shuttles. From dawn to dusk, commuters can catch a flight almost every half hour between these cities. As sociologist John Palen (1981) says, city-to-city air shuttles often offer more frequent and faster transportation than the service available between some parts of a single metropolitan area.

Regional Planning

As the fate of one city merges with that of others, new regional governing structures are developing. They attempt to match in scope the areas that are governed, superseding the boundaries of their many urban units. Although cities and suburbs find it difficult to give up their autonomy, many work together through county boards in an endeavor called *regional planning*. They establish regulations that incorporate the larger regions, especially those concerning transportation, environmental control, housing, and policing. Cooperation does not come about without struggle, as each smaller urban unit clings to its historical rights, granted by state charter, and thinks of itself as independent. With profits at stake, there is little doubt about the outcome of such struggles: The larger governing unit will win out.

Edge Cities

Expansion beyond traditional political boundaries is also indicated by the appearance of *edge cities*. This term refers to a clustering of buildings and services near the intersection of major highways (Garreau 1991a, 1991b). This clustering of shopping malls, hotels, office parks, and residential areas overlaps political boundaries and includes parts of several cities or towns. Although edge cities are not cities, they do provide a sense of place to those who live or work there. Many of the nation's new jobs are developing in edge cities (Lagerfeld 1991).

Restratification: Regional Shifts in Wealth and Power

Another major change in U.S. cities is **restratification**, a shift in the cities' relative population, wealth, and power. Figure 12-4 depicts this dramatic shift. Our ten fastest-growing cities are in the West and South. Of the ten cities that lost the most population, only two are in the South and none in the West. Table 12-2 illustrates this restratification on a *regional* basis. Since 1970, the South and the West account for almost all the increase in the U.S. population. About half the country's total population growth occurred in just the western states.

The political implications of this regional shift are enormous, for only during one other period of U.S. history—the Civil War—has the balance of power among the states undergone such rapid and deep transformation. As their population grows, the tax base and congressional representation of the West and South become stronger, while those of the Northeast and Midwest weaken.

Emerging Problems in the Sun Belt

The rapid growth in the sun belt has created the same problems the older urban centers faced: traffic congestion, air pollution, urban sprawl, and pressures on educational systems. The capital and human resources flowing from the old industrial

Table 12-2 Population Changes in U.S. Regions

	Millions of People					Increase in Millions	Percentage Increase
	1970	1980	1990	1997	2000	1970–2000	1970–2000
Northeast	49	49	51	52	54	5	10.2
Midwest	57	59	60	63	64	7	12.2
South	63	75	85	94	100	37	59
West	35	43	53	59	63	28	80

Source: U.S. Census Bureau (2001) *Population Change and Distribution,* 2000 Census Brief, Table 1.

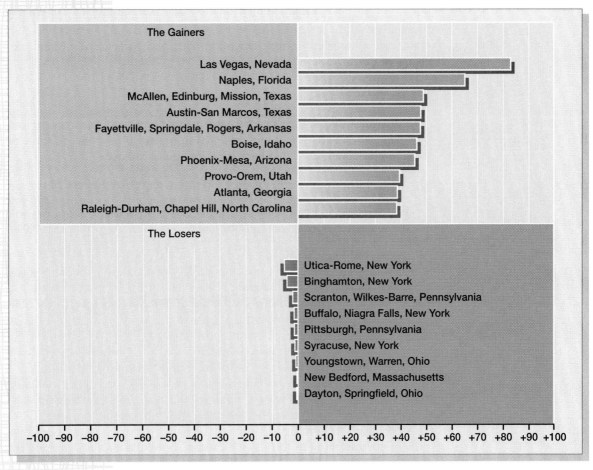

The Gainers

- Las Vegas, Nevada
- Naples, Florida
- McAllen, Edinburg, Mission, Texas
- Austin-San Marcos, Texas
- Fayettville, Springdale, Rogers, Arkansas
- Boise, Idaho
- Phoenix-Mesa, Arizona
- Provo-Orem, Utah
- Atlanta, Georgia
- Raleigh-Durham, Chapel Hill, North Carolina

The Losers

- Utica-Rome, New York
- Binghamton, New York
- Scranton, Wilkes-Barre, Pennsylvania
- Buffalo, Niagra Falls, New York
- Pittsburgh, Pennsylvania
- Syracuse, New York
- Youngstown, Warren, Ohio
- New Bedford, Massachusetts
- Dayton, Springfield, Ohio

−100 −90 −80 −70 −60 −50 −40 −30 −20 −10 0 +10 +20 +30 +40 +50 +60 +70 +80 +90 +100

FIGURE 12-4
Large U.S. Metro Areas that Gained or Lost the Most Population, 1990–2000
(*Source: Statistical Abstract of the United States*, 2001:Table 31.)

The Essential Condition for Success: Establishing Community

centers to the sun-belt states, however, have given them the resources to solve their urban problems. As in the older cities, many problems in these newly expanding urban areas mostly affect the poor—and few leaders are willing to devote many resources to helping the poor.

Let's look at the potential for improving life in U.S. cities.

◆ Social Policy ◆

Many despair that the crises facing our cities can be solved. Some feel that the government has simply shuffled money from one fashionable urban program to another, with little, if anything, to show for it. Some even insist that government programs have made the problems worse. A few have given up on cities, saying their problems are too great, and we should disperse the urban population throughout the countryside, to new, planned-from-scratch small cities with designated maximum populations (Webber 1973).

Short of such an extreme approach, whose outcome would be uncertain, what steps are reasonable? Sociologists stress that the essential focus of urban policy must be to create a sense of community (Karp et al. 1991). If it does not do this, it is doomed. To create community, we must focus on the preservation and development of neighborhoods. Keeping this focus will help us avoid ill-conceived "urban renewal" programs that destroy neighborhoods and social relationships, no matter what appealing names they may be given.

SPECIFIC PROGRAMS

Six Programs with Promise:

Programs that hold special promise are urban homesteading, working with landlords/landladies, enterprise zones, regional authority, job deconcentration, and condominium in-filling. Let's first look at urban homesteading.

> Paul Gasparotti bought two abandoned adjacent houses from the city for a dollar each. After tearing everything out but the exterior bricks, roof rafters, and floor joists, he connected the two houses and dug out the basement. Under a low-interest loan program, Gasparotti put $42,000 into the home, now worth over $100,000. (Kirkpatrick 1981)

1. Urban Homesteading

Urban homesteading is sometimes called "sweat equity," because people invest toil rather than money in a building (Chandler 1988). In this program, a city sells (usually for $1) derelict housing that it has acquired by tax foreclosure. The buyer agrees to stay for a minimum time, ordinarily at least three years, and to bring the house up to code within eighteen months (Conway 1977; Williams 1977). As the mayor of Wilmington, Delaware, said, "We are not trying to provide housing for people. We are trying to find people for [abandoned] housing."

This program aims to stabilize neighborhoods by inspiring confidence (Rohe 1991). The idea is that salvaging buildings will encourage residents to stay and to improve their own properties. Deterioration will stop, neighborhoods will be rebuilt, and people will be lured back from the suburbs. Despite its promise, however, a study of homesteading in forty-two locations showed that it did *not* stabilize neighborhoods (Varady 1986).

Urban homesteading is a mixed blessing, because it does not include the very poor. Only people with good incomes and credit can undertake the rehabilitation of buildings. How can the poor repay the loans, unless they have jobs? Even if times are prosperous and the unskilled poor get jobs, what happens when they are fired when the economy slows? Urban homesteading threatens to be another displacer of the poor, for as a neighborhood is upgraded, rent and property values increase.

2. Working with Landlords/ Landladies

Another approach to abandoned housing would aim to solve the problem *before* it becomes a problem. Landlords do not want to abandon buildings. Walking away from a property means losing money. City officials could work with landlords to maintain neighborhoods. When landlords improve their properties, taxes could be reduced or held steady (instead of being raised, as is current policy). Improving police and other city services to the area would help attract renters who have jobs, and would benefit the area's current residents. Some may object that this policy helps landlords, but it also makes landlords a vehicle for improving and maintaining neighborhoods. Everyone wins. Social policies that penalize landlords sow seeds of neighborhood destruction.

3. Enterprise Zones

Although the socialistic management of cities is appealing to some, it has failed in the countries that have tried it. Cuba's cities, for example, are rotting, and only now that private investment is being tentatively allowed in some areas are its neglected buildings being restored. Following capitalist principles, then, the third program, **enterprise zones** (also known as empowerment zones) is being tried by most states (Cisneros 1993). The general principles of enterprise zones are:

1. Businesses that locate in a designated zone—a rundown area with high unemployment—receive tax credits for each full-time, qualified employee they hire.
2. Businesses in the enterprise zone that improve their facilities receive credits on their property tax.
3. Low-interest loans are available.

Enterprise zones are designed to stimulate economic growth and generate employment (Kemp 1990; O'Brien 1992; Wartzman and Harwood 1992). A danger is that enticing businesses to move from other sites may create blighted areas in the zones they leave behind. Another problem is that subsidizing some businesses in this fashion may create unfair competition for businesses not in the zone.

Supporters of enterprise zones claim that this policy has created thousands of jobs. Detractors scoff and suggest that if any *new* jobs have been formed, they are few and heavily tax subsidized (Guskind 1990). Researchers have not been able to determine how many jobs have been created or what the cost of those jobs is (Funkhouser and Lorenz 1987).

4. Regional Authority

More *regional planning* is needed. Metropolitan areas are fragmented into numerous small, competing political divisions. Each jealously guards its own turf against other jurisdictions. Overarching regional governments responsible for regional development can be created without abolishing the individual, smaller governments. States, from which cities receive their charter to operate, can force cities to give up some authority to regional bodies (such as water and sewer systems, police and fire protection, and building codes). These agencies would then implement policies for the region as a whole.

5. Job Deconcentration

Job deconcentration is another promising policy. It presupposes a regional master plan and a regional authority to enforce it. Toronto has such a plan. Factories, offices, shopping centers, and housing subdivisions can be built only in specified areas adjacent to the city. This allows rational planning and helps control urban and suburban sprawl. Job deconcentration also lets planning bodies develop public transportation that serves workers outside the central city. Lack of regional authority, however, makes such a policy impossible. As policy analyst Jan Newitt said to me, "Can't you just see New York City adopting a policy of putting jobs in the suburbs!"

6. Condominium In-filling

The exodus of the young middle class is the snow-belt cities' major loss. To reverse this migration, Newitt proposes **condominium in-filling,** building small energy-efficient condominiums for older urban home-owners. Because many older people stay in the homes in which they reared their children, they often have more room than they need and more maintenance than they can handle. Building condominiums in the neighborhoods in which people reared their children—where many older people wish to remain—would give these older people a place to move to, while allowing them to remain in the area and help stabilize the neighborhood. The larger, older housing they vacate would be available to younger families with children, who have energy and enthusiasm to maintain and improve such homes. More younger adults would then remain in the city, often in the same neighborhood where they spent their childhood. Of all programs, this has the most exciting potential, because it meets the sociological requirement to foster a sense of community.

To be successful, however, any urban program must confront one of our major failures, the education of the poor. As Gans (1968:292) says:

> The public-school system has never learned how to teach poor children, mainly because it has not needed to do so. In the past, those who could not or would not learn what the schools taught dropped out quietly and went to work. Today, such children drop out less quietly, and they cannot find work. Consequently, the schools have to learn how to hold them, not only when they drop out physically, but long before, in the early elementary grades, when they begin to drop out in spirit.

Principles for Success

Good schools for the poor require more than new buildings. Their curriculums must nourish the motivation to learn, which poor children are not lacking when they begin school. As they stay in school, however, urban poor children often see the public school system as irrelevant to their lives and future. To meet this need, Gans (1968) says that our schools will have to:

1. Hire motivated and dedicated teachers.
2. Develop new teaching methods.
3. Require smaller classes.
4. Develop innovative curriculums that build on the ideas and aspirations of inner-city youth.
5. Develop a more decentralized and less bureaucratized school system.
6. Adopt work-study programs.
7. Make scholarships available to encourage adult dropouts to return to school.

Violence and gang activity must also be reduced—or, better, eliminated—to produce an effective learning environment (Boyd 1991; Toby 1992).

ABC

ABC (A Better Chance) is a successful program in Boston. Financed by corporations, foundations, and individuals, it gives highly promising, stellar-performing inner-city youngsters scholarships to exclusive preparatory schools, such as Phillips Academy in Andover, Massachusetts, and Cate Preparatory School in Carpinteria, California. The program is so successful that all graduates have gone to college or studied abroad (Holden 1994).

The Potential vs. Short-Term Solutions

This program reaches only a few, though. We need to touch the lives of most poor children. As the Thinking Critically box on educating for success on the next page shows, we can design and implement successful programs. While they appear expensive, such programs would be cheap in the long run. They would pay back their cost many times over: Former students would pay taxes, and costs of crime and punishment would decrease. The initial cost, however, would be high, and the basic question is where this money would come from. Both our leaders and the public have a short-term view of educating the poor, and show little interest in solving fundamental problems.

The Basic Solution

In conclusion, if we have learned anything from the recent past, it is that *replacing buildings does not cure urban ills.* The basic social problems of the city are not dilapidated buildings. Those are only surface appearances. The real problems are street crime, poverty, unemployment, broken families, gang violence, riots, arson, drug addiction, mental illness, and juvenile delinquency—conditions whose origins are not local and that fixing or replacing old buildings does not solve (Webber 1977). As sociologist William Julius Wilson (1987) says, the key to solving urban problems is a

THINKING CRITICALLY ABOUT SOCIAL PROBLEMS

Educating for Success:
Reestablishing Community in the Learning Process

Education is in crisis. Children are being promoted from one grade to another whether they learn or not. Some students graduate from high school illiterate. Budgets are cut, programs trimmed, teachers burned out, and students unmotivated.

"Sow the wind and reap the whirlwind," said Hosea, an Old Testament prophet. And sowing a future of children having babies, unemployment, welfare dependency, crime, and despair will bring a whirlwind of shattered community—which can destroy a society.

Can education make a difference? How about for the most impoverished of society, the children of the inner city? To find out, the Yale Child Study Center School Development Team worked with the staff and parents in two grade schools in New Haven, Connecticut. The schools were in low-income neighborhoods that were 99 percent black and marked by the usual inner-city problems. Student achievement, which had been the lowest in the city, soared to the third and fourth highest. As measured on standardized tests, the students' achievement levels jumped to nine months above their grade level in one school, and twelve months ahead in the other. Attendance and behavior also improved dramatically.

How was this accomplished? First, the team made a radical assumption—that the problem was not "poor students," but, rather, the educational system. This put the responsibility on the shoulders of the staff—they had to meet the needs that the children's background created. Second, the staff fostered a feeling of common cause. They transferred leadership from a central office to the grass roots, to mature participants who worked on problems and made decisions together. Third, parents, staff, and students interacted frequently. This allowed students to identify with adults who valued and encouraged learning, reflecting a solid educational principle that learning is based on modeling and imitation. Fourth, a sense of community was engendered as trust, mutual respect, and a sense of common cause developed among teachers, administrators, parents, and students.

How would you apply these principles to change a troubled school in your area? What other principles from this text would you use?

Based on Comer 1986.

---

revitalized economic system that offers work to all. There is a balance here: More equal access to jobs, housing, education, and justice will reduce urban problems, but problems of the cities will persist to the same degree that inequalities in these areas persist.

◆ The Future of the Problem ◆

Thirteen Trends Likely to Continue

Based on current trends, I foresee the following:

1. The continued segregation of poor and minorities in the inner city.

2. Further development of downtown areas in response to their potential for profit.

3. The slum areas adjacent to downtown areas remaining slums with the same problems they have now.

The United States is experiencing one of its largest waves of immigration (approximately a million immigrants a year). A primary pattern of adjustment of earlier immigrants was to form ethnic enclaves in which they maintained customs from their homeland while they adjusted to the norms of their new land. Today's immigrants are following this same pattern.

The Homeless

4. Poor young males still being attracted to gangs.

5. More young females joining gangs and committing street crime.

6. High rates of school violence.

7. High rates of street crimes that continue to make parts of the city unsafe for visitors and residents.

8. Continued fear and avoidance of the inner city by the middle class.

9. Sporadic riots in our major cities.

10. More middle-class flight to the suburbs, by both whites and minorities.

11. Maintenance of racial and ethnic neighborhoods.

12. More migration from the snow belt to the sun belt.

13. Financial crises for city governments and deteriorating services.

An urgent problem is a reduced tax base in the face of rising costs and demands for services. Our cities depend on federal money to finance many programs, from urban transit to rehabilitating buildings and even supervising playgrounds. Some of that federal money has dried up. Caught in a financial squeeze, many cities have cut back on education, street cleaning, library hours, recreation programs, and activities for children and the elderly. Because reducing services upsets voters, urban governments have postponed maintenance—a cutback that is less visible and less subject to voter outcry. Deferred maintenance, however, borrows from the future, for the hidden deterioration of structures such as bridges and sewers continues. Deferred maintenance is one of the most severe crises U.S. cities face.

The maintenance of racial and ethnic neighborhoods flies in the face of predictions sociologists used to make. As John Palen (1977) pointed out, for decades sociologists have been predicting the imminent disappearance of ethnic neighborhoods—but no one apparently told the people who live there. Neighborhoods based on race, ethnicity, and social class will continue to provide a sense of community for their residents.

Skid rows used to mark all our cities. Now many have faded away because the skid row population is recruited primarily from unskilled migratory workers, a dwindling group. In addition, speculators have seen the value of this urban real estate and have converted many skid rows into high-rise office buildings, upscale shops, and hotels. The reclaiming of New York's Times Square from winos and pornographers by developers is such an example. The demise of skid row may be more appearance than substance, however, for its residents don't disappear, but, instead, resurface in adjacent areas, less visible because they are dispersed.

The homeless, who will continue their sorry presence on our city streets, will encounter persecution from city officials. To foster tourism and profits, politicians will disperse the homeless. This will create outcry—not at the existence of such miserable poverty but at the presence of pitiful people in areas that the better-off would like to enjoy without having their consciences pricked. There will be calls to remove the homeless from sight, to put them in "asylums" somewhere, as though hiding them might solve the problem.

Pressures on Housing

Two major forces will increase the demand for and cost of housing. First, each year about 4 million Americans turn age 30, the typical first-time home-buying age (*Statistical Abstract* 2001:Table 13). Second, the American dream of building one's own home continues to be nourished by developers and financial institutions. Middle-aged Americans, although they have so few children, are insisting that their new homes be larger and have more amenities (whirlpool baths, hot tubs, and so on). These two factors, which obviously depend on times being prosperous, will feed urban sprawl and inflate the cost of housing.

Potential In-Migration

Higher home and commuting costs, however, could lead to a turnaround for our cities. As couples face the high cost of commuting to the city for work, the lower-priced, solid houses in deteriorated areas of the city become attractive. Gentrification holds the potential of reversing the exodus from the city. It may also signal another major racial-ethnic change, for it may increase the proportion of whites in our central cities. Gentrification, of course, will fuel another controversy, for it will mean accommodating the middle class at the expense of the poor, who are displaced (Anderson 1990; Smith 1996).

Restratification and Regional Welfare

The future of the city depends on what city we are talking about. Because our cities are undergoing restratification, their future will be region-oriented. Sun-belt cities hold the brightest future. With their influx of capital, jobs, and workers, along with an expanding tax base, they appear best equipped to weather problems.

Principles for Successful Social Policy to Mold the Future

I need to stress that no particular future is inevitable. The future of our cities depends on trends yet unknown and on the social policies we adopt. The following four principles provide a solid foundation for shaping that future:

1. As a cultural center of work and play, the city offers vast potential for human happiness.

2. The city is a social creation, and so are its negative features. As such, they can be overcome.

3. Urban problems center on basic human needs.

4. To design a future that overcomes urban problems, our policies must incorporate basic human needs—social, psychological, physical, and spiritual.

The Potential for Our Urban Future

We can use these principles to forge a future that enhances the quality of life, maximizes human potential, and creates urban areas that satisfy the human need for community. Or we can ignore sound principles and long-term planning, deal with problems on a piecemeal, haphazard basis, and leave a failed legacy to future Americans. The choice is ours.

As a final note, I want to stress that if we do not solve the problem of the many miserably poor who are isolated in the inner city—desperate people with little hope, who descend into drugs and crime, turning savagely on one another and on anyone within their reach—the city is doomed. U.S. cities will go up in flames.

◆Summary

1. The world is seeing an urban explosion. In 1900, about 13 percent of the world's population lived in *cities*. Today about 50 percent do. The U.S. figure is about 75 percent.

2. Symbolic interactionists emphasize that an area that appears undesirable, disorganized, and threatening to outsiders may be a viable community to its inhabitants. Slums are worlds in miniature, with their own hierarchies of status, standards, and controls over behavior. It takes an insider's frame of reference to understand such worlds.

3. According to functionalists, specialized zones naturally develop as a city grows. Each zone meets certain needs of a city's residents, and people with distinctive characteristics live there. Antagonisms result from the *invasion-succession cycle*, as one group displaces another. Urban problems are generally associated with the area adjacent to the central business district.

4. According to the conflict perspective, business leaders caused the decline of the inner city. They influenced politicians to subsidize the relocation of their businesses to the suburbs and to build a transportation system to move their products. Suburban development came at the city's expense; it reduced its tax base and spurred the flight of the middle class.

5. Many people find cities alienating and experience intense problems in them. Some people, however, find in cities islands of intimacy that yield high personal satisfaction.

6. With the poor locked out of opportunities, *redlining*, the abandonment of buildings, and arson, the quality of life in our cities deteriorated. Older suburbs and sun-belt cities also have problems.

7. Violence is such a major problem that youth gangs even control some areas of our major cities. Violence is also common in our urban schools. Poverty and discrimination remain background factors, but riots require a *precipitating incident*.

8. The replacement of the *political machine* by a professional bureaucracy created its own problems, such as department loyalty and lack of coordinated planning. Ethnic minorities are gaining political clout in our urban areas, and the transition of power is going smoothly. *Megalopolises*, interconnected metropolitan centers that were once a series of smaller towns and cities, have emerged. The move to the sun belt is forcing *restratification* of U.S. cities in terms of capital, human resources, and political power.

9. To meet human needs better, urban policy can preserve existing neighborhoods and encourage new ones. Social policies with high potential include *urban homesteading, enterprise zones*, regional authority, *job deconcentration*, and *condominium in-filling*. To succeed, an urban policy must develop a sense of community and meet the needs of the poor.

10. Our cities have a troubled future. Their current problems are likely to get worse. We are now at the crossroads in making decisions that will affect future generations.

◆Key Terms

Chicago school of sociology   An approach to research that originated with the Department of Sociology at the University of Chicago in the 1920s, with an emphasis on participant observation, symbolic interactionism, and seeing things from an insider's point of view.

City   A large number of people who are permanently based and do not produce their own food.

Commodity riot   Collective violence that involves extensive looting.

Communal riot   Collective violence between the residents of two areas for control of a contested area.

Community   People identifying with an area and with one another, sensing that they belong and that others care about what happens to them.

Concentric zone theory   A theory developed by Ernest Burgess suggesting that cities develop outward from their center, resulting in areas, or zones, that have specialized functions. The area closest to the central business district—the zone in transition—demonstrates the most severe urban problems.

Condominium in-filling   An urban policy in which condominiums for older people are built in vacant areas of a neighborhood, while the larger homes they vacate are taken over by younger families.

Disinvestment   Withholding investments from an area.

Enterprise zones   An urban policy that attempts to encourage private enterprise in a designated area of a city by reducing taxes and government regulations.

Gemeinschaft   A group of people characterized by bonds of intimacy combined with a sense of tradition and belonging. See *Gesellschaft*.

Gentrification   The relatively affluent displacing the poor and renovating their homes.

Gesellschaft   A group of people characterized by impersonality and the pursuit of self-interest. See *Gemeinschaft*.

Hit A form of youth gang violence in which a small raiding party seeks out individual members of a rival gang.

Housing unit A place of residence normally occupied by a family, individual, or group of people. Examples are a detached house, a mobile home, or an individual apartment or condominium.

Invasion-succession cycle One group moving into an area already inhabited by a group with different characteristics. Moving in represents the invasion; dominating the area, the succession.

Job deconcentration An urban policy that moves jobs to specified areas adjacent to a city.

Machine See *Political machine*.

Megalopolis The "overspill" of urban areas onto one another, making them an interconnected metropolitan region.

Political machine A political organization that distributes government jobs or favors among its members. Essential to its operation is an informal, behind-the-scenes working arrangement that circumvents the official ways of handling a city's business.

Precipitating incident A specific incident that triggers a riot.

Redlining The refusal to service a designated area, such as a bank not offering mortgages or an insurance company not writing insurance.

Restratification A shift in the relative wealth and power of various sections of a society. The gains recently made by the sun belt are an example.

Rumble An encounter between fairly large numbers of rival gang members.

Skid row An area of the city inhabited by the poor, the homeless, and the social institutions catering to their needs, such as rescue missions and shelters.

Suburban sprawl The disappearance of open areas as the suburb expands into the countryside.

Urban crisis The interrelated critical problems of governing and financing our cities, including their poverty, violence, crime, and deterioration of services.

Urban homesteading An urban policy whereby a city gives tax-foreclosed property to an individual who agrees to bring it into compliance with city codes and to live in it for a designated period of time.

Urban sprawl The expansion of a city onto adjacent farmland.

◆Critical Thinking Questions

1. Which of the theoretical perspectives (symbolic interactionism, functionalism, or conflict theory) do you think does the best job of explaining urban problems? Explain.

2. If a bank finds that a certain community within a city contains an abundance of "risky" investments and makes a business decision to "redline" the area, generally refusing to give loans to people who live or work in the area, do you think it is proper for government to ban such a practice? Explain.

3. What are the political implications of the changes in the racial–ethnic makeup of U.S. cities? As these changes occur, who will benefit? Who will lose? Why?

4. Which of the following programs do you think are the most appropriate and helpful responses to urban decay?
   • urban homesteading
   • enterprise zones
   • job deconcentration
   • condominium in-filling
   Why?

Population
and
Food

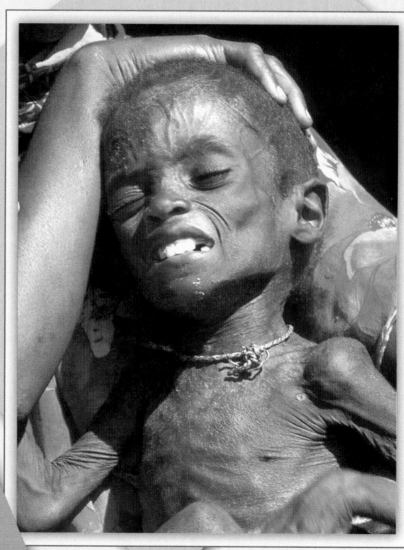

With her varicose veins and her blackened and missing teeth, Celia, only 30 years old, looked like an old woman. She beamed as she pointed to her distended stomach, indicating that her thirteenth child was on its way. Looking at her smiling face, it was hard to imagine how she could be more delighted—even if she were expecting her first.

"The rich get richer—and the poor get children," we thought, as we looked around the tiny palapa, the single-room hut that housed this large family. We saw straw mats on the dirt floor where the older children slept, a double bed for the parents and younger children, and, for the oldest, a hammock strung between the poles that supported the thatched roof. The only furnishings were a stove, a cabinet where Celia stored her dishes and cooking utensils, and a table in the cooking area.

There were no chairs. This really startled us: The family was so poor that they could not afford even a single chair.

We found it difficult to swallow, as we ate the posole, swollen corn tasting something like hominy, that Celia and her husband, Angel, generously offered us. "Surely the children are not receiving enough food on Angel's daily wage of $5," we thought. And the family obviously could not afford adequate medical care. They had lost one child to polio, while their oldest daughter had been left badly disfigured by an injury to her right eye. Vainly trying to conceal her disfigurement, this 13-year-old would constantly sweep stringy locks of hair over the ghastly eye.

We were living in Armeria, Mexico, and we had come to accept many things. But Celia's situation was depressing. We looked at the haggard face of her oldest son. Only 14 years old, he had already begun to work in the fields with the men. Each day we watched these men, machetes in hand, dragging themselves home at twilight. This was his fate, to labor exhaustingly in fields for pennies a day. But Celia could not have been more proud of him. He was doing his part to help pay for the family's needs. She was as thrilled about her son's working as a U.S. mother is when her child graduates from college.

And then there was the coming child. Celia and her husband were genuinely delighted about this latest pregnancy. We congratulated them on the coming blessed event and decided we still had much to learn about this culture. "Why is their thinking so different from ours?" we wondered.

◆ The Problem in Sociological Perspective ◆

What Is Demography?

The textbook definition of **demography,** the study of the size, composition, growth, and distribution of human populations, makes it sound like a pretty dry subject. Yet this subdiscipline of sociology is anything but dry, for demographers focus on some of the most far-reaching changes occurring in the world. Some say these changes threaten to engulf us and our children and destroy our way of life.

Demographers find changes in population especially important. For example, for most of history, Europe's population increased at a snail's pace. By 1750, all of Europe had only about 140 million inhabitants. During the next fifty years, Europe's population grew by 48 million. Fifty years later, by 1850, it had increased by another 68 million, reaching a total of 256 million. What caused such an abrupt change?

Why Did Europe's Population Surge from 1750 to 1850?

In 1926, G. T. Griffith argued that the increase was due to improved public health. Better medical knowledge, hospitals, housing, water, and sanitation, he said, lowered the *death rate*, the number of deaths per 1,000 people. More people lived longer, and the population grew.

While Griffith's view is the most widely accepted, some demographers disagree. Thomas McKeown (1977), for example, claimed that the population of Europe remained low until 1750 because Europeans practiced **infanticide,** killing infants shortly after birth. This practice declined after 1750, he said.

If McKeown is right, why did infanticide decline? His answer is surprising—because of the potato! McKeown's explanation goes like this: Europeans had been practicing infanticide because their food supply could not support more people. Infanticide kept their population in balance with their food supply. Then their food supply suddenly changed.

During their sixteenth-century conquest of South America, the Spanish discovered the potato, which was cultivated in the Andean highlands. When they brought it back home with them, Europeans at first viewed the potato with suspicion. Some grew it as a curiosity, but gradually Europeans began to see the potato as a good food, and they started to grow it in quantity. Their change in attitude was so sweeping that by 1800 the potato had become the principal food of the poor in northern and central Europe. This "miracle" vegetable enlarged Europe's food supply, allowing the population almost to double in a century.

Demography, then, emphasizes the relationship between population and environment. If a population increases dramatically, demographers look for changes in a people's customs. Such changes may be as complicated as new medical and sanitation practices, or as simple as a better diet.

The Gloomy Prophet: Thomas Malthus

To Thomas Malthus, an English economist, Europe's surge in population was a sign of coming doom. In 1798 he wrote *An Essay on the Principle of Population*, arguing that while population grows geometrically, that is, from 2 to 4 to 8 to 16 and so forth, the food supply increases only arithmetically, that is, from 1 to 2 to 3 to 4 and so on. This means, he said, that if births go unchecked, the population of a country, or even of the world, will outstrip its food supply.

The Pessimists: The New Malthusians

Demographers still debate whether Malthus was right. One group, the "New Malthusians," insists that he was. We are still in the early stages of the process Malthus identified, they say, and today's situation is as grim, if not grimmer, than he ever imagined. Indeed, the world's population is out of control. It is following an **exponential growth curve.** This means that if growth doubles during approximately equal intervals of time, it suddenly accelerates.

To illustrate the implications of exponential growth, sociologist William Faunce (1981:84) told a parable about a man who saved a rich man's life. The rich man, of course, was very grateful, and he offered a reward:

> The man said he would like his reward to be spread out over a four-week period, with each day's amount being twice what he received on the preceding day. He also said he would be happy to receive only one penny on the first day. The rich man handed over the penny and congratulated himself on how cheaply he had gotten by. At the end of the first week, the rich man checked to see how much he owed and was pleased to find that the total was only $1.27. By the end of the second week he owed only $163.83. On the 21st day, however, the rich man was surprised to find that the total had grown to $20,971.51. When the 28th day arrived the rich man was shocked to discover that he owed $1,342,177.28 for that day alone and that the total reward had jumped to $2,684,354.56!

This is precisely what alarms the New Malthusians. They say that we have just entered the "fourth week" of an exponential growth curve. Figure 13-1 shows why

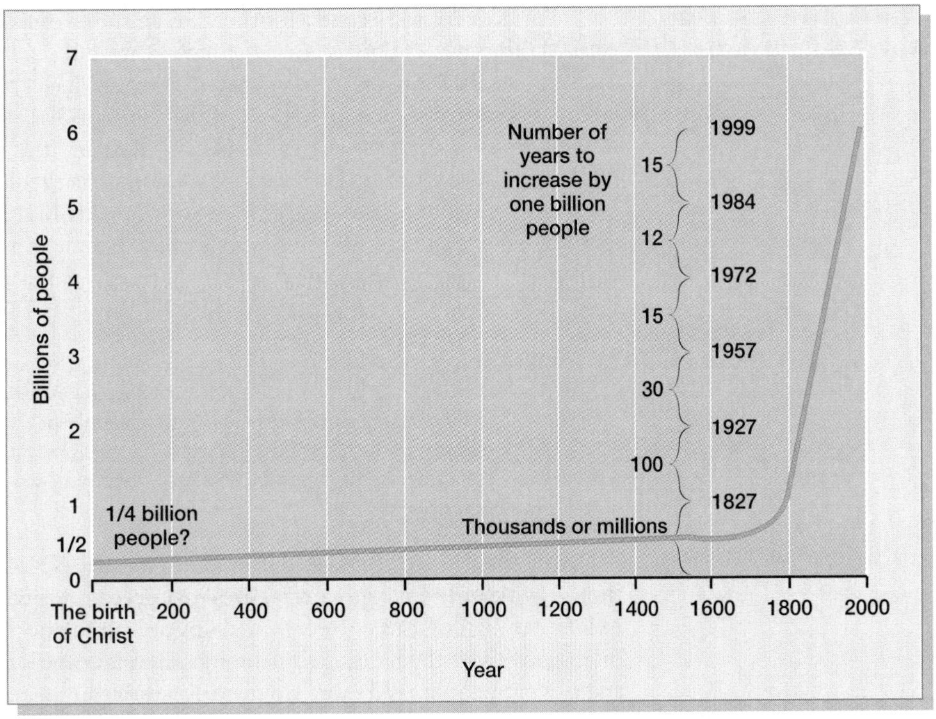

FIGURE 13-1

The World's Population Is Following an Exponential Growth Curve.
(*Source:* Modified from Piotrow 1973:4.)

Number of years to increase by one billion people

15 — 1999
15 — 1984
12 — 1972
15 — 1957
30 — 1927
100 — 1827

1/4 billion people?

Thousands or millions

Billions of people

7
6
5
4
3
2
1
1/2
0

The birth of Christ   200   400   600   800   1000   1200   1400   1600   1800   2000

Year

FIGURE 13-2

How Fast Is the World's Population Growing?
(*Source:* McFalls 1998.)

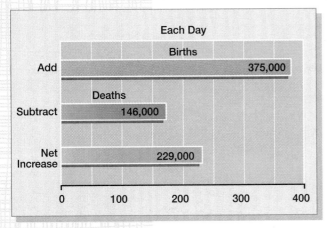

Each Day

Add — Births — 375,000

Subtract — Deaths — 146,000

Net Increase — 229,000

0   100   200   300   400

they think the day of reckoning is just around the corner. They point out that it took thousands, some say millions, of years for the world's population to reach its first billion, around 1827. Remarkably, it took only about 100 years to add the second billion (1927), 30 years to reach the third billion (1957), 15 years to reach the fourth billion (1972), and just 12 years (1984) to reach the fifth billion. Fifteen years later, in 1999, we reached the sixth billion. The population of the world has doubled in the past 40 years.

On average, every minute of every day, 261 babies are born. As Figure 13-2 shows, at sunset the world has 229,000 more people than it did the day before. In one year this amounts to an increase of 84 million people. In just three and one-half years, the world adds the equivalent of the entire U.S. population (McFalls 1998; *Statistical Abstract* 2001:Table 1327). You might think of it this way: *In just the next fifteen years the world's population will increase as much as it did during the first 1,800 years after the birth of Christ.*

These figures terrify the New Malthusians. They believe we are heading toward a showdown between population and food. India, Pakistan, and Bangladesh—whose pitiful, starving children we have seen on television—are expected to grow from their current 1.2 billion people to 1.5 billion by the year 2010 (Haub and Cornelius 1999). By 2025, these three countries are expected to reach 1.8 billion— more than the entire world's population 100 years ago. We will soon run out of food if we do not curtail population growth.

The Optimists: The Anti-Malthusians

"You're wrong!" replies another, much more optimistic group, which I call the Anti-Malthusians. "This is just so much scare talk," claims this group. "Ever since Malthus reached his faulty conclusions, people have been claiming that the sky is falling—it is only a matter of time until the world is overpopulated and everybody starves. Year after year, the New Malthusians do the same song and dance, and, frankly, we're tired of it. Let's be realistic for a change."

And what is the counterargument of the Anti-Malthusians? They first point out that the way the New Malthusians perceive people is wrong, for the New Malthusians think of people as being comparable to germs that breed in a bucket:

> Assume there are two germs in the bottom of a bucket, and they double in number every hour. . . . If it takes one hundred hours for the bucket to be full of germs, at what point is the bucket one-half full of germs? A moment's thought will show that after ninety-nine hours the bucket is only half full. The title of this volume [*The 99th Hour*] is not intended to imply that the United States is half full of people but to emphasize that it is possible to have "plenty of space left" and still be precariously near the upper limit. (Price 1967:4)

Anti-Malthusians scoff at this image. They say fitting the world's current population growth onto an exponential growth curve and then projecting it into the future indefinitely is not the correct way to figure population growth. It ignores people's intelligence and their rational planning when it comes to having children. To understand what people really do, we need to study the historical record. Here we see an encouraging principle at work: People generally limit reproduction to match their available food. And that principle applies today, as shown in the Global Glimpse box on the next page. The current "explosion" in world population, then, is a hopeful sign. It means the world is producing *more food* than ever before. As the Europeans did with the potato, people are simply reacting to this increased capacity to support them.

To understand the future, continue the Anti-Malthusians, consider Europe's **demographic transition.** As diagrammed in Figure 13-3, Stage I consists of a fairly stable population—high death rates offset the high birth rates. Most of Europe's

FIGURE 13-3
The Demographic Transition

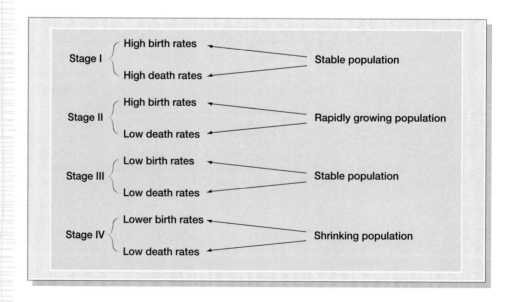

A GLOBAL GLIMPSE

"I'd Like to Have Twenty Children"

In 1976, an anthropologist, who was making a documentary of an African village in Kenya, asked a 26-year-old mother of two, whose stomach was bulging, how many children she wanted. The woman giggled and said, "I'd like to have twenty children."

The documentary then went into a freeze frame, with a subtitle stating that the woman had given birth to twins.

This image haunted John Tierney. "What was wrong with her?" he wondered. "What would become of her family?" Ten years later he went to Kenya to follow up the story. He found the woman, Fanisi Kalusa, living in the same hut, the twins healthy, She was now 36, with seven children, aged 4 to 16.

When Tierney asked about her wanting twenty children, Fanisi laughed, and said, "I've rejected that idea because there is not enough food to meet the demand."

Most African men dislike birth control, but her husband had agreed to limit their family. He had his mother put a curse on his wife to make her barren—a standard practice in the area.

Fanisi went along with the curse—but without telling her husband, she visited a clinic for a free IUD.

Having twenty children made sense when children meant labor on the farm and support in old age. But now, children have become expensive in Kenya. For each child, parents must pay $10 a year in tuition, a burden in this poor land. In addition, many children are moving to the city, breaking the close family bonds and threatening the custom of adult children providing support for their aged parents.

Fanisi told her 16-year-old daughter to have only six children. Fanisi's daughter told Tierney that she thought four would be about right.

What do you think? Will Africa successfully make the demographic transition? The Anti-Malthusians point to Fanisi Kalusa as evidence that they will. But the New Malthusians retort that Kenya is growing at 2.1 percent each year. Its population will double in just 33 years.

Based on Tierney 1986; Haub and Cornelius 1999.

---

history was characterized by Stage I. Then came the "population explosion" of about 1750, and Europe entered Stage II. The population surged because death rates declined rapidly but birth rates remained high. Europe then entered Stage III. Its population stabilized as people brought their birth rates in line with their lower death rates.

The demographic transition was so successful that European countries now worry about *not having enough babies*. Having moved into Stage IV of the demographic transition, Western Europe fears **population shrinkage,** not producing enough children to replace people who die. Italy was the first country in the world to have more people over age 65 than children under age 15 (Haub and Cornelius 1999). The transition has been like a small stream that turns into a raging river. Of the 42 countries of Europe, 40 no longer produce enough children to maintain their populations (McDonald 2001). They all fill more coffins than cradles.

The Anti-Malthusians predict that this demographic transition will also occur in the poorer nations of the world. Their current rapid growth indicates that they are in the second stage of the demographic transition. But already their growth rate has slowed. Recall how it took the world's population 12 years to go from four to five billion, but then 15 years to go from five to six billion. This slowing of growth is exactly what we would expect. These nations are just now penetrating the third stage of the demographic transition, and soon we will be wondering what all the fuss was about.

✦ The Scope of the Problem ✦

How the New Malthusians See the Scope of the Problem

Let's suppose that the world's population doubles during the next 49 years, which it will if present growth rates continue (Haub and Cornelius 1999). Can the world support twice its present population? The New Malthusians say the answer lies in how the world is doing with its current population. They note that famine and malnutrition stalk the earth. About one of every five people on earth lives in absolute poverty (Livernash and Rodenburg 1998). Most of these people are malnourished and go to bed hungry each night. In some of the world's poorest nations, such as Bangladesh, *half* the population does not eat enough protein. Every year thousands of people in Africa, Asia, and Latin America are born deaf-mutes because of iodine deficiency. Several hundred million people survive on *less* than $200 a year. (The *average* income in Ethiopia, which has one of the highest birth rates in the world, is just $110 for the entire year [Haub and Cornelius 1999]).

As bad as it is now, add the New Malthusians, the future looks even bleaker. Urban sprawl is devouring productive farmlands at a furious pace. Each year in the United States alone, developers turn about 3 million acres of farmland into subdivisions and businesses. That is enough land to form a corridor a mile and a half wide stretching from San Francisco to New York. The land chewed up by urban sprawl is lost to food production, further sealing the fate of the world's malnourished.

How the Anti-Malthusians See the Scope of the Problem

"It isn't like that at all," object the Anti-Malthusians. The idea that the United States is being "paved over" is absurd, argued economist Julian Simon (1981). The United States has about 2 billion acres. All the land taken up by cities, highways, roads, railroads, and airports amounts to only 75 million acres—less than 4 percent of our total land. We are in no danger of running out of farmland.

Urban sprawl has not even slowed food production, continue the Anti-Malthusians, nor is it taking food out of the mouths of starving children, as the New Malthusians would have us believe. The problem is neither that the earth has too many people, nor that the earth fails to produce sufficient food. The amount of food available for every person on earth has actually been *increasing*, not decreasing. Every country records how much food it produces. As Figure 13-4 shows, *despite the billions that have been added to the earth's population, more food is available per person now than in the past.* The United States produces so much food that our problem is what to do with it all. The government sometimes even pays its farmers *not* to farm some land. Americans eat so much that obesity has become a major health problem. The bottom line is that efforts to reduce the world's population are misdirected.

If it isn't too many people or not enough food, then what causes starvation? The earth's abundance, continue the Anti-Malthusians, is not adequately distributed. In fact, if we were to redistribute a mere 3 to 5 percent of the grain of the Most Industrialized Nations, we could prevent *all* the malnutrition and starvation in the entire world (Conti 1980).

The African famines that upset the world do *not* occur because there are too many people, but because of drought and civil war. Africa, a continent rich in resources, has *fewer* people per square mile than Europe or the United States (*Statistical Abstract* 2001:Table 1327). Those alarming images of starving children—little bony arms, protruding stomachs, and flies crawling over their faces—are due to civil wars that disrupt food production and block humanitarian aid from reaching the dying (Gibbons 1991; MacKenzie 1998; Nelan 1998). The suffering shown in this

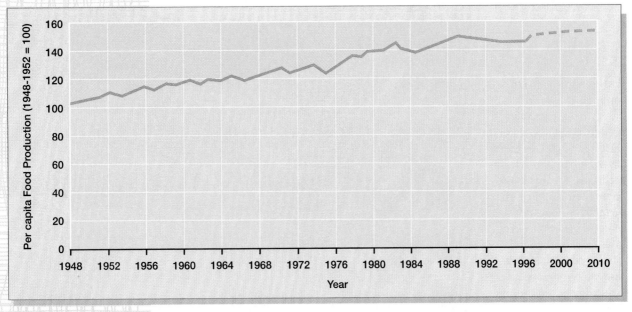

FIGURE 13-4
How Much Food Does the World Produce Per Person?

(*Source*: U.S. Department of Agriculture. Simon 1981:58; *Statistical Abstract* 1988:Table 1411; 1998:Tables 1380, 1381, 1382, 1383, recomputed to 1948–52 base.)
Note: Projections from 1997 are the author's.

In Sum

chapter's opening photo is totally unnecessary. There is plenty of food to feed this child—and all others like her.

To look at the problem as too many people or insufficient food misses the mark entirely. The problem is a combination of agricultural inefficiency, inadequate incentives, political corruption, maldistribution of the earth's abundance, poor governments, and war—not too little food in the world.

Simon (1981) stressed that today's famines are even a sign that food production and distribution have improved. *Fewer* people starve today, he pointed out, than at any other point in history for which we have reasonable estimates. This means that the food supply for the poor is more stable than at any time in the past two or three centuries.

As far as those statistics about deaf-mutes go, the Anti-Malthusians agree that those are horrible figures. They point out, however, that these people are born deaf-mutes because they lack iodized food, not because they are "excess" people. Their situation has nothing to do with the earth being overpopulated. The problem is how to get iodized food to people, not how to reduce population.

The New Malthusians and the Anti-Malthusians draw different conclusions from the same evidence. Much like the pessimist who considers half a glass of water half empty, the New Malthusians conclude that we are about to run out of land and food. Like the optimist who considers the same glass of water half full, the Anti-Malthusians conclude that our era enjoys the greatest abundance and hope that the world has ever known. The scope of the population problem depends on one's focus—whether one sees the glass as half empty or half full.

No one can settle this for you. You will have to read the evidence and make up your own mind. As you do so, remember the symbolic interactionist principle that *facts never interpret themselves:* To interpret something, we always place it within a framework that gives it meaning. As we consider issues of population and food in the coming pages, we will return to this basic principle from time to time. For now, let's look at the frameworks of understanding called sociological theories.

With political conflicts common, the world is awash in refugees, who need to be fed, clothed, and sheltered. Their care is usually a temporary matter, as in this scene from Albania, but in some instances the turmoil continues or the refugees' government refuses to allow them back into the country. In that case the "temporary" arrangement can continue for decades.

✦ Looking at the Problem Theoretically ✦

As usual, our three theoretical lenses provide different views of this social problem. We will use symbolic interactionism to better understand why the population of the Least Industrialized Nations is increasing so fast. Functionalism illuminates the relationship between modern medicine and the twin problems of population and food. Finally, conflict theory yields a controversial analysis of food, profits, and international relations. Together, these perspectives help us understand the whole.

SYMBOLIC INTERACTIONISM

Why Do the Poor Have So Many Children?

Let's start with something that doesn't seem to make sense. Look at Figure 13-5. The population of the Least Industrialized Nations is increasing fast, that of the Most Industrialized Nations hardly at all. You can see that almost all of the increase in the world's population is coming from the Least Industrialized Nations.

It seems obvious that if you are poor, you should have fewer children. Why wouldn't hunger and disease, starvation and death, convince poor people to have fewer children? One possibility is that they are unfamiliar with birth control. Perhaps people in the Least Industrialized Nations *want* to have fewer children, but do not know how to prevent them. This, however, is not the case. Cheap and effective birth control techniques are available, but many of the poor won't use them. They continue to have many children because they want large families (Burns 1994).

The focus of symbolic interactionism—trying to grasp people's perspective, to see the world as they see it—helps explain this. Our ideas about what seems to be irrational behavior change when we examine what children *mean* for people in the Least Industrialized Nations.

Taking the Role of the Other

Recall Celia and Angel in the chapter's opening vignette. As you could tell, my wife and I had difficulty understanding Celia's joy at being pregnant with her thirteenth child. We saw her situation from our framework, not as she and her husband

Chapter 13   Population and Food

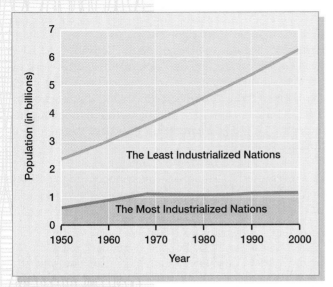

FIGURE 13-5
Where Is the World's Population Growth Taking Place?
(*Source*: World Population Profile 1985; 1986:1.)

As stressed in the text, events in life do not come with built-in meanings. All of us use frameworks of thought to interpret life's events. How do New Malthusians and Anti-Malthusians interpret this scene in Pushkar, India? Why do they see things so differently?

saw it. Only by **taking the role of the other**—that is, seeing things from someone's perspective—can we make sense of people's experiences.

To understand Celia's and Angel's desire for more children, then, and the desires of millions of poor people like them, we must move beyond our own culture. We need first to see that in the Least Industrialized Nations people's identities center around their children. Motherhood is the most exalted status a woman can achieve. Through childbearing, she finds fulfillment. The more children she bears, the more she has fulfilled the purpose for which she was born. Similarly, a man proves his manhood by fathering many children, especially sons. Through them, his name lives on.

There is more to the explanation, though: Such people live in small communities of shared values, in which they identify with one another. It is here that they are given or denied the status that matters—their rank in the family and among friends and acquaintances. Having many children is taken as a sign of God's blessing. As people produce more children, then, the community grants them higher status. The barren woman, not one with a dozen children, is to be pitied.

These are strong motivations for bearing many children. But there is another: For the poor in the Least Industrialized Nations, children are economic assets. This, too, is difficult for us to grasp. We live in an urbanized, industrialized society where children have become economic liabilities. Long ago, we left the agrarian world where children helped on the family farm. In the industrialized world, children have become luxuries. They are expensive, and with longer education, they remain so for many years. Parents consider having children in much the same way that they consider buying a new car: "Can we afford one?" or "Should we put it off until later?"

How, then, can poor people afford to have many children, and why do they see them as economic assets? There is no social security or medical and unemployment insurance in the Least Industrialized Nations. This provides a motivation to have *more* children, not fewer, for when parents become too sick or too old to work or when no work is available, they rely on their families to take care of them. The more children they have, the broader their support. Moreover, supporting a family usually requires many workers. Like the oldest son of Celia and Angel, children begin contributing to the family income at a young age. Figure 13-6 illustrates this aspect of parenting in the Least Industrialized Nations.

For us, of course, it would be irrational to have many children. From the framework of the people involved, however—the essence of the symbolic interactionist position—having many children is rational. The contrast is drawn sharply in this incident, reported by a worker for the Indian government:

> A water carrier . . . Thaman Singh. . . . welcomed me inside his home, gave me a cup of tea (with milk and "market" sugar, as he proudly pointed out later), and said: "You were trying to convince me . . . that I shouldn't have any more sons. Now, you see, I have six sons and two daughters and I sit at home in leisure. They are grown up and they bring me money. One even works outside the village as a laborer. *You told me I was a poor man and couldn't support a large family. Now, you see, because of my large family I am a rich man.*" (Italics added) (Mamdani 1973:109)

In Sum

Our ideas of the right number of children and their role make sense for us, for our ideas match our life situation. To superimpose our ideas onto people in a different culture is to overlook their situation and their perspective. To understand the behavior of any group we must see things as they see them, including behavior that appears irrational to us.

FUNCTIONALISM

As we look at the functionalist perspective, keep in mind that functionalists want to determine the functions or consequences of events objectively and do not judge those functions. As we saw in the instances of poverty, rape, heroin addiction, and

FIGURE 13-6

Why the Poor in the Least Industrialized Nations Want Many Children

Surviving children are an economic asset in the Least Industrialized Nations. Based on a survey in Indonesia, this figure shows that boys and girls can be net income earners for their families by the age of 9 or 10.
(*Source:* U.N. Fund for Population Activities.)

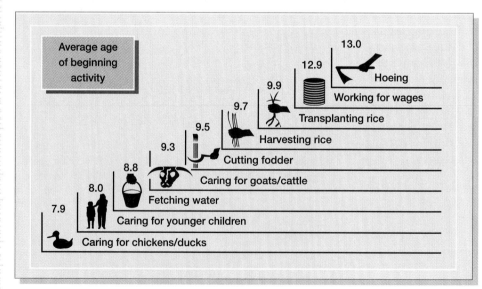

Chapter 13 Population and Food

Catastrophes
Are Functional

The Latent
Dysfunctions
of Modern Medicine
and Public Health
Practices

Population
Pyramids

ethnic discrimination, functionalists find that even deviant, illegal, or abhorrent events have functions. With regard to the problem of population and food, functionalists stress that war, natural disasters, disease, and famine are functional. These mass killers have held the world's population down to manageable levels, ensuring that humans did not outstrip their food supply.

Modern medicine, however, has upset the precarious balance between population and food. It attacked the major killers: smallpox, diphtheria, typhoid, measles, and other communicable diseases. With better nutrition, sanitation, and modern drugs, the high death rates of the Least Industrialized Nations plunged. Their birth rates, however, remained high. Millions who otherwise would have died now survive to reproduce. This has forced the Least Industrialized Nations into the difficult second stage of the demographic transition.

Countries at different stages in the demographic transition have different proportions of their population at various age levels. To illustrate how different rates of growth produce different "shapes" of populations, demographers use **population pyramids,** such as Figure 13-7, which contrasts Mexico, in Stage II of the demographic transition, and the United States, in advanced Stage III.

Population growth in the Least and Most Industrialized Nations contrasts sharply. The population growth of the Most Industrialized Nations averages 0.1 percent per year; it will take 583 years for their population to double. The Least Industrialized Nations are growing *fifteen times faster*; they will double in just 40 years

FIGURE 13-7
**Population
Pyramids of
Mexico and the
United States**
(*Source:* U.S. Bureau of the Census, International Data Base, Table 94.)

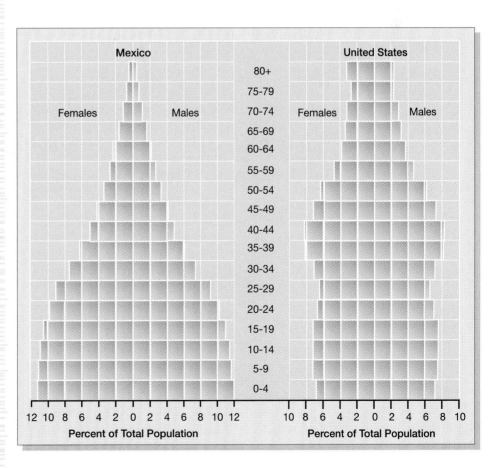

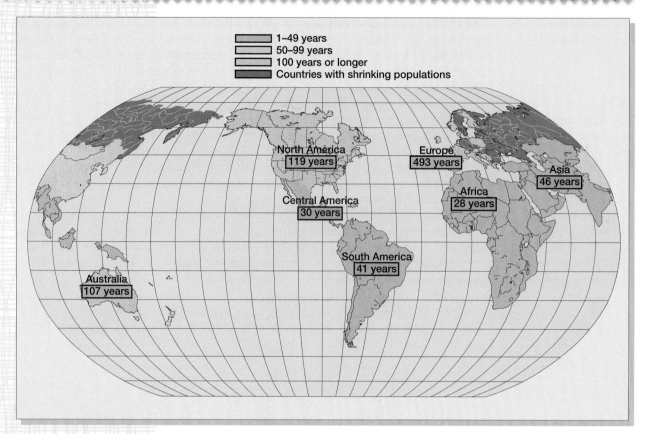

1–49 years
50–99 years
100 years or longer
Countries with shrinking populations

North America
119 years

Europe
493 years

Asia
46 years

Africa
28 years

Central America
30 years

South America
41 years

Australia
107 years

FIGURE 13-8
Social Map: How Long Will It Take for Population to Double?
(*Source:* Haub and Cornelius 1999.)

Implications of a Doubled Population

The Contrast

Latent Dysfunctions of Medicine

(Haub and Cornelius 1999). The doubling time of the world's nations is shown on the Social Map above. Some of the extremes are shown in Table 13-1. Consider two countries with the same population: At current growth rates, Chad will double its population in just 21 years, but it will take Austria 2,310 years to do so.

The implications of a doubled population are mind-boggling. *Just to stay even* a country must double its food production and factories; its medical and educational capacity; its transportation, communication, water, gas, sewer, and electrical systems; its housing, churches, civic buildings, theaters, stores, and parks; its automobiles, electronics, and household appliances; as well as jobs and all else that constitutes "decent living standards." If not, a society's standard of living falls.

The Least Industrialized Nations, then, appear destined to fall still farther behind the industrialized nations, for they start with less and their swelling numbers drain their limited financial resources. In contrast, the Most Industrialized Nations, such as the United States, *can spend much more on fewer people.* With an annual growth rate of 0.9 percent, the United States is at the low end of the world's growth rate but at the high end of the rate for the Most Industrialized Nations. One third of the U.S. increase is due to immigration. The U.S. rate of natural increase (growth without immigration) is 0.6 percent (*Statistical Abstract* 2001:Table 4; Haub and Cornelius 1999).

Functionalists analyze how modern medicine and public hygiene tipped a delicate balance. Introducing modern medicine and public hygiene to the Least Industrialized Nations led to malnutrition, mass starvation, and political unrest. Be-

Table 13-1 How Long Will It Take a Country to Double Its Population?

Some Most Industrialized Nations

Country	Population (in millions)	Births (per 1,000 women)	Deaths (per 1,000 population)	Annual Natural Increase	Years It Takes to Double
United States	273	15	9	0.6	116
Canada	31	11	7	0.4	162
Japan	127	10	7	0.2	318
Great Britain	59	12	10	0.2	423
Denmark	5	12	11	0.1	472
Belgium	10	11	10	0.1	693
Austria	8	10	10	Slightly over 0	2,310

Some Least Industrialized Nations

Country	Population (in millions)	Births (per 1,000 women)	Deaths (per 1,000 population)	Annual Natural Increase	Years It Takes to Double
Chad	8	50	17	3.3	21
Nicaragua	5	38	6	3.2	22
Ethiopia	60	46	21	2.5	28
Algeria	31	30	6	2.4	29
Mexico	100	27	5	2.2	32
India	987	28	9	1.9	37
China	1,254	16	7	1.0	73

Source: Haub and Cornelius 1999.

cause such consequences were not anticipated or intended, sociologists call them **latent dysfunctions.**

But Could These Difficulties Actually Be Functional?

Where others see dysfunctions, the Anti-Malthusians see functions. They believe that in the long run the increase in the world's population is functional. The Least Industrialized Nations are just in the difficult second stage in their demographic transition; they will enter the third stage and limit their populations. Some already have begun to do so. Their growing populations will stimulate them to industrialize and to apply technology to farming. Consequently, warnings to reduce world population are unwarranted, and what some now find so upsetting will turn out to be functional for humanity.

CONFLICT THEORY

The Problem is a Product of Power: Political and Economic Arrangements that Favor the Most Industrialized Nations

Conflict theorists focus on the global distribution of power and resources. They stress that social and economic arrangements, not nature, produce poverty, hunger, malnutrition, and starvation. The Least Industrialized Nations have problems feeding their populations not because of Malthusian inevitabilities but because they have too little income. As sociologist Michael Harrington (1977) stressed, their income is restricted because political and economic arrangements favor the rich nations.

Conflict theorists point out that the Most Industrialized Nations exploit the Least Industrialized Nations today just as the European powers used to exploit their colonies. They control the international markets so they can extract the mineral and agricultural wealth of the Least Industrialized Nations at the lowest possible cost. Manipulating commodity markets, they determine what they will pay for tin from Bolivia, copper from Peru, sugar from Cuba, coffee from Brazil, and so forth.

The poor nations even contribute to the diet of the rich nations. For example, each year the United States imports about $39 billion of food, much of it from the Least Industrialized Nations (*Statistical Abstract* 2001:Table 818). Although the ultimate consumers of these foods pay dearly for them, the poor countries themselves receive little of that amount. As Harrington (1977) pointed out, international arrangements benefit the wealthy elite of the industrialized world. The real profits go to middlemen in the Most Industrialized Nations.

The United States also exports about $52 billion of food (*Statistical Abstract* 2001:Table 818). Like other grain-exporting nations, it treats food as a money-making enterprise, not as a means of dealing with world hunger (Seaborg 1985). The United States and Canada, which control about 60 percent of the world's wheat market, sell their wheat surpluses first to those that can pay the highest prices, not to the most needy (Conti 1980).

Food Politics

Why does the U.S. government pay farmers billions of dollars *not* to grow crops even though people in some nations are starving? Conflict theorists say that the answer is "food politics," manipulating food production to control food prices. By paying farmers to leave their land fallow, they create an artificial shortage and drive up grain prices. They also avoid running up high charges for storing grain, and cater to the farm vote by keeping grain prices high. Food politics, they stress, is pursued for political ends, with no concern for its moral implications.

Conflict theorists conclude that food is a tool in the U.S. diplomatic kit. The food crisis affecting the undernourished masses of the world is the result of food politics, not Malthusian inevitabilities (Harrington 1977). Conflict theorists think in terms of a grain cartel, which the United States and Canada control, and which is as damaging to the Least Industrialized Nations as the OPEC oil cartel was to the industrialized world before the United States bombed it into submission. The United States, say conflict theorists, is engaged in a struggle of "agripower against petropower."

◆ Research Findings ◆

Let's first examine the position of the New Malthusians: the harm to fisheries, forests, and grasslands; the threat of plant disease and the intensification of natural disasters; and the built-in momentum in world population growth. Then we'll consider the views of the Anti-Malthusians, and conclude by examining why it is so difficult to predict population growth accurately and whether the United States has a population problem.

THE NEW MALTHUSIANS

Pressures on the Earth's Three Natural Systems:

The New Malthusians are convinced that the world is outstripping its food supply. The world's huge population has put unsustainable pressure on the earth's three natural systems—its fishing grounds, forests, and grasslands—on which we all depend

1. The Fishing Grounds

for food. Each has a *carrying capacity*, limits fixed by nature, and we are straining those limits.

It is folly to view the ocean, as some do, as an infinite source of food that only needs better harvesting techniques. Biologists Paul and Anne Ehrlich (1972) note that 90 percent of the ocean is a biological desert. The upper layer of open sea, which gets enough sunlight for photosynthesis, lacks nutrients for high productivity. Close to shore are the areas that supply us with virtually all our fish, but these are also the most polluted. Modern fishing fleets equipped with echo sounders and sonar are devastating these fragile fish populations.

2. The Forests

The second natural system, the forests, seems eternally renewable. On one level, this is true. For every tree cut down, a tree can be planted. Each year, however, the world's forest areas shrink by an area the size of Cuba. In Peru and Chile, for example, vast areas have been cut for firewood and farming. With the soil unprotected against wind and rain, some hills are as barren as the moon. Pressure on the world's forests will increase even further, as the demand for newsprint and packaging soars worldwide. Incredibly, it takes about 850 acres of timber to produce just the Sunday edition of the *New York Times* (Waddington 1978).

3. The Grasslands

The third global life-support system, the grasslands, is also under mounting pressure. Many U.S farmers in the Midwest, for example, have bulldozed their windrows, the row of trees planted between their fields. By reducing the force of the wind, windrows keep topsoil from blowing away. Now that many are removed, some fear a repeat of the dust bowl of the 1930s. Back then, Oklahoma was the main victim; this time, much of the Midwest would be hit.

Much of the agricultural production of the Midwest and the West depends on the Ogallala aquifer, an extensive underground water system. Irrigation is rapidly depleting this reservoir. Wells are running dry, as we shall see in the next chapter. Soon we will have to curtail this extensive irrigation, which underlies much of the high productivity of the western United States.

Around the world, this pressing need for food is pushing into production land that is basically unsuitable for cultivation (Little and Horowitz 1987). The steep hillsides of Indonesia are being eroded, while slash-and-burn agriculture is destroying tropical forests in many countries, including Brazil and the Philippines. Attempts to apply farming techniques from the temperate zone to the tropical soils of Brazil and Sudan have caused **laterization,** the transformation of soils into laterite, a rocklike material. This occurs when certain soils are exposed to the air through cultivation.

Two Major Dangers:

1. Disease of Specialized Strains

In addition to pressure on the world's three natural systems, the rapidly expanding population of the world faces two other dangers. First, the world's agricultural system now depends on only a few specialized strains of crops. In the quest for higher yields, a few specifically bred, high-yield strains have replaced the world's wide range of traditional varieties of wheat and rice. While these high-yield varieties allow farmers to produce more food, they also increase the probability of widespread crop failure from insects and disease.

Biologists John Holdren and Paul Ehrlich (1974) warned that what happened in Ireland during the last century could indicate what our generation might experience on a much larger scale:

> The Irish potato famine of the last century is perhaps the best-known example of the collapse of a single agricultural ecosystem. The heavy reliance of the Irish population on a single, high productive crop led to 1.5 million deaths when the potato monoculture fell victim to a fungus.

In other words, if the right pest or plant disease comes along, we can have a worldwide calamity. Our extensive cultivation of single high-yield grains is "an accident waiting to happen." The benefits it now yields may come at the future cost of epidemic starvation, malnutrition, and disease.

2. Intensification of Natural Disasters

The second danger arises from the intensification of natural disasters. As human populations grow, they expand into areas less likely to protect them from the elements. The Ehrlichs (1972:243) provided this account of how overpopulation intensifies natural disasters:

> In November of 1970, a huge tidal wave driven by a cyclone swept over the Ganges Delta of East Pakistan. There a large, mostly destitute population lived exposed on flat lowland, in spite of the ever-present danger of climatic disaster for which the region is famous. They live in constant jeopardy because in grossly overpopulated East Pakistan the choice of places for them is greatly restricted. In November, 1970, 300,000 people died who need not have died if their nation had not been over-populated. This cataclysm has been described as the greatest documented national disaster in history.

In this poor, overcrowded nation, now called Bangladesh, evacuation was impossible. Because it was already nutritionally marginal, after the disaster people began to starve.

An Amazing Statistic

Now consider this statistic, which underscores the New Malthusians' point. Despite this huge death toll, in only five or six weeks new births made Bangladesh's population as large as it was before the catastrophe (Waddington 1978). In May 1991, a cyclone and its aftermath claimed about 200,000 Bangladeshi (Crossette 1991). It would take just a month to replace this number.

Thus the New Malthusians conclude that humanity must stop its population growth. Outstripping our food supply, they warn, will bring the worst catastrophe the world has ever known. Some are so pessimistic that they say even an increased food supply will not buy much time. It would allow us to postpone, but not avoid, the inevitable disaster. The only solution is to stabilize world population (Miles 1970).

Zero Population Growth

Suppose that we miraculously achieve **zero population growth**—that is, adults reproduce only enough children to replace themselves. It seems obvious that the world's population problem would disappear, right? The obvious, however, is not true. *The momentum built into the world's population would keep it growing for 50 to 70 years before it leveled off.* Why? Because there are more people in the younger age groups than in the older age groups. For example, 43 percent of Africa's people are not yet age 15 (Haub and Cornelius 1999). Thus, more people will enter the reproductive ages each year than will leave them. Although the growth *rate* would fall during this 50- to 70-year period, population would increase before it eventually stabilized.

Even World Peace is Threatened

The future looks desperate. The world faces famine, malnutrition, starvation, as well as pollution and environmental destruction (which we discuss in Chapter 14). The world's swelling population also threatens world peace. When the governments of the Least Industrialized Nations cannot feed their people, civil disorder will ensue. Governments will topple, threatening the precarious balance of international power.

THE ANTI-MALTHUSIANS

Larger Populations Are Good

The Anti-Malthusians, of course, draw different conclusions. They insist that, in the long run, more people are good for a country; larger populations lead to *higher* standards of living (Simon 1977, 1982, 1991). This seems to fly in the face of reality.

The world's population is growing rapidly. It has just reached 6 billion. Food production, however, has increased faster than population growth, and today the average person has more food than when the world had billions fewer people. New and Anti-Malthusians disagree sharply on what this means.

Food Production Is Outpacing Population Growth

How can they take this position? All we have to do is look at India, Bangladesh, and China. To support their position, they make four points. First, population growth forces countries to use its land more efficiently, thereby increasing productivity. Second, a growing population means that more geniuses will be born, who will contribute to everyone's welfare. Third, larger populations create larger markets. This promotes more efficient manufacturing, lowering the production cost per unit. More goods become available more cheaply. Fourth, a larger population makes many social investments profitable, especially railroads, highways, irrigation systems, and ports. These factors spur productivity and increase a country's capacity to deliver that productivity to its people.

The Anti-Malthusians stress that we should not lose sight of how the world has increased its food production. (Recall Figure 13-4 on page 441). Food production has actually *outpaced* population growth, and now there is more food for each person in the entire world than there was 25, 50, 100 years ago. Moreover, per capita food increased while the world's population "exploded" and the "breadbasket of the world" decreased its farm acreage. As Figure 13-9 shows, the United States now has *less* land under the plow than in 1930 and in 1960.

If the population increase is dramatic, then this food increase is more dramatic still. Even in the Least Industrialized Nations, agricultural productivity has outpaced population growth. India, for example, produces more food per capita than it did 20 years ago (Stevens 1994). As productivity in the Least Industrialized Nations increases even more, they, too, will need less land to feed even more people (Simon 1981).

When it comes to fishing grounds, the Anti-Malthusians say that the numbers tell the story there, too. The world's fish harvest has not fallen, as one would expect from the New Malthusians' alarms. According to official U.S. government figures, it now is 60 percent *higher* than it was in 1980 (*Statistical Abstract* 1998:Table 1341; 2001:Table 1358). This, of course, does not make good headlines and does not

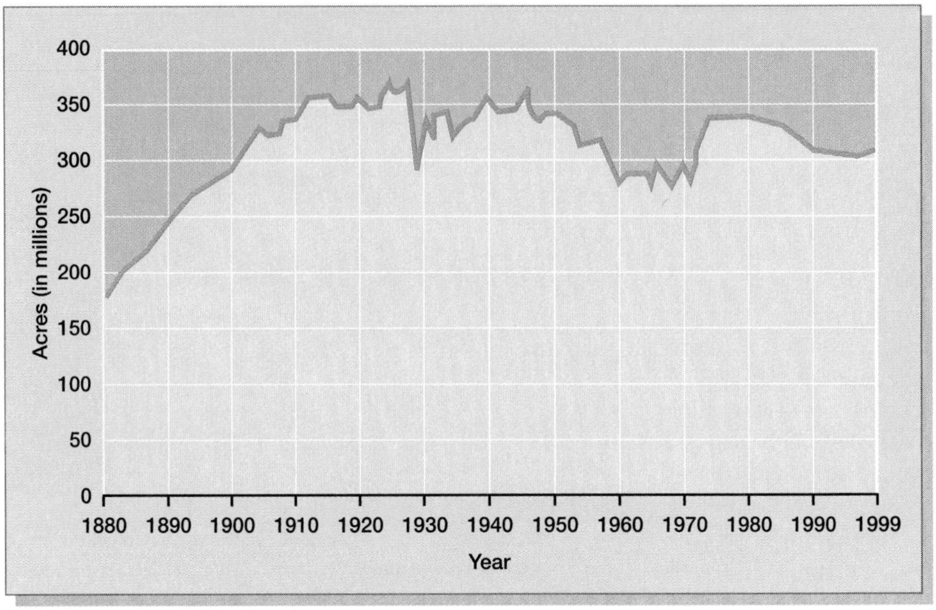

FIGURE 13-9
Cropland Harvested in the United States
(*Source: Statistical Abstract* 1991:Table 1154; 1998:Table 1126; 2001:Table 796.)

spread fear. Therefore, the good news is ignored by the mass media that make their billions by screaming the end of the world.

Not Even a Land Shortage

And running out of land? Not in any realistic future, say the Anti-Malthusians. According to the U.N. Food and Agricultural Organization, more than two billion acres of rain-fed land go unfarmed (Livermore and Rodenburg 1999). Contrary to common belief, then, the world contains enough land to feed even more people. If we should ever farm all this unused land, and need more, then we could reclaim wasteland and make it productive. The best example is Holland, whose success shows the potential of human endeavor. Originally Holland belonged more to the sea than the land; one would expect it to be filled with lagoons and dominated by sea fowl and migratory birds. Instead, it is a prosperous country with one of the highest population densities in Europe.

HAS THE POPULATION EXPLOSION PEAKED?

The Anti-Malthusians

The Anti-Malthusians point out that the world's rate of growth is slowing. The world's population grew 2 percent a year between 1965 and 1975. Then it dropped to 1.7 percent a year during the 1980s. Now it has dropped to 1.3 percent (*Statistical Abstract* 1991:Table 1434; Haub and Cornelius 1999; U.S. Bureau of the Census 2000, International Data Base, 5-10-00). This means that the world's population is growing 30 percent slower than it was just 30 years ago. This slowdown has occurred not only in the industrialized nations of Europe and North America but also in the poorer nations on all continents. Even Africa, which long refused to budge, has started the transition. The growth is still speeding along, but it is slowing—just as we would expect according to the demographic transition. Perhaps the most startling statistic is this: In the 1950s, the average woman in the Least Industrialized Nations gave birth to 6.2 children. Today she has just 3.4 children (Livernash and Rodenburg 1998).

The New Malthusians

The advocates of zero population growth reply that these figures indicate only that even though the *rate* has slowed, the world's population is still exploding. They emphasize that in absolute numbers the world's population is soaring beyond anything history has ever seen; we are still adding about 84 million people a year to our planet.

PROBLEMS IN FORECASTING POPULATION GROWTH

The Pessimistic Prophets

To forecast population growth is to invite yourself to be wrong (Conner 1990). Consider this:

> During the depression of the late 1920s and early 1930s, birth rates plunged as unemployment reached unprecedented heights. Demographers then issued warnings about the dangers of depopulation almost as alarmist as some of today's forecasts of overpopulation (Waddington 1978). Because each year fewer and fewer females would enter the childbearing years, they felt that the population of countries such as Great Britain would shrink.

Why Demographers Hedge Their Bets

Instead, with the end of the depression and the outbreak of World War II, the birth rate rose. After the war, both the United States and Britain saw a "baby boom." The inaccuracy of the pessimistic prophecies of the 1930s should make us skeptical of demographic forecasts. Population growth depends on people's attitudes and behavior, and how can anyone know what those will be? Today, demographers hedge their bets. They make several predictions, each based on different assumptions. Figure 13-10 shows three of their projections about the U.S. population.

Which projection will prove most accurate? As we saw, unforeseen trends upset population projections. Because some children die, for our population to stay even every 1,000 women must give birth to 2,100 children. For decades, the U.S. birth rate has dropped (recall Figure 11-1 on page 364), and now, at 14.5 per 1,000 population, it is the lowest in our history (*Statistical Abstract* 2001:Table 70). At some point, we will not reproduce our population.

FIGURE 13-10

Three Projections of the U.S. Population
(*Source: Statistical Abstract* 2001:Table 3)

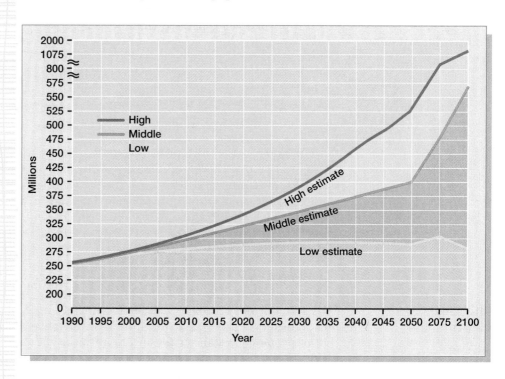

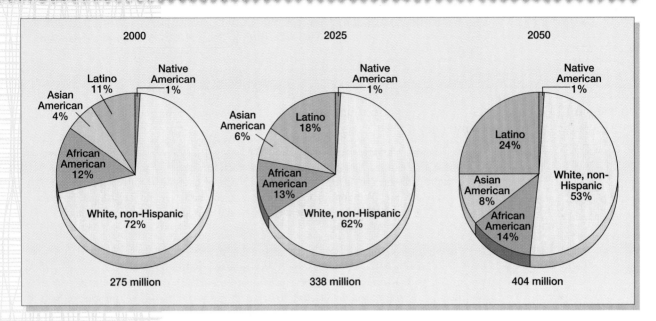

FIGURE 13-11

U.S. Population by Race and Ethnic Group, 2000, 2025, and 2050

(*Source*: U.S. Bureau of the Census, *Current Population Reports* P25-1130 [1996]; 2000:NP-TS-A.)

Do Immigrants Pay Their Way?

Unlike the population of such countries as Italy and Spain, however, ours will not shrink. Our low rate of childbearing is more than offset by immigration. Each year, about 3/4 million immigrants enter the United States legally (*Statistical Abstract* 2001:Table 6), and perhaps even more do so illegally. This vast immigration will have dramatic effects on the United States. Figure 13-11 shows one of them, how immigration (combined with the natural increase due to births minus deaths) is expected to affect the U.S. racial-ethnic makeup.

People worry that immigrants depress wages and take jobs away from citizens. Concerns that they are a drain on taxpayers motivated a 1997 law that made immigrants ineligible for federal welfare benefits (Martin and Midgley 1999). Some economists claim that after subtracting what immigrants collect in welfare and adding what they produce in jobs and taxes, they make a positive contribution to the economy (Simon 1986). Others find an "immigrant deficit," concluding that immigrants are a drain on taxpayers (Huddle 1993).

The situation is complicated, but the key seems to be education (Smith and Edmonston 1997). The fairest summary is that immigrants with low education collect more in benefits than they pay in taxes, while those with high education pay more in taxes than they collect in benefits. On average, adult immigrants who have less than a high school education impose a net cost of $89,000 over their lifetime. Those with more than 12 years of schooling provide a $105,000 lifetime gain (Martin and Midgley 1999).

DOES THE UNITED STATES HAVE A POPULATION PROBLEM?

The Anti-Malthusians

Let's conclude this section by considering whether the United States has a population problem. As Table 13-2 shows, in terms of available space and absolute numbers of people, it is difficult for anyone to make the case that we do. The Anti-Malthusians stress that even if Americans started to have larger families, the country

Table 13-2   Density of Selected Countries

Country	Number of Persons per Square Mile
Monaco	41,235
Singapore	17,849
Bangladesh	2,539
Taiwan	1,796
Barbados	1,658
South Korea	1,224
Holland	1,200
India	897
Japan	832
Israel	757
Philippines	720
Haiti	655
Great Britain	632
Germany	614
Italy	500
Pakistan	481
Switzerland	474
North Korea	457
Nigeria	360
China	354
Poland	329
Denmark	327
Indonesia	324
Guatemala	310
Portugal	285
Hungary	283
France	283
Cuba	261
Austria	255
Turkey	223
Greece	210
Spain	208
Egypt	181
Morocco	178
Ethiopia	152
Ireland	144
Iraq	139
Mexico	137
Afghanistan	107
Nicaragua	106
Iran	105
South Africa	92
United States	79
Venezuela	70
Sweden	56
Peru	56
Brazil	53
Chile	53
Norway	38
New Zealand	37
Argentina	35
Saudi Arabia	27
Angola	22
Russia	22
Congo	22
Canada	9
Libya	8
Suriname	7
Australia	7
Botswana	7
Mongolia	4

Source: Statistical Abstract 2001:Table 1327.

would have enough room, industry, and food to satisfy them. In fact, a larger population would prove an economic boom to the United States, because industries would have to supply what they needed. In short, say the Anti-Malthusians, the United States does *not* have *enough* people, and we ought to increase immigration, especially of skilled people (Simon 1991).

The New Malthusians

The New Malthusians look at the same set of statistics differently, of course. They maintain that we do have a population problem. It is not inadequate space, food, or industry, or even too many people, but, instead, the rate at which Americans deplete the world's resources and pollute the environment. The average American uses 5 times more energy than the average person in the world, 30 times more energy than a citizen of India (*Statistical Abstract* 2001:Table 1369). If each American costs the earth as much as 21 Indians, then in terms of energy our approximately 275 million inhabitants use the same amount as 6 billion Indians. Put somewhat differently, if the population of India multiplied until it was as large as the earth's total population, only then would India put as much pressure on the earth's resources as we Americans do.

The Anti-Malthusians

This analogy, reply the Anti-Malthusians, is irrelevant. We need to focus on what Americans contribute to the earth. Our science, technology, and industry give the world the capacity to increase production and enhance the standard of living of even the poorest nations. If we had more people, we would have more geniuses, spurring even more creativity. We would then develop more of our potential, increase our capacity for production, including food, and help the poorer nations even more (Simon 1981).

How should we look at the matter? As with the optimist and the pessimist, the question again depends on definitions and viewpoints. These clashing views highlight the relevance of symbolic interactionism, for conclusions on both sides depend on interpreting facts. While the facts may be objective, what we choose to stress is not. Accordingly, the conclusions of both the New Malthusians and the Anti-Malthusians are biased.

◆ Social Policy ◆

When it comes to social policy, the New and Anti-Malthusians again have differing viewpoints.

EXPORTING WESTERN AGRICULTURE

Our agricultural techniques are so efficient that, as discussed, our problem is what to do with excess production. Since we have such advanced technology, why can't we solve the world's food problem once and for all by exporting our agricultural techniques to the Least Industrialized Nations? Everyone knows the old proverb, "Give a man a fish and you feed him for a day. Teach him to fish, and you feed him for a lifetime." If these nations adopt our techniques, which are tried and proven, couldn't they produce food in abundance? What works for us ought to work for them.

This solution has initial appeal, but it is unworkable. The **green revolution**—the rapidly expanded food production that occurred in the 1950s and 1960s—originated during a period of cheap energy and seemingly unlimited amounts of fresh water. The development of high-yield wheat and rice, coupled with effective fertilizers, raised hopes that impoverished nations could abolish famine. The U.S. Midwest could be reproduced in India, China, and Africa.

It didn't happen. Water and fertilizer, essential to these high-yield plants, are in short supply in the poor nations. To maximize yields, fields must be dosed with up to 150 pounds of nitrogen fertilizer per acre, and they also require massive amounts of water to keep the fertilizer from burning up the crops.

Nitrogen fertilizer is expensive. Some U.S. farmers find its cost prohibitive, and few farmers in the poor nations can afford it at all. Rural poverty in the Least Industrialized Nations is difficult for Americans to imagine. Many farmers cannot afford even the gasoline or electricity to irrigate their fields:

> "Oh, yes, we know about the green revolution," said Patal Mukherjee, a primary-school teacher in India who farms a few acres of rice and wheat. "But it does not change anything here. We are too poor."

Mukherjee's primitive farming methods are typical of India's 600 million village dwellers. He knows that different fertilizers will increase crops. And he knows how to apply them. But he rarely has the money to buy them. He is locked into an endless cycle of defeat. When he most needs fertilizers—to make up for a bad harvest—he cannot afford to buy them. Thus, skimpy harvests often follow bad harvests (Wallace 1980).

Another factor also prevents the exportation of Western farming methods. As functional analysts emphasize, food production is only one item in an interconnected system. Abundance is not enough; it must be distributed quickly to consumers or it rots. Our vast network of railway and trucking units, many of them refrigerated, allows us to do this. Our superhighways are subsidized by the federal government, which, in turn, depends on a vast system of tax collection. We also have an intricate system of supermarkets. Simply to export one or two pieces of our agricultural system to a poor nation would be ineffective. Instead, it would require an elaborate and expensive support system of production, processing, and distribution (Harrington 1977).

Exporting our agricultural techniques is not the answer. Let's look at the policies that follow from the Anti-Malthusian and New Malthusian positions.

POLICY IMPLICATIONS OF THE ANTI-MALTHUSIANS

While both the New and the Anti-Malthusians want to increase food production, they differ in most other respects.

Not all Anti-Malthusians will like the policy implications of their position (Simon 1982), but if larger populations are good for the world, then it follows that social policy ought to encourage larger families, or at least not discourage people from having children. Accordingly, the following steps could be taken:

Encouraging Population Growth

and

More Technology and Development

1. Establish incentives for women to become mothers, such as reduced taxes, paid maternity leave, subsidized housing, and free education and medical care— even cash bonuses, with larger bonuses for each successive child.

2. Criminalize abortion and birth control.

3. Establish incentives to encourage education, medicine, science, technology, industry, and agriculture.

4. Export Western medicine, public health techniques, and technical assistance for building schools, hospitals, roads, railroads, and heavy industry to the Least Industrialized Nations.

POLICY IMPLICATIONS OF THE NEW MALTHUSIANS

Many New Malthusians are also unlikely to be pleased with the implications of their position. Because their views are more widely held, let's examine their policy implications in more detail.

Malthus' Machiavellian Proposal

Although Malthus' main suggestion for limiting population was sexual abstinence, in *An Essay on the Principle of Population* (1798) he proposed a solution that most would find outrageous:

> We should . . . encourage . . . destruction. . . . Instead of recommending cleanliness to the poor, we should encourage contrary habits. In our towns we should make the streets narrower, crowd more people into the houses, and court the return of the plague. In the country, we should build villages near stagnant pools, and particularly encourage settlements in all marshy and unwholesome situations . . . . But above all, we should reprobate (abandon, reject) specific remedies for ravaging diseases.

If we were to take Malthus' recommendations seriously, we would withdraw modern medicine from the Least Industrialized Nations, especially vaccines and antibiotics. We would also refuse to train students from the Least Industrialized Nations and withhold food from the starving.

Today's Workable but Generally Unacceptable Solutions

Other unacceptable policies include:

1. Infanticide
2. Requiring a license to have children
3. Forced abortions for women who become pregnant without a license

4. Encouraging homosexual unions, since they are childless

5. Sterilizing enough baby girls to assure zero population growth

6. Sterilizing each woman who gives birth to a second child

7. Abortion on demand (more acceptable to many than most of the above, but, for many others, just as morally repugnant)

Today's Gloomy Prophet

Pentti Linkola, a Finnish botanist, suggests that we annihilate most of the human race (Milbank 1994). He compares humanity to a sinking ship with 100 passengers and a lifeboat that can hold only 10. He says, "We need to end aid to the Third World, stop giving asylum to refugees—and a war would be good, too." He adds, "If there were a button I could press that meant millions of people would die, I would gladly sacrifice myself."

For Dictators, Machiavelli Still Lives: The Example of China

Although most of these solutions seem too far-fetched to be implemented, we can note that legal abortion in the United States was once unthinkable; it now is commonplace. Similarly, homosexual relations were once punished by law; they now are supported by law. The other policy implications of the New Malthusians can similarly become accepted over time. Consider China, where the government launched a national campaign to reduce its population. The policy is simple: "One couple, one child." Steven Mosher (1983), an anthropologist who did fieldwork in China, found the implementation of this policy severe:

> "Each population unit, such as a rural collective, is limited to a certain number of births per year, which it allots to couples who have yet to have children." Women who have had their allotted quota of 1 who get pregnant "are forced to attend round-the-clock 'study courses' until they submit to an abortion." In some cases abortions are physically forced on resisting women, some of whom are nine months pregnant. (Erik 1982)

He also reports that

> families who actually have a second child must pay heavy fines, up to $2,000— several year's wages in mainland China—and run the risk of demotion or assignment to less desirable work as well.

One consequence is female infanticide:

> Among the peasants, especially, sons are more valued, as they still provide for their aged parents in a society that has no old-age security insurance. A daughter, in contrast, takes up residence with her husband's family upon marriage, severing all economic ties with her natal family. The birth of a son signals a relaxed and secure old age, while the arrival of a daughter portends poverty in one's declining years. Consequently, many peasants decide in favor of their own security, and trade the infant's life for their own.

The authorities not only overlook female infanticide but practice it. Mosher provides this example:

> A young woman pregnant for the first time gave birth to twin boys. What should have been an occasion for rejoicing quickly turned tragic as the cadres (government representatives on the local level) present asked her which one she wanted. Both of them, she replied, but to no avail. One of the babies—she could not and would not choose which—was taken from her and put to death.

In other words, to solve social problems, leaders of an autocratic state can take steps that are out of bounds in a democracy. Remember that Hitler's murder of millions of Jews was his solution to what he saw as a social problem. Citizens of any nation ruled by dictators, or any group not subject to the will of the people, are subject to the *leaders' views of reality*. Although our system is far from perfect, it prevents leaders from enacting many policies that the people strongly oppose.

Zero Population Growth

The New Malthusians usually support zero population growth. This is no simple matter, however, for as we saw with Celia and Angel, strong reasons for wanting many children are built into peasant society. There, children are intricately interwoven with identity and security, and few can comprehend the attitudes toward children that are common in the industrialized nations. They consider those ideas selfish and shortsighted—refusing what God wants to give in order to maintain a higher standard of living. Nor can they connect their desire to reproduce with some apocalyptic vision of an overpopulated, starving world. Most people decide to have fewer children not because of the world's population—but because of their attitudes, beliefs, and values (Hickey 1979).

A Change in Perception

For zero population growth to occur in the Least Industrialized Nations, adults must believe that smaller families are workable. They must be confident that they do not need their children to take care of them when they are sick or old. This appears unlikely without the system that underlies our views: retirement programs, medical and disability insurance, and old-age assistance. Except for a few oil-rich nations such as Qatar, such a support system would require industrial development.

Specific Proposals

Ways to achieve zero population growth include (Miles 1970; Bird 1977; Specter 1998):

1. Encouraging women to work and to have careers. Careers reduce commitment to motherhood—women find satisfactions in their careers, and their families become dependent on their income for a higher standard of living.

2. Distributing free or low-cost birth control devices.

3. Teaching zero population growth to schoolchildren.

4. Awarding cash payments to people who undergo sterilization. The payment can be small, as $20 or $30 goes a long way for people whose annual incomes are $200.

5. Providing no medical intervention in the poor nations that is not accompanied by measures to simultaneously lower birth rates.

6. Providing no food aid that is not tied to agricultural reform.

This last principle was tried successfully in the 1960s. India faced mass starvation, and the United States used food to force agricultural reform: Each month's shipments depended on progress in meeting monthly goals. Today India can feed itself (Brown 1985).

The Least Industrialized Nations have the potential to produce enough food to feed themselves. Asia used to have famines that killed millions. Now it *exports* excess food. China broke up its communal farms and, using capitalist (profit-oriented) incentives, produces more food than it needs for its billion-plus people (Critchfield 1986).

Not a Panacea

Paul and Anne Ehrlich (1972) pointed out that population control is not a panacea. If the world's population were to stabilize exactly where it is, virtually all other human problems would remain—poverty, urban blight, drug addiction, violence, discrimination, and environmental decay. The New Malthusians, however, believe that to try to solve these problems is a lost cause without population control.

Some New and Anti-Malthusians agree that the root of the problem is poverty, and that to eradicate it we need to restructure international markets. This means, however, that the rich nations would have to redistribute their wealth (Burch 1971; Frank 1979; Wallerstein 1974, 1979, 1984). Why would they do this? Their people do not want to lower their standard of living.

Michael Harrington (1977) suggested a more moderate program to redress the imbalance in international trade that forces the poor nations into crushing debt. Harrington called for canceling their debt, increasing trade with them, and giving technical assistance to increase their food production. He also pointed out how nations with specialized economies suffer from fluctuations in the price they receive for their commodities. To stabilize prices, he said that we should create a world organization to buy commodities when the price dips below a specified level and to sell them when they rise to a certain point. He also suggested indexing, keying the costs of industrial products that the poor nations buy from the rich to the return they receive for their own primary products. Indexing could lower the price the poor nations pay for manufactured goods.

Such proposals require altruism on the part of the Most Industrialized Nations, which are more likely to act from short-term self-interest. Note, however, that genuine self-interest is not always obvious. For example, it may well be in the self-interest of the wealthy nations to restructure the international markets, for these nations may face a more hostile world if they do not. The Iraqi invasion of Kuwait may have had more to do with an attempt by a Least Industrialized Nation to restructure international markets than anything else. The invasion by the Western nations under the leadership of the United States (Desert Storm) may also have had more to do with maintaining the structure of international markets than anything else. As more Least Industrialized Nations gain access to nuclear weapons, attempts to restructure markets and relationships will be more difficult to thwart.

◆ The Future of the Problem ◆

The future of food and population problems is murky. Demographers cannot even agree what the future population of a given country will be, much less the future population of the world. With this caveat, let's plunge into the unknown.

THE NEW MALTHUSIAN VIEWPOINT

If the New Malthusians are right, our future will one day mean wall-to-wall people. Perhaps the life portrayed in the Global Glimpse box on the next page on population density in Hong Kong is to be the fate of the world.

If population outstrips food production, as the New Malthusians seem convinced it will, supply and demand will push the price of food upward. Many Americans already find food expensive, but the burden on the Least Industrialized Nations will be greater. Oppressed by debt to the Most Industrialized Nations, they have little left to spend to import food.

If the New Malthusians are right, the famines of Africa are an omen for other parts of the world. Millions of people will starve each year, and the world will face a flood of international refugees. Neither the Least Industrialized Nations nor the Most Industrialized Nations will be willing to accept the social strain of allowing hundreds of thousands of poor, uneducated, culturally foreign people to enter their

Where Wall-to-Wall Means People

The Mong Kok section of Hong Kong may be the densest area on the face of the earth. Here, 200,000 people live in a bit more than half a square mile—a density rate of 300,000 people per square mile.

Officials have left a little strip of grass and a few wispy trees. People stand and stare at them. The trees are fenced off from the public.

How do the people feel about the crowding?

Winnie Choi, a hairdresser, says, "It's very crowded, but people like to live here because it's very convenient. It's a popular neighborhood." She adds that her family of five lived with two other families because her parents rented out two of the three rooms in their tiny apartment. Thirteen people shared one bathroom and a closet kitchen. "But we didn't think we were crowded. The other families each stayed in their rooms, and we had ours."

Lee Chi-Kwong, a successful merchant, could move out of Mong Kok if he wanted to. But he says, "I don't mind crowds. Crowds mean prosperity."

When asked about crowding, some residents just gave a quizzical look. They had difficulty understanding what the interviewer was trying to get at.

Based on Basler 1988.

---

lands. Consequently, huge numbers of dislocated people will live in "temporary" camps.

Revolution and Repression

If efforts to stave off famine fail, or if there is insufficient food to feed the rural masses flocking to the cities in search of work, the Least Industrialized Nations will face revolution. In response, these governments, run by their wealthy elites, will become more repressive. Because political and civil disorders could upset the international balance, the Most Industrialized Nations may well encourage such repression.

THE ANTI-MALTHUSIAN VIEWPOINT

The Optimistic View: The Future Is What We Make It

The Anti-Malthusians, of course, see a different future. The idea that famines are inevitable if the world's population grows is a bogeyman designed to scare people into having fewer children and to raise money for political purposes (Simon 1981). The earth can support several times more people than it does now. Whether famines will be avoided, however, depends on political and economic arrangements. The future is what we make it.

The Potential of Abundance

Biotechnology

Poorly managed, the earth's renewable resources can collapse, losing much of their productivity and bringing unmitigated suffering. Carefully managed, however, they can produce all that the world, even a growing one, will ever need. Biotechnology can produce new strains of pest-resistant plants, some of which will be able to produce their own fertilizers. Gene splicing will allow us to develop new varieties of cereal that replace nitrogen in the soil. Farmers will be able to avoid expensive petroleum-based fertilizers.

If any of this seems far-fetched, we only have to note that the biotechnological future has already begun. Not only can we clone animals, but we have already produced the first "designer animals," gene-spliced farm animals that produce more meat and milk. We will produce low-fat cows that turn fodder into meat more efficiently, and chickens that lay several eggs a day. Developed from existing animals, entire new breeds of farm animals are on the drawing boards. Not only can the

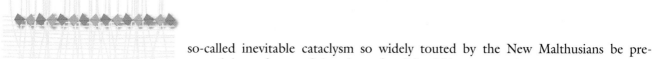

so-called inevitable cataclysm so widely touted by the New Malthusians be prevented, but a future of abundance for all is within our capacity.

THE LONG-TERM ANTI-MALTHUSIAN VIEWPOINT

The Fourth Stage of the Demographic Transition Creates Controversy

To see the long term, we need to consider the nations that are in the latter stages of the demographic transition. As we saw earlier in this chapter, some nations have entered the fourth stage of the demographic transition and face population shrinkage. They confront a dilemma. Because of their low birth rates, they don't produce enough workers for their factories, and masses of unemployed, hungry young people in the Least Industrialized Nations want those jobs. But their immigration means an influx of people who have different customs, which can upset a society. Germany and France, which have a lot of workers from Turkey, are experiencing this now. There, immigration has become a political issue. Because Germany is mindful of the Holocaust, it remains quiet about the controversy. Without such historical baggage, France is more open in its opposition to immigrants. One political party, whose slogan is "France for the French," has even made anti-immigration its cornerstone. Some of its candidates have been elected to office.

Fearful of a shrinking population and a political backlash, the French government has embarked on a policy that will avoid the need of having immigrants. It has initiated **pronatalist policies,** policies that encourage women to bear children. It is trying to build public attitudes and a political consensus that will increase fertility. If French women bear more children, there will be more French to operate the offices and factories. Because the factors that created a low birth rate are so firmly in place, however, it is unlikely that government policy will deflect them. (See the Global Glimpse box on Sweden, on the next page.)

You can see why it is perilous to predict the future of populations. A nation may turn inward and exile immigrants, or it may welcome them. A nation may establish effective pronatalist policies. Any of these actions will affect its future. If the United States did not welcome immigrants, its population would be stagnant or shrinking. Only its million immigrants a year keep it growing. The United States, however, is one of the largest countries in the world, and as we have seen, it is relatively unpopulated. Few countries face similar conditions.

This is a potential future—today's Least Industrialized Nations follow the Western world. They reach the fourth stage of the demographic transition; their population levels off and then declines as women do not bear enough children to replace those who die. Governments that now despair over too many children one day will have to offer incentives for women to give birth.

WHICH WILL IT BE?

Contradictory Potential Outcomes

Will the earth be filled with famine and suffering? Will such conditions spur vast political unrest that topples governments if they do not curtail population growth? Is African-style famine the world's fate? Or, without curtailing population growth, can the nations manage their resources, feed and clothe themselves, and even provide a high standard of living for everyone? Could the problem of the future be not enough people?

I have no crystal ball. Like others, I must await the outcome. It certainly appears that the world has the potential to meet its nutritional needs, but this would require the Most Industrialized Nations to cooperate to meet the challenge. Perhaps they will rise to the occasion.

A GLOBAL GLIMPSE

The Lopsided Society: Pronatalism in Sweden

"What is happening now has simply never happened before in the history of the world," said Nicholas Eberstadt, a demographer (Specter 1998). Never before has a country's birth rate plunged so low that its population shrank. But now the populations of several European countries are shrinking.

Is this a brand new occurrence in the history of the world? How could that be? Certainly there have been instances in the past when a country's leaders thought their nation had too few children. Usually this was because many young men had been killed in war, and they wanted to replace them quickly. They would then initiate *pronatalism*, policies that favor or promote births. They were successful. Men and women responded to the rewards and had more children.

Today, we face a different situation. Populations are shrinking not because of war but because women are having so few children that they aren't replacing the people who die. Sweden, one of these countries, helps us understand what is happening—and why pronatalism is failing.

If any country is pronatalistic, it is Sweden. Health care for mothers and children is free. Maternity centers offer free health checks and free courses in preparation for childbirth. When a child is born, the parents are eligible for fifteen months' leave of absence with pay. They can divide the leave between them any way they want, as long as the father gets at least one of the months. When a child is sick, either parent can stay home to care for it and receive full pay for missed work—up to sixty days a year per child (The Swedish Institute 1992; Froman 1994).

Births should be booming, families growing larger, the baby carriage industry prosperous. Instead, Sweden is becoming a lopsided society, one in which there are more old people than young, one in which there will not be enough workers to pay for the health care and pensions of the elderly.

The culprit is prosperity and freedom. Women are staying in school longer, putting more emphasis on work, marrying later—and having fewer children. Sweden's birth rate is the same as Japan's—and dropping.

Throughout western Europe, people are developing different ideas about children and about what they want out of life.

"People want their freedom. They see children as a burden, as an inconvenience."

"It's a sacrifice to have a child."

"Children cost more than they used to. Today you have to bring them to the pool, and you need to get a nanny, and they have to learn a foreign language. Children have more needs. Parents just didn't think of all these things before."

Ninni Lundblad, a biologist who works in Stockholm, said, "Did your parents sit down with a spreadsheet and figure out whether they could afford to have two or three children?"

No, they didn't. They just had them. But Ninni Lundblad, who said this so derisively, has no children (Specter 1998).

So why don't Sweden's generous pronatalist policies work? Perhaps this statement by Jan Delanor of Stockholm best sums it up:

"I am supposed to have an extra child to help the system? Nonsense. I'll have a child if and when it makes sense to me, not because the government thinks it's a good idea."

Swedes are finding so much more that makes sense to them—education, travel, career, money, spending time with friends. All these things come before having children.

I wonder who is going to live in Sweden after the Swedes are gone? The government is wondering, too.

1. *Demographers* study the size, composition, growth, and distribution of human populations. They disagree as to why Europe's population surged after 1750. They cite improved public health or a change in diet.

2. In 1798, Thomas Malthus predicted that the world's population would outstrip its food supply. His prediction is still controversial. The New Malthusians fear that the population of the world is entering the latter stages of an *exponential growth curve,* and most of this growth is in the nations least able to afford it. They favor an immediate cutback in population. The Anti-Malthusians claim that the world is producing more than enough food; the problem is the maldistribution of food due to political arrangements.

3. By applying symbolic interactionism, we can see why the birth rate is higher in the Least Industrialized Nations. There, children are seen as a blessing from God, they give the parents status in the present, and they provide security for the future.

4. By applying functionalism, we can see that introducing the Most Industrialized Nations' medicine and public health techniques upset the balance between birth and death rates in the Least Industrialized Nations. This *latent dysfunction* has intensified their problems.

5. Conflict theorists stress that food problems are due to political and economic arrangements that favor the Most Industrialized Nations. Food politics creates and intensifies problems in the Least Industrialized Nations.

6. Demographers who take a New Malthusian position stress pressures on the earth's three natural systems: fishing grounds, forests, and grasslands. Two dangers are the threat of famine as the result of our dependence on specialized strains of grains and the intensification of natural disasters. Even if we attain zero population growth, it would still take 50 to 70 years to stabilize the world's population.

7. Demographers who take an Anti-Malthusian position argue that the earth can support more people than it has now. Food production is outpacing population growth, fewer people are dying from famines, and much land remains uncultivated. A growing population can spur us to greater productivity.

8. Because of many cross-trends, demographers cannot forecast population growth accurately.

9. The United States is not overpopulated, but Americans place relatively great pressures on the earth's resources.

10. The New Malthusians recommend social policies to curb population. The Anti-Malthusians advocate policies that encourage (or do not discourage) population growth. Both sides agree that agricultural development should be stimulated. Exporting Western agricultural techniques to the Least Industrialized Nations is not viable, because it requires a vast support system that these nations cannot afford.

11. The New and Anti-Malthusians envision different futures. The New Malthusians anticipate widespread famine in the Least Industrialized Nations, which may lead to more repression. The Anti-Malthusians stress that the world's nations hold the potential for meeting human needs, that one day the world's problem will be population shrinkage.

◆Key Terms

Demographic transition A three-stage historical process of population growth. The first is high birth rates and high death rates; the second is high birth rates and low death rates; the third is low birth rates and low death rates. A fourth stage appears to have emerged: Population shrinkage due to even lower birth rates.

Demography The study of the size, composition, growth, and distribution of human populations.

Exponential growth curve As growth doubles during approximately equal intervals, it accelerates in the latter stages.

Green revolution The world's rapidly expanded food production during the 1950s and 1960s as the result of new fertilizers and high-yield strains of wheat and rice.

Infanticide Killing infants shortly after birth, usually as a form of population control.

Latent dysfunctions Unplanned results that have negative or harmful effects.

Laterization The tendency of certain tropical soils to become laterite, a rocklike material, when exposed to the air through cultivation.

Population pyramid A graphic representation of a population, divided, by sex, into age levels (see Figure 13-7 on page 453).

Population shrinkage A country's population shrinking because the

birth rate and immigration are too low to replace those who die.

Pronatalist policies Social policies that encourage women to bear children.

Taking the role of the other Putting yourself in someone else's shoes so you can see things as that person sees them.

Zero population growth Women bearing only enough children to replace the adults.

✦Critical Thinking Questions

1. Which side do you agree with—the New Malthusians or the Anti-Malthusians? Explain.

2. Do you believe that the United States should use its foreign policy to change internal social and economic policies of other countries?
   - If yes, under what conditions and for what reasons?
   - If no, under what conditions would you change your mind?

3. Do you think that Russia, Germany, or any other nation should use its foreign policy to change the internal social and economic policies of the United States?
   - If yes, under what conditions and for what reasons?
   - If no, under what conditions would you change your mind?
   - If your answer to this question is different from your answer to question #2, why the differences?

4. Which perspective (symbolic interactionism, functionalism, or conflict theory) do you think best explains the world problems of population and food? Explain.

5. What is your reaction to Pentti Linkola's suggestion that we annihilate most of the human race to save the rest of the world? If such a policy were enacted, who would choose who lives and who doesn't?

The Environmental Crisis

I hadn't been teaching very long at Southern Illinois University, Edwardsville, when I decided that I wanted to move to a farm. I had purchased a small trailer and had been living in a low-rent, working-class mobile home park. By living there and driving a junker, for the first time in my adult life I had a money surplus.

I advertised for a farm in the county papers. When I visited the third one, I knew I had found what I was looking for. It was remote ("in the boonies," as the phrase goes here), filled with trees and pastures, with its own pond for swimming and fishing. (The pond was also our water source.) At $150 an acre, I knew I couldn't go wrong. My fellow professors were paying as much for a house as I would for the entire 165 acres.

Being a town boy, I had a lot to learn about farm life. Eventually, I owned a dog, a horse, a sheep, and twenty-five head of cattle. My inexperience led to several humorous events (at least I can laugh at them now): the sharpie farmer sticking me with the runt of his herd, the horse I bought refusing to let me ride her, the cattle breaking through the fence and running away.

One of my most insightful lessons came one Saturday morning, when I went to a cattle auction. This is where area farmers bring their excess cattle, and fellow farmers—and meat companies, as it turned out—bid on them.

Standing amidst men wearing hats emblazoned with "Allis-Chalmers," "John Deere," and "Nutra-Feeds," I felt myself entering a new culture. I was enjoying the moment, lost in reverie as I observed the auctioneer and the bidding. When one group of animals was brought into the ring, the auctioneer said, "Them's red-tagged, boys. Them's red-tagged."

I asked a man standing next to me what that meant. He said, "You can't buy 'em. They've got some disease. You can't take 'em back to your farm."

I nodded, then asked, "What happens to 'em, then?"

He replied, "Only guys from the meat packing plant can bid on 'em."

I let this sink in, relieved that I didn't eat much sandwich meat.

Then I recalled something my grandfather had told me when I was a child. He farmed on Minnesota's brutally cold Canadian border, and to earn money to buy his farm he had worked at a meat packing plant in St. Paul, Minnesota. I noticed that he always refused sandwich meat, and had asked him about it. He said that it was because of what he had seen.

I suppose I was too young for my grandfather to explain his revulsion, but I think I felt something similar on that Saturday morning. Animals too diseased to live on farms were, under our government's supervision, judged perfectly acceptable to be turned into lunch meat.

◆ The Problem in Sociological Perspective ◆

**Romantic Imagery:
The Myth of the
Noble Savage**

Before modern history, humans lived in harmony with their environment. They considered themselves one with the water, earth, sky, animals, and plants. Unlike modern people, who greedily destroy their environment, primitive people used their resources wisely. Their presence did not disrupt the earth's natural systems. An old woman of the Wintu tribe explained:

> The White people never cared for land or deer or bear. When we Indians kill meat, we eat it all up. When we dig roots, we make little holes. . . . We shake down

acorns and pine nuts. We don't chop down trees. We only use dead wood. But the White people plow up the ground, pull up the trees, kill everything. . . . How can the spirit of the earth like the White man? . . . Everywhere the White man has touched it, it is sore. (Lee 1959:163)

Many people agree with this view. It evokes a warmth about some primitive past that is a part of us all. The problem is that it just isn't true. Sociologist William Burch (1971) calls the image of primitive people as "noble savages" a myth. He says that the social sciences should stop perpetuating romanticized views of the past and set the matter straight.

Let's try. The destruction of the environment is not new. It has been going on as long as humans have lived on earth. In Australia, carnivorous kangaroos, giant lizards, and horned turtles the size of automobiles disappeared about the time humans arrived there. Environmental historians believe that the humans destroyed these animals by setting fire to trees and shrubs to keep warm or to clear the land (Hotz 1999). The same thing happened in North America. As early humans burned forests for game management, mosquito control, or even for pleasure, they wiped out three-fourths of the animals weighing more than 100 pounds (Lutz 1959; Martin 1967; Hotz 1999). Prehistoric hunters may have exterminated more large animal species than people have since then.

Human destruction of the environment in the past may even have destroyed entire civilizations. The fall of Mesopotamia, located in the lush river basin of the Tigris and Euphrates, in what is now Iraq, has usually been attributed to invaders. Environmental stress, however, may have been the cause (Jacobsen and Adams 1958). An irrigation system provided abundant food for the Mesopotamians, and their civilization flourished. Their irrigation system did not allow for drainage, however, and with constant evaporation, the water that seeped into the earth grew saltier. Over centuries, the underground water table rose, making the land too salty for crops. The agriculture collapsed, and with it, their civilization.

The great Mayan civilization of what is today Guatemala and Yucatan may have met a similar fate. This civilization developed for seventeen centuries, reaching its peak in agriculture, architecture, and science in 900 A.D. Then, within decades, a population of about 5 million dropped to fewer than half a million. Environmental destruction may have been the cause. Samples from lake beds indicate heavy soil erosion. As their population increased, the Maya cleared the land of trees. The topsoil washed from the denuded land, and with it went the agricultural productivity on which their civilization depended (Deevey et al. 1979).

The story was the same for the Anasazi Indians in what are now Arizona and New Mexico (Budiansky 1987). They built roads, irrigation channels, and pueblos of stone and masonry; some pueblos were four or five stories high, and had 800 rooms. They also deforested the canyons until they had to travel fifty miles or more to gather wood for fuel. Having outstripped the forest's ability to replenish itself, their civilization, too, collapsed.

Far from gentle conservationists, then, earlier humans were like us. They, too, destroyed thoughtlessly. Because our civilizations are larger, however, our capacity

Many of our ideas of the past are shrouded in myth and portrayed in idyllic terms. An example is the common view of the early Native Americans' relationship to the environment: human life in harmonic balance with nature. The text explains why this view is a myth. Native Americans today treat the environment in the same thoughtless ways that most other Americans do. When I visited an Indian settlement on an Arizona mesa, I peered behind the houses. There, at the bottom of the ravine, lay piles of garbage—easier to dump down the hillside than to discard properly.

for destruction is greater. Many hope there is another difference, too—that, having advance information about the destruction of the environment on which our civilizations depend, we will act before it is too late.

Unfortunately, self-interest (or selfishness, if you prefer) works against the logic of environmental protection. Biologist Garrett Hardin (1968) used to tell a parable known as *the tragedy of the commons.*

> Let us picture a pasture open to everyone. The number of cattle exactly matches the amount of available grass. Each herdsman, however, will seek to maximize his own gain. He thinks to himself: "If I add a cow to my herd, I will receive *all* the proceeds from the sale of this additional animal. The little overgrazing that this extra animal causes will be shared by all the other herdsmen."

Naturally, the herdsman adds another animal to his herd. He eventually adds another . . . and another. And every other herdsman sharing the commons does the same. Each is locked into a system that rewards him for increasing the size of his herd. And therein lies the tragedy. The pasture is limited, and additional

The reason for the collapse of the Mayan civilization is uncertain, but one theory is that it was due to the destruction of their environment. Shown here are Mayan ruins in Chichen Itza, Mexico.

stress eventually causes it—and the civilization dependent on it—to fail. As each pursues his own interest, all rush to their collective ruin.

In sum, an irony of human existence is that our attempt to improve life can destroy the very environment upon which life depends. Even the ancients confronted this dilemma, and our environmental destruction joins a line that stretches into prehistory. Today, however, with new technology, demands for an ever-rising standard of living, and more people on earth than ever before, we have magnified our destructive capacity.

◆ The Scope of the Problem ◆

"Everything Is Connected to Everything Else"

None of us is isolated. Although the connections between ourselves and others may not be apparent, we all are part of a system that interrelates humanity, technology, and the environment. To think in terms of individual small units ignores reality. For example, although my grandfather, whom I mentioned in the opening vignette, lived on a remote, northern Minnesota farm, his actions had international consequences. He sprayed his fields with DDT, the practice at the time. The excess would run from his fields into a creek. The creek ran into a local river, and the river ran into the Mississippi. From there, the chemicals flowed into New Orleans, helping to give its residents extraordinarily high rates of cancer, and then into the Atlantic, where it affected other nations.

The Need to See the Environmental Crisis in Global Terms

Because we all are part of a worldwide interdependent system, we need to see the environmental crisis in global terms. The population explosion, industrialization, and the drive for higher living standards are upsetting our planet's precarious balance. If we deplete the earth's natural resources, as some civilizations of the past did, ours, too, will collapse. This is the fear of some ecologists, scientists who study **ecology**—the relationship between living things and their environment.

Pollution

Defining Pollution

Pollution Does Not Depend on Ideology

For many, the primary concern is pollution. While pollution by humans is not new—it occurred when the first fires were lit for warmth, cooking, or visual delight—it has intensified beyond anything the world has ever seen. Although the industrializing nations are placing strain on the environment (Farley 1999), its main polluters are the world's industrial giants.

We all know what pollution is, but it is hard to define. A common definition of pollution is the accumulation in the air, water, and land of substances harmful to living things. This, however, would make nature itself a polluter: It would include every active volcano and pollen scattered by the wind. We need to look at pollution in *social* terms. Like all *social* problems, it is people who say that something is polluted, that they do not like what they see, and that they want to change it. Consequently, we can define **pollution** as the presence of substances that interfere with socially desired uses of the air, water, land, or food (Davies and Davies 1975).

As the tragedy of the commons reveals that the depletion of resources is due to shortsighted self-interest, so, too, is pollution. Ideology makes no difference. In the former Soviet Union, pollution was treated as a state secret (Feshbach 1992). Scientists and journalists could not even mention pollution in public; to demonstrate against it, even peacefully, could bring two years in prison. With protest stifled, no environmental protection laws, and rigid production quotas, pollution was rampant. Russian citizens and those of the former Soviet states have been left a legacy of death—from abandoned factories that had manufactured chemical and germ weapons to billions of pounds of nuclear waste that was simply dumped into holes in the ground (Garelik 1996; Miller 1999). Is the term "legacy of death" too strong? Consider this: Birth defects in Russia have jumped, and life expectancy has dropped. (The life expectancy of Russian men is now 57 years, compared to 77 in the United States.)

Environmental decay in Russia is extensive. Shown here is one of the many leaks in the decrepit trans-Siberian oil pipe. The environmental costs of this pipeline, which is inadequate for withstanding the tremendous freezing and thawing conditions of this region, may not be known for generations.

Humans have destroyed many animal species. Some have been extinguished without remorse. When the magnificent whales were threatened, however, an international movement developed to save them. With whaling banned, whales are now increasing in numbers. Shown here are two humpback whales enjoying life.

Defining the environmental crisis is not easy, however, because even experts disagree about its essential aspects. As we examine this social problem, we will look at conflicting opinions that surround it.

◆ Looking at the Problem Theoretically ◆

Each of our three theoretical perspectives helps us understand the environmental crisis. Using symbolic interactionism, we will examine how concerns about the environment arose and how the environment became a social problem. Through functionalism, we will focus on the interdependence of people and their environment. Through conflict theory, we will examine the conflicting interests of environmentalists and those who pollute.

SYMBOLIC INTERACTIONISM

The Natural History of Environmental Problems: The Creation of a Social Problem

How did the environment become a social problem? As we saw in Chapter 1, even if objective conditions are widespread and injurious, they are not automatically considered social problems. Objective conditions must be translated into subjective concerns.

This translation did not come easily. In the 1800s, when hundreds of steel plants in the United States polluted the air, no one considered it a social problem. Since the automobile was invented, people have discarded worn-out tires in gullies and creeks, but only recently have these actions been regarded as part of a social problem. This was also true with the disappearance of animal species, which began millennia ago:

Many welcomed the near extinction of the bison, seeing it as a way to defeat the Indians. The passenger pigeon, during its mass annual migration, used to darken the skies for days. Its extinction in 1914 was seen as unfortunate—an interesting bit of history, perhaps, but not tragic.

Today, in contrast, people who have never seen a tropical rain forest are upset that they are disappearing. Around the world, people are bothered by the harm that is done to whales, seals, dolphins, owls, and by the loss of plants and animals whose names they can't pronounce. A worldwide protest movement has evolved.

How did we decide that environmental decay and destruction are a pressing, worldwide social problem? Sociologists Clay Schoenfeld, Robert Meier, and Robert Griffin (1979) investigated this question. They found that the 1960s were not the first time that Americans became concerned about the environment. Around 1900, Theodore Roosevelt (U.S. president from 1901 to 1909) spearheaded a conservation movement. He was concerned about vanishing wildlife in our wilderness areas (Morrison et al. 1972; Gale 1972). Roosevelt, who, ironically, roamed the United States and Africa killing big game, supported bills that established our national park system, setting aside millions of acres for public use. There is a vast difference, however, between conserving wilderness areas to make certain that hunters do not run out of moving targets and being concerned about the quality of our food, air, and water.

How did "conservation" change to "environmental concern"? Schoenfeld, Meier, and Griffin found that the change began with professionals and ended with an aroused public. Here are the five steps involved:

First, *professionals* became troubled by the environment. Knowing that we depend on natural resources, some of them concluded that the situation was critical. In 1959, geographers began to write about environmental problems in their journals

How Did Attitudes Change?

The Conservation Movement

From Conservation to Environmental Concern

Five Steps in This Change

Concerned about a decline in wildlife, Theodore Roosevelt, 25th president of the United States (1901–1909), launched a conservation movement. Though it seems ironic today, Roosevelt, who supported legislation to establish our extensive national park system, setting aside millions of acres for public use, was an avid hunter who roamed the United States and Africa in search of animals to kill. As explained in the text, the way our environmental concerns changed from wanting to "conserve" wilderness areas in order to prevent hunters from running out of moving targets to what our environmental concerns are today represents an extensive sociological process.

and to present papers at their conventions. Then *interest groups* began to form around specific issues. Third, *government agencies,* aroused by the activities of the interest groups, began to issue environmental reports. Fourth, the *news media* discovered the issue. At first, reporters had difficulty understanding and communicating the idea that people, resources, and technology are all part of a larger system. They tended to see things in terms of single, unrelated news items, such as an oil spill. Gradually, they understood that "everything is connected to everything else," and they began to connect events.

Fifth, *the public* was aroused by the stories in the mass media. Three stories were significant. The first was Rachel Carson's *The Silent Spring,* published in 1962. Focusing on the dangers of pesticides, this blockbuster alerted Americans to environmental hazards. It was, however, a single-issue approach. People, including the media, still did not yet perceive interconnections among events. Then, in January 1969, an oil well erupted off the coast of Santa Barbara, California. For weeks, environmental destruction riveted America's attention. Each day, 20,000 gallons of oil poured into the water. National headlines reported its drift to the coast, and people were outraged as twenty miles of beautiful beaches were blackened (Davies and Davies 1975). Later that same year came the single most effective environmental message of the century—the view from the moon of earth as a fragile, finite "spaceship." That first glimpse of us from the "outside" made it clear that we all are partners on a small planet.

In Sum

Thus a social problem was "created," for over the course of these five steps people's perceptions changed. The general public began to see individual events as interconnected parts of the same problem. The idea of an **ecosystem,** that all life on the planet is interconnected in the finely balanced cycles of the dynamic layer of the earth's surface, has transformed our opinions of ourselves, our relationship with other living things, and even our place in the universe. This change in how we symbolize our world is still in process; only gradually are we coming to connect what we do with a distant future.

FUNCTIONALISM

Seeing Interconnections

The idea that everything is connected to everything else is becoming part of our intuitive understanding. We all know that though we are individuals, we are part of a larger group. We also know that the small groups to which we each belong are parts of a larger society, and that our nation is part of a global network. Slowly, we are coming to grasp that we all are part of a global social system, that what each of us does—whether individual, group, or nation—affects the others.

This picture of humanity forming a global network is a functional analysis. Each unit is part of a larger structure, with the activities of one part having functional or dysfunctional consequences for the other parts.

An Ecosystem

Both biologists and sociologists working on environmental problems emphasize the interconnections between people and the earth's resources. No matter where we live on this globe, we need air, water, and soil to survive. We all are enmeshed in an intricate ecosystem. We have multiplied and expanded into every habitable region of the globe. Our cultures have permitted us to adapt to mountains and plains, to deserts and oceans, even to ice-bound regions. Our intelligence has allowed us to dominate the earth. We have domesticated plants and animals. To improve our lives, we have harnessed the energy of animals, rivers, and the wind.

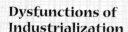

Dysfunctions of Industrialization

The steam engine increased productivity on a scale unknown in history. As we saw in Chapter 11, the industrial revolution that followed created countless new jobs and great wealth. Because of it, the average person today enjoys a standard of living that was previously attained only by the wealthy.

Industrialization, however, also brought dysfunctional consequences for the earth's ecosystem. Production of our material wealth damaged the air, water, and soil on which we depend. Our industrial wastes are toxic. In our drive to expand our industrial systems and create a better life, we are damaging the environment that allows us life in the first place.

Although we still have problems conceptualizing it, we have begun to think in terms of our being part of a complex, living machine called the environment. Our survival depends on the ecosystem. Green plants produce oxygen for human and animal life. Plants, animals, and microorganisms purify the water in lakes and streams. Biological processes in the soil provide food and fuel. Anything that disrupts the earth's ecosystem threatens these finely balanced cycles.

As with earlier civilizations such as the Mesopotamians, the Maya, and the Anasazi, our economic and political systems depend on an ecosystem that is mostly invisible to us. If it fails, our society will collapse.

CONFLICT THEORY

The Basic Conflict

Opposing sides are lining up. Some see us on the verge of catastrophe, and they act politically to protect the environment. Others resist what they consider arbitrary and irrational controls over their right to pollute. No one ever defends dirty water or filthy air, of course, for clean air and water have become like motherhood and apple pie. Nevertheless, some groups fight efforts to reduce pollution. Let's look at this conflict.

On One Side: Environmental Groups

On one side are the environmental action groups—organizations such as the National Wildlife Federation, the Izaak Walton League, the Sierra Club, Americans for Safe Food, and Earth First!—that fight environmental threats. The official policy of the Izaak Walton League expresses this position:

> There is no sound justification for water pollution. The people of the United States are entitled to wholesome water, usable for all human needs. . . . The public goal should be maximum removal of pollutants from all streams, rather than use of streams to carry an "acceptable maximum" load of wastes. (Davies and Davies 1975:89)

These groups have become a powerful force. With chapters across the nation, they maintain Washington lobbyists, aggressively promote legislation, and hire lawyers to fight environmental cases in the courts. Many politicians support their efforts.

On the Other Side: Polluters

Other groups oppose pollution control. At their core are the industrial polluters. Their dilemma is obvious. Pollution control is expensive and adds nothing to the value of their products. Manufacturers must compete with foreign businesses, which already have the advantage of low-cost labor. These foreign corporations gain an additional edge from not having to pay for pollution controls in the manufacturing process.

Making It Profitable to Pollute

Manufacturers can't take a public stand in favor of pollution, of course. But they know how to work behind the scenes, and they have deep pockets. They, too, lobby in Washington, guiding legislation. As the box on the next page illustrates, in some instances they even have enough clout to pass laws so they can make a hefty profit

TECHNOLOGY AND SOCIAL PROBLEMS

How to Get Paid to Pollute: Corporate Welfare and Big Welfare Bucks

Welfare is one of the most controversial topics in the United States, arousing the ire of many wealthy and middle-class Americans. They view the poor who collect welfare as parasites. But have you heard about corporate welfare?

Corporate welfare refers to handouts given to corporations. A state offers a company tax breaks so it will relocate within the state, or remain in the state if it has threatened to leave. A state may even provide land and factories at bargain prices. The reason: jobs.

Corporate welfare even goes to companies that foul the land, water, and air. Borden Chemicals in Louisiana is a case in point. Its plant has released hazardous chemicals so thick that several times the police have had to shut down the highway that runs near the plant. The company has also burned hazardous wastes without a permit; and it contaminated groundwater beneath the plant site, threatening the aquifer that provides drinking water for residents of Louisiana and Texas. Borden's pollution cost them dearly: $3.6 million in fines, $3 million to clean up the groundwater, and $400,000 for local emergency response units. The company didn't make out so badly, though: It was awarded corporate welfare—$15 million in reduced and canceled property taxes (Bartlett and Steele 1998). That's a net gain of $8 million. And that's not counting the savings the company racked up by not having to properly dispose of their toxic wastes in the first place.

Louisiana has added a novel twist to its corporate welfare program. It offers an incentive program to help start-up companies. This itself isn't novel; the owners of that little "mom and pop" grocery store on your corner may have gotten some benefits when they first opened. Louisiana's twist is how it counts start-up operations. You may have heard of some of them. One of these little start-up companies is called Exxon Corp. Although Exxon opened for business about 120 years ago, it had $213 million in property taxes canceled under this program. Another little company that the state figured could use a little nudge to get going was Shell Oil Co., which had $140 million slashed from its taxes (Bartlett and Steele 1998). Then there were International Paper, Dow Chemical, Union Carbide, Boise Cascade, Georgia Pacific, and another tiny one called Procter & Gamble.

Of course, you can always improve welfare programs, and if the recipients themselves get to design them, you can be certain they'll come up with some good ones. Let's suppose poor people were polluting, and the state issued them credits for reducing their pollution. They could then spend those credits to continue to pollute or sell them to others, giving them the right to pollute.

Naw, too far-fetched.

Yet that is just what United States industry has arranged. According to a treaty negotiated in Kyoto, Japan, by the year 2008 the United States must reduce its emissions of greenhouse gases. U.S. industries grew concerned about the cost, but they hit on a novel way to reap billions of dollars. They proposed a new corporate welfare law, that the government would issue credits to companies that reduce their emissions early—and even for reductions that took place years before the treaty. The companies could then use the credits to continue to pollute—or they could sell them for billions of dollars to companies that have not reduced their emissions, allowing them to continue to pollute (Cushman 1999). Now that's a great way to clean up—without cleaning up.

The spectre of having to reduce emissions, however, proved too great a threat to U.S. capitalists, and in 2001 President George W. Bush rejected the Kyoto Treaty.

The Power of U.S. Industry

from their pollution. They also try to get around the law by using lawyers who specialize in finding loopholes in pollution controls. Consider the automobile industry:

> The story began back in 1951 when it was discovered that automobiles were the major cause of smog in Los Angeles. The suggestion was made to develop electric cars. The auto industry formed a committee to study this proposal. The White House stacked the committee with representatives from the auto and oil industries,

The most extensive polluters are the wealthy, those who own the factories, but the poor are most frequently the victims. One consequence is environmental racism, discussed in the text. Shown here is a child in Matamoros, Mexico, playing in a drainage ditch. Most of this pollution comes from U.S. companies.

The Fearful Discovery

and the "surprising" conclusion was a recommendation against research on electric vehicles (Davies and Davies 1975).

While the car manufacturers were opposing the control of automobile emissions, another group of manufacturers tried to pass laws that would require pollution control devices. This group was made up of the businesses that manufacture the pollution control equipment. For them, the more regulation the better—more stringent laws mean more profit in their pockets.

The automobile industry's fight against pollution controls and alternative transportation illustrates a basic principle of conflict theory—that society is composed of competing groups whose interests often collide. The interests of one business group may conflict with those of another.

The efforts of environmentalists to eliminate what they see as dangers to the public welfare conflict with what other groups see as their inherent right—to make profits regardless of pollution. Those who campaign to develop what they consider to be a more livable, healthy, sane society run head on into the interests of powerful groups who see the cure as worse than the illness. This basic conflict runs throughout the environmental crisis.

Conflict and unequal power have led to what sociologists call **environmental racism**—that pollution is more likely to hurt minorities (Moberg 1999). This is because polluting industries locate where land is cheaper, places where the wealthy do not live. As a result, low-income communities, often inhabited by minorities, have higher levels of exposure to pollution. Sociologists have studied, formed, and joined environmental justice groups that fight to stop polluting plants and to block construction of polluting industries.

◆ Research Findings ◆

How badly has our environment deteriorated? To answer this question, we will first examine the pollution of our air, land, water, and food. Then we will look at energy and resources, and finally, we'll consider why some say the whole matter is exaggerated.

AIR POLLUTION

A mixture of fog and smoke settled over Donora, Pennsylvania, during the last five days of October 1948. By Sunday, October 31, wind and rain finally cleared the smog.

Of the 12,300 people who lived in this steel mill town, about half (5,910) soon became sick. Another 1,440 were "severely affected." Seventeen died.

Front-page news stories compared Donora to the Meuse Valley in Belgium, where 60 people died in 1930. Both were heavily industrialized, and both had a **thermal inversion,** a layer of cold air sealing in a lower layer of warm air. Thermal inversions trap smoke, exhaust, and particles.

By Tuesday, November 2, most of Donora's dead were buried. The residents' reactions sound hauntingly familiar. The local doctor described the deaths as murder. An air pollution expert from a nearby university said the lungs of the people in the valley had suffered chronic damage. The superintendent of the steel factory, however, said, "I can't conceive how our plant has anything to do with the condition. There has been no change in the process we use since 1915." The workers, who saw the dense smoke and fog as part of their way of life, said, "That smoke coming out of those stacks is putting bread and butter on our tables." And most of the public shrugged their shoulders and went about their business. (Bowen 1972)

A few years later, in 1952, a "killer smog" settled on London. In just four days, 4,000 people were dead (Carr 1972). People became fearful. Slowly, facts about air pollution emerged. Air pollution is essentially a poison that accumulates in the human body. Besides causing eye, nose, and throat irritations, it causes bronchitis, emphysema, and lung cancer, which lead to a slow, agonizing death.

What causes air pollution? The main cause is the burning of fossil fuels, that is, substances derived from living things—wood, coal, petroleum, and natural gas. To produce our electricity and the goods we consume, power plants and factories pour pollutants into the air. The worst polluter, however, is the internal combustion engine. The exhausts of cars, trucks, and buses emit poisons—sulfur dioxide, nitrogen oxide, hydrocarbons, and carbon monoxide. The vehicles also leave behind a **carcinogenic** (cancer-causing) trail from the asbestos particles in their brake linings.

On occasion, pollution is the result of deliberate, spiteful acts. The most dramatic example occurred in 1991, when Iraqi troops ignited 600 oil wells, storage tanks, and refineries in Kuwait. The soot from the fires circled the globe (Naj 1992).

Waste incineration is a second major source of air pollution. Burning plastics is especially damaging to our health because it creates PCBs (polychlorinated biphenyls), a potent toxin. Plastics are not **biodegradable;** that is, they do not disintegrate after being exposed to normal bacteria. Unlike even steel, which rusts, plastics endure almost indefinitely. Consequently, we burn them.

A third source of air pollution is fluorocarbon gases. These gases are suspected of damaging the **ozone shield,** the layer in the earth's upper stratosphere that screens out much of the sun's ultraviolet rays. High-intensity ultraviolet radiation harms most life forms. In humans, it causes skin cancer and cataracts; in plants, it reduces growth and causes genetic mutations. When the danger was realized, the use of fluorocarbon gases in aerosol cans, refrigerators, and air conditioners was reduced or eliminated, and the damage to the ozone is expected to be repaired (U.S. Department of State 1997).

Air pollution may lead to what is known as the **greenhouse effect.** Carbon dioxide and water vapor form an invisible blanket around the globe that allows the sun's light to enter, but traps the heat. Without this blanket, temperatures would plummet, and the earth would be unable to support life. If the blanket is too thick, however, it traps too much heat, which can have devastating consequences for our environment.

Because of the industrial revolution, we burn more fossil fuels than humans did in the past, releasing more carbon dioxide into the air. Atmospheric carbon dioxide is now 30 percent higher than it was before the industrial revolution (Singer 1994). In effect, the carbon dioxide has smudged the atmospheric window through which our earth's daily heat escapes to outer space. The blanket is growing thicker.

Scientists are severely divided on this issue. Some claim that the result is **global warming.** They say that the earth's temperature is getting warmer, and by the year 2100 the earth may be 2 to 6 degrees Fahrenheit warmer (Stevens 1998a). This will disrupt the earth's climate and biological system (Smith and Tirpak 1988; Thomas 1988; Stevens 1995, 1998b, 1998c), and we can expect the following consequences:

Three Main Sources of Air Pollution:

1. Burning of Fossil Fuels

2. Waste Incineration

3. Fluorocarbon Gases

The Greenhouse Effect

Scientists Don't Agree

Chapter 14   The Environmental Crisis

1. Climate boundaries will move about 400 miles north, resulting in a longer growing season in the United States, Canada, and Russia.

2. The oceans will rise about 26 inches as the polar ice caps melt.

3. The world's shorelines will erode. (Most of the beaches on the U.S. east coast will be gone in 25 years.)

4. Some small island nations will be destroyed, and the United States will lose an area of land the size of Massachusetts.

5. Coastal fisheries will be damaged.

6. Summers will be hotter, increasing the demand for electricity.

7. There will be more forest fires, droughts, floods, and outbreaks of pests.

8. There will be outbreaks of diseases—malaria, dengue fever, cholera.

9. Many species of plants and animals will become extinct.

10. The Least Industrialized Nations will have more extensive problems, as they have fewer resources to meet the crisis.

Other scientists say that global warming is not occurring (Robinson and Robinson 1997; Stevens 1998). They conclude that during the past 3,000 years the earth has had five extended periods that were warmer than today. Atmospheric temperatures are rising, but they have been rising for 300 years (from a cold period called "the Little Ice Age"); they remain below the 3,000 year average. Some even conclude that if carbon dioxide increases, it may *lower* sea levels (Singer 1997). A warmer earth would increase evaporation from the warmer oceans, and more rain would fall over Greenland and the Antarctic; this would thicken the polar ice caps, removing vast amounts of water from the oceans.

In 1998, 15,000 scientists signed a petition asking that the United States revoke agreements to cut emissions of carbon dioxide. The petition was accompanied by a letter from a former president of the National Academy of Sciences who said that not only was there no climatic threat, but higher carbon dioxide would benefit the world. It would increase plant growth and be "a wonderful and unexpected gift from the industrial revolution" (Stevens 1998). Confused, members of Congress called the National Academy of Sciences, and its current president assured them that the greenhouse effect poses a threat to the world.

At this point, we do not know if global warming is occurring or not. Scientists who examine the same data disagree. We will have to await more data.

With today's pollution control devices and the agitation of environmentalists, is our air getting cleaner? Figure 14-1 shows some striking improvements we have made. The change in the amount of lead in our air is stunning; it is now only 2 percent of what it was in 1970. The primary factor for this welcome change is lead-free gasoline. But results are mixed: We now have slightly more nitrogen dioxide in our air than in 1970 (*Statistical Abstract* 2001:Table 356). Our air still contains 188 chemicals that have been linked to cancer, birth defects, and other serious health problems (Getter 1999).

LAND POLLUTION

It was such a beautiful day that Tamara and Bill decided to skip their social problems class and have a picnic on the beach. As they walked hand in hand, they found that they had to step around sewage that had washed ashore the night before.

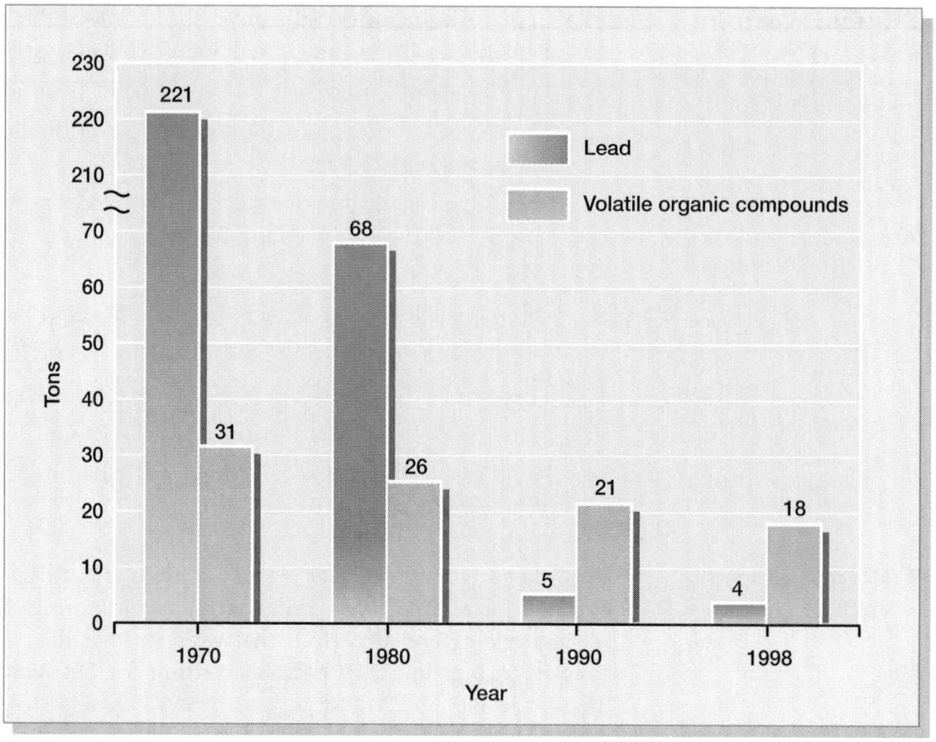

FIGURE 14-1
U.S. Air Quality: The Emission of Pollutants
(Source: Statistical Abstract 2001:Table 356.)

Their stomachs turned when they saw blood samples and contaminated needles that must have come from a hospital. All they could think of was AIDS.

They left hastily—without eating their lunch.

Cities and towns across the nation have to dispose of their waste. From Figure 14-2, which shows how much solid waste each American generates each year, you can see how our garbage has increased. The plateau we have reached is likely to be temporary, as others have been in the past. At 4.6 pounds of solid waste per American per day, we produce *460 billion pounds* of garbage each year (*Statistical Abstract* 2001:Table 359).

Humans have always dumped their wastes around them. For example, we can identify many Stone Age villages by the mounds of oyster and mussel shells their inhabitants left behind. But modern industrial civilization produces so much waste that we no longer know what to do with it. Some can be burned in incinerators, but this creates air pollution. Gullies and swampy areas are sometimes used as dumping grounds, but areas convenient to urban centers are filling up—and groundwater contamination has become a problem. The land seems incapable of constantly absorbing our garbage, and few want to turn the Grand Canyon into a giant landfill.

Many cities burn their waste. No longer can they simply throw it in a pit and light it, as they once did. Now they must use EPA-approved garbage incinerators—renamed resource recovery plants. These facilities solve the problem of what to do with waste, and they partly pay for themselves. Federal regulations require utilities to buy power from generators, such as garbage-burning plants. However,

> even with state-of-the-art pollution-control devices, garbage-burning plants still emit dangerous amounts of toxic gases such as dioxin. . . . As these toxic materials disperse on land and in air and water, they can become concentrated in the flesh of

The Problem of Garbage

FIGURE 14-2
Ounces of Solid Waste Each American Generates Each Day
These totals are based on postconsumer residential and commercial solid wastes, which comprise the major portion of municipal trash collections. The totals do not include mining, agricultural, and industrial processing, demolition and construction wastes, sewage sludge, nor junked autos and obsolete equipment wastes.
(Source: Statistical Abstract 1994:Table 370; 1998: Table 402; 2001:Table 359.)

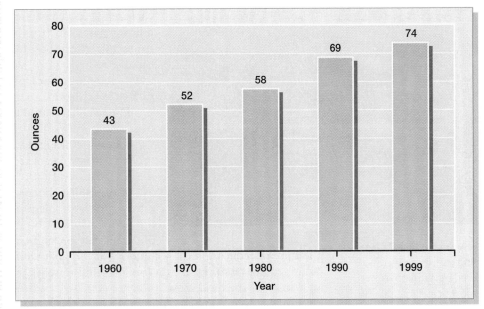

fish, wildlife and humans. . . . Ultimately, a plethora of ailments can result, including cancer, birth defects. (Paul 1986)

As a consequence, the EPA has tightened its rules, threatened legal action against those who operate the incinerators it once approved, and is requiring multimillion-dollar pollution controls. Unable to afford this bill, many communities have abandoned their incinerators (Schneider 1994).

Some states tried to solve the problem by shipping their garbage to other states. Their shipments were refused, and the case went to the Supreme Court. When the Court ruled that they had to accept them, landfills across the Midwest were opened to the hard-pressed, more populated eastern states (Bailey 1992). As a result, some midwestern states are becoming giant "garbage cans" for other states.

Strip Mining

Strip mining, which occurs where coal lies so close to the surface that it can be retrieved by stripping away the soil, has scarred more than 5 million acres of U.S. land. West Virginia was a special target. Vast tracts of this state can no longer be farmed because, stripped bare of forest and plant life, salt from the coal poisoned the land. Although current federal regulations require mining companies to return land to its original condition, many believe that this is impossible. Today the western areas of the United States are vulnerable, for vast amounts of shale and coal lie just beneath the surface.

WATER POLLUTION

Acid Rain

A silent spring has fallen over parts of the western Adirondacks. Brook trout have vanished from Big Moose Lake—along with crayfish and frogs, loons, kingfishers, and most of the swallows.

Pollutants from Midwest factories, borne by rain, wind, and snow, have left more than 300 lakes devoid of fish. The acid rain is also killing the trees. (Blumenthal 1981; Ehrlich and Ehrlich 1981; Stevens 1996)

How do factory emissions in the Midwest destroy lakes in Canada and our northeastern states? Death at long distance begins when power plants in the Midwest burn

The Taj Mahal in Uttar Pradesh, India, is considered by many to be the most beautiful building in the world. This mausoleum built by Shah Jehan in 1630–1648 for himself and his favorite wife, Mumtaz Mahal, is made of white marble inlaid with semi-precious stones. Along with other architectural masterpieces the world over, the Taj Mahal is threatened by acid rain.

Drinking Water

Lakes

coal and oil to generate electricity. Burning fossil fuels releases gases, such as sulfur dioxide and nitrogen oxide, into the atmosphere. Moisture in the air turns these emissions into sulfuric and nitric acid. After traveling hundreds of miles, they fall to the earth's surface as **acid rain.**

Humans have produced acid rain ever since they began to burn fossil fuels. Ice samples from glaciers show heavy concentrations of acids 350 years ago, probably from volcanic activity and organic decomposition (LaBastille 1979; Lynch 1980). Our intensified use of fossil fuels, however, has transformed acid rain into a global problem. Coal-burning utility companies in the Midwest built more than 175 smokestacks 500 feet tall or higher. These "megastacks" do a good job of reducing local pollution, but the pollutants do not magically disappear; disgorged high into the air, they remain aloft for days and even weeks before becoming part of a "chemical soup."

Canadians are upset by this "airborne sewer" spilling across their border. Acid rain has destroyed the fish and normal plant life of about 200 lakes in Ontario. Authorities there say that it threatens 48,000 of their more than 180,000 lakes. The strongest opponents of tighter controls are the major polluters, in this instance U.S. utility and coal companies.

Acid rain damages crops and forests around the world, as well as such historic landmarks as the Colosseum in Rome, the Taj Mahal in India, the Parthenon in Athens, and the Lincoln Memorial in Washington. Even more important, acid rain threatens human health. Apparently, it produces chemical reactions that release toxic metals into the water table. From there, they end up in the public water supply.

Pollution also contaminates groundwater, the source of drinking water for millions (Lewis 1990; Raloff 1990; Bartlett and Steele 1998). Some of our drinking water contains arsenic, asbestos, benzene, carbon tetrachloride, chloroform, mercury, PCBs, and other chemical wastes. Some wells on which large populations depend have had to be closed. For example, a well in the San Gabriel Valley of California supplying drinking water to 400,000 persons was closed because it had become contaminated with the solvent TCE. Large portions of the water supplies of southern Michigan are so polluted that state officials have suggested that it might be "cheaper to simply write off the ground water supplies" than to try to clean up the problem.

The Mississippi River is a special case in point. Thousands of industries discharge their wastes into this river, yet hundreds of cities pump their drinking water directly out of this putrid cesspool. To "purify" the water they send to their customers, the water companies add more chemicals, a senseless process that one day must end.

The pollution of the Great Lakes is of special concern, for this giant network of waterways—Erie, Superior, Michigan, Huron, and Ontario—contains *one of every five gallons of the entire world's surface fresh water.* More than 900 toxic chemicals have been found in the Great Lakes (Ashworth 1987; Pearse 1987; Gorrie 1990). The pollution of these formerly pristine waters by industry is so bad that people are warned not to eat bottom-feeding fish (which are exposed to heavier concentrations of poisons in the lakes' sediment). Congress has mandated that the EPA report its progress in cleaning up these lakes, and improvements are being made (EPA 1994, 1998).

Oil Spills

Like a junkie, our industrial machine demands a continuous supply of oil. Transportation of those vast quantities of oil is risky. Although industry and government assured environmentalists that they could handle oil spills, those promises proved hollow in 1989 when the *Exxon Valdez*, a 1,000-foot-long supertanker, ran aground and ruptured. It spewed 11 million gallons of crude oil into the pristine waters of Alaska's Prince William Sound, soiling 1,300 miles of coastline (Wells and McCoy 1989; Rosen 1999). Left dead were 250,000 sea birds, 2,800 sea otters, 300 harbor seals, 250 bald eagles, 22 killer whales, and vast numbers of fish (Rosen 1999). Although Exxon spent over $2 billion to try to clean up the mess (Wells 1990), Prince William Sound, which looks as lovely as ever, is forever changed: The birds are gone, and the waters no longer teem with fish (Rosen 1999).

Unfortunately, oil spills in Russia dwarf the Exxon spill (Rosett 1994; Garelik 1996). In 1994, a cross-country oil pipeline burst in Siberia, dumping 300 million gallons onto the tundra and into rivers—27 times more oil than in the Exxon spill. Russia's rusting oil pipes continue to spew oil.

TOXIC CHEMICALS

The pollutions we have discussed so far all involve chemicals. Chemicals are so poisonous to land, air, and water that it is difficult to overstate the extent to which they threaten our well-being.

Love Canal

Perhaps the most infamous case of chemical pollution in the United States is Love Canal, New York, where

> hundreds of families unwittingly purchased homes adjacent to a covered-over waste dump. Deadly poisons seeped into their homes over the years. Neurological damage was common. So were urinary tract infections, kidney damage, swollen joints, sleepiness, clumsiness, headaches, fragile bones, irritability, and loss of appetite. One third of Love Canal residents suffered chromosome damage (Brown n.d.). One child was born with two rows of teeth, another with one kidney, and a third with three ears (Shribman 1989).
>
> Eventually the federal government ordered all pregnant women and children under age 2 to move out (Brody 1976; Brown n.d.). In 1978, 239 families abandoned their homes, and in 1980 the federal government and the state of New York relocated another 710 families. Two hundred twenty-eight homes were bulldozed (Shribman 1989).

What led up to this event?

> Beginning in the early 1940s, Hooker Chemical Company buried and covered with clay 44 million pounds of chemical wastes in a canal it owned (Mokhiber and Shen 1981). When Niagara Falls officials unwittingly chose the covered-over canal as the site for an elementary school, Hooker said that they had chosen a "desirable site" for the school and deeded the land to the city for a token $1. The company warned no one about the chemicals, but the deed stated that Hooker was not liable for any injuries or deaths that might occur at this site (Brown 1979).
>
> "That account of what happened," replied Hooker, "is only partly fact, combined with a good mixture of lies." The truth, claimed Hooker, is that "we warned the board about the risk. We even told them on what part of the property to locate the school so they would not disturb the buried chemicals." Moreover, when the board considered selling part of the property, Hooker sent an attorney to the board meeting to warn them that the buried chemicals could have a "serious deleterious effect on foundations, water lines, and sewer lines" and that it was "quite possible that personal injuries could result from contact therewith." The attorney also stated

that "only the surface of the land" should be used because "the subsoil conditions make it very undesirable and possibly hazardous if excavations are to be made therein" (Wilcox 1957).

Despite these warnings, Niagara Falls' Board of Education approved that dirt be removed from the canal for top grading, the city constructed a storm sewer through the landfill, and the Department of Transportation built an expressway across part of the site. It was these construction projects that disturbed properly buried industrial wastes and caused the resulting damage, said Hooker.

Whoever is to blame—and there seems to be plenty of negligence and culpability to go around—Love Canal illustrates the danger of burying chemical wastes, the lack of adequate controls over these hazards, and the necessity of proper safeguards to prevent harm to people.

One Solution: Keep Doing What You've Been Doing, But Give It a New Name

How to dispose of chemical wastes properly is an enormous problem. U.S. industries produce about 200 billion pounds of hazardous chemical wastes each year (Brown n.d.). Just as it used to be convenient to discharge wastes into the air and dump them into rivers and the oceans, it is now convenient to bury them. To help us feel better about it, we have changed the name from dump to landfill. The containers buried in landfills slowly disintegrate, allowing lethal chemical wastes to rise to the surface or to leach into the groundwater.

The Profit Potential Has Attracted Organized Crime

The crackdown surrounding the proper disposal of toxic wastes has opened up new opportunities for greedy, careless money-grubbers—including members of organized crime (Brown n.d.). While legal disposal of a tankful of chemical wastes would cost $40,000, underworld firms show no compunction about offering to do it for half that amount. They drive an 8,000-gallon tank truck full of waste to a wooded area and dump it in eight minutes flat. The industrial company that produced the waste (a legitimate business) feigns ignorance. On 21 acres of marshlands on Staten Island, men "well known to law enforcement agents" deposited 700,000 gallons of waste oil in tanks. In North Carolina one "midnight dumper" simply opened the spigots on a tankload of PCBs and then drove until the tank was empty.

Time Bombs

With inadequate disposal and thousands of toxic dump sites, chemical wastes are a time bomb—and the fuse is lit. The Social Map on page 493 shows the *worst* of the hazardous wastes sites in the United States, those designated as needing *immediate* attention.

NUCLEAR POLLUTION

The Kyshtym Disaster

In 1980, Zhores Medvedev, a Russian biologist and dissident who had fled his country, published a book in which he claimed that a devastating nuclear accident had occurred in 1957 in Kyshtym, in Russia's Ural River Valley. The Soviet government denied that an accident had taken place, and would not allow Medvedev's book to be published in the Soviet Union. Some Western nuclear scientists also derided Medvedev, calling his account "science fiction." Medvedev was right, however, and the Russian government has now acknowledged the accident (Clines 1998).

The Russians chose this remote area of the Urals to develop their first atomic bomb. They built a nuclear reactor to obtain plutonium, which produced millions of gallons of liquid waste. Accounts vary as to how the Soviets disposed of this nuclear waste. Some say they bored holes into the ground, and poured down the liquid wastes (Solomon and Rather 1980). Others report that they piled the waste onto a dry lake bed (Clines 1998). In either case, a chemical reaction occurred, and in the

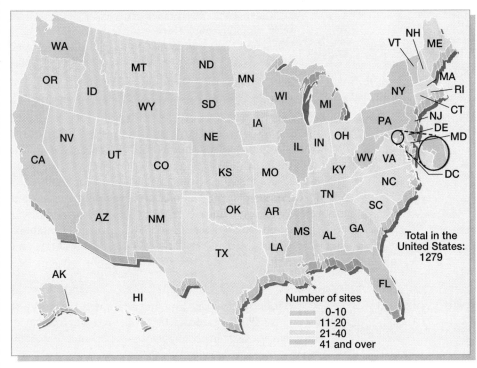

FIGURE 14-3
Social Map: Hazardous Waste Sites
(Source: Statistical Abstract 1998:Table 407; 2000:Table 365.)

winter of 1957 the waste exploded. Radioactive dust and materials shot high into the sky.

The fallout was devastating. Maps of the area before 1958 show 30 villages and towns around Kyshtym. On maps printed after 1958, those communities have disappeared. Thousands of people had to be evacuated permanently from a 1,000-square-kilometer area.

Three Mile Island

By comparison, the worst nuclear accident in the United States was puny. It occurred at Three Mile Island, Pennsylvania, in 1979. When a reactor leaked, 100,000 residents fled in panic (Rabinovitz 1998). The contamination was minimal, and today people live nearby the defunct reactor. While some say this accident may cause up to 50 people to die from cancer (Milvy 1979), Edward Teller (1980), the "father of the hydrogen bomb," claimed that "one person at some later time—one single person—may develop cancer." He added that this "single case has only 10 percent probability of occurring." Others even claim that the accident was simply a minor loss of coolant that exposed people to less radiation than they receive from their dentists (Williams 1980).

The Chernobyl Disaster

Then there was Chernobyl, a nightmare that shocked the former Soviet Union in 1986:

> *Meltdown.* The word froze in the mouth of the operating engineer. No one wanted to even think it could happen. Yet the evidence was undeniable. An explosion had blown a 1,000-ton steel cover plate off of a nuclear reactor. The containment structure was obliterated.
>
> It was too late to flee; the deadly radiation could not be outrun. The world had no choice but to watch the drama and destruction play out. For ten days the fire raged, spewing a radioactive plume into the air.

Chernobyl's cloud of radioactive gases slowly traveled around the world. In two weeks, airborne radioactivity was detected in the United States and Tokyo (Flavin 1987). Canadians were advised not to drink rain water, and even today some farms in Great Britain are under orders not to produce certain crops because of radioactive fallout from Chernobyl. (Dufay n.d.)

About 135,000 people were evacuated. Despite emergency transplants of bone marrow and fetal liver cells by an international medical team, 30 people died during the first months. In Russia and the rest of Europe, the Chernobyl disaster will account for perhaps 15,000 to 135,000 cancer cases and up to 35,000 deaths.

About 12,000 square miles of farm- and forestlands were made worthless for human use for at least two generations. Fearful that other reactors may explode, the Most Industrialized Nations are providing money and engineers to improve the safety of Soviet nuclear plants (U.S. Department of State 1997). Unfortunately, about 600 elderly have moved back into the contaminated area around Chernobyl. They know the risk, but they still call it home (Dufay n.d.).

FOOD POLLUTION

Two Types of Food Pollution

A form of pollution that you and I face daily is **food pollution.** There are two types: disease-causing organisms in food, and chemicals added to food to process it, lengthen its shelf life, enhance its appearance, or alter its taste. Let's look at both types.

1. Disease

We can illustrate the first by noting how poultry becomes contaminated during processing (Ingersoll 1990a). Slaughter lines run so fast that inspectors have two seconds to scrutinize each carcass, inside and out, for signs of disease and feces. "After a while, it gets to be a blur," says one inspector.

Processing chickens actually *increases* contamination. In one plant, 57 percent of chickens arrived at the plant contaminated with disease-causing bacteria such as salmonella, but 76 percent went out infected. The two primary sources of bird-to-bird contamination are automatic disemboweling knives, which spread fecal matter, and vats of chilled water in which the chickens are dipped before going into the freezer. Says a microbiologist, "Even if you chlorinate the chill water, it's still like soaking birds in a toilet." To this, industry officials reassuringly reply, "It may spread bacteria from bird to bird, but it also dilutes the overall dose level."

Why Not Use Alternative Techniques?

Why doesn't the U.S. poultry industry switch to blasts of cold air, like in Europe? The reason is profits. Federal regulations allow each carcass to soak up to 8 percent of its weight in this filthy water, allowing the sale of hundreds of thousands of gallons of disease-ridden water at poultry prices.

These sorts of standards make it easier to understand why many European nations refuse to import food from the United States. For other reasons, see the Technology and Social Problems box on the next page.

The Danger Is Real

It isn't just chickens, of course, that present such a threat to our health. When hot dogs produced by a subsidiary of Sara Lee were contaminated with listeria monocytogenes, 20 people died. Jalisco brand soft cheese, also contaminated with listeria, killed 40 people (Burros 1999). A plant in Arkansas, which was producing 400,000 pounds of hot dogs a day, was shut down due to listeria contamination—but the contaminated meat had already been shipped nationwide and to South Korea and Russia (Associated Press, January 23, 1999). After eating Swan's ice cream, 224,000 Americans became sick. The ice cream was tainted with salmonella, which was traced to trucks that carried ice cream mix in the same tanks used to transport

TECHNOLOGY AND SOCIAL PROBLEMS

"Do You Eat Plastic Food?"
Why Europeans Don't Like U.S. Food

I didn't know what to say when a friend in Spain asked me if Americans ate plastic food. I was amused by the phrase, and perplexed by not knowing how to answer.

The reason for the question became apparent as I became more familiar with Spanish food. My wife and I noticed that the egg yolks were brighter, almost orange. Fruits and vegetables are picked ripe, and sold and eaten fresh. The meat is more tender and tasty. It doesn't come prepackaged or frozen. Each grocery store has it own butcher; in small ones, the butcher is also the owner. Bread is freshly baked, often purchased that morning at the local bakery. The Spanish use a lot of fresh herbs—especially garlic and parsley. They also cook with olive oil—always.

All of these things account for the better taste of Spanish food. And, as scientists have discovered, Spanish food is healthier. But plastic? A rumor had spread throughout Europe that U.S. food companies do a lot of strange things to our food, that it had become synthetic. The term *plastic* may have been my friend's, but, unfortunately, it is not too far off the mark.

It isn't only the common folk who wonder about our food. (My friend, who asked this question, runs one of the thousands of mom-and-pop bar-restaurants on Spain's many beaches.) Officials of the European Union (EU) are also suspicious about U.S. food. EU

scientists claim that a hormone our farmers feed cattle to make them grow faster is carcinogenic. The EU has banned any beef with 17-beta-oestradiol. 17-beta oestradiol? I don't like the sound of that one. EU scientists haven't cleared the other five growth-promoting hormones the farmers use, either—they just don't have enough data yet to call them carcinogens (Wolf 1999).

Why don't our lawmakers insist that meat laced with carcinogens be labeled as such? They claim that European test results are "bad science" (Bahree 1999). Maybe. I don't have the expertise to judge those results. But I do know this: As conflict theorists remind us, politicians are concerned not about our health, but about how much money the food industry pumps into their political campaigns.

Some European countries refuse to import our genetically-engineered grains as well. Their scientists say these biofoods aren't safe. We don't get a label on those either.

The U.S. food industry isn't taking European resistance to its beef and biofoods lying down, of course. Its political arm, the U.S. government, has slapped millions of dollars of punitive import taxes on goods imported from Europe (Bahree 1999). Guess that'll show 'em that our food is healthy.

raw eggs (Neergaard 1998). Apple juice produced by Odwalla was infected with e.coli bacteria—14 children developed a life-threatening disease that ravages kidneys, and a 16-month-old girl died (Belluck 1998). Overall, each year in the United States food-borne diseases account for *30 million illnesses and 9,000 deaths* (Burros 1998).

2. Chemical Additives

Let's turn to the second type of food pollution. Food companies depend on artificial additives. Just to flavor our foods, they use 2,000 different chemical compounds. The "cherry" flavor in soft drinks, pies, and shakes, for example, requires 13 different chemicals.

The relationship of food additives to safety is not reassuring. The U.S. agency charged with overseeing the safety of food additives, the Food and Drug Administration (FDA), has a sad history in this field. For example, Red Dye No. 2 used to be the most common food coloring in the United States. Because it enhances colors, the food industry added more than a million pounds to our food each year. In 1970, researchers discovered that rats and mice fed this dye developed cancer. It took five years for the FDA to ban this dye—and only after the agency was flooded with petitions from public interest groups.

Many find little comfort in knowing that Red Dye Nos. 3, 8, 9, 19, 37, and 40 replaced No. 2 to color food. Some of these dyes have also been shown to cause cancer in animals—yet the FDA allows them to be used (Brooks 1985, 1987). Red dye #40, for example, has been banned in Austria, Belgium, France, Germany, Norway, Sweden, and Switzerland—yet it continues to be sprinkled into our foods (Hanssen 1997).

The sulfites provide another example:

> The food industry has found sulfites to be a handy chemical, for they are antioxidants. Because they keep foods from discoloring, they are spread over raw fruits and vegetables, especially at salad bars, to keep them "looking fresh." Sulfites are also added to beer, wine, and bakery goods, sprinkled over shrimp and fish, mixed with dairy and grain products, and added to fruit juices and frozen potatoes.
>
> The problem is that the sulfites also make some people sick. A few even die from allergic reactions. Sulfites have been linked to deaths involving pizza, wine, and beer, and they pose a special danger to asthmatics. After years of complaints—and no regulation—the FDA decided to limit the amount of sulfites in our food, and to require a warning label. (Dingell 1985; Ingersoll 1988; FDA 1994)

The Strange Case of Saccharin

To be fair to the Food and Drug Administration, its hands are tied when Congress speaks. And sometimes Congress utters some strange words. Saccharin, an artificial sweetener, is known to cause cancer, and the FDA banned it (FDA 1988; Smolinske 1992; Hanssen 1997). But Congress "granted it a special exemption," and saccharine is still sold in food stores. Little cancer packets are also found in restaurants, conveniently placed next to the sugar. A label, of course, warns consumers that they may be killing themselves. It wouldn't be too harsh to assume that Congress's "special exemption" had something to do with campaign contributions from the food industry, would it?

The Problem of Synergism

Because they are **synergistic,** that is, they interact with one another, chemical food additives are a complicated hazard. For example, the nitrites that give hot dogs, ham, and bacon their inviting red color appear to be safe in and of themselves. In the presence of amines, however, nitrites become nitrosamines—potent carcinogens. Every organ in every species of experimental animal ever exposed to the nitrosamines has shown cancer. Amines are commonly added to beer, wine, cereals, tea, fish, cigarettes, streptomycin, Librium, and Contac. Thus, hot dogs and beer are an unhealthy combination, as are a ham sandwich and a cup of tea. See Figure 14-4 for another illustration of polluted food.

The Problem of Cumulative Effects

Many chemical additives build up in our bodies. They appear harmless until they reach a certain level; then they begin to destroy tissues and organs.

Why Not Use Alternative Techniques?

Although chemical additives are convenient for the food industry, they are not necessary. We have a long *food chain*—that is, getting food from grower to consumer is a lengthy process—but we have alternative techniques to preserve food. These include older techniques such as pickling, smoking, salting, canning, freezing, and drying, as well as newer forms such as freeze-drying, vacuum packing, and irridation. The food industry adulterates our food with chemicals not because it is necessary but because it is profitable. The chemicals retard spoilage and increase sales by making food appealing to the public's conditioned taste and sight. From a conflict perspective, we can say that those who control the food industry put profits ahead of health.

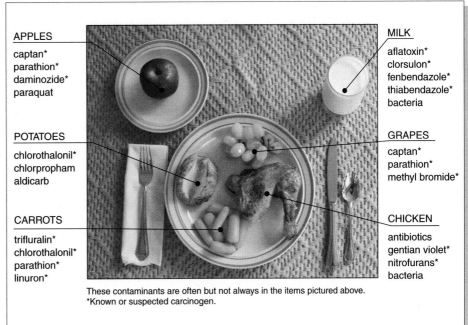

APPLES

captan*
parathion*
daminozide*
paraquat

POTATOES

chlorothalonil*
chlorpropham
aldicarb

CARROTS

trifluralin*
chlorothalonil*
parathion*
linuron*

MILK

aflatoxin*
clorsulon*
fenbendazole*
thiabendazole*
bacteria

GRAPES

captan*
parathion*
methyl bromide*

CHICKEN

antibiotics
gentian violet*
nitrofurans*
bacteria

These contaminants are often but not always in the items pictured above.
*Known or suspected carcinogen.

FIGURE 14-4
Bon Appetit?

The Extent of Food Pollution

Some of our food is polluted before it is processed and marketed. Many animals are fed antibiotics, hormones, and growth-promoting drugs that end up in our bodies when we eat them or their products, such as milk and cheese. Similarly, fruits and vegetables are coated with chemicals to prevent insect damage, some of which we consume because it is absorbed into fruits and vegetables.

High Stakes

The stakes are high. Food is the largest industry in the United States. Sales in our 250,000 retail foodstores amount to about $460 billion a year (*Statistical Abstract* 2001:Table 1031). Adulterating our food is so profitable that our food industry adds more than 1 billion pounds of chemicals to our food each year—about five pounds of chemicals for every man, woman, and child in the United States. Researchers associate these chemicals with our high incidence of cancer.

POLLUTION IN THE INDUSTRIALIZING NATIONS

Although most pollution occurs in the industrialized nations, those that are industrializing also contribute to this problem. The air in Mexico City, for example, some of the worst in the world, is so bad that 25 percent of the children have symptoms of asthma (U.S. Department of State 1997). For a snapshot of how harmful conditions can get in these nations, see the Global Glimpse box on the next page.

Four Factors that Increase Pollution in the Industrializing Nations

1. Use of Dangerous Chemicals

Four factors underlie pollution in the industrializing nations: First, chemicals that are outlawed in the industrialized nations remain legal in many of the industrializing countries. Our chemical companies still manufacture these chemicals, although they cannot be used here. They ship them to the industrializing nations, where workers who cannot read the warnings on the label use them. The chemicals poison the workers, the land, and the water. In a strange twist, they also often poison the food that you and I eat, for they return to us in our coffee, fruit, nuts, and so on.

A GLOBAL GLIMPSE

Where New Life Brings Death

"The factories, they give us life, but they kill us at the same time," sighs Maria Alves, who awakens at night to the sounds of her six children gagging in the polluted air. "It isn't fair, but what can we do? We need to work."

This is Cubatao, Brazil, a village nestled in the Serr do Mar mountains. It was pretty 20 years ago. Today the people call it "the valley of death."

As nations rush to industrialize, they often leave health and safety standards behind. Their problems with hazardous chemicals don't grab the world's attention, but they still kill.

Cubatao is one of the most polluted cities on earth. With factory pollutants and the worst acid raid ever recorded, half its 100,000 people have respiratory ailments.

A benzene gas leak caused hundreds of workers to develop leukopenia, an abnormality of the blood cells. Three developed leukemia and died. The company was fined $4,000.

When the fertilizer factories emit phosphates, it looks like winter. Little white chemical flakes flutter down, burning the skin.

Adimar dos Santos Lima, who works in a steel plant for $70 a month, and is happy to have a job, says, "I make a living. But I live in a sewer."

A slum neighborhood blew up after gasoline leaked from an underground pipe owned by Petrobras, the national oil company. They found 90 bodies. About 500 were incinerated without a trace.

Based on Schuster 1985.

The EPA banned domestic use of the pesticide ethylene dioromide (EDB) because it causes cancer. The State Department, whose concern is foreign relations, fearing bad relations with Mexico and Haiti, and, not incidentally, damages to U.S.-financed mango growers in Belize and Guatemala, pressured the EPA to allow foreign mango growers to continue using the pesticide. (Meier 1987a)

2. The Manufacture of Dangerous Chemicals

Second, the industrializing nations manufacture chemicals that the United States bans or that can be made cheaper in those nations—often in factories that U.S. corporations own. Those factories mean jobs, and if an industrializing nation insisted on stringent safeguards in manufacturing or in pollution controls, it would cut its own economic throat. Other nations would welcome the company—without the safeguards.

These operations, however, produce goods at a high price. Consider Bhopal:

It was an unseasonably cold night in Central India. In the shantytowns of Bhopal, thousands of poor families were asleep. At a nearby railway station, a scattering of people waited for early-morning trains. At the local Union Carbide plant, a maintenance worker spotted a problem. A storage tank holding methyl isocyanate (MIC), a chemical used in making pesticides, was showing a dangerously high pressure reading. The worker heard rumbling in the tank, then the sound of cracking concrete. The plant superintendent was notified, and he sounded an alarm. But it was too late. A noxious white gas had started seeping from the tank, spreading through the region on the northwesterly winds. At the Vijoy Hotel near the railroad, sociologist Swapan Saha, 33, woke up with a terrible pain in his chest. "It was both a burning and a suffocating sensation," he said. "It was like breathing fire."

Wrapping a damp towel around his nose and mouth, Saha went outside to investigate. Scores of victims lay dead on the train-station platform. "I thought at first there must have been a gigantic railway accident," he recalled. Then he noticed a pall of white smoke on the ground, and an acrid smell in the air. People were running helter-skelter, retching, vomiting, and defecating uncontrollably. Many collapsed and died. Dogs, cows, and water buffaloes also lay on the ground, shuddering in death throes. Saha made his way to the railway office, only to find the stationmaster slumped over his desk. For a moment, he thought that an atom bomb had hit Bhopal. Staggering back to the hotel, half blind himself by now, he sat down to write a farewell letter to his wife.

Saha survived. More than 2,500 others did not. (Whitaker 1984; Spaeth 1989)

This accident took place in India, but it could happen here. "The only reason we haven't had a release with the same disastrous effect is that we've been lucky," said one EPA official (Beck 1984). An expert on workplace safety put it this way, "It's like a giant roulette wheel. This time the marble came to a stop in a little place in India. But the next time it could be the United States" (Whitaker 1984).

The third factor is the pollution these nations produce as they, too, industrialize. China and India, for example, will account for much of the growth in carbon dioxide emissions over the next several decades (Livernash and Rodenburg 1998).

Fourth, the industrialized nations dump hazardous toxic wastes in the nations that have not industrialized. They make deals with dictators and weak governments and ship them chemical wastes that under our regulations are expensive to dispose of (Bartlett and Steele 1998). We even send them the ships we are discarding. In Alang, India, 35,000 men work for $1.50 a day breaking up ships whose parts are laden with asbestos, PCBs, lead, and toxic sludge (Englund and Cohn 1997b). The men work unprotected, and almost every day a worker dies from some type of accident. It is almost impossible to grasp the conditions under which people in these nations live, unless you visit them yourself. Despite being paid only $1.50 for a full day's toil under primitive conditions and the smell of death that hovers over his work, one man described the situation this way: "It is better to work and die than starve and die."

GETTING THE OTHER SIDE

Some experts say that the negative aspects of the environment have been exaggerated by alarmist doomsayers. Isolated incidents such as Bhopal, although tragic, have been blown out of proportion. If we take a more realistic, dispassionate view, they say, we will see that things are not so bad.

This group believes that improved technology will solve whatever threat pollution may pose to the environment. We have had predictions of disaster in the past, they argue, and our technology has always seen us through. The present is no exception. Some of them point to a situation in 1900. At that time, many cities had trouble dealing with the large amounts of horse manure that were piling up on their streets. Then that problem disappeared when horses were replaced by automobiles, trucks, and streetcars. The present is no different, and we will develop technology to counter threats to our environment.

People who believe this also claim that the environmentalists' proposals can do more harm than good. Edward Teller (1980), the man most responsible for the hydrogen bomb, said that strict environmental regulations not only are expensive but also create poverty and disease in the poor nations. He pointed out that when DDT was removed from Sri Lanka, 2 million people came down with malaria before DDT was reintroduced. He said, "I challenge anybody to show me a case where lack of environmental protection has made 2 million people as seriously sick as the disease caused by the environmentalists."

Life Expectancy as an Indicator That the Environment Is Improving

The optimists also stress that the best single indicator of the condition of the environment is life expectancy. When the environment deteriorates, life expectancy drops, such as is happening in Russia. If an environment improves, life expectancy increases. Figure 14-5 shows the change in U.S. life expectancy. Americans are living longer because our environment has improved, not deteriorated (Simon 1981b). We should stop worrying about what *may* go wrong, much less twist reality in order to match a woeful view of life.

IN SUM

Three Essential Aspects of Pollution

Whether we take the optimistic or pessimistic view, we confront three aspects of environmental pollution (Faunce 1981):

1. Pollutants are being introduced at an exponential rate.
2. The earth has a finite capacity to absorb pollutants.
3. A long delay often occurs between the introduction of a pollutant and indications that it is doing harm.

Reasonable Concerns: The Extinction of Species

We need not be alarmists to see that, at a minimum, we must deal with toxic wastes, provide wholesome food, and learn how to preserve, create, or—at least—not destroy a healthy environment. We also need not be alarmists to be concerned

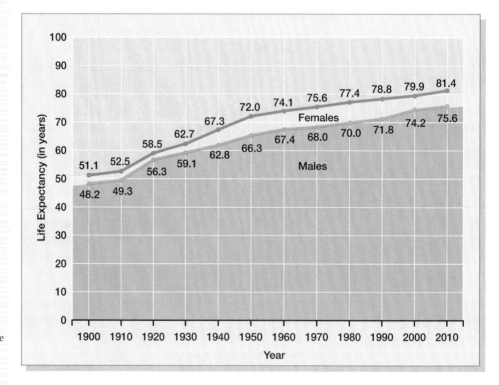

FIGURE 14-5
Life Expectancy in the United States, by Year of Birth
(Source: Statistical History 1976: Table B 116, 117; Statistical Abstract 1998: Table 128; 2001: Table 96.)

The Tropical Rain Forests and the Future of Humanity

The Pessimistic Ecologists

Ecotourism has developed to educate people about the environment and to generate profits to help sustain the environment. Shown here is a guide in the Sabah Rainforest of the Danum Valley, Malaysia.

about the extinction of plant and animal species. The destruction of the tropical rain forests is especially ominous for humanity's future.

The rain forests have been called the lungs of the world (Wolfensohn and Fuller 1998). Like our lungs, they help to regulate the earth's exchange of oxygen and carbon dioxide; they absorb carbon gases that create global warming and release oxygen into the air. They also help keep the earth's climate in balance by giving off water vapor that keeps the ground from drying out. Those lungs are gasping, and, if action is not taken soon, they will collapse.

Although the rain forests cover just 7 percent of the earth's land area, they are home to *one third to one half* of all plant and animal species. Many species of plants, still unstudied, possess medicinal or nutritional value (Durning 1990; Linden 1991; Cheng 1995). Some of the discoveries from the rain forests have been astounding: A flower from Madagascar is used in the treatment of leukemia, and a frog in Peru produces a painkiller more powerful, but less addictive, than morphine (Wolfensohn and Fuller 1998).

Despite our knowledge that the rain forests are essential for humanity's welfare, we seem bent on destroying them. For the sake of timber and farms, we clear them at a rate of 2,500 acres *each hour* (McCuen 1993). In the process, we extinguish thousands of plant and animal species. Some estimate that we destroy 10,000 species each year—about 1 *per hour* (Durning 1990). Others say that this number is conservative, that we extinguish 100 plant and animal species a day, *4 per hour* (Wolfensohn and Fuller 1998). Whatever the number, as biologists remind us, a species once lost is gone forever.

Like Esau who exchanged his birthright for a bowl of porridge, we exchange our future for some lumber, farms, and pastures.

Let's turn to resource depletion. Here we find more disagreement among the experts.

ENERGY AND RESOURCES

Americans used to hold the idea that energy was limitless. We even had "gas wars," and to attract people to buy their gas, stations gave premiums (glasses, dishes, and coupons). This ended abruptly in the late 1970s when OPEC surprised the West with an oil embargo. Overnight, long lines appeared at U.S. gas stations, and Americans, for a moment, became acutely aware of how fragile their energy supply was. But only for a moment. Although a few changes were permanent, such as more fuel-efficient cars and better-insulated homes, when the embargoes were removed, we mostly went back to our old habits.

How concerned should we be about energy and resources? It depends on whom you listen to. Let's examine the views.

One group of experts feels that we are facing energy shortages that will shatter the foundations of the industrialized world (Catton 1980). Our civilization depends on materials whose supply is limited. In

1950, one third of the energy used in the United States came from petroleum and natural gas, but now over two thirds does. One day we shall run out of these finite substances.

This group is also disturbed by how quickly we are depleting water and minerals. While fresh water appears to be endless, 97 percent of all the water on earth is salt water. A little over 2 percent is frozen in glacial ice. This leaves about 1 percent for all agricultural, industrial, and personal uses. Industrial societies are making huge demands on this limited supply of fresh water.

The Ogallala aquifer illustrates the coming crisis. The aquifer, shown in Figure 14-6, runs from South Dakota to Texas. It waters nearly 12 percent of the nation's corn, cotton, grain sorghum, and wheat (Frazier and Schlender 1980; Brown 1987). This area fattens almost half the nation's cattle. Yet we are depleting this underground formation. Broader natural forces may also be at work to dry out this region; the natural condition of much of this area, now in pasture and farmlands, may be Sahara-like desert, with giant sand dunes (Stevens 1996). Frank Popper, the head of the Department of Urban Studies at Rutgers University, says this region may become depopulated. He suggests that the federal government buy huge chunks of the land, replant the native prairie grasses, reintroduce the buffalo, and turn off the lights (Farney 1989).

Pessimistic ecologists conclude that our needs may soon outpace our water supply. They also foresee a bleak outlook for essential minerals. While the quantities of minerals are finite, their demand is growing exponentially. We have moved from an era of abundance to an era of scarcity, and soon we will run out of the metals we need to maintain our societies.

We are facing the end of the industrialized world. Although substitute materials may buy us some time, we are reaching limits that will curtail expansionary industrialism. As Barry Commoner (1972) warned, we are playing out a fundamental paradox of human life: Our civilization has a built-in tendency to grow, but its growth depends on irreplaceable, essential resources—and these are not growing. We're cruising along at 90 mph, with the top down and the radio tuned to our favorite station—and we don't see the brick wall ahead.

Such a view misreads and distorts the evidence, reply the optimists. Economist Julian Simon, for example, insisted that raw materials are *not* getting scarcer. This led to one of history's famous bets, which is recounted in the Thinking Critically box on the next page. Simon said that when something in demand grows scarce, its price increases. To see if raw materials are becoming scarcer, look at their price. The long-term trend is lower prices, which means *less scarcity* (1980:11):

The cost trends of almost every natural resource— whether measured in labor time required to produce

**FIGURE 14-6
The Ogallala
Aquifer**

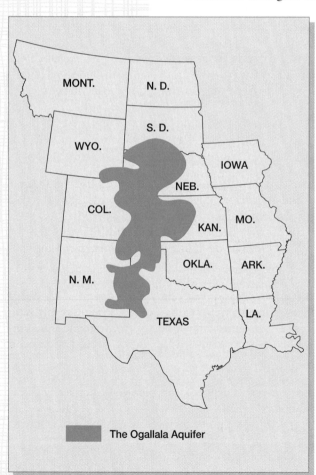

The Ogallala Aquifer

THINKING CRITICALLY ABOUT SOCIAL PROBLEMS

Put Your Money Where Your Mouth Is: The Simon-Ehrlich Bet

To say that Professors Julian Simon and Paul Ehrlich didn't like each other would be to understate matters a bit. *Detest* would be a more appropriate word. Simon was an economist who taught at the University of Maryland. Ehrlich, a demographer and ornithologist, taught at Stanford.

Ordinarily, their paths would not have crossed. They worked in different fields, and they lived a continent apart.

But then life changed for both of them.

Ehrlich came out swinging. In 1968, he wrote the book that scared millions of people and fueled the environmental movement. As populations grew, there would be scarcity of food. Prices would soar, and life expectancy would drop. *The Population Bomb* sold three million copies, scared the American public, and made Ehrlich rich. He appeared on talk shows, and Johnny Carson made him even more famous.

Fame and fortune. A good job at Stanford. How could that be spoiled?

Simon appeared on the scene. He started grumbling in public, saying that Ehrlich's book was a piece of, well, rotten codfish. Simon claimed that the opposite was true—larger populations would mean more abundance. Prices would drop, and life expectancy would increase.

The two began to call each other names and to write nasty comments about one another in academic journals.

Ehrlich still had the public. He kept repeating his predictions of doomsday. He was a founder of Earth Day, where he spoke to a crowd of 200,000.

Simon was there, too, but he had an audience of 16.

Simon didn't like this, but there wasn't much he could do about the public latching on to Ehrlich's ideas, not his.

Then Simon hit upon a bright idea. He challenged any New Malthusian to a bet (Toth 1990). They could select any commodity, and Simon would bet that its price would drop. "After all," he said, "contrary to common sense, resources are growing more plentiful, and they will drop in price."

"Put your money where your mouth is," Simon boasted, none too gently.

This was too much for Ehrlich. In October 1980, he grabbed the bet, and did a little boasting of his own. He said, "I'll accept Simon's astonishing offer before other greedy people jump in" (Tierney 1990).

The bet—on chrome, copper, nickel, tin, and tungsten—was a public affair. If the prices were higher in 10 years, Ehrlich would win; if they were lower, Simon would win. To be sure there were no misunderstandings, the two signed a contract.

During the 1980s, Ehrlich and Simon kept attacking each other, and the world's population kept growing—until it had increased by more than 800 million, the greatest increase in history.

Ten years later to the day, the two checked prices.

Ehrlich was chagrined. The price of all five metals had dropped. He quietly sent Simon a check; he enclosed no letter.

Simon gloated publicly. "Now you know who's right," he said. "And if you think this was just a fluke, let's do it again. And this time, let's put up some real money. How about $20,000?"

Ehrlich refused, saying that the matter was of minor importance.

Simon laughed, and continued to poke fun at Ehrlich.

Julian Simon died at age 65 in 1990. Paul Ehrlich stayed on at Stanford, where he still teaches. The two never reconciled.

the resource, or even in the price relative to other consumer goods—have been downward over the course of recorded history.

An hour's work in the United States has brought increasingly more of copper, wheat, and oil (representative and important raw materials) from 1800 to the present. . . . These trends imply that the raw materials have been getting increasingly available and less scarce relative to the most important and most fundamental element of life, human work time.

The Optimistic Ecologists

To illustrate how the prices of raw materials have been falling relative to wages, Simon used the example of copper. As Figure 14-7 illustrates, it takes less and less time to earn enough to buy a pound of copper.

The optimists also count on technology (Singh 1999). If we should ever exhaust a particular resource, our technology will produce a substitute. New technology will exploit materials that were useless to older technology. In fact, technology is rushing so headlong into the future that it even produces new materials before the old ones are threatened. A recent example is how fiber optic cable is replacing copper wire for the transmission of sound and images. Just a few years ago, they point out, the pessimists were saying that we would run out of copper. Take another look at Figure 14-7.

And energy? Simon again stressed that the answer is in long-term price trends. Short-term trends often yield a distorted picture. The escalation of oil prices in the 1970s, for example, did not indicate scarcity, but the futile attempt of a cartel to control prices. OPEC saw its chance at monopoly and took it. As Figure 14-8 makes clear, OPEC's effort was but a blip on a long-term trend of declining oil prices. That the world's reserves are increasing, not decreasing, supports the optimists' position (Singh 1999). The same is true for electricity and coal. Their long-term price is downward, too, indicating an increasing and stable supply of energy.

THE COMING RESOLUTION

Frameworks of Interpretation

As with population and food, the experts fall into opposing camps. As symbolic interactionists stress, the framework into which we fit data affects our conclusions—and that applies to "experts" and "nonexperts" alike. If we assume that the environment is deteriorating and our vital resources disappearing, we interpret data one way. If we do not, other interpretations follow.

What usually happens in science is that, barring political interference, opposing sides present their evidence, air their views, try to disprove the other, and the best data win out. This isn't always the case, mind you, but usually it is. As environmental issues are aired and more scientists produce more data, the exaggerations of each side should become apparent, and the position the data best support should be evident.

The Need for Continued Debate

Meanwhile, we must draw our own conclusions—which affect our perception of the problem and its solutions. On an individual level, they color our choices about energy use and lifestyles. For governments, the conclusions have greater ramifications, because the well-being of millions of people depend on them—including future generations. It is to everyone's benefit that this debate continue, unencumbered by politics, so that governmental policies can be soundly based. We now turn to social policies.

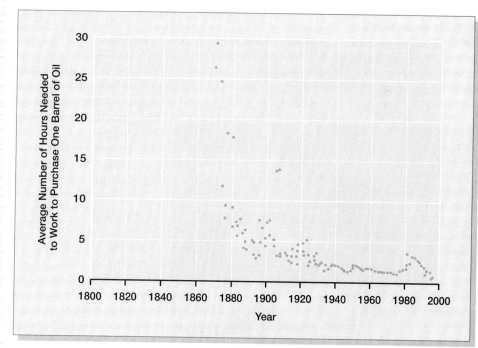

FIGURE 14-7
The Price of Copper Relative to Wages
(Source: Historical Statistics of the U.S.: Colonial Times to 1970, 1976; Statistical Abstract 1998: Table 1171.)

FIGURE 14-8
The Price of Oil Relative to Wages
(Source: Historical Statistics of the U.S.: Colonial Times to 1970, 1976; Statistical Abstract, various years, including 1998: Tables 754, 1177.)

Comparing the Pessimists and the Optimists

Before we examine specific social policies, let's look at an overarching solution that the pessimists propose. It is folly, they say, to expect the world's economies and our standards of living to increase endlessly. We must develop a **steady state society;** that is, stabilize industrial output approximately where it is now. If we stop industrial growth, we will decrease the rate at which we pollute the environment and use up resources. To do this, we must curb our appetite for the material goods that support our current lifestyles.

Other pessimists go further. They urge that we must reduce industrial output. Only after we have cut back to an optimal level can we move to a steady state society. This will require sacrifice; all of us, except the most poor, must reduce our standard of living. To become less dependent on rapidly depleting fossil fuels, we must scale back our expectations and live simpler, less materialistic lives.

The optimists counter that we can solve the environmental crisis and create a world of even greater material abundance—while enjoying an even higher standard of living. A steady state society would deny billions of people a better life. Moreover, it is unnecessary and foolish.

Regardless of the position one takes on a steady state or scaled-back society, we need social policies for pollution and energy. Let's consider them.

To save the environment, some insist that we must drastically reduce the world's population and our standard of living. Few of us, however, want to live like this hermit in Desolation Canyon of southern Utah. There must be a balance that we can strike between population, standard of living, and the environment.

POLLUTION

Four Potential Policies for Pollution:

1. Preventing the Misuse of Toxic Chemicals

A pressing problem is the misuse of toxic chemicals. As the Global Glimpse box on the next page highlights, it is not enough to ban the use of a chemical in the United States. It will return to us by way of a food chain that stretches back to us from the Least Industrialized Nations. We need to prohibit U.S. companies and their subsidiaries from manufacturing chemicals whose use is banned in the United States. Because other countries also produce toxic chemicals, the United States can call a summit to enact international controls.

To prevent misuse, industry must be held accountable. To protect the people of the industrializing nations, where many harmful chemicals are used in food production, all chemicals need to be labeled in the language of the country to which they are shipped, their dangers clearly stated in plain words. To make industry accountable, Congress passed the Community Right to Know law in 1986. It requires companies to make annual listings of the hazardous chemicals they release. Some environmentalists want to expand the "right to know," requiring that both business and government disclose when they use, release, or transport hazardous materials (Harrison 1987).

A GLOBAL GLIMPSE

The Circle of Poison

In U.S. ports from Gulfport, Mississippi, to Oakland, California, you can watch forklifts loading 55-gallon drums onto the decks of vessels bound for Central and South America.

What's in the drums? Heptachlor, chlordane, BHC, and other chemicals on their way to the plantations of Latin America.

These pesticides are banned or severely restricted in the United States, but U.S. and European companies manufacture and market them in the industrializing countries. Studies link such pesticides to cancer and sterility. But even though banned or restricted in the United States, they flow freely from our factories to the industrializing nations.

It is legal to make heptachlor, chlordane, and BHC and sell them abroad. In the industrializing nations, most workers who handle these chemicals cannot read the warning instructions on the labels. Yet they, their family, and their food will be contaminated.

Then these chemicals poison us—when the fruit grown in these countries appears on our dining tables. *Pesticides, although banned here, come back to haunt us.* BHC comes back in your coffee. DDT applied to cotton in El Salvador shows up in beef carcasses imported through Miami. Nearly half of the green coffee beans we import are contaminated with pesticides, potential carcinogens. In all, about 5 percent of the 33 billion pounds of fruits and vegetables the United States imports each year are contaminated.

Based on a newsletter from
Frances Moore Lappe, founder
of Food First; Ingersoll 1990b; Allen 1991.

Some environmentalists want a more comprehensive policy for toxic chemicals (Pearse 1987). In this "cradle-to-grave" approach, all toxic chemicals would be approved for sale and use, registered as they entered the marketplace, and monitored throughout their lifetime.

2. Preventing Food Pollution

A second pressing problem is food pollution. Recall the chapter's opening vignette. No compelling reason exists to allow diseases to be transmitted in foods. With our alternative forms of food processing and preservation, there also is no compelling reason to adulterate food chemically to make it look or taste better, to make its transportation easier, or to lengthen its shelf life. At a minimum, no chemicals should be added to our food until they are proven safe for human consumption. State-of-the-art testing procedures can be used to detect banned chemicals in our food, whether imported or domestic. We can shut down U.S. companies that violate chemical restrictions and ban food imports from countries that do so. To be effective, the legal penalties need to be directed against the *managers and directors* of companies that chemically adulterate food.

3. Disposing of Industrial Wastes

A third pressing problem is how to safely dispose of the unwanted by-products of industrialization. We already know how to detoxify most industrial wastes. We probably could learn to detoxify the rest. Recycling waste products is especially promising because it turns noxious waste into safe and usable products. To develop better technology to recycle and detoxify, we could establish a superfund to finance cooperative research by scientists. Through a crash program—a "Manhattan Project" of industrial wastes—we might be able to decontaminate the world's chemical time bombs before they go off.

Scattered across the nation are thousands of hazardous waste sites where we have discarded oil, battery acid, PCBs, pesticides, paint, and radioactive wastes. The

Callous disregard for the environment, and for people's health, has led to environmental degradation. These smokestacks can be found on Zug Island in Detroit, Michigan.

EPA has drawn up a National Priority List of the most dangerous waste sites. As we saw earlier, these are shown on Figure 14-3 (page 493). Table 14-1 ranks the states on the basis of the number of priority waste sites they contain. Congress established a superfund to clean up these sites, and has spent $20 billion to begin the cleanup. The total bill may run $500 billion. That's roughly $2,000 for every person in the United States.

The Special Problem of Nuclear Wastes

Because they stay lethal for hundreds of thousands of years, left-over plutonium and other nuclear wastes have especially perplexed the experts. For decades, while scientists debated how to store something that was beyond humanity's experience, *millions* of pounds of radioactive waste were kept in temporary containers (Campbell 1987; Schneider 1992). Their new home will be near Carlsbad, New Mexico, in chambers carved from an ancient salt bed, nearly half a mile below ground. Geologists assure us that this salt deposit has been stable for 250 million years (Brooke 1999). Critics point out that this may be so, but the waste is stored in stainless steel containers. No one knows if those containers will last a thousand years, much less hundreds of thousands of years.

4. Solving the Greenhouse Effect

The greenhouse effect is a fourth pressing problem. As we discussed earlier, global warming is embroiled in controversy. Some scientists even deny that it exists. If it does, however, it will affect everyone on earth. An immediate and direct step would be to plant vast numbers of trees around the world, for they thrive on carbon dioxide. Because of the potential threat, in 1997 in Kyoto, Japan, diplomats from 160 nations approved the world's most sweeping environmental treaty. The Most Industrialized Nations must cut emissions of greenhouse gases to about 7 percent below their 1990 levels (Fialka 1997). As of this writing, the U.S. Senate has not ratified the treaty.

Protecting the Rain Forests

For this same purpose, the destruction of the world's rain forests needs to stop. I propose that the industrialized nations *purchase the rights to not develop the rain forests.* Since most of the rain forests are in nations that have not industrialized, those funds could pay off their huge debts, thus helping to solve another problem. This

Table 14-1 How the States Rank in Number of Hazardous Waste Sites on the National Priority List

State	Number of Sites	State	Number of Sites
1. New Jersey	113	26. Louisiana	16
2. California	99	27. Alabama	15
3. Pennsylvania	97	28. Georgia	15
4. New York	88	29. Kentucky	15
5. Michigan	69	30. Montana	14
6. Florida	53	31. Tennessee	14
7. Washington	48	32. Arkansas	12
8. Illinois	44	33. Kansas	12
9. Wisconsin	41	34. Maine	12
10. Texas	38	35. New Mexico	12
11. Ohio	35	36. Oklahoma	12
12. Massachusetts	33	37. Oregon	12
13. Virginia	31	38. Rhode Island	12
14. Indiana	29	39. Arizona	10
15. Minnesota	25	40. Nebraska	10
16. Missouri	25	41. Idaho	9
17. North Carolina	25	42. West Virginia	9
18. South Carolina	25	43. Vermont	8
19. Utah	20	44. Alaska	7
20. New Hampshire	19	45. Hawaii	3
21. Maryland	18	46. Mississippi	3
22. Colorado	17	47. South Dakota	2
23. Delaware	17	48. Wyoming	2
24. Connecticut	16	49. Nevada	1
25. Iowa	16	50. North Dakota	0
		Total	**1,278**

Source: Statistical Abstract 2001:Table 365.

policy would preserve millions of acres and thousands of plant and animal species for future generations. The rights would extend indefinitely and be overseen by an international watchdog agency.

Is the United States Preparing to Invade Other Nations to Enforce Environmental Policies?

No social policy is simple, of course, and policies concerning the rain forests bring their own complications. Brazil, for example, which has extensive rain forests, knows that the United States prospered by cutting down most of its forests for farmland. Brazilian officials find it ironic that the United States wants them to preserve Brazil's forests for the benefit of Americans. Brazilian officials fear that the concern the United States has expressed is a prelude to an invasion, and they are training jungle forces to repel it (Goering 1998). Paranoia? With the history of U.S. intervention in Latin America, their fears are easy to understand.

The Overarching Solution

An overarching solution is to produce less of what harms the environment (Ball 1999; Dye 1999). We can do this by changing our production techniques and equipment, redesigning our products, and doing more in-process recycling. We have the capacity, but we must be convinced that our fragile environment is being harmed and that it is worth the effort and cost to change our ways.

**Two Types
of Solutions:**

**1. Finding
Alternatives**

2. Conservation

Aside from discovering new deposits of gas and petroleum, only two types of solutions for energy exist: alternative forms of energy and energy conservation.

Let's first consider alternative forms of energy. One alternative to oil and petroleum has already been mentioned—coal. We have enough coal in the United States to satisfy our energy needs for centuries. We can transform coal into liquids and gases. South Africa operates a coal liquefaction plant that produces a fuel competitive with petroleum.

"Synfuels" can be developed from garbage, sawdust, and other waste. The decay of organic substances, such as sewage and straw, produces methane and methanol, gases that motors can burn efficiently. One day we may solve two problems at once: the disposal of our organic garbage and the production of alternative fuels. We may see fields of common milkweed turned into flourishing "petroleum farms" as factories extract hydrocarbons—the backbone of motor fuels, lubricants, turpentine, and rubber—from those plants.

Hydrogen, too, holds great potential. As a basic component of air and water, it is available in limitless amounts. Other alternative sources include the sun, wind, ocean tides, geothermal energy (heat from beneath the earth's crust), and nuclear fusion (combining atoms, as opposed to nuclear fission, which splits atoms). The most promising alternative is harnessing the sun. Solar power is infinite, and technologies, such as the photovoltaic cell, which changes sunlight into electricity, can trap it. Alternative sources of energy are promising, but the political climate is not. After the oil embargo of the 1970s, the U.S. government funded many prototypes for producing alternative energy. After that threat dissipated, the government lost interest and withdrew its funding.

Another step is to conserve energy. This involves everything from insulating homes, businesses, and factories to working four ten-hour shifts instead of five eight-hour shifts a week. Such a change in working patterns would cut commuting expenses by 20 percent and allow factories to fire up their boilers less often. The potential of conservation is dramatic, but it does involve changing strongly ingrained patterns of behavior.

Our homes and cars have become more energy efficient, but we still have a long way to go. The "Lo-Cal" house, developed at the University of Illinois, can cut fuel bills by about two thirds. It makes these savings through its design, without help from solar equipment. About 85 percent of the total window area in the house faces south, the house is heavily insulated, and it has a 30-inch-overhang roof that lets sun in during the winter but excludes it during the summer. Another home design is the "solar envelope." The house is built within a second set of walls that provide a "skin" to trap and distribute the sun's heat. Even in northern climates, a furnace is needed on only the cloudiest days of winter. Its ingenious design also cools the house in the summer by drawing in cool air from a chamber under the house.

Another form of conservation is **cogeneration,** producing electricity as part of normal operations, such as generating electricity from the heat that industrial boilers produce. This is not a new idea. In 1900, cogenerators produced more than half of the nation's electricity. Now they produce only about 3 percent. To encourage their construction, federal law requires that utility companies purchase a firm's excess production at the utility's standard costs (Paul 1987).

Alternative forms of energy and conservation should guarantee that we never run out of energy. Solar energy, for example, is endless. We need only harvest it. We must keep in mind, however, what conflict theorists stress: Both conservation and alternative forms of energy threaten politically powerful oil companies—and they do not take threats to their profits lightly.

Again, the Optimists

Finally, we should note that if the optimists are right, developing alternative forms of energy and even conserving energy are unnecessary because we are in no danger of running out of energy. If we run out of one form of energy, our technologies will develop alternative sources. Leave everything to market forces, they say, and the balance will occur naturally (Simon 1986).

DETERMINING NATIONAL PRIORITIES

No Perfect Solutions

As with all social policy, every choice exacts its costs. So it is with resources and energy. Each choice forgoes some alternative. No choice is *the* perfect solution. All choices are limited by technology, politics, and imperfect knowledge. No society is a heaven on earth, where all pollution and poverty, brutality and evil, have been eliminated. And I do not foresee such a society as ever existing on earth.

The Need for Global Cooperation

The Technological Fix

Because the environmental problem is global, its solution requires global cooperation. If the industrialized nations dedicate their resources, we can solve our environmental problems. Consider the potential of technology.

Some technology that can solve environmental problems sounds as though it is straight out of science fiction: Already we can grow a fungus that eats the heavy metals (mercury, uranium, lead, nickel, silver, and zinc) that pollute our waterways (Roberts 1987; Naj 1988b, 1989a, 1989b; Siwolop 1988). By genetically altering strains of bacteria, we can develop "superbugs" to neutralize hazardous wastes, even radioactive wastes (Daly and Minton 1998). We can convert cellulose, a common waste product of many manufacturing processes, into an acid that can be used to produce fuels and fertilizer (Dye 1999).

Fuel-Cell Powered Cars

Dethroning the king of power, the internal combustion engine, even seems within our grasp. Although the automobile industry dragged its feet, after California mandated that 10 percent of the vehicles sold in that state be essentially pollution free by 2003, car companies began researching alternatives in earnest. Soon cars with fuel cells will be sold. Fuel cells work by mixing hydrogen and oxygen from the air to produce electricity (Ball 1999). If fuel-cell powered cars and trucks become economically competitive, and standards of pollution control become stricter, the internal combustion engine will become obsolete. Fuel-cell power will even reduce global warming, because water will flow out of the exhaust of these vehicles, instead of carbon dioxide.

Taking the Lead and Determining Policies

The Dilemma

The United States can take the lead in solving environmental problems by proposing international legislation to benefit all nations. This, however, may conflict with the individual sovereignty of nations, and some may reject such legislation as violating their national interest. This will bring us face to face with a basic, philosophical, moral problem. Is there a fundamental right of some nations to enforce their will on others? If so, what is the basis of that right? Some "greater good" for the world's benefit? If so, who decides what that greater good is and how it should be enforced? Assumptions of a "greater good," as conflict theorists remind us, can be excuses for world bullying by the Most Industrialized Nations.

Establishing National Priorities

The best social policy may be to set an example. For this, we need to establish national priorities. Without them, we follow current dictates of the market, which are circular; that is, public demand is based on advertising, which, in turn, is based on the need of selling what we produce. To establish national priorities requires a vision of the future, and I'm not certain that we have much agreement of where our destination should be.

◆ The Future of the Problem ◆

As we discussed social policy, we touched on the future. At this point, let's first examine energy conservation and pollution. Then we'll again look through the eyes of the pessimists and optimists.

The Outlook for Energy

In the 1970s, when the Arab oil embargoes made Americans aware of the limitations of their oil-based economy, energy conservation became a patriotic duty. Today, we have forgotten that warning. The average size of a new home has risen from 1,600 square feet to 2,100—even as the average household has shrunk to 3 people from 3.6. We also furnish our homes with more energy-eating appliances. In the 1970s, 40 percent of new homes had central air conditioning; now 80 percent do (Myerson 1998). Dishwashers have gone from being luxuries to being "necessities." Although our cars get better mileage, we burn gasoline as though there were no tomorrow—with more fuel being used per person than was used in the 1970s (Myerson 1998). The conservation movement has stagnated, and without another embargo or some other external threat we and the rest of the industrialized world will continue our energy-wasteful ways.

But why not? The most likely future will bring oil in abundant supply. In the United States, gasoline is cheaper than bottled water. The Gulf War of 1991 demonstrated that the industrialized nations will not let the petroleum-rich nations threaten their oil supply. Bombs proved mightier than a dictator, or a cartel. If we have energy shortages, they will be artificial, markets manipulated to raise prices and profits.

For energy, the future is rosy. We possess vast coal and oil reserves, and we are still discovering new oil fields. We could use technology to harness alternative forms of energy, lowering their price and making them even more widely available. Doubtless, the international oil companies will turn the alternative forms into profitable enterprises.

The Outlook for Pollution

The picture for pollution is less positive. Our measures are inadequate. We are merely working on an emergency basis: When the leaching of a chemical dump becomes too public to ignore, we apply an environmental Band-Aid. We have no overarching plan for chemical and nuclear pollution that ensures the long-range health of our population. Local businesses and industrial giants are still not adequately concerned about their wastes.

If bringing pollution under control required only law and technology, we could assume a future that becomes ever more pollution-free. But more is required—particularly a national determination to make our environment as free of pollution as possible. While this depends on public awareness, which ebbs and flows, it also depends on politics; any administration can strengthen or weaken standards.

The Greens

Environmentalists in Germany have formed their own political party. The Green Party, as it is called, holds seats in the German parliament, and in several of Germany's states it has become a key player in coalition governments. The United States, too, has a Green Party, but the most it can claim is a municipal judge in New Mexico (Steinmetz and Rohwedder 1998). That the U.S. Greens have not been able to muster strong political support does not mean that this will continue indefinitely. Some unexpected event may etch the environment into the consciousness of Americans, making it a top political issue.

Out of environmental degradation, and the potential that conditions will worsen, has arisen an international environmental movement. Some feel that people who use extreme measures to get their message across are crazy, while many environmentalists feel that people who put profits ahead of the world's health are crazy. Greenpeace uses news-exploiting tactics to get its message to the world.

An Unfolding Coalition of Interests

The Picture Painted by the Pessimists

The Picture Painted by the Optimists

As conflict theorists would predict, the future of pollution depends on the balance of power among groups whose interests collide. The environmental movement may be picking up key strength at this point in our history, however. A coalition of religious groups is making the environment a top priority (Watanabe 1998). With missionary zeal, Christians and Jews are joining forces under the banner "Creation Care." They stress that "we are called to be stewards, not exploiters, of the earth."

Finally, let's look at the future through the eyes of the two groups who see practically nothing alike. The pessimists paint a gloomy future, of course. Pollution will continue with only superficial improvements here and there, and the depletion of resources will accelerate. The countdown has already begun, and "PD Day" (Pollution-Depletion Day) is on its way—the day when pollution has gone so far that we can't fix it, and we have depleted our vital resources. With its industrial base undermined, modern society will disintegrate. Desperate, people will flee. But to where? Even the countryside will be too polluted to support anything but a minimum of life.

Can this gloomy future be averted? Yes, reply the pessimists, but only if we develop a steady state society. But reducing our energy consumption and eliminating much of our material gadgetry will be like weaning an alcoholic from the bottle. Our adjustment will be upsetting, because we have built a society on the assumption of inexhaustible resources. But once we recover from the initial shock of having our lifestyle drastically changed, we may find that a simpler way of life is rewarding: we will be less rushed, enjoy social relationships more, and feel less need to own things.

The optimists, in contrast, paint a rosy future. A steady state society not only would be ill advised, but it also would require a torturous and unnecessary adjustment. Our present path is fine. The more industry grows, the greater the demand for resources. This, in turn, increases the motivation to locate new supplies of resources and to develop substitutes for those in use. We already have more resources than we need for the foreseeable future—and that means for thousands of years (Simon 1981b). Scientists are even making breakthroughs in hydrogen storage and fusion that hold the potential for energy in unlimited quantities, capable of meeting all the world's needs now and in the future (Bishop and Wells 1989; Stevens 1989).

Pollution is not a fearsome problem either. It will be solved as people demand a cleaner environment and are willing to pay for prevention and cleanup. The environment is already getting cleaner, and it will continue to improve. Consequently, the future promises a better environment, an even higher standard of living, and a continued lengthening of our life expectancy.

Who Is Right?

Who is right? What *is* the future of the environmental crisis? Is humanity at a crossroads, as the pessimists insist, with our current course destining us to destruction? Or are the optimists right, and our current course is taking us to a delightful future? Could the future turn out to be even gloomier than imagined, with nuclear war, the worst pollution of all, destroying our ecosystem—and humanity? We consider that possibility in the following chapter.

We who are audience—and either beneficiaries or victims—of this unfolding drama will have to await its outcome.

◆ Summary

1. The destruction of the environment began millennia ago and may even have destroyed ancient civilizations. Industrialization has intensified this process.
2. The nations of the world are part of a common *ecosystem*. The environmental crisis is a global matter: Individual acts of *pollution* can have international consequences. Pollution comes primarily from industrialization, and is not dependent on ideology. Pollution is common in capitalist nations, the former Soviet Union, and China.
3. Symbolic interactionists have studied how the environment became a social problem, how objective environmental conditions were translated into subjective concerns. Concerns began with professionals, were picked up by interest groups and government agencies, and then by the press, which aroused the public.
4. Functionalists stress that all life on earth is interdependent. We all are part of a huge, complex living machine called the environment. Industrialization has dysfunctional consequences for the ecosystem.
5. Conflict theorists stress the conflict between environmentalists who battle to reduce environmental threat and industrial leaders who fight for the right to pollute while earning a profit.
6. Some measures of air and water pollution show improvement, but the results are mixed, and pollution continues. The *greenhouse effect* could cause climatic change that would have far ranging consequences for humanity. Some scientists, however, doubt that the problem even exists.
7. Strip mining and the disposal of solid wastes despoil the land. Industrial wastes threaten our drinking water and many of our lakes and rivers. *Acid rain* imperils animal and plant life.
8. Chemical pollutants pervade our environment. Industrial accidents and leaching from landfills are extensive. Nuclear pollution is ominous, as illustrated by the Kyshtym and Chernobyl disasters. Food additives are another form of pollution.
9. Alarmed at the environmental crisis, pessimists advocate a *steady state society*—one based on no economic growth or even controlled shrinkage of the economy. Optimists are convinced that the environmental crisis is exaggerated; they believe that we can solve environmental problems through technology and continued industrial growth. Regardless of who is right, pollution is a global problem that requires international social policies.
10. With our reserves, technology, and alternative forms of energy, our energy future looks positive. The outlook for pollution, however, is less positive. Chemical pollution especially will plague us.

◆ Key Terms

Acid rain   Rain with heavy concentrations of sulfuric and nitric acids.

Biodegradable   Capable of disintegrating in outdoor weather.

Carcinogen   A cancer-causing substance.

Cogeneration   Producing electricity as a by-product of one's ordinary operations.

Corporate welfare   Handouts given to corporations, usually in the form of tax breaks; may also be bargain-priced real estate or rents.

Ecology   The study of the relationship between living things and their environment.

Ecosystem   The interconnection of life on the planet's outer surface.

Food pollution   (also called food contamination) The transmission of disease during food processing and the adding of chemicals to food to help process it, lengthen its shelf life, or enhance its appearance or taste.

Greenhouse effect   The concentration of gases in the atmosphere that allows sunlight to enter but inhibits the release of heat. It is thought to hold the potential of warming the earth's climate.

Ozone shield   A layer of earth's upper stratosphere that screens out a high proportion of the sun's ultraviolet rays.

Pollution   The presence of substances that interfere with socially desired uses of the air, water, land, or food.

Steady state society   A society in which the economy does not grow or shrink.

Synergistic   (literally, "working together") Applied to chemicals, it refers to their interactions.

Thermal inversion   A layer of cold air sealing in a lower layer of warm air.

◆ Critical Thinking Questions

1. Which of the perspectives (symbolic interactionism, functionalism, or conflict theory) do you think does the best job of explaining environmental pollution? Explain.

2. How far do you think the government should go to reduce pollution? Should individuals who run polluting corporations be jailed? Should the government be more willing to shut down polluters? What else could or should the government do?

3. The scientists represented by, among others, the conservative think tank the Heritage Foundation, argue that environmental and scarcity problems are best solved by free enterprise. They believe that free enterprise is much more likely and better equipped than governments to solve these problems. What do you think of their position? Explain.

4. Do you think that U.S. corporations should be allowed to export their environmentally questionable products or production processes to foreign countries to avoid U.S. environmental regulations? Explain.

5. Do you think the U.S. government has the power or authority to demand a steady state society? Do you think it is advisable? Why or why not?

War, Terrorism, and the Balance of Power

Most of us can vividly remember where we were on September 11, 2001, a day that has become emblazoned on our own memories—and seared into the national consciousness. This day, which began like so many before it—a bright dawn, shining sun, and people going about their everyday lives—was destined to change the United States. No longer would our assumptions about life be the same.

When the commercial passenger planes that had been transformed into speeding missiles struck the Twin Towers and the Pentagon, the United States was shaken to its roots. At dawn, these global symbols of capitalism and military power had stood tall and proud. Just a few hours later, the one had been destroyed, the other crippled.

Americans shook their heads in dismay and confusion. Why had they been attacked? And by what enemy? As confusion turned into anger, and the face of the enemy was beamed to Americans and the world, the response of the United States was swift and violent. Amidst missiles directed from remote locations, along with the direct intervention of U.S. Special Forces, al-Qaida was quickly routed from Afghanistan.

The United States declared war on terrorism—as it steeled itself against further attacks by an enemy that hit suddenly and without warning. Where would this unseen enemy strike next? The White House? Some nuclear plant? A professional football game? Even the local mall?

Just as in 1941, a surprise attack had resulted in war. This time, though, it was different. There is no particular country to counterattack. The enemy consists of small groups in many countries. There are sleeper cells within the United States. An attack could come at any time, from almost anywhere.

And how will we know when this war has ended? After all, will there ever be an end to those who hold grudges against the United States? And powerful weapons proliferate. Will the United States have to track down groups around the world, without end?

It's a strange war—and strange times we live in.

◆ The Problem in Sociological Perspective ◆

The Magnitude of Today's Threat

From the end of World War II in 1945 until the end of the 1980s, the Soviet Union and the West were caught up in an **arms race.** Each furiously developed and produced new weapons, trying to match each other's war capabilities. During these decades, they built an arsenal of nuclear weapons that still has the capacity to destroy the world many times over. Although the **Cold War,** the protracted hostilities between these nations, thawed, these nuclear weapons still threaten human existence. They could instantaneously reduce major cities to ash and transform world powers into barren deserts. All of the catastrophes the world has experienced throughout history would pale in comparison with nuclear war.

Why Is War Common?

Although the magnitude of the threat is new, war itself is not. Human groups have always fought each other. Since war has been common in human history, some anthropologists have suggested that humans have an instinct for aggression. Konrad Lorenz (1966) said that aggressive energy accumulates inside us. Like steam in a closed container, it builds up pressure and demands release. Long ago, Lorenz says, this instinct helped ensure that only the fittest survived. It also forced humans to

Why Men Fight: The Yanomamö

Yanomamö men often attack neighboring villages, killing the males and stealing the women. They also fight with one another. Fights often begin about sex: infidelity, seductions, or failure to give a promised girl in marriage. Sometimes the men challenge one another to a duel. One man gets to hit the other once in the chest or pound him over the head with a long wooden club. Then the other gets a turn. This continues until one man can no longer return the blow. At other times they use axes and machetes and neglect to await their turn. When relatives are drawn in, fights turn into brawls. These games can trigger feuds between villages. When someone is killed, relatives seek revenge. A feud is self-feeding, for each killing requires more retaliation.

Why do the men fight like this? Anthropologist Napoleon Chagnon, who has lived with the Yanomamö, believes that access to women is the basic reason. He found that the men in this northern Venezuelan jungle who have killed at least one other person have more wives and children than those who have never killed. An especially successful warrior may have six wives.

It works this way: Because violence is the mark of a true man, a reputation for violence gives a Yanomamö male high status. This makes him an attractive candidate for arranged marriages—which the men arrange.

"How primitive they are!" we might say. The Yanomamö are not that different from us, however, as Chagnon points out. While we don't reward our war heroes with additional wives, we do give them medals, seats in the U.S. Senate, and even the presidency. Chagnon points out that the military experience of candidates is important in U.S. political races.

Are we any different from the Yanomamö—aside from being more indirect in rewarding "war behaviors"?

Based on Allman 1988; Chagnon 1988.

The Sociological Perspective: Societies Channel Aggression

colonize the whole world as they fled from one another's innate aggression. Today, however, as Lorenz puts it, this instinct is a "hereditary evil of modern society."

To find the answer to warfare, sociologists and most anthropologists do not look *within* people. Whether humans have an instinct for aggression is not the point. Conflicts always arise among people who live together. *What is significant are the norms that groups establish to deal with those conflicts.* Let's look at two extremes. One is the nourishment of aggression. The Yanomamö, discussed in the Global Glimpse box above, represent this extreme. The other is represented by the Eskimos of East Greenland. Instead of fighting, their norms require that hostile individuals engage in a song duel:

> The singing style is highly conventionalized. The successful singer uses the traditional patterns of composition which he attempts to deliver with such finesse as to delight the audience to enthusiastic applause. He who is most heartily applauded is "winner." . . . One of the advantages of the song duel carried on at length is that it gives the public time to come to a consensus about who is correct or who should admit guilt in the dispute. . . . Gradually more people are laughing a little harder at one of the duelist's verses than at the other's, until it becomes apparent where the sympathy of the community lies, and then opinion quickly becomes unanimous and the loser retires. (Fromm 1973)

Some groups channel aggression into ritualistic violence. Here is an example of a spear-throwing duel among the Tiwi of north Australia:

The origins of warfare go back to the origins of history. Because war is so common, some theorists suggest that humans have an instinct for aggression. If so, it is socially channeled into cultural forms. Shown here are men of a Yanomamo tribe competing with spears while wearing traditional body paint.

When a dispute is between an accuser and a defendant, which is commonly the case, the accuser ritually hurls the spears from a prescribed distance, while the defendant dodges them. The public can applaud the speed, force, and accuracy of the accuser as he hurls his spears, or they can applaud the adroitness with which the defendant dodges them. After a time unanimity is achieved as the approval for one or the other's skill gradually becomes overwhelming. When the defendant realizes that the community is finally considering him guilty, he is supposed to fail to dodge a spear and allow himself to be wounded in some fleshy part of his body. Conversely, the accuser simply stops throwing the spears when he becomes aware that public opinion is going against him. (Fromm 1973)

War Is Not Universal

While hostilities, aggression, and even murder characterize all human groups, war does not. War is one option that groups choose to settle disagreements, and not all societies choose this option. The Mission Indians of North America, the Arunta of Australia, the Andaman Islanders of the South Pacific, and the Eskimos of the Arctic, for example, have ways to handle quarrels, but they do not have organized battles that pit one tribe against another. These groups have no word for war (Lesser 1968).

War—an organized form of aggression that involves armed conflict between politically distinct groups—is often part of national policy. Why do some groups choose war to handle disputes when less drastic measures are available?

Three Essential Conditions of War

Sociologist Nicholas Timasheff became interested in this question. After studying armed conflicts, he (1965) identified three essential conditions of war. The *first* is a cultural tradition of war. This shapes people's thinking, helping them to see war as a way to resolve conflict with another nation. The *second* is an antagonistic situation in which states confront incompatible objectives—for example, each wants the same land or resources. A cultural tradition for war and an antagonistic situation are not enough. There also has to be a *third* condition—a fuel that ignites this tinder,

something that moves the nations from thinking about war to actually engaging in it.

To find these fuels, Timasheff studied wars throughout history. He found seven "fuels" that, poured onto the antagonistic situation, explode into war. They are the opportunity to

Seven "Fuels" of War

1. Get revenge (to settle "old scores" from previous conflicts).
2. Dictate one's will to a weaker nation.
3. Protect or enhance prestige (to save the nation's "honor").
4. Unite rival groups within one's country.
5. Protect or exalt the nation's leaders.
6. Satisfy the national aspirations of ethnic groups (to bring "our people" who are living in another country into our borders).
7. Convert others to religious and ideological beliefs.

In Sum: The Sociological Perspective

In sum, to understand war, sociologists do not look for factors within humans. Instead, they look for social causes—factors in society that encourage or discourage aggression and shape aggression into organized combat between nations.

◆ The Scope of the Problem ◆

War in the History of the West

The evening news always seems to include a war somewhere. And the United States always seems to be sending troops somewhere, sometimes to countries we can't even pronounce or spell, and, frankly, don't care about. Did countries fight this much in the past?

In Medieval times in Europe, war was considered a gentlemen's exercise, a grand game fought according to established rituals. This painting from about 1250 shows knights who are ready to engage in combat. Note the child musicians who accompanied them.

To find out how common war has been, sociologist Pitirim Sorokin (1937) listed the wars in Europe from 500 B.C. to A.D. 1925. He identified 967 wars, an average of one war every two to three years. Counting years or parts of a year in which a country was at war, Germany had the least warfare, at 28 percent; Spain had the highest, at 67 percent.

Sorokin found that Russia, the land of his birth, had experienced only one peaceful quarter century during the previous 1,000 years. Since

William the Conqueror took power in 1066, England had been at war for 56 of each 100 years. Spain had fought even more often.

The United States: One of the Most Warlike Nations in the World

And the United States? Since 1850, we have intervened militarily around the world more than 150 times (Kohn 1988). It won't be long until the total reaches 200. Although we were "at war" with no nation, in recent years we have "intervened" in Grenada, Panama, Afghanistan, Iraq, Somalia, Haiti, Bosnia, Sudan, Kosovo—and then back in Afghanistan again. Military operations from our declared war on terrorism, then, are not new, but, rather, the continuity of a longstanding pattern.

Measuring Wars in Terms of Deaths

War may be hell, as an unknown pundit said, but some wars are more hellish than others. Consider the killing. Since 1829, there have been approximately

80 wars in which 3,000 to 30,000 people died.

40 wars in which 30,000 to 300,000 people died.

11 wars in which 300,000 to 3,000,000 people died.

2 wars (World War I and II) in which 3,000,000 to 31,000,000 people died (Richardson 1960; updated).

The Growing Capacity to Kill

If your father or mother dies in a war, of course, it matters little that there were 30,000 or 3 million others. On a personal level, we measure things by how they affect us.

Nevertheless, it is important to know how industrialization has increased our capacity to kill. Consider bombs. During World War I, of every 100,000 people in England and Germany, fewer than 3 died from bombs. During the next twenty years, however, scientists "advanced" this technique of human destruction, and during World War II about 300 of every 100,000 English and Germans died from bombs (Hart 1957). Our technology in killing has "advanced" much farther since then, and if nations were to use nuclear weapons, such as those described in this chapter's opening vignette, the deaths of past wars would seem as nothing. Some weapons, even more "advanced," supposedly have the capacity to destroy every living thing on earth.

The Continuing Slaughter

What about education? As education has expanded, one might suppose that war would have become a relic of a primitive past. We should have reached a more advanced state, able now to look back uncomprehendingly, and with a bit of smug superiority, at how humans used to slaughter one another. As we all know, however, this doesn't even come close to describing our situation. A generation ago, the United States fought in Vietnam for about seven years—at a cost of 38,000 American lives and a couple of hundred thousand Vietnamese. The death toll of the Soviet Union's nine-year war in Afghanistan ran about 1 million Afghanistani and perhaps 20,000 Soviet soldiers (Armitage 1989). Iran and Iraq fought an eight-year war at a cost of 400,000 lives.

In Sum

War, then, as Sorokin sadly concluded, is normal. That is, war is a regular part of the world's history. Sorokin added that we are living in one of the bloodiest, most turbulent periods in the history of Western civilization—and perhaps in the history of humanity. Our era certainly provides no reason to correct Sorokin's judgment We recently saw Serbs kill Bosnians, and Bosnians kill Serbs—each claiming rightful revenge for atrocities of years past. After generations and even hundreds of years, they claim the right to hate eternally—and to pass this nasty heritage to their children. Israelis and Palestinians do the same. They, too, continue to kill one another—each absolutely convinced that its views are just and God is on its side. As I write this, India and Pakistan, claiming their right to perpetuate old hatreds, are again threatening to nuke one another to hell.

✦ Looking at the Problem Theoretically ✦

Let's use our theoretical perspectives to focus on the problem of war. Using symbolic interactionism, we will examine the symbolic basis of the nuclear arms race. Using functionalism, we will consider why nations go to war. Through conflict theory, we will explore how conflicting interests and the desire for more territory lead to war.

SYMBOLIC INTERACTIONISM

The Role of Perceptions

Symbolic interactionists emphasize how significant *perceptions* are in war. They stress how leaders evaluate their own nation's strengths relative to those of the enemy, and how they see the odds for winning or losing.

During the Cold War, the United States and the Soviet Union had to decide which weapons to build and how much to spend on them. To underestimate the enemy could prove fatal, so each magnified the evil intentions and destructive capability of the other. Without hard information, each had to guess what the other intended, and they then used their guesses to choose what seemed to be the most practical response.

This led to an arms race. When one superpower thought that the other might build a certain weapon, it began to build that weapon itself. Sometimes, however, the other nation had no intention of building the weapon, and the "countermeasure" turned out to be an aggressive step that forced the other nation to build the weapon. Robert McNamara explained how mistaken perceptions forced the Soviet Union to build more nuclear warheads (Kurth 1974).

> In 1961 when I became Secretary of Defense, the Soviet Union possessed a very small operational arsenal of intercontinental missiles. However, they did possess the technological and industrial capacity to enlarge that arsenal very substantially over the succeeding several years. We had no evidence that the Soviets did plan, in fact, fully to use that capability. But, as I have pointed out, a strategic planner must be conservative in his calculations; that is, he must prepare for the worst plausible case and not be content to hope and prepare merely for the most probable.
>
> Since we could not be certain of Soviet intentions, since we could not be sure that they would not undertake a massive buildup, we had to insure against such an eventuality by undertaking ourselves a major buildup of the Minuteman and Polaris forces. . . . But the blunt fact remains that if we had more accurate information about planned Soviet strategic forces, we simply would not have needed to build as large a nuclear arsenal as we have today.

Symbols Are Central to Human Behavior—Including War

This event illustrates a primary principle of symbolic interactionism—symbols are central to human behavior. Based on how we perceived Soviet plans, we decided to build intercontinental ballistic missiles (ICBMs). Our decision, in turn, became a signal to the Soviets that they needed to build ICBMs right away. The nuclear arms race was based on symbolic interpretations of what the enemy might do.

Symbols Determine Reality

This example also shows us that *symbols can take on a life of their own;* how, once put into play, symbols wield power over human affairs. Although McNamara's initial perception of Soviet intentions may have been wrong, our buildup of missiles became proof to the Soviets that they needed to build more missiles. This, in turn, became proof to us that our interpretation was right—and that we needed to build even more powerful weapons. *Perception, not facts, usually guide human behavior.*

Symbolic interaction underlies war in another way. As long as two rival nations perceive war as a no-win situation, they are likely to avoid it. If there is hatred and fear between them, however, and one nation thinks that striking first can destroy the other's capacity to strike back, that nation is encouraged to strike first. During the Cold War, U.S. Air Force generals advocated a "first-strike" if it meant that they could win the war (Kurth 1974). Apparently Soviet generals did the same. You can see how tense and dangerous the situation was. Each nation felt that it had to let the other know that it could not win, that a first strike would be foolish. As a result, both the Soviet Union and the United States would let information slip about their new weapons, or defense systems like "Star Wars." It is scary to think that our lives—and those of the world—depended on mutual fear and the correct interpretation of one another's signals!

FUNCTIONALISM

In 1939, the world was in turmoil. Hitler's tanks and *Luftwaffe* were rampaging through Europe. Japan had invaded China and was threatening the South Pacific. His sociological imagination piqued, Robert Park (1941) decided to analyze war's social functions. He surveyed the literature on war and found that the world's countries (or states) had been born in war. Our countries came about as one group extended its political boundaries by subjugating other groups. What is today's United States, for example, would not exist if it weren't for the Indian wars, and wars against France, Great Britain, Spain, and Mexico. A major function of war, said Park, is the *extension of territory,* an enlargement of a group's political power.

Another function of war is *social integration.* If a country has groups in conflict, war can give them a mutual outside enemy. The factions close ranks and cooperate in order to repel the common threat (Coser 1956; Timasheff 1965; Shibutani 1970; Blainey 1973). After the war, the factions turn back to unfinished business and try to settle old scores. Afghanistan's bitterly divided groups cooperated to repel the Soviets, but after the Soviet defeat they turned on one another—based on their prewar religious, class, tribal, and clan loyalties. Today, the United States looks in dismay as it tries to produce from the territory of Afghanistan a country in its own image.

Sociologist Georg Simmel (1904) identified *social change* as a third function of war. Warfare can stimulate the development of science and technology. Five centuries ago, for example, Leonardo da Vinci designed war machines for his patron. Today, we owe our interstate highways to war. (In case the Soviets attacked, President Eisenhower wanted to be able to rapidly move soldiers, weapons, and supplies.) War has also prompted aerodynamic designs, the harnessing of nuclear energy, surgical techniques, satellites, and the Internet.

Even losers can benefit from the changes stimulated by war. The Japanese, for example, after their defeat in World War II, embraced Western technology. This not only increased their standard of living and life expectancy, but also it gained them the world leadership that they had failed to win by war. No social change is without its dysfunctions, however, and Japan's, too, has come at a price: the disruption of its traditional ways of life.

A fourth function of war is *economic gain:* access to treasure, raw materials, trade routes, markets, and outlets for investment (Pruitt and Snyder 1969). This was the primary function of Desert Storm: To protect its source of cheap oil, an alliance of industrialized

War has many motives, and they are often mixed together in a war. Religion, land, riches, revenge, and glory became intermixed in one of the world's strangest wars, the Crusades, which were fought between the 11th and 13th centuries. The Christians' stated purpose was to recover the Holy Land, particularly Jerusalem, from the Muslims, but these other motives became intertwined. In 1212, the Children's Crusade took place. In this, the most pathetic of the Crusades, thousands of children set out from France for the Holy Land. The ships' captains sold them to the Muslims as slaves. German children met a different fate. Going overland, they died of hunger and disease.

5. Ideology
6. Vengeance
7. Military Security
8. Establish Credibility

Functions for Individuals

No War Serves a Single Function

nations bombed Iraq. Industrialization has put a new twist on this function—increasing business, profits, and employment. The best example is how World War II put millions to work and helped lift the United States out of the Depression. Even the threat of war can bring economic gain. As sociologist C. Wright Mills (1958) noted back in the 1950s, "war readiness" requires high spending that benefits big corporations. This is still true today.

A fifth function of war is *ideological*—advancing a political or religious system or suppressing an opposing one. An example is the Crusades by European Christians between the eleventh and fourteenth centuries to recover the Holy Land from Islam. A sixth function is *vengeance* or *punishment*—teaching another nation "a lesson" or avenging an injury or insult (Pruitt and Snyder 1969). Much of the warfare in Bosnia and Kosovo, including the rapes and other atrocities, serves this function. A seventh function is to increase *military security*. That is, a nation does not desire an asset in and of itself, but attacks to prevent an enemy from using that asset against it. This is why Israel bombed Iraq's nuclear plants in 1981. An eighth function of war is to *increase the credibility* of a nation's threats or guarantees. By going to war, other nations will see that a nation means what it says.

War also has functions for soldiers and leaders. Soldiers often report that battle presented them with a challenge to "see what I'm made of." Some even report an excitement that verges on sexual arousal. More significant, however, are the satisfactions that war brings its leaders. Although most leaders bemoan war, much of this is self-posturing, done for the sake of a public image. Those who plan battles derive intense satisfactions from outmaneuvering the enemy, gaining advantage through surprise attacks, being the acclaimed victor of pitched battles, and so forth. Since no one wants to be seen as a loser, such personal functions also play a role. In addition, for its successful leaders, war can be an avenue of social mobility. Generals George Washington, Ulysses S. Grant, and Dwight D. Eisenhower, for example, moved from generalships in the Army to the presidency of the United States. Colin Powell moved from the same position to Secretary of State, one of the most powerful positions in the world.

No war serves a single function. The same war can involve territory, revenge, ideology, and military security. If war is drawn out, functions can even change. The

Crusades began in 1095 when Pope Urban II exhorted Christians to go to war, promising that their journey to the Holy Land would ensure forgiveness of sins. Ideological purposes may have dominated at first, but the Crusades also functioned to provide treasure and territory. Nine Crusades and 200 years later, all functions of war were present.

War Is Usually Functional for the Victors

Traditionally, war has been highly functional for the victors. Rome, for example, conquered most of the known world, subjugating one people after another and exploiting their resources. Generals would return victoriously to Rome, laden with bullion, to the acclaim of citizens and Caesar alike. They also brought with them thousands of captives, slaves to do the drudge work for Rome's elite—or, in the case of the educated slaves they brought back from Greece, men to be turned into tutors for the elite's children. In the latter part of the empire, the slaves provided drama, their deaths in the Coliseum yielding pleasure for Rome's jaded and bloodthirsty citizens.

Dysfunctions of War

Standing in stark contrast are the dysfunctions of war. Defeat is the most well known dysfunction. Rome never recovered from its defeat of 2,000 years ago. Even military victory, however, can be dysfunctional. The victor can become dependent on the exploitation of subjugated peoples, and when that control ends, as it inevitably does, the economic pain is severe. Spain experienced this dysfunction when it lost its colonies in the 1820s. It has never fully recovered from that experience. Russia is undergoing this same dysfunction today. No longer can bureaucrats send an order from Moscow, and the designated resources unquestioningly flow. The spigot has been turned off.

Today, war carries a greater threat of dysfunction than it ever has. As our opening vignette pinpoints, nuclear weapons hold the capacity to destroy the earth.

CONFLICT THEORY

Four Causes of War

Conflict theorists provide four major explanations of the cause of war. Ibn Khaldun of Tunis proposed the first explanation in the 1300s. He stressed that all human groups struggle to survive. As they compete for scarce resources and strive to expand their power, they inevitably conflict with one another. War is simply one form that human conflict takes.

1. Conflict over Resources

2. Conflicting Interests of the Bourgeoisie

The second explanation is based on what conflict theorists see as the central force in human history. In each society, some group takes control. This group, which they call the *bourgeoisie*, uses the resources of society to keep itself in power and to exploit the powerless. As the bourgeoisie expand their power beyond their country, they come into conflict with one another. As a result, they sometimes decide to go to war. The bourgeoisie don't fight, of course. They hold the power, so they send the exploited (the poor, the workers, the *proletariat*) to battle for them. The German's term for the young men of the poor who died in such outrageous numbers in their wars was "cannon fodder."

3. Imperialism

The third explanation focuses on the expansion of markets. In 1902, John Hobson, an economist, said that capitalist nations develop surplus capital, and business leaders want to expand their markets so they can invest this capital. They then persuade the government to go to war and take over other lands. The result is **imperialism,** the pursuit of unlimited expansion by war and threat of war.

4. A Military Machine

Another economist, Joseph Schumpeter, proposed a fourth explanation in 1919. He said (1955) that the military and political elite want war because it brings them power and prestige. To prepare for war, they build a strong military machine. This in itself encourages war, because the military is there to be used, and its use brings more prestige to the elite.

Conflict Theorists Build on These Ideas: The War Machine

Today's conflict theorists have built on these explanations. They, too, stress how a war machine has increased the threat of war. They note that after World War I we dismantled our military, and our war industries returned to their peacetime pursuits (Barber 1972). World War II, however, was a turning point. When it was over, we did not dismantle our war machine (Eisenhower 1972). Instead, we kept a large armed force and pumped vast amounts of money into upgrading its weapons and equipment. The Soviet Union, Great Britain, France, and others did the same. The telling moment came after the fall of the Soviet Union. With its enemy weakened and supposedly transformed into a capitalist ally, the West has continued to pay and arm millions of soldiers. It has now even incorporated Russia into NATO, the organization it founded to fight the Soviets.

Using the War Machine to Promote Global Capitalism

To understand this, conflict theorists stress that we need to look at the top levels of power. There we see the *power elite*—the military, business, and politicians. And if we look closely, we can see how their interests have merged. The military always wants a powerful military machine, as greater power bolsters its position in society. It also perceives enemies on every side, so it has endless rationalizations for expansion. This isn't new—but global capitalism is. To protect their far-flung investments, business leaders, too, want a powerful military. They may need armed intervention at home—or on the other side of the globe. Politicians are sensitive to what the business elite wants, because, as conflict theorists stress, they owe their positions to the business elite. If business withdraws its support, they have little chance of being re-elected. Consequently, they find it in their interest to support a strong military, and in the name of national security (an effective phrase at budget time), politicians levy taxes to finance the military machine.

Today, stress conflict theorists, the U.S. military machine is used to advance capitalism around the world. When you see U.S. armed forces in action, alone or sometimes accompanied by the United States' international capitalist partners—Great Britain, France, and Germany—you can be sure that the world is being made safe for capitalism. The result, says Mills (1958:2), is that "war is no longer an interruption of peace; in our time, peace itself has become an uneasy interlude between wars. . . ."

◆ Research Findings ◆

With war so common—and with today's weapons jeopardizing even the existence of humanity—what factors reduce the likelihood that nations will go to war? After looking at this question, we will then examine the costs of war, both economic and human, and the U.S. military machine. Finally, we'll consider the possibility of accidental war, biological and chemical warfare, and terrorism.

WHAT REDUCES WAR? AN OVERVIEW OF FINDINGS

Seven Major Findings About War and Peace

Quincy Wright (1942), a professor of international law, looked at war throughout history and tallied the important battles. His findings, combined with those of physicist-mathematician Lewis Richardson (1960), are not encouraging. They can be summarized this way (Nettler 1976):

1. Type of religion does not reduce warfare. A nation in which Christianity is dominant is not any more pacifistic than a nation in which Islam is dominant.

2. Type of government does not reduce warfare. Democracies and republics are neither more nor less peaceful than dictatorships and monarchies.

3. Prosperity does not reduce warfare. Prosperous nations are neither more nor less peaceful than poor nations. Nor do periods of prosperity reduce fighting.

4. A shared religion does not reduce warfare between nations.

5. A common language does not reduce warfare.

6. Being "neighbors" does not reduce warfare. The opposite is true: Shared boundaries stimulate fights over territory, and war increases in proportion to the number of boundaries that countries share.

7. Education does not reduce warfare. Education does not create an "enlightened" preference for peace; countries with high education are as likely to go to war as those with low education.

No Trend Toward Peace

When we attempt to discover what reduces war, then, we are forced to conclude that we don't know. Contrary to common sense, religion, democracy, prosperity, and education don't reduce war. Experts can make up fancy sounding terms such as "conflict resolution," but the world's nations aren't becoming more peaceful. Instead, wars have become more intense, killing more people than ever. As sociologist Gwynn Nettler (1976) ruefully observed, the Nobel Peace Prize usually goes to a citizen of a nation with a long history of recent war. He said that perhaps we should consider this prize as awarded on the basis of need, rather than as a recognition of achievement.

THE COSTS OF WAR

What the United States Spends on War

It is no exaggeration to say that war is costly. Consider what the United States has spent on its nine major wars (see Table 15-1). This huge amount does not include the billions of dollars spent on Desert Storm or on U.S. incursions in places such as

Table 15-1	What Has the United States Spent on Its Wars?
War of 1812	$615,000,000
Mexican War	$1,076,000,000
American Revolution	$1,918,000,000
Spanish–American War	$5,961,000,000
Civil War	$45,990,000,000
Korean War	$262,062,000,000
World War I	$369,580,000,000
Vietnam War	$553,088,000,000
World War II	$2,953,716,000,000
Total	$4,194,006,000,000

Note: In the source, the costs are listed in 1967 dollars. To account for inflation, I increased these amounts by 350 percent, and added the costs of service-connected benefits. Where a range was listed, the mean was used.

The costs of the many "military interventions" such as in Grenada, Panama, Somalia, and Haiti are not listed in the source, nor is the more expensive "military intervention" on behalf of Kuwait. These costs do not include interest payments on war loans, nor are they reduced by the financial benefits to the United States, such as the acquisition of California and Texas in the Mexican War.

Source: Statistical Abstract 1993:Table 553; this table was dropped after 1993.

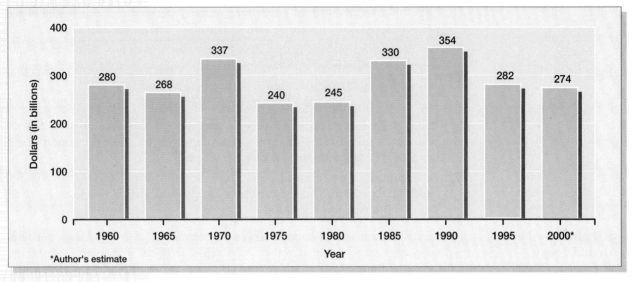

FIGURE 15-1

How Much Does the United States Spend on Its Military? (in Constant [1996] Dollars)

(*Source: Statistical Abstract* 2001:Table 490.)

Bosnia, Kosovo, and Afghanistan. Figure 15-1 shows how many tax dollars Americans pay each year to support the U.S. military. The totals are in constant dollars, so you can easily compare one period to another. The highest spending, 1970 and 1985–1990, represents expenditures for the war in Vietnam and the ICBM defense called Star Wars. Today's spending has dropped back to the 1960 level.

The expenditures shown in Figure 15-1 include the costs of veterans' benefits, but a more realistic total of what we spend on war and preparing for war would also include the costs of running the Central Intelligence Agency, the National Aeronautics and Space Administration, and the Agency for International Development. A case could also be made to include what we spend on the Overseas Private Investment Corporation, the International Monetary Fund, and the World Bank (Greenberger 1994).

On average, since 1960 we have spent $270 billion a year on what is euphemistically called national defense. Such numbers roll easily off the tongue—with little realization of what they mean. This is because the concept of 1 billion of anything is beyond our experience. To gain an idea of how much we are spending, consider this (Shaffer 1986):

> If we were to lay a million dollar bills end to end, we could just about cover the distance from New York to Philadelphia. If we laid a billion dollar bills end to end, we would circle the earth four times around the equator.

Now if we laid the dollar bills of our average annual defense budget end to end, they would circle the earth 1,100 times!

Another way to measure our military expenditures is to compare them with what else we could buy with the same money. I could not find a comparison with today's dollars, and have to rely on costs from the 1980s, but the same principle applies:

The Cost of War Preparations in Terms of Alternative Purchases

1. For the price of one aircraft carrier, we could build 12,000 high schools.

2. For the price of one naval weapons plant, we could build twenty-six 160-bed hospitals.

3. For the price of one jet bomber, we could provide school lunches for 1 million children for a year.

4. For the price of one new prototype bomber, we could pay the annual salaries of 250,000 teachers (de Silva 1980).

Money goes a lot further in the Least Industrialized Nations. There, the price of one tank would buy 1,000 classrooms. One can dream of a world in which military dollars go to education, medicine, and the enlightenment of nations, but we do not live in such a world.

Money spent on the military represents alternative purchases that we did not make. Our armed forces employ about 1.4 million military personnel and more than another million civilians. Add the 1.5 million men and women in the reserves and national guard, and the total comes to 4 million people (*Statistical Abstract* 2001:Tables 502, 510, 511).

Like other nations, the United States finds itself boxed in. While the military is costly in money spent and benefits foregone, not spending this money would leave us vulnerable. In light of the world's bellicose history, an assumption of danger appears well founded. Only if all nations miraculously become pacifists and all dangers of attack ceased would military preparedness become unnecessary. No such miracle seems in the offing.

The nations of the world spend about $865 billion a year to arm themselves (*Statistical Abstract* 2001:Table 495). The good news is that this is less than they spent ten years ago. The bad news is that this is 2.6 percent of the entire world's gross national product—$294 a year for every man, woman, and child in the entire world. Laid end to end, those dollars would stretch around the earth 3,460 times. If you wished, you could lay them end to end and reach the moon—and then you could make that round trip a couple of hundred times!

Table 15-2 shows which countries spend the most and least on their military. The table holds some surprises. On a per capita basis, Singapore outspends the United States. Sweden, hardly a bellicose nation, is in the top ten of spenders. As you can see, the nations that spend the least have little industrialization. Although what they spend for their military on a per capita basis is tiny (in the extreme, just a thousandth of the biggest spender), these are very poor nations, and they need every dollar they can get for basic necessities.

War's greatest cost, of course, is not dollars, but lives lost. During the 1700s, wars were fought according to aristocratic ideals. Small professional armies waged short, limited campaigns. In battle, the soldiers marched in formation, accompanied by flags, drums, and other musical instruments. War was like a chess game, with generals matching wits with opponents who came from similar economic backgrounds, and who sometimes had even been trained in the same military schools. They considered warfare a test of bravery, and referred to battle as the "field of honor."

Napoleon changed this when he initiated **total war,** "no-holds-barred" warfare (Finsterbusch and Greisman 1975). This came home to us with the American Civil War. During four brutal years, 620,000 Americans died, more than in all our other wars combined, from the Revolution to the present. No longer is there a field of honor, if ever there was one. U.S. civilians were shocked by the actions of the U.S. military in Vietnam, and their protests led to a shortening of that brutal war. In Kosovo, U.S. planes bombed civilian targets in order to undermine support for the country's regime. The war was too short to initiate anything but feeble protest. With

The Incredible Amounts the World's Nations Spend on War

The Costs of War in Terms of Deaths

Table 15-2 What Countries Spend on Their Military

What Countries Spend the Most on Their Military?

Rank	Country	Per Capita	As a Percentage of Gross National Product
1.	Israel	$1,690	9.7
2.	Singapore	$1,650	5.2
3.	Kuwait	$1,510	7.5
4.	United States	$1,030	5.3
5.	Saudi Arabia	$1,050	14.5
6.	France	$708	3.0
7.	Sweden	$626	2.5
8.	Slovenia	$617	5.2
9.	Taiwan	$602	4.6
10.	United Kingdom	$600	2.7

What Countries Spend the Least on Their Military?

Rank	Country	Per Capita	As a Percentage of Gross National Product
1.	Tanzania	$3	1.3
2.	Bangladesh	$5	1.4
3.	Congo	$5	5.0
4.	Kenya	$7	2.1
5.	India	$11	2.8
6.	Philippines	$17	1.5
7.	Nigeria	$19	1.4
8.	Indonesia	$23	2.3
9.	Pakistan	$26	5.7
10.	Sri Lanka	$41	5.1

Source: Statistical Abstract of the United States 2001:Table 1391.

World War I brought the worst destruction the world had ever seen. Trenches were dug across France and Germany, with opposing armies dug in on each side. The armies were fairly balanced in strength and munitions, and for months there would be relative calm. Then in a feverish attempt to overrun the enemy, tens of thousands of young men would die in a single battle, with only yards of terrain changing hands. This picture was taken October 17, 1918, in Molain, France.

today's mass armies, and the capacity to deliver wholesale death, with industries spewing out weapons, and with civilians not spared, an image of pageantry and games is far from reality.

Most fearful of all, today's weapons are so destructive that they threaten human existence itself. Although killing in the past was inefficient, since 1700 over 100 million people have died in war (Gartner 1988). Today, that many could die from just one nuclear blast. If ever there were another world war, deaths could number in the hundreds of millions—if, indeed, anyone were left to count them.

The costs of war in terms of quality of life. While we can measure war in terms of money and deaths, war involves more than such gross measures. Among

The Costs of War in Moral Terms: Dehumanization

war's other costs is a loss in people's "quality of life." This is impossible to measure accurately, but at the very minimum war increases insecurity, paranoia, fear, and worry. Even everyday life becomes uncertain, as war breaks down the norms that regulate human behavior. It becomes difficult to plan for the future, and the ordinary expectations of what life is like begin to unravel.

Morality is also part of our "quality of life," and war erodes this, too. Soldiers who are exposed to brutality and killing tend to become **dehumanized.** They come to see the enemy as objects, not as people. This removes the obligation to treat them as human beings. Consciences become so numbed that participants can dissociate even acts of torture from their "normal self." Torture and killing, though remaining perhaps disagreeable, become "dirty work" that has to be done. They think of themselves as having the duty to obey orders, not to question them. "Those who make the decisions are responsible, not I, a simple soldier who does my duty."

Four Characteristics of Dehumanization

The process of dehumanization is fascinating, as physicians Viola Bernard, Perry Ottenberg, and Fritz Redl (1971) found out. They identified these four characteristics of dehumanization:

1. *Increased emotional distance from others.* A person stops identifying with others, seeing them as lacking basic human qualities. They become not people, but an object called "the enemy."

2. *An emphasis on following procedures.* Regulations become all-important. A person does not question them, even if they involve atrocities. A person will say, "I don't like it, but it's necessary," or "We all have to die some day."

3. *Inability to resist pressures.* Fears of losing one's job or the respect of one's group, or of having one's integrity and loyalty questioned become more important than morality.

4. *Diminished personal responsibility.* One sees oneself as a small cog in a large machine. One is not responsible, because one has no choice. One is simply obeying orders. One's superiors know best. They have the information to judge what is right and wrong. One uses the reasoning, "Who am I to question this?"

The Symbolic Transformation of the Struggle

Sociologist Tamotsu Shibutani (1970) pointed out that dehumanization is helped along by the tendency for prolonged conflicts to be transformed into a struggle between good and evil. We don't want to do these things, but because the survival of good (democracy, freedom, the nation) hangs in the balance, we must suspend moral standards. War, then, exalts treachery, brutality, and killing—and we give medals to glorify behavior that we would otherwise condemn.

World War II: The Nazis and the Japanese

To participate in such acts, soldiers must distance themselves from their earlier socialization. They must neutralize the morality they learned as children. This often is effective. For instance, it enabled ordinary Germans to staff the concentration camps. Surgeons who had been educated at top universities, whose profession called for them to be highly sensitive to people's needs, denied that the inmates they experimented on were fully human. Methodically and dispassionately, they mutilated patients just to study the results. Some doctors immersed Jews in vats of ice water in freezing weather, considering their deaths insignificant because the results of the studies would be used to save the lives of German pilots shot down over the North Atlantic (Gellhorn 1959).

Despite the horrors of the Nazis, the Japanese matched their atrocities with prisoners of war. They beheaded U.S. prisoners of war, and buried others alive (Watanabe 1999). They also tortured prisoners and performed medical experiments on them (Davis 1994). In one experiment, Japanese doctors pumped U.S. prisoners full of horse blood. In another, they injected them with typhus, typhoid, smallpox, and other diseases. In one test, they lined up ten prisoners "behind a protective screen with their naked buttocks exposed while a fragmentation bomb was detonated" (Leighty 1981). In China, the Japanese conducted germ warfare experiments, killing perhaps hundreds of thousands of Chinese with anthrax, typhoid, and plague (Harris 1994).

The War in Vietnam: The Americans

The Germans and Japanese carried dehumanization to horrifying limits, but they were not unique. U.S. soldiers in Vietnam also dehumanized their victims. The Vietnamese became less than people; they became "gooks," "dinks," "slants." Shooting into villages and shooting at mothers trying to flee with their babies were dissociated from the self. It was better not to question the morality of the act, better to think of the act as part of the larger scheme of things, saving a people from communism—or as rightful retaliation for buddies who had been killed: "I don't like this, but, after all, this is war."

When Dehumanization Fails

Although such techniques can protect the self, they are not foolproof, and their failure can lead to crippling guilt. Tim, for example, who is quoted below, was a Marine interrogator in Vietnam. Beating prisoners to elicit information became a way of life for him. When beating did not work, he would use electric shocks, attaching "two wires of a field telephone usually to the earlobe or the cheek or the temple, sometimes the balls or the crotch" (Smith 1980:27). Tim did not enjoy his work, and one day as he was beating a 16- or 17-year-old girl, he began to think:

> Why are we killing all these people? These aren't soldiers. I'm beating on this girl—and it all hit me. I'm beating up this girl, what for? Who am I? . . . It was as if for the first time I was looking at myself. Here's this guy, slapping, beating on this girl—for what?
>
> No longer seeing this prisoner as an object, Tim insightfully added: "For the first time I was looking at this person, a detainee, as a real human being, not as a source of information." This change of perspective directly affected Tim's job performance. As he said: "I wasn't a very good interrogator from that time on. I lost all motivation."

Being surrounded by army buddies who agree that the enemy is less than human helps maintain definitions that justify cruelty. After returning home, however, the former soldiers are resocialized into more routine norms, and these definitions tend to break down. As a result, many former soldiers are disturbed by what they did in the war. Before putting a bullet in his head, a soldier from California wrote:

> I can't sleep anymore. When I was in Vietnam, we came across a North Vietnamese soldier with a man, a woman, and a 3- or 4-year-old girl. We had to shoot them all. I can't get the little girl's face out of my mind. I hope that God will forgive me. I hope the people in this country who made millions of dollars off the men, women, and children that died in that war can sleep at night (I can't, and I didn't make a cent). (Smith 1980:15)

In an unusual development, some Japanese soldiers, who kept quiet for fifty years, have publicly confessed their mass rapes and killings. Their neutralization techniques, too, failed.

Let's turn from what has been a symbolic interaction analysis to a conflict perspective and examine how organizations and profit underlie modern warfare.

This is Hamburg, Germany, in July of 1943, following Allied bombing. The real destruction of war, however, is the loss of human lives, and the toll from World War II was about 31 million men, women, and children. When I visited Hamburg for an international sociology conference a few years ago, my hosts escorted me through the city. It has been meticulously restored.

The Cold War

The Military as a Powerful Economic Force

"Pentagon Capitalism"

THE MILITARY-INDUSTRIAL COMPLEX

As we discussed, the United States did not disarm after World War II. During the protracted period of hostilities known as the Cold War, the West and the Soviet Union tried to "contain" one another's influence on the world. Our leaders were convinced, as were theirs, that to prevent an attack we had to possess the most advanced weapons and show a willingness to use them.

The military requires a vast industrial backup. Those industries that specialize in armaments—the guidance systems, bombs, missiles, tanks, planes, guns, ships, submarines, and other weapons—have become a powerful force in the U.S. economy. Military weapons are like personal computers; they quickly become obsolete, forcing their continuous replacement with a new generation of even more highly sophisticated and expensive ones. About twenty percent of all the money spent by the federal government is consumed by the Department of Defense and the Department of Veterans' Affairs (*Statistical Abstract* 2001:Table 490).

Like other U.S. businesses, the corporations that manufacture our armaments want to increase their profits. Unlike other U.S. businesses, however, their main customer is the Department of Defense. To make sure that it has inside connections to that customer, the defense industry hires retired top-ranking military officers. They know the military system and even some of the people in charge of military purchases. Some of those in charge of purchasing may themselves be eyeing well-paying jobs in the defense industry after their own retirement.

With their interests merged, the military and defense industries have become a power to be reckoned with by Congress. The **military-industrial complex,** as it is known, pressures key members of Congress to increase military spending. Congress listens, because the Defense Department can channel lucrative contracts into their districts. Seymour Melman (1970) called this interlocking relationship between Pentagon armaments and U.S. business **pentagon capitalism.**

Table 15-3 shows how important "defense" industries have become to the U.S. economy. Ten states receive at least $3 billion each in military contracts. The several hundred thousand employees paid by the military also spend huge sums for local

Table 15-3 Where Defense Contracts Go: The Top 20 Winners

Rank	State	Amount of Contracts	Military Personnel	Civilian Employees*	Payroll
1.	California	$18,100,000,000	146.3	60.8	$11,362,000,000
2.	Virginia	$13,637,000,000	133.3	79.6	$11,407,000,000
3.	Texas	$12,145,000,000	109.9	39.3	$8,659,000,000
4.	Florida	$6,470,000,000	60.9	26.4	$6,887,000,000
5.	Maryland	$4,977,000,000	30.4	32.0	$3,726,000,000
6.	Massachusetts	$4,737,000,000	2.3	6.9	$826,000,000
7.	Arizona	$4,547,000,000	21.3	8.2	$1,995,000,000
8.	Missouri	$4,508,000,000	16.2	9.4	$1,604,000,000
9.	Pennsylvania	$3,967,000,000	3.1	25.7	$2,217,000,000
10.	New York	$3,839,000,000	19.6	11.1	$1,776,000,000
11.	Georgia	$3,665,000,000	66.0	30.4	$4,934,000,000
12.	Alabama	$3,298,000,000	11.1	20.2	$2,376,000,000
13.	Ohio	$3,077,000,000	6.8	23.4	$2,189,000,000
14.	New Jersey	$2,944,000,000	8.5	14.2	$1,518,000,000
15.	Colorado	$2,214,000,000	29.1	11.0	$2,395,000,000
16.	Washington	$2,192,000,000	48.9	23.1	$4,035,000,000
17.	Connecticut	$2,177,000,000	6.5	2.6	$541,000,000
18.	Louisiana	$1,938,000,000	15.5	8.6	$1,403,000,000
19.	DC	$1,899,000,000	13.0	12.6	$1,218,000,000
20.	Indiana	$1,611,000,000	1.1	9.3	$929,000,000

*These are civilians directly employed by the military. The totals do not include workers in the defense industries who fulfill the military contracts listed in column 3.

Source: Statistical Abstract 1998:Table 573; 2001:Table 494.

purchases. Consider how Virginia, an average-size state (7 million people), brings in almost $10 billion in military contracts. Its 178,000 workers who are paid by the "defense" industry net another $11 billion a year. The threat to close a military base unites local governments, Chambers of Commerce, and unions. They send lobbyists to Washington to fight to keep the base. "Now that the Cold War is over, it's okay to close unneeded bases—but not mine" has been heard across the country. NIMBY (Not In My Back Yard) has changed to KIMBY (Keepit In My Back Yard).

Growing Efficiency in Death

During the arms race, the West and the Soviet Union feverishly stockpiled nuclear weapons, continuously increasing their explosive power and the efficiency of their delivery systems. Our capacity for inflicting death grew so sharply that *if a bomb the size of the one dropped on Hiroshima had been exploded every single day from the birth of Christ until now, the total force of those bombs would be less than the destructive capacity of the United States* (Melman 1970).

That's just the United States. To this, we can add the nuclear weapons of Russia, France, Great Britain, and others. It is almost impossible to grasp the destructive capacity of the nuclear powers, but imagery sometimes helps. Consider this. The explosive energy of nuclear weapons is measured in megatons. If you had 1 million tons of TNT, you would have one **megaton.** The United States has over 3,000 megatons of explosive power. Think of a freight train filled with gunpowder that stretches from earth to the moon. Now *triple* that—make the train 925,000 miles long—and you have an image of the destructive power of the United States (see *Nucleus* 1981).

The length of the U.S. train is a matter of alarm for many. But then there is also this statistic: Russia's train is even longer. France and Great Britain also have trains, although theirs are shorter. Israel, India, Pakistan, China, and a few other nations have them as well. Still other nations, envious that they aren't in the nuclear club, are frantically trying to build their own trains.

The Cold War has bequeathed us trains that are running along the edge of a cliff. There has been a downpour, and a washout may be ahead. Yet the trains steam forward full speed into the darkness. At any time, one of them may hit a washout, plunge off the cliff, and obliterate humanity.

A Glimmer of Hope?

In the midst of this dark futility lies a glimmer of hope. Like a train's engineer who has seen the washout ahead and is furiously waving a warning lantern, the superpowers are heeding the danger. They have negotiated agreements to eliminate ICBMs with multiple warheads and to reduce their nuclear stockpiles. No longer do Russia and the United States target each other's major cities. (A skeptic might wonder, however, just where those ICBMs are targeted—and a realist knows that it takes little time to retarget nuclear warheads.) Although a few weapons have been destroyed, this is not disarmament. This is really only *a reduction of excess capacity:* After all, each nation can still destroy the other many times over.

Political Instability in Russia Spells Greater Nuclear Danger

Not only do we still face the possibility of nuclear warfare, but it may be that the likelihood of nuclear exchange has actually *increased.* The rise of democracy in Russia is certainly welcome, but the country's political instability makes it difficult to know whose finger is on the trigger of its nuclear weapons. Ethnic conflicts have also resurfaced. The former Soviet Union suppressed ethnic conflicts with an iron hand. As its empire broke up, throughout its former borders those simmering ethnic rivalries and hatreds erupted. At the same time, militant fundamentalism and terrorism have grown. All this is accompanied by nuclear proliferation and the capacity to smuggle nuclear weapons across borders.

Is it any wonder that some see our civilization ending in one gigantic mushroom cloud? Before we examine that possibility, look at the Social Map on pages 528–529. There you can see the major sources of this danger.

THE POSSIBILITY OF ACCIDENTAL WAR

The Reality of the Possibility of Accidental War

Only with disarmament, which we discuss later, will the world be safe from nuclear destruction. As things now stand, we face not only the potential of some leader launching a nuclear attack, but also the possibility of missiles being unleashed accidentally. Consider how close we have come in the past:

Computer Failure

> Back in 1980, a computer reported that Russia had fired missiles at the United States. The United States immediately went to red alert. U.S. bombers plotted courses toward preselected targets in the Soviet Union, and we prepared our missiles for launching. The countdown toward nuclear devastation had begun. (*U.S. News & World Report,* June 24, 1980)

Russia had not launched its missiles. A computer had given a wrong signal. It's a chilling thought—the end of the world due to a computer malfunction.

Operator Failure

Or the obliteration of humanity could come from a simple human error. Here's another real-life event:

> On October 28, 1962, the North American Defense Command was informed that Cuba had launched a nuclear missile. It was about to hit Tampa, Florida. The U.S. began a countdown for its retaliatory strike. Then someone noticed that there had been no explosion in Tampa (Sagan 1994).

COUNTRIES KNOWN TO HAVE NUCLEAR WEAPONS

1. United States
Tests: Over 1,000, more than the rest of the world combined.
Warheads: 12,000
Range: 8,100 miles
Is able to reach any country in the world.
Has missiles on submarines.

2. Russia
Tests: 715
Warheads: 22,000
Range: 6,800 miles
Is able to reach any country in the world.
Has missiles on submarines.

3. France
Tests: 210
Warheads: 500
Range: 3,300 miles

4. Great Britain
Tests: 45
Warheads: 380
Range: 7,500 miles

5. China
Tests: 45
Warheads: 450
Range: 6,800 miles
Is rapidly developing more powerful weapons and advanced guidance systems based on secrets stolen from the U.S. Los Alamos Laboratories.

6. Israel
Tests: Unknown
Warheads: about 100
Range: 930 miles

7. India
Tests: About 10
Warheads: 65
Range: 1,550 miles

8. Pakistan
Tests: About 10
Warheads: About 25
Range: 930 miles

COUNTRIES SUSPECTED OF HAVING NUCLEAR WEAPONS PROGRAMS

9. Iraq
Its nuclear program was halted by Desert Storm and U.N. inspections. At this writing, Hussein has refused more inspections.

10. Iran
Believed to be developing nuclear weapons.

11. North Korea
Believed to be developing nuclear weapons. Has tested missiles over Japan and soon may have two warheads.

12. Libya
A U.N. embargo has stopped its nuclear weapons program.

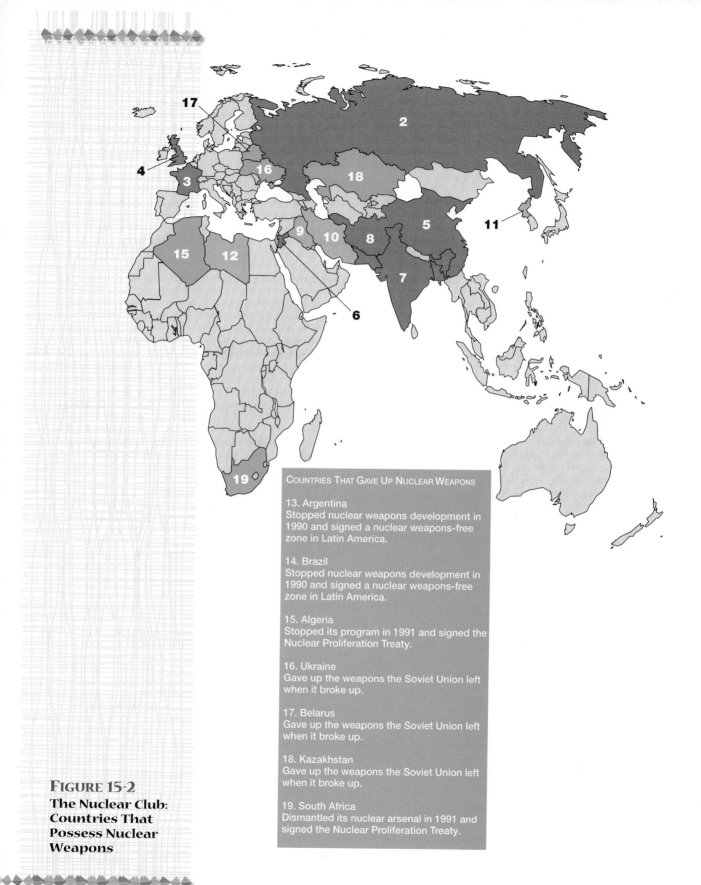

FIGURE 15-2
The Nuclear Club: Countries That Possess Nuclear Weapons

It turned out that a radar operator had accidentally inserted into the system a test tape that simulated an attack from Cuba. If the United States had launched immediately, instead of waiting a few minutes, the Soviet Union may have responded to a missile attack on Cuba with salvos of its own—and you probably would not be here to read this book.

Nuclear Accidents

Or the end may come because a nuclear weapon detonates accidentally. Consider these accidents that Rear Admiral Gene LaRocque, U.S. Navy (retired) summarized:

> The *George Washington*, a missile submarine, ran into a Japanese ship and sank it.
>
> The *Scorpion* and the *Thresher*, two other nuclear attack submarines, sank in the ocean.
>
> When a mechanic dropped a wrench in a missile silo in Arkansas, a missile was launched.
>
> Several nuclear weapons have fallen out of planes, through open bomb bays.
>
> A nuclear weapon fell from a plane into a swamp in the Carolinas. The Air Force was unable to find it. The Defense Department bought the land, put a fence around it, and, in Orwellian fashion, called it a "nuclear safety area." (Keyes n.d.)

In none of these incidents did a nuclear weapon detonate. We have no assurance that similar accidents will not happen again, and, if they occur, that the weapons will not explode.

Nuclear Sabotage

The U.S. government has repeatedly assured us—and the world—that a missile cannot be launched without proper authorization. Any talk to the contrary, they say, is alarmist. This event shows such assurances to be lies:

> The year was 1962. Kennedy had backed down in the Bay of Pigs invasion of Cuba, and the Soviet military thought that Kennedy would be a pushover. Khrushchev, the premier of the Soviet Union, decided to ship missiles to Cuba. The CIA reported that the missiles would be capable of destroying the Pentagon, New York City, and other U.S. cities. Kennedy warned Khrushchev to order the ships back, and set up a blockade to intercept them. The world waited tensely, television reporting the movement of the ships as they neared the blockade.

All of the above is well known. What is not well known is this:

> At the height of the Cuban crisis, officers at Malmstrom Air Force Base in Montana, who also doubted the resolve of President Kennedy to give the order to bomb the Soviets, did what was supposedly impossible: They jerry-rigged their Minutemen missiles so they could launch them on their own.
>
> After the crisis, the Air Force investigated the jerry-rigging. It then altered the evidence to prevent higher authorities from learning that officers at Malmstrom had given themselves the ability to launch missiles. (Sagan 1994)

The Significance of Symbolic Interaction

This hair-raising event demonstrates the significance of symbolic interaction. To have meaning, all events in life must be interpreted. If a missile were launched, or a city destroyed, as could happen with a computer malfunction or an unauthorized launch, this question would have to be answered: Is this an accident, an unauthorized attack by a madman, or the opening of an orchestrated attack? On that interpretation hangs the fate of the world.

Fortunately, the United States and Russia have agreed to notify the other if either spots a missile—and to help each other track and destroy it (Greenberger

1992). Their intention is to protect one another against missile attacks by third nations, but such cooperation also helps prevent accidental nuclear war.

The proliferation of nuclear weapons, however, has expanded the possibility of accidental war. India and Pakistan, two neighbors with a history of warfare and continued unresolved territorial disputes, joined the nuclear club some years ago. Each hates and fears the other, and each sees the other's possession of nuclear weapons as a direct threat to its own existence. Although they know that their weapons can destroy each other, India and Pakistan continue to hurl threats across the thin line that separates them.

BIOLOGICAL AND CHEMICAL WARFARE

The Origin of This Type of Warfare

It sometimes is difficult to fathom the human mind. One of the strangest quirks in human thinking is this: To kill by bullets and bombs is considered normal. To kill by gas is considered abnormal. During World War I, the French and Germans shocked the world by using poison gas, and, after the war, in 1925, the major powers met in Geneva, where they signed an agreement banning the use of poison gases in warfare. In 1972, they agreed not to use biological weapons (Seib 1981). In 1989, 145 nations met to try to ban chemical weapons (Revzin 1989). They failed.

The Use of These Weapons

A few nations have used biological and chemical weapons. In the 1980s, Iran and Iraq used mustard gas on each other. In the 1960s and 1970s, the United States rained chemical defoliants on the jungles of Vietnam. These chemicals were intended to destroy crops and clear terrain. Spraying stopped when Vietnamese women began giving birth to deformed babies, such as the children shown in the photo on the next page.

Agent Orange

After the war, thousands of U.S. Vietnam veterans claimed that Agent Orange had damaged their health. The Veterans Administration (VA) insisted that the defoliant was not the cause of the "cancer, birth defects in their children, miscarriages by their wives, impotency, respiratory problems, and liver, skin, nerve, and emotional disorders" (Feinsilber 1981). The VA claimed that Agent Orange caused only a "severe skin rash." When the Department of Health and Human Services investigated the matter, it found that the United States had dropped 12 million gallons of Agent Orange on Vietnam. In 41 emergency situations, Agent Orange was dumped "directly over or near U.S. air bases and other military installations." In 1989, each soldier who had sued the government was awarded about $12,000.

Afghanistan and Laos

The Soviets may have used chemicals in Afghanistan and Laos, not against plants but against people (Douglass 1998). Here is one account:

> The biplane came out of a clear sky at 9:30 one morning. It made a single run over the Laotian village of Va Houng, unleashing a stream of yellow gas that fell like rain along a one-kilometer strip and formed droplets on the ground. To the villagers, it smelled like burning peppers.
>
> According to Gnia Pao Vang, a subdistrict chief in Vientiane Province, the gas killed 83 of the 473 residents of Va Houng, as well as all village animals.
>
> The people died in pain, usually after two or three days of intense diarrhea and vomiting. Like other survivors, Mr. Gnia suffered for weeks from headaches and dizziness, impaired vision, a runny nose, painful breathing and a swollen throat. For days he spit phlegm and blood. (Wain 1981)

The former Soviet Union denies the allegations.

It seems well documented that Saddam Hussein used poison gas against the Kurds. Hussein denies the charge.

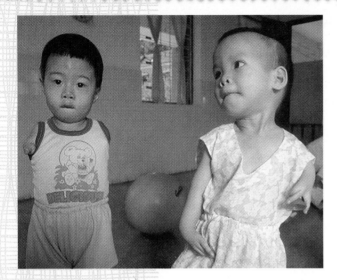

The human costs of war far outnumber the soldiers who are killed and maimed. Shown here are two victims of Agent Orange, a defoliant used by U.S. troops in Vietnam to clear the forests and disrupt the movement of troops and supplies from the north. Birth defects, especially the absence of vital organs (brains, eyes, kidneys, and so on) were a major factor in terminating the massive use of chemical defoliants during this war.

The justification for producing the most powerful biological and chemical weapons was the same that the West and the Soviet Union gave for producing nuclear weapons. The Pentagon would tell Congress: "The Soviet Union has achieved a dangerous advantage over the United States." Congress would then fund a new program to "catch up." At one point, the Pentagon reported that we were behind in **binary chemical weapons.** These are shells or bombs in which two benign chemicals are kept in separate chambers. When the weapon is detonated, the chemicals mix, releasing a lethal agent. We caught up, of course. And, of course, the Soviet Union then had to rush to catch up, producing even more destructive agents. This, in turn, forced us to move into even higher gear—and so the weapons race has been given push after push.

The research for even worse weapons continues. Because the Pentagon does not have money of its own, it has to go to Congress to finance its weapons. In true Orwellian fashion, the Pentagon once told Congress that chemical weapons could help bring about peace. If we can develop more powerful chemical weapons, they said, this might force the Soviets to agree to "a complete and verifiable ban on the development, production, and stockpiling of chemical weapons by dangling the threat of retaliation over the heads of the Soviets" (*Wall Street Journal,* February 9, 1982). Apparently, the irony of producing chemical weapons in order to stop the production of chemical weapons was lost on Congress, the Pentagon, and the Politburo.

Although the Cold War has ended, the United States and Russia have not destroyed their stockpiles of biological weapons. They have also continued their mad research to develop even more lethal agents. Russia has announced that it has genetically engineered a new anthrax microbe that attacks blood cells. Current vaccines are useless against it (Broad and Miller 1998). A defector reported that Russia has ICBMs with warheads loaded with plague, anthrax, and smallpox intended for delivery against U.S. cities (Douglass 1998). One can assume that the United States is doing the same—its missiles pointed the other way, of course. With Russia now a part of NATO, we would hope that this race toward biological destruction will stop. It is likely, however, that the ICBM warheads will merely be directed toward other targets.

A major danger is that terrorists will get their hands on some of these weapons. Let's consider this possibility.

POLITICAL TERRORISM

Terrorism is today's nightmare. Hostages and kidnappings used to be the main worries, but with 9-11 the world changed. Americans are concerned that terrorists lurk unsuspectingly around the corner, that they will again turn some routine item into a weapon of destruction. Nuclear plants may become atomic bombs, and stadiums filled with spectators may be blown up. Boarding a plane used to be a simple matter, but no longer. Armed security scrutinize our baggage and person, while screening devices do the same. Billions of dollars have been spent to fortify our embassies around the world, and yet they remain subject to attack.

Political terrorism is similar to warfare. Although it is not war between nations, **political terrorism** is the use of the means of war—intimidation, coercion, threats

Three Types of Political Terrorism:

Chapter 15 War, Terrorism, and the Balance of Power

of harm, and violence—to achieve political objectives (Boston et al. 1977). Political terrorists use violence to sow fear. They do not recognize civilians as "noncombatants." On the contrary, they often target civilians because they are easier to reach, and the apparent randomness of the attack creates fear. The three types of political terrorism are revolutionary, repressive, and state-sponsored. Let's look at each.

1. Revolutionary Terrorism

In **revolutionary terrorism,** enemies of the state use terrorism to try to overthrow the political system. Walter Laqueur (1977), a political scientist, found these background factors in revolutionary terrorism:

1. Existence of a self-conscious, segregated, ethnic, cultural, or religious minority
2. Perceptions of being deprived or oppressed
3. Unemployment or inflation
4. External encouragement (often from an ethnic, cultural, or religious counterpart living elsewhere)
5. An historical "them" (a group they blame for their oppressed condition)
6. Frustrated elites who provide leadership and justify ideological violence

The Goals of Revolutionary Terrorism

The first act of terrorism doesn't appear in a vacuum. The group (whichever it is) has usually tried legal channels to change its situation. It has found the government unresponsive. Turning to revolutionary terrorism, the group chooses targets designed to

1. Publicize the group and its grievances.
2. Demonstrate the government's vulnerability.
3. Force political and social change.

Because publicity is often a key objective of a terrorist act, terrorism is sometimes called "political theater." As political scientist Brian Jenkins (1987) put it: "Terrorists want a lot of people watching, not a lot of people dead." Consequently, terrorists choose targets that will attract the media. Of course, it sometimes takes a lot of dead people to attract the media and their audiences.

Communist terrorists have a fourth purpose. They believe that the masses are deluded by "false consciousness" and don't see that they are oppressed. What Trotsky called the "theater of terrorism" is designed to provoke the capitalist rulers to overreact. The harshness and brutality of their reaction will then expose the repressive system and arouse the masses (Rubenstein 1987).

Why Revolutionary Terrorism and Not Guerrilla Warfare?

Revolutionary terrorism occurs mostly in the industrialized nations because old-fashioned guerrilla warfare is not possible in them. The industrialized countries lack the inaccessible rural areas and disaffected peasant populations on which revolutionaries depend for support. Urban guerrillas choose terrorism as their alternative, making the city their base of operations (Sterling 1981).

For Americans, the most shocking act of terrorism of the 1990s occurred in Oklahoma City in 1995 when a truck bomb destroyed a federal building. The deaths of almost 200 unsuspecting people, including 19 children in a daycare center, destroyed the innocence of Americans. Up to that time, they assumed that terrorism only happened "over there."

Then, as recounted in this chapter's opening vignette, an even more shocking act of terrorism on U.S. soil was the destruction of the World Trade Center in New York City on September 11, 2001. This attack, accompanied by the simultaneous

Convictions of Moral Superiority Underlie Revolutionary Terrorism

2. Repressive Terrorism

Shown here is the Pentagon after the attack on September 11, 2001. War and terrorism take many forms. The availability of powerful bombs along with men and women who are willing to die for "the cause" have turned former sanctuaries into dangerous places.

attack on the Pentagon in Washington, caused several thousand deaths. These two targets were not random choices. The leaders of al–Qaida chose the World Trade Center because it symbolized the dominance of U.S. capitalism around the globe. They chose the Pentagon because it is a symbol of the U.S. military. To strike at the heart of two major symbols exposed the vulnerability of the United States. It struck fear in Americans, for they knew that nothing was safe.

The attack of 9/11 also served as theater, in precisely the way that analysts had indicated. The timing—a Tuesday morning—meant that a huge audience would gather immediately. The act went beyond the terrorists' dream, of course, for none could have anticipated the dramatic collapse of the Twin Towers. Yet they did collapse, and, in even more dramatic fashion, took with them several hundred fire fighters. The message could not have been clearer, nor an audience so large as quickly summoned.

While the terrorists' acts of bloodshed are immoral to outsiders and victims, to their perpetrators they are righteous acts. Using a neutralization technique we reviewed in Chapter 6, terrorists appeal to a higher morality to justify their acts. While their actions are criminal, terrorists are convinced of their moral superiority. As they see it, their "cause" justifies any act.

It is this conviction—that the cause (seeming so righteous) justifies any act (no matter how heinous)—that makes revolutionary terrorists such formidable opponents of the established order. Some revolutionaries become as dedicated to "the cause" as any monk to his god. Listen to Karari Mjama, a Mau Mau insurgent:

> No one can serve two masters. In order to become a strong faithful warrior who would persevere to the last minute, one had to renounce all worldly wealth, including his family. . . . In fact, I had said to my wife . . . not to expect any sort of help from me for at least ten years' time. I had instructed her to take care of herself and our beloved daughter. I had trained myself to think of the fight, and the African Government; and nothing of the country's progress before independence. I had learned to forget all pleasures and imagination of the past. I confined my thoughts (to) the fight only—the end of which would open my thoughts to the normal world. (Schreiber 1978:32)

As with 9/11, terrorists often strike without warning. Japan had prided itself on being a "community nation" that was insulated from the "profane" social problems of the West. Its soothing, self-serving myth was shattered by a renegade religious leader who launched a poison gas attack on Tokyo subways. Twelve people died, and 5,000 were injured (Miller and Broad 1999). The gas, sarin, can be manufactured from chemicals used in pesticides that you can buy at your local hardware store. Other frightening recipes for poisons have turned up on the Internet—a sort of Betty Crocker cookbook on how to poison the world (Greenberger and Bishop 1995).

Repressive terrorism, a second type, is terrorism waged by a government against its own citizens. For example:

Diana, a dedicated Christian, worked among the poor in Buenos Aires. One midnight, soldiers broke down her door, rushed in, and knocked her to the floor. They blindfolded her and beat her across the head. They then threw her into a car and drove to a building with an underground chamber. Here she was threatened, tortured, and interrogated for six straight hours about church leaders, the Vatican Council, and the Jews.

Beaten beyond all tears, she suddenly blurted, "Good God, aren't you Christians?"

Abrupt silence followed. One of the soldiers grabbed her hand and pressed her fingers to a metal cross on his chest. Afterward, they seemed to give up on her. "I'm convinced that small incident saved my life," she says. "The man apparently wanted to be recognized as a person rather than a torturer. He couldn't have that recognition without making me a person, too, rather than an object to be disposed of."

Diana was later taken back to her apartment and held there for two more days by four officers who took turns raping her. The police then released her. (Cornell 1981)

The Case of Argentina

The reason for the massive brutality and killing in Argentina was typical of repressive terrorism: The government felt weak and vulnerable, unable to respond to social change. Fearful of its own collapse, it became afraid of ideas. Like Diana, thousands of Argentines were arrested, tortured, and executed. Some bodies were dumped in public places, a mute warning to others. Most, however, were burned in secret places, with tens of thousands of relatives never knowing what happened to their child or parent.

The Case of Cambodia

Pol Pot, the dictator of Cambodia, directed perhaps the most ruinous terrorism that any government has ever inflicted on its people (Markusen 1995). The extent of his regime's devastation is mind boggling. For almost four years, from April 1975 to January 1979, Cambodia was Pol Pot's slaughterhouse. On an average day, 1,500 Cambodians died. In just forty-five months, the government killed about 2 million Cambodians (Wain 1981). Death often came by rubber hoses and bamboo sticks. Some victims were chained to beds, and then lowered upside down into vats of water. *All* intellectuals were marked for death, for they represented an elite, and the Pol Pot government was supposedly ushering in a classless society (Miles 1980). Being able to speak a foreign language was enough to merit execution. In one area of Cambodia, members of the ruling group, the Khmer Rouge, could count only to 10. Anyone who could count higher was an "intellectual." To ferret them out, the Khmer Rouge would have someone count other people—they executed those who counted to 20, instead of counting two groups of 10. Only 50 of Cambodia's 800 doctors survived.

The Case of the Soviet Union

To dictators, who hold power uneasily and have few checks on their behavior, repressive terrorism is attractive. It allows them to silence criticism and suppress ideas they don't like. Soviet officials were sensitive to criticism of any sort, and they even persecuted poets who expressed "incorrect" political thought. They also felt threatened by religion, and party leaders referred to the Church as "the enemy within" (Ra'anan et al. 1986). Andrei Sakharov (1977), a dissenter who drew attention to "the persecution of Baptists, of the True Orthodox church, of Pentecostals, and uniates, and others" said:

It is a common practice of the Russian government to take children away from parents who are evangelical; that is, they believe that Jesus of Nazareth is God incarnate or the Savior who should be placed ahead of the State. Pastors of underground churches are regularly arrested, beaten, tortured, and killed.

3. State-Sponsored Terrorism

In the third type of terrorism, **state-sponsored,** a government finances, trains, and arms terrorists. Colonel Moammar Gadhafi of Libya sees terrorism as a legitimate extension of the state. He has bankrolled terrorist groups and provided training camps for them. And he nurses a strong grudge because the U.S. Air Force tried to kill him by bombing his palace (Seib and Greenberger 1992). Osama bin Laden, the terrorist most wanted by the U.S. government, declared war on the United States. He has sworn to kill U.S. civilians no matter where they are. Bin Laden operated under the protection of the Taliban government of Afghanistan, which harbored hatred for the United States (Richter 1999). Bin Laden's safe haven was disrupted when the United States attacked Afghanistan in retaliation for 9-11 and destroyed the Taliban government.

Criminal Terrorism

In addition to political terrorism, there is **criminal terrorism.** The most widely known example today of criminals using terrorism to attain their objectives is the Russian Mafia. To maintain their control, these gangsters intimidate and kill anyone who opposes them. They terrorize both the public and government into submission. The Russian Mafia guns down bankers who won't launder money for them, and, as the executions of reporters, prosecutors, and judges attest, quick death is likely for anyone who dares investigate them.

Narco-Terrorism

Narco-terrorism is criminal terrorism that centers on drugs. Some narco-terrorists have political goals, and drug dealing is simply a way to earn money to reach them. Mehemet Ali Agca, for example, sold drugs in order to finance his attempted assassination of Pope John Paul II (Oakley 1985; Ehrenfeld 1990). For other narco-terrorists, the primary objective is to make money; they use terrorism to protect their drug operations. In Colombia, international drug dealers hired thugs to assassinate the justices of the Colombian supreme court. They also terrorized the Colombian government to cancel its extradition treaty with the United States.

A development in narco-terrorism that worries officials is the uniting of the sophisticated Russian Mafia with the Colombian drug cartel (Farah 1997). The Russian Mafia, with former KGB (Russian secret police) agents and members with Ph.D.s, has opened banks in the Caribbean to launder Colombian drug money. It also has sold the Colombian drug cartel sophisticated weapons—AK-47 assault rifles, rocket-propelled grenades, helicopters, and surface-to-air missiles.

Nuclear and Biological Terrorism

Nuclear and *biological terrorism* are in a class by themselves. Let's look at each.

Because plutonium can be used to manufacture nuclear weapons, you would think it would be guarded extremely carefully. This will sound as though I am making it up, but about 5,000 pounds—two and a half tons—of plutonium are missing from U.S. nuclear facilities. A former security agent reported that protective measures at the Rocky Flats weapons factory near Denver were so lax that it was "like having a window in a bank vault" (Hosenball 1999). When the missing plutonium was made public, officials took a cavalier attitude. "What's to worry?" they asked. After all, the plutonium "probably got stuck in pipes and manufacturing tools." The solution? Simple. They suspended the individual who had complained about the missing plutonium.

In light of 9-11, such a cavalier attitude can be taken as a sign of gross incompetence, one that can lead to the destruction of tens of thousands of lives.

The danger of nuclear terrorism has grown worse since the breakup of the Soviet empire. Seeing its opportunity, the "Russian Mafia" stepped into the void of legitimate power. With apparently no morality to hold their desires in check, these gangsters stole plutonium and uranium and offered them for sale to Iraq and other dictatorships ("The Wild Wild East" 1995). The United States is helping to make Russia's nuclear material more secure, but problems abound in keeping it out of the hands of terrorists. The Soviet Union produced 1,300 tons of enriched uranium and 220 tons of plutonium, which are scattered throughout the former Soviet Union at 40 to 50 locations (Gordon 1996).

This terrorist threat is amplified by Russia's dire economic situation. Conditions have deteriorated to the point that guards at some nuclear facilities have abandoned their posts to forage for food (Gordon 1998a). Many of Russia's nuclear scientists are unemployed, while others work for wages paid to common laborers—and even these go unpaid for months at a time. Both U.S. and Russian leaders fear that tempting offers from Iraq or some other state may lead some nuclear scientists to defect. To prevent this, the United States has sent Russia money to pay these scientists, to retrain them in business ventures, and to turn nuclear production facilities into factories to manufacture automobiles and other consumer items.

One nightmare facing the West is that a dictatorship will develop nuclear-tipped missiles, and, unrestrained by the checks and balances built into democracies, terrorize an entire region—and, with advanced delivery systems, perhaps the world. One scenario is that North Korea, an iron-fisted dictatorship whose rulers have proved willing to sacrifice millions of their people to starvation, will blackmail the West by threatening to destroy Seoul and Tokyo (Ricks 1999). Another scenario is that Iraq will develop nuclear weapons and Saddam Hussein, regardless of the consequences for Iraq, will bomb Israel. China, by stealing nuclear secrets from an incredibly insecure Los Alamos, has been able to miniaturize its nuclear warheads and develop precise guidance systems. It now is able to threaten the world's nations, including the United States and the countries of Europe (Risen and Gerth 1999). At the moment, the nuclear weapons picture is as grim, if not grimmer, as it was during the Cold War.

Pictured here is Osama bin Laden, the man most feared, hated, and hunted by U.S. authorities. Even before he masterminded 9/11, Bin Laden had financed other attacks against the United States, such as the bombing of the U.S. embassies in Nairobi and Dar Al Salam. Bin Laden wants to reclaim Arab grandeur and power and drive the United States and other Western nations from the Mideast.

The nightmare grows. Because the potential destruction is so huge, nuclear terrorists could hold the U.S. government captive. Without even possessing advanced delivery systems, terrorists could smuggle nuclear weapons into the country. With miniaturization of nuclear weapons, this is not unimaginable. What would U.S. officials do if terrorists threatened to detonate a nuclear weapon in the heart of New York City? The thought of nuclear weapons in the hands of Moammar Gadhafi, Saddam Hussein, or the likes of Slobodan Milosevic sends chills down the back of the industrialized nations.

Biological terrorism presents perhaps an even greater threat. Biological weapons such as anthrax, smallpox, and the plague are cheaper to produce, their components are easier to come by, and they can be transported in tiny containers. Terrorists could infiltrate the United States or any other country and simultaneously release anthrax or other killer germs in several cities. If this occurs in the United States, a large proportion of Americans could die. As I write this, the perpetrator of the anthrax scare through the U.S. mail remains unknown. That this anthrax attack occurred so soon after 9/11 has made some suspect Al Queda and Osama bin Laden. Eventually, the fingerprint

TECHNOLOGY AND SOCIAL PROBLEMS

Our Future:
Biological Terrorism in the Twenty-First Century

Consider this scenario:

Over a period of years, agents of a nation whose leader hates the United States and has a score to settle quietly infiltrate the United States. Most gain admission as students at universities around the country. All have been highly trained by their country's secret police. On a predetermined day, at a specified hour, they release anthrax and smallpox into the air of twenty major cities. Within days, a third of Americans are dead.

This scenario haunts U.S. officials. No safeguards exist to protect against it, and some think such an attack has already been planned and may soon be carried out. There will be no warning, no attempt to hold the United States hostage in order to extort billions of dollars. Money is not the goal. The motive is revenge for humiliation suffered at U.S. hands. The goal will be no less than to wipe out the United States itself.

The secret agents know that they will sacrifice their lives, for they, too, will be infected by the diseases they release. But they have been assured that they will obtain immediate entry into heaven, for they will become martyrs for a holy cause. Just in case that promise is insufficient motivation, they've been assured that their families will be tortured and killed if they change their minds.

U.S. officials are scared. They fear that such a scenario is not theoretical. The White House conducted a secret exercise to play out what would happen if terrorists struck with genetically modified germs. The president and other officials were alarmed at the results (Broad and Miller 1998). How seriously officials are taking this threat is indicated by the federal budget: Over $1 billion has been earmarked for civil defense in the event of such an attack (Richter 1999). Officials have begun to stockpile vaccines around the country (Broad and Miller 1998), and emergency medical teams are being trained in major cities. All 2.4 million military personnel, including National Guard and reserve units, are being vaccinated against anthrax. All military personnel who refuse to be vaccinated are punished and discharged (Myers 1999).

The president and his cabinet have held secret meetings, and the president has issued secret directives. Top officials have developed plans, not to evacuate populations, but to block roads and stop people at gunpoint from fleeing cities and spreading the disease. The president wants Congress to approve a military takeover of state and local governments to fight the chaos that would result from such an attack (Miller and Broad 1999). Reading between the lines, it is certain that the secret directives include Pentagon control of the continental United States.

An ancient Chinese proverb says: "May you live in exciting times." This simple saying is actually a curse, for it expresses the hope that an enemy's life will be made chaotic. We live in exciting times. Let's hope that the curse with which we live—nuclear weapons, hatreds engendered by foreign domination, and retaliatory action by terrorists—does not mean our destruction.

of the anthrax should reveal the laboratory in which it was produced, and, from there, telltale clues should point to the killer.

As the Technology box above discusses, biological terrorism remains a very real threat.

◆ Social Policy ◆

Let's look at social policies on the two major problems we have reviewed in this chapter, nuclear war and political terrorism.

POLITICAL TERRORISM

The Need to Avoid Encouraging Terrorists

The first principle for dealing with terrorists is to not give in to their demands. As one analyst said, "You cannot permit terrorism to become a profitable tactic unless you want more of it" (Bremer 1988). To give in to terrorism is to encourage terrorists.

Legal and government experts suggest the following as effective social policies (Oakley 1985; Bush 1986; Bremer 1988; Clawson 1988; Ehrenfeld 1990; FBI 1998):

Eight Promising Policies

1. Promise anything during negotiations. Promises made under threat are not valid.

2. Make no distinction between terrorists and their state sponsors. States that sponsor terrorists are not neutral and should not be treated as neutrals. This principle allows both retaliatory and preemptive acts.

3. Use economic and political sanctions to break the connection between terrorists and the states that provide them weapons, financing, safe houses, training areas, and identity documents in return for terrorism done on their behalf.

4. Treat terrorists as war criminals. Track them, arrest them, and punish them. Bomb them, if that is what it takes. Make certain customs agents watch for known terrorists.

5. Discourage media coverage because publicity is a prime terrorist goal. It should be illegal for the media to pay terrorists for interviews.

6. Establish an international extradition or prosecution agreement: If terrorists are caught anywhere, they would be extradited or tried.

7. Develop an international organization solely to combat terrorism. Such a group would coordinate worldwide intelligence and advise nations. It would also direct international teams to respond to specific events—such as freeing hostages or locating evidence that pinpoints the sponsoring group.

8. Offer large rewards for information leading to the disabling of known terrorists. Just as in the old West, rewards can be paid on a "dead-or-alive" basis. With rewards of $50,000, or $1 million, or $5 million, terrorists will never know if associates can be trusted. Informants should also be offered new identities.

NUCLEAR WARFARE AND THE ELUSIVE PATH TO PEACE

The Strange Path to Peace

The primary policy that the United States and the former Soviet Union pursued after World War II was **mutual deterrence**—using threats and the fear of mutual destruction to prevent the other from striking first. Each was afraid to use its nuclear arsenal, because each had developed doomsday safeguards—that is, if a country were attacked and destroyed, even out of the ashes missiles would be launched that would destroy the other. Since neither country would survive, there was no benefit to attacking the other. The resulting balance of power was called Mutual Assured Destruction (MAD).

MAD

The path to peace, then, has been a strange one. Each superpower armed itself to the teeth, stockpiled nuclear, chemical, and biological weapons, and signaled to its counterpart that it would unleash those weapons if necessary. Thus the superpowers struck a balance of power—or terror—that kept them from attacking each other. Sociologist Nicholas Timasheff (1965:291) explained how it worked:

Each party may consider that it has a fair chance to win, but each party also knows that the cost of victory would be prohibitive; physical destruction of 90–95 percent of the total population, almost complete destruction of industrial equipment, transformation of almost the total territory into an uninhabitable area because of radiation, contamination of air, water, plants and animals and other natural resources. Under these circumstances victory can be worse than the most crucial defeat before this atomic age. Each of the parties to the possible conflict has full reason to refrain from attack.

G7 and the Precarious Balance of World Domination

1. Spreading Nuclear Capacity

G7, the world's seven most powerful industrialized nations, is working out a new balance of power—sometimes called the New World Order. The balance, however, is precarious. Of its many sources of disequilibrium, perhaps the most disturbing is the proliferation of nuclear weapons. Poor nations may not be able to make it to G7's bargaining table, but if they join the nuclear club, G7 will listen to them. With many poor nations now possessing or building nuclear weapons, the nuclear balance of power is precarious. India has developed a missile system that can be fired from mobile launchers. India's missiles can not only hit any target in Pakistan, its neighboring enemy, but also they can reach Beijing and Shanghai (Bearak 1999a). A nuclear arms race is apparently being set off in this region. Look at the Social Map on pages 528–529.

2. Spreading Conflicts

Even local conflicts can upset G7's balance of power. If a local conflict heats up, other nations may become involved. This is one reason that NATO (North Atlantic Treaty Organization) was so quick to take action against Serbia. Bombs speak louder than words, as Milosevic discovered. If a minor, hostile power even comes close to possessing nuclear weapons, as in the case of Hussein's Iraq, G7 will bomb now and ask questions later.

3. Gross Incompetence

Our current balance of power is more fragile than most of us realize. It could even be upset by incompetence at a low level. Consider this event from the 1970s:

> For nearly four years the public library of the Los Alamos Scientific Laboratory in New Mexico had on its shelves a report that provided precise details of the devices that trigger hydrogen bombs (Mintz 1979). Only a few pages of the report

Six weeks after terrorist attacks, President Bush signs the anti-terrorism bill into law during a ceremony in the White House East Room. The law gives police unprecedented authority to secretly search people's homes and business records and to eavesdrop on telephone and computer conversations. The government says it will begin using the new powers immediately.

were supposed to have been declassified, but through a "clerical error" the entire report was made available to the public, both Americans and foreigners, for inspection and copying. A nuclear expert, Dimitri Rotow, who copied this report, was quoted as saying: "It was easier than getting something out of the Library of Congress. At the Library of Congress, they at least check your briefcase" (AP May 25, 1979).

Three Potential Policies: 1. Disarmament

Policies that could help ensure peace include disarmament, interlocking networks of mutual interests, and international law. Let's look at each.

Proponents of disarmament are of two major types. Some propose **bilateral disarmament;** that is, both sides agree to disarm simultaneously. Others favor **unilateral disarmament:** One nation would announce its intention to disarm, and begin to dismantle some weapons system. When its antagonist sees that it has made itself more vulnerable, it supposedly would begin to disarm, too. Just as each step of armament led to the escalation and proliferation of weapons systems, so each step of disarmament would reduce and ultimately eliminate that stockpile.

Another group argues that only a strong military and the will to use it can make a nation secure. Those who favor this position oppose disarmament. While full military preparedness may indeed prevent war (Kagan 1995), extremists carry this argument to logical absurdities. They argue that the nuclear powers should help other nations build nuclear weapons (Sagan 1994). Since nuclear weapons kept the superpowers from attacking one another, they will also restrain smaller nations. The more the merrier!

Russia and the United States have signed treaties to reduce their stockpiles of nuclear weapons. This is not disarmament, however, as neither intends to rid itself of nuclear weapons, just to reduce the number it possesses. The huge cost of maintaining these weapons, however, has led some of the top military to favor unilateral reduction. Maintaining them is taking money from other projects the military favors (Myers 1998).

2. Interlocking Networks of Mutual Interests

Some feel that the key to peace is to develop interlocking networks of mutual interest. It is thought that the more a nation depends on another for its own well-being, the less likely it will be to destroy that nation. The principle is sound, but the route to such dependence may come as a surprise, for it involves global capitalism. The expansion of capitalism has produced a **global economy,** one that links the world's nations to one another. As a nation's trading partners increase, its affairs become more linked to those nations. To develop further interlocking interests, then, we should encourage trade among the world's nations. To stimulate peace, we also would encourage communication, including travel and scientific and cultural exchanges.

3. International Law

International law is essential for world peace. If each nation is a law unto itself and feels free to wage war when its goals are frustrated, we can never have peace. The major obstacle to implementing international law is the unwillingness of nations to yield sovereignty to an international organization. The rule of law, as represented by the United Nations, was dealt a severe blow when NATO bombed Kosovo. Despite the official reason given for the bombing, with which most of us can agree—to prevent further ethnic slaughter—NATO placed itself above international law by attacking without the approval of the United Nations. It has been dealt a further blow by the refusal of the United States to submit to the World Court of the United Nations. Officials of the United States fear that they could be charged with war crimes. This is not so far-fetched, for "one person's freedom fighter is another person's terrorist."

The Mutual Benefit of Survival

In the end, perhaps the desire for self-preservation is what will prevent the nuclear annihilation of humanity. Leaders don't want themselves, their families, or their own country destroyed by warfare. Unfortunately, there are exceptions—madmen who want to dominate the world and, failing to do so, want to destroy it. As Albert Speer (1970), one of Hitler's close associates, noted, Hitler held onto the illusion of victory until the end. When he saw that the war was lost, he blamed failure on a lack of will on the part of the Germans, and he wanted to destroy his country. If Hitler had had nuclear bombs, the history of the world may have been written with a different hand.

The Need to Focus on This Problem

Most of us ignore the proliferation of nuclear weapons and the threat of nuclear war. We have enough concerns in our daily lives without trying to shoulder problems of world peace. Besides, this problem is scary, and we would rather think about pleasant things. Yet, I suggest that because the survival of humanity hangs in the balance, we need to think about it—and to do what we can to halt nuclear and biological destruction and proliferation. If we don't, who will?

◆ The Future of the Problem ◆

More Wars

The International Arms Trade

There is no sign whatsoever that war will disappear. On the contrary, indications are that it will continue indefinitely. Look at Table 15-4, which lists the top merchants of death. The United States takes an easy lead, selling five times as many weapons as its nearest competitor. With borders in jeopardy, and dictators needing to prop up their sagging regimes, there is no end to eager buyers. Where profit comes in, for some, morality goes out. With greed being what it is, it is unlikely that this profitable merchandising in death will diminish—regardless of the destruction of human life that ensues.

As Table 15-4 also shows, poor nations pay huge amounts for arms. Some purchasers, such as Egypt and Malaysia, are dirt poor. They are using money that they need to feed, house, and educate their people.

More Political Terrorism

Ethnic Antagonisms Unleashed

What about political terrorism? Indications are that it will increase. The unshackling of the central dictatorship in the former Soviet Union unleashed ethnic antagonisms that are rooted in centuries of animosity and that had been bottled up for decades. Groups that we had never heard of are at each other's throats. In the former Yugoslavia, for example, Serbs, Croats, Muslims, and Albanians tried to eliminate each other. Today,

After the September 11, 2001 attacks on New York City and Washington, D.C., a new form of environmental terrorism affected many parts of the country. Anthrax poisoning was spread via packages sent through the U.S. mail. In their continuing testing for anthrax contamination, these hazardous materials workers are preparing to enter a mail facility in Washington, D.C.

Table 15-4　The Global Arms Trade: Buying and Selling the Weapons of Death

The Top Exporters	Amount Sold
1. United States	$31,800,000,000
2. United Kingdom	$6,600,000,000
3. France	$5,900,000,000
4. Russia	$2,300,000,000
5. China: Mainland	$1,100,000,000
6. Sweden	$900,000,000

The Top Importers: The Most Industrialized Nations	Amount Purchased
1. China, Taiwan	$9,200,000,000
2. Japan	$2,600,000,000
3. United Kingdom	$2,100,000,000
4. United States	$1,600,000,000
5. Israel	$1,100,000,000
6. Australia	$925,000,000
7. Germany	$750,000,000
8. Netherlands	$460,000,000
9. Spain	$430,000,000
10. Italy	$430,000,000

The Top Importers: The Industrializing and Least Industrialized Nations	Amount Purchased
1. Saudi Arabia	$11,600,000,000
2. Kuwait	$2,000,000,000
3. Turkey	$1,600,000,000
4. Egypt	$1,600,000,000
5. United Arab Emirates	$1,400,000,000
6. Korea, South	$1,100,000,000
7. Thailand	$950,000,000
8. Greece	$850,000,000
9. Iran	$850,000,000
10. Malaysia	$725,000,000

Source: Statistical Abstract of the United States 2001:Table 496.

More Revolutionary Terrorism

groups in India and Pakistan fight one another—both killing and dying over the same sliver of disputed land.

Revolutionary terrorists, such as those who bombed the World Trade Center in New York in 2001, will acquire more sophisticated weapons. Available on the black market are shoulder-fired, precision-guided surface-to-air missiles that can bring down jumbo jets. Terrorists will even acquire systems that can target cars in a motorcade several miles away, and few political leaders will be safe (Jenkins 1985). That we will face nuclear and biological weapons is also likely. With advances in genetic engineering, the potential of biological weapons that could launch global plagues haunts humanity.

The Wild Card: Russia

Despite democratic crosscurrents, repressive terrorism will continue, particularly in China and Central and South America. Government repression, in turn, will stimulate resistance groups—and the bloody struggles will continue.

Russia holds fascinating prospects. After seven decades of persecution, its people have gained freedom of speech, press, politics, education, religion, and the arts. Increased trade and cultural exchanges with the West have reduced suspicions and hostilities on both sides. The acceptance of Russia into NATO, albeit as a junior partner at first, also allows us to visualize a better future. Nothing about Russia is certain, however. Its leaders may slap their repressive hats firmly on their heads. The arduous experiment with democracy may prove too threatening—inflation, poverty, the Russian Mafia, and open criticism and even defiance of leaders. On one side are the hard-liners, straining to seize power and make repression state policy. They are restrained only with difficulty. On the other side is the potential for anarchy. If the government fails to regain control, and to legitimate its authority, the state may dissolve. With an arsenal of nuclear weapons hanging in the balance, either hardliners or anarchy threatens world peace.

◆ Summary

1. Three essential conditions of war are a cultural tradition for *war,* an antagonistic situation, and a "fuel" that sets off the war. War is common in history, but today's wars are much more destructive.

2. Symbolic interactionists analyze how symbols (meanings) underlie war. The West and the Soviets saw each other as mortal enemies arming for deadly combat. Each felt obliged to arm itself, setting off a nuclear arms race. Nuclear weapons are intended not to be used, but to symbolize a country's capacity to destroy an enemy.

3. Functionalists identify these functions of war: the extension of political boundaries, social integration, economic gain, social change, ideology, vengeance, military security, and credibility. The dysfunctions of war are defeat, dependence, and destruction.

4. Conflict theorists identify four causes of war: competition for resources, a conflict of interests, a surplus of capital, and the dominance of a military machine.

5. Humans are no more peaceful today than in earlier times. The following do *not* diminish the chances of warfare: the type of government, the dominant religion, prosperity, a common language, shared political boundaries, or level of education.

6. Modern weapons are expensive, and come at the cost of alternative benefits. A major cost of war is *dehumanization.*

7. Both the military and business gain from producing, selling, and using weapons. The *military-industrial complex* is a powerful force in promoting war.

8. One of the more serious threats facing humanity is biological and chemical warfare. Unless international agreements and effective controls are put into place, these weapons will proliferate, one day leading to vast destruction. Today's nations are vulnerable to these forms of terrorism.

9. *Political terrorism,* that is, the use of war to achieve political objectives, is of three types: *revolutionary terrorism,* waged by individual groups against the state; *repressive terrorism,* waged by the state against its own people; and *state-sponsored terrorism,* waged by one state against another. *Criminal terrorism* cuts across these types.

10. Disarmament, international law, and more interlocking interests among the nations of the world could increase the chances for peace.

11. The future holds more terrorism and war. All-out nuclear war is unlikely because of mutual destruction. Revolutionary terrorism will continue. This, in turn, will stimulate repressive terrorism. The unleashed ethnic antagonisms in the former Soviet Union will lead to more terrorism. The Russian Mafia is likely to be brought under control, but political instabilities may bring hardliners back into power. Control of Russia's nuclear weapons hangs in the balance.

Arms race   The attempt by the West and the Soviets to match one another's war capabilities.

Bilateral disarmament   Two or more nations disarming simultaneously.

Binary chemical weapons   Shells or bombs in which two benign chemicals are kept in separate chambers in the weapon. Upon detonation, they mix, forming a lethal agent.

Cold War   A period of protracted hostilities between the former Soviet Union and nations of the West.

Criminal terrorism   Organized crime using terrorism to achieve its objectives.

Dehumanization   Viewing and treating a person as an object that does not deserve the treatment ordinarily accorded humans.

Global economy   The economic interdependence of the nations of the world such that economic events are no longer isolated but have far-reaching ramifications on many nations.

Imperialism   The pursuit of unlimited geographic expansion.

Megaton   The explosive power of 1 million tons of TNT.

Military-industrial complex   The combined interests of the military and business to produce armaments. The military-industrial complex has become a potent political force in the contemporary world.

Mutual deterrence   Preventing a first strike by making the enemy fear that a massive retaliation would also destroy them.

Narco-terrorism   The combining of drug dealing and terrorism.

Pentagon capitalism   A term coined by Seymour Melman to refer to the influence of the Pentagon's armaments programs on the economy of the United States. Roughly equivalent to the military-industrial complex.

Political terrorism   Using the means of war to try to achieve political objectives. It is of four types: repressive terrorism, revolutionary terrorism, state-sponsored terrorism, and criminal terrorism.

Repressive terrorism   Terrorism directed by a government against its own citizens.

Revolutionary terrorism   Terrorism used in the attempt to bring about change in the political structure.

State-sponsored terrorism   A country supporting terrorism against another nation.

Total war   No-holds-barred warfare.

Unilateral disarmament   One nation disarming itself. When used to refer to a social policy, it generally means one nation taking some dramatic step in disarmament in order to encourage a similar step by the enemy.

War   Violent armed conflict between countries.

◆Critical Thinking Questions

1. Using the three essential conditions of war identified by sociologist Nicholas Timasheff, along with the seven "fuels" that explode into war, analyze three wars that the United States participated in during the twentieth century. In these three examples, what were the fuels?

2. Which of the three perspectives (symbolic interactionism, functionalism, or conflict theory) do you think best explains why countries go to war? Explain.

3. The functions of war are summarized on pages 515–517. Apply these functions to the U.S. war on terrorism. How about the dysfunctions?

4. Do you think that the United States would ever be able to trust the other nuclear countries of the world if a worldwide treaty to destroy all nuclear weapons were signed? How would we be able to protect ourselves if just one country decided to secretly retain their weapons?

5. Do you think it's justified for the United States to intervene in another country to protect our economic or political interests? Under what conditions is intervention justified? Explain.

6. Do you think it is justified for another country to intervene in the United States to protect its economic or political interest? Under what conditions is intervention justified? Explain.

7. Do you agree that nuclear war is more likely now than it was during the Cold War? Explain.

Bibliography

"AA Fact File." 1998. Alcoholics Anonymous. Online.

ACHENBAUM, W. ANDREW, 1978. *Old Age in the New Land: The American Experience Since 1970*. Baltimore: Johns Hopkins University Press.

ACKER, JOAN, 1973. "Women and Social Stratification: A Case of Intellectual Sexism." *American Journal of Sociology, 78,* January, 936–945.

ADLER, STEPHEN J. 1991. "Lawyers Advise Concerns to Provide Precise Written Policy to Employees." *Wall Street Journal,* October 9, B1, B4.

ALDER, CHRISTINE. 1992. "Violence, Gender, and Social Change." *International Social Science Journal, 44,* 132, May, 267–276.

ALIHAN, MILLA A. 1938. *Social Ecology.* New York: Columbia University Press.

ALLEN, BRANDT. 1975. "Embezzler's Guide to the Computer." *Harvard Business Review, 53,* July–August, 79–89.

ALLEN, CHARLOTTE LOW. 1988. "Anti-Abortion Movement's Anti-Establishment Face." *Wall Street Journal,* December 8, A14.

ALLEN, FRANK EDWARD. 1991. "Environment." *Wall Street Journal,* May 28.

ALLEN, MARILYN H. 1991. *New Woman, 21,* 2, February, 112–113.

ALLEN, MIKE. 1998. "New York Begins to Raid and Close Adult Businesses." *New York Times Bulletin,* August 2.

ALLPORT, GORDON. 1954. *The Nature of Prejudice.* Reading, Mass.: Addison-Wesley.

ALTMAN, LAWRENCE K. 1998. "At AIDS Conference, a Call to Arms Against 'Runaway Epidemic.'" *New York Times,* June 29.

ALTMAN, LAWRENCE K. 1992a. "Deadly Strain of Tuberculosis Is Spreading Fast, U.S. Finds." *New York Times,* January 24, A1, A10.

ALTMAN, LAWRENCE K. 1992b. "Drug-Resistant TB Makes U.S. Rethink Elimination Program." *New York Times,* January 28, B6.

American Civil Liberties Union. 1996. "ACLU Says Court Case Exposes America's Dirty Little Secret: The Criminal Justice System is Racially Biased." "Freedom Network." Online. February 26.

American Savings Education Council. 1999. "Personal Savings Rate, 1929–1998. Online.

AMOTT, TERESA, AND JULIE MATTHAEL. 1991. *Race, Gender, and Work: A Multicultural Economic History of Women in the United States.* Boston: South End.

AMSELLE, JORGE. 1995. "HUD's Battle Against English Only." *Wall Street Journal,* August 21, A8.

ANDERSEN, MARGARET L. 1988. *Thinking About Women: Sociological Perspectives on Sex and Gender.* New York: Macmillan.

ANDERSON, ELIJAH. 1978. *A Place on the Corner.* Chicago: University of Chicago Press.

ANDERSON, ELIJAH. 1990. *Streetwise: Race, Class, and Change in an Urban Community.* Chicago: University of Chicago Press.

ANDERSON, ELIJAH. 1995. "Streetwise." In *Down-to-Earth Sociology: Introductory Readings,* 8th ed., James M. Henslin (ed.). New York: Free Press, 168–177.

ANDERSON, JACK. 1980. "Mob's Latest Interest: Dumping Toxic Wastes." Syndicated column, November 15.

ANDERSON, JACK. 1995. "Chicago's Public Housing Official Tries to Thwart Gangs." *Alton Telegraph,* March 24, A6.

ANDERSON, JACK, AND JAN MOLLER. 1998. "Gorton Under Republican Fire for Indian Wars." January.

ANDERSEN, MARGARET L. 1988. *Thinking About Women: Sociological Perspectives on Sex and Gender.* New York: Macmillan.

ANDERSON, NELS. 1923. *The Hobo.* Chicago: University of Chicago Press.

ANDERSON, ROBERT T. 1965. "From Mafia to Cosa Nostra." *American Journal of Sociology, 71,* November, 302–310.

ANDERSON, TERESA A. 1985. "The Best Years of Their Lives." *Newsweek,* January 7, 6.

ANSLINGER, HARRY J., AND COURTNEY RYLEY COOPER. 1937. "Marijuana: Assassin of Youth." *American Magazine,* July.

ARCHER, DANA, AND ROSEMARY GARTNER. 1984. *Violence and Crime in Cross-Cultural Perspective.* New Haven, Conn.: Yale University Press.

ARÍAS, JESÚS. "La Junta rehabilita en Grenada casas que deberá tirar por ruina." *El Pais,* January 2, 1993:1.

ARIES, PHILIPPE. 1962. *Centuries of Childhood: A Social History of Family Life.* Robert Baldick (trans.). New York: Vintage.

ARLACCHI, P. 1980. *Mafia, Peasants and Great Estates: Society in Traditional Calabria.* Cambridge: Cambridge University Press.

ARRIOLA, ELVIA ROSALES. 1990. "Sexual Identity and the Constitution: Homosexual Persons as a Discrete and Insular Minority." *Women's Rights Law Reporter, 10,* 2–3, Winter, 143–176.

ASHLEY, RICHARD. 1975. *Cocaine: Its History, Uses, and Effects.* New York: St. Martin's.

ASHWORTH, WILLIAM. 1987. "The Great and Fragile Lakes." *Sierra,* November–December, 42–50.

ASSOCIATED PRESS. 1995. "Father's Persistence Pays Off." February 12.

ASSOCIATED PRESS. 1999. "Clinton Will Announce Welfare Rolls Are at Their Lowest Levels in 30 Years." *Wall Street Journal,* January 25.

ASSOCIATED PRESS. 1999. "Gun Deaths Still High Among Youths." January 2.

ASSOCIATED PRESS. 1999. "Possible Listeria Contamination Prompts Meat and Poultry Recall." January 23.

ASTON, G., AND V. FOUBISTER. 1998. "MD and Physician Extender Turf War." *The American Medical News, 41,* 27, 9–10.

ATCHLEY, ROBERT C. 1975. "Dimensions of Widowhood in Later Life." *The Gerontologist, 15,* April, 176–178.

ATHENS, LONNIE H. 1980. *Violent Criminal Acts and Actors: A Symbolic Interactionist Study.* Boston: Routledge.

AUERBACH, JUDITH D. 1990. "Employer-Supported Child Care as a Women-Responsive Policy." *Journal of Family Issues, 11,* 4, December, 384–400.

BAGNE, PAUL. 1992. "High-Tech Breeding." In *Marriage and Family in a Changing Society,* 4th ed., James M. Henslin (ed.). New York: Free Press, 226–234.

BAHR, HOWARD M. 1973. *Skid Row: An Introduction to Disaffiliation.* New York: Oxford University Press.

BAHREE, BHUSHAN. 1999. "U.S., Canada Can Penalize EU Over Its Ban on Beef." *Wall Street Journal,* July 13.

BAILEY, JEFF. 1992. "Economics of Trash Shift as Cities Learn Dumps Aren't So Full." *Wall Street Journal,* June 2, A1, A7.

BAILEY, WILLIAM C. 1990. "Murder, Capital Punishment, and Television: Execution Publicity and Homicide Rates." *American Sociological Review, 55,* October, 628–633.

BAI, MATT. 1999. "Anatomy of a Massacre." *Newsweek,* May 3, 25–31.

BALL, JEFFREY. 1999. "Auto Makers Race to Sell Cars Powered by Fuel Cells." *Wall Street Journal,* March 15.

BANDURA, ALBERT, AND RICHARD H. WALTERS. 1963. *Social Learning and Personality Development.* New York: Holt.

BARBANEL, JOSH. 1992. "From L.I. Teller Machines to Gas Stations, Suburban Robberies Are on the Rise." *New York Times,* February 18, B7.

BARDWICK, JUDITH M. 1971. *Psychology of Women: A Study of Bio-Cultural Conflicts.* New York: Harper & Row.

BARNES, EDWARD, AND WILLIAM SHEBAR. 1987. "Quitting the Mafia." *Life,* December, 108–112.

BARNES, JOHN A. 1990. "Canadians Cross Border to Save Their Lives." *Wall Street Journal,* December 12, A14.

BARON, LARRY. 1987. "Immoral, Inviolate or Inconclusive?" *Society,* July/August, 6–12.

BARR, ROBERT. 1998. "Report Says 33 Million Have HIV." Associated Press, November 24.

BART, PAULINE B., LINDA FREEMAN, AND PETER KIMBALL. 1985. "The Different Worlds of Women and Men: Attitudes Toward Pornography and Responses to *Not a Love Story*—A Film About Pornography." *Women's Studies International Forum, 8,* 4, 307–322.

BART, PAULINE B., AND PATRICIA H. O'BRIEN. 1984. "How the Women Stopped Their Rapes." *Signs, 10.*

BART, PAULINE B., AND PATRICIA H. O'BRIEN. 1985. *Stopping Rape: Successful Survival Strategies.* New York: Pergamon.

BARTLETT, DONALD L., AND JAMES B. STEELE. 1998. "Paying a Price for Polluters." *Time,* November 23, 72–80.

BARTOI, MARLA GREEN, AND BILL N. KINDER. 1998. "Effects of Child and Adult Sexual Abuse on Adult Sexuality." *Journal of Sex & Marital Therapy, 24,* 75–90.

BAUM, DAN. 1993. "Medical Marijuana." *Village Voice, 38,* 28, July 13, 15–16.

BAYER, RONALD. 1978. "Heroin Decriminalization and the Ideology of Tolerance: A Critical View." *Law and Society Review, 12,* Winter, 301–318.

BEALS, RALPH L., AND HARRY HOIJER. 1965. *An Introduction to Anthropology,* 3rd ed. New York: Macmillan.

BEARAK, BARRY. 1999a. "India Tests Missile Able to Hit Deep Into Neighbor Lands." *New York Times,* April 12.

BEARAK, BARRY. 1999b. "India and Pakistan Agree to Reduce Risk of Nuclear War." *New York Times,* February 22.

BEARDSLEY, JIM. 1988. "Getting Warmer." *Scientific American,* July, 32.

BECK, MELINDA. 1984. "Could It Happen in America?" *Newsweek,* December 17, 38, 40, 44.

BECKER, HOWARD S. 1966. "Editor's Introduction." In *Social Problems: A Modern Approach.* Howard S. Becker (ed.). New York: Wiley, 1–31.

BECKER, HOWARD S. 1967. "History, Culture, and Subjective Experience: An Exploration of the Social Bases of Drug Induced Experiences." *Journal of Health and Social Behavior, 7,* June, 163–176.

BEIRNE, PIERS, AND RICHARD QUINNEY (eds.). 1982. *Marxism and Law.* New York: Wiley.

BELL, ALAN P., MARTIN S. WEINBERG, AND SUE KIEFER HAMMERSMITH. 1981. *Sexual Preference: Its Development in Men and Women.* Bloomington: Indiana University Press.

BELL, DANIEL. 1960. *The End of Ideology.* New York: Free Press.

BELL, DAVID A. 1991. "An American Success Story: The Triumph of Asian-Americans." In *Sociological Footprints: Introductory Readings in Sociology,* 5th ed., Leonard Cargan and Jeanne H. Ballantine (eds.). Belmont, Calif.: Wadsworth, 308–316.

BELLUCK, PAM. 1998. "First-Ever Criminal Conviction Levied in Food Poisoning Case." *New York Times,* July 24.

BELLUCK, PAM. 1998. "Forget Prisons: Americans Cry Out for the Pillory." *New York Times,* October 4.

BENGTSON, VERN L., GERARDO MARTI, AND ROBERT E. L. ROBERTS. 1991. "Age-Group Relationships: Generational Equity and Inequity." In *Parent-Child Relations Throughout Life,* Karl Pillemer and Kathleen McCartney (eds.). Hillsdale, N.J.: Lawrence Erlbaum Associates, 253–278.

BENGTSON, VERN L., CAROLYN ROSENTHAL, AND LINDA BURTON. 1990. "Families and Aging: Diversity and Heterogeneity." In *Handbook of Aging and the Social Sciences,* 3rd ed., Robert H. Binstock and Linda K. George (eds.). San Diego: Academic Press, 263–287.

BENSON, IAN, AND JOHN LLOYD. 1983. *New Technology and Industrial Change: The Impact of the Scientific-Technical Revolution on Labour and Industry.* New York: Nichols.

BENSON, MICHAEL L. 1985. "Denying the Guilty Mind: Accounting for Involvement in White-Collar Crime." *Criminology, 23,* November, 585–607.

BERGSTRÖM, HANS. 1992. "Pressures Behind the Swedish Health Reforms." *Viewpoint Sweden, 12,* July, 1–5.

BERNARD, JESSIE. 1971. *Women and the Public Interest: An Essay on Policy and Protest.* Chicago: Aldine-Atherton.

BERNARD, VIOLA W., PERRY OTTENBERG, AND FRITZ REDL. 1971. "Dehumanization: A Composite Psychological Defense in Relation to Modern War." In *The Triple Revolution Emerging: Social Problems in Depth,* Robert Perucci and Marc Pilisuk (eds.). Boston: Little, Brown, 17–34.

BERNSTEIN, DEBORAH S. 1996. "Expanding the Split Labor Market Theory: Between and Within Sectors of the Split Labor Market of Mandatory Palestine." *Comparative Studies in Society and History, 38,* 2, April, 243–266.

BERNSTEIN, Nina 2000. "Studies Dispute 2 Assumptions About Welfare Overhaul", *New York Times,* December 12.

BERRY, BRIAN J. L., AND JOHN D. KASARDA. 1977. *Contemporary Urban Ecology.* New York: Macmillan.

BIRD, DAVID. 1977. "Population: Winning the War." *New York Times,* January 30, Section 12, 22.

BISHOP, JERRY E. 1988b. "Study Discovers Biochemical Difference Between Some Alcoholics, Non-Alcoholics." *Wall Street Journal,* December 12, B2.

BISHOP, JERRY E. 1990. "Attempt to Confirm Link Between Gene and Alcoholism Fails in Federal Study." *Wall Street Journal,* December 26, 11.

BISHOP, JERRY E., AND KEN WELLS. 1989. "Two Scientists Claim Breakthrough in Quest for Fusion Energy." *Wall Street Journal,* March 24, A1, A5.

BISHOP, KATHERINE. 1992. "Marijuana Still a Drug, Not a Medicine." *New York Times,* March 22, 5.

BLACKSTONE, SIR WILLIAM. 1899. *Commentaries on the Laws of England,* 4th ed., Thomas M. Cooley (ed.). Chicago: Callaghan and Co.

BLAINEY, GEOFFREY. 1973. *The Causes of War.* New York: Free Press.

BLAKELY, MARY KAY. 1985. "Is One Woman's Sexuality Another Woman's Pornography?" *Ms.,* April, 37–47.

BLAU, FRANCINE D. 1975. "Women in the Labor Force: An Overview." In *Women: A Feminist Perspective,* Jo Freeman (ed.). Palo Alto, Calif.: Mayfield, 211–226.

BLAU, FRANCINE D., AND LAWRENCE M. KAHN. 1992. "The Gender Earnings Gap: Some International Evidence." Working Paper No. 4224, National Bureau of Economic Research, December.

BLOCK, RICHARD, AND WESLEY G. SKOGAN. 1982. "Resistance and Outcome in Robbery and Rape: Nonfatal, Stranger to Stranger Violence." Mimeo.

BLOK, ANTON. 1974. *The Mafia of a Sicilian Village: A Study of Violent Peasant Entrepreneurs.* New York: Harper Torchbooks.

BLUM, RICHARD H., AND ASSOCIATES. 1969. *Drugs I, Society and Drugs: Social and Cultural Observations.* San Francisco: Jossey-Bass.

BLUM, RICHARD H., EVA BLUM, AND E. GARFIELD. 1976. *Drug Education: Results and Recommendations.* Lexington, Mass.: Heath.

BLUMBERG, ABRAHAM S. 1967. "The Practice of Law as Confidence Game: Organizational Cooptation of a Profession." *Law and Social Review, 1,* 15–39.

BLUMEMTHAL, RALPH. 1981. "Polluted Midwest Rain Is Killing New York Lakes." *Alton Telegraph,* June 8.

BLUMSTEIN, ALFRED, AND JACQUELINE COHEN. 1987. "Characterizing Criminal Careers." *Science, 237,* August, 985–991.

BOGUE, DONALD J. 1963. *Skid Row in American Cities.* Chicago: University of Chicago Press.

BOOT, MAX. 1998. "Your Money or Your Life? That Depends." *Wall Street Journal,* March 4, A18.

BOOTH, ALAN, AND JAMES M. DABBS, Jr. 1993. "Testosterone and Men's Marriages." *Social Forces, 72,* 2, December: 463–477.

BOWE, CLAUDIA. 1992. "Women and Depression: Are We Being Overdosed?" *Redbook,* March, 43–44, 47, 78.

BOWEN, CROSSWELL. 1972. "Donora, Pennsylvania." In *Society and Environment: The Coming Collision,* Rex R. Campbell and Jerry L. Wade (eds.). Boston: Allyn & Bacon, 163–168.

BOYD, WILLIAM LOWE. 1991. "What Makes Ghetto Schools Succeed or Fail?" *Teachers College Record, 92*, 3, Spring, 331–362.

BRANNIGAN, AUGUSTINE. 1987. "Is Obscenity Criminogenic?" *Society,* July/August, 12–19.

BRECHER, EDWARD M., and the Editors of *Consumer Reports.* 1972. *Licit and Illicit Drugs.* Boston: Little, Brown.

BREMER, L. PAUL III. 1988. "Terrorism: Myths and Reality." *Department of State Bulletin,* May, 63.

BROAD, WILLIAM J., AND JUDITH MILLER. 1998. "Rocky Start for U.S. Plan to Stockpile Vaccines to Fight Germ Warfare." *New York Times,* August 7.

BROCKERHOFF, MARTIN. 1996. "'City Summit' to Address Global Urbanization." *Population Today, 24,* March, 4–5.

BRODY, ELAINE M. 1978. "The Aging of the Family." *Annals of the American Academy of Political and Social Science, 438,* July, 13–27.

BRODY, JANE E. 1976. "1,100 Tested in Michigan for Effects of Toxin That Poisoned Food in '73." *New York Times,* November 5.

BROFF, NANCY. 1989. Statements supplied to the author from NARAL, January.

BROOKE, JAMES. 1999. "Deep Desert Grave Awaits First Load of Nuclear Waste." *New York Times,* March 26.

BROOKS, JACK. 1985. *HHS' Failure to Enforce the Food, Drug, and Cosmetic Act: The Case of Cancer-Causing Color Additives.* Eleventh Report of the Committee on Government Operations. Washington, D.C.: U.S. Government Printing Office.

BROOKS, JACK 1987. *FDA Continues to Permit the Illegal Marketing of Carcinogenic Additives.* Twenty-fifth Report of the Committee on Government Operations. Washington, D.C.: U.S. Government Printing Office.

BROOKS, VIRGINIA R. 1982. "Sex Differences in Student Dominance Behavior in Female and Male Professors' Classrooms." *Sex Roles, 8, 7,* 683–690.

BROWN, JANET WELSH. n.d. *Environmental Defense Fund Letter.* New York.

BROWN, LESTER R. 1985. "'Human Element,' Not Drought, Causes Famine." *U.S. News & World Report,* February 25, 71–72.

BROWN, LESTER R. 1987. "Food Growth Slowdown: Danger Signal for the Future." In *Food Policy: Integrating Supply, Distribution, and Consumption,* J. Price Gittinger, Joanne Leslie, and Caroline Hoisington (eds.). Baltimore: Johns Hopkins University Press, 89–102.

BROWN, MICHAEL H. 1979. "Love Canal and the Poisoning of America." *The Atlantic, 235,* December, 33–47.

BROWN, RICHARD MAXWELL. 1969. "Historical Patterns of Violence in America." In *Violence in America: Historical and Comparative Perspectives.* Hugh Davis Graham and Ted Robert Gurr (eds.). New York: Bantam.

BROWNFIELD, DAVID, AND ANN MARIE SORENSON. 1993. "Self-Control and Juvenile Delinquency: Theoretical Issues and an Empirical Assessment of Selected Elements of a General Theory of Crime." *Deviant Behavior, 14,* July–September, 243–264.

BROWNMILLER, SUSAN. 1975. *Against Our Will: Men, Women, and Rape.* New York: Simon & Schuster.

BROWNSTEIN, RONALD. 1999. "Extra Serving of Surplus to Elderly Raises Eyebrows." *Los Angeles Times,* February 2.

BRYANT, TIM. 1990. "Settlement Payments Ready in Chrysler Odometer Case." *St. Louis Post-Dispatch,* January 6, 3A.

BUCK, K. J. 1998. "Recent Progress Toward the Identification of Genes Related to Risk for Alcoholism." *Mamm Genome. 12,* December 9, 927–928.

BUDIANSKY, STEPHEN A. 1987. "The Trees Fell—And So Did the People." *U.S. News & World Report,* February 9, 75.

BUFF, STEPHEN A. 1987. "Lois Lee Takes Back Children from the Night." *ASA Footnotes, 15,* 5, May, 1, 2.

BULKELEY, WILLIAM M. 1995. "Untested Treatments, Cures Find Stronghold on On-Line Services." *Wall Street Journal,* February 27, A1, A7.

BULLOCK, HENRY A. 1961. "Significance of the Racial Factor in the Length of Prison Sentences." *Journal of Criminal Law, Criminology, and Police Science, 52,* September–October, 411–417.

BURCH, WILLIAM R., JR. 1971. *Daydreams and Nightmares: A Sociological Essay on the American Environment.* New York: Harper & Row.

BURGESS, ANN WOLBERT, AND LYNDA LYTLE HOLMSTROM. 1974. "Rape Trauma Syndrome." *American Journal of Psychiatry, 131,* 981–986.

BURGESS, ERNEST W. 1925. "The Growth of the City: An Introduction to a Research Project." In *The City,* Robert E. Park, Ernest W. Burgess, and Roderick D. McKenzie (eds.). Chicago: University of Chicago Press (pages 47–62 in the 1967 edition).

BURGESS, ERNEST W., AND HARVEY J. LOCKE. 1945. *The Family: From Institution to Companionship.* New York: American Book.

BURLEIGH, MICHAEL. 1991. "Racism as Social Policy: The Nazi 'Euthanasia' Programme, 1939–1945." *Ethnic and Racial Studies, 14,* 4, October, 453–473.

BURNS, JOHN F. 1994. "Bangladesh, Still Poor, Cuts Birth Rate Sharply." *New York Times,* September 13, A10.

BURROS, MARIAN. 1999. "Experts Worry About the Return of a Deadly Germ in Cold Cuts." *New York Times,* March 14.

BURROS, MARIAN. 1998. "Clinton Pressures Congress for Money to Ensure Safety of Food." *New York Times,* July 4.

BURROUGHS, WILLIAM. 1975. "Excerpts from 'Deposition: Testimony Concerning a Sickness.'" In *Drugs in Amer-*

ican Life, Morrow Wilson and Suzanne Wilson (eds.). New York: Wilson, 133–158.

BURTON, VELMER S., JR., FRANCIS T. CULLEN, T. DAVID EVANS, LEANNE FIFTAL ALARID, AND R. GREGORY DUNAWAY. 1998. "Gender, Self-Control, and Crime." *Journal of Research in Crime and Delinquency, 35,* 2, May, 123–147.

BUSH, GEORGE. 1986. *Public Report of the Vice President's Task Force on Combatting Terrorism.* Washington, D.C.: U.S. Government Printing Office, February.

BUTTERFIELD, FOX. 1999. "Prison Population Increases as Release of Inmates Slows." *New York Times,* January 11.

BYLINSKY, GENE. 1973. "New Clues to the Causes of Violence." *Fortune,* January, 134–146.

CAHALAN, D., I. A. CISIN, AND H. M. CROSSLEY. 1969. *American Drinking Practices: A National Study of Drinking Behavior and Attitudes.* New Brunswick, N.J.: Rutgers Center for Alcohol Studies.

CAIN, GLEN G., AND DOUGLAS A. WISSOKER. 1990. "A Re-analysis of Marital Stability in the Seattle-Denver Income-Maintenance Experiment." *American Journal of Sociology, 95,* 5, March, 1235–1269.

CAMPBELL, DUNCAN. 1995. "Electronic Tagging May be Used for Prisoners Released on Parole." *The Guardian,* August 12.

CAMPBELL, JOHN L. 1987. "The State and the Nuclear Waste Crisis: An Institutional Analysis of Policy Constraints." *Social Problems, 34,* 1, February, 18–33.

"Canada Tries to Bar Pro-Nazi View on the Internet." 1998. *New York Times,* August 2.

CANTRIL, ALBERT H., AND SUSAN DAVIS CANTRIL. 1994. *Live and Let Live.* New York: American Civil Liberties Union Foundation.

CAPLOW, THEODORE. 1982. *Middletown Families: Fifty Years of Change and Continuity.* Minneapolis: University of Minnesota Press.

CARLSON, KENNETH, AND JAN CHAIKEN. 1987. "White Collar Crime." Special Report of the Bureau of Justice Statistics. Washington, D.C.: U.S. Department of Justice, September.

CARLSON, LEWIS H., AND GEORGE A. COLBURN. 1972. *In Their Place: White America Defines Her Minorities, 1850–1950.* New York: Wiley.

CARLSON, RICK J. 1975. *The End of Medicine.* New York: Wiley.

CARNEVALE, MARY LU. 1990. "New Jolt for Nynex: Bawdy 'Conventions' of Buyers, Suppliers." *Wall Street Journal,* July 12, A1, A6.

CARR, DONALD E. 1972. "The Disasters." In *Society and Environment: The Coming Collision,* Rex R. Campbell and Jerry L. Wade (eds.). Boston: Allyn & Bacon, 129–134.

CARROLL, PETER N., AND DAVID W. NOBLE. 1977. *The Free and the Unfree: A New History of the United States.* New York: Penguin.

CARTER, TIMOTHY J., AND DONALD CLELAND. 1979. "A Neo-Marxian Critique, Formulation and Test of Juvenile Dispositions as a Function of Social Class." *Social Problems, 27,* October, 96–108.

CARTON, BARBARA. 1994. "At Jenny Craig, Men Are Ones Who Claim Sex Discrimination." *Wall Street Journal,* November 29, A1, A7.

CASS, VIVIENNE C. 1979. "Homosexual Identity Formation: A Theoretical Model." *Journal of Homosexuality, 4,* Spring, 219–235.

CASTANEDA, CARLOS. 1968. *The Teachings of Don Juan: A Yaqui Way of Knowledge.* New York: Ballantine.

CASTANEDA, CARLOS. 1971. *A Separate Reality: Further Conversations with Don Juan.* New York: Simon & Schuster.

CASTANEDA, CARLOS. 1974. *Tales of Power.* New York: Simon & Schuster.

CASTELLS, MANUEL. 1977. *The Urban Question: A Marxist Approach.* Alan Sheridan (trans.). Cambridge, Mass.: MIT Press.

CASTELLS, MANUEL. 1983. *The City and the Grass Roots.* Berkeley: University of California Press.

CASTELLS, MANUEL. 1989. *The Informational City.* Oxford, England: Blackwell.

CATANZARO, RAIMONDO. 1992. *Men of Respect: A Social History of the Mafia.* New York: Free Press.

CATES, JIM A., AND JEFFREY MARKLEY. 1992. "Demographic, Clinical, and Personality Variables Associated with Male Prostitution By Choice." *Adolescence, 27,* 107, Fall, 695–706.

CATTON, WILLIAM R., JR. 1980. *Overshoot: The Ecological Basis of Revolutionary Change.* Urbana: University of Illinois Press.

Centers for Disease Control. 1994. "HIV/AIDS Surveillance Report," 5, 4.

CHACKO, ARUN. 1977. "Birth of Girl Often Sad Event in India." *Los Angeles Times,* October 7, VII, 636.

CHAFETZ, JANET SALTZMAN. *Gender Equity: An Integrated Theory of Stability and Change.* Newbury Park, Calif.: Sage, 1990.

CHAFETZ, MORRIS E. 1990. "Alcohol and Innocent Victims." *Wall Street Journal,* March 5, A10.

CHAMBLISS, WILLIAM J. 1995. "The Saints and the Roughnecks." In *Down-to-Earth Sociology: Introductory Readings,* 8th ed., James M. Henslin (ed.). New York: Free Press, 254–267.

CHAMBLISS, WILLIAM J. 1999. "The Saints and the Roughnecks." In *Down-to-Earth Sociology: Introductory Readings,* 10th ed., James M. Henslin, ed. New York: Free Press, 260–274.

CHANDLER, MITTIE O. 1988. *Urban Homesteading: Programs and Policies.* Westport, CT.: Greenwood Press.

CHENG, V. 1995. "328 Useful Drugs Are Said to Lie Hidden in Tropical Forests." *New York Times,* June 27, C4.

CHESLER, MARK A., BARBARA CHESNEY, AND BENJAMIN GIDRON. 1990. "Israel and U.S. Orientations Toward Self-Help Groups for Families in Crisis." *Non-profit and Voluntary Sector Quarterly, 19,* 3, Fall, 251–262.

CHILMAN, CATHERINE S. 1988. "Public Policies and Families." In *Mental Illness, Delinquency, Addictions, and Neglect,* Elam W. Nunnally, Catherine S. Chilman, and Fred M. Cox (eds.). Newbury Park, Calif.: Sage, 189–197.

CHURCHILL, WARD, AND JIM VANDER WALL. 1990. *Agents of Repression: The FBI's Secret Wars Against the Black Panther Party and the American Indian Movement.* Boston: South End Press.

CISNEROS, HENRY G. (ed.). 1993. *Interwoven Destinies: Cities and the Nation.* New York: W. W. Norton.

"Citibank Thieves Transferred $12M." 1995. Online.

CLAUSING, JERI. 1998. "Senate Adds Internet Proposals to Spending Bill." *New York Times Bulletin,* July 22.

CLAWSON, PATRICK. 1988. "Terrorism in Decline?" *Orbis, 32,* Spring, 263–276.

CLEAVER, ELDRIDGE. 1968. *Soul on Ice.* New York: McGraw-Hill.

CLINARD, MARSHALL B. 1990. *Corporate Corruption: The Abuse of Power.* New York: Praeger.

CLINARD, MARSHALL B., PETER C. YEAGER, JEANNE BRISETTE, DAVID PETRASHEK, AND ELIZABETH HARRIES. 1979. *Illegal Corporate Behavior.* Washington, D.C.: U.S. Department of Justice.

CLINES, FRANCIS X. 1998. "Soviets Now Admit '57 Nuclear Blast." *New York Times,* June 18.

CLINTON, HILLARY RODHAM. 1997. *It Takes a Village: And Other Lessons Children Teach Us.* New York: Touchstone Books.

CLOWARD, RICHARD A., AND LLOYD E. OHLIN. 1960. *Delinquency and Opportunity: A Theory of Delinquent Gangs.* New York: Free Press.

COCKERHAM, WILLIAM C. 1991. *This Aging Society.* Englewood Cliffs, N.J.: Prentice Hall.

COCKERHAM, WILLIAM C. 1997. "The Social Determinants of the Decline of Life Expectancy in Russia and Eastern Europe: A Lifestyle Explanation." *Journal of Health and Social Behavior, 38,* June, 117–130.

COHEN, ADAM. "The Great American Welfare Lab." *Time,* April 21, 1997:74–76, 78.

COHEN, ALBERT K. 1955. *Delinquent Boys: The Culture of the Gang.* New York: Free Press.

COHEN, ELIZABETH. 1997. "Shrinks Aplenty Online, But Are They Credible." *New York Times,* January 17.

COHEN, JACQUELINE. 1978. "The Incapacitative Effect of Imprisonment: A Critical Review of the Literature." In *Deterrence and Incapacitation: Estimating the Effects of Criminal Sanctions on Crime Rates,* Alfred Blumstein, Jacqueline Cohen, and Daniel Nagin (eds.), Washington, D.C.: National Academy of Sciences.

COHEN, MORRIS R. 1940. "Moral Aspects of the Criminal Law." *Yale Law Journal, 49,* April, 1009–1026.

COHEN, MURRAY, THEOHARIS SEGHORN, AND WILFRED CALAMAS. 1969. "Sociometric Study of the Sex Offender." *Journal of Abnormal Psychology, 74,* April, 249–255.

COHEN, STEVEN M. 1990. "Hey NCR—We're the Shareholders, You Work for Us." *Wall Street Journal,* December 19, A16.

COHN, GARY. 1998. "Shipbreaker Gets 2 1/2–Year Term for Safety Violations." *Baltimore Sun,* February 14.

COLEMAN, JAMES WILLIAM. 1989. *The Criminal Elite: The Sociology of White Collar Crime.* New York: St. Martin's.

COLEMAN, JAMES WILLIAM. 1995. "Politics and the Abuse of Power." In *Down-to-Earth Sociology: Introductory Readings,* 8th ed., James M. Henslin (ed.). New York: Free Press, 442–450.

COMMONER, BARRY. 1972. *The Closing Circle: Nature, Man, and Technology.* New York: Bantam.

COMONS, MARLENE. 1999. "Scientists Study Gender Gap in Drug Response." *Los Angeles Times,* June 6.

"Congress Looks to Fund Efforts to Beat Back Fetal Alcohol Syndrome." 1994. *The Nation's Health, 24,* 3, March, 5.

CONNER, ROGER L. 1990. "Demographic Doomsayers: Five Myths About Population." *Current,* February, 21–25.

CONRAD, PETER. 1975. "The Discovery of Hyperkinesis: Notes on the Medicalization of Deviant Behavior." *Social Problems, 23,* October, 12–21.

CONRAD, PETER. 1995. "Learning to Doctor: Reflections on Medical School." In *Down-to-Earth Sociology: Introductory Readings,* 8th ed., James M. Henslin (ed.). New York: Free Press, 420–430.

CONTI, MASSIMO. 1980. "The Famine Controversy." *World Press Review, 27,* January, 56.

CONVENSKY, MILTON. 1980. "Postindustrial Society and the Family." University of California, University Extension, Courses by Newspapers, San Diego.

CONWAY, WILLIAM G. 1977. "'People Fire' in the Ghetto Ashes," *Saturday Review,* July 23, 15–16.

COOPER, AARON. 1989–1990. "No Longer Invisible: Gay and Lesbian Jews Build a Movement." *Journal of Homosexuality, 18,* 3–4, 83–94.

CORCORAN, MARY, GREG J. DUNCAN, GERALD GURIN, AND PATRICIA GURIN. 1985. "Myth and Reality: The Causes and Persistence of Poverty." *Journal of Policy Analysis and Management, 4,* 4, 516–536.

CORNELL, GEORGE W. 1981. "Modern Persecutions Mirror Those of Jesus." AP, April 13.

CORSON, DAVID J. 1992. "Language, Gender, and Education: A Critical Review Linking Social Justice and Power." *Gender and Education, 4,* 3, October, 229–254.

CORZINE, JAY, AND RICHARD KIRBY. 1977. "Cruising the Truckers: Sexual Encounters in a Highway Rest Area." *Urban Life, 6,* July, 171–192.

COSE, ELLIS. 1999. "The Good News About Black America." *Newsweek,* June 7, 29–40.

COSER, LEWIS A. 1956. *The Functions of Social Conflict.* New York: Free Press.

COSER, LEWIS A. 1967. *Continuities in the Study of Social Conflict.* New York: Free Press.

COSER, LEWIS A. 1977. *Masters of Sociological Thought: Ideas in Historical and Social Context.* New York: Harcourt.

County and City Data Book. Washington, D.C.: U.S. Government Printing Office, annual.

COWELL, ALAN. 1994. "Affluent Europe's Plight: Graying." *New York Times,* September 7.

COWLEY, JOYCE. 1969. *Pioneers of Women's Liberation.* New York: Merit.

COX, MEG. 1986. "Clearer Connections." *Wall Street Journal,* March 24, 200.

CRESSEY, DONALD R. 1953. *Other People's Money.* New York: Free Press.

CRESSEY, DONALD R. 1967. "Methodological Problems in the Study of Organized Crime as a Social Problem." *Annals of the American Academy of Political and Social Science, 347,* November, 101–122.

CRESSEY, DONALD R. 1969. *Theft of the Nation: The Structure and Operations of Organized Crime in America.* New York: Harper & Row.

CRESSEY, PAUL C. 1932. *The Taxi-Dance Hall: A Sociological Study in Commercialized Recreation and City Life.* Chicago: University of Chicago Press.

CRIDER, RAQUEL. 1986. "Phencyclidine: Changing Abuse Patterns." In *Phencyclidine: An Update,* Doris H. Clouet (ed.). Rockville, Md.: National Institute on Drug Abuse, 163–173.

CRISP, ANTHONY D. 1980. "Making Substance Abuse Prevention Relevant for Low-Income Black Neighborhoods." *Journal of Psychedelic Drugs, 12,* January–March, 13–19.

CRITCHFIELD, RICHARD. 1986. "China's Agricultural Success Story." *Wall Street Journal,* January 13, 25.

CROSSETTE, BARBARA. 1991. "Official Toll Reaches 92,000 in Bangladesh Cyclone." *New York Times,* May 4, A1.

CUMMING, ELAINE, AND WILLIAM E. HENRY. 1961. *Growing Old: The Process of Disengagement.* New York: Basic Books.

CURRIE, ELLIOTT. 1985. *Confronting Crime: An American Challenge.* New York: Pantheon.

CURWIN, E. CECIL, AND GUDMOND HART. 1961. *Plough and Pasture.* New York: Collier.

CUSHMAN, JOHN H. 1999. "Industries Press Plan for Credits in Emissions Control." *New York Times,* January 3.

DABBS, JAMES M., Jr. and ROBIN MORRIS. "Testosterone, Social Class, and Antisocial Behavior in a Sample of 4,462 Men." *Psychological Science, 1,* 3, May 1990: 209–211.

DAHL, ROBERT. 1961. *Who Governs?* New Haven, Conn.: Yale University Press.

DAHRENDORF, RALF. 1959. *Class and Class Conflict in Industrial Society.* Stanford: Stanford University Press.

DAHRENDORF, RALF. 1973. "Toward a Theory of Social Conflict." In *Social Change: Sources, Patterns, and Consequences,* Amitai Etzioni and Eva Etzioni (eds.). New York: Basic Books.

DALY, MARTIN, AND MARGO WILSON. 1988. *Homicide.* New York: Aldine de Gruyter.

DALY, MICHAEL, AND KENNETH MINTON. 1998. "Conan the Bacterium." *The Sciences.* July–August.

DANDOY, SUZANNE. 1990. *Journal of the American Medical Association, 263,* 19, May 18, 2674–2675.

DANIELS, ROGER. 1975. *The Decision to Relocate the Japanese Americans.* Philadelphia: Lippincott.

DAO, JAMES. 1999. "U.S. Government Joins Oneida Indians' Suit Against New York State." *New York Times,* January 13.

DASH, LEON. 1990. "When Children Want Children." *Society, 27,* 5, July–August, 17–19.

DAVIES, J. CLARENCE III, AND BARBARA S. DAVIES. 1975. *The Politics of Pollution,* 2nd ed. Indianapolis, Ind.: Bobbs-Merrill.

DAVIS, ANGELA. 1974. *Angela Davis: An Autobiography.* New York: Random House.

DAVIS, KINGSLEY. 1937. "The Sociology of Prostitution." *American Sociological Review, 2,* October, 744–755.

DAVIS, KINGSLEY. 1966. "Sexual Behavior." In *Contemporary Social Problems,* 2nd ed., Robert Merton and Robert Nisbet (eds.). New York: Harcourt.

DAVIS, KINGSLEY, AND WILBERT MOORE. 1945. "Some Principles of Stratification." *American Sociological Review, 10,* April, 242–249.

DAVIS, NANCY J., AND ROBERT V. ROBINSON. 1988. "Class Identification of Men and Women in the 1970s and 1980s." *American Sociological Review, 53,* February, 103–112.

DAVIS, NANETTE J. 1978. "Prostitution: Identity, Career, and Legal-Economic Enterprise." In *The Sociology of Sex: An Introductory Reader,* James M. Henslin and Edward Sagarin (eds.). New York: Schocken, 297–322.

DAVIS, NATALIE ZEMON. 1980. "Families in the Past." University of California, San Diego, Courses by Newspaper, University Extension.

DAWS, GAVIN. 1994. *Prisoners of the Japanese: POWs of World War II in the Pacific.* New York: Morrow.

DAY, CHARLES R., JR. 1990. "Tear Up the Tracks." *Industry Week, 239,* 5, March 5, 5.

DE BEAUVOIR, SIMONE. 1953. *The Second Sex.* New York: Knopf.

DEEVEY, E. S., DON S. RICE, PRUDENCE M. RICE, H. H. VAUGHAN, MARK BRENNES, AND M. S. FLANNERY. 1979. "Mayan Urbanism: Impact on a Tropical Karst Environment." *Science,* October 19, 298–306.

DELPH, EDWARD WILLIAM. 1978. *The Silent Community: Public Homosexual Encounters.* Beverly Hills, Calif.: Sage.

DE MOTT, BENJAMIN. 1980. "The Pro-Incest Lobby." *Psychology Today, 13,* March, 11–12, 15–16.

DENES, MAGDA. 1976. *In Necessity and Sorrow: Life and Death in an Abortion Hospital.* New York: Basic Books.

DENNEY, NANCY W., AND DAVID QUADAGNO. 1992. *Human Sexuality,* 2nd ed. St. Louis, Mo.: Mosby.

DEPARLE, JASON. 1999. "Wisconsin's Welfare Plan Justifies Hopes and Some Fear." *New York Times,* January 15.

DERIOS, MARLENE DOBKIN, AND DAVID E. SMITH. 1977. "Drug Use and Abuse in Cross-Cultural Perspective." *Human Organization, 36,* 14–21.

DIAZ-CALDERON, JOSEPH. "Letters to the author." September 1996 and March 1997.

DICKSON, DONALD T. 1968. "Bureaucracy and Morality: An Organizational Perspective on a Moral Crusade." *Social Problems, 16,* Fall, 143–156.

DIEUGENIO, JAMES. 1997. "The Posthumous Assassination of JFK, Part II." *Probe, 5,* 1, November-December.

DIIULIO, JOHN J., JR. 1992. "The Value of Prisons." *Wall Street Journal,* May 13, A16.

DINGELL, JOHN D. 1985. *Sulfites: Hearing Before the Subcommittee on Oversight and Investigations of the Committee on Energy and Commerce, House of Representatives.* Washington, D.C.: U.S. Government Printing Office, March 27.

DOBYNS, HENRY F. 1983. *Their Numbers Became Thinned: Native American Population Dynamics in Eastern North America.* Knoxville: University of Tennessee Press.

DOERNER, WILLIAM G. 1978. "The Index of Southernness Revisited: The Influence of Wherefrom upon Whodunnit." *Criminology, 16,* May, 47–56.

DOHRENWEND, BRUCE P. 1975. "Sociological and Social-Psychological Factors in the Genesis of Mental Disorders." *Journal of Health and Social Behavior, 16,* December, 365–392.

DOLLARD, JOHN, NEAL E. MILLER, LEONARD W. DOOB, O. H. MOWRER, AND ROBERT R. SEARS. 1961. *Frustration and Aggression.* New Haven, Conn.: Yale University Press (originally published in 1939).

DOMHOFF, G. WILLIAM. 1967. *Who Rules America?* Englewood Cliffs, N.J.: Prentice Hall.

DOMHOFF, G. WILLIAM. 1974. *The Bohemian Grove and Other Retreats: A Study in Ruling-Class Cohesiveness.* New York: Harper & Row.

DOMHOFF, G. WILLIAM. 1978a. *The Powers That Be.* New York: Random House.

DOMHOFF, G. WILLIAM. 1978b. *Who Really Rules?* New Brunswick, N.J.: Transaction.

DOMHOFF, G. WILLIAM. 1990. *The Power Elite and the State: How Policy Is Made in America.* New York: Aldine de Gruyter.

DOMHOFF, G. WILLIAM. 1998. *Who Rules America? Power and Politics in the Year 2000,* 3rd ed. Mountain View, CA.: Mayfield Publishers.

DORITY, BARBARA. 1993. "Americans in Cages." *Humanist, 53,* 6, November–December, 36–37.

DOROZYASKI, ALEXANDER. 1993. "Grapes of Wrath." *Psychology Today, 26,* 1, January, 18.

DOUGHERTY, WILMA HOLDEN, AND ROSALIND E. ENGEL. 1987. "An 80s Look for Sex Equality in Caldecott Winners and Honor Books." *Reading Teacher, 40,* 4, January 394–398.

DOUGLASS, JOSEPH D. 1998. "A Biological Weapons Threat Worse Than Saddam." *Wall Street Journal,* March 10, A22.

DOUVAN, ELIZABETH. 1980. "Is the American Family Obsolete?" University of California, University Extension, Courses by Newspaper, San Diego.

DOVE, ADRIAN. n.d. "Soul Folk 'Chitling' Test or the Dove Counterbalance Intelligence Test." Mimeo.

DOWIE, MARK. 1977. "Pinto Madness." *Mother Jones, 2,* September–October, 18–32.

DOWIE, MARK. 1977. "The Corporate Crime of the Century." *Mother Jones, 4,* November, 23–25, 37.

DRAPER, R. 1986. "The History of Advertising in America." *New York Review of Books 33,* June 26, 14–18.

Drug Dependence in Pregnancy: Clinical Management of Mother and Child. 1979. Rockville, Md.: U.S. Department of Health, Education, and Welfare.

DUBAR, HELEN. 1980. "American Discovers Child Pornography." In *Human Sexuality 80/81,* James R. Barbour (ed.). Guilford, Conn.: Dushkin.

DUFAY, JOANNE. n.d. "Ten Years After Chernobyl: A Witness to the Devastation." Greenpeace online.

DURKHEIM, EMILE. 1951. *Suicide,* John A. Spaulding and George Simpson (trans.). New York: Free Press (originally published in 1897).

DURKHEIM, EMILE. 1964. *The Division of Labor in Society,* George Simpson (trans.). New York: Free Press (originally published in 1893).

DURKHEIM, EMILE. 1965. *Elementary Forms of the Religious Life,* Joseph Weld Swain (trans.). New York: Free Press (originally published in 1912).

DURNING, ALAN. 1990. "Cradles of Life." In *Social Problems 90/91,* Leroy W. Barnes (ed.). Guilford, Conn.: Dushkin, 231–241.

DUSTER, TROY. 1970. *The Legalization of Morality: Law, Drugs, and Moral Judgment.* New York: Free Press.

DUSTER, TROY. 1988. "From Structural Analysis to Public Policy." *Contemporary Sociology, 17,* 3, May, 287–290.

DYE, LEE. 1999. "Tiny Firm Sees Process as Big Answer to Waste." *Los Angeles Times*, March 1.

EASTLAND, TERRY. 1992. "Weed and Seed: Root Out Crime, Nurture Poor." *Wall Street Journal*, May 14, A14.

EBERSTADT, NICK. 1988. *The Poverty of Communism*. New Brunswick, N.J.: Transaction.

EBOMOYI, EHIGIE. 1987. "The Prevalence of Female Circumcision in Two Nigerian Communities." *Sex Roles, 17,* 3/4, 139–151.

EDGERTON, ROBERT B. 1992. *Sick Societies: Challenging the Myth of Primitive Harmony*. New York: Free Press.

EFRON, SONNI. 1999. "Japanese Choke on American Biofood." *Los Angeles Times*, March 14.

EGAN, TIMOTHY. 1991. "Life, Liberty, and Maybe Marijuana." *New York Times,* February 5, A16.

EHRENFELD, RACHEL. 1990. *Narcoterrorism*. New York: Basic Books.

EHRENFELD, RACHEL, AND MICHAEL KAHAN. 1986. "The Narcotic-Terrorism Connection." *Wall Street Journal,* February 10, 14.

EHRENREICH, BARBARA, AND DEIRDRE ENGLISH. 1973. *Witches, Midwives, and Nurses: A History of Women Healers*. Old Westbury, N.Y.: Feminist Press.

EHRLICH, ELIZABETH. 1989. "The Mommy Track." *Business Week*, March 20, 126–134.

EHRLICH, PAUL R., AND ANNE H. EHRLICH. 1972. *Population, Resources, and Environment: Issues in Human Ecology,* 2nd ed. San Francisco: Freeman.

EHRLICH, PAUL R., AND ANNE H. EHRLICH. 1981. *Extinction: The Causes and Consequences of the Disappearance of Species*. New York: Random House.

EISENHART, R. WAYNE. 1975. "You Can't Hack It, Little Girl: A Discussion of the Covert Psychological Agenda of Modern Combat Training." *Journal of Social Issues, 31,* Fall, 13–23.

EISENHOWER, DWIGHT D. 1972. "From 'Farewell Address to the Nation,' January 17, 1961." In *The Military and American Society: Essays and Readings,* Stephen E. Ambrose and James A. Barber, Jr. (eds.). New York: Free Press, 61–63.

EISINGER, PETER K. 1980. *The Politics of Displacement: Racial and Ethnic Transition in Three American Cities*. Campbell Calif.: Academic Press.

"Electric Kool-Aid Viagra." 1998. *New York Times,* August 12.

ELLIS, HAVELOCK. 1897. "Mescal: A New Artificial Paradise." *Annual Report of the Smithsonian Institution, 52,* 547–548.

ELLIS, HAVELOCK. 1902. "Mescal: A Study of a Divine Plant." *Popular Science Monthly, 61,* 52–71.

ENGELMAYER, PAUL A. 1983. "Violence by Students, from Rape to Racism, Raises College Worries." *Wall Street Journal,* November 21, 1, 18.

ENGLUND, WILL, AND GARY COHN. 1997a. "Scrapping Ships, Sacrificing Men." *Baltimore Sun*, December 7.

ENGLUND, WILL, AND GARY COHN. 1997b. "A Third World Dump for America's Ships?" *Baltimore Sun*, December 9.

Environmental Protection Agency. 1994. "The Great Lakes: Report to Congress on the Great Lakes Ecosystem." February.

Environmental Protection Agency. 1998. "Reduction of Toxic Loadings to the Niagara River From Hazardous Waste Sites in the United States." November.

EPSTEIN, CYNTHIA FUCHS. 1986. "Inevitabilities of Prejudice." *Society*, September–October, 7–13.

EPSTEIN, CYNTHIA FUCHS. 1988. *Deceptive Distinctions: Sex, Gender, and the Social Order*. New Haven, Conn.: Yale University Press.

EPSTEIN, CYNTHIA FUCHS. 1989. Letter to the author, January 26.

EPSTEIN, SAMUEL S. 1999. "International Scientific Committee Warns of Serious Risk of Breast and Prostate Cancer from Monsanto's Hormonal Milk." Press Release, March 21.

ERIK, JOHN. 1982. "China's Policy on Births." *New York Times,* January 3, IV, 19.

ESPENSHADE, THOMAS J. 1990. "A Short History of U.S. Policy Toward Illegal Immigration." *Population Today,* February, 6–9.

ETZIONI, AMITAI. 1998. "Letter to the Editor: Porn Filters Are a Net Benefit." *Wall Street Journal*, November 3, A23.

ETZKOWITZ, HENRY, CAROL KEMELGOR, MICHAEL NEUSCHATZ, AND BRIAN UZZI. 1992. "Athena Unbound: Barriers to Women in Academic Science and Engineering." *Science and Public Policy, 19,* 3, June, 157–179.

FAISON, SETH, JR. 1991. "Friend Says Girl Killed on Train Resisted Robbery of Other Girls." *New York Times,* September 22, 34.

FAMIGHETTI, ROBERT (ed.). 1999. *The World Almanac and Book of Facts*. Mahwah, New Jersey: World Almanac Books.

FARAH, DOUGLAS. 1997. "Russian Gangs Amplify Drug Threat." *The Seattle Times*, September 29.

FARAH, JUDY. 1995. "Crime and Creative Punishment." *Wall Street Journal*, March 15, A15.

FARIS, R. E. L., AND W. W. DUNHAM. 1939. *Mental Disorders in Urban Areas*. Chicago: University of Chicago Press.

FARLEY, MAGGIE. 1999. "The City With the Grittiest Air on Earth." *Los Angeles Times*, June 15.

FARNEY, DENNIS. 1989. "On the Great Plains, Life Becomes a Fight for Water and Survival." *Wall Street Journal,* August 16, A1, A12.

FARNEY, DENNIS. 1994. "Gay Rights Confront Determined Resistance from Some Moderates." *Wall Street Journal,* October 7, A1, A4.

FARNEY, DENNIS. 1998. "They Hold the Cards, But After All, They Do Own the Casino." *Wall Street Journal,* February 5, A1, A6.

FAUNCE, WILLIAM A. 1981. *Problems of an Industrial Society,* 2nd ed. New York: McGraw-Hill.

FAUPEL, CHARLES E., AND CARL B. KLOCKARS. 1987. "Drugs-Crime Connections: Elaborations from the Life Histories of Hard-Core Addicts." *Social Problems, 34,* 1, February, 54–68.

FBI Uniform Crime Reports. Washington, D.C.: U.S. Government Printing Office, annual.

Federal Bureau of Investigation. 1998. *Terrorism in the United States, 1997.* Washington, D.C.: U.S. Department of Justice.

FELDMAN, HARVEY M. 1985. "Background and Purpose of the Ethnographers' Policymakers' Symposium." In *Ethnography: A Research Tool for Policymakers in the Drug and Alcohol Fields,* Karl Akins and George Beschner (eds.). Rockville, Md.: Department of Health and Human Services.

FELSENTHAL, EDWARD. 1998. "Justices' Ruling Further Defines Sex Harassment." *Wall Street Journal,* March 5, B1, B2.

FERGUSON, TIM W. 1991. "Good for the Walkers." *Barron's,* January 7, 12.

FERRARO, KATHLEEN J., AND JOHN M. JOHNSON. 1992. "Battered Wives." In *Marriage and Family in a Changing Society,* 4th ed., James M. Henslin (ed.). New York: Free Press, 333–343.

FERRI, ENRICO. 1913. *The Positive School of Criminology.* Chicago: Kerr.

FESHBACH, MURRAY. 1981. "Health in Russia: Statistics and Reality." *Wall Street Journal,* September 14, 30.

FESHBACH, MURRAY. 1992. "Russia's Farms, Too Poisoned for the Plow." *Wall Street Journal,* May 14, A14.

FESHBACH, MURRAY, AND ALFRED FRIENDLY, JR. 1992. *Ecocide in the USSR: Health and Nature Under Siege.* New York: Basic Books.

FIALKA, JOHN J. 1988. "Pentagon Outlines Plans to Use Troops to Join Border 'War' Against Drugs." *Wall Street Journal,* February 23, A10.

FIALKA, JOHN J. 1997. "Global Warming Treaty Is Approved." *Wall Street Journal,* December 11, A2.

FIELDS, GEORGE. 1986. "Racism Is Accepted Practice in Japan." *Wall Street Journal,* November 10, 19.

FIELD, MARK G. 1998. "The Health Crisis in the Former Soviet Union: A Report from the 'Post-War' Zone. In *Readings in Medical Sociology,* William C. Cockerham, Michael Glasser, and Linda S. Heuser, eds. Upper Saddle River, New Jersey: Prentice Hall, 506–519.

FINCKENAUER, JAMES O. 1982. *Scared Straight and the Panacea Phenomenon.* Englewoods Cliffs, N.J.: Prentice Hall.

FINCKENAUER, JAMES O., AND ELIN WARING. 1999. *The Russian Mafia in America: Immigration, Culture, and Crime.* Boston: Northeastern University Press.

FINKELHOR, DAVID. 1980. "Long-Term Effects of Childhood Sexual Victimization in a Non-Clinical Sample." Unpublished, October 2.

FINKELHOR, DAVID, AND LINDA MEYER WILLIAMS. 1988. *Nursery Crimes: Sexual Abuse in Day Care.* Newbury Park, Calif.: Sage.

FINKELHOR, DAVID, AND KERSTI YLLO. 1983. *License to Rape: Sexual Abuse of Wives.* New York: Holt.

FINKELHOR, DAVID, AND KERSTI YLLO. 1989. "Marital Rape: The Myth versus the Reality." In *Marriage and Family in a Changing Society,* James M. Henslin (ed.). New York: Free Press, 382–391.

FINSTERBUSCH, KURT, AND H. C. GREISMAN. 1975. "The Unprofitability of Warfare in the Twentieth Century." *Social Problems, 22,* February, 450–463.

FIRESTONE, SHULAMITH. 1970. *The Dialectic of Sex: The Case for Feminist Revolution.* New York: Morrow.

FISCHER, CLAUDE S. 1976. *The Urban Experience.* New York: Harcourt.

FISHER, GORDON M. 1998. "Setting American Standards of Poverty: A Look Back." *Focus, 19,* 2, Spring 47–52.

FISHER, IAN. 1992. "Gay Groups Call Police Decoys Ineffective." *New York Times,* January 1, 35A.

FISHER, SUE. 1986. *In the Patient's Best Interest: Women and the Politics of Medical Decisions.* New Brunswick, N.J.: Rutgers University Press.

FISSE, BRENT, AND JOHN BRAITHWAITE. 1987. "The Impact of Publicity on Corporate Offenders: Ford Motor Company and the Pinto Papers." In *Corporate and Governmental Deviance: Problems of Organizational Behavior in Contemporary Society,* 3rd ed., M. David Ermann and Richard J. Lundman (eds.). New York: Oxford University Press, 244–262.

FLAVIN, CHRISTOPHER. 1987. "Reassessing Nuclear Power." In *State of the World,* Lester R. Brown (ed.). New York: Norton, 57–80.

FODERARO, LISA W. 1998. "Affluent Blacks Drawn to Harlem by Property Bargains and History." *New York Times,* September 18.

Food and Drug Administration. 1994. "Food Allergies—Rare But Risky." *FDA Consumer,* May.

Food and Drug Administration. 1988. "A Primer on Food Additives."

FORD, CLELLAN S., AND FRANK A. BEACH. 1972. *Patterns of Sexual Behavior.* New York: Harper Colophon.

"The Former Soviet Union." 1994. *World Press Review, 41,* 1, January, 26.

FORNEY, MARY ANN, JAMES A. INCIARDI, AND DOROTHY LOCKWOOD. 1992. "Exchanging Sex for Crack-Cocaine: A Comparison of Women from Rural and Urban Communities." *Journal of Community Health, 17,* 2, April, 73–85.

FORREST, JACQUELINE DARROCH, CHRISTOPHER TIETZE, AND ELLEN SULLIVAN. 1978. "Abortion in the United States, 1976–1977." *Family Planning Perspectives, 10,* September–October, 271–279.

FORWARD, SUSAN, AND CRAIG BUCK. 1978. *Betrayal of Innocence: Incest and Its Devastation.* New York: Penguin.

FOX, EDWARD WILLIAM. 1980. Personal correspondence to Donald W. Light, Jr., September 30.

FOX, JOHN W. 1990. "Social Class, Mental Illness, and Social Mobility: The Social Selection-Drift Hypothesis for Serious Mental Illness." *Journal of Health and Social Behavior, 31,* 4, December, 344–353.

FRANK, ANDRE GUNDER. 1979. *Dependent Accumulation and Underdevelopment.* New York: Monthly Review.

FRAZIER, STEVE, AND BRENTON R. SCHLENDER. 1980. "Huge Area in Midwest Relying on Irrigation Is Depleting Its Water." *Wall Street Journal,* August 6, 1.

FREED, ANNE O. 1994. "How Japanese Families Cope with Fragile Elderly." In *Perspectives in Social Gerontology,* Robert B. Enright, Jr. (ed.). Boston: Allyn & Bacon, 76–86.

FREEDMAN, ALIX M. 1994. "How a Tobacco Giant Doctors Snuff Brands to Boost Their 'Kick.'" *Wall Street Journal,* October 26, A1, A6.

FRIEDAN, BETTY. 1963. *The Feminine Mystique.* New York: Norton.

FRIEDL, ERNESTINE. 1990. "Society and Sex Roles." In *Conformity and Conflict: Readings in Cultural Anthropology.* James P. Spradley and David W. McCurdy (eds.). Glenview Ill.: Scott, Foresman, 229–238.

FREIDSON, ELIOT. 1961. *Patient's Views of Medical Practice.* New York: Russell Sage.

"Frequent Tobacco Use Among U.S. Youth Declines." 1992. *Smokers' Advocate,* February.

FREUND, MATTHEW, NANCY LEE, AND TERRI LEONARD. 1991. *Journal of Sex Research, 28,* 4, November, 579–591.

FROHMANN, LISA. 1991. "Discrediting Victim's Allegation of Sexual Assault: Prosecutorial Accounts of Case Rejections." *Social Problems, 38,* 2, May, 213–226.

FROMAN, INGMARIE. 1994. "Sweden for Women." *Current Sweden, 407,* November, 1–4.

FROMM, ERICH. 1973. *The Anatomy of Human Destructiveness.* New York: Holt.

FULLER, REX, AND RICHARD SCHOENBERGER. 1991. "The Gender Salary Gap: Do Academic Achievement, Internship Experience, and College Major Make a Difference?" *Social Science Quarterly, 72,* 4, December, 715–726.

FUNKHOUSER, RICHARD, AND EDWARD LORENZ. 1987. "Fiscal and Employment Impacts of Enterprise Zones." *Atlantic Economic Journal,* July, 62–76.

GALBRAITH, JOHN KENNETH. 1979. *The Nature of Mass Poverty.* Cambridge, Mass.: Harvard University Press.

GALE, RICHARD P. 1972. "From Sit-In to Hike-In: A Comparison of the Civil Rights and Environmental Movements." In *Social Behavior, Natural Resources, and the Environment,* William R. Burch, Jr., Neil H. Cheek, Jr., and Lee Taylor (eds.). New York: Harper & Row, 280–305.

GALINSKY, ELLEN, JAMES T. BOND, AND DANA E. FRIEDMAN. 1993. *The Changing Workforce: Highlights of the National Study.* New York: Families and Work Institute.

GALINSKY, ELLEN, AND PETER J. STEIN. 1990. "The Impact of Human Resource Policies on Employees: Balancing Work/Family Life." *Journal of Family Issues, 11,* 4, December, 368–383.

GALLESE, LIZ ROMAN. 1980. "Blue-Collar Women." *Wall Street Journal,* July 28.

GALLIHER, JOHN R., AND ALLYN WALKER. 1977. "The Puzzle of the Social Origins of the Marihuana Tax Act of 1937." *Social Problems, 24,* February, 367–376.

GALLUP, GEORGE. 1976. "Economic Woes Haunt the Developing Nations." Gallup Poll, November 25.

GANS, HERBERT J. 1962. *The Urban Villagers.* New York: Free Press.

GANS, HERBERT J. 1968. *People and Plans: Essays on Urban Problems and Solutions.* New York: Basic Books.

GANS, HERBERT J. 1973. *More Equality.* New York: Pantheon.

GANS, HERBERT J. 1991. "The Way We'll Live Soon." *Washington Post,* September 1, BW3.

GANS, HERBERT J. 1991. *People, Plans, and Policies: Essays on Poverty, Racism, and Other National Urban Problems.* New York: Columbia University Press.

GANS, HERBERT J. 1999. "The Uses of Poverty: The Poor Pay All." *Social Policy,* July-August 1971:20–24. Reprinted in *Down to Earth Sociology: Introductory Readings,* 10th ed., James M. Henslin, ed. New York: Free Press, 336–342.

GARBARINO, MERWIN S. 1976. *American Indian Heritage.* Boston: Little, Brown.

GARDNER, SANDRA. 1992. "Coping with a Daughter's Murder." *New York Times.* January 5, NJ3.

GARELIK, GLENN. 1996. "Russia's Legacy of Death." *National Wildlife,* June–July.

GARREAU, JOEL. 1991a. *Edge City: Life on the New Frontier.* New York: Doubleday.

GARREAU, JOEL. 1991b. "Life on the Edge." *Washington Post, September 8, C1.*

GARRETT, LAURIE. 1999. "Global Warning." *Los Angeles Times,* March 1.

GARTNER, MICHAEL. 1988. "A Dream of Peace, the Reality of Never-Ending Wars." *Wall Street Journal,* December 22, A13.

GATTARI, P., L. SPIZZICHINO, C. VALENZI, M. ZACCARELLI, AND G. REZZA. 1992. "Behavioural Patterns and HIV Infection Among Drug Using Transvestites Practising Prostitution in Rome." *AIDS Care, 4,* 1, 83–87.

GAY, JILL. 1985. "The 'Patriotic' Prostitute." *The Progressive,* February, 34–36.

GAY, WILLIAM, AND MICHAEL PEARSON. 1987. *The Nuclear Arms Race.* Chicago: American Library Association.

GAYLIN, WILLARD. 1974. *Partial Justice: A Study of Bias in Sentencing.* New York: Knopf.

GELLES, RICHARD I. 1980. "The Myth of Battered Husbands and New Facts About Family Violence." In *Social Problems 80–81,* Robert L. David (ed.). Guilford, Conn.: Dushkin.

GELLHORN, MARTHA. 1959. *The Face of War.* New York: Simon & Schuster.

GEMME, ROBERT. 1993. "Prostitution: A Legal, Criminological, and Sexological Perspective." *Canadian Journal of Human Sexuality, 2,* 4, Winter, 227–237.

GERBNER, GEORGE. 1998. "The 1998 Screen Actors Guild Report: Casting the American Scene." Online. December.

GERLIN, ANDREA. 1994. "Quirky Sentences Make Bad Guys Squirm." *Wall Street Journal,* August 4, B1, B2.

GERSHMAN, CARL. 1980. "A Matter of Class." *New York Times Magazine,* October 5, 24, 92–98, 102–104.

GEST, TED. 1987. "Teaching Convicts Real Street Smarts." *U.S. News & World Report,* May 18, 72.

GETTER, LISA. 1999. "Cancer Risk From Air Pollution Still High, Study Says." *Los Angeles Times,* March 1.

"Getting the Message." 1997. Children Now. Online.

GIBBONS, ANN. 1991. "Famine: Blame Policy, Not Nature." *Science, 254,* 5033, November 8, 790.

GIBBS, NANCY. 1999. "In Sorrow and Disbelief." May 3, 25–36.

GIDDENS, ANTHONY. 1969. "Georg Simmel." In *The Founding Fathers of Social Science,* Timothy Raison (ed.). Baltimore: Penguin, 165–173.

GIELE, JANET ZOLLINGER. 1978. *Women and the Future: Changing Sex Roles in Modern America.* New York: Free Press.

GILHAM, STEVEN A. 1989. "The Marines Build Men: Resocialization in Recruit Training." In *The Sociological Outlook: A Text with Readings,* 2nd ed., Reid Luhman (ed.). San Diego, Calif.: Collegiate Press, 232–244.

GILMARTIN-ZENA, PAT. 1985. "Rape Impact: Immediately and Two Months Later." *Deviant Behavior, 6,* 347–361.

GILMORE, DAVID G. 1990. *Manhood in the Making: Cultural Concepts of Masculinity.* New Haven, Conn.: Yale University Press.

GIULIANI, RUDOLPH W. 1999. "The Welfare Reform Battle Isn't Over Yet." *Wall Street Journal,* February 3.

GLABERSON, WILLIAM. 1991. "One-Fourth of Stonypoint Police Face Drug Tests Under New Plan." *New York Times,* December 29, 26.

GLADSTONE, NEIL. 1999. "Brotherly Love and Hate." *New York Times,* January 3.

GLASER, DANIEL. 1978. *Crime in Our Changing Society.* New York: Holt.

GLASSNER, BARRY, AND BRUCE BERG. 1980. "How Jews Avoid Alcohol Problems." *American Sociological Review, 45,* August, 647–664.

GOAD, G. PIERRE. 1999. "G-7 Will Focus on Ways to Predict Market Behavior." *Wall Street Journal,* February 19.

GOERING, LAURIE. 1998. "Paranoia Pervasive in Amazon." *Seattle Times,* August 28.

GOLDBERG, DAVE. 1981. "Official Attitudes Changing Toward Indian Claims." AP, August 24.

GOLDBERG, STEVEN. 1974. *The Inevitability of Patriarchy,* rev. ed. New York: Morrow.

GOLDBERG, STEVEN. 1986. "Reaffirming the Obvious." *Society,* September–October, 4–7.

GOLDBERG, STEVEN. 1989. Letter to the Author. January 18.

GOLDBERG, SUSAN, AND MICHAEL, LEWIS. 1969. "Play Behavior in the Year-Old Infant: Early Sex Differences." *Child Development, 40,* March, 21–31.

GOLEMAN, DANIEL. 1987. "Girls and Math: Is Biology Really Destiny?" *New York Times,* August 2, 42–44, 46.

GOODE, ERICH. 1989. *Drugs in American Society,* 3rd ed. New York: Knopf.

GORDON, MICHAEL R. 1996. "Russia Struggles in Long Race to Prevent an Atomic Theft." *New York Times,* April 20.

GORDON, MICHAEL R. 1998a. "Hard Times at Russia's Once-Pampered Nuclear Centers." *New York Times,* November 18.

GORDON, MICHAEL R. 1998b. "Russia and U.S. Plan to Guard Atom Secrets." *New York Times,* September 23.

GORDON, MILTON. 1964. *Assimilation in American Life.* New York: Oxford University Press.

GORRIE, PETER. 1990. "Great Lakes Clean-Up at Critical Turning Point." *Canadian Geographic, 110,* 6, December, 44–57.

GOSCH, MARTIN A., AND RICHARD HAMMER. 1975. *The Last Testament of Lucky Luciano.* New York: Dell.

GOTTFREDSON, MICHAEL, AND TRAVIS HIRSCHI. 1990. *A General Theory of Crime.* Stanford, CA.: Stanford University Press.

GOTTMANN, JEAN MEGALOPOLIS. 1964. *The Urbanized Northeastern Seaboard of the United States.* Cambridge, Mass.: MIT Press.

"GPS Creates Global Jail." 1998. Online, April 8.

GRADY, DENISE. 1999. "Bacteria Resistant to Powerful Antibiotics Are Discovered in Chicken Feed." *New York Times,* February 26.

GRASSO, K. L. 1994. *Criminal Child Sexual Abuse and Exploitation Laws in Eight Midwestern States: Recommendations for Legislative Change.* Washington, D.C.: The Center.

GRAVEN, KATHRYN. 1990. "Sex Harassment at the Office Stirs Up Japan." *Wall Street Journal,* March 21, B1, B7.

GREEN, EDWARD. 1961. *Judicial Attitudes in Sentencing.* London: Macmillan.

GREEN, GARY S. 1993. "White-Collar Crime and the Study of Embezzlement." *Annals of the American Academy of Political and Social Sciences, 525,* January, 95–106.

GREEN, WAYNE E. 1988. "Environmental Lawyers Are Finding a Silver Lining in Hazardous Waste." *Wall Street Journal,* October 10, 5B.

GREENBERG, DAVID F. 1975. "The Incapacitative Effect of Imprisonment: Some Estimates." *Law and Society Review, 9,* Summer, 541–579.

GREENBERG, LARRY M. 1994. "Take Two Tablespoons of Mustard and Call if You Don't Feel Better." *Wall Street Journal,* February 22, B1.

GREENBERGER, ROBERT S. 1992. "U.S., Russia Will Explore Joint System for Early Warning of Missile Attacks." *Wall Street Journal,* February 19, A7.

GREENBERGER, ROBERT S. 1994. "U.S., Russia Agree to Faster Timetable for Destruction of Nuclear Arsenals." *Wall Street Journal,* September 29, A22.

GREENFIELD, LAWRENCE A. 1991. "Capital Punishment 1990." *Bureau of Justice Statistics Bulletin,* September.

GREENHOUSE, STEVEN. 1999. "Doctors, Under Pressure from H.M.O.'s, Are Ready Union Recruits." *New York Times,* February 4.

GREER, GERMAINE. 1972. *The Female Eunuch.* New York: Bantam.

GREGG, ALAN. 1955. "A Medical Aspect of the Population Problem." *Science,* May 13, 681–682.

GRELLA, CHRISTINE E. 1990. "Irreconcilable Differences: Women Defining Class after Divorce and Downward Mobility." *Gender and Society, 4,* 1, March, 41–55.

"Guardian of Brazil Indians Faces Many Foes." 1997. Reuters online, June 10.

GUDKOV, YURI. 1980. "The 'Respectable' Mafia." *World Press Review, 27,* January, 51.

GUSFIELD, JOSEPH R. 1963. *Symbolic Crusade: Status Politics and the American Temperance Movement.* Urbana: University of Illinois Press.

GUSKIND, ROBERT. 1990. "Enterprise Zones: Do They Work?" *Journal of Housing,* January–February, 47–54.

HAAS, JACK, AND WILLIAM SHAFFIR. 1993. "The Cloak of Competence." In *Down-to-Earth Sociology: Introductory Readings,* 7th ed., James M. Henslin (ed.). New York: Free Press.

HABERMAN, PAUL W., AND GEETHA NATARAJAN. 1986. "Trends in Alcoholism and Narcotics Abuse from Medical Examiner Data." *Journal of Studies on Alcohol, 47,* 4, 316–321.

HACKER, HELEN MAYER. 1951. "Women as a Minority Group." *Social Forces, 30,* October, 60–69.

HACKETT, GEORGE. 1988. "Kids: Deadly Force." *Newsweek,* January 11, 18–19.

HADDEN, JEFFREY K., AND JOSEF J. BARTON. 1973. "An Image That Will Not Die: Thoughts on the History of Anti-Urban Ideology." In *The Urbanization of the Suburbs,* Louis H. Masoti and Jeffrey K. Hadden (eds.). Beverly Hills, Calif.: Sage, 79–116.

HAKANSSON, STEFAN. 1994. "New Ways of Financing and Organizing Health Care in Sweden." *International Journal of Health Planning and Management, 9,* 1, January, 103–124.

HALE, MARION. 1980. "In Courts, Defendant's Color Counts." *Fort Lauderdale News,* October 3.

HALL, SUSAN. 1972. *Gentleman of Leisure: A Year in the Life of a Pimp.* New York: New American Library.

HAMER, DEAN H., STELLA HU, VICTORIA L. MAGNUSON, NAN HU, AND ANGELA M. L. PATTATUCCI. 1993. "A Linkage Between DNA Markers on the X Chromosome and Male Sexual Orientation." *Science, 261,* July 16, 321–327.

HANSON, DAVID J. 1995. *Preventing Alcohol Abuse: Alcohol, Culture, and Control.* Westport, Conn.: Praeger.

HANSON, KITTY. 1977. "Victims of Violence." *Daily News,* October 3, 4, and 5.

HANSSEN, M. 1997. *The New Additive Code Breaker.* Port Melbourne, Australia: Lothian Books.

HARDIN, GARRETT. 1968. "The Tragedy of the Commons." *Science, 162,* December, 1243–1248.

HARRINGTON, MICHAEL. 1962. *The Other America: Poverty in the United States.* New York: Macmillan.

HARRINGTON, MICHAEL. 1977. *The Vast Majority: A Journey to the World's Poor.* New York: Simon & Schuster.

HARRIS, CHAUNCY, AND EDWARD ULLMAN. 1945. "The Nature of Cities." *Annals of the American Academy of Political and Social Science, 242,* November, 7–17.

HARRIS, MARVIN. 1977. "Why Men Dominate Women." *New York Times Magazine,* November 13, 46, 115, 117, 123.

HARRIS, SHELDON H. 1994. *Factories of Death.* New York: Routledge.

HARRISON, BRUCE. 1987. "Pressing or Passe?" *Public Relations Journal, 43,* March, 4–6.

HART, HORNELL. 1957. "Acceleration in Social Change." In *Technology and Social Change,* Francis R. Allen, Hornell Hart, Delbert C. Miller, William F. Ogburn, and Meyer F. Nimkoff (eds.). New York: Appleton.

HAUB, CARL, AND DIANA CORNELIUS. 1999. "World Population Data Sheet." Population Reference Bureau.

HAUSER, PHILIP, AND LEO SCHNORE (eds.). 1965. *The Study of Urbanization.* New York: Wiley.

HAVEMAN, ROBERT H., AND JOHN KARL SCHOLZ. 1994–95. "The Clinton Welfare Reform Plan: Will It End Poverty as We Know It?" *Focus, 16,* 2, Winter, 1–11.

HAYES, ARTHUR S. 1991. "How the Courts Define Harassment." *Wall Street Journal,* October 11, B1, B3.

HECKATHORN, DOUGLAS D. 1990. "Collective Sanctions and Compliance Norms: A Formal Theory of Group-Medicated Social Control." *American Sociological Review, 55,* June, 366–384.

HEINS, MARJORIE. 1991. "The War on Nudity, Continued." *Playboy,* November, 53.

HEINTZ, KATHERINE E. 1987. "An Examination of Sex and Occupational-Role Presentations of Female Characters in Children's Picture Books." *Women's Studies in Communication, 10,* 2, Fall, 76–78.

HELLINGER, DANIEL, AND DENNIS R. JUDD. 1991. *The Democratic Facade.* Pacific Grove, Calif.: Brooks/Cole.

HELMER, J. 1975. *Drugs and Minority Oppression.* New York: Seabury.

HENDIN, HERBERT, CHRIS RUTENFRANS, AND ZBIGNIEW ZYLICZ. 1977. "Physician-Assisted Suicide and Euthanasia in the Netherlands: Lessons from the Dutch." *Journal of the American Medical Association, 277,* 21, June 4.

HENRIQUES, FERNANDO. 1966. *Prostitution and Society.* New York: Grove.

HENSLIN, JAMES M. 1970. "Guilt and Guilt Neutralization: Response and Adjustment to Suicide." In *Deviance and Respectability: The Social Construction of Moral Meanings,* Jack D. Douglas (ed.). New York: Basic Books.

HENSLIN, JAMES M. 1971. "Criminal Abortion: Making the Decision and Neutralizing the Act." In *Studies in the Sociology of Sex,* James M. Henslin (ed.). New York: Appleton-Century-Crofts, 113–135.

HENSLIN, JAMES M. 1988. "Individualism and Structuralism in Deviance Theory." *Deviant Behavior, 9,* 211–223.

HENSLIN, JAMES M. 1992. "Centuries of Childhood." In *Marriage and Family in a Changing Society,* 4th ed., James M. Henslin (ed.). New York: Basic Books, 214–225.

HENSLIN, JAMES M. 1993. Introduction to Article. In *Down-to-Earth Sociology: Introductory Readings,* 7th ed., James M. Henslin (ed.), New York: Free Press, 365.

HENSLIN, JAMES M. 1995a. "On Becoming Male: Reflections of a Sociologist on Childhood and Early Socialization." In *Down to Earth Sociology: Introductory Readings,* 8th ed., James M. Henslin (ed.). New York: Free Press, 126–136.

HENSLIN, JAMES M. 1995b. *Sociology: A Down-to-Earth Approach,* 2nd ed. Boston: Allyn & Bacon.

HENSLIN, JAMES M. 1996. *Essentials of Sociology: A Down-to-Earth Approach.* Boston: Allyn & Bacon.

HENSLIN, JAMES M. n.d. "Study of Real Estate Discrimination Practices in an All White Midwestern Community." Unpublished.

HENSLIN, JAMES M. 1999. *Sociology: A Down-to-Earth Approach,* 4th ed. Boston: Allyn and Bacon.

HENSLIN, JAMES M. 2000. *Essentials of Sociology, A Down-to-Earth Approach,* 3rd ed. Boston: Allyn and Bacon.

HENSLIN, JAMES M., AND MAE A. BIGGS. 1995. "Behavior in Public Places: The Sociology of the Vaginal Examination." In *Down-to-Earth Sociology: Introductory Readings,* 8th ed., James M. Henslin (ed.). New York: Free Press, 201–212.

HERBERT, BOB. 1988. "The Hate Virus." *New York Times,* August 10.

HERBERT, BOB. 1998. "Don't Flunk the Future." *New York Times,* August 13.

HEYL, BARBARA SHERMAN. 1979. *The Madam as Entrepreneur: Career Management in House Prostitution.* New Brunswick, N.J.: Transaction.

HIBBERT, CHRISTOPHER. 1963. *The Roots of Evil: A Social History of Crime and Punishment.* New York: Minerva.

HICKEY, MARY FRANCES. 1979. "Population: Under Control?" *News Focus, Newsweek.*

"High Anxiety." 1993. *Consumer Reports,* January, 19–24.

HILLS, STUART L. 1980. *Demystifying Social Deviance.* New York: McGraw-Hill.

HILLS, STUART L. (ed.). 1987. *Corporate Violence: Injury and Death for Profit.* Totowa, N.J.: Rowman & Littlefield.

HILTZ, STARR ROXANNE. 1969. "Widowhood." In *Marriage and Family in a Changing Society,* James M. Henslin (ed.). New York: Free Press, 521–531.

HIMMELHOCH, JEROME, AND SYLVIA FLEIS FAVA (eds.). 1955. *Sexual Behavior in American Society: An Appraisal of the First Two Kinsey Reports.* New York: Norton.

HINDELANG, MICHAEL J. 1978. "Race and Involvement in Common Personal Crimes." *American Sociological Review, 43,* February, 93–109.

HINDELANG, MICHAEL J., AND BRUCE J. DAVIS. 1977. "Forcible Rape in the United States: A Statistical Profile." In *Forcible Rape: The Crime, the Victim, and the Offender,* Duncan Chappell, Robley Geis, and Gilbert Geis (eds.). New York: Columbia University Press, 87–114.

HIRSCHI, TRAVIS. 1969. *Causes of Delinquency.* Berkeley: University of California Press.

HOBSON, JOHN A. 1939. *Imperialism: A Study,* rev. ed. London: G. Allen (first published in 1902).

HOCHSCHILD, ARLIE, AND ANNE MACHUNG. 1995. "Men Who Share 'The Second Shift.'" In *Down-to-Earth Sociology: Introductory Readings,* 8th ed., James M. Henslin (ed.). New York: Free Press, 383–397.

HOFFMAN, ALBERT. 1968. "Psychotomimetic Agents." In *Drugs Affecting the Central Nervous System* (vol. 2). New York: Marcel Dekker.

HOLDEN, BENJAMIN A. 1994. "In Elite Schools, Students See Hope of a Ticket Out." *Wall Street Journal,* August 15, B1, B4.

HOLDREN, JOHN P., AND PAUL R. EHRLICH. 1974. "Human Population and the Global Environment." *American Scientist, 62,* May–June, 282–292.

HOLMAN, RICHARD L. 1994. "World Wire." *Wall Street Journal,* July 28, A10.

HOLMS, JOHN PYNCHON, AND TOM BURKE. 1994. *Terrorism.* New York: Windsor.

HOLMES, STEVEN A. 1998. "AIDS Deaths in U.S. Drop by Nearly Half as Infections Go On." *New York Times,* October 8.

HOLMSTROM, LYNDA LYTLE, AND ANN WOLBERT BURGESS. 1989. "Rape and Everyday Life." In *Deviance in American Life,* James M. Henslin (ed.). New Brunswick, N.J.: Transaction, 349–371.

HOLTZMAN, ABRAHAM. 1963. *The Townsend Movement: A Political Study.* New York: Bookman.

HOMBLIN, DORA JANE. 1973. *The First Cities.* Boston: Little, Brown, Time-Life Books.

HOOKER, EVELYN. 1957. "The Adjustment of the Male Overt Homosexual." *Journal of Projective Techniques, 21,* March, 18–31.

HOOKER, EVELYN. 1958. "Male Homosexuality in the Rohrschach." *Journal of Projective Techniques, 22,* March, 33–54.

HOOTON, EARNEST A. 1939. *Crime and the Man.* Cambridge, Mass.: Harvard University Press.

HOPE, CHRISTINE A., AND RONALD G. STOVER. 1987. "Gender Status, Monotheism, and Social Complexity." *Social Forces, 65,* 1132–1138.

HORNBLOWER, MARGOT. 1993. "The Skin Trade." *Time,* June 21, 45–51.

HOROWITZ, RUTH. 1983. *Honor and the American Dream: Culture and Identity in a Chicano Community.* New Brunswick, N.J.: Rutgers University Press.

HOSENBALL, MARK. 1999. "A Plutonium Mystery." *Newsweek,* May 3, 62–64.

HOTCHKISS, SANDY. 1978. "The Realities of Rape." *Human Behavior, 12,* December, 18–23.

HOTZ, ROBERT LEE. 1999. "Early Humans' Fire Use Linked to Extinctions." *Los Angeles Times,* January 8.

HOWARD, JAN, AND ANSELM STRAUSS (eds.). 1975. *Humanizing Health Care.* New York: Wiley.

HOYT, HOMER. 1939. *The Structure and Growth of Residential Neighborhoods in American Cities.* Washington, D.C.: U.S. Federal Housing Administration.

HSU, FRANCIS L. K. 1971. *The Challenge of the American Dream: The Chinese in the United States.* Belmont, Calif.: Wadsworth.

HUBER, JOAN. 1990. "Micro-Macro Links in Gender Stratification." *American Sociological Review, 55,* February, 1–10.

HUDDLE, DONALD. 1993. "The Net National Cost of Immigration." Washington, D.C.: Carrying Capacity Network.

HUDSON, CHRISTOPHER G. 1988. "The Social Class and Mental Illness Correlation: Implications of the Research for Policy and Practice." *Journal of Sociology and Social Welfare, 15* (1), March, 27–54.

HUDSON, ROBERT B. 1978. "The 'Graying' of the Federal Budget and Its Consequences for Old-Age Policy." *The Gerontologist, 18,* October, 428–440.

HUFF-CORZINE, LIN, JAY CORZINE, AND DAVID C. MOORE. 1986. "Southern Exposure: Deciphering the South's Influence on Homicide Rates." *Social Forces, 64,* 906–924.

HUFF-CORZINE, LIN, JAY CORZINE, AND DAVID C. MOORE. 1991. "Deadly Connections: Culture, Poverty, and the Direction of Lethal Violence." *Social Forces, 69,* 3, March, 715–732.

HUGGINS, MARTHA K. 1993. "Lost Childhood: Assassinations of Youth in Democratizing Brazil." Paper presented at the annual meetings of the American Sociological Association.

HULL, JON D. 1987. "Life and Death with the Gangs." *Time,* August 24, 21–22.

HUMPHREYS, LAUD. 1970. *Tearoom Trade.* Chicago: Aldine. (Expanded version, Chicago: Aldine-Atherton, 1975.)

HUMPHRIES, DREW, JOHN DAWSON, VALERIE CRONIN, PHYLLIS KEATING, CHRIST WISNIEWSKI, AND JENNINE EICHFELD. 1992. "Mothers and Children, Drugs and Crack: Reactions to Maternal Drug Dependency." *Women and Criminal Justice, 3,* 2, 81–99.

HUXLEY, ALDOUS. 1954. *The Doors of Perception.* New York: Harper & Row.

IANNI, FRANCIS A. J., AND ELIZABETH REUSS-IANNI (eds.). 1976. *The Crime Society: Organized Crime and Corruption in America.* New York: New American Library.

INCIARDI, JAMES A. 1986. *The War on Drugs: Heroin, Cocaine, Crime, and Public Policy.* Mountain View, Calif.: Mayfield.

INCIARDI, JAMES A., AND ANNE E. POTTIEGER. 1994. "Crack-Cocaine Use and Street Crime." *Journal of Drug Issues, 24,* 2, Winter, 273–292.

INCIARDI, JAMES A., AND DUANE C. MCBRIDGE. 1990. "Debating the Legalization of Drugs." In *Handbook of Drug Control in the United States,* James A. Inciardi (ed.). New York: Greenwood.

INGERSOLL, BRUCE. 1988. "FDA Is Proposing Limits on Sulfites in Range of Foods." *Wall Street Journal,* December 20, C21.

INGERSOLL, BRUCE. 1990a. "Faster Slaughter Lines Are Contaminating Much U.S. Poultry." *Wall Street Journal,* November 16, A1, A6.

ISBELL, HARRIS. 1969. "Historical Development of Attitudes Toward Opiate Addiction in the United States." In *Man and Civilization: Conflict, and Creativity,* Seymour M. Farber and Roger H. L. Wilson (eds.). New York: McGraw-Hill, 154–170.

JACOBS, DAVID. 1978. "Inequality and the Legal Order: An Ecological Test of the Conflict Model." *Social Problems, 25,* June, 515–525.

JACOBSEN, THORKILD, AND ROBERT M. ADAMS. 1958. "Salt and Silt in Ancient Mesopotamian Agriculture." *Science,* November 21, 1251–1258.

JAFFE, JEROME H. 1965. "Drug Addiction and Drug Abuse." In *The Pharmacological Basis of Therapeutics,* Louis S. Goodman and Alfred Gilmann (eds.). New York: Macmillan, 285–311.

JAMES, JENNIFER, AND NANETTE J. DAVIS. 1982. "Contingencies in Female Sexual Role Deviance: The Case of Prostitution." *Human Organization, 41,* 4, Winter, 345–350.

JAMES, J., AND J. 1977. MEYERDING. 1977. "Early Sexual Experiences in Prostitution." *Archives of Sexual Behavior, 7,* 31–42.

JANOWOTZ, MORRIS. 1970a. "The Twentieth-Century Race Riot, Commodity Type: The Summer of 1967." In *American Violence,* Richard Maxwell (ed.). Englewood Cliffs, N.J.: Prentice Hall, 147–155.

JANOWITZ, MORRIS. 1970b. "The Twentieth-Century Race Riot, Communal Type: Chicago, 1919." In *American Violence,* Richard Maxwell (ed.). Englewood Cliffs, N.J.: Prentice Hall, 126–136.

JEFFERSON, THOMAS. 1977. *Notes on the State of Virginia,* Bernard Wishy and William C. Leuchtenburg (eds.). New York: Harper & Row.

JEKIELEK, SUSAN M. 1998. "Parental Conflict, Marital Disruption and Children's Emotional Well-Being." *Social Forces, 76,* 3, March, 905–935.

JENKINS, BRIAN MICHAEL. 1985. "Future Trends in International Terrorism." *Symposium on International Terrorism.* Washington, D.C.: Defense Intelligence Agency, December 2–3.

JENNESS, VALERIE. 1990. "From Sex as Sin to Sex as Work: COYOTE and the Reorganization of Prostitution as a Social Problem." *Social Problems, 37,* 3, August, 103–120.

JOFFE, CAROLE. 1978. "What Haven? For Whom?" *Social Policy, 9,* May–June, 58–60.

JOHNSON, BRUCE, KEVIN ANDERSON, AND ERIC D. WISH. 1988. "A Day in the Life of 105 Drug Addicts and Abusers: Crimes Committed and How the Money Was Spent." *Sociology and Social Research, 72,* 3, April, 185–191.

JOHNSON, BRUCE D., PAUL J. GOLDSTEIN, EDWARD PREBLE, JAMES SCHMEIDLER, DOUGLAS S. LIPTON, BARRY SPUNT, AND THOMAS MILLER. 1985. *Taking Care of Business: The Economics of Crime by Heroin Abusers.* Lexington, Mass.: Lexington Books.

JOHNSON, DANNY R. 1992. "Tobacco Stains: Cigarette [...] African-American Groups." *The Progres- [...]cember, 26–28.*

JOHNSON, DIRK. 1987. "Fear of AIDS Stirs New Attacks on Homosexuals." *New York Times,* April 24, 8.

JOHNSON, DIRK. 1988. "Murder Charges Are Met by Cries of Compassion." *New York Times,* August 8, A14.

JOHNSON, TERRY R., RANDALL J. POZDENA, AND GARY STEIGER. 1979. *The Impact of Alternative Negative Income Tax Programs on Non Durable Consumption.* Menlo Park, Calif.: SRI International, October.

JOHNSTON, LLOYD D., PATRICK M. O'MALLEY, AND JERALD G. BACHMAN. 1998. *National Survey Results on Drug Use from The Monitoring the Future Study, 1975–1997.* Washington, D.C.: U.S. Department of Health and Human Services.

JOSEPHY, ALVIN M., JR. 1970. "Indians in History." *Atlantic Monthly,* June, 67–72.

Juvenile Justice Bulletin. 1988. Washington, D.C.: U.S. Government Printing Office.

KAGAN, DONALD. 1995. *On the Origins of War and the Preservation of Peace.* New York: Doubleday.

KAIN, JOHN F., AND JOHN R. MEYER (eds.). 1971. *Essays in Regional Economics.* Cambridge, Mass.: Harvard University Press.

KAISERMAN, MURRAY J., AND BYRON ROGERS. 1991. "Tobacco Consumption Declining Faster in Canada Than in the US." *American Journal of Public Health, 81, 7,* July, 902–094.

KAL, CLAUDIA. 1998. "Now, a Scary Strain of Drug-Resistant HIV." *Newsweek,* July 13.

KAMIN, LEON. 1981. "Schizophrenia." Unpublished. Princeton University, Department of Psychology.

KANTOR, GLENDA KAUFMAN, AND MURRAY A. STRAUS. 1987. "The 'Drunken Bum' Theory of Wife Beating." *Social Problems, 34,* 3, June, 213–230.

KAPLAN, CARL. S. 1998. "Anti-Porn Law Enters Court; Delay Soon Follows." *New York Times,* November 20.

KAPLAN, SIDNEY. 1990. "Historical Efforts to Encourage White-Indian Intermarriage in the United States and Canada." *International Social Science Review, 65,* 3, Summer, 126–132.

KARLEN, ARNO. 1978. "Homosexuality: The Scene and Its Students." In *The Sociology of Sex: An Introductory Reader,* rev. ed., James M. Henslin and Edward Sagarin (eds.). New York: Schocken, 223–248.

KARLEN, NEAL, AND BARBARA BURGOWER. 1985. "Dumping the Mentally Ill." *Newsweek, 105,* January 7, 17.

KARMEN, ANDREW. 1980. "The Narcotics Problem: Views from the Left." In *Is America Possible? Social Problems from Conservative, Liberal, and Socialist Perspectives,* 2nd ed., Henry Etzkowitz (ed.). St. Paul, Minn.: West, 171–180.

KARP, DAVID A., GREGORY P. STONE, AND WILLIAM C. YOELS. 1991. *Being Urban: A Sociology of City Life,* 2nd ed. New York: Praeger.

Bibliography

KARP, DAVID A., AND WILLIAM C. YOELS. 1990. "Sport and Urban Life." *Journal of Sport and Social Issues, 14,* 2, 77–102.

KARR, ALBERT R. 1995. "Fed Study Challenges Notion of Bias Against Minorities in Mortgage Lending." *Wall Street Journal,* January 26, A13.

KATZ, MICHAEL B. 1989. *The Undeserving Poor: From the War on Poverty to the War on Welfare.* New York: Pantheon.

KATZENSTEIN, LARRY. 1994. "Alcohol for the Heart." *American Health, 13,* 4, May, 9.

KAYSON, CARL. 1972. "The Computer That Printed W*O*L*F." *Foreign Affairs, 50,* July, 662–666.

KEANS, CARL. 1991. "Socioenvironmental Determinants of Community Formation." *Environment and Behavior, 23,* 1, January, 27–46.

KEATING, FRANK. 1998. Memo released by the Governor of Oklahoma. Online.

KEIL, THOMAS J., AND GENNARO F. VITO. 1989. "Race, Homicide Severity, and Application of the Death Penalty: A Consideration of the Barnett Scale." *Criminology, 27,* 3, 511–535.

KELLEY, KITTY. 1988. "The Dark Side of Camelot." *People Magazine,* February 28, 107–114.

KEMP, JACK. 1990. "Tackling Poverty: Market-Based Policies to Empower the Poor." *Policy Review, 51,* Winter, 2–5.

KEOWN, JOHN, AND GERRIT VAN DER WAL. 1999. "Assessment of Physician-Assisted Death by Members of the Public Prosecution in the Netherlands." *Journal of Medical Ethics. 25,* February 16, 8–15.

KERNER, OTTO. 1968. *Report of the National Advisory Commission on Civil Disorders.* Washington, D.C.: U.S. Government Printing Office.

KETTL, DONALD F. 1991. "The Savings-and-Loan Bailout: The Mismatch Between the Headlines and the Issues." *PS, 24,* 3, September, 441–447.

KILBORN, PETER T. 1998. "Reality of H.M.O. System Does Not Live Up to Hopes for Health Care." *New York Times,* October 5.

KIMBALL, M. M. 1986. "Television and Sex-Role Attitudes." In *The Impact of Television: A Natural Experiment in Three Communities,* T. M. Williams (ed.). Orlando, Fla.: Academic Press.

KING, MARTIN LUTHER, JR. 1958. *Stride Toward Freedom: The Montgomery Story.* New York: Harper.

KING, RALPH T., JR. 1994. "Some Mortgage Firms Neglect Black Areas More Than Banks Do." *Wall Street Journal,* August 9, A1, A6.

KING, WAYNE. 1979. *The New York Times,* March 15.

KINSEY, ALFRED C., WARDELL B. POMEROY, AND CLYDE E. MARTIN. 1948. *Sexual Behavior in the Human Male.* Philadelphia: Saunders.

KINSEY, ALFRED C., WARDELL B. POMEROY, CLYDE E. MANTIN, AND PAUL H. GEBHARD. 1953. *Sexual Behavior in the Human Female.* New York: Saunders.

KIRKHAM, GEORGE L. 1971. "Homosexuality in Prison." In *Studies in the Sociology of Sex,* James M. Henslin (ed.). New York: Appleton, 325–349.

KIRKPATRICK, MELANIE. 1992. "On the Abortion Barricades." *Wall Street Journal,* April 23, A14.

KIRKPATRICK, TERRY. 1981. "A New Breed of Pioneers Are Homesteading America's Cities." *Alton Telegraph.* June 26.

KITANO, HARRY H. L. 1974. *Race Relations.* Englewood Cliffs N.J.: Prentice Hall.

KLECK, GARY, AND SUSAN SAYLES. 1990. "Rape and Resistance." *Social Problems, 37,* 2, May, 149–162.

KLEIMAN, MARK. 1985. "We Can't Stop Friend or Foe in the Drug Trade." *Wall Street Journal,* April 9, 30.

KLEIN, STEPHEN, JOAN PETERSILIA, AND SUSAN TURNER. 1990. "Race and Imprisonment Decisions in California." *Science, 247,* 4944, February 16, 812–816.

KLEINFIELD, N. R. 1999. "Days on Methadone, Bound by Its Lifeline." *New York Times,* January 2.

KLEINMAN, PAUL H., ERIC D. WISH, SHREEY DEREN, GREGORY RAIMONE, AND ELLEN MOREHOUSE. 1987. "Daily Marijuana Use and Problem Behaviors Among Adolescents." *International Journal of the Addictions, 22* (12).

KNIGHTS, ROGER. 1999. "Electronic Tagging in Practice." *Teleconnect,* January 22.

KNOWLES, LOUIS L., AND KENNETH PREWITT. 1969. *Institutionalized Racism in America.* Englewood Cliffs, N.J.: Prentice Hall.

KOHN, ALFIE. 1988. "Make Love, Not War." *Psychology Today,* June, 35–38.

KOMISAR, LUCY. 1971. "The Image of Woman in Advertising." In *Woman in Sexist Society: Studies in Power and Powerlessness.* Vivian Gornick and Barbara K. Moran (eds.). New York: Basic books, 207–217.

KORDA, MICHAEL. 1973. *Male Chauvinism: How It Works.* New York: Random House.

KORNHAUSER, WILLIAM. 1961. "'Power Elite' or 'Veto Groups'?" In *Culture and Social Character,* Seymour Martin Lipset and Leo Lowenthal (eds.). Glencoe, Ill.: Free Press, 252–267.

KOTLOWITZ, ALEX. 1988. "Chicago Street Gangs Treat Public Housing as Private Fortresses." *Wall Street Journal,* September 30, 1, 2.

KOZEL, NICHOLAS J. 1996. *Epidemiologic Trends in Drug Abuse. Community Epidemiology Work Group.* Bethesda, Maryland: National Institutes of Health, June.

KOZOL, JONATHAN. 1995. "Savage Inequalities." In *Down-to-Earth Sociology: Introductory Readings,* 8th ed., James M. Henslin (ed.). New York: Free Press, 315–323.

KOZOL, JONATHAN. 1999. "Savage Inequalities." In *Down-to-Earth Sociology: Introductory Readings,* 10th ed., James M. Henslin, ed. New York: Free Press, 343–351.

KRIEGER, LISA. 1985. "Abortion Foes, Proponents Intensify Battle." *American Medical News, 28,* June 7, 2–3.

KUCZYNSKI, JURGEN. 1946. *A Short History of Labour Conditions Under Industrial Capitalism in the United States of America, 1789–1946,* 2nd ed. New York: Barnes & Nobel.

KURTH, JAMES R. 1974. "American Military Policy and Advanced Weapons." In *Social Problems and Public Policy: Inequality and Justice,* Lee Rainwater (ed.). Chicago: Aldine, 336–352.

KUSUM. 1993. "The Use of Pre-natal Diagnostic Techniques for Sex Selection: The Indian Scene." *Bioethics, 7,* 2–3, April, 149–165.

KUTCHINSKY, BERL. 1973. "The Effects of Easy Availability of Pornography on the Incidence of Sex Crimes in Copenhagen: The Danish Experience." *Journal of Social Issues, 29,* 163–181.

LA BARRE, WESTON. 1954. *The Human Animal.* Chicago: University of Chicago Press.

LA GORY, MARK, RUSSELL WARD, AND THOMAS JURAVICH. 1980. "The Age Segregation Process." *Urban Affairs Quarterly, 16,* 59–80.

LaBASTILLE, ANNE. 1979. "The Deadly Toll of Acid Rain: All of Nature Is Suffering." *Science Digest, 86,* October, 61–66.

LABI, NADYA. 1998. "The Choirboy." *Time,* April 6, 29–34.

LACAYO, RICHARD. 1991. "Crusading Against the Pro-Choice Movement." *Time,* October 21.

LaDOU, JOSEPH. 1991. "Deadly Migration: Hazardous Industries' Flight to the Third World." *Technology Review, 94,* 5, July, 46–53.

LaFREE, GARY D. 1980. "The Effect of Sexual Stratification by Race on Official Reactions to Rape." *American Sociological Review, 45,* October, 842–854.

LAGERFELD, STEVEN. 1991. "A Look at the Urban Future." *Wall Street Journal,* October 2, A10.

LAMAR, JACOB V., JR. 1986. "An Inmate and a Gentleman." *Time,* August 11, 17.

LAMAR, JACOB V. 1988. "A Bloody West Coast Story." *Time,* April 18, 32.

LAMBERT, WADE. 1994. "Appeals Court Upholds Ban on Gays in Military." *Wall Street Journal,* November 23, B2.

LANDES, DAVID S. 1998. *The Wealth and Poverty of Nations: Why Some Are Rich and Some So Poor.* New York: W.W. Norton.

LANDRIGAN, PHILIP J., AND DEAN B. BAKER. 1991. "The Recognition and Control of Occupational Disease." *Journal of the American Medical Association, 266,* 5, August 7, 676–680.

LANG, KURT, AND GLADYS LANG. 1968. "Racial Disturbances as Collective Protest." In *Riots and Rebellion: Civil Violence in the Urban Community,* Louis H. Masotti, and Don R. Bowen (eds.). Beverly Hills, Calif.: Sage, 121–130.

LANGAN, PATRICK A. 1985. "Racism on Trial: New Evidence to Explain the Racial Composition of Prisons in the United States." *Journal of Criminal Law and Criminology,* Fall, 666–683.

LANGAN, PATRICK A., AND MARK A. CUNNIFF. 1992. "Recidivism of Felons on Probation, 1986–1989." Bureau of Justice Statistics Special Report, Washington, D.C., February.

LANNIN, DONALD R. 1998. "Cocaine Overdose Deaths Higher in Hot Weather." *Journal of the American Medical Association, 279,* June 10, 801–1808.

LAQUEUR, WALTER. 1977. *Terrorism.* Boston: Little, Brown.

LARNED, DEBORAH. 1977. "The Epidemic in Unnecessary Hysterectomies." In *Seizing Our Bodies: The Politics of Women's Health,* Claudia Dreyfus (ed.). New York: Random House.

LASCH, CHRISTOPHER. 1977. *Haven in a Heartless World: The Family Besieged.* New York: Basic Books.

LASLETT, BARBARA. 1980. "Family, Social Change Can Often Spell Trouble." University of California, University Extension, Course by Newspaper, San Diego.

LAUMANN, EDWARD O., JOHN H. GAGNON, ROBERT T. MICHAEL, AND STUART MICHAELS. 1994. *The Social Organization of Sexuality: Sexual Practices in the United States.* Chicago: University of Chicago Press.

"Law Enacted to Protect Ainu Culture, Tradition." 1997. Foreign Press Center of Japan, June 19.

LAW, SYLVIA. 1988. "Homosexuality and the Social Meaning of Gender." *Wisconsin Law Review, 2,* 187–235.

LAWSON, PAUL E., AND C. PATRICK MORRIS. 1991. "The native American Church and the New Court: The Smith Case and Indian Religious Freedoms." *American Indian Culture and Research Journal, 15,* 1, 79–91.

LEE, DOROTHY. 1959. *Freedom and Culture.* Englewood Cliffs, N.J.: Prentice Hall.

LEE, REX E. 1980. *A Lawyer Looks at the Equal Rights Amendment.* Provo, Utah: Brigham Young University Press.

LEE, SHARON M. 1998. "Asian Americans: Diverse and Growing." *Population Bulletin, 53,* 2, June, 1–39.

LEIGHTY, KEITH E. 1981. "Germ Testing by Japanese Killed POWs." AP, October 31.

LENDER, MARK EDWARD, AND JAMES KIRBY MARTIN. 1982. *Drinking in America: A History.* New York: Free Press.

LENZ-ROMEISS, FELIZITAS. 1973. *The City: New Town or Home Town?* Edith Kustner and J. A. Underwood (trans.). New York: Praeger.

LEONARD, REBECCA, AND DON C. LOCKE. 1993. "Communication Stereotypes: Is Interracial Communication Possible?" *Journal of Black Studies, 23,* 3, March, 332–343.

LERNER, GERDA. 1986. *The Creation of Patriarchy.* New York: Oxford University press.

LERNER, ROBERT, ALTHEA K. NAGAI, AND STANLEY ROTHMAN. 1990. "Abortion and Social Change in America." *Society, 2, 27,* January–February, 8–15.

LESSER, ALEXANDER. 1968. "War and the State." In *War: The Anthropology of Armed Conflict and Aggression,* Morton Fried, Marvin Harris, and Robert Murphy (eds.). Garden City, N.Y.: Natural History.

LESTER, DAVID. 1972. "Incest." *Journal of Sex Research, 8,* November, 268–285.

LeVAY, SIMON. 1993. *The Sexual Brain.* Cambridge, Mass.: MIT Press.

LEVIN, JACK, AND JAMES ALAN FOX. 1985. *Mass Murder: America's Growing Menace.* New York: Plenum.

LEVIN, LOWELL S., ALFRED H. KATZ, AND ERIK HOLST. 1976. *Self-Care: Lay Initiatives in Health.* New York: Prodist.

LEVINE, ART. 1986. "Drug Education Gets an F." *U.S. News & World Report,* October 13, 63–64.

LEVITAN, SAR A., AND ISAAC SHAPIRO. 1987. *Working but Poor: America's Contradiction.* Baltimore: Johns Hopkins University Press.

LEWIN, TAMAR. 1998. "1 in 8 Boys of High-School Age Has Been Abused, Survey Says." *New York Times,* June 26.

LEWIS, DAVID L. 1996. "Bias in Drug Sentences." *National Law Journal,* February 5.

LEWIS, JACK. 1990. "The Ogallala Aquifer: An Underground Sea." *EPA Journal, 16, 6,* November, 42–44.

LEWIS, KAREN J. 1988. "Abortion: Judicial Control." Washington, D.C.: Congressional Research Service, American Law Division. Mimeo. September 13.

LEWIS, OSCAR. 1959. *Five Families.* New York: Basic Books.

LEWIS, OSCAR. 1966. "The Culture of Poverty." *Scientific American, 115,* October, 19–25.

LEWIS, OSCAR. 1968. *La Vida.* New York: Vintage.

LEWIS, PETER W., AND KENNETH D. PEOPLES. 1978. *The Supreme Court and the Criminal Process: Cases and Comments.* Philadelphia: Saunders.

LIAZOS, ALEX. 1981. "Corporate Crime and Capitalism." Paper presented at the annual meeting of the Society for the Study of Social Problems.

Library of Congress, Federal Research Division, *Russia: A Country Study, 1999.* online.

LIGHT, DONALD W., JR. 1973. "Treating Suicide: The Illusions of a Professional Movement." *International Social Science Journal, 25,* 473–488.

LIGHT, DONALD W. 1992. "Perestroika for Russian Health Care." *Footnotes, 20, 3,* March, 7, 9.

LIGHTFOOT-KLEIN, H. 1989. "Rites of Purification and Their Effects: Some Psychological Aspects of Female Genital Circumcision and Infibulation (Pharaonic Circumcision) in an Afro-Arab Society (Sudan)." *Journal of Psychological Human Sexuality, 2,* 61–78.

LINDEN, EUGENE. 1991. "Lost Tribes, Lost Knowledge." *Time,* September 23, 46, 48, 50, 52, 54, 56.

LINTON, RALPH. 1936. *The Study of Man.* New York: Appleton.

LINZ, DANIEL, EDWARD DONNERSTEIN, AND STEVEN PENROD. 1987. "The Findings and Recommendations of the Attorney General's Commission on Pornography: Do the Psychological 'Facts' Fit the Political Fury?" *American Psychologist,* October, 946–953.

LIPTON, MICHAEL. 1979. *Why Poor People Stay Poor: Urban Bias in World Development.* Cambridge, Mass.: Harvard University Press.

LITTLE, PETER D., AND MICHAEL M. HOROWITZ (EDS.). 1987. *Lands at Risk in the Third World: Local-Level Perspectives.* Boulder, Colo.: Westview.

LIVERNASH, ROBERT, AND ERIC RODENBURG. 1998. "Population Change, Resources, and the Environment." *Population Bulletin, 53, 1,* March, 1–40.

LLOYD, ROBIN. 1976. *For Money or Love: Boy Prostitution in America.* New York: Ballantine.

LOLLI, GIORGIO. 1958. *Alcohol and Italian Culture.* New York: Free Press.

LOMBROSO, CESARE. 1911. *Crime: Its Causes and Remedies,* H. P. Horton (trans.). Boston: Little, Brown. "The Long Losing Battle Against Drugs." 1988. *The Economist.* March 5, 23–24.

LOPEZ, ADALBERTO (ed.). 1980. *The Puerto Ricans: Their History, Culture, and Society.* Cambridge, Mass.: Schenkman.

LORBER, JUDITH. 1980. "Beyond Equality of the Sexes: The Question of Children." In *Marriage and Family in a Changing Society,* James M. Henslin (ed.). New York: Free Press, 522–533.

LORENZ, KONRAD. 1966. *On Aggression.* New York: Harcourt.

LOWENSTEIN, SOPHIE FREUD. 1980. "Understanding Lesbian Women." *Social Casework, 61,* January, 29–38.

LOWI, THEODORE J. 1977. "Machine Politics—Old and New." In *City Scenes: Problems and Prospects,* J. John Palen (ed.). Boston: Little, Brown.

LUBLIN, JOANN S. 1991. "Sexual Harassment Is Topping Agenda in Many Executive Education Programs." *Wall Street Journal,* December 2, B1, B5.

LUBLIN, JOANN S. 1992. "Corporate Efforts to Fight Harassment Face Credibility Gap, Survey Finds." *Wall Street Journal,* May 15, A5B.

LUCKENBILL, DAVID F. 1986. "Deviant Career Mobility: The Case of Male Prostitutes." *Social Problems 33, 4,* April, 283–296.

LUKER, KRISTEN. 1975. *Taking Chances: Abortion and the Decision Not to Contracept.* Berkeley: University of California Press.

LUNDBERG, OLLIE. 1991. "Causal Explanations for Class Inequality in Health: An Empirical Analysis." *Social Science and Medicine, 32, 4,* 385–393.

LUTZ, HAROLD J. 1959. *Aboriginal Man and White Man as Historical Causes of Fires in the Boreal Forest, with Particular Reference to Alaska.* New Haven, Conn.: Yale University School of Forestry. No. 65 [as referenced in Burch 1971].

LUY, MARY LYNN M. 1977. "Rape: Not a Sex Act—A Violent Crime, An Interview with Dr. Dorothy J. Hicks." *Modern Medicine.* February 15, 36–41.

LYNCH, MITCHELL C. 1980. "Old Ice Indicates Acid Was Present in Rain Long Ago." *Wall Street Journal,* September 18, 13.

LYND, ROBERT S., AND HELEN M. LYND. 1929. *Middletown.* New York: Harcourt.

LYND, ROBERT S., AND HELEN M LYND. 1937. *Middletown in Transition.* New York: Harcourt.

LYNCH, JOHN W., GEORGE A. KAPLAN, AND SARAH J. SHEMA. 1997. "Cumulative Impact of Sustained Economic Hardship on Physical, Cognitive, Psychological, and Social Functioning." *New England Journal of Medicine, 337,* 26, December 25, 1889–1895.

MACKENZIE, DORIS LAYTON, AND DALE G. PARENT. 1991. "Shock Incarceration and Prison Crowding in Louisiana." *Journal of Criminal Justice, 19,* 225–237.

MACKENZIE, HILARY. 1998. "Enmeshed in Conflict and Drought, Southern Sudan Starves." *New York Times,* July 22.

MACKINNON, CATHARINE A. 1979. *Sexual Harassment of Working Women: A Case of Sex Discrimination.* New Haven, Conn.: Yale University Press.

MACKLIN, ELEANOR D. 1974. "Cohabitation in College: Going Very Steady." *Psychology Today, 8,* 53–59.

MACNAMARA, DONAL E. J., AND EDWARD SAGARIN. 1977. *Sex, Crime, and the Law.* New York: Free Press.

MADIGAN, LEE, AND NANCY GAMBLE. 1991. *The Second Rape: Society's Continued Betrayal of the Victim.* New York: Free Press.

MAHRAN, M. 1978. *Proceedings of the Third International Congress of Medical Sexology.* Littleton, Mass.: PSG.

MAHRAN, M. 1981. "Medical Dangers of Female Circumcision." *International Planned Parenthood Federation Medical Bulletin, 2,* 1–2.

MAMDANI, MAHMOOD. 1973. *The Myth of Population Control: Family, Caste, and Class in an Indian Village.* New York: Monthly Review [as contained in Simon 1981].

Manpower Report to the President. 1971. Washington, D.C.: U.S. Department of Labor, Manpower Administration, April.

MANSKI, CHARLES F. 1992–93. "Income and Higher Education." *Focus, 14,* 3, Winter, 14–19.

MARGER, MARTIN N. 1987. *Elites and Masses: An Introduction to Political Sociology,* 2nd ed. Belmont, Calif.: Wadsworth.

MARKUSEN, ERIC. 1995. "Genocide in Cambodia." In *Down-to-Earth Sociology: Introductory Readings,* 8th ed., James M. Henslin (eds.). New York: Free Press, 355–364.

MARSIGLIO, WILLIAM. 1993. "Attitudes Toward Homosexual Activity and Gays as Friends: A National Survey of Heterosexual 15- to 19-Year-Old Males." *Journal of Sex Research, 30,* 1, February, 12–17.

MARTIN, PAUL SCHULTZ. 1967. "Prehistoric Overkill." In *Pleistocene Extinctions: The Search for a Cause,* Paul Schultz Martin and H. E. Wright, Jr. (eds.). New Haven, Conn.: Yale University Press.

MARTIN, PHILIP, AND ELIZABETH MIDGLEY. 1999. "Immigration to the United States." *Population Bulletin, 54,* 2, June, 1–43.

MARX, KARL. 1967. *Das Kapital.* New York: International (originally published in 1867–1895).

MARX, KARL, AND FRIEDRICH ENGELS. 1906. *Capital: A Critique of Political Economy,* E. Aveling (trans.). Chicago: Charles Kerr.

MARX, KARL, AND FRIEDRICH ENGELS. 1964. *The Communist Manifesto,* S. Moore (trans.). New York: Washington Square (originally published in 1848).

MASTERS, WILLIAM, AND VIRGINIA JOHNSON. 1979. *Homosexuality in Perspective.* Boston: Little, Brown.

MAUGH, THOMAS H., II. 1998. "AIDS Care Costs Overstated, Says Rand Study." *Los Angeles Times,* December 25.

MAYNARD, DOUGLAS W. 1984. *Inside Plea Bargaining: The Language of Negotiation.* New York: Plenum.

MAYNE, SUSAN TAYLOR, DWIGHT T. JANERICH, PETER GREENWALD, SHERRY CHOROST, CATHY TUCCI, MUHAMMAD B. ZAMAN, MYRON R. MELAMED, MAUREEN KIELY, AND MARTIN F. MCKNEALLY. 1995. "Dietary Beta Carotene and Lung Cancer Risk in U.S. Nonsmokers." *Journal of the National Cancer Institute, 86,* 1, January 5, 33–38.

MCCARTHY, BILL, AND JOHN HAGAN. 1992. "Mean Streets: The Theoretical Significance of Situational Delinquency Among Homeless Youths." *American Journal of Sociology, 98,* 3, November, 597–627.

MCCORMICK, JOHN. 1999. "Change Has Taken Place." *Newsweek,* June 7, 34.

MCCUEN, GARY E. (ed.). 1993. *Ecocide and Genocide in the Vanishing Forest: The Rainforests and Native People.* Hudson, Wis: GEM.

MCDONALD, PETER. "Low Fertility Not Politically Sustainable." *Population Today,* August–September 2001:3, 8.

MCDOWELL, BART. 1984. "Mexico City: An Alarming Giant." *National Geographic, 166,* 139–174.

MCFALLS, JOSEPH A., JR. 1998. "Population: A Lively Introduction." *Population Bulletin, 53,* 3, September, 1–45.

MCGEARY, JOHANNA. 1998. "Nukes . . . They're Back." *Time,* May 25, 34–40.

MCGARIGLE, BILL. 1997. "Satellite Tracking for House Arrest." *Geo Info,* May.

McGINLEY, LAURIE. 1999. "Health-Care Debate Heats Up Over Control of Medical Decisions." *Wall Street Journal,* February 18.

McINTYRE, JENNIE, THELMA MYINT, AND LYNN CURTIS. 1979. "Sexual Assault Outcomes: Completed and Attempted Rapes." Paper presented at the annual meeting of the American Sociological Association. Boston.

McKEOWN, THOMAS. 1977. *The Modern Rise of Population.* New York: Academic Press.

McKEOWN, THOMAS. 1980. *The Role of Medicine: Dream, Mirage, or Nemesis?* Princeton, N.J.: Princeton University Press.

McMANUS, MICHAEL J. 1986. "Introduction." In *Final Report of the Attorney General's Commission on Pornography.* Nashville, Tenn: Rutledge Hill, ix—l.

McNEELY, R. L., AND CARL E. POPE. 1981. "Socioeconomic and Racial Issues in the Measurement of Criminal Involvement." In *Race, Crime, and Criminal Justice,* R. L. McNeely and Carl E. Pope (eds.). Beverly Hills, Calif.: Sage, 31–47.

MEDVEDEV, ZHORES. 1980. *Nuclear Disaster in the Urals.*

Meese Commission. 1986. *Final Report of the Attorney General's Commission on Pornography.* Washington, D.C.: U.S. Department of Justice.

MEIER, BARRY. 1987a. "As Food Imports Rise, Consumers Face Peril from Use of Pesticides." *Wall Street Journal,* March 26, 1, 25.

MEIER, BARRY. 1987b. "Health Studies Suggest Asbestos Substitutes Also Pose Cancer Risk." *Wall Street Journal,* May 12, 1, 21.

MEIER, BARRY. 1999. "Tobacco Windfall Begins Tug-of-War Among Lawmakers." *New York Times,* January 10.

MELLOAN, GEORGE. 1994. "Europe Struggles with the Burdens of Old Age." *Wall Street Journal,* December 12, A15.

MELMAN, SEYMOUR. 1970. *Pentagon Capitalism.* New York: McGraw-Hill.

MELODY, G. F. 1969. "Chronic Pelvic Congestion in Prostitutes." *Medical Aspects of Human Sexuality, 3,* November, 103–104.

MENDELS, PAMELA. 1998. "Judge Rules Against Filters at Library." *New York Times,* November 23.

MENDELS, PAMELA. 1998. "Rights Group Develops 'Hate' Filter." *New York Times,* November 11.

MERTON, ROBERT K. 1968. *Social Theory and Social Structure,* enlarged ed. New York: Free Press.

MERTON, ROBERT K., AND ROBERT NISBET (eds.). 1976. *Contemporary Social Problems,* 4th ed. New York: Harcourt.

MERWINE, MAYNARD H. 1993. "How Africa Understands Female Circumcision." *New York Times,* November 24.

MESSNER, STEVEN F. 1983. "Regional and Racial Effects on the Urban Homicide Rate: The Subculture of Violence Revisited." *American Journal of Sociology, 88,* 997–1007.

MEYER, H. 1954. *Old English Coffee Houses.* Emmaus, Pa.: Rodale.

MIALL, CHARLENE E. 1986. "The Stigma of Involuntary Childlessness." *Social Problems, 33,* 4, April, 268–282.

MICHELMAN, KATE. 1988. As quoted in "NARAL," pamphlet published by the National Abortion Rights Action League, 1.

MILBANK, DANA. 1994. "In His Solitude, A Finnish Thinker Posits Cataclysms." *Wall Street Journal,* May 20, A1, A8.

MILES, RUFUS E., JR. 1970. "The Population Challenge of the 70's: Achieving a Stationary Population." In *The Crisis of Survival,* editors of *The Progressive* (eds.). Glenview, Ill.: Scott Foresman, 122–140.

MILES, STEVEN. 1980. "Intellectualism Meant Death in Cambodia." *St. Louis Post-Dispatch,* April 8, D3.

MILLAR, HEATHER. 1997. "For 'Neurosis,' Press 'Enter.'" *Business Week,* October 27.

MILLER, JUDITH. 1999. "U.S. and Uzbeks Agree on Chemical Arms Plant Cleanup." *New York Times,* May 25.

MILLER, JUDITH, AND WILLIAM J. BROAD. 1999. "Clinton Describes Terrorism Threat for 21st Century." *New York Times,* January 22.

MILLER, MICHAEL W. 1994a. "Quality Stuff: Firm Is Peddling Cocaine, and Deals Are Legit." *Wall Street Journal,* October 27, A1, A8.

MILLER, MICHAEL W. 1994b. "Survey Sketches New Portrait of the Mentally Ill." *Wall Street Journal,* January 14, B1, B10.

MILLER, WALTER B. 1958. "Lower-Class Culture as a Generating Milieu of Gang Delinquency." *Journal of Social Issues, 14,* 5–19.

MILLER, WALTER B. 1975. *Violence by Youth Gangs and Youth Groups as a Crime Problem in Major American Cities.* Washington, D.C.: U.S. Government Printing Office.

MILLETT, KATE. 1970. *Sexual Politics.* Garden City, N.Y.: Doubleday.

MILLETT, KATE. 1973. *The Prostitution Papers: A Candid Dialogue.* New York: Avon.

MILLS, C. WRIGHT. 1958. *The Causes of World War Three.* New York: Simon & Schuster.

MILLS, C. WRIGHT. 1959a. *The Power Elite.* New York: Oxford University Press.

MILLS, C. WRIGHT. 1959b. *The Sociological Imagination.* New York: Oxford University Press.

MILLS, KAREN M., AND THOMAS J. PALUMBO. 1980. *A Statistical Portrait of Women in the United States: 1978.* Washington, D.C.: U.S. Government Printing Office.

MILNER, CHRISTINA, AND RICHARD MILNER. 1972. *Black Players.* Boston: Little Brown.

MILVY, PAUL. 1979. "Cancer from the Radiation." *New York Times,* April 12, 19.

"Minneapolis Judge Lets Victim Set Punishment." 1989. *Jet, 17,* January 30, 24.

MINTZ, MORTON. 1979. "Error Placed H-Bomb Secrets on Library Shelf." *St. Louis Globe-Democrat,* May 18, 5a.

MOBERG, MARK. 1999. "Strategies of a Multiracial Environmental Coalition in Southern Alabama." *Enviro-Tech,* Spring, 4–8.

MOKHIBER, RUSSELL, AND LEONARD SHEN. 1981. "Love Canal." In *Who's Poisoning America: Corporate Polluters and Their Victims in the Chemical Age,* Ralph Nader, Ronald Brownstein, and John Richard (eds.). San Francisco: Sierra Club Books, 268–310.

MONTAGU, M. F. ASHLEY. 1960. *Introduction to Physical Anthropology,* 3rd ed. Springfield, Ill.: C. C. Thomas

MONTAGU, M. F. ASHLEY. 1964. *The Concept of Race.* New York: Free Press.

MOORE, GWEN. 1979. "The Structure of a National Elite Network." *American Sociological Review, 44,* October, 673–691.

MOORE, JOAN W. 1978. *Homeboys: Gangs, Drugs, and Prison in the Barrios of Los Angeles.* Philadelphia: Temple University Press.

MOORE, STEPHEN D., AND RON WINSLOW. 1993. "Health-Care Systems in 12 Countries Near Crisis, Drug Maker Study Says." *Wall Street Journal,* September 15, B6.

MORASH, MERRY A., AND ETTA A. ANDERSON. 1978. "Liberal Thinking on Rehabilitation: A Work-Able Solution to Crime." *Social Problems, 25,* June 556–563.

MORASH, MERRY, AND LILA RUCKER. 1990. "A Critical Look at the Idea of Boot Camp as a Correctional Reform." *Crime and Delinquency, 36,* 2, April, 204–222.

MORGAN, M. 1982. "Television and Adolescents' Sex-Role Stereotypes: A Longitudinal Study." *Journal of Personality and Social Psychology, 43,* 947–955.

MORGAN, M. 1987. "Television, Sex-Role Attitudes, and Sex-Role Behavior." *Journal of Early Adolescence, 7,* 3, 269–282.

MORGAN, PATRICIA A. 1978. "The Legislation of Drug Law: Economic Crisis and Social Control." *Journal of Drug Issues, 8,* Winter, 54–62.

MORRISON, DENTON E., KENNETH E. HORNBACK, AND W. KEITH WARNER. 1972. "The Environmental Movement: Some Preliminary Observations and Predictions." In *Social Behavior, Natural Resources, and the Environment,* William R. Burch, Jr., Neil H. Cheek, Jr., and Lee Taylor (eds.). New York: Harper & Row, 259–279.

MORSE, EDWARD V., PATRICIA M. SIMON, HOWARD J. OSOFSKY, PAUL M. BALSON, AND H. RICHARD GAUMER. 1991. "The Male Street Prostitute: A Vector for Transmission of HIV Infection into the Heterosexual World." *Social Science and Medicine, 32,* 5, 535–539.

MOSHEN, STEVEN W. 1983. "Why Are Baby Girls Being Killed in China?" *Wal Street Journal,* July 25, 9.

"Movie Spurs Jamaica Tourism." 1998. Associated Press, December 13.

MUECKE, MARJORIE A. 1992. "Mother Sold Food, Daughter Sells Her Body: The Cultural Continuity of Prostitution." *Social Science and Medicine, 35,* 7, October, 891–901.

MUEHLENHARD, CHARLENE L., AND MELANEY A. LINTON. 1987. "Date Rape: Familiar Strangers." *Journal of Counseling Psychology, 34,* 186–196.

MULVIHILL, DONALD J., MELVIN M. TUMIN, AND LYNN A. CURTIS. 1969. *Crimes of Violence: A Staff Report to the National Commission on the Causes and Prevention of Violence.* Washington, D.C.: U.S. Government Printing Office.

MURDOCK, GEORGE PETER. 1937. "Comparative Data on the Division of Labor by Sex." *Social Forces, 15,* 1937:551–553.

MURPHY, KIM. 1999. "Last Stand of an Aging Aryan." *Los Angeles Times,* January 10.

MYDENS, SETH. 1991. "Bullets and Crayons: Children Learn Lessons of the 90s." *New York Times,* June 16, 14.

MYERS, MARTHA A., AND SUSETTE M. TALARICO. 1986. "The Social Contexts of Racial Discrimination in Sentencing." *Social Problems, 33,* 3, February, 236–251.

MYERS, STEVEN LEE. 1999. "Airman Discharged for Refusal to Take Anthrax Vaccine as Rebellion Grows." *New York Times,* March 11.

MYERS, STEVEN LEE. 1998. "Pentagon Ready to Shrink Arsenal of Nuclear Bombs." *New York Times,* November 23.

MYERSON, ALLEN R. 1998. "U.S. Splurging on Energy After Falling Off Its Diet." *New York Times,* October 22.

MYRDAL, GUNNAR. 1944. *An American Dilemma.* New York: Harper.

NAJ, AMAL KUMAR. 1988b. "Battle Against Toxic PCBs Gains Ground as Bacteria Are Found That Eat Them." *Wall Street Journal,* November 9, B5.

NAJ, AMAL KUMAR. 1989a. "Lab Notes." *Wall Street Journal,* February 1, B1.

NAJ, AMAL KUMAR. 1989b. "'Super' Microbes Offer Way to Treat Hazardous Waste." *Wall Street Journal,* January 25, B1.

NAJ, AMAL KUMAR. 1992. "Kuwait Oil-Well Fires Did Little Damage to the Global Environment, Study Says." *Wall Street Journal,* May 15, B5.

NASAR, SYLVIA. 1992. "Fed Gives New Evidence of 80's Gains by Richest." *New York Times,* April 21.

NASH, GARY B. 1979. *The Urban Crucible.* Cambridge, Mass.: Harvard University Press.

National Institute of Justice Research Report. 1996. "Drug Use Forecasting: Annual Report on Adult and Juvenile Arrestees." Washington, D.C.

National Women's Political Caucus. 1998. "News & Opinions: 1998 Election Results." November 5.

NAVARRO, MIREYA. 1998. "Miami Restores Gay Right Law." *New York Times,* December 2.

NAZARIO, SONIA L. 1990. "Alcoholism Is Linked to a Gene." *Wall Street Journal,* April 18, B1.

NEERGAARD, LAURAN. 1998. "Strong Tainted Food Warnings Urged." Associated Press, December 31.

NELAN, BRUCE W. 1998. "Sudan: Why Is This Happening Again?" *Time,* July 27, 29–32.

NETTLER, GWYNN. 1974. "Embezzlement Without Problems." *British Journal of Criminology,* 14, January, 70–77.

NETTLER, GWYNN. 1976. *Social Concerns.* New York: Mc-Graw-Hill.

NEUHAUS, RICHARD JOHN. 1990. "Freedom and Democracy; Church, State, and Peyote." *National Review, 42,* June 11, 40–44.

NEWDORF, DAVID. 1991. "Bailout Agencies Like to Do It in Secret." *Washington Journalism Review, 13,* 4, May, 15–16.

NEWMAN, DONALD J. 1966. *Conviction: The Determination of Guilt or Innocence Without Trial.* Boston: Little, Brown.

NEWMAN, DOROTHY K., NANCY J. AMIDEI, BARBARA L. CATER, DAWN DAY, WILLIAM J. KRUVANT, AND JACK S. RUSSELL. 1978. *Protest, Politics, and Prosperity: Black Americans and White Institutions, 1940–1975.* New York: Pantheon.

New York Times. 1991. "First Death Sentence Under New Drug Law." May 15, A24.

1969 Handbook on Women Workers. 1969. Washington, D.C.: U.S. Department of Labor, Woman's Bureau.

NIEVES, EVELYN. 1998. "Homelessness Tests San Francisco's Ideals." *New York Times,* November 13.

NISHIO, HARRY KANEHARU. 1994. "Japan's Welfare Vision: Dealing with a Rapidly Increasing Elderly Population." In *The Graying of the World: Who Will Care for the Frail Elderly?* New York: Haworth, 233–260.

NORC (National Opinion Research Center). 1994. *General Social Survey.* Chicago, University of Chicago Press.

Nucleus: A Report to Union of Concerned Scientists Sponsors. 1981. 3, Spring–Summer.

NULAND, SHERWIN. 1995. "The Debate over Dying." *USA Weekend,* February 3–5, 4–6.

NULLIS, CLARE. "U.N.: Worst of AIDS Epidemic Is Still Ahead." Associated Press, June 28, 2000.

OAKLEY, ROBERT B. 1985. "Combating International Terrorism." *Department of State Bulletin,* June, 73–78.

O'BRIEN, TIMOTHY L. 1992. "Bush Proposal for Enterprise Zones Draws Skepticism." *Wall Street Journal,* June 4, B2.

O'CONNELL, PAMELA LICALZI. 1998. "Web Erotica Aims for New Female Customers." *New York Times,* August 13.

OGBURN, WILLIAM F. 1933. "The Family and Its Functions." In *Recent Social Trends in the United States, Report of the President's Research Committee on Social Trends.* New York: McGraw-Hill, 661–708.

O'HARE, WILLIAM P. 1992. "America's Minorities: The Demographics of Diversity." *Population Bulletin, 47,* 4, December, 1–47.

OLESKER, MICHAEL. 1997. "School's Resegregation Portends an 'Us vs. Them.'" *Baltimore Sun,* September 30.

OLIVER, MELVIN L., AND THOMAS M. SHAPIRO. 1995. *Black Wealth/White Wealth: A New Perspective on Racial Inequality.* New York: Routledge.

OLIVO, ANTONIO. 1999. "Doctor Shortage Severe in Poor Areas." *Los Angeles Times,* April 19.

OLSON, JAMES S., MARK BAXTER, JASON M. TETZLOFF, AND DARREN PIERSON. 1997. *Encyclopedia of American Indian Civil Rights.* Westport, Conn.: Greenwood Press.

OLSON, LAURA KATZ. 1994. "Public Policy and Privatization: Long-Term Care in the United States." In *The Graying of the World: Who Will Care for the Frail Elderly?* New York: Haworth, 25–58.

O'MALLEY, JEFF. 1988. "Sex Tourism and Women's Status in Thailand." *Society and Leisure, 11,* 1, Spring, 99–114.

Organized Crime: Report of the Task Force on Organized Crime, 1976. Washington, D.C.: National Advisory Committee on Criminal Justice Standards and Goals.

ORTEGA, SUZANNE T., AND JAY CORZINE. 1990. "Socioeconomic Status and Mental Disorders." *Research in Community and Mental Health, 6,* 149–182.

OTTEN, ALAN L. 1994. "People Patterns." *Wall Street Journal,* September 23, B1.

OTTEN, ALAN L. 1995. "People Patterns." *Wall Street Journal,* January 27, B1.

OYSERMAN, DAPHNA, AND HAZEL MARKUS. 1990. "Possible Selves in Balance: Implications for Delinquency." *Journal of Social Issues, 46,* 2, 141–157.

PADDOCK, RICHARD C. 1999. "Patient Deaths Point to Depth of Russian Crisis." *Los Angeles Times,* March 13.

PAE, PETER. 1989. "To Catch an Embezzler, Best Be Nimble, Be Quick." *Wall Street Journal,* August 3, B1.

PAGELOW, MILDRED DALEY. 1992. "Protecting the Fetus From Its Mom: A New Form of Social Control." Paper presented at the annual meeting of the society for the Study of Social Problems.

PALEN, J. JOHN. 1977. *City Scenes: Problems and Prospects.* Boston: Little, Brown.

PALEN, J. JOHN. 1981. *The Urban World,* 2nd ed. New York: McGraw-Hill.

PALEN, J. JOHN., AND LEO F. SCHNORE. 1965. "Color Composition and City-Suburban Status Difference." *Land Economics, 41,* February, 87–91.

PALLEY, HOWARD A., AND DANA A. ROBINSON. 1988. "Black on Black Crime." *Society,* July–August, 59–62.

PAMUCK, ELSIE. 1998. A study for the National Centre for Health Statistics, as reported in America Online, "Rich Get Richer, Poor Get Sicker in U.S." July 30.

PARK, ROBERT E. 1941. "The Social Function of War." *American Journal of Sociology, 46,* January, 551–570.

PARTINGTON, DONALD H. 1965. "The Incidence of the Death Penalty for Rape in Virginia." *Washington and Lee Law Review, 22,* 43–75.

PASSELL, PETER. 1996. "Race, Mortgages and Statistics." *New York Times,* May 10, D1, D4.

PAUL, BILL. 1986. "Burning Trash is Becoming Big Business." *Wall Street Journal,* October 13, 6.

PAUL, BILL. 1987. "Cogeneration Is Rapidly Coming of Age." *Wall Street Journal,* March 2, 6.

PAUL, WILLIAM, JAMES D. WEINRICH, JOHN C. GONSIOREK, AND MARY E. HOTVEDT. 1982. *Homosexuality: Social, Psychological, and Biological Issues.* Beverly Hills, Calif.: Sage.

PEARSE, PETER H. 1987. "The Environment Revisited." *Au Courant, 7,* Winter, 7.

PEELE, STANTON. 1987. "The Addiction Experience." In *Social Problems: A Critical Thinking Approach,* Paul J. Baker and Louis E. Anderson (eds.). Belmont, Calif.: Wadsworth, 210–218.

PENN, STANLEY. 1982. "Organized Crime Finds Rich Pickings in Rise of Union Health Plans." *Wall Street Journal,* October 5, 1, 26.

PEPLAU, LETITIA ANNE, AND HORTENSIA AMARO. 1982. "Understanding Lesbian Relationships." In *Homosexuality: Social, Psychological and Biological Issues.* William Paul, James D. Weinrich, John C. Gonsiorek, and Mary E. Hotvedt (eds.). Beverly Hills, Calif.: Sage, 233–247.

PEREIRA, JOSEPH. 1993. "Toys 'R' Us Decides to Pull Night Trap from Store Shelves." *Wall Street Journal,* December 17, A9A.

PERSELL, CAROLINE HODGES, SOPHIA CATSAMBIS, AND PETER W. COOKSON, JR. 1992. "Family Background, School Type, and College Attendance: A Conjoint System of Cultural Capital Transmission." *Journal of Research on Adolescence, 2,* 1, 1–23.

PERSELL, CAROLINE HODGES, AND PETER W. COOKSON, JR. 1985. "Where the Power Starts." *Signature,* August, 51–57.

PETERSILIA, JOAN. 1983. *Racial Disparities in the Criminal Justice System.* Santa Monica, Calif.: Rand, June.

PETERSON, RUTH D., AND WILLIAM C. BAILEY. 1991. "Felony Murder and Capital Punishment: An Examination of the Deterrence Question." *Criminology, 29,* 3, 367–393.

PETTIGREW, THOMAS. 1976. "How the People Really Feel." *The Center Magazine, 9,* January–February 35.

PHELPS, ORME WHEELOCK. 1939. *The Legislative Background of the Fair Labor Standards Act: A Study of the Growth of National Sentiment in Favor of Government Regulation of Wages, Hours, and Child Labor.* Chicago: University of Chicago Press.

PILIAVIN, IRVING, AND SCOTT BRIAR. 1964. "Police Encounters with Juveniles." *American Journal of Sociology, 70,* September, 206–214.

PILLEMER, KARL, AND DAVID W. MOORE. 1989. "Abuse of Patients in Nursing Homes: Findings from a Survey of Staff." *The Gerontologist, 29,* 3, 314–320.

PIOTROW, PHYLIS TILSON. 1973. *World Population Crisis: The United States' Response.* New York: Praeger.

PISTONO, STEPHEN P. 1988. "Susan Brownmiller and the History of Rape." *Women's Studies, 14,* 265–276.

PITTMAN, DAVID J. 1971. "The Male House of Prostitution." *Transaction, 8,* March–April, 21–27.

PIVEN, FRANCES FOX, AND RICHARD A. CLOWARD. 1971. *Regulating the Poor.* New York: Vintage.

PIVEN, FRANCES FOX, AND RICHARD A. CLOWARD. 1977. *Poor People's Movements: Why They Succeed, How They Fail.* New York: Pantheon.

PIVEN, FRANCES FOX, AND RICHARD A. CLOWARD. 1982. *The New Class War: Reagan's Attack on the Welfare State and Its Consequences.* New York: Pantheon.

PIVEN, FRANCES FOX, AND RICHARD A. CLOWARD. 1989. *Why Americans Don't Vote.* New York: Random House.

PIVEN, FRANCES FOX, AND RICHARD A. CLOWARD. 1997. *The Breaking of the American Social Compact.* New York: New Press.

PLATT, ANTHONY M. 1969. *The Child Savers.* Chicago: University of Chicago Press.

PODOLSKY, DOUG. 1990. "Saved from the Knife." *U.S. News & World Report, 109,* 20, November 19, 76–77.

POLENBERG, RICHARD. 1980. *One Nation Divisible: Class, Race, and Ethnicity in the United States Since 1938.* New York: Penguin.

POLLAY, RICHARD W. 1997. "Hacks, Flacks, and Counter-Attacks: Cigarette Advertising, Sponsored Research, and Controversy." *Journal of Social Issues, 53,* 1, 43–74.

POPE, CARL E. 1988. "The Family, Delinquency, and Crime." In *Mental Illness, Delinquency, Addictions, and Neglect,* Elam W. Nunnally, Catherine S. Chilman, and Fred M. Cox (eds.). Newbury Park, Calif.: Sage, 108–127.

POTTERAT, JOHN J., DONALD E. WOODHOUSE, JOHN B. MUTH, AND STEPHEN Q. MUTH. 1990. *Journal of Sex Research, 27,* 2, May, 233–243.

POZDENA, RANDALL J., AND TERRY R. JOHNSON. 1979. *Income Maintenance and Asset Demand.* Menlo Park, Calif.: SRI International, March.

PRATHER, JANE E. 1980. "The Mystique of Minor Tranquilizers." *Use and Misuse of Benzodiazepines: Hearing Before the Subcommittee on Health and Scientific Research of the Committee on Labor and Human Resources, September 10, 1979.* Washington, D.C.: U.S. Government Printing Office, 438–458.

PRICE, DANIEL O. (ed.). 1967. *The 99th Hour*. Chapel Hill: University of North Carolina Press (as contained in Simon 1981).

PROVENZO, EUGENE. 1991. *Video Kids: Making Sense of Nintendo*. New York: Harvard University Press.

PRUITT, DEAN G., AND RICHARD C. SNYDER, 1969. "Motives and Perceptions Underlying Entry into War." In *Theory and Research on the Causes of War*, Dean G. Pruitt and Richard C. Synder (eds.). Englewood Cliffs, N.J.: Prentice Hall.

PRUS, ROBERT, AND STYLLIANOSS IRINI. 1988. *Hookers, Rounders, and Desk Clerks: The Social Organization of the Hotel Community*. Salem, Wis.: Sheffield.

RA'ANAN, URI, ROBERT L. PFALTZGRAFF, JR., RICHARD H. SHULTZ, ERNST HALPERIN, AND IGOR LUKES (eds.). 1986. *Hydra of Carnage: The International Linkages of Terrorism and Other Low-Intensity Operations, The Witnesses Speak*. Lexington, Ky.: Lexington Books.

RABINOVITZ, JONATHAN. 1998. "For Sale: Used Nuclear Reactor." *New York Times,* July 7.

RAKOW, LANA F. 1992. "'Don't Hate Me Because I'm Beautiful': Feminist Resistance to Advertising's Irresistible Meanings." *Southern Communication Journal, 57,* 2, Winter, 132–142.

RALOFF, JANET. 1990. "The Colloid Threat." *Science News, 137,* 11, March 17, 169–170.

RATCLIFF, JOHN. 1981. "Enterprise Zones in the United Kingdom." *Urban Land, 40,* September, 14–17.

RAVENHOLT, R. T. 1990. "Tobacco's Global Death March." *Population and Development Review, 16,* 2, June, 213–240.

RAY, OAKLEY. 1978. *Drugs, Society, and Human Behavior,* 2nd ed. St. Louis, Mo.: Mosby.

RAY, OAKLEY. 1996. *Drugs, Society, and Human Behavior,* 7th ed. St. Louis, Mo.: Mosby.

REASONS, CHARLES E. (ed.). 1974. *The Criminologist: Crime and the Criminal*. Pacific Palisades, Calif.: Goodyear.

RECKLESS, WALTER C. 1973. *The Crime Problem,* 5th ed. New York: Appleton.

REDLICH, FRITZ, AND STEPHEN R. KELLERT. 1978. "Trends in American Mental Health." *American Journal of Psychiatry, 135,* January, 22–28.

REED, RALPH. 1994. *Politically Incorrect: The Emerging Faith Factor in American Politics*. Dallas: Word.

REICH, MICHAEL. 1972. "The Economics of Racism." In *The Capitalist System*, Richard C. Edwards, Michael Reich, and Thomas E. Weiskopf (eds.). Englewood Cliffs, N.J.: Prentice Hall, 313–326.

REICH, MICHAEL. 1981. "The Economic Impact in the Postwar Period." In *Impacts of Racism on White Americans,* Benjamin P. Bowser and Raymond G. Hunt (eds.). Beverly Hills, Calif.: Sage, 165–176.

REICHERT, LOREN D., AND JAMES H. FREY. 1985. "The Organization of Bell Desk Prostitution." *Sociology and Social Research, 69,* 4, July, 516–526.

REINIG, TIMOTHY W. 1990. "Sin, Stigma, and Society: A Critique of Morality and Values in Democratic Law and Policy." *Buffalo Law Review, 38,* 3, Fall, 859–901.

REISS, ALBERT J. 1961. "The Sociological Integration of Queers and Peers." *Social Problems, 9,* Fall, 102–120.

RESSLER, ROBERT K., AND TOM SHACHTMAN. 1992. *Whoever Fights Monsters*. New York: St. Martin's.

REVZIN, PHILIP. 1986. "Seveso: 10 Years After the Dioxin Leak." *Wall Street Journal,* July 8, 34.

REVZIN, PHILIP. 1989. "U.S. Claims Progress at Global Meeting Discussing Ban on Chemical Weapons." *Wall Street Journal,* January 9, A3.

REYNOLDS, JANICE. 1973. "The Medical Institution: The Death and Disease-producing Appendage." In *American Society: A Critical Analysis,* Larry T. Reynolds and James M. Henslin (eds.). New York: McKay, 198–224.

REYNOLDS, JANICE. 1976. "Rape as Social Control." In *Social Problems in American Society,* 2nd ed., James M. Henslin and Larry T. Reynolds (eds.). Boston: Holbrook, 79–86.

RICHARDSON, LEWIS F. 1960. *Statistics of Deadly Quarrels*. Chicago: Quadrangle.

RICHTER, PAUL. 1999. "CIA Director Warns of Terrorist Threat." *Los Angeles Times,* February 3.

RICKS, THOMAS E. 1999. "Prospect of Nuclear Rogue State Makes North Korea Worrisome." *Wall Street Journal,* February 3.

RIESEL, VICTOR. 1982a. "Crackdown on Mobsters." Syndicated column, January 16.

RIESEL, VICTOR. 1982b. "Racketeers Infest New Jersey Construction Trade." Syndicated column, January 25.

RIESMAN, DAVID, NATHAN GLAZER, AND REUEL DENNEY. 1951. *The Lonely Crowd: A Study of the Changing American Character*. New Haven, Conn.: Yale University Press.

RILEY, NANCY E. 1997. "Gender, Power, and Population Change." *Population Bulletin, 52,* 1, May, 1–47.

RILEY, K. JACK. 1998. "Crack, Powder Cocaine, and Heroin. Drug Purchase and Use Patterns in Six U.S. Cities." National Institute of Justice, online, December 12.

RISEN, JAMES, AND JEFF GERTH. 1999. "China Stole Nuclear Secrets From Los Alamos, U.S. Officials Say." *New York Times,* March 6.

ROBINSON, ARTHUR B., AND ZACHARY W. ROBINSON. 1997. "Science Has Spoken: Global Warming Is a Myth." *Wall Street Journal,* December 4, A22.

ROBINSON, J. P., AND G. GODBEY. 1996. "The Great Showdown." *American Demographics, 18,* 42–46.

ROBERTS, LESLIE. 1987. "Discovering Microbes with a Taste for PCBs." *Science, 237,* August 28, 975–977.

ROBERTS, SAM. 1994. "Hispanic Population Outnumbers Blacks in Four Major Cities as Demographics Shift." *New York Times,* October 9. 34.

ROBINSON, JAMES C. 1991. "HMO Market Penetration and Hospital Cost Inflation in California." *Journal of the*

American Medical Association, 19, November 20, 2719–2723.

ROCKETT, IAN R. H. 1994. "Population and Health: An Introduction to Epidemiology." *Population Bulletin, 49,* 3, November, 1–47.

ROCKWELL, DON. 1972. "Social Problems: Alcohol and Marijuana." *Journal of Psychedelic Drugs, 5,* Fall, 49–55.

ROE, KATHLEEN M. 1989. "Private Troubles and Public Issues: Providing Abortion Amid Competing Definitions." *Social Science and Medicine, 29,* 10, 1191–1198.

ROGERS, JOSEPH W. 1977. *Why Are You Not a Criminal?* Englewood Cliffs, N.J.: Prentice Hall.

ROHE, WILLIAM M. 1991. "Expanding Urban Homesteading: Lessons from the Local Property Demonstration." *Journal of the American Planning Association, 57,* 4, Autumn, 444–455.

ROLO, MARK ANTHONY. n.d. "Marked Media." *The Circle.* Online.

ROSALDO, MICHELLE ZIMBALIST. 1974. "Women, Culture, and Society: A Theoretical Overview." In *Women, Culture, and Society,* Michelle Zimbalist Rosaldo and Louise Lamphere (eds.). Stanford: Stanford University Press.

ROSE, FREDRICK. 1992. "Los Angeles Tallies Losses: Curfew Is Lifted." *Wall Street Journal,* May 5, A3, A18.

ROSEN, LAWRENCE, LEONARD SAVITZ, MICHAEL LALLI, AND STANLEY TURNER. 1991. "Early Delinquency, High School Graduation, and Adult Criminality." *Sociological Viewpoints, 7,* Fall, 37–60.

ROSEN, YERETH. 1999. "Exxon Valdez Oil Spill of 1989 Crippled Sound, Alaskans Say." Reuters, March 14.

ROSENBERG, CHARLES E. 1987. *The Care of Strangers: The Rise of America's Hospital System.* New York: Basic Books.

ROSENFELD, RACHEL A., AND ARNE L. KALLEBERG. 1990. "A Cross-National Comparison of the Gender Gap in Income." *American Journal of Sociology, 96,* 1, July, 69–106.

ROSENTHAL, ELISABETH. 1999. "Suicides Reveal Bitter Roots of China's Rural Life." *New York Times,* January 24.

ROSETT, CLAUDIA. 1994. "Big Oil-Pipeline Spill in Russia May Be a Sign of Things to Come." *Wall Street Journal,* October 27, A14.

ROSZAK, BETTY, AND THEODORE ROSZAK. 1969. *Masculine/Feminine: Readings in Sexual Mythology and the Liberation of Women.* New York: Harper & Row.

ROTHMAN, DAVID J. 1971. *The Discovery of the Asylum.* Boston: Little, Brown.

ROTHMAN, DAVID J., AND SHEILA M. ROTHMAN. 1972. *On Their Own.* Reading, Mass.: Addison-Wesley.

ROTHSCHILD, N. 1984. "Small Group Affiliation as a Mediating Factor in the Cultivation Process." In *Cultural Indicators: An International Symposium,* G. Melischek, K. E. Rosengren, and J. Strappers (eds.). Vienna: Österreichischen Akademie der Wissenschaften.

ROYKO, MIKE. 1971. *Boss: Richard J. Daly of Chicago.* New York: Dutton.

RUBENSTEIN, RICHARD E. 1987. *Alchemists of Revolution: Terrorism in the Modern World.* London: I. B. Tauris.

RUGGLES, PATRICIA. 1989. "Short and Long Term Poverty in the United States: Measuring the American 'Underclass.'" Washington, D.C.: Urban Institute, June.

RUGGLES, PATRICIA. 1990. *Drawing the Line: Alternative Poverty Measures and Their Implication for Public Policy.* Washington, D.C.: Urban Institute.

RUGGLES, PATRICIA. 1992. "Measuring Poverty." *Focus, 14,* 1, Spring, 1–5.

RUMBAUT, RUBEN G., AND JOHN R. WEEKS. 1994. "Unraveling a Public Health Enigma: Why Do Immigrants Experience Superior Perinatal Health Outcomes?" Paper presented at the annual meeting of the American Public Health Association.

RUSSELL, DIANA E. H. 1977. "On Pornography." *Chrysalis, 4,* 11–15.

RUSSELL, DIANA E. H. 1979. *The Politics of Rape: The Victim's Perspective.* New York: Scarborough.

RUSSELL, DIANA E. H. 1980. "Rape in Marriage: A Case Against Legalized Crime." Paper presented at the annual meeting of the American Society of Criminology.

RUSSELL, DIANA E. H. 1986. *The Secret Trauma: Incest in the Lives of Girls and Women.* New York: Basic Books.

RUSSELL, DIANA E. H. n.d. "Preliminary Report on Some Findings Relating to the Trauma and Long-Term Effects of Intrafamily Childhood Sexual Abuse." Unpublished.

RUSSO, ETHAN B. 1998. "Cannabis for Migraine Treatment: A Historical and Scientific Review." *Pain,* June.

RYBCZYNSKI, WITOLD. 1999. "The Virtues of Suburban Sprawl." *Wall Street Journal,* May 25.

SAGAN, SCOTT D. 1994. "The Perils of Proliferation: Organization Theory, Deterrence Theory, and the Spread of Nuclear Weapons." *International Security, 18,* 4, Spring, 66–107.

SAGARIN, EDWARD. 1980. Communication to the author. April 7.

SAKHAROV, ANDREI. 1977. "Text of Sakharov Letter to Carter on Human Rights." *New York Times,* January 29.

SALAS, ROSALINDA. 1996. "Letter to the author." May.

SAMPSON, CATHERINE. 1992. "Corrupt Care." *World Press Review, 39,* 5, May, 46.

SAMUELSON, ROBERT J. 1988. "The Elderly Aren't Needy." *Newsweek,* March 21, 68.

SAWHILL, ISABEL V. 1988. "Poverty in the U.S.: Why Is It So Persistent?" *Journal of Economic Literature, 26,* 3, September, 1073–1119.

SCHAEFER, RICHARD T. 1979. *Racial and Ethnic Groups.* Boston: Little, Brown.

SCHLAFLY, PHYLLIS. 1979. "The Phyllis Schlafly Report." 13, November.

SCHMALLEGER, FRANK. 1999. *Criminology Today: An Integrative Introduction*. Upper Saddle River, New Jersey: Prentice Hall.

SCHMIDT, GUNTER, AND VOLKMAR SIGUSCH. 1970. "Sex Differences in Response to Psychosexual Stimulation by Films and Slides." *Journal of Sex Research, 6,* November, 268–283.

SCHMITT, RICHARD B. 1982. "Some Towns Jail Indigents Illegally and Get Free Labor." *Wall Street Journal,* February 2, 1, 16.

SCHNEIDER, KEITH. 1992. "Nuclear Disarmament Raises Fear on Storage of 'Triggers.'" *New York Times,* February 26, A1.

SCHNEIDER, KEITH. 1994. "Burning Trash for Energy: Is It an Endangered Industry?" *New York Times,* October 11, A18.

SCHOENFELD, A. CLAY, ROBERT F. MEIER, AND ROBERT J. GRIFFIN. 1979. "Constructing a Social Problem: The Press and the Environment." *Social Problems, 27,* October, 38–61.

SCHOTTLAND, CHARLES I. 1963. *The Social Security Plan in the U.S.* New York: Appleton.

SCHRAG, PETER, AND DIANE DIVOKY. 1975. *The Myth of the Hyperactive Child and Other Means of Child Control.* New York: Pantheon.

SCHREIBER, JAN. 1978. *The Ultimate Weapon: Terrorists and the World Order.* New York: Morrow.

SCHRIEKE, BERTRAM J. 1936. *Alien Americans.* New York: Viking.

SCHUMPETER, JOSEPH A. 1955. *The Sociology of Imperialism.* New York: Meridian (first published in 1919).

SCHWARTZ, FELICE N. 1989. "Management Women and the New Facts of Life." *Harvard Business Review, 89,* 1, January–February, 65–76.

SCHWENDINGER, JULIA R., AND HERMAN SCHWENDINGER. 1983. *Rape and Inequality.* Beverly Hills, Calif.: Sage.

SCHWIDROWSKI, KLAUS. 1980. "Italy's Mafia Blight." *World Press Review, 17,* March, 56.

SCIENTISTS' COMMITTEE FOR RADIATION INFORMATION. 1962. "The Effects of a 20-Megaton Bomb." *New University Thought,* Spring.

SCULLY, DIANA. 1990. *Understanding Sexual Violence: A Study of Convicted Rapists.* Boston: Unwin Hyman.

SCULLY, DIANA. 1994. "Negotiating to Do Surgery." In *Dominant Issues in Medical Sociology,* 3rd ed. Howard D. Schwartz (ed.). New York: McGraw-Hill, 146–152.

SCULLY, DIANA, AND JOSEPH MAROLLA. 1999. "'Riding the Bull at Gilley's': Convicted Rapists Describe the Rewards of Rape." In *Down-to-Earth Sociology: Introductory Readings,* 10th ed., James M. Henslin, ed. New York: Free Press, 45–60.

SEABORG, DON. 1985. "Agriculture in the United States and Canada." In *1985 Yearbook of Agriculture: U.S. Agriculture in a Global Economy 1985,* Larry B. Morton (ed.).

Washington, D.C.: U.S. Department of Agriculture, 68–80.

SEIB, GERALD F. 1981. "U.S. Aides Say Toxins on a Cambodian Leaf Hint at Chemical War." *Wall Street Journal,* September 15, 22.

SEIB, GERALD F., AND ROBERT S. GREENBERGER. 1992. "U.N. Sanctions on Libya Have Changed Rules of Warfare Against Terrorism." *Wall Street Journal,* April 24, A10.

SEIDMAN, STEVEN A. 1992. "An Investigation of Sex-Role Stereotyping in Music Videos." *Journal of Broadcasting and Electronic Media,* Spring, 210–216.

SELIGMANN, JEAN. 1984. "The Date Who Rapes." *Newsweek,* April 9, 91–92.

SELLIN, THORSTEN. 1928. "The Negro Criminal: A Statistical Note." *Annals of the American Academy of Political and Social Sciences, 140,* Part II, November, 52–64.

Seventh Special Report to the U.S. Congress on Alcohol and Health. 1990. Rockville, Md.: U.S. Department of Health and Human Services.

SHAFFER, HARRY G. 1986. "$1,000,000,000,000." *Republic,* May, 24.

SHAFIR, GERSHON, AND YOAV PELED. 1998. "Citizenship and Stratification in an Ethnic Democracy." *Ethnic and Racial Studies, 21,* 3, May, 408–427.

SHAFIR, GERSHON. 1995. "Split Labor Market and the Sources of National Separatism in the Israeli-Palestinian Conflict." In *Racism and the Labour Market: Historical Studies,* Marcel Van Der Linden and Jan Lucassen, eds. Bern: Peter Lang, 437–456.

SHAPIRO, JOSEPH P. 1997. "Euthanasia's Home: What the Dutch Experience Can Teach Americans about Assisted Suicide." *U.S. News Online,* January 17.

SHAW, SUE. 1987. "Wretched of the Earth." *New Statesman, 20,* March, 19–20.

SHEEHY, GAIL. 1973. *Hustling: Prostitution in Our Wide-Open Society.* New York: Dell.

SHELLENBARGER, SUE. 1994. "Companies Help Solve Day-Care Problems." *Wall Street Journal,* July 22, B1.

SHELLENBARGER, SUE. 1995. "Sales Offers Women Fairer Pay, but Bias Lingers." *Wall Street Journal,* January 24, B1, B14.

SHEPPARD, NATHANIEL, JR. 1980. "Chicago Project Dwellers Live Under Siege." *New York Times,* August 6, A14.

SHIBUTANI, TAMOTSU. 1970. "On the Personification of Adversaries." In *Human Nature and Collective Behavior,* Tamotsu Shibutani (ed.). Englewood Cliffs, N.J.: Prentice-Hall, 223–233.

SHILTS, RANDY. 1987. *And the Band Played On: People, Politics and the AIDS Epidemic.* New York: St. Martin's.

SHIM, KELLY H., AND MARSHALL DEBERRY. 1988. *Criminal Victimization in the United States, 1986.* Washington, D.C.: U.S. Department of Justice, Bureau of Justice Statistics, August.

SHINNAR, REVEL, AND SHLOMO SHINNAR. 1975. "The Effects of the Criminal Justice System on the Control of Crime: A Quantitative Approach." *Law and Society Review, 9,* Summer, 581–611.

SHIVELY, JOELLEN. 1999. "Cowboys and Indians." In *Down-to-Earth Sociology: Introductory Readings,* 10th ed., James M. Henslin, ed. New York: Free Press, 104–116.

SHRIBMAN, DAVID. 1989. "Even After 10 Years, Victims of Love Canal Can't Quite Escape It." *Wall Street Journal,* March 9, A1, A8.

SIEGEL, KAROLYNN, LAURIE J. BAUMAN, GRACE H. CHRIST, AND SUSAN KROWN. 1988. "Patterns of Change in Sexual Behavior Among Gay Men in New York City." *Archives of Sexual Behavior, 17,* 6, December, 481–497.

SIEGEL, KAROLYNN, AND MARC GLASSMAN. 1989. "Individual and Aggregate Level Change in Sexual Behavior and Gay Men at Risk for AIDS." *Archives of Sexual Behavior, 18,* 1, August, 335–348.

SIGNORIELLI, NANCY. 1989. "Television and Conceptions About Sex Roles: Maintaining Conventionality and the Status Quo." *Sex Roles, 21,* 5/6, 341–360.

SIGNORIELLI, NANCY. 1990. "Children, Television, and Gender Roles: Messages and Impact." *Journal of Adolescent Health Care, 11,* 50–58.

SILBERMAN, CHARLES E. 1978. *Criminal Violence, Criminal Justice.* New York: Random House.

SILBERT, MIMI H., AND AYALA M. PINES. 1982. "Entrance into Prostitution." *Youth and Society, 13,* 4, June, 471–500.

SILBERT, MIMI H., AND AYALA M. PINES. 1983. "Early Sexual Exploitation as an Influence in Prostitution." *Social Work, 28,* July–August, 285–289.

SILVA, REX DE. 1980. "Developing the Third World." *World Press Review,* May, 48.

SILVER, JONATHAN M. 1979. "Medical Terms—A Two-Way Block?" *Colloquy: The Journal of Physician-Patient Communications,* November, 4–10.

SILVERMAN, DEIDRE. 1981. "Sexual Harassment: The Working Women's Dilemma." *Building Feminist Theory: Essays from Quest.* New York: Longman, 84–93.

SIMMEL, GEORG. 1904. "The Sociology of Conflict." *American Journal of Sociology, 9,* January, 490–525; March, 672–689; and May, 798–811.

SIMON, DAVID R. 1981. "The Political Economy of Crime." In *Political Economy: A Critique of American Society,* Scott G. McNall (ed.). Glenview, Ill.: Scott Foresman, 347–366.

SIMON, JULIAN L. 1977. *The Economics of Population Growth.* Princeton, N.J.: Princeton University Press.

SIMON, JULIAN L. 1980. "Global Confusion, 1980: A Hard Look at the Global 2000 Report." *Public Interest, 62,* Winter, 3–20.

SIMON, JULIAN L. 1981. *The Ultimate Resource.* Princeton, N.J.: Princeton University Press.

SIMON, JULIAN L. 1982. Conversation with the author. March 23.

SIMON, JULIAN L. 1986. *Theory of Population and Economic Growth.* New York: Blackwell.

SIMON, JULIAN L. 1991. "The Case for Greatly Increased Immigration." *The Public Interest, 102,* Winter, 89–103.

SIMPSON, GEORGE EATON, AND J. MILTON YINGER. 1972. *Racial and Cultural Minorities: An Analysis of Prejudice and Discrimination,* 4th ed. New York: Harper & Row.

SINDLER, ALLAN P. 1978. *Bakke, De Funis, and Minority Admissions: The Quest for Equal Opportunity.* New York: Longman.

SINGER, S. FRED. 1994. "Benefits of Global Warming." In *Social Problems 94/95,* Harold A. Widdison (ed.). Guilford, Conn.: Dushkin, 220–226.

SINGER, S. FRED. 1997. "The Sky Isn't Falling, and the Ocean Isn't Rising." *Wall Street Journal,* November 10, A22.

SINGH, MOHINDER. 1999. "Will petrol pumps ever run dry?" *Science Tribune* (Chandigarh, India), February 4.

SITOMER, CURTIS J. 1986. "Fencing Out Pornography Without Fencing in Free Speech." *Christian Science Monitor,* March 13, 23.

SIWOLOP, SANA. 1988. "Developments to Watch." *Business Week,* April 11, 123.

Sixth Special Report to the U.S. Congress on Alcohol and Health. 1987. Washington, D.C.: U.S. Department of Health and Human Services.

SKINNER, B. F. 1948. *Walden Two.* New York: Macmillan.

SKINNER, B. F. 1953. *Science and Human Behavior.* New York: Macmillan.

SKINNER, B. F. 1971. *Beyond Freedom and Dignity.* New York: Knopf.

SLIKKER, WILLIAM, JR. 1992. "Behavioral, Neurochemical, and Neurohistological Effects of Chronic Marijuana Smoke Exposure in the Nonhuman Primate." In *Marijuana Cannabinoids Neurobiology and Neurophysiology,* Laura Murphy and Andrzej Bartke, eds. Boca Raton, Florida: CRC Press.

SMITH, BARBARA ELLEN. 1987. *Digging Our Own Graves: Coal Miners and the Struggle over Black Lung Disease.* Philadelphia: Temple University Press.

SMITH, CLARK. 1980. "Oral History as 'Therapy': Combatants' Accounts of Vietnam War." In *Strangers at Home: Vietnam Veterans Since the War,* Charles R. Figley and Seymore Leventman (eds.). New York: Praeger, 9–34.

SMITH, COLIN, AND SHYAM BHATIA. 1980. "Stealing the Bomb for Pakistan." *World Press Review, 27,* March, 26–28.

SMITH, DOUGLAS A., AND CHRISTY A. VISHER. 1981. "Street-Level Justice: Situational Determinants of Police

Arrest Decisions." *Social Problems, 29,* December, 167–177.

SMITH, HAROLD, 1986. "A Colossal Cover-Up." *Christianity Today,* December, 16–17.

SMITH, JAMES P., AND BARRY EDMONSTON, EDS. 1997. *The New American: Economic, Demographic, and Fiscal Effects of Immigration.* Washington, D.C.: National Academy Press.

SMITH, JOEL B., AND DENNIS A. TIRPAK. 1988. *The Potential Effects of Global Climate Change on the United States.* Washington, D.C.: U.S. Environmental Protection Agency, October.

SMITH, KRISTEN F., AND VERN L. BENGTSON. 1979. "Positive Consequences of Institutionalization: Solidarity Between Elderly Parents and Their Middle-Aged Children." *The Gerontologist, 19,* October, 438–447.

SMITH, NEIL. 1996. *The New Urban Frontier: Gentrification and the Revanchist City.* New York: Routledge.

SMITH, TOM W. 1990. "The Polls—A Report: The Sexual Revolution." *Public Opinion Quarterly, 54,* 415–435.

SMITH, TOM W. 1998. "Public Opinion on Abortion." National Opinion Research Center.

SMITH, WESLEY J. 1999. "Dependence or Death? Oregonians Make a Chilling Choice." *Wall Street Journal,* February 25.

SMITH-LOVIN LYNN, AND CHARLES BRODY. 1989. "Interruptions in Group Discussions: The Effects of Gender and Group Composition." *American Sociological Review, 54,* 424–435.

SMOLINSKE, S. 1992. *Handbook of Food, Drug, and Cosmetic Excipients.* Boca Raton, Florida: CRC Press.

SNELL, TRACY L. 1998. "Capital Punishment 1997." Washington, D.C.: Bureau of Justice Statistics.

SNIPP, C. MATTHEW, AND ALAN L. SORKIN, 1986. "American Indian Housing: An Overview of Conditions and Public Policy." In *Race, Ethnicity, and Minority Housing in the United States,* Jamshid A. Momeni (ed.). New York: Greenwood, 147–175.

SNOW, RONALD W., AND ORVILLE R. CUNNINGHAM. 1985. "Age, Machismo, and the Drinking Locations of Drunken Drivers: A Research Note." *Deviant Behavior, 6,* 57–66.

SNYDER, CHARLES R. 1958. *Alcohol and the Jews.* New York: Free Press.

SNYDER, HOWARD. 1988. *Court Careers of Juvenile Offenders.* Washington, D.C.: Office of Juvenile Justice and Delinquency Prevention.

SOLOMON, JEANNE, AND DAN RATHER. 1980. "The Kyshtym Disaster." A segment of *60 Minutes,* November 9 (Jean Solomon, producer, and Dan Rather, interviewer).

SOLOMON, JOLIE. "Companies Try Measuring Cost Savings from New Types of Corporate Benefits." *Wall Street Journal,* December 29, 1988:B1.

SORENSEN, JESPER B. 1990. "Perceptions of Women's Opportunity in Five Industrialized Nations." *European Sociological Review, 6,* 2, September, 151–164.

Sourcebook of Criminal Justice Statistics. Washington, D.C.: U.S. Government Printing Office, annual.

SPAETH, ANTHONY. 1989. "Court Settlement Stuns Bhopal Survivors." *Wall Street Journal,* February 22, A10.

SPECTER, MICHAEL. 1992. "TB Carriers See Clash of Liberty and Health." *New York Times,* October 14, A1, A20.

SPECTER, MICHAEL. 1995. "Plunging Life Expectancy Puzzles Russians." *New York Times,* August 1, A1, A6.

SPECTER, MICHAEL. 1998. "Population Implosion Worries a Graying Europe." *New York Times,* July 10.

SPECTER, MICHAEL. 1998. "Zimbabwe's Descent into AIDS Abyss: Little Hope, Much Despair." *New York Times,* August 6.

SPEER, ALBERT. 1970. *Inside the Third Reich,* Richard and Clara Winston (trans.). New York: Avon.

SPITZER, STEVEN. 1975. "Toward a Marxian Theory of Deviance." *Social Problems, 22,* June, 608–619.

SPIVAK, JONATHAN. 1980. "Israel's Discrimination Problem." *Wall Street Journal,* December 3, 28.

SQUIRES, GREGORY D., ED. 1997. *Insurance Redlining: Disinvestment, Reinvestment, and the Evolving Role of Financial Institutions.* Washington, D.C.: Urban Institute Press.

SRISANG, KOSON. 1989. "The Ecumenical Coalition on Third World Tourism." *Annals of Tourism Research, 16,* 1, 119–121.

SROLE, LEO, ET AL. 1978. *Mental Health in the Metropolis: The Midtown Manhattan Study.* New York: New York University Press.

St. Petersburg Press. 1995. "Guilty Plea by Alleged Levin Aide." Online.

STAFFORD, LINDA, SONYA R. KENNEDY, JOANNE E. LEHMAN, AND GAIL ARNOLD. 1986–87. "Wealth in America." *ISR Newsletter,* Winter.

STANFORD, SALLY. 1968. "Madambood as a Vocation." In *In Their Own Behalf: Voices from the Margin,* Charles H. McCaghy, James K. Skipper, Jr., and Mark Lefton (eds.). New York: Appleton, 204–207.

STANLEY, ALESSANDRA. 1990. "All Ganged Up." *Time, 135,* 25, June 18, 50–52.

STARR, MARK. 1985b. "Violence on the Right." *Newsweek,* March 4, 23, 25–26.

STARR, MARK, AND FRANK MAIER. 1985. "Chicago's Gang Warfare." *Newsweek,* January 28, 32.

Statistical Abstract of the United States. Washington, D.C.: U.S. Bureau of the Census, annual.

The Statistical History of the United States: From Colonial Times to the Present. 1976. New York: Basic Books.

STEACY, ANNE, MAUREEN BROSNAHAN, CLAIRE FRASER, AND DEREK WOLFF. 1989. *Maclean's 102,* 33, August 14, 48.

STEFFENSMEIER, DARRELL J., AND ROBERT M. TERRY. 1986. "Institutional Sexism in the Underworld: A View from the Inside." *Sociological Inquiry 56,* 3, Summer, 304–323.

STEIN, MAURICE. 1971. *Eclipse of Community.* Princeton, N.J.: Princeton University Press.

STEIN, PETER J. 1992. "The Diverse World of Single Adults." In *Marriage and Family in a Changing Society,* 4th ed., James M. Henslin (ed.). New York: Free Press, 93–103.

STEINHAUER, JENNIFER. 1999. "For Women in Medicine, a Road to Compromise, Not Perks." *New York Times,* March 1.

STEINHAUER, JENNIFER. 1999. "Angry at Managed Care, Doctors Start Fighting Back." *New York Times,* January 10.

STEINHOFF, PATRICIA G., AND MILTON DIAMOND. 1977. *Abortion Politics: The Hawaii Experience.* Honolulu: University Press of Hawaii.

STEINITZ, MARK S. 1987. "Insurgents, Terrorists and the Drug Trade." In *The Terrorism Reader: A Historical Anthology,* rev. ed., Walter Laqueur and Yonah Alexander (eds.). New York: Penguin, 327–337.

STEINMETZ, GEORGE. 1992. "The Preventable Tragedy: Fetal Alcohol Syndrome." *National Geographic, 181,* 2, February, 36–39.

STEINMETZ, GREG, AND CACILIE ROHWEDDER. 1998. "Green Party Grows Strong on Soil Peculiar to Germany." *Wall Street Journal,* April 20, A15.

STEINMETZ, SUZANNE K. 1988. *Duty Bound: Elder Abuse and Family Care.* Newbury Park, Calif.: Sage.

STEINMETZ, SUZANNE K., AND MURRAY A. STRAUS (eds.). 1974. *Violence in the Family.* New York: Dodd Mead.

STERLING, CLAIRE. 1981. *The Terror Network: The Secret War of International Terrorism.* New York: Holt.

STEVENS, AMY. 1992. "Sensible Victims Will Be Hoping Their Burglar Drives Up in a Rolls." *Wall Street Journal,* April 8, B1.

STEVENS, AMY, AND SARAH LUBMAN. 1992. "Deciding Moment of the Trial May Have Been Five Months Ago." *Wall Street Journal,* May 1, A6.

STEVENS, CHARLES W. 1980. "Integration Is Elusive Despite Recent Gains; Social Barriers Remain." *Wall Street Journal,* September 29, 1.

STEVENS, CHARLES W. 1989. "Advance in Hydrogen Storage May Make Use of Abundant Element More Practical." *Wall Street Journal,* March 8, B4.

STEVENS, ROSEMARY. 1971. *American Medicine and the Public Interest.* New Haven, Conn.: Yale University Press.

STEVENS, WILLIAM K. 1994. "Green Revolution Is Not Enough, Study Finds." *New York Times,* September 6.

STEVENS, WILLIAM K. 1995. "Scientists Say Earth's Warming Could Set Off Wide Disruptions." *New York Times,* September 18.

STEVENS, WILLIAM K. 1996. "Great Plains or Great Desert?" *New York Times,* May 28.

STEVENS, WILLIAM K. 1998a. "As Alaska Melts, Scientists Consider the Reasons Why." *New York Times,* August 18.

STEVENS, WILLIAM K. 1998b. "Linking Health Effects to Changes in Climate." *New York Times,* August 10.

STEVENS, WILLIAM K. 1998c. "Science Academy Disputes Attack on Global Warming." *New York Times,* April 22.

STIPP, DAVID. 1994. "New Study Indicates How Alcohol Use May Reduce the Risk of Heart Attacks." *Wall Street Journal,* September 28, B4.

STOCKARD, JEAN, AND MIRIAM M. JOHNSON. 1980. *Sex Roles: Sex Inequality and Sex Role Development.* Englewood Cliffs, N.J.: Prentice Hall.

STOLBERG, SHERYL GAY. 1998. "AIDS Is Becoming an Epidemic of Silence Among Blacks." *New York Times,* June 29.

STOLBERG, SHERYL GAY. 1998. "Superbugs." *New York Times,* August 2.

STONE, ALAN A., AND HARVEY M. STEIN. 1968. "Psychotherapy of the Hospitalized Suicide Patient." *American Journal of Psychotherapy, 22,* January, 15–25.

STOUFFER, SAMUEL A., ARTHUR A. LUMSDAINE, MARION HARPER LUMSDAINE, ROBIN M. WILLIAMS, JR., M. BREWSTER SMITH, IRVING L. JANIS, SHIRLEY A. STAR, AND LEONARD S. COTTRELL, JR. 1949. *The American Soldier: Combat and Its Aftermath,* vol. 2. New York: Wiley.

STRAUS, MURRAY A. 1980. "Victims and Aggressors in Marital Violence." *American Behavioral Scientist, 23,* May–June, 681–704.

STRAUS, MURRAY A. 1992. "Explaining Family Violence." *Marriage and Family in a Changing Society,* 4th ed., James M. Henslin (ed.). New York: Free Press, 344–356.

STRAUS, MURRAY A., AND RICHARD J. GELLES. 1988. "Violence in American Families: How Much Is There and Why Does It Occur?" In *Troubled Relationships,* Elam W. Nunnally, Catherine S. Chilman, and Fred M. Cox (eds.). Newbury Park, Calif.: Sage, 141–162.

STRAUS, MURRAY A., RICHARD J. GELLES, AND SUZANNE K. STEINMETZ. 1980. *Behind Closed Doors: Violence in the American Family.* New York: Anchor/Doubleday.

STROBEL, LEE. 1980. *Reckless Homicide: Ford's Pinto Trial.* South Bend, Ind.: And Books.

"Suit Settled by Neil Bush." 1992. *New York Times,* March 29, A43.

SUTHERLAND, EDWIN H. 1937. *The Professional Thief.* Chicago: University of Chicago Press.

SUTHERLAND, EDWIN H. 1947. *Principles of Criminology,* 4th ed. Philadelphia: Lippincott.

SUTHERLAND, EDWIN H. 1949. *White Collar Crime.* New York: Dryden.

SUTTLES, GERALD D. 1968. *The Social Order of the Slum: Ethnicity and Territory in the Inner City.* Chicago: University of Chicago Press.

SUZUKI, BOB H. 1985. "Asian-American Families." In *Marriage and Family in a Changing Society,* 2nd ed., James M. Henslin (ed.). New York: Free Press, 104–119.

SWEDISH INSTITUTE, THE. 1992. "Fact Sheets on Sweden." February.

SYKES, GRESHAM M. 1978. *Criminology.* New York: Harcourt.

SYKES, GRESHAM M., AND DAVID MATZA. 1957. "Techniques of Neutralization: A Theory of Delinquency." *American Sociological Review, 22,* December, 664–670.

SZASZ, THOMAS. 1961. *The Myth of Mental Illness.* Harper & Row.

SZASZ, THOMAS. 1975. *Ceremonial Chemistry: The Ritual Persecution of Drugs, Addicts, and Pushers.* Garden City, N.Y.: Anchor.

TANNEN, DEBORAH. 1990. *You Don't Understand: Women and Men in Conversation.* New York: Morrow.

TANOUYE, ELYSE. 1998. "Price Markups on Generic Can Top Brand-Name Drugs." *Wall Street Journal,* December 31.

TEAFORD, JOHN. 1986. *The Twentieth Century American City.* Baltimore: Johns Hopkins University Press.

TELLER, EDWARD. 1980. "The Energy Crisis: No Contingency Plan." San Diego, Calif.: World Research.

TERESA, VINCENT, WITH THOMAS C. RENNER. 1973. *My Life in the Mafia.* Greenwich, Conn.: Fawcett.

"Terror, but Not Terrorism." 1985. *The Economist,* January 5, 18–19.

THAYER, FREDERICK C. 1997. "The Holy War on Surplus Americans+ Soviet Dogma, Old-time Religion and Classical Economics." *Social Policy, 28,* 1, Fall, 8–18.

THIO, ALEX. 1978. *Deviant Behavior.* Boston: Houghton Mifflin.

"33 Million Penalty Notices." 1995. *Wall Street Journal,* April 17, A12.

THOMAS, PAULETTE. 1988. "EPA Predicts Global Impact from Warming." *Wall Street Journal,* October 21, B5.

THOMAS, PAULETTE. 1992. "Boston Fed Finds Racial Discrimination in Mortgage Lending Is Still Widespread." *Wall Street Journal,* October 9, A3.

THOMPSON, HUNTER. 1967. *Hell's Angels.* New York: Random House.

THORNTON, RUSSELL. 1987. *American Indian Holocaust and Survival: A Population History Since 1492.* Norman: University of Oklahoma Press.

THRASHER, FREDERIC M. 1927. *The Gang.* Chicago: University of Chicago Press.

TIERNEY, JOHN. 1986. "The Population Crisis Revisited." *Wall Street Journal,* January 20, 16.

TIERNEY, JOHN. 1990. "Betting on the Planet." *New York Times.* December 2.

TIGER, LIONEL, AND ROBIN FOX. 1971. *The Imperial Animal.* New York: Holt.

TIMASHEFF, NICHOLAS S. 1965. *War and Revolution.* Joseph F. Scheuer (ed.). New York: Sheed & Ward.

TIMERMAN, JACOBO. 1981. *Prisoner Without a Name, Cell Without a Number.* New York: Knopf.

TOAI, DOAN VAN, AND DAVID CHANOFF. 1984. "Vietnam Turns to Narcotics to Pay Its Bills." *Wall Street Journal,* March 8, 30.

TOBY, JACKSON. 1992. "To Get Rid of Guns in Schools, Get Rid of Some Students." *Wall Street Journal,* March 23, A12.

TOFFLER, ALVIN. 1971. *Future Shock.* New York: Bantam.

TOLCHIN, MARTIN. 1991a. "Mildest Possible Penalty Is Imposed on Neil Bush." *New York Times,* April 19, D2.

TOLCHIN, MARTIN. 1991b. "Fund Established to Help Pay Legal Fees for President's Son." *New York Times,* June 9, 1–31.

TONNIES, FERDINAND. 1957. *Community and Society.* East Lansing: Michigan State University (originally published in 1887).

TOTH, MIKE. 1998. "According to Professor Ehrlich, Shouldn't the World Be Over By Now?" *Stanford Review,* March 10.

TREASTER, JOSEPH B. 1991a. "Agency Says Marijuana Is Not Proven Medicine." *New York Times,* March 19, B11.

TREASTER, JOSEPH B. 1991b. "Doctors in Survey Support Marijuana Use by Cancer Patients." *New York Times,* May 1, D22.

TREBACH, ARNOLD S. 1987. *The Great Drug War: And Radical Proposals That Could Make America Safe Again.* New York: Macmillan.

TRUST, CATHY. 1986. "Presidential Panel Says 4 Major Unions Have Connections to Organized Crime." *Wall Street Journal,* January 15, 48.

TURNER, JONATHAN H. 1972. *American Society: Problems of Structure.* New York: Harper & Row.

TURNER, JONATHAN H. 1978. *The Structure of Sociological Theory.* Homewood, Ill.: Dorsey.

ULLMAN, SARAH E. 1998. "Does Offender Violence Escalate When Rape Victims Fight Back?" *Journal of Interpersonal Violence, 13,* 2, April, 179–192.

United States Department of State. 1997. "Environmental Diplomacy: The Environment and U.S. Foreign Policy," April 22.

United Press International. 1998. "Vegetables More Effective Than Vitamins Against Heart Disease." November 30.

Use and Misuse of Benzodiazepines: Hearing Before the Subcommittee on Health and Scientific Research of the Committee on Labor and Human Resources, September 10,

1979. 1980. Washington, D.C.: U.S. Government Printing Office.

USEEM, MICHAEL. 1979. "The Social Organization of the American Business Elite." *American Sociological Review, 44,* August, 553–572.

USEEM, MICHAEL. 1984. *The Inner Circle: Large Corporations and the Rise of Business Political Activity in the U.S. and U.K.* New York: Oxford University Press.

VALOCCHI, STEVE. 1994. "The Racial Basis of Capitalism and the State, and the Impact of the New Deal on African Americans." *Social Problems, 41,* 3, August, 347–362.

VAN DEN HAAG, ERNEST. 1975. *Punishing Criminals: Concerning a Very Old and Painful Question.* New York: Basic Books.

VAN DEN HAAG, ERNEST, AND JOHN P. CONRAD. 1983. *The Death Penalty: A Debate.* New York: Plenum.

VAN DER KWAAK, ANKE. 1992. "Female Circumcision and Gender Identity: A Questionable Alliance." *Social Science and Medicine, 35,* 6, September, 777–787.

VANDE BERG, LEAH R., AND DIANE STRECKFUSS. 1992. "Prime-Time Television's Portrayal of Women and the World of Work: A Demographic Profile." *Journal of Broadcasting and Electronic Media,* Spring, 195–208.

VARADY, DAVID. 1986. *Neighborhood Upgrading: A Realistic Assessment.* Albany: SUNY Press.

VATZ, RICHARD E. 1994. "Attention Deficit Delirium." *Wall Street Journal,* July 27, A14.

VEEVERS, JEAN E. 1973. "Voluntarily Childless Wives." *Sociology and Social Research, 57,* April, 356–366.

VEEVERS, JEAN E. 1980. *Childless by Choice.* Toronto: Butterworths.

VERESPEI, MICHAEL A. 1992. "Drug Users, Not Testing, Anger Workers." *Industry Week, 241,* 4, February 17, 33–34.

VETTER, BETTY M., AND ELEANOR L. BABCO. 1986. *Professional Women and Minorities.* Washington, D.C.: Commission on Professionals in Science and Technology, February.

VIDAL, DAVID. 1977. "Bilingual Education Is Thriving but Criticized." *New York Times,* January 30.

WADDINGTON, CONRAD H. 1978. *The Man-Made Future.* New York: St. Martin's.

WAGLEY, CHARLES, AND MARVIN HARRIS. 1958. *Minorities in the New World.* New York: Columbia University Press.

WAGMAN, ROBERT. 1981. "Is Japanese Mafia Threat to U.S.?" Syndicated column, November 27.

WAIN, BARRY. 1981. "Cambodia: What Remains of the Killing Ground." *Wall Street Journal,* January 29, 24.

WAITZKIN, HOWARD, AND BARBARA WATERMAN. 1974. *The Exploitation of Illness in Capitalist Society.* New York: Bobbs-Merrill.

WALD, PATRICIA M. 1974. "Making Sense Out of 12 Rights of Youth." *Human Rights, 4,* Fall, 13–29.

WALKER, ALICE, AND PRATIBHA PARMAR. 1993. *Warrior Marks: Femal Genital Mutilation and the Sexual Binding of Women.* New York: Harcourt Brace.

WALLACE, JAMES N. 1980. "Green Revolution Hits Double Trouble." *U.S. News & World Report,* July 28, 37, 40.

WALLERSTEIN, IMMANUEL. 1974. *The Modern World System: Capitalist Agriculture and the Origins of the European World-Economy in the Sixteenth Century.* New York: Academic Press.

WALLERSTEIN, IMMANUEL. 1979. *The Capitalist World-Economy.* New York: Cambridge University Press.

WALLERSTEIN, IMMANUEL. 1984. *The Politics of the World-Economy: The States, the Movements, and the Civilizations.* Cambridge: Cambridge University Press.

WALSH, MARK. 1996. "Supreme Court Refuses to Weigh Race-Based College Admissions." *Education Week on the WEB,* July 10.

WARD, RUSSELL A. 1991. "Patient-Provider Ties and Satisfaction with Health Care." *Research in the Sociology of Health Care, 9,* 169–190.

WARR, MARK. 1985. "Fear of Rape Among Urban Women." *Social Problems, 32,* 3, February, 238–250.

WARTZMAN, RICK, AND JOHN HARWOOD. 1992. "Congress, Bush Back Enterprise Zones for Inner Cities, Need Compromise First." *Wall Street Journal,* May 13, A3.

WATANABE, TERESA. 1998. "The Green Movement Is Getting Religion." *Los Angeles Times,* December 25.

WAX, MURRAY L. 1971. *Indian Americans: Unity and Diversity.* Englewood Cliffs, N.J.: Prentice Hall.

WAX, MURRAY L., AND ROSALIE H. WAX. 1964. "Cultural Deprivation as an Educational Ideology." *Journal of American Indian Education, 3,* January 15–18.

WAX, MURRAY L., AND ROSALIE H. WAX. 1965. "Indian Education for What?" *Midcontinent American Studies Journal, 6,* Fall, 164–170.

WAX, ROSALIE H. 1967. "The Warrior Dropouts." *Trans-Action, 4,* May 40–46.

WEBBER, MELVIN M. 1973. "Urbanization and Communications." In *Communications Technology and Social Policy; Understanding the New Cultural Revolution.* George Gerbner, Larry P. Gross, and William H. Melody (eds.). New York: Wiley.

WEBBER, MELVIN M. 1977. "The Post-City Age." In *City Scenes: Problems and Prospects.* J. John Palen (ed.). Boston: Little, Brown 307–319.

WEBSTER, WILLIAM H. 1978. *FBI Uniform Crime Reports.* Washington, D.C.: U.S. Government Printing Office.

WEINBERG, S. KIRSON, AND HENRY AROND. 1952. "The Occupational Culture of the Boxer." *American Journal of Sociology, 57,* March, 460–469.

WEISSBOURD, R. 1996. *The Vulnerable Child: What Really Hurts America's Children and What We can Do About It.* Reading, Mass.: Addison-Wesley.

WEITZ, ROSE. 1991. *Life with AIDS*. New Brunswick, N.J.: Rutgers University Press.

WEITZ, ROSE, AND DEBORAH A. SULLIVAN. 1986. "The Politics of Childbirth: The Re-Emergence of Mid-Wifery in Arizona." *Social Problems, 33,* 3, February, 163–175.

WEITZMAN, LENORE J. 1985. *The Divorce Revolution: The Unexpected Social and Economic Consequences for Women and Children in America*. New York: Free Press.

WEITZMAN, LENORE J., DEBORAH EIFLER, ELIZABETH HOKADA, AND CATHERINE ROSS. 1972. "Sex Role Socialization in Picture Books for Pre-School Children." *American Journal of Sociology, 77,* May, 1125–1150.

WELLS, JOHN WARREN. 1970. *Tricks of the Trade*. New York: New American Library.

WELLS, JOSEPH. 1998. "Report to the Nation on Occupational Fraud and Abuse." Association of Certified Fraud Examiners.

WELLS, KEN. 1990. "Hazelwood Is Acquitted of Most Charges." *Wall Street Journal*. March 23, A3, A4.

WELLS, KEN, AND CHARLES MCCOY. 1989. "Exxon Says Fast Containment of Oil Spill in Alaska Could Have Caused Explosion." *Wall Street Journal,* April 5, A3.

WENNEKER, MARK B., AND ARNOLD M. EPSTEIN. 1989. "Racial Inequalities in the Use of Procedures for Patients with Ischemic Heart Disease in Massachusetts." *Journal of American Medical Association, 261,* 2, January 13, 253–257.

WERMIEL, STEPHEN. 1986a. "Justices Uphold Georgia's Law Barring Sodomy." *Wall Street Journal,* July 1, 4.

WERMIEL, STEPHEN. 1986b. "Supreme Court Refuses to Hear Exxon Appeal." *Wall Street Journal,* January 28, 3.

WERTHEIMER, DAVID M. 1988. "Victims of Violence: A Rising Tide of Anti-Gay Sentiment." *USA Today,* January, 52–54.

WEST, CANDACE, AND ANGELA GARCIA. 1988. "Conversational Shift Work: A Study of Topical Transitions Between Women and Men." *Social Problems, 35,* 551–575.

WEST, RICHARD W., AND GARY STEIGER. 1980. *The Effects of the Seattle and Denver Income Management Experiments on Alternative Measures of Labor Supply*. Menlo Park, Calif.: SRI International Research Memorandum, 72, May.

WESTLEY, WILLIAM A. 1953. "Violence and the Police." *American Journal of Sociology, 59,* July, 34–41.

WHITAKER, JENNIFER SEYMOUR. 1988. *How Can Africa Survive?* New York: Harper & Row.

WHITAKER, MARK. 1984. "'It Was Like Breathing Fire . . .'" *Newsweek,* December 17, 26–32.

WHITBECK, LES B., AND RONALD L. SIMONS. 1990. "Life on the Streets: The Victimization of Runaway and Homeless Adolescents." *Youth and Society, 22,* 1, September, 108–125.

WHITE, HELENE RASKIN. 1991. "Marijuana Use and Delinquency: A Test of the 'Independent Cause' Hypothesis." *Journal of Drug Issues, 21,* 2, Spring, 231–256.

WHITE, SAMMIS B. 1981. "Displacement: Is It the Real Enemy?" *Urbanism: Past and Present, 6,* Summer–Fall, 21–26.

WHITEHURST, CAROL A. 1977. *Women in America: The Oppressed Majority*. Santa Monica, Calif.: Goodyear.

WHITMAN, DAVID. 1987. "For Latinos, a Growing Divide." *U.S. News & World Report,* August 10, 47–49.

WHYTE, WILLIAM FOOTE. 1943. *Street Corner Society*. Chicago: University of Chicago Press.

WILCOX, ANSLEY II. 1957. Letter from Hooker Electrochemical Company to the President of the Niagara Falls Board of Education, November 21.

"The Wild Wild East." 1995. CNN, March 12.

WILL, GEORGE. "AIDS Crushes a Continent." Newsweek, January 10, 2000:64.

WILLHELM, SIDNEY M. 1980. "Can Marxism Explain America's Racism?" *Social Problems, 28,* December, 98–112.

WILLIAMS, J. ALLEN, JOETTA A. VERNON, MARTHA C. WILLIAMS, AND KAREN MALECHA. 1987. "Sex Role Socialization in Picture Books: An Update." *Social Science Quarterly, 68,* 1, March, 148–156.

WILLIAMS, ROBERT C. 1980. "Three Mile Island as History." *Washington University Magazine, 50,* October, 56, 58–59, 61–63.

WILLIAMS, ROGER M. 1977. "The New Urban Pioneers: Homesteading in the Slums." *Saturday Review,* July 23, 9–14.

WILLIAMS, TERRY M., AND WILLIAM KORNBLUM. 1985. *Growing Up Poor*. Lexington, Mass.: Lexington Books.

WILLIAMSON, JOHN B., JUDITH A. SHINDUL, AND LINDA EVANS. 1985. *Aging and Social Policy: Social Control or Social Justice?* Springfield, Ill.: Charles C. Thomas.

WILSON, JAMES Q. 1975. "Lock 'Em Up and Other Thoughts on Crime." *New York Times Magazine,* March 9, 11, 44–48.

WILSON, WILLIAM JULIUS. 1978. *The Declining Significance of Race: Blacks and Changing American Institutions*. Chicago: University of Chicago Press.

WILSON, WILLIAM JULIUS. 1987. *The Truly Disadvantaged: The Inner City, the Underclass, and Public Policy*. Chicago: University of Chicago Press.

WILSON, WILLIAM JULIUS. 1992. Scholar in Residence Lecture at Southern Illinois University, Edwardsville, June 14.

WINICK, CHARLES. 1961. "Physician Narcotic Addicts." *Social Problems, 9,* Fall, 174–186.

WINICK, CHARLES, AND PAUL M. KINSIE. 1971. *The Lively Commerce: Prostitution in the United States*. Chicago: Quadrangle.

WINSBERG, MORTON. 1991. "The Mean Streets Get Meaner: City and Suburb." *Population Today, 19,* 4, April 1, 4–5.

WINSLOW, RON. 1990. "Homicide Study Highlights Issue of Public Health." *Wall Street Journal,* June 27, B5.

WINSLOW, RON. 1991. *Wall Street Journal,* February 7, B4.

WINSLOW, RON. 1995a. "Heroin Remedy to Be Marketed for Alcoholism." *Wall Street Journal,* January 17, B1, B5.

WINSLOW, RON. 1995b. "Employer Costs Slip as Workers Shift to HMOs." *Wall Street Journal,* February 14, A3, A5.

WIRTH, LOUIS. 1938. "Urbanism as a Way of Life." *American Journal of Sociology, 44,* July, 1–24.

WIRTH, LOUIS. 1945. "The Problem of Minority Groups." In *The Science of Man in the World Crisis,* Ralph Linton (ed.). New York: Columbia University Press.

WOLF, DEBORAH GOLEMAN. 1979. *The Lesbian Community.* Berkeley: University of California Press.

WOLF, JULIE. 1999. "EU Scientists Contend Hormone Fed to U.S. Cattle Is Carcinogenic." *Wall Street Journal,* May 4.

WOLFENSOHN, JAMES D., AND KATHRYN S. FULLER. 1998. "Making Common Cause: Seeing the Forest for the Trees." *International Herald Tribune,* May 27, 11.

WOLFGANG, MARVIN E. 1958. *Patterns in Criminal Homicide.* Philadelphia: University of Pennsylvania Press.

WOLFGANG, MARVIN, E., AND MARC REIDEL. 1975. "Rape, Race, and the Death Penalty." *American Journal of Orthopsychiatry, 45,* July, 658–668.

"Women in the Riksdag." 1998. Online, December 7.

WORD, RON. 1998. "Woman Executed in Florida Electric Chair." Associated Press, March 30.

World Population Profile. Washington, D.C.: Bureau of the Census, U.S. Department of Commerce, various years.

"The World's Wars." 1988. *The Economist,* March 12, 19–22.

WREN, CHRISTOPHER S. 1998. "Methadone Use Emerged in City Where It Is Now Challenged." *New York Times,* October 3.

WRIGHT, ERIK OLIN. 1979. *Class Structure and Income Determination.* New York: Academic Press.

WRIGHT, QUINCY. 1942. *A Study of War,* 2 vols. Chicago: University of Chicago Press.

YABLONSKY, JUDY. 1981. "Survey Finds World Trend Toward More Liberal Abortion Laws." AP, May 20.

YARDLEY, JIM. 1998. "Abortion Provider Killed by Sniper's Bullet." *New York Times,* October 25.

YEAKEY, CAROL CAMP, AND CLIFFORD T. BENNETT. 1990. "Race, Schooling, and Class in American Society." *Journal of Negro Education, 59,* 1, Winter, 3–18.

YOUNG, T. R. 1985. "Social Problems: A Radical Agenda for the 80's and 90's." *SSSP Newsletter, 16,* Summer, 7–11.

YUAN, D. Y. 1963. "Voluntary Segregation: A Study of New York Chinatown." *Phylon, 24,* Fall, 255–265.

ZABLOCKI, BENJAMIN, ANGELA AIDALA, STEPHEN HANSELL, AND HELENE RASKIN WHITE. 1991. "Marijuana Use, Introspectiveness, and Mental Health." *Journal of Health and Social Behavior, 32,* 1, March, 65–79.

ZAWITZ, MARIANNE W. (ed.). 1988. *Report to the Nation on Crime and Justice,* 2nd ed. Washington, D.C.: U.S. Department of Justice, Bureau of Justice Statistics, July.

ZIMBARDO, PHILIP G. 1972. "The Pathology of Imprisonment." *Society, 9,* 6, April, 4–8.

ZIMBARDO, PHILIP G. 1995. "The Pathology of Imprisonment." In *Down-to-Earth Sociology: Introductory Readings,* 8th ed., James M. Henslin, ed. New York: Free Press, 278–283.

Photo Credits

CHAPTER 1: *1,* Soqui Ted/Corbis/Sygma; *6,* Roberts Rugh/UPI/Corbis; *11,* Collection, The Supreme Court Historical Society/Richard Strauss, Smithsonian Institute; *12,* Lynn Johnson/Aurora & Quanta Productions; *14,* Bob Daemmrich/Stock Boston; *16,* Ron Heflin/AP/Wide World Photos.

CHAPTER 2: *24,* Ronnie Kaufman/Corbis; *29,* Bertrand Rieger/Getty Images, Inc.–Stone; *31,* I. Burgham/ P. Boorman/ Getty Images, Inc.–Stone; *38,* Brown Brothers; *43 (top),* Pauline Lubens/Detroit Free Press, Inc.; *43 (bottom),* Bob Daemmrich/Stock Boston.

CHAPTER 3: *48,* Reuters/Peter Morgan/Getty Images Inc.–Hulton Archive Photos; *50,* Archeological Museum, Athens, Greece/Bridgeman Art Library/SuperStock, Inc.; *56,* Churchill & Klehr Photography; *58,* Michael Goldman/Getty Images, Inc.–Taxi; *61,* Jana Birchum; *65,* Richard B. Levine/Frances M. Roberts; *69,* Rasmussen/ SIPA Press; *73,* Alan Schein/ Corbis/Stock Market; *78,* Mark Mellett/Stock Boston; *82,* Globe Photos, Inc.

CHAPTER 4: *86,* Larry Mulvehill/Photo Researchers, Inc.; *88,* James D'Addio/Corbis/Stock Market; *91,* The Granger Collection, New York; *98,* Eugene Richards/ Magnum Photos, Inc.; *100,* AP/Wide World Photos; *106,* National Archives and Records Administration; *110,* Tom & DeeAnn McCarthy/Corbis/Stock Markey; *115,* Suzi Moore/Woodfin Camp & Associates; *119,* Garry Sussman/AP/Wide World Photos; *124,* Bebeto Matthews/AP/Wide World Photos.

CHAPTER 5: *130,* AP/Wide World Photos; *132,* PhotoEdit Inc.; *139,* Davis Barber/PhotoEdit; *146,* Lee Celano/Corbis/SABA Press Photos, Inc.; *150,* Tracy Weisheit/TLW Stock & Assignment Photography; *151,* PhotoEdit Inc.; *156,* Les Stine/Corbis/Sygma; *159,* © Greg Gilbert/Reuters NewMedia, Inc./CORBIS.

CHAPTER 6: *166,* Bob Daemmrich/The Image Works; *170,* Haviv/Corbis/SABA Press Photos, Inc.; *176,* Parker & Hart/Creators Syndicate, Inc.; *181,* Alon Reininger/Contact Press Images, Inc.; *185,* Carolyn Cole/Los Angeles Times Syndicate; *188,* George Widman/AP/Wide World Photos; *190,* AP/Wide World Photos; *192,* Jim Argo/The Daily Oklahoman/ Corbis/SABA Press Photos, Inc.; *194,* Mark Foley/ AP/Wide World Photos; *200,* Mark Peterson/ Corbis/SABA Press Photos, Inc.; *201,* AP/Wide World Photos.

CHAPTER 7: *211,* Gabe Kirchheimer/Black Star; *213,* Josef Beck/Getty Images, Inc.; *219,* Karen Kasmausk/ Matrix International, Inc.; *220,* AP/Wide World Photos; *224,* Jean Higgins/New England Stock Photo; *229,* Bob Daemmrich/Stock Boston; *230,* Chris Minerva/Index Stock Imagery, Inc.; *231,* Sarah Leen/Matrix International, Inc.; *240,* Brown Brothers.

CHAPTER 8: *247,* Rafael Macia/Photo Researchers; *251,* The Granger Collection; *255,* Ariel Skelley/Corbis/ Stock Market; *261,* AP/Wide World Photos; *267,* John Bazemore/AP/Wide World Photos; *270,* Jeff Greenberg/Lonely Planet Images/Photo 20-20; *273,* Russell Lee/The Granger Collection; *277,* Getty Images, Inc.–Hulton Archive Photos.

CHAPTER 9: *285,* Bob Daemmrich/Stock Boston; *287,* Najlah Feanny/Corbis/SABA Press Photos, Inc.; *296,* AP/Wide World Photos; *301,* AP/Wide World Photos; *302,* F. Trapper/Corbis/Sygma; *307,* Esbin/Anderson/ Omni-Photo Communications, Inc.; *309 (left),* Kim Kulish/SABA Press Photos, Inc.; *309 (right),* Scott Applewhite/AP/Wide World Photos.

CHAPTER 10: *319,* PhotoEdit; *324,* Elise Amendola/AP/ Wide World Photos; *325,* Steve Lehman/Corbis/SABA Press Photos, Inc.; *329,* Bob Kramer/Stock Boston; *336,* Betty Press/Woodfin Camp & Associates; *345,* Lew Merrim/Science Source/Photo Researchers, Inc.; *354,* Robin Nelson/Black Star; *358,* Sam Ogden/Science Photo Library/Photo Researchers, Inc.

CHAPTER 11: *361,* T. & D. McCarthy/Corbis/Stock Market; *365,* Jason Grow/Corbis/SABA Press Photos, Inc.; *367,* David P. Hall/Corbis Sharpshooters; *371,* Peter Beck/Corbis/Stock Market; *372,* Richard B. Levine/Frances M. Roberts; *374,* Alain Evrard/Getty Images, Inc.–Liaison; *378,* The Granger Collection, New York ; *381,* Bob Daemmrich/Stock Boston; *385,* Zefa London Corbis/ Stock Market; *388,* Joseph Schuyler/Stock Boston.

CHAPTER 12: *398,* Comstock Images; *410,* Lee Snider/The Image Works; *413,* R. Lord/The Image

Works; *414,* Cameramann/The Image Works; *416,* Jonathan Elderfield/Getty Images, Inc.–Liaison; *418,* The Granger Collection, New York ; *430,* John Nordell/ The Image Works.

CHAPTER 13: *434,* Les Stone/Corbis/Sygma; *442,* Goddard/Corbis/Sygma; *443,* Mark Graham/Getty Images, Inc.–Liaison; *451,* D. H. Hessel/Stock Boston.

CHAPTER 14: *467,* Ben Osborne/Tony Stone Images; *469,* Christie's Images, New York/SuperStock; *470,* T. Savino/The Image Works; *471,* Greenpeace/ Warford/Corbis/Sygma; *489,* James M. Henslin; *472,* Sanford/Agliolo/Corbis/Stock Market; *473,* Corbis; *477,* L. Dematteis/The Image Works; *482,* Alvaro De Leiva/GettyImages, Inc.–Liaison; *493,* Greg Girard/ Contact Press Images, Inc.; *498,* ©Buddy Mays/Corbis; *500,* Robert Eckert/Stock Boston; *505,* ©Tom Salyer/Corbis.

CHAPTER 15: *508,* AP/Wide World Photos; *511,* Napoleon A. Chagnon, *512,* The Granger Collection, New York ; *516,* E. F. Skinner/Mary Evans Picture Library Ltd.; *522,* Owen/Black Star; *525,* Keystone/ Getty Images, Inc.–Liaison; *532,* Stephanie Hollyman/ Getty Images, Inc.–Liaison; *537,* AFP Photo/Corbis; *534,* AP/Wide World Photos; *540,* AP/Wide World Photos; *542,* AP/Wide World Photos.

Photo Credits

Name Index

Hakansson, S., 352
Hale, M., 194
Hall, S., 53
Halperin, E., 535
Hamer, D. H., 70
Hammer, R., 191
Hammersmith, S. K., 71
Hammurabi, 161
Hansell, S., 101
Hanson, D. J., 105
Hanson, K., 162
Hanssen, M., 488
Hardin, G., 470
Harlan, C., 167
Harries, E., 187
Harrington, M., 220, 236, 448,
    458, 461
Harris, C., 407
Harris, E., 131
Harris, M., 248, 287, 291–292
Harris, S. H., 524
Harrison, B., 498
Hart, C. W., 25–26
Hart, G., 400
Hart, H., 513
Harwood, J., 427
Haub, C., 437, 439, 440, 446,
    447, 450, 452
Hauser, P., 399
Haveman, R. H., 243
Hawthorne, N., 199
Hayakawa, S. I., 271
Hayes, A. S., 311
Hayes, J., 8
Heche, A., 82
Heckathorn, D. D., 177
Heins, M., 76
Heintz, K. E., 301
Helmer, J., 96
Hendin, H., 357
Henley, E. W., 159
Hennard, G., 158
Henriques, F., 50
Henry, P., 267
Henry, W. E., 33
Henslin, J. M., 30, 44, 250, 268,
    289, 291, 352, 355, 374
Henslin, L., 145
Herbert, B., 228, 256
Heyl, B. S., 53, 56

Hibbert, C., 201
Hickey, M. F., 460
Hicks, D., 142
Hills, S. L., 145, 184
Hiltz, S. R., 387
Himmelhoch, J., 67
Hindelang, M. J., 149, 194
Hippocrates (Greek Physician), 87
Hirschi, T., 140, 177, 370
Hitler, A., 248, 251–252, 459,
    541–542
Hobson, J. A., 517
Hochschild, A., 307, 378
Hoffman, A., 116
Hoffman, C., 241
Hoijer, H., 385
Holden, B. A., 428
Holdren, J. P., 449–450
Holman, R. L., 5
Holmes, S. A., 340
Holmstrom, L. L., 149, 163
Holtzman, A., 37
Homblin, D. J., 399
Homer, W., 212
Hooker, E., 70
Hooton, E. A., 136
Hope, C. A., 292
Hornback, K. E., 473
Hornblower, M., 57
Horowitz, M. M., 449
Horowitz, R., 138
Hosenball, M., 536
Hotchkiss, S., 145
Hotvedt, M. E., 70
Hotz, R. L., 469
Howard, J., 355
Hoyt, H., 407
Hsu, F. L. K., 277
Hu, N., 70
Hu, S., 70
Huber, J., 292
Huberty, J., 158
Huddle, D., 454
Hudo, B., 383–384
Hudo, C., 383–384
Hudson, C. G., 343
Hudson, R. B., 37, 40
Huff-Corzine, L., 158
Huggins, M., 236
Hull, J. D., 399, 416

Humphreys, L., 68–69
Humphries, D., 113
Hussein, S., 537, 540
Huxley, A., 115

◆ I ◆

Ianni, F. A. J., 191
Ibn Khaldun, 517
Inciardi, J. A., 51, 89, 112, 118,
    171
Ingersoll, B., 486, 488, 499
Irini, S., 53, 56, 72
Isbell, H., 89

◆ J ◆

Jackson, A., 223
Jacobs, D., 178
Jacobsen, T., 469
Jaffe, J. H., 119
James, J., 58
James, King of England, 88
James, W., 28
Janerich, D. T., 351
Janowitz, M., 418, 419
Jefferson, T., 403
Jekielek, S. M., 366
Jenkins, B. M., 533, 543
Joffe, C., 390, 392
John Paul II, Pope, 536
Johnson, B. D., 117, 118
Johnson, D., 65, 121
Johnson, D. R., 109
Johnson, J. M., 383
Johnson, L. B., 76, 216, 220, 419
Johnson, M. M., 298, 302
Johnson, T. R., 243
Johnson, V., 70
Johnston, L. D., 103, 110
Jones, P., 309
Jong, E., 78
Josephy, A. M., Jr., 268

◆ K ◆

Kagan, D., 541
Kahan, M., 98
Kahn, L. M., 306
Kaiserman, M. J., 122
Kalb, C., 342
Kalleberg, A. L., 307

Lowie, R. H., 49
Lublin, J. S., 311
Lubman, S., 282
Lucas, H. L., 159
Luciano, "Lucky,", 191
Luckenbill, D. F., 60
Luker, K., 16–17, 18, 19
Lukes, I., 535
Lundberg, O., 343
Lundblad, N., 464
Lutz, H. J., 469
Luy, M. L. M., 142
Lynch, J. W., 343
Lynch, M. C., 482
Lynd, H. M., 388
Lynd, R. S., 388

◆ M ◆

McBride, D. C., 112
McCarthy, B., 183
McCormick, J., 421
McCorvey, N., 16
McCoy, C., 483
McCuen, G. E., 493
McDowell, B., 402
McFalls, J. A., Jr., 437
McGarigle, B., 204
McGinley, L., 348
McGlocklin, B., 248
Machung, A., 307
McIntyre, J., 145, 149
MacKenzie, D. L., 202
MacKenzie, H., 440
McKenzie, R. D., 406
McKeown, T., 338, 340, 436
MacKinnon, C. A., 308–311
Macklin, E. D., 379
McKneally, M. F., 351
McManus, M. J., 77
MacNamara, D. E. J., 79
McNamara, R., 514
McNeely, R. L., 144
McVeigh, T., 192
Madigan, E., 150
Magnuson, V. L., 70
Mahoney, L., 121
Mahran, M., 293
Maier, F., 417
Malecha, K., 301
Malthus, T., 436, 458–459

Mamdani, M., 444
Manski, C. F., 220
Marger, M. N., 234
Mariana, A., 112
Markley, J., 61
Markus, H., 177
Markusen, E., 535
Marolla, J., 142, 143, 145, 146, 148
Marsiglio, W., 62
Martin, J. K., 93
Martin, P., 454
Martin, P. S., 469
Marx, K., 36, 140, 224
Masters, W., 70
Matthaei, J., 277
Matza, D., 181–182
Maugh, T. H., 340
Maynard, D. W., 192
Mayne, S. T., 351
Mead, G. H., 28
Medvedev, Z., 484
Meier, B., 108, 329, 490
Meier, R. F., 473
Melamed, M. R., 351
Melloan, G., 42
Melman, S., 525, 526
Melody, G. F., 53
Mendels, P., 83, 256
Merton, R. K., 20, 32, 139–140, 175, 421–422
Merwine, M. H., 293
Messner, S. F., 158
Meyer, H., 88
Meyerding, J., 58
Miall, C. E., 380
Michelman, K., 12
Midgley, E., 454
Milbank, D., 459
Miles, R. E., Jr., 450, 460, 535
Millar, H., 347
Miller, J., 471, 532, 534, 538
Miller, M. W., 112, 343
Miller, T., 118
Miller, W. B., 416
Millett, K., 53, 60, 142
Mills, C. W., 2, 231, 233, 234, 282, 365, 516, 518
Mills, K. M., 305
Milner, C., 60

Milner, R., 60
Milosevic, S., 537, 540
Milvy, P., 485
Minton, K., 503
Mintz, M., 540
Mjama, K., 534
Moberg, M., 476
Moiser, I., 399
Moiser, K., 399
Mokhiber, R., 483
Moller, J., 269
Montagu, M. F. A., 253
Moore, B. T., 159
Moore, D. C., 158
Moore, D. W., 34
Moore, G., 234, 235
Moore, J. W., 182
Moore, S. D., 353
Moore, W., 223
Morash, M. A., 202, 203
Morehouse, E., 111
Morgan, M., 301
Morgan, P. A., 96
Morris, C. P., 115
Morris, R., 297
Morrison, D. E., 473
Morse, E. V., 61
Moseley-Braun, C., 303
Mosher, S. W., 459
Muecke, M. A., 57
Muehlenhard, C. L., 147, 148
Muhammad, K. A., 256
Mukherjee, P., 457
Mulvihill, D. J., 137
Murdock, G. P., 287
Murphy, K., 248, 256
Muth, J. B., 51
Muth, S. Q., 51
Mydens, S., 417
Myers, M. A., 195
Myers, S. L., 538, 541
Myerson, A. L., 504
Myint, T., 145, 149
Myrdal, G., 282, 286

◆ N ◆

Nagai, A. K., 14
Naj, A. K., 478, 503
Nasar, S., 233
Nash, G. B., 238

Rimland, I., 256
Risen, J., 537
Robb, T., 248
Roberts, L., 503
Robinson, A. B., 479
Robinson, D. A. , 135
Robinson, J. C., 348
Robinson, J. P., 316
Robinson, R. V., 215
Robinson, Z. W., 479
Rockwell, D., 95, 106
Rodenburg, E., 440, 452, 491
Roe, K. M., 6
Rogers, B., 122
Rogers, C., 121
Rogers, J. W., 177
Rohe, W. M., 426
Rohwedder, C., 504
Rolo, M. A., 270
Roosevelt, F. D., 38, 238, 244, 276
Roosevelt, T., 473
Rosaldo, M. Z., 288
Rose, F., 282
Rosen, L., 180–181
Rosen, Y., 483
Rosenberg, C. E., 324, 342
Rosenfeld, R. A., 307
Rosenthal, C., 363, 387
Rosett, C., 483
Rothman, D. J., 223, 238
Rothman, S., 9
Rothman, S. M., 223
Rothschild, N., 301
Rotow, D., 541
Royko, M., 422
Rubenstein, R. E., 533
Rucker, L., 202
Ruggles, P., 216, 230
Rumbaut, R. G., 328
Russell, D. E. H., 78, 146, 150, 384, 385
Russell, J. S., 258
Russo, E. B., 111
Rutenfrans, C., 357
Rybczynski, W., 413, 420

◆ S ◆

Sagan, S. D., 527, 530, 541
Sagarin, E., 57, 79

Saha, S., 490–491
Sakharov, A., 535
Salas, R., 270
Samoset, 93
Sampson, C., 353
Sanders, H., 421
Sanger, M., 167–168
Sappho (Greek poet), 72
Savitz, L., 180–181
Sawhill, I. V., 230
Sayles, S., 145
Schaefer, R. T., 267, 277
Schlafly, P., 393
Schlender, B. R., 494
Schmalleger, F., 149
Schmeidler, J., 118
Schmidt, G., 76
Schmitt, R. B., 171
Schneider, K., 481, 500
Schnore, L. F., 399, 407
Schoenberger, R., 306–307
Schoenfeld, A. C., 473
Scholz, J. K., 243
Schottland, C., 38
Schrag, P., 101
Schreiber, J., 534
Schrieke, B. J., 277
Schumpeter, J. A., 517–518
Schuster, L., 490
Schwartz, F. N., 307
Schwendinger, H., 143, 144, 146
Schwendinger, J. R., 143, 144, 146
Schwidrowski, K., 191
Scully, D., 142, 143, 145, 146, 148, 312, 337
Seaborg, D., 448
Seghorn, T., 145
Seib, G. F., 531, 536
Seidman, S. A., 302
Seligmann, J., 147
Sellin, T., 194
Shachtman, T., 159
Shaffer, H. G., 219, 520
Shaffir, W., 334
Shafir, G., 264
Shapiro, J. P., 356, 357
Shapiro, T. M., 243, 258
Shaw, S., 57
Shebar, W., 138

Sheehy, G., 51
Shellenbarger, S., 307, 395
Shema, S. J., 343
Shen, L., 483
Shepard, M., 65
Sheppard, N., Jr., 412
Shibutani, T., 515, 523
Shilts, R., 340
Shim, K. H., 194
Shindul, J. A., 39
Shinnar, R., 204
Shinnar, S., 204
Shively, J., 269
Shribman, D., 483
Shultz, R. H., 535
Siegel, K., 72
Signorielli, N., 302
Sigusch, V., 76
Silberman, C. E., 176
Silbert, M. H., 58
Silver, J. M., 334
Silverman, D., 309
Simmel, G., 37, 515
Simmons, B., 121
Simon, D. R., 191
Simon, J. L., 440, 441, 450, 451, 454, 456, 458, 462, 492, 494, 495, 496, 503, 506
Simon, P. M., 61
Simpson, G. E., 250–251, 261, 268, 420
Sindler, A. P., 280
Singer, S. F., 478, 479
Singh, M., 496
Singh, T., 444
Sitomer, C. J., 76
Siwolop, S., 503
Skinner, 137
Skogan, W. G., 145
Slikker, W., Jr., 111
Smith, A., 316
Smith, B. E., 321
Smith, C., 524
Smith, D., 316
Smith, D. A., 194
Smith, D. E., 87
Smith, H., 106
Smith, James, 219
Smith, J. B., 478
Smith, John, 412

Walters, R. H., 137
Ward, R. A., 348
Waring, E., 190
Warner, W. K., 473
Warr, M., 142
Wartzman, R., 427
Washington, G., 516
Watanabe, T., 505, 523–524
Waterman, B., 337
Wax, M. L., 268
Wax, R. H., 268
Webber, M. M., 425, 428
Weeks, J. R., 328
Weinberg, M. S., 71, 72
Weinberg, S. K., 263
Weinrich, J. D., 70
Weissbourd, R., 366
Weitz, R., 71, 334
Weitzman, L. J., 301, 366
Welch, M., 409–410
Wells, J., 184
Wells, J. W., 53
Wells, K., 483, 506
Wenneker, M. B., 259
Wermiel, S., 64, 184
Wertheimer, D. M., 67
West, C., 298
West, R. W., 243
Westley, W. A., 173
Whitaker, M., 491
White, H. R., 101, 111
Whitehurst, C. A., 295, 296, 298–299, 300

Whitman, C., 158
Whyte, W. F., 404
Wilcox, A., 484
Willhelm, S. M., 265
Williams, J. A., 301
Williams, L. M., 362
Williams, M. C., 301
Williams, R. C., 485
Williams, R. M., 426
Williams, T. M., 58
Williams, W., 159
Williamson, J. B., 39
William the Conquerer, 513
Wilson, B., 417
Wilson, J., 204
Wilson, M., 157
Wilson, W., 171
Wilson, W. J., 158, 216, 230, 275–276, 282, 428–429
Winick, C., 51, 118
Winsberg, M., 413
Winslow, R., 104, 135, 321, 348, 353
Wirth, L., 249, 404, 410
Wish, E. D., 111, 118
Wisniewski, C., 113
Wissoker, D. A., 243
Wolf, D. G., 72
Wolf, J., 487
Wolfensohn, J. D., 493
Wolff, Derek, 105
Wolfgang, M. E., 138, 195
Woodhouse, D. E., 51

Word, D., 409–410
Word, R., 195
Wren, C. S., 123
Wright, E. O., 226
Wright, Q., 518
Wuornos, A., 159

◆Y◆

Yablonsky, J., 16
Yano, V., 8
Yardley, J., 11
Yeager, P. C., 187
Yeakey, C. C., 176
Yeldell, J., 171
Yinger, J. M., 250–251, 261, 268, 420
Yllo, K., 142, 148, 384
Yoels, W. C., 411, 425
Young, T. R., 20
Yuan, D. Y., 277

◆Z◆

Zablocki, B., 102
Zaccarelli, M., 60
Zaman, M. B., 351
Zawitz, M. W., 135, 158, 161, 171, 172, 193
Zimbardo, P. G., 167, 197
Zinn, M. B., 379
Zorbaugh, H., 404
Zundel, E., 256
Zylicz, Z., 357

Subject Index

Executive Order 9066 (1942), 276
Experimental group, 18
Experiments, 18
Exponential growth, 436
Extended families, 386
Exxon Corporation, 476, 483
Exxon Valdez, 483

False class consciousness, 224, 265
Families. *see also* Children; Divorce;
 Marriage
 and aging, 386–87
 changes in, 362–65, 390
 child rights, 393
 childless, 380–81
 cohabitation, 379
 day care, 362
 decline of, 388–89
 and divorce. *see* Divorce
 extended, 386
 functionalist perspective, 375–77
 functions, changing, 363,
  375–77
 future of, 394–95
 headed by women, 226–28
 homosexuality, as a threat, 62, 73
 household size, 388
 incest, 385–86
 industrialization, effects of,
  362–63, 376
 intervention versus interference,
  390, 392
 marital rape, 148, 384–85
 nuclear, 386
 and poverty, 392
 professional intrusion into,
  389–90
 and reproduction, 376–77
 runaway children, 371
 single-parent, 226–28, 368–71
 unwed motherhood, 367, 369
 violence, 312, 371–72, 381–84
Family of orientation, 372–73
Family of procreation, 373
Family Protection Act, 393
Family types
 African Americans, 368
 and elderly poverty rate, 45

Latinos, 368
 and poverty of children, 226–28
 in U.S., 391
FBI Uniform Crime Reports, 148
Federal Housing Authority (FHA),
 258
Federal Trade Commission (FTC),
 177, 178
Fee-for-service system, 322–23,
 335
Female circumcision, 293
Female feticide, 5
Female infanticide, 5, 286, 459
Feminist perspectives
 prostitution, 53
 rape, 142–43
 sex discrimination, 313
Feminization of poverty, 227, 229,
 230, 239
Fetal alcohol syndrome (FAS),
 104–05
Fetal narcotic syndrome, 118
Feticide. *see* Abortion
Feudal societies, 231
Fictive kinship, 189
Field studies, 18
Food
 the biotechnological future,
  462–63
 chain, 488
 chemical additives, 487–88
 crops, specialized strains of, 449
 fish harvest, 451
 functionalist perspective, 457–58
 the green revolution, 457
 international trade imbalance,
  461
 lateralization, 449
 limiting reproduction based on
  supply, 438
 natural systems, carrying capacity
  of, 449
 Ogallala aquifer, 449, 494
 politics, 448
 pollution, 486–89
 the potato famine, 449–50
 production out pacing need,
  451–52
 production per person, 441
 slash-and-burn agriculture, 449

Western farming methods,
 exporting, 457–58
 windrows, bulldozing of, 449
Food and Drug Administration
 (FDA), 487, 488
Food politics, 448
Food pollution, 486
Forced assimilation, 250
Forcible rape, 141
Ford Motor Company, 184–85
Foreign Miner's Act (1850), 277
Fourteenth Amendment, 316
Freebasing, 113
Freedom of Access to Clinic
 Entrances Act (1993), 13
Frustration-aggression, 136
Functional analysis. *see*
 Functionalism
Functional theory. *see*
 Functionalism
Functionalism
 defined, 31
 disengagement theory, 33
 dysfunctions, 31–32
 function and structure, 32
 society, interrelated parts of, 31
Functionalist perspectives
 aging, 31–37
 crime, 174–77
 discrimination, 262–64, 262–64
 drugs, 94–95
 families, 375–77
 food, 457–58
 homosexuality, 62
 medical care, 334–36
 murder, 154, 157–58
 pimps, 59
 population and food, 444–47
 poverty, 223–24, 225, 226
 prostitutes, 59
 prostitution, 51–53
 sexism, 291–92
 urban problems, 406–07
 violence, 139–40, 141, 163
 war, 515–17
Functions
 defined, 32
 discrimination, 262, 263
 of drugs, 94
 nursing homes, 33

killing and compartmentalization, 262
lives lost, 513
Village endogamy, 189
Violence. *see also* Murder; Rape
and anomie, 139
atavism, 135
biological theories, 135–36
and class oppression, 140–41
conflict perspective, 140–41, 163
continuation of, 163
defined, 131
differential association and group interaction, 137–38
family, 371–72, 381–84
fear of, 133
frequency of, 132–33
frustration-aggression theory, 136
functionalist perspective, 139–40, 141, 163
growth of, in U.S., 135, 136
and manliness, connection between, 138
modeling and learning theory, 137
normal, 139
objective conditions, 133–35
offenders, dealing with, 160–61
preventing, 162–63
psychological theories, 137
rates, amongst different groups, 134–35
retributionists versus reformists, 160
ritualistic, 510–11
in schools, 417
social heredity of, 382–83
sociological question of, 131
southern subculture of, 158
strain theory, 139–40
structural changes, need for, 163
subcultural theory, 138
subjective concerns, 132–33
symbolic interactionist perspective, 137–39, 141, 163
types of, 132
urban gangs, 416–17

U.S., compared with other countries, 134, 135
victims, dealing with, 161–62
against women, 312
Voting Rights Act (1965), 274

◆ **W** ◆

Walk-in stations, 332
War
accidental, possibility of, 527–31
aggressive instinct for, 509–10
arms race, 509, 514–15
binary chemical weapons, 532
biological and chemical, 531–32
causes of, 517–18
channeling aggression, 510–11
Cold War, 509
conditions of, 511–12
conflict perspective, 517–18
costs of, 519–24
death, capacity to inflict, 526–27
deaths attributed to, 513, 521–22
defined, 511
and dehumanization, 523–24
disarmament, 541
dysfunctions of, 517
and education, 513
fuels of, 512
functionalist perspective, 515–17
functions of, 515–17
future of, 542–44
and the global economy, 541
global expenditures, 521, 522
ICBMs, 514
imperialism, 517
and industrialization, 513
international arms trade, 542, 543
international law, 541
military machine, 517–18
the military-industrial complex, 525–27
mutual deterrence, 539–40
the Nuclear Club, 528–29
pentagon capitalism, 525
preparations versus alternative purchases, 520–21
and quality of life, 522–23
reduction of, 518–19

ritualistic violence, 510–11
"Star Wars" system, 515
symbolic interactionist perspective, 514–15
total, 521
in U.S. history, 513
in Western history, 512–13
women, as rewards, 510
War on poverty, 216–17, 220
Watergate, 192
Wealth
culture of, 234–35
defined, 218
distribution of, 218–19, 239
and power, 235
progressive taxation, 239
Webster v. Reproductive Services, 12–13
Welfare, 240, 241, 242–43
Welfare wall, 243
White Anglo-Saxon Protestants, 232
White flight, 274–75
White-collar crimes
on behalf of a corporation, 184–85
against a corporation, 185–86
cost of, 184
embezzlement, 185–86
future of, 207
and gender, 186
illegitimate opportunity structure for, 176
the "Pinto case," 184–85
theft by computer, 186, 189
types of, 184
U.S. savings and loan industry, looting of, 186
Widowhood, 387
Windrows, 449
Withdrawal, 92
Women. *see also* Sex discrimination; Sexism
drug use, during pregnancy, 113
earnings, compared to men, 306–07
and family roles, 363
and family violence, 381, 382, 383
female circumcision, 293

SINGLE PC LICENSE AGREEMENT AND LIMITED WARRANTY

READ THIS LICENSE CAREFULLY BEFORE OPENING THIS PACKAGE. BY OPENING THIS PACKAGE, YOU ARE AGREEING TO THE TERMS AND CONDITIONS OF THIS LICENSE. IF YOU DO NOT AGREE, DO NOT OPEN THE PACKAGE. PROMPTLY RETURN THE UNOPENED PACKAGE AND ALL ACCOMPANYING ITEMS TO THE PLACE YOU OBTAINED THEM [[FOR A FULL REFUND OF ANY SUMS YOU HAVE PAID FOR THE SOFTWARE]]. *THESE TERMS APPLY TO ALL LICENSED SOFTWARE ON THE DISK EXCEPT THAT THE TERMS FOR USE OF ANY SHAREWARE OR FREEWARE ON THE DISKETTES ARE AS SET FORTH IN THE ELECTRONIC LICENSE LOCATED ON THE DISK:*

1.   GRANT OF LICENSE and OWNERSHIP: The enclosed computer programs <<and data>> ("Software") are licensed, not sold, to you by Pearson Education, Inc. publishing as Prentice Hall ("We" or the "Company") and in consideration [[of your payment of the license fee, which is part of the price you paid]] [[of your purchase or adoption of the accompanying Company textbooks and/or other materials,]] and your agreement to these terms. We reserve any rights not granted to you. You own only the disk(s) but we and/or our licensors own the Software itself. This license allows you to use and display your copy of the Software on a single computer (i.e., with a single CPU) at a single location for <u>academic</u> use only, so long as you comply with the terms of this Agreement. You may make one copy for back up, or transfer your copy to another CPU, provided that the Software is usable on only one computer.

2.   RESTRICTIONS: You may <u>not</u> transfer or distribute the Software or documentation to anyone else. Except for backup, you may <u>not</u> copy the documentation or the Software. You may <u>not</u> network the Software or otherwise use it on more than one computer or computer terminal at the same time. You may <u>not</u> reverse engineer, disassemble, decompile, modify, adapt, translate, or create derivative works based on the Software or the Documentation. You may be held legally responsible for any copying or copyright infringement that is caused by your failure to abide by the terms of these restrictions.

3.   TERMINATION: This license is effective until terminated. This license will terminate automatically without notice from the Company if you fail to comply with any provisions or limitations of this license. Upon termination, you shall destroy the Documentation and all copies of the Software. All provisions of this Agreement as to limitation and disclaimer of warranties, limitation of liability, remedies or damages, and our ownership rights shall survive termination.

4.   LIMITED WARRANTY AND DISCLAIMER OF WARRANTY: Company warrants that for a period of 60 days from the date you purchase this SOFTWARE (or purchase or adopt the accompanying textbook), the Software, when properly installed and used in accordance with the Documentation, will operate in substantial conformity with the description of the Software set forth in the Documentation, and that for a period of 30 days the disk(s) on which the Software is delivered shall be free from defects in materials and workmanship under normal use. The Company does <u>not</u> warrant that the Software will meet your requirements or that the operation of the Software will be uninterrupted or error-free. Your only remedy and the Company's only obligation under these limited warranties is, at the Company's option, return of the disk for a refund of any amounts paid for it by you or replacement of the disk. THIS LIMITED WARRANTY IS THE ONLY WARRANTY PROVIDED BY THE COMPANY AND ITS LICENSORS, AND THE COMPANY AND ITS LICENSORS DISCLAIM ALL OTHER WARRANTIES, EXPRESS OR IMPLIED, INCLUDING WITHOUT LIMITATION, THE IMPLIED WARRANTIES OF MERCHANTABILITY AND FITNESS FOR A PARTICULAR PURPOSE. THE COMPANY DOES NOT WARRANT, GUARANTEE OR MAKE ANY REPRESENTATION REGARDING THE ACCURACY, RELIABILITY, CURRENTNESS, USE, OR RESULTS OF USE, OF THE SOFTWARE.

5.   LIMITATION OF REMEDIES AND DAMAGES: IN NO EVENT, SHALL THE COMPANY OR ITS EMPLOYEES, AGENTS, LICENSORS, OR CONTRACTORS BE LIABLE FOR ANY INCIDENTAL, INDIRECT, SPECIAL, OR CONSEQUENTIAL DAMAGES ARISING OUT OF OR IN CONNECTION WITH THIS LICENSE OR THE SOFTWARE, INCLUDING FOR LOSS OF USE, LOSS OF DATA, LOSS OF INCOME OR PROFIT, OR OTHER LOSSES, SUSTAINED AS A RESULT OF INJURY TO ANY PERSON, OR LOSS OF OR DAMAGE TO PROPERTY, OR CLAIMS OF THIRD PARTIES, EVEN IF THE COMPANY OR AN AUTHORIZED REPRESENTATIVE OF THE COMPANY HAS BEEN ADVISED OF THE POSSIBILITY OF SUCH DAMAGES. IN NO EVENT SHALL THE LIABILITY OF THE COMPANY FOR DAMAGES WITH RESPECT TO THE SOFTWARE EXCEED THE AMOUNTS ACTUALLY PAID BY YOU, IF ANY, FOR THE SOFTWARE OR THE ACCOMPANYING TEXTBOOK. BECAUSE SOME JURISDICTIONS DO NOT ALLOW THE LIMITATION OF LIABILITY IN CERTAIN CIRCUMSTANCES, THE ABOVE LIMITATIONS MAY NOT ALWAYS APPLY TO YOU.

6.   GENERAL: THIS AGREEMENT SHALL BE CONSTRUED IN ACCORDANCE WITH THE LAWS OF THE UNITED STATES OF AMERICA AND THE STATE OF NEW YORK, APPLICABLE TO CONTRACTS MADE IN NEW YORK, AND SHALL BENEFIT THE COMPANY, ITS AFFILIATES AND ASSIGNEES. HIS AGREEMENT IS THE COMPLETE AND EXCLUSIVE STATEMENT OF THE AGREEMENT BETWEEN YOU AND THE COMPANY AND SUPERSEDES ALL PROPOSALS OR PRIOR AGREEMENTS, ORAL, OR WRITTEN, AND ANY OTHER COMMUNICATIONS BETWEEN YOU AND THE COMPANY OR ANY REPRESENTATIVE OF THE COMPANY RELATING TO THE SUBJECT MATTER OF THIS AGREEMENT. If you are a U.S. Government user, this Software is licensed with "restricted rights" as set forth in subparagraphs (a)-(d) of the Commercial Computer-Restricted Rights clause at FAR 52.227-19 or in subparagraphs (c)(1)(ii) of the Rights in Technical Data and Computer Software clause at DFARS 252.227-7013, and similar clauses, as applicable.

Should you have any questions concerning this agreement or if you wish to contact the Company for any reason, please contact in writing: Social Sciences Media Editor, Prentice Hall, One Lake Street Upper Saddle River, NJ 07458.